RACIAL
AND
ETHNIC
RELATIONS

RACIAL AND ETHNIC RELATIONS

second edition

JOE R. FEAGIN
University of Texas

PRENTICE-HALL, INC., Englewood Cliffs, New Jersey 07632

Library of Congress Cataloging in Publication Data

FEAGIN, JOE R.
  Racial and ethnic relations.

  Includes bibliographical references and index.
  1. Minorities—United States. 2. United States—
Race relations. 3. United States—Ethnic relations.
4. Assimilation (Sociology) I. Title.
EL84.AlF38   1984   305.8'00973   83-13829
ISBN 0-13-750125-0

Editorial/production supervision and
  interior design: Fred Bernardi
Cover design: Diane Saxe
Manufacturing buyer: John Hall

Prentice-Hall Series in Sociology
Neil J. Smelser, Editor

© 1984, 1978 by Prentice-Hall, Inc., Englewood Cliffs, New Jersey 07632

Printed in the United States of America

10 9 8 7 6 5 4

ISBN: 0-13-750125-0

Prentice-Hall International, Inc., *London*
Prentice-Hall of Australia Pty. Limited, *Sydney*
Editora Prentice-Hall do Brasil, Ltda., *Rio de Janiero*
Prentice-Hall Canada Inc., *Toronto*
Prentice-Hall of India Private Limited, *New Delhi*
Prentice-Hall of Japan, Inc., *Tokyo*
Prentice-Hall of Southeast Asia Pte. Ltd., *Singapore*
Whitehall Books Limited, *Wellington, New Zealand*

Contents

CHAPTER 3   ENGLISH AMERICANS
AND THE ANGLO-SAXON CORE CULTURE   50

CHAPTER 6   JEWISH AMERICANS   139

CHAPTER 7   NATIVE AMERICANS ("INDIANS")   175

CHAPTER 8   BLACK AMERICANS   212

CHAPTER 9   MEXICAN AMERICANS   260

CHAPTER 10   PUERTO RICANS   298

Preface

This revised edition of *Racial and Ethnic Relations* is designed for social sciences courses variously titled "minority groups," "minority relations," "race relations," and "racial and ethnic relations," as well as a variety of "ethnic studies" courses in college and noncollege settings. My purpose is to provide the reader with access to the social science literature on race and ethnic groups in the United States. I have drawn on a broad array of sources, including articles, books, and other data analyses by sociologists, political scientists, social psychologists, historians, economists, journalists, and legal scholars. After two decades of research work in this field, I have come to the conclusion that much interesting, provocative, and revealing material on race and ethnic groups is buried in government reports, technical analyses in scholarly books (many of which are now unavailable), and in journals. Using these sources, I have tried to put together well-researched and theoretically informed accounts of U.S. racial and ethnic groups.

I have focused on a modest number of major racial and ethnic groups, preferring to accent depth rather than breadth. And I have chosen to concentrate on groups primarily important in the United States, rather than to work up an analysis comparing race and ethnic relations in countries around the globe. That latter task deserves more attention than it has received, but I remain convinced that a major task is to dig deeper into race and ethnic relations in specific countries. Overview analyses of the United States have just begun to dig deeper into the "what," "why," and "how" of racial and ethnic relations here, particularly relations involving such little-studied groups as the Italian Americans, Cuban Americans, and Puerto Ricans. Until we do that analytical and descriptive task well, it is difficult to compare the situation in the United States with that in other countries. I have here set myself this task: an exploration of the diversity, depth, and significance of racial and ethnic relations in one country—the United States.

This second edition of *Racial and Ethnic Relations* is thoroughly revised and updated. The first two chapters have been revised to include ideas and theories which have appeared in recent years; for example, new power-conflict approaches such as the split labor market approach, are now discussed in Chapter 2. A new chapter (Chapter 10) has been added on Puerto Ricans. The other substantive chapters have been rewritten to include recent studies and data on specific racial and ethnic groups. A mostly new final chapter has been added, one which deals with the character of, and debates over, the new waves of immigrants to U.S. shores and with the debates over affirmative action and equal opportunity programs. In addition, the first edition manuscript has been corrected and polished in line with helpful suggestions from students, teachers, and reviewers.

I am indebted to a long list of insightful readers and colleagues whose help, advice, and suggestions have made this a better book than it otherwise would have been: Graham Kinloch, Edward Murguía, the late Louis Schneider, Nestor Rodríguez, Gilberto Cardenas, David Roth, John S. Butler, Andrew M. Greeley, Joseph Lopreato, Clairece Booher Feagin, Anthony Orum, Eric Woodrum, Lester Hill, Edna Bonacich, Chad Oliver, Marcia A. Herndon, Rogelio Nuñez, Tom Walls, Samuel Heilman, Phylis Cancilla Martinelli, José Limon, Devon Peña, Diana Kendall, and Robena Jackson. I am also indebted to Neil J. Smelser for his penetrating suggestions and continuing support for this book, to Karen E. Predow, Department of Sociology, Rutgers University, and Harry H. Bash, Department of Sociology, the University of Missouri-St. Louis for their helpful reviews of the manuscript, and to Ed Stanford and Susan Taylor at Prentice-Hall for shepherding this project through from idea to reality.

RACIAL AND ETHNIC RELATIONS

The Racial
and
Ethnic Mosaic
CHAPTER 1

INTRODUCTION

Just two hundred years ago this fledgling nation took its leave from Mother Europe. Born in revolution, the new nation has been portrayed as forging an era of patriotic unity and intense dedication to freedom and equality. Over the next two centuries a complex and vigorous nation would emerge, with great racial and ethnic diversity. Yet the new society had its seamy side as well. Racial and ethnic oppression and conflict—these too were imbedded in the founding period and in the unfolding history of the new republic. Thus by the end of the seventeenth century the enslavement of black Africans was fundamental to the economy of the North American colonies, and slave revolt was a recurrent problem. Other nonwhite peoples, such as Chinese Americans and Japanese Americans, would eventually suffer similar yokes of oppression.

But non-Europeans were not the only ones to face oppressive conditions. Discrimination against later white immigrant groups was part of the sometimes forgotten history of both the pre- and postrevolutionary periods. In the earliest period the colonial population on the prospering Atlantic coast was predominantly English in its origins and basic social institutions.

With a voracious appetite for raw materials and new markets, England later encouraged non-English immigration to the colonies as well. Yet there was popular opposition, verbal and violent, to the long line of new white immigrants. "Foreigners" soon became a negative category for the colonists. As Dinnerstein and Jaher note, "despite the need for new settlers English colonials had mixed feelings about foreign arrivals. Anglo-Saxon mobs attacked Huguenots in Frenchtown, Rhode Island, and destroyed a Scotch-

Irish frontier settlement in Worcester, Massachusetts."[1] In the 1700s colonies such as Virginia, Pennsylvania, and Rhode Island attempted to put serious roadblocks in the way of non-British immigrants.[2]

Institutionalized Racism

The basic documents of the new republic reflect its patterns of race relations and racial subordination, and some of the republic's first laws were aimed at hampering groups of non-English origin. An early draft of the radical Declaration of Independence, prepared by Thomas Jefferson, accused King George of pursuing slavery, of waging "cruel war against human nature itself, violating its most sacred rights of life and liberty in the persons of a distant people who never offended him, captivating them and carrying them into slavery in another hemisphere, or to incur miserable death in the transportation thither."[3] Jefferson noted that the king had not attempted to prohibit the slave trade and, furthermore, had even encouraged the slaves to "rise in arms" against white colonists.

Because of pressure from slaveholding interests in the South and slave-trading interests in New England, this critique of slavery was omitted from the final version of the Declaration. Even in this revolutionary period the doctrine of liberty could not be extended to the black population, for criticism of King George was in fact criticism of the North American economic system. Ironically, Jefferson himself was a slaveholder whose wealth was tied to an oppressive agricultural system.

The Constitution explicitly recognized race subordination in three places. First, as a result of a famous compromise between northern and southern representatives to the Constitutional Convention, Article I originally stipulated that three-fifths of a given state's slave population was to be counted among the total in apportioning the legislative representation and taxes—that is, each slave was officially three-fifths of a person. Interestingly, in this case southern slaveowners pressed for full inclusion of the slaves in the population count, while northern interests were opposed. In addition, a section was added to Article I permitting the slave trade to continue until 1808. The Constitution also incorporated a fugitive-slave provision requiring the return of runaway slaves to their owners, a provision opposed by very few at the time.[4] Neither the statement in the Declaration of Independence that "all men are created equal" nor the Constitution's Bill of Rights was seen as applying to what was a very large proportion of the population at that time—citizens of African descent. Black slavery, strangely enough, would last much longer in the new republic than in imperial Britain.[5]

Blacks were not the only group to suffer from government action. Numerous other non-English groups continued to find themselves less than equal under the law. Anti-immigrant legislation in the late 1700s and early 1800s included the Alien, Sedition, and Naturalization Acts.[6] Irish, German, and French immigrants were growing in number by the late eighteenth century, and concern with the political sentiments of these and other immigrants was acute. The Naturalization Act stiffened residency requirements for citizenship from five to fourteen years, while an Alien Act gave the president the power to expel foreigners. President Adams was frequently pressed to issue exclusion warrants and did so in two cases. Shiploads of foreign immigrants left the country out of fear of exclusion.[7]

Inequality

Inequality in life chances along racial and ethnic lines was a fundamental fact of the new nation's institutions. At first the image of liberty and justice seemed in reality to be for British males only. Yet this situation did not go unchallenged. By the late eighteenth century many Irish and German immigrants had come into the colonies. Indeed, a significant proportion of the four million persons enumerated in the first United States Census were of non-English origins. Over the next two centuries English domination was slowly modified to include other northern Europeans. These groups in turn were challenged by a series of southern and eastern European and nonwhite groups trying to move up in the social, economic, and political systems. Gradually the new nation became a complex and unprecedented mixing of peoples.

Most in the non-British immigrant groups came to adopt the English language and institutions, which comprised the core of American society and culture. Most groups adapted, in part or in whole, to the dominant culture and ways, with some gaining substantial power and status in the process. Yet other groups remained more or less in a subordinate position both politically and economically. Thus racial and ethnic diversity and inequality became early and continuing dimensions of the foundation of this society. Intergroup relations were not always peaceful, nor was equality a basic fact of group life. In some cases, racial and ethnic stratification intensified, with some groups taking precedence over others. These dual themes of adaptation and stratification will recur throughout this book.

AN OVERVIEW

What is race? What is ethnicity? What is assimilation? What is racial stratification? Answers to these questions will be developed in this chapter and in Chapter 2. The next section will explore definitions; Chapter 2 will introduce conceptual frameworks which have been influential in the analysis of racial and ethnic issues.

After probing definitions and conceptual frameworks, we will move on in the next nine chapters to a detailed analysis of nine racial and ethnic groups which have played important roles in this nation's development. The first groups are of European origin—English Americans, Irish Americans, Italian Americans, and Jewish Americans. Of these, the first three have received little or no attention in previous textbooks. Next we will move on to a consideration of five primarily non-European groups—Native Americans ("Indians"), black Americans, Mexican Americans, Puerto Ricans, and Japanese Americans, groups that have substantial roots in the Americas, Africa, and Asia.

In the chapters which follow, the history and experiences of sizable groups (such as Scandinavian Americans, Scottish Americans, and Chinese Americans) receive fleeting or no attention. At least several dozen groups have a good claim to inclusion in a comprehensive treatment of race and ethnic relations in North America, but that would entail an encyclopedia rather than a workable textbook. Thus I have chosen to give intensive attention to a modest number of groups selected to suggest the broadest possible range of experiences, rather than to provide more superficial coverage of many groups.

The white groups discussed in this text illustrate not only important contributions and diverse experiences, but also different times of entry. The English were the core group, although they have received remarkably little attention in the literature on race and ethnicity. The Irish were in the first great immigration waves in the eighteenth and nineteenth centuries and included the first large waves of non-Protestants. The Italians entered later in massive numbers, at the end of the nineteenth and the beginning of the twentieth century. The Jews, a composite group including several nationalities, came in three major waves, the largest of which roughly coincided with the immigration of the Italians. Other major groups covered here include the four always listed among the most oppressed—blacks, Puerto Ricans, Native Americans, and Mexican Americans. These groups have substantial and growing research literatures for an author to draw on. Japanese Americans were chosen to illustrate the experiences of an important representative of the growing Asian groups in the United States and one with the unique experience of imprisonment in American concentration camps a few decades back. An explicit contrast will be drawn between experiences of white and nonwhite groups.

Each group's entry into North American history and its subsequent experiences will be examined. In general, I have attempted to analyze the following dimensions of the experiences of each group: migration; conflict with other groups; prejudice and stereotyping; experiences in such major institutional sectors as the economy, politics, and education; and the usefulness of theoretical models in interpreting each group's role in this society. Following an examination of these dimensions for the chosen groups, a concluding chapter explores current issues in race and ethnic relations, including new immigrant groups from Cuba and Asia and government remedial policies such as Affirmative Action.

BASIC TERMS IN THE STUDY OF RACE-ETHNIC RELATIONS

A logical place to start in making sense out of this dynamic mosaic of groups is with basic terms and concepts. Such terms as *ethnic groups* and *prejudice* have often been used without specifying their meaning. Since these terms signify basic concepts in the study of intergroup relations, we need to analyze them in some detail.

Race

Both *racial group* and the common term *race* have been used in a number of different senses in social science and popular writings. *Human race, Jewish race, Negro race*—such terms in the literature suggest a range of different meanings. The earliest use of race in sixteenth- and seventeenth-century Europe was in the sense of descendants of a common ancestor, emphasizing kinship linkages or generation.[8]

It was only in the late eighteenth century that the term race came to mean a distinct category of human beings with *physical* characteristics transmitted by descent.[9] Prior to the late eighteenth century, however, humans were being categorized by Europeans on physical grounds. In the late 1600s François Bernier was one of the first Europeans to sort out human beings into a number of basic and distinctive categories, relying heavily on facial character and skin color.[10] Soon a hierarchy of groups (not yet termed races) came to be accepted, with white Europeans at the top. The Negro or black African category was usually relegated to the bottom, in part because of black Africans' color and allegedly "primitive" culture, but primarily because they were then best known as slaves to Europeans. Economic subordination meant a "lower" position in the classification system.

Immanuel Kant's use of the German phrase for "races of mankind" in the 1770s was probably the first explicit use of the term in the sense of biologically or physically distinctive categories of human beings.[11] The use of the term race by physical anthropologists in the late eighteenth and nineteenth centuries was with this biological meaning. Basic to the increasingly prevalent view was the idea of a set number of genetic groups with distinctive physical characteristics, together with the idea that these characteristics made for a hierarchy of groups. By the late nineteenth century numerous European and American writers were systematically distinguishing and downgrading all peoples not of northern European origin as inferior "races," particularly southern and eastern Europeans.[12]

Racism

It was in this context that ideological "racism" emerged. Although this term has been used loosely, for our purposes we can define *racism* specifically as *an ideology which considers a group's unchangeable physical characteristics to be linked in a direct, causal way to psychological or intellectual characteristics, and which on this basis distinguishes between superior and inferior racial groups.*[13] The "scientific racism" of such European writers as Count de Gobineau in the midnineteenth century was used to morally justify the imperialism of northern European states in Asia, Africa, and the Americas. A long line of "scientific racists" followed in de Gobineau's footsteps, including German Nazi leaders. In their hands the ideology of racial inferiority was broadly applied to culturally distinct white European groups, such as the Jews; in this perspective, real or alleged physical characteristics were coupled with cultural traits.

This extended to the U.S. as well. In 1935 an influential University of Virginia professor wrote that

> . . . the size of the brain in the Black Race is below the medium both of the Whites and the Yellow-Browns, frequently with relatively more simple convolutions. The frontal lobes are often low and narrow. The parietal lobes voluminous, the occipital protruding. The psychic activities of the Black Race are a careless, jolly vivacity, emotions and passions of short duration, and a strong and somewhat irrational egoism. Idealism, ambition, and the co-operative faculties are weak. They love amusement and sport but have little initiative and adventurous spirit.[14]

We see in this ideological racism the linking of physical and personality characteristics. While this portrait often passed for science prior to World War II—and in some racist organizations much of it still does—it is really pseudoscience. For the most part the ideological racists assumed the stereotyped characteristics traditionally applied to black Americans to be true; they did not scientifically prove their assertions. Modern biologists and anthropologists have demonstrated the wild-eyed irrationality of much of this racist mythology. The basic tenet of racist thinking is that physical differences such as skin color or nose shape are intrinsically tied to meaningful differentials in intelligence or culture. Since no convincing scientific support for this assumed linkage exists, many social scientists have come to reject attempts at constructing complex typologies of inferior and superior racial categories. But the lack of scientific support has hardly lessened the tremendous impact of racist ideologies.

Montagu has noted that this ideological racism is dangerous, a view shaped in part by his observation of the German Nazi ideology, which argued for distinctive Aryan and Jewish races.[15] That ideology was linked to the killing of millions of European Jews in the 1930s and 1940s. As a result, a 1950 *UNESCO Statement on Race,* prepared by a distinguished group of social scientists, pointed out that race, even from a strict biological standpoint, could *at most* refer to a group with certain distinctive gene concentrations. Whatever categorization social scientists apply to human beings, the document further asserts, they should never include "mental characteristics as part of those classifications."[16] The UNESCO statement goes on to point out that inherited genetic factors are not the major forces shaping cultural or intellectual differences among human groups. Environment is far more important.

Racial Group

In the last few decades a major concern among social scientists has been with the *social* definition of race and racial groups. In 1947 Cox was one of the first to underscore this perspective by defining a race as "any people who are distinguished, or consider themselves distinguished, in social relations with other peoples, by their physical characteristics."[17] From the social-definition perspective characteristics such as skin color have *no unique or self-evident meaning*; rather, they primarily have *social* meaning, so much so that one might even speak of "social races." Similarly, racial group has been defined by van den Berghe as a "human group that defines itself and/or is defined by other groups as different from other groups by virtue of [presumed] innate and immutable physical characteristics."[18] This definition relates to the everyday use of racial distinctions in the social world.

A person's race is most typically determined by and important to certain outsiders, although a group's self-definition can also be important. Thus *a racial group is not something which is naturally generated as part of the self-evident order of the universe, but is a social group which persons inside or outside the group have decided is important to single out as inferior or superior, typically on the basis of real or alleged physical characteristics subjectively selected.*

In the United States a number of groups would fit into this definition. As we will see in a later chapter, black Americans have been defined as racially different by white groups for several centuries on the basis of certain physical characteristics. Asian Americans, Native Americans ("Indians"), and Mexican Americans have also seen certain physical characteristics, such as skin color and eye shape, singled out as badges of racial inferiority. Note too that some social groups defined at an earlier point in time as racial groups, as physically and mentally inferior groups, are no longer defined that way. In later chapters we will see the way the Irish and the Italians were at one time defined as *inferior racial groups* by Anglo-Saxon Protestants. Later on, definition as a racial group was replaced by definition as an *ethnic* group, a term which will be examined below. After a while, it became clear that there were no significant physical differences between the Irish, or the Italians, and Anglo-Saxon Americans.

Why are some physical characteristics, such as skin color, selected as a basis for distinguishing human groups, while other characteristics, such as eye color, are seldom used to distinguish groups from one another? These questions can be answered, not simply in biological terms, but primarily by historical and sociological analysis. Such characteristics as skin color are, of course, as Banton has argued, "easily observed and ordered in the mind."[19] But such characteristics as skin color become highlighted in a social interaction process. More important than ease of observation is the way in which economic or political exploitation often leads to the need for the identification of the exploited group in a certain way. The real (or alleged) physical characteristics singled out to typify the exploited group often become seen as inferior racial characteristics in the process of justifying exploitation. Technological differences in military firepower between European and African peoples facilitated the subordination of Africans as slaves in the English and other European colonies. In turn, darker skin color and selected other physical differences became signals indicating the different obligations and privileges of the two groups. Skin color characteristics had no inherent meaning; in the intergroup interaction process they became important only because they could be used easily to classify most members of the dominant and subordinate groups.

Knowledge of descent and of one's kinship and relatives sometimes affects one's assignment to a racial group, particularly for those who do not have the obvious physical characteristics. People have been distinguished not only on the basis of their own physical characteristics but also on the basis of a socially determined "rule of descent."[20] Descent is not typically determined scientifically, but on the basis of social perception of ancestry. With regard to black Americans, for example, as the clear-cut color characteristic accented in the early phases of colonial development became more problematical over time, the ancestry aspect became more critical in the identification process. Pettigrew has noted that "black" Americans in the United States today "evidence an unusually wide range of physical traits. Their skin color extends from ebony to a shade paler than many 'whites'; their nose-shape from extremely flat to aquiline; their stature from basketball giant to dwarf."[21]

In some communities, particularly in the southern United States, the *social* aspect of the defining process becomes obvious when a light-skinned person without some of the physical traits usually associated with blacks is treated as black partly because one of his or her ancestors or relatives is remembered to have been of dark color and of African ancestry. Even in the case of groups which have traditionally been distinguished on the basis of physical characteristics, ambiguity often arises in the actual defining process. Moreover, since the distinctive physical characteristics of subordinate racial groups are assumed to be linked to intellectual or cultural characteristics, dominant groups regularly mix their racial definitions with notions about intelligence and even about cultural distinctiveness. For example, in an employment situation a black applicant may suffer discrimination not only because of his darker color but also because he or she dresses or speaks oddly in the view of a white personnel interviewer.

Ethnic Group

The term *ethnic group* has been used by social scientists in two different senses, one narrow and one broad. Some definitions of the term are general enough to include socially defined racial groups. For example, in Gordon's broad definition an ethnic group is a social group distinguished "by race, religion, or national origin."[22] As in the case of racial group, here is a notion of set-apartness. But here the distinctive characteristics can be physical or cultural, and language and religion are seen as critical signs of ethnicity even where there is no physical distinctiveness. Glazer has expressed this inclusive view of the ethnic group:

> Thus one possible position on ethnicity and race, and the one I hold, is that they form part of a single family of social identities—a family which, in addition to races and ethnic groups, includes religions (as in Holland), language groups (as in Belgium), and all of which can be included in the most general term, ethnic groups, groups defined by descent, real or mythical, and sharing a common history and experience.[23]

These two definitions illustrate the broad definition of an ethnic group. Other analysts have preferred a narrower definition of ethnic group, one which omits groups defined *primarily* in terms of racial characteristics and limits the term to groups distinguished *primarily* on the basis of cultural or nationality characteristics. Indeed, the word *ethnic* comes from the Greek *ethnos*, originally meaning "nation." In its earliest English usage the word ethnic referred to culturally different "heathen" nations (those not Christian or Jewish). Apparently the first usage of ethnic group in terms of national origin developed in the period of heavy immigration from southern and eastern European nations to the United States in the early twentieth century. Since the 1930s and '40s a number of prominent social scientists have suggested that the narrower definition of ethnic group, in line with the literal Greek meaning, may make the term more useful.[24]

Warner distinguished between ethnic group, which he saw as characterized by cultural differences, and racial group, characterized by physical differences. The greater the cultural and racial differences are between a group and the core society, the slower the assimilation into the core society.[25] More recently, other scholars have also preferred the narrower usage. In van den Berghe's succinct translation of this view, ethnic groups are "socially defined but on the basis of cultural criteria."[26] When the term *ethnic group* is used in this book, the usual meaning will be the narrower one—that of *a group which is socially distinguished or set apart, by others and/or by itself, primarily on the basis of cultural or nationality characteristics.*

Reviewing different definitions of ethnic group, one soon sees that the definitions sometimes vary because of different assumptions underlying them—or, alternatively, because they are intended to suggest different conclusions on group experiences. Those who prefer the broader definition often argue that the experiences of people defined as nonwhite are essentially similar to the experiences of white groups.* Some have argued that, in the United States, the situation and experiences of nonwhite Americans are essentially similar in kind to those of white immigrant groups. Often a further assumption is that the experiences of both white and nonwhite groups are adequately explained using the same theoretical framework—usually an assimilationist framework.[27] Analysts who prefer the narrower definition, who see ethnic groups typically as in a category separate from racial groups, usually have different underlying assumptions. These include the view that the experiences of non-European racial groups have been distinctively different from those of European groups.[28]

Whether ethnic group is defined in a narrow or a broad sense, ancestry is important. Perception of common ancestry, both real and mythical, has been important both to outsiders' definitions and to ethnic groups' self-definitions. Max Weber saw ethnic groups broadly as "human groups that entertain a subjective belief in their common descent—because of similarities of physical type or of customs or both, or because of memories of colonization or migration—in such a way that this belief is important for

---

*In this book the term "nonwhite" will ordinarily refer to groups basically of non-European origin, such as black Americans. The term "white" will be used for groups basically of European origin and often will encompass different ethnic groups. Both terms relate to the social definition of groups.

the continuation of the nonkinship communal relationships."[29] Gordon has described an ethnic group as one having a shared sense of being one people.[30] Consciousness of one's own kind is accented.

The social definitions of racial group and ethnic group get us away from a biological determinism that sees groups as self-evident and genetically fixed with unchanging physical or mental characteristics. People themselves, both outside and inside differentiated groups, determine when certain physical or cultural characteristics are important enough to single out a group for social interest, whether for good or for ill. Admittedly, this social definition approach is not as neat as that of those with lists of categories of "natural" races. But it is more accurate.

A given social group may be viewed by different outsiders or at different points in time as a racial or an ethnic group. And some groups have been defined by the same outsiders as important on the basis of both physical and cultural criteria. Jews, for example, were spoken of as a "race" in Nazi Germany, in part because of both real and alleged differences in physical characteristics. However, in Nazi Germany, routine identification of specific Jews for persecution was based more on ethnic characteristics—on cultural characteristics such as religion or language and on genealogical ties to Jewish ancestors—than on physical characteristics. Nonetheless, as later chapters should make clear, outsiders have frequently placed more emphasis on one or the other of these sets of socially distinguished criteria—physical or cultural characteristics—in defining a given group's societal position.

Minority and Majority Groups

Other terms have been used for racial and ethnic groups. Prominent among these has been the term *minority group*.[31] Louis Wirth explicitly defined a minority group in terms of subordinate position as "a group of people who, because of their physical or cultural characteristics, are singled out from others in the society in which they live for differential and unequal treatment and who therefore regard themselves as objects of collective discrimination."[32] Wagley and Harris have provided a definition of minority groups as:

1. suffering discrimination and subordination within a society;
2. set apart in terms of physical or cultural traits disapproved of by the dominant group;
3. which are units with a sense of collective identity and common burdens;
4. whose membership is determined by the socially invented rule of descent;
5. characterized by marriage within the group.[33]

The term minority group implies the existence of a "majority group," a dominant group with superior rights and advantages. These concepts point up racial and ethnic *stratification*, a ranking system whose shape takes the form of a hierarchy of more and less powerful groups. It would seem more accurate to use the term *dominant group* for majority group, as well as *subordinate group* for minority group, since the "majority group" can be numerically a minority, as with white Europeans who have ruled in a number of African countries. The "minority groups" in these situations are actually numerical majorities. In this book the terms dominant and subordinate group will be the preferred designations wherever possible for groups in a hierarchy.

Prejudice and Stereotyping

Another common term is *prejudice,* a term which in popular discourse is tied to negative attitudes. Understanding how and why negative attitudes develop is best approached by first defining *ethnocentrism,* which was long ago described by Sumner as the "view of things in which one's own group is the center of everything, and all others are scaled and rated with reference to it."[34] Members of social groups develop, on the one hand, "positive ethnocentrism," a loyalty to the values, beliefs, and members of one's own group. This positive ethnocentrism, however, often becomes linked with negative views of outgroups, views manifested in prejudices and stereotypes. Such negative views, which seem to grow out of the constant evaluating of outgroups in terms of one's own values and ways, are inextricably linked to social, economic, and political interaction among groups.[35]

Prejudice has been defined by Allport as "thinking ill of others without sufficient warrant."[36] The term comes from the Latin word *praejudicium,* which referred to a judgment made on the basis of prior experience. In English the word evolved from meaning "hasty judgment" to the present connotation of unfavorableness that goes with the meaning of an unsupported or biased judgment. While prejudice can theoretically apply to biases favoring a group, its current meaning in both popular usage and social science analysis is almost exclusively in terms of negative views. Prejudice can be defined more precisely as *"an antipathy based upon a faulty and inflexible generalization. It may be felt or expressed. It may be directed toward a group as a whole, or toward an individual because he [or she] is a member of that group."*[37] Prejudice is here viewed as involving both a negative feeling or attitude toward the outgroup and an inaccurate belief as well; it has both emotional and cognitive aspects. An example might be "I hate black people, because black people always smell worse than whites." The first part of the sentence expresses the negative feeling (the hatred), while the last part indicates an inaccurate generalization. This latter cognitive aspect has been termed a *stereotype*—that is, *an overgeneralization associated with a racial or ethnic category that goes beyond existing evidence.*

One television show, *All in the Family,* has been popular for a long time. In that show the prominent character, Archie Bunker, is supposed to be an example of a white bigot who verbally attacks outgroups, who calls blacks "jungle bunnies," and who worries deeply about white women marrying blacks. Supposedly only the blue-collar people of America, such as Bunker, are bigots. But that is simply not the case. Prejudices and stereotypes aimed at nonwhites are common among all classes of white America; social science surveys have found prejudiced people at all levels of this society.

Why do some people stereotype others? Why have Irish Americans for so long been stereotyped as lazy drunkards? Why have blacks been depicted as indolent, violent, and oversexed? Why have Italians been stereotyped as crime-oriented "Mafia" types? Why have the Japanese been stereotyped as treacherous Orientals? This forces us to examine the role that prejudices and stereotypes play in the lives of individuals and groups. In this regard sociologically oriented analysts tend to emphasize the group pressures on the individual for conformity or rationalization, while psychological analysts tend to stress individual irrationality or personality defectiveness. Much sociopsychological research and analysis has underscored the expressive function of prejudice for the individual. Frustration-aggression theories, psychoanalytic theories, and authoritarian personality perspectives focus on the *externalization* function of prejudice—the transference of an individual's internal psychological problem onto an external object as a solution to that internal problem. Many psychologically oriented interpretations stress "sick" or "abnormal" individuals whose race or ethnic prejudice is intimately linked to special emotional problems in their internal psychological life-economy, such as hatred of their own fathers.[38] In a classic study of prejudice and personality, *The Authoritarian Personality*, Adorno et al. argue that persons who hate Jews or blacks differ from tolerant persons in central personality traits—specifically, that they exhibit "authoritarian personalities."[39] Those with authoritarian personalities differ from others in their greater submission to authority, tendency to stereotyping, superstition, and concern for social status. They view the world as sinister and threatening, a view easily linked to intolerant views of outgroups in subordinate positions in the social world around them.

Some scholars have raised serious questions about this traditional stress on the expressive function of prejudice and of stereotypes. Williams and Pettigrew have suggested that *conformity* may be a much more important factor. Most people seem to accept their own social and community situation as given and to hold the prejudices which they have been taught at home and at school. Conformity to prevailing beliefs is thus seen as a major source of prejudice. From this perspective prejudices are not so much individually determined preferences, but rather shared social definitions of selected racial and ethnic groups. This points to the social-adjustment function of prejudice. Indeed, most of us can think of numerous situations in which northerners or southerners have had to adjust to new racial beliefs as they moved from one region to another or from one setting to another.[40] As Schermerhorn notes, "prejudice is a product of *situations*," not "a little demon that emerges in people simply because they are depraved."[41]

These explanations partly explain why people hold prejudices and stereotypes; an additional factor is that stereotypes help rationalize a subordinate group's position. While prejudice goes back deep into human history, stereotyping in the form of a fully developed racist ideology may be a relatively recent development, perhaps developing with the rise of the European colonization of peoples of color around the world. Prejudice,

Cox argues, "is a divisive attitude seeking to alienate dominant group sympathy from an 'inferior' race, a whole people, for the purpose of facilitating its exploitation."[42]

In the process of subordinating a people, as in the case of white enslavement of black Africans in the American colonies or in the case of restrictive quotas for Jews in American medical schools, stereotypes developed, at least in part, to justify that subordination. Indeed, the ideological racism noted previously can be viewed as a complex set of stereotypes aimed at rationalizing the imperialism of certain white European nations exploiting southern and eastern European immigrants and expanding at the expense of non-European peoples. Stereotyping continues to be a weapon in group conflict.

Discrimination: Distinguishing Dimensions

Discussions of discrimination and of government programs which attempt to eradicate discrimination are often confusing, in part because the dimensions of discrimination are not distinguished. As a first step in sorting out discrimination, I suggest the diagram in Figure 1-1. The dimensions of discrimination include (a) motivation, (b) discriminatory action, (c) effects, (d) the relation between motivation and action, (e) the relation between action and effects, (f) the immediate institutional context, and (g) the larger societal context.[43] For example, a given set of discriminatory acts—such as the legalized exclusion of black children from all-white schools from the nineteenth century to the 1960s—can be looked at in terms of these dimensions. One can ask what the motivation was for this legalized discrimination. Was it prejudice, or what? One can also ask what form the

FIGURE 1–1 The Dimensions of Discrimination

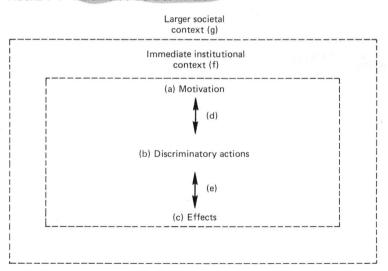

Larger societal
context (g)

Immediate institutional
context (f)

(a) Motivation

(d)

(b) Discriminatory actions

(e)

(c) Effects

exclusionary practices actually took. In some cases principals refused black children entrance into their school buildings. Also of importance are the effects of these practices. One effect was the poorer education many black children received. But these practices were often not the isolated actions of principals and other administrators. They were part of an institution-alized pattern of segregated education, the persisting effects of which are still a part of U.S. society. Finally, such legalized patterns of school dis-crimination have been part of a larger social context of general racial subordination of black Americans in many institutional areas. Discrimi-nation is a multidimensional problem.

Traditional Research on Prejudice and Discrimination

Much research and discussion on discrimination has focused on one type of motivation (*a* in Figure 1–1)—prejudice—to the virtual exclusion of other types of motivation. Much traditional analysis emphasizes the relation between prejudice and discrimination (*d* in Figure 1–1), with prej-udice seen as the critical causal factor underlying discriminatory treatment of a singled-out group. For example, Gordon Allport suggested that few prejudiced people keep their prejudices entirely to themselves, but rather act out their feelings in a variety of ways, ranging from speaking against an outgroup to discriminating against an outgroup to exterminating an outgroup.[44] In his classic study, *An American Dilemma* (1944), Gunnar Myrdal saw race prejudice as "the whole complex of valuations and beliefs which are behind discriminatory behavior on the part of the majority group."[45] A few years later Robert K. Merton argued that discrimination might be practiced even by an unprejudiced person who was afraid of the prejudices of others.[46]

Over the last several decades laboratory research studies have also focused on the relationship between prejudice and discrimination. This research has tried to determine if prejudiced people do in fact discriminate and to see how prejudice is linked to discrimination. In these research studies prejudice is typically determined by means of simple questions on administered questionnaires.[47] Discriminatory action is often measured in a weak or questionable way, as, for example, by the readiness of a white subject to sign a release form indicating a willingness to be photographed with blacks. Such studies have found a low positive correlation between expressed prejudice and the measured discriminatory behavior, that is, knowing how prejudiced a subject is often does not help predict his or her actions. The weakness of this correlation has been explained in various ways. One problem may be the wording or character of the questions on attitudes; another may be the mild form of discrimination measured in the laboratory. Racial discrimination in the outside world is usually far more substantial than that measured in the lab. Moreover, much social-psycho-logical research on the prejudice-discrimination linkage emphasizes indi-vidualistic explanations; the research seldom considers the important variables other than the experimental subject's personality or immediate reference group.[48]

Institutional and Individual Discrimination

The heavy emphasis on prejudice and bigoted individuals in assessments of discrimination, reflecting attitudes conspicuous in American history, has been questioned in recent years by those concerned with privilege theories of discrimination and with institutional discrimination. Some authors, for example, have pointed out that the intent to harm lying behind much discrimination may not reflect prejudice or antipathy but simply a desire to protect one's own privileges. Some people discriminate because they gain economically or politically from racial restrictions on the competition. In the historical struggle over resources, systems of race stratification were established in which the dominant groups, such as whites, benefitted economically, politically, and psychologically. They strive to maintain their privileges, whether or not they rationalize the striving in terms of prejudice. Wellman has argued for the view that discrimination is a "rational response to struggles over scarce resources." In the struggle over resources a system of stratification was established in which the dominant group benefitted economically, politically, and psychologically.[49]

A related issue is the institutionalization of privilege and thus of discrimination. Hamilton and Carmichael apparently were the first to develop the concepts of "individual racism," exemplified by the actions of white terrorists bombing a black church, and, in contrast, "institutional racism," illustrated by societal practices which lead to large numbers of black children suffering constantly because of inadequate food and medical facilities.[50] The book by Hamilton and Carmichael, *Black Power*, represents an attempt to move beyond a focus on individual bigots. Institutional racism can involve actions in which people have "no intention of subordinating others because of color, or are totally unaware of doing so."[51] In his analysis of racism and mental health, Pettigrew distinguishes between "direct" and "indirect" racial discrimination, the latter applying to situations where restrictions in one area are shaped by racial discrimination in yet another.[52]

Drawing on this literature, one can define discrimination without including prejudice or intent to harm in the definition.[53] The working definition of discrimination in this book is as follows: *actions carried out by members of dominant groups, or their representatives, which have a differential and harmful impact on members of subordinate groups*. The dominant and subordinate groups here are racial and ethnic groups. Thus discrimination involves actions, as well as one or more discriminators acting and one or more victims on the receiving end. The distinction between *intentional* (motivated by prejudice or intent to harm) and *unintentional* (not motivated by prejudice or intent to harm) is useful for distinguishing basic types of discrimination.

Drawing particularly on these two dimensions of scale and of intention, I would suggest four basic types of discriminatory practices, as listed in the boxed figure on page 16. Type A, *isolate discrimination*, refers to harmful action taken intentionally by an individual member of a dominant group against members of a subordinate racial or ethnic group, without that action being socially imbedded in the larger organizational or com-

---

Type A—Isolate discrimination
Type B—Small-group discrimination
Type C—Direct institutionalized discrimination
Type D—Indirect institutionalized discrimination

---

munity context. An example of this type of discrimination might be a white police officer who implements antiblack hostility by beating up black prisoners at every opportunity, even though police department regulations specifically prohibit such actions. (If the majority of officers in that department behaved in this fashion, these beatings would no longer fall into this category.) The term *isolate* should not be taken to mean that Type-A discrimination is rare in the United States, for it is indeed commonplace. Rather, the term can be used to indicate an individual's action taken without the immediate support of norms (standards of conduct) in a large group or organizational context.

Type B, *small-group discrimination*, refers to harmful actions taken intentionally by a small number of dominant group individuals acting in concert against members of subordinate racial and ethnic groups, without the support of the norms or rules of a larger organizational or community context. The bombing of Irish Catholic churches in the 1800s or of the homes of black families in northern cities by small Ku Klux Klan–type groups in the 1960s might be viewed as examples of this type.

Type C, *direct institutionalized discrimination*, refers to organizationally prescribed or comunity-prescribed actions which by intention have a differential and negative impact on members of subordinate race and ethnic groups. Typically, these actions are not episodic or sporadic, but are routinely carried out by a large number of individuals guided by the norms of a large-scale organization or community. With type C we come to the *institutionalization* of discrimination. Historical examples of this type include the intentional segregation of black or Jewish persons in inferior facilities or jobs. Currently, Type C discrimination can be seen in the "steering" practices of real estate companies which channel blacks away from white housing areas, practices documented by Diana Pearce in a study of Detroit.[54] A recent study of minority medical students by Diana Kendall has also demonstrated the persistence of institutionalized patterns of informal discrimination which batter the lives of nonwhite Americans.[55]

Type D, *indirect institutionalized discrimination*, refers to practices having a negative and differential impact on members of subordinate race and ethnic groups even though the organizationally prescribed or community-prescribed norms or regulations guiding those actions have been established, and are carried out, with no intent to harm the members of those groups. For example, intentional discrimination institutionalized in the education and training of subordinate groups has often handicapped their attempts to compete with dominant group members in the employment sphere, where hiring and promotion standards often incorporate educational requirements. Many nonwhite workers have suffered indirect discrimination in recent years because of seniority practices which usually were established with no intent to harm them. For example, in businesses that were intentionally segregated in the past, recently hired members of subordinate groups consequently have little seniority; thus, when a recession comes, they are the first to be laid off.

Various combinations of these four types of discrimination can coexist in a given organizational or community setting. Members of subordinate groups can suffer both from institutionalized regulations intended to have a harmful effect and from those not so intended, as well as from the flamboyant actions of bigots who focus their hostility on racial or ethnic targets within their reach. From a broader point of view, the sets of patterns of discrimination interlocking political, economic, and social organizations in this society might even be termed systematic discrimination. For a given victimized group oppression can be interlocking and cumulative, involving many institutional sectors.

Contrary to some views of more conservative analysts of American racial patterns, racial discrimination has not disappeared from U.S. society; nor does it seem to be dying away rapidly. In a fall 1979 survey, the Mathematica survey research firm interviewed 3,000 black households nationwide. Two-thirds of these heads of households felt black Americans were still discriminated against "a great deal" in this country.[56]

SUMMARY

After a brief introduction and overview, this chapter concluded with an examination of key terms: *race, racial group, racism, ethnic group, minority (subordinate) group, majority (dominant) group, prejudice, stereotyping,* and *discrimination.* These are critical concepts which loom large in discussions of race and ethnic issues. More than a century of discussion of these concepts lies behind the voyage we have set out on here and in the following chapters. We must carefully think through the meaning of such terms as *race* and *racial group,* because such concepts themselves have been used in the shaping of ethnic and race relations.

Indeed, ideas about race and racial groups have been dangerous for human beings, playing an active role in the triggering, or the convenient rationalizing, of societal processes costing millions of lives. Ideas can have an impact. The sharp cutting edge of race, as in "racial inferiority" theorizing, can be seen in the actions involving the enslavement by white Europeans of black Africans between the seventeenth and nineteenth centuries or in actions taken by German non-Jews against Jews in the 1930s and 1940s. Sometimes it is easy to consider words and concepts as harmless abstractions. However, a moment's reflection on recent and distant Western history gives the lie to this naive view. The concept may not be "mightier than the sword," to adapt an old cliché, but it is indeed mighty.

Intergroup Contact
and its Outcomes
CHAPTER 2

INTRODUCTION

How do racial and ethnic groups develop? How do they come into contact in the first place? And how do they adjust to one another in and beyond the initial stage? A number of theories try to explain how intergroup contact leads to initial patterns of racial and ethnic interaction and stratification. Other theories explore the persistence of these patterns. Issues of group control and stratification, as well as of intergroup conflict, are critical issues in these racial and ethnic theories.

There is a diversity of racial and ethnic groups in this society. As in the 1790s, in the 1980s the number of racial and ethnic groups in North America remains impressive, although the exact mix varies from that in the eighteenth century. Diversity seems omnipresent in the history of this society.

Yet diversity, as the common terms "majority group" and "minority group" suggest, has often been linked to a racial and ethnic *hierarchy*. Human beings organize themselves in a number of different ways; there is, for example, organization for earning a living, for religious rituals, and for governing. Among the important features of social organization are ranking systems. Such systems rank categories of people, not just individuals; several ranking systems coexist, shaped by differences in such aspects as race or ethnic group, sex, and economic class position. In most societies there are a number of categories in each ranking system. Rewards parallel these categories. Some categories in these ranking systems have greater privileges and resources than others; these ranked classifications may persist from one generation to the next. Class stratification in Western capitalist countries has been a focus of concern since the middle of the nineteenth century, exemplified in the distinction between the proletariat and the capitalist classes. Racial and ethnic stratification refers to a ranking system where ascribed group characteristics such as race or ethnicity are major criteria for social position and social rewards. Class stratification and race-ethnic stratification, as we will see in the chapters that follow, are sometimes overlapping systems and sometimes differentiated and contrasting systems.[1]

A Ladder of Groups

The image of a ladder will make the concept of hierarchy clearer. In Figure 2–1 the positions of five racial and ethnic groups at specific points in time are diagrammed on a ladder. Some groups are higher than others, suggesting that they have greater privileges than lower groups. The privileges can be thought of in terms of economic privileges, political privileges, and social or cultural prestige. A group substantially higher than another on an important dimension is usually viewed as a dominant group; one substantially lower than another is seen as a subordinate group. Given a number of groups in a society, the image becomes more complex, with middle groups standing in a relation of dominance to some groups and in a relation of subordination to others.

FIGURE 2–1 A Ladder of Dominance: The United States as of 1790

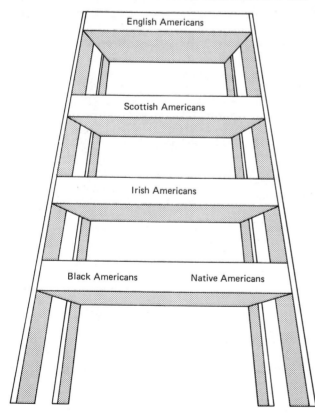

Slave importation includes the forcible removal of Africans to the North and South American colonies, while contract labor transfer includes the migration of indentured Irish servants to the English colonies and of Japanese and Chinese laborers to western North America. Indeed, some Asian contract labor migration came close to forced labor. The displaced persons category is exemplified in the streams of refugees which have come to the United States in the wake of wars. Voluntary migration would cover the great Atlantic migration of European groups to the English colonies, and later to the United States, a migration stream which has varied in voluntariness depending on the severity of economic and political circumstances in the countries of origin.

Another important type of migration often precedes the types just examined. This is the voluntary migration of colonizers, sometimes termed *colonization migration*. Unlike the types of migration just noted, this involves the *control* of an indigenous people by a more powerful group coming from the outside. External colonization can be seen in the English trading companies whose employees founded early American colonies, which led to the eventual engulfing of an indigenous Native American ("Indian") population.[8]

PATTERNS OF RACIAL AND ETHNIC ADAPTATION

The Initial Contact

What happens once different human groups come into contact as the result of migration? Are there typical end results on contact? Are there typical stages of adaptation beyond the initial stage? A close look at racial and ethnic contact reveals a variety of different outcomes. In the initial stage the range of outcomes includes:

1. Exclusion or genocide
2. Egalitarian symbiosis
3. A hierarchy or stratification system.

Genocide refers to one group killing off the other, a common outcome of contacts between British settlers and Native Americans on the Atlantic Coast of North America. Egalitarian symbiosis refers to two groups coming into contact, with the result being rough economic and political equality for the two groups. While a few examples of this outcome can be found in the history of world migrations, it is rare, especially in North America. A possible example might be the migration of Scots to the English colonies in the eighteenth century. However, the most common result of migration and contact seems to be some sort of hierarchy or stratification system. Lieberson has listed two possible hierarchies that can result from intergroup contact. *Migrant superordination* occurs when the group migrating into a new territory, usually because of superior weapons and organization, imposes its will on indigenous groups. The Native American ("Indian") populations of the United States and Canada were subordinated in this fashion.

Indigenous superordination occurs when groups immigrating into a new society become subordinate to groups already there, as in black slave importation to North America.[9]

Later Adaptation Patterns

It is useful to distinguish between the initial stabilization of relations
between social groups which have come into contact and the later period
of intergroup adaptation. Beyond the initial period, the range of outcomes
of intergroup contact broadens a bit to include:

1. Continuing genocide
2. Continuing egalitarian symbiosis
3. Stratification replaced by inclusion among "Anglo-conformity" lines
4. Stratification replaced by inclusion along cultural pluralism lines
5. Continuing stratification with some acculturation, ranging from moderate to
   extreme exploitation of the subordinate race/ethnic group.

One type of outcome can be a continuing thrust by the dominant
group to kill off the subordinate group. Some Native American groups
experienced this situation until the early twentieth century. Egalitarian
symbiosis can also persist in the later period. The initial hierarchy can be
modified in the later period in the direction of full assimilation or inclusion
of the incoming migrant group within the core culture and society. This
can take two forms. In the first, inclusion in the dominant sphere is along
conformity lines, with the incoming group conforming to the dominant
group. Here rough equality is attained by surrender of most of one's heritage, though some retention of in-group ties may remain. Some have
argued that North European immigrant groups, such as Scandinavian
Americans, gained rough equality in this way. Others, in contrast, might
argue that the initial stratification can also be replaced by rough egalitarian
inclusion along cultural pluralism lines, and thus that the eventual outcome
for certain white immigrant groups (such as Irish Catholics and Jews) was
substantial socio-economic and political assimilation with retention of major
cultural and primary-group distinctiveness. That is, according to this view
adaptation or assimilation was not so complete that major ethnic distinctiveness did not remain, but the absorption trend was in essential economic
or political matters, moving in the direction of rough equality.

A fifth outcome of continuing intergroup contact is persisting racial
or ethnic subordination and stratification. The extent of the stratification
can vary, but for many nonwhite groups in the United States political and
economic inequality has remained so great that it has been described as a
type of colonialism. Even here, however, partial assimilation usually occurs
in the area of adaptation to the core culture (e.g., language).

Types of Theories

Explanatory theories in the study of racial and ethnic relations have
been concerned with patterns of migration and of adaptation. Most theories
can be classified into two categories: "order" theories and "power-conflict"

cific processes often suggested in less systematic form in earlier analyses of assimilation. Gordon distinguishes between seven different assimilation processes which occur as the general adaptation of one group to the core society proceeds:

1.	Cultural assimilation	Change of cultural patterns to those of the core society
2.	Structural assimilation	Penetration into cliques and associations of the core society at the primary-group level
3.	Marital assimilation	Significant intermarriage
4.	Identification assimilation	Development of a sense of identity linked to the core society
5.	Attitude receptional assimilation	Absence of prejudice and stereotyping
6.	Behavior receptional assimilation	Absence of intentional discrimination
7.	Civic assimilation	Absence of value and power conflict[14]

Gordon has systematized the framework suggested previously by Park. What seems to be a simple idea of assimilation is complex; different levels of assimilation are underscored. In the several chapters which follow we will find Gordon's summary of the assimilationist tradition here useful for concrete applications.

However, several modifications of this Park-Gordon model will be made. First, this typology lists structural assimilation as relating to primary group relations, as in friendship groups and kinship groups or cliques and clubs in larger organizations. It seems a serious omission not to highlight explicitly, as a separate type of structural assimilation, the movement of a new group into what sociologists term "secondary groups" in the core or host society—that is, the penetration of a new group into preexisting employing organizations, such as businesses or public bureaucracies, as well as penetration of educational and political institutions. Indeed, we will underscore the secondary-organization penetration (or lack of it) of various race and ethnic groups in the rest of this book. Penetration of the core society's secondary organizations, as in the employment sphere, does not necessarily mean penetration of the preexisting primary groups, such as friendship cliques. In addition, the dimension called "civic assimilation" is here somewhat confusing, since it includes "values," which are really part of the cultural assimilation dimension, and "power," which is really an aspect of structural assimilation at the secondary-group level.

In his later work Gordon has admitted neglecting the power and conflict issues in his model of assimilation and has proposed to bring them into the model. But his subsequent analysis of power and conflict has been brief. In one major book, for example, although he mentions in passing the different resources available to competing racial and ethnic groups and refers briefly to black-white conflict, he gives no serious attention to economic power, material resource inequalities, or capitalistic economic history in examining U.S. racial and ethnic relations. Indeed, a discussion of the fundamental class structure and inequality of U.S. capitalism is missing. The importance of these omissions will become clear later in this chapter.[15]

Nonetheless, Gordon carried assimilation analysis beyond Park's rougher formulations. Particularly important is Gordon's distinction between cultural and structural assimilation, which Park had earlier suggested. Unlike Park, who saw structural (primary group) assimilation as inevitably flowing from cultural assimilation, Gordon underscores the real possibility that this linkage may not be inevitable. While acculturation is an inevitable outcome of initial contact for Gordon, structural (primary group) assimilation or marital assimilation is not.

Focusing on the millions of European immigrants and on their adjustment to the core culture, Gordon also places an emphasis on *generational* changes. From this perspective substantial acculturation to the dominant Anglo-Saxon core culture, though partial in the first generation, has often been completed by the second or third generation for many European immigrant groups. The first generation formed protective immigrant communities and associations, but children of those first-generation immigrants were considerably more exposed to Anglo-conformity pressures, in the mass media and in the public school system.[16]

Gordon suggests that substantial assimilation along other dimensions, such as the civic, behavior-receptional, and attitude-receptional dimensions, has substantially occurred for numerous white European groups. (Most have made considerable headway in the direction of equality at the structural-secondary level, in employment and politics, although this dimension is not named and is barely touched in his discussion.) Structural assimilation at the primary-group level is another matter altogether. Indeed, the facts sometimes suggest that structural integration at the primary-group level is limited even in present-day America for certain white European immigrant groups, particularly for non-Protestant groups. Gordon introduces the idea of substantially complete cultural assimilation with structural (primary-group) pluralism as a characteristic pattern of adaptation for certain white ethnic groups in the United States, although even in that structural pluralism there is a strong tendency for merging informal ties within the three bounded religious communities, Protestant, Catholic, and Jewish.[17] He terms this limited diversity "structural pluralism," rejecting the idea that any significant cultural pluralism persists.[18]*

Other assimilation analysts have looked at the adaptive patterns of ethnic groups in a somewhat different light. A few have accented an assimilation model which questions whether Anglo-conformity cultural assimilation was actually as comprehensive as theorists like Park and Gordon

---

*Gordon does recognize the existence of an internal stratification system, even to the point of introducing the concept of "ethclass." *Ethclass* refers to groups such as lower-class Italian Americans. The various ethnic groups are composed of divisions on the basis of social status. Here we have a focus on status divisions *within* race/ethnic groups. Power-conflict theorists emphasize economic class divisions, such as those between capitalists and workers (see pp. 39–42).

pull of the old culture, which was usually strongest in the first generation, while the second generation was scissored between the parentally monitored cultural background and the new pressures in the schools and the media. Historians have written about "second generation rejection" as though there were an iron law dictating absolute cultural rejection for most of the children of immigrants. This theory has been coupled with a view of a "third generation return," the notion that what the children of immigrants rejected the grandchildren returned to. Generational differences in the assimilation process will become clear in later chapters.

A number of recent field studies have documented the persistence of distinctive white ethnic groups such as Irish Americans, Italian Americans, and Polish Americans in U.S. cities, not just in New York and Chicago, but in San Francisco, New Orleans, and Tucson as well. For example, the research by Yancey and associates in Philadelphia revealed the persistence of numerous Jewish and Catholic neighborhoods and related organizational networks. Ethnic Catholics were disproportionately concentrated in "urban villages," that is, intimate urban neighborhoods. Based on Philadelphia research, Yancey and associates have suggested the idea that ethnicity is an "emergent phenomenon"—that is, its importance in cities depends a lot on the specific social and economic situations. The time in history that a group entered the United States and the dominant industries at that time shaped how groups such as the Irish and Italians developed, determined what jobs they took, and shaped where they lived. Thus how strong, how "ethnic," their communities became was partially an effect of time of entry.[25]

Problems with Assimilation Theories

Most assimilation theorists usually have in mind as their main examples white European groups migrating more or less voluntarily. But what of the adaptation and assimilation of non-European groups beyond the initial contact stage? Some assimilation analysts include nonwhite Americans in their framework, although modest attention has been given to problems that arise from such a classification. Some analysts have argued that assimilation, cultural and structural, is the inevitable or necessary answer to the race problem in the United States—and the likely result of the long-term trend as well.

One prominent writer on race relations, Gunnar Myrdal, has argued that as a practical matter it is "to the advantage of American Negroes as individuals and as a group to become assimilated into American culture, to acquire the traits held in esteem by the dominant white Americans."[26] In Myrdal's view there is a fundamental ethical dilemma, a contrast between the democratic principles of the Declaration of Independence and the subordination of groups such as black Americans. For Myrdal this represents a "lag of public morals," a problem solved in principle but still being worked out.

Gordon has underscored the progressive cultural assimilation of black

Americans, particularly those above the poverty level, to the Anglo-Saxon core culture. However, structural (primary-group) assimilation is recognized as difficult for black Americans. More optimistically, other analysts have emphasized the progressive inclusion process, which will eventually provide nonwhites with full citizenship. Those with an assimilation or inclusion perspective have often assumed that all racial and ethnic groups, including nonwhites, desire assimilation and will, in fact, be assimilated.

Nathan Glazer and Talcott Parsons stress the egalitarianism in the institutions of the United States and the progressive emancipation of nonwhites. Full membership for black Americans seems the inevitable goal, for "the only tolerable solution to the enormous tensions lies in constituting a single societal community with full membership for all."[27] The importance of racial stratification is expected to decline as powerful, universalistic societal forces wipe out the vestiges of earlier value systems. Racial stratification is not fundamental. From this viewpoint white immigrants have desired substantial assimilation, and most have been absorbed. The same is expected to happen for such non-European groups as black Americans. In many applications of assimilation or inclusion theories to nonwhite Americans, the phrase *Anglo-Saxon core culture and society* is used in the broad sense of *white core culture and society*.

Both the traditional views of assimilation and the cultural pluralism perspective of such analysts as Andrew Greeley emphasize the cultural aspects of ethnic groups, such as language, religion, and basic values. For traditional assimilationists, ethnic characteristics are corroded by the ongoing industrialization and urbanization processes of a modern society such as the United States. Numerous social scientists have long argued that the ascribed characteristics of peoples, such as race, become less important than achieved characteristics under an industrial system. From this point of view, ethnicity must decline the longer an immigrant group stays in a highly industrial, urbanized society. However, Greeley disagrees, arguing that ethnicity has dramatically resisted eradication by ongoing industrial and urban processes.

Assimilation theories have been criticized as having an establishment bias, as not distinguishing carefully enough between what *has* happened to a given group and what the establishment at some point felt *should* have happened. For example, a number of Asian American scholars and leaders have reacted vigorously against the application of the concept "assimilation" to Asian Americans, arguing that such a concept originated in the period (1890–1925) of intense attacks by white Americans on Asian Americans. However neutral the term may seem, they argue, it was tainted from the beginning by its association with the dominant group's ideology that asserted that the only "good groups" were those which assimilated (or could assimilate) in slavish Anglo-conformity fashion. Such a criticism must be taken seriously, since assimilation ideologies have often been pressed vigorously on new groups entering. Anglo-conformity assimilation was what they "ought" to do, insofar as the dominant group permitted such assimilation.

the white and black castes were separated by a prohibition on intermarriage. Warner was also critical of the heavy emphasis on prejudice traditional in race and ethnic relations analysis. Prejudice, he believed, did not capture the systemic character or complexity of southern race patterns.[32]

Another early analyst who contributed to the emergence of a power-conflict perspective is Oliver C. Cox, a brilliant black scholar whose work has been neglected. Cox was one of the first to analyze systematically the economic distinctiveness of black slave migration and the oppressiveness of the later economic adjustment patterns of blacks. In his view racial (black-white) stratification arose out of the growth and expansion of the European economic system of profit-oriented *capitalism*. The African slave trade, beginning with Spain and Portugal, was in his view "a way of recruiting labor for the purpose of exploiting the great natural resources of America"; the color of Africans was not important, for they were chosen "simply because they were the best workers to be found for the heavy labor in the mines and plantations across the Atlantic."[33] European prejudice did not generate modern race relations. Rather, a desire for cheap labor by a profit-oriented capitalist class led to a system of race subordination. Capitalistic expansion thus accounts in large part for both the origin of white-black stratification and its initial stabilization in the United States.

Recent Power-Conflict Analysis

Since the 1960s several theorists have given greater attention to power and inequality issues. For example, Donald Noel has suggested that for the emergence of racial and ethnic stratification, three conditions must be present: ethnocentrism, competition, and differential power. Ethnocentrism (see Chapter I) means that one's own group is preferred; other groups tend to be downgraded or rejected. But ethnocentrism alone is not enough to produce racial-ethnic stratification. Around the world many groups have lived in peace with one another even though they are ethnocentric. Noel emphasizes that competition for the same resources along race-ethnic lines is also required for stratification to develop. If two groups are striving for the same land or the use of the same labor, that competition often encourages the development of inequality and hierarchy.[34]

But for Noel the most important factor in generating racial or ethnic stratification is differential power and resources. Differential power can mean that one group has greater military firepower (guns, ships, etc.) and better military organization than another, as was often the case in the early contacts between Europeans and Africans. This greater power and resources makes it possible for one group (for instance, Europeans) to establish dominance and to impose subordination on the other (for instance, Africans).

Internal Colonialism

A number of scbolars and other analysts have adopted the term *internal colonialism* to describe their model of intergroup adaptation in the United States. An emphasis on power and resource inequalities is at the heart of this model. Traditional assimilation models are inadequate to the task of describing what has happened to nonwhite Americans. It is not enough to see nonwhites as slowly assimilating, or even as cases of stalled assimilation. A basic idea here is that nonwhite Americans were brought into the emerging economic and political system initially by *force*. And subsequent adaptation was along nonegalitarian lines, with continuing elements of coercion and systematic oppression.

The internal-colonialism framework owes a debt to the analysts of "external" colonialism. Extensive analysis has been undertaken of the imperialism of European nations. In the 1950s Balandier noted the impact of capitalistic expansion on non-European peoples since the fifteenth century: "Until very recently the greater part of the world's population, not belonging to the white race (if we exclude China and Japan), knew only a status of dependency on one or another of the European colonial powers."[35] Covering hundreds of millions of individuals, external colonialism extended into Africa, Asia, and the islands of the great oceans. Raw materials from these external colonies sustained the technological development of the mother countries in Europe.[36]

External colonialism becomes internal colonialism when the control and exploitation of subordinate groups passes to dominant groups within the newly independent society, when the white colonists and settlers "run the show" themselves. Nonwhite groups entering *later* are also viewed in internal-colonialism terms. Internal colonialism emerges out of classical European colonialism and imperialism, but it takes on a life of its own. It is a system grounded in the sharp differentiation of white and nonwhite labor, in economic exploitation under capitalist auspices.[37]

The historical origin and initial stabilization of internal colonialism in North America predates the Revolutionary War. Early white-nonwhite contact, beginning with migration, is a focal point. The process of systematic subordination of non-Europeans began, according to Bailey and Flores, with "genocidal attempts by colonizing settlers to uproot native populations and force them into other regions."[38] Native Americans were killed or driven off desirable lands. Later, Asians and Pacific peoples were imported as indentured workers or annexed in an expansionist period of United States development. Slave labor from Africa was a cheap source of labor for capital accumulation in both the pre- and postrevolutionary situations.

Robert Blauner, a colonialism theorist, notes that agriculture in the South depended on black labor; in the Southwest, Mexican agricultural development was taken over by force by European settlers; and later agricultural development was based to a substantial degree on cheap Mexican labor coming into what was once northern Mexico.[39] Moreover, groups such as the Japanese and Hawaiians have been brought in as contract labor, a process connected with the fact that their homelands were United States possessions. Bailey and Flores argue that the "colonial expansionism by which the U.S. absorbed vast territories paved the way for the incorporation of its nonwhite colonial labor forces."[40] In this process of exploiting the labor of nonwhite people, who were made slaves or were paid low wages,

jobs that the dominant groups in the society are not eager to do. For example, in the face of exclusion from mainstream employment, many Jewish and Japanese Americans became small-scale peddlers, tailors, restaurant operators, or gardeners. Thus these groups occupy "a distinctive class position that is of special use to the ruling [capitalist] class." They "act as a go-between to society's subordinate classes."[44]

In this position "middleman minorities," such as the Jewish merchants, often become the targets of hostility from less well-off groups, such as poor blacks. Pre-existing ethnic solidarity supports the small-scale trading, but the trading also reinforces ethnic solidarity. Strong ethnic bonds make the "middleman" group a more effective competitor. Yet even white Anglo-Saxon capitalists may develop hostility toward a white immigrant "middleman" minority which is a too-effective competitor. Thus Jewish Americans have suffered from the negative views of the better-off Anglo-Saxon merchants, who had the power to discriminate against Jews, as well as from poor blacks who dealt with Jews as landlords and merchants.

Recurring Themes in Power-Conflict Theories

Even though power-conflict theories are more diverse than assimilation theories, there are a number of recurring themes:

1. A central concern for racial and ethnic inequalities in power and resources
2. An emphasis on the economic roots of racial inequalities and hierarchies
3. A major concern with the economic history and class structure (for instance, capitalists versus workers) of capitalism
4. A rejection of the idea of values shared across major racial lines
5. An emphasis on value and group conflict.

Let us examine these themes.

Most power-conflict theories emphasize racial and ethnic inequalities and the deep-lying roots of these inequalities in the U.S. economy. Assimilation theories tend to neglect the economic roots of today's race-ethnic hierarchies. Assimilation theorists are more concerned with cultural adaptations (changes in language, dress, and values) and with primary-group adaptation (interracial friendship ties and intermarriage) than with adaptation in the economic and political spheres. Assimilation theorists tend to neglect or play down the fact that nonwhites, such as black Americans, have remained in disproportionate numbers in the "dirty work" sectors of the economy for centuries, while white (ethnic) immigrants have tended to move out of those sectors in a few decades. When they do deal with employment issues, assimilation theorists tend to see the situations of blacks and other nonwhites as similar to those of earlier white immigrants. In contrast, most power-conflict theories recognize the persisting, deep roots of black and other nonwhite subordination in U.S. society.

White domination of Afro-Americans, for example, has its roots in the expansion of capitalism around the world in the fifteenth through nineteenth centuries. Expansionist in orientation, white British merchants pursued overseas colonization. Robert Allen argues that, wherever capitalism went, the native population was reorganized into a capitalist labor system, with an organized, subordinate work force pressed into plantations, mining operations, and factories. Local self-sufficient agriculture was turned into commercial agriculture for export; native peoples were moved and placed on plantations or in mines; forced work, including slavery, was the rule. Allen notes that "the colonized societies were forcibly brought into the worldwide system of commodity circulation, contributing their economic 'surplus' to the growing capital of Europe."[45] British colonies in the Americas had their origin in violence and exploitation. The relations between whites and Afro-Americans were exploitative because of the labor needs of a rapidly expanding capitalist system.

External European colonialism became locally controlled when the control and exploitation of less powerful nonwhite groups passed to dominant white groups within newly independent societies, as in the United States when the white colonists and settlers came to "run the show" themselves. In the United States the landed slaveowners of the preindustrial agricultural South, together with northern shipping and trading interests, created a racist social structure with black Americans at the bottom. Moreover, even the (later) industrial capital in the northern United States came, in part, from the merchant capital which had been gained from trade in cotton, tobacco, and slaves.[46]

Many power-conflict theories emphasize this important political-economic background of capitalism and the class relations and class conflict which this capitalistic system creates. The classes emphasized in these theories can be diagrammed as follows.

1. Capitalists—that small group of people who control the means of production (such as factories and offices) and who buy the labor of many others
2. Managers—that modest-sized group of people who work for the capitalists but who have been granted control over the work of others
3. Petit bourgeoisie—that small group of traders and merchants who control their own businesses and who do most of their work themselves, thus buying little of the labor power of others
4. The working class—that huge group of blue-collar and white-collar workers who sell their labor power to employers in return for wages and salaries (and who do not own or control the means of production).

The dominant class in the U.S. political-economic system is the capitalist class.

The working class is further divided into major fractions along racial lines. Thus black and other nonwhite workers have often filled the least desirable of the jobs carried out by working-class people. They have been the poorest fraction of the working class. Since the days of slavery, several groups have benefited from the presence of a large group of subordinate black workers. Large capitalist employers benefit from the lower wages of black workers and from the divisions created between black and white workers, divisions reducing the likelihood of large working-class unions.

conditions encountered by black immigrants moving up from the South to the cities of the North. Recent research by Theodore Hershberg, William Yancey, and their associates has underscored the importance of a power-conflict approach emphasizing economic roots and deeplying inequalities. Their research strongly suggests that economic conditions at the *time of entry* into cities and the level of racism at that time made the experiences of blacks far more oppressive and difficult than those of the white ethnic groups in Northern cities. In the case of white immigrant groups, and of their children and grandchildren, group mobility was possible because

1. Most arrived at a point in time when jobs were available, when capitalism was expanding and opportunities were more abundant
2. Most faced far less severe employment and housing discrimination than blacks did
3. Most found housing, however inadequate, reasonably near the workplaces.[56]

In the critical periods of white immigration most major U.S. cities (for example, New York, Philadelphia, Boston, and Chicago) were rapidly industrializing. Central cities were expanding centers of manufacturing. Factories were booming. Blue-collar jobs were increasing and available, if not plentiful, in this critical period of industrial capitalism. Upward mobility was possible. It was into these booming areas that many European immigrants migrated. In the mid-nineteenth century Irish and German immigrants were attracted to cities, where most found jobs in the industrializing economy or in supporting service sectors. This was also a period of expansion in government jobs, so it is not surprising that groups such as Irish immigrants moved into government. And these white immigrants could live near their workplaces. Research on cities such as Philadelphia has made it clear that Irish and German immigrants were clustered into neighborhoods with other immigrants, but that they did not live in highly segregated Irish or German ghettos. Half the people in such areas where they lived were not of their own ethnic background. They were not nearly as segregated from the native white population as blacks were then or now.[57]

In the period extending from 1890 to 1930, newer immigrant groups (such as the Italians, Poles, and Russian Jews) came in large numbers to the cities, sometimes to the same cities as earlier immigrant groups, sometimes to newer cities emerging in this period. Central to the location decisions was a desire to go where expanding job opportunities were. One recent study notes that "the Italian concentration in construction and the Polish in steel were related to the expansion of these industries as the groups arrived."[58] And Jewish involvement in the textile industry was not accidental. When Jewish immigrants entered in large numbers around 1900, the clothing industry was moving into a large-scale mass production stage with plenty of low-wage jobs and chances for small-scale entrepreneurs. The new immigrants often resided within a mile or so of their workplaces, many of them crowded into tenement housing. Capitalistic workplaces were becoming larger and more concentrated in cities, thus encouraging immigrants to settle in congested residential areas near their employment.

However, as American capitalism became ever more concentrated in ever larger corporations, transportation systems changed to reflect the needs of those companies. Many white ethnic Americans, over the next few decades, followed industrial plants to suburbs. This left central cities with a disproportionate number of lower-wage employers. It was into this new employment situation that nonwhite Americans—blacks, Puerto Ricans, Chicanos, and Native Americans—moved in the growing waves of migration after World War II. Often many of the best job opportunities had moved away. Thus the economic situation for nonwhites was (and is) quite different from the situation for large segments of the white immigrant groups. Nonwhites took over areas abandoned by industry and by the more affluent children of the earlier German, Irish, and Italian immigrants. While the earlier waves of European immigrants found varying employment opportunities—sometimes good, sometimes declining—their opportunity structure was far better than that of blacks and other nonwhites four or five decades later. Moreover, many blacks already in the cities from 1880 to 1920, prior to the great waves of black migration, often lived near the new manufacturing jobs being created in the factories, but they were rarely hired. In Philadelphia, for example, blacks were excluded from the better-paying jobs; and they were even forced out of their traditional unskilled jobs, which became the preserves of new white immigrants.[59]

Nonwhites have also faced much greater discrimination in housing and schooling than did earlier immigrant groups. For a century or more, racial segregation in housing has been more severe for nonwhites than for white immigrants. A major Philadelphia study found the following segregation indexes (the higher the number, the greater the segregation) for the years 1850 to 1970 for several urban immigrant groups relative to the native-born whites in the city (an index number of 40 or more means very substantial segregation):

	1850	1880	1930	1940	1950	1970
Blacks	47	52	61	68	71	75
Irish-born	30	32	28	32	29	n.a.
German-born	33	36	32	35	31	n.a.

Clearly, the black population in Philadelphia was very segregated from native-born whites in every year listed above, while the Irish and German immigrants were much less segregated than blacks even in the first generation. And, strikingly, the black population was more segregated in 1970 than in any previous year.[60]

The view that urban blacks are much like the earlier white immigrant groups is wrong. Black immigrants in the decades after World War II differed dramatically in their structural conditions and historical experiences from white groups. First, the white immigrants faced a much better economic opportunity structure. They arrived when the expanding capitalist-directed industry was expanding in core cities. Later, blacks and other nonwhites arrived when many jobs, particularly better-paying jobs, were

[2]William M. Newman, *American Pluralism* (New York: Harper & Row, 1973), pp. 30–38.

[3]See ibid., p. 50.

[4]Ernest A. T. Barth and Donald L. Noel, "Conceptual Frameworks for the Analysis of Race Relations: An Evaluation," *Social Forces* 50 (March, 1972): 336.

[5]Charles Tilly, *Migration to an American City* (Wilmington: University of Delaware Agricultural Experiment Station, 1965).

[6]Barth and Noel, "Conceptual Frameworks," pp. 337–39.

[7]R. A. Schermerhorn, *Comparative Ethnic Relations* (New York: Random House, 1970), p. 98.

[8]Ibid., p. 99.

[9]Stanley Lieberson, "A Societal Theory of Racial and Ethnic Relations," *American Sociological Review* 26 (December 1961): 902–10.

[10]Robert E. Park, *Race and Culture* (Glencoe, Ill.: Free Press, 1950), p. 150. See also p. 103.

[11]Robert E. Park and Ernest W. Burgess, *Introduction to the Science of Society* (Chicago: University of Chicago Press, 1924), p. 735.

[12]Janice R. Hullum, "Robert E. Park's Theory of Race Relations" (M.A. thesis, University of Texas, 1973), pp. 81–88; Park and Burgess, *Introduction to the Science of Society*, p. 760.

[13]Milton M. Gordon, *Assimilation in American Life* (New York: Oxford University Press, 1964), pp. 72–73.

[14]Ibid., p. 71.

[15]Milton M. Gordon, *Human Nature, Class, and Ethnicity* (New York: Oxford University Press, 1978), pp. 67–89.

[16]Gordon, *Assimilation in American Life*, pp. 78–108.

[17]See Will Herberg, *Protestant—Catholic—Jew*, revised edition (Garden City, N.Y.: Doubleday Anchor Books, 1960).

[18]Gordon, *Assimilation in American Life*, p. 159. See also pp. 110–11.

[19]Milton R. Konvitz, "Horace Meyer Kallen (1882–1974): Philosopher of the Hebraic American Idea," in *American Jewish Year Book, 1974–1975*, ed. Morris Fine and Milton Himmelfarb (Philadelphia: Jewish Publication Society of America, 1974), pp. 65–67; Horace M. Kallen, *Culture and Democracy in the United States* (New York: Boni and Liveright, 1924), pp. 124–25.

[20]Gordon, *Assimilation in American Life*, pp. 141–59.

[21]Nathan Glazer and Daniel P. Moynihan, *Beyond the Melting Pot* (Cambridge: Harvard University Press and MIT Press, 1963).

[22]Andrew M. Greeley, *Ethnicity in the United States* (New York: John Wiley, 1974), p. 293.

[23]Ibid., pp. 295–301.

[24]Ibid., p. 309.

[25]Ibid., pp. 290–317; William L. Yancey, E. P. Ericksen, and R. N. Juliani, "Emergent Ethnicity: A Review and Reformulation," *American Sociological Review* 41 (June 1976): 391–93.

[26]Gunnar Myrdal, *An American Dilemma* (New York: McGraw-Hill, 1964), 2:929.

[27]Talcott Parsons, "Full Citizenship for the Negro American? A Sociological Problem," in *The Negro American*, ed. Talcott Parsons and Kenneth B. Clark (Boston: Houghton Mifflin, 1965–66), p. 740.

[28]Gordon, *Human Nature, Class, and Ethnicity*, pp. 73–78.

[29]Pierre L. van den Berghe, *The Ethnic Phenomenon* (New York: Elsevier, 1981).

[30]Edna Bonacich, "Class Approaches to Ethnicity and Race," *The Insurgent Sociologist* 10 (Fall 1980): 11.

[31]W. Lloyd Warner, "Introduction," in Allison Davis et al., *Deep South* (Chicago: University of Chicago Press, 1941), pp. 4–6: W. Lloyd Warner and Leo Srole, *The Social Systems of American Ethnic Groups* (New Haven: Yale University Press, 1945), pp. 295–96.

[32]cf. Robert Blauner, *Racial Oppression in America* (New York: Harper & Row, 1972), p. 7.

[33]Oliver C. Cox, *Caste, Class, and Race* (Garden City, N.Y.: Doubleday, 1948), p. 332.

[34]Donald Noel, "A Theory of the Origin of Ethnic Stratification," *Social Problems* 16 (Fall 1968): 157–72.

[35]G. Balandier, "The Colonial Situation: A Theoretical Approach," in *Social Change*, ed. Immanuel Wallerstein (New York: John Wiley, 1966), p. 35.

[36]Ronald Bailey and Guillermo Flores, "Internal Colonialism and Racial Minorities in the U.S.: An Overview," in *Structures of Dependency*, ed. Frank Bonilla and Robert Girling (Stanford, Calif.: privately published by Stanford faculty-student seminar, 1973), pp. 151–53.

[37]Pablo Gonzalez-Casanova, "Internal Colonialism and National Development," in *Latin American Radicalism*, ed. Irving L. Horowitz et al. (New York: Random House, 1969), p. 130; Bailey and Flores; "Internal Colonialism," p. 156.

[38]Bailey and Flores, "Internal Colonialism," p. 156.

[39]Blauner, *Racial Oppression in America*, p. 55. This analysis of internal colonialism draws throughout on Blauner's provocative discussion.

[40]Bailey and Flores, "Internal Colonialism," p. 150.

[41]Guillermo B. Flores, "Race and Culture in the Internal Colony: Keeping the Chicano in His Place," in Bonilla and Girling, *Structures of Dependency*, p. 192.

[42]Joan W. Moore, "American Minorities and 'New Nation' Perspectives," *Pacific Sociological Review* 19 (October 1976): 448–55.

[43]Bonacich, "Class Approaches to Ethnicity and Race," p. 14.

[44]Ibid., pp. 14–15.

[45]Robert L. Allen, *Reluctant Reformers* (Washington, D.C.: Howard University Press, 1974), p. 255.

[46]Michael Perelman, *Farming for Profit in a Hungry World* (New York: Universe Books, 1977), p. 26.

[47]See Parsons, "Full Citizenship for the Negro American?".

[48]Shibutani and Kwan, *Ethnic Stratification*, p. 242: Robin M. Williams, Jr., "Prejudice and Society," in *The American Negro Reference Book*, ed. John P. Davis (Englewood Cliffs, N.J.: Prentice-Hall, 1966), p. 728.

[49]Newman, *American Pluralism*, p. 110.

[50]Ralf Dahrendorf, *Class and Class Conflict in Industrial Society* (Stanford, Calif.: Stanford University Press, 1959), pp. 135, 183–222.

[51]R. A. Schermerhorn, *Comparative Ethnic Relations* (New York: Random House, 1970), pp. 81–87.

[52]Irving Kristol, "The Negro Today Is Like the Immigrant of Yesterday," *New York Times Magazine*, September 11, 1966, pp. 50–51, 124–42.

[53]Nathan Glazer, "Blacks and Ethnic Groups: The Difference, and the Political Difference It Makes," *Social Problems* 18 (Spring 1971): 459.

[54]Ibid., pp. 458–59.

[55]*New York Times*, November 5, 1978, p. 6; as reported in Theodore Hershberg et al., "A Tale of Three Cities: Blacks, Immigrants, and Opportunity in Philadelphia: 1850–1880, 1930, 1970," in *Philadelphia*, ed. Theodore Hershberg (New York: Oxford University Press, 1981), p. 486.

[56]Ibid., pp. 462–64.

[57]Ibid., pp. 473–83.

[58]Yancey, Ericksen, and Juliani, "Emergent Ethnicity," p. 393.

[59]Hershberg, "A Tale of Three Cities," pp. 469–80.

[60]Ibid., p. 468.

English Americans
and the
Anglo-Saxon Core Culture
CHAPTER 3

Cleveland Amory tells a story about prominent English families in Massachusetts. A Chicago banking firm wrote a Boston investment company for a letter of recommendation on a young Bostonian. Eloquently praising the young man's virtues, the company's letter pointed out that his mother was a member of the Lowell family, his father a member of the Cabot family, and his other relatives members of other prominent New England families. The bank wrote back, thanking them for the letter, but noting that this was not the type of letter of recommendation they had in mind. They replied, "We were not contemplating using Mr. _____ for breeding purposes."[1] Apocryphal or not, this story illustrates the elite status of the "proper Bostonians." Their wealth and prominence in the history of New England are suggested.

The story underscores the importance of inbreeding, descent, and interlocking family ties over generations. Ethnicity involves cultural or nationality characteristics which are distinguished by the group itself or by important outgroups, but lines of descent are the channels for passing along ethnic characteristics to later generations.

Who are these English Americans? What is their significance? The phrase English Americans itself may sound a bit strange. We hear discussions of Mexican Americans, of black Americans, even of Irish Catholics, but few speak of English Americans. One reason for this is that other labels are used to designate the group. Perhaps the most common are "Anglo-Saxon" and "White-Anglo-Saxon Protestant." Although in-depth analyses of this group are rare, numerous authors have commented on the central importance of the Anglo-Saxons. For example, a prominent historian of immigration takes the impact of the Anglo-Saxon group for granted: "Our American culture, our speech, our laws are basically Anglo-Saxon in origin."[2]

Milton Gordon's view of the shaping impact of this first large group of European immigrants on the *core culture* of the United States has already been noted: "If there is anything in American life which can be described as an overall American culture which serves as a reference point for immigrants and their children, it can best be described . . . as the middle-class cultural patterns of, largely, white Protestant, Anglo-Saxon origins."[3] These comments suggest the importance of the core culture in the adaptation process faced by later immigrant groups. To take another example, Herberg has noted the influence of this Anglo-Saxon group on the self-image of Americans: "It is the *Mayflower*, John Smith, Davy Crockett, George Washington, and Abraham Lincoln that define the American's self-image, and this is true whether the American in question is a descendant of the Pilgrims or the grandson of an immigrant from southeastern Europe."[4] This is the result of an essentially one-way cultural assimilation process, whereby everyone adapts to the English core culture.

Two troubling problems come to mind here. One is the question of why no social science analyst has undertaken a comprehensive analysis of these English Americans, the group which is of paramount importance. Why has this English American group been among the most neglected? The answer is unclear. A second question regards the term *Anglo-Saxon*. Numerous sources use the term loosely for persons or institutions of English extraction. In one sense, Anglo-Saxon is an inadequate designation for those immigrants who came from England and their descendants. The term derives etymologically from the names for the Germanic tribes, the Angles and the Saxons, which came to the geographical area now called England in the fifth and sixth centuries A.D. But there were other people there already, the Celts; and the Germanic tribes were followed by the Normans from France. By the time of the American colonies the English settlers were the result of several centuries of fusion of nationality types.[5] So, at best, the term Anglo-Saxon is shorthand for complex heritages.

Some authors use Anglo-Saxon and such related terms as "old-stock Americans" in two broader senses. The terms are sometimes used in a loose way to include British groups other than the English—the Scots and the Welsh. In addition, certain other closely related white north European groups which substantially assimilated to the English core culture—particularly Scandinavian and German Protestants—are sometimes included in the Anglo-Saxon terminology. In any event, when the terms Anglo-Saxon and British are used, English Americans and the core culture they generated are often at the heart of the discussion.

THE ENGLISH MIGRATIONS

Some Basic Data

What was the origin of those English Americans whose company now numbers in the tens of millions? As every schoolboy and schoolgirl probably knows, it was migration. Although the English were not the first to come to North America, they were the first to colonize in large numbers. Only rough estimates exist for the number of English migrants prior to the early 1800s, because no records were kept. By the early eighteenth century there were approximately 350,000 English and Welsh colonists in North America. At the time of the Revolution the number of British colonists in North America had increased to between one and two million.[6]

Much of this growth seems to have been from colonial birth rates rather than from migration. Migration to the American colonies was very heavily English until 1700, after which time English migration receded. Migration remained at modest levels in the few decades after the Revolution. "Most people who have studied the history of the period and whatever local records were available," note the Taeubers, "believe that something less than a quarter of a million white immigrants entered the country in the 30 years from 1790 to 1819."[7] Most of these came from Britain and Germany.

Nearly three million English persons migrated to the United States between 1820 and 1950, with the two decades between 1880 and 1900 seeing the heaviest flow. The English migration to the colonies, and later to the United States, was one of the largest population flows in this period. The English were not only the first sizeable European group in what was to become the United States; they continued to be an important part of the migration flow until World War I.[8]

The First Colonial Settlements

The migration of the English settlers in the seventeenth century, together with the establishment of settlements, was different from later European migration streams. This migration can be viewed as *colonization*. Colonization, unlike other types of migration, involves the subordination of native people. Unlike the French and Spanish, who also explored North America, the English had come to establish permanent colonies. A range of economic interests was involved.[9] The colonies developed under the auspices of the English king and his merchants and were often viewed as an extension of the mother country.

Why did the English Crown become interested in North American colonies? Why were colonies developed at all? Various explanations for colonial development were put forth by English advocates in the colonial period. Commercial objectives were often mentioned; much attention was given to the need for trading posts and for new sources of raw materials. Emphasis was placed on the creation of new markets for English goods.[10] Other colonial advocates emphasized Protestant missionary objectives, the search for a passage to Asia, the need to stop Spanish and French expansion, and the need for some place for surplus English population and for criminals and other undesirables. Nonetheless, the central objective of colonization was economic gain: "What England primarily looked for in colonies was neither expansion of territory *per se* nor overseas aggregations of Englishmen, but goods and markets."[11]

The colonization process had dire consequences for Native American ("Indian") tribes. Geographical expansion proceeded rapidly. Native

Americans were perceived as a threat. The French were interested in the fur trade, but the English wanted land for economic colonization and farming.[12] At first, some attempt was made to convert the "heathen" natives and certain tribes were treated in a friendly fashion. The settlers, small in numbers at first, soon gained superiority over the Native Americans, forcing them into frontier areas or killing them.[13] Few settlers seemed concerned over the genocidal consequences of colonialism. In Massachusetts a plague had wiped out many Native Americans prior to the *Mayflower*'s landing. The famous minister Cotton Mather commented: "The woods were almost cleared of those pernicious creatures, to make room for a better growth."[14]

The English established large settlements in North America. The first joint-stock companies were formed by merchants under the auspices of James I of England in the early 1600s. The southern company settled Jamestown, a colony where the primary goal was economic. The settlers were employees of the company. This was the English colony which bought Africans from a Dutch ship in 1619, laying the foundation for racial oppression. The northern settlement was under the auspices of another royal company. In 1620 its first settlers took root in the Massachusetts area; these settlers, the famous Pilgrims, were separatists who had seceded from the Anglican Church.[15]

Both settlements nearly expired in the early years because of disease and starvation. The development of tobacco agriculture and the granting of private property to settlers saved Jamestown. Thousands of English immigrants came to Jamestown, and a healthy and vigorous agricultural settlement gradually developed. The Plymouth colony managed to survive with the aid of friendly Native Americans. By 1640 there were thousands of English colonists in the New England area. It was the New England colonists who first regarded themselves as English *Americans*.[16]

What was the racial and ethnic mix of this colonial population? As late as the 1740s the English still made up the majority of immigrants to North America.[17] By the mid-eighteenth century immigration from England had become less central. The fears of overpopulation and the political dissent which had originally fueled the large outmigration had lessened by the late seventeenth century in England because of better economic conditions, and outmigration was now discouraged. The Irish and the Germans came to dominate the migration flow by the 1760s.[18]

The American Historical Association has developed estimates of the national stocks of the white population in 1790 based on a surname analysis:[19]

English	60.1%
Scotch, Scotch-Irish	14.0
German	8.6
Irish (Free State)	3.6
Dutch	3.1
French, Swedish	3.0
Other	7.6
Total	100.0%

Estimates give the English the primary position, with a significant proportion of the population composed of other British groups. In most states the English constituted more than half the white population. Of course, the largest single group in the South was the black African group. Slaves made up one-fifth of the total population in revolutionary America.[20]

The Nineteenth-Century Migration: Capital and Workers

There was a modest flow of immigrants from the British Isles and the rest of Europe in the period between the Revolution and 1820, but the century following 1820 was the century of the greatest Atlantic migration in history. The English and other British contributions to this nineteenth-century migration have been neglected.[21] This neglect underscores the ease with which the later English immigrant blended in. Nearly 3 million came between 1820 and 1950. Yet by the 1910s the great English migration stream had declined significantly.[22]

Economic motives were of paramount importance for the nineteenth-century immigrants. There were numerous depressions, and thus widespread unemployment, in the textile industry, the largest employer in Britain. Emigration came to be seen as one solution to unemployment.[23] The skills of these workers facilitated their mobility. As with their predecessors, this group attained a relatively successful position in a country just beginning to industrialize. Their skills spurred the dramatic industrialization in the nineteenth century. In the United States the English received high wages in the iron and copper mining and silk industries; together with other British groups, English workers were top wage earners in many other industries. They moved in large numbers from British manufacturing and mining industry to comparable positions in American industry.[24]

When English workers were eventually displaced by machines or later immigrant groups, they often moved up into managerial and technical positions. A similar pattern occurred with English and other British workers in the mining and metal industries. With their help, American industry had surpassed the industry of the mother industrial society. The English immigrants were not just skilled blue-collar workers. Some were unskilled laborers; some were professionals; some were farmers. But all of these workers were welcomed and generally did well.[25]

Was adaptation to the core culture difficult for these English immigrants? The ease with which many moved into industry indicates the swiftness of assimilation at the level of secondary organizations. Their skills kept most from the poverty that usually faced other immigrants. Larger numbers moved into clerical and professional jobs than was the case with most other white immigrant groups. Acculturation was easy for the English immigrants. Facility with the English language meant they would be more readily hired where the ability to speak English was important. These English immigrants avoided most of the anti-immigrant agitation others faced. Indeed, new English immigrants often shared the ethnocentric or racist views of previous English settlers, including the stereotyping of Jews, hostility toward blacks, and hatred of southern Europeans. The English immigrants encountered relatively little prejudice or discrimination. Structural assimilation in the primary relations sphere, to use the concept developed by Milton Gordon, proceeded rapidly for the new English immigrants. Intermarriage between these immigrants and citizens was common. Kinship and friendship ties were easily developed. Enforced residential segregation did not develop for these immigrants.[26]

Ties to the homeland were immediately severed. The monarch was widely revered. British taverns flourished in American cities. English newspapers were published for immigrants, although they seldom lasted more than a year or two. Charitable societies such as the St. George's Society were created to aid destitute English settlers, and there were also social clubs. However, the organizations for preserving English culture were fewer in number and less exclusive than similar organizations among other immigrant groups. Many of the children of these immigrants left the immigrant organizations. Berthoff quotes a young son of a Chicago Englishman who was reviewing the Revolutionary War for his father: "You had the King's army, and we were only a lot of farmers, but *we* thrashed you!"[27] Here the pinnacle of identificational assimilation has been reached, even in the second generation; the son's identity is English *American*.

Twentieth-Century Migration

Smaller numbers of English immigrants have come to the United States in the decades since 1910—only 11,000 a year in the late 1920s. In the 1930s, indeed, more people returned to England than came in as immigrants. Between the 1950s and the 1980s one distinctive aspect of English migration has been the so-called "brain drain." A large proportion of immigrants in this period was composed of managerial, professional, and technical workers, including physicians and academics. While relatively small in numbers compared with the immigrants of earlier decades, these immigrants generated a controversy in Great Britain over the "brain drain," the costly loss of highly skilled workers.[28]

Other Protestant Immigrants

Because the term Anglo-Saxon has been used to include not only the English but also the Scots, the Welsh, and even Scandinavian and German groups, we need to touch briefly on these groups. The Welsh entered the colonies in relatively small numbers, beginning in the early 1600s. The total number who came has been estimated at just over 100,000, with many going into industrial jobs or into farming. The first generations retained their customs, language, and distinctive communities, but they were soon assimilated to the core society, becoming a part of the white Protestant mainstream.[29]

In terms of power the Scots were perhaps the closest to the dominant English group from the first century onward, although they would feel Anglo-conformity pressures. Scottish Highlanders and Lowlanders, as well as Scottish immigrants by way of Ireland, came to the new nation in its formative centuries. By the late eighteenth century there were perhaps 250,000 Scots, a number to be supplemented over the next century by three-quarters of a million migrants. Many were merchants, clerks, soldiers, and middle-income farmers in the colonial period, although the majority probably were servants, laborers, and poor farmers. Assimilation to the English core culture accompanied inclusion in the economic system, so that by the early 1800s the Scots had probably moved up to near parity with the English. They too became an important segment of the white Protestant mainstream.

German immigrants made up the largest non-British group. Germans were perhaps 9 percent of the colonists in the eighteenth century; in the century after 1820 several million would come to the United States. Some were Catholics and Jews, but the largest proportion was Protestant. Many became farmers, laborers, merchants, and, later, industrial workers. Over several generations much, but by no means all, of the German culture was reshaped by the well-established Anglo-American patterns. Cultural assimilation, together with substantial mobility in the economic and political spheres, came in a few generations for these Protestants. Yet some distinctiveness did persist, in the form of German communities.

Scandinavian immigrants, such as Swedes and Norwegians, did not enter in really large numbers until the 1870s and 1880s. Perhaps two million came. Many immigrants entered as farmers and laborers, but the next generation moved up into skilled blue collar and white collar positions. Here too substantial assimilation to the core culture and society came in a few generations, and much of their ethnic distinctiveness was lost as they became part of the Anglo-Saxon Protestant mainstream. Yet some community distinctiveness persists to the present day.

These Protestant groups, together with other groups, assimilated relatively rapidly to the dominant core culture, particularly in the cultural, economic, and political spheres. Although maintaining some communal distinctiveness, such as in informal group life, most became part of the Protestant mainstream by the early twentieth century.

Yet this assimilation was not always peaceful. In earlier periods some of these Protestant groups suffered physical attacks and cultural pressure from the established English group. By the nineteenth century English Americans were intermarrying with other British Americans, some even with Scandinavians and Germans. So it is not surprising that by the early twentieth century the "white Anglo-Saxon Protestant" designation increasingly came to blur over the distinction between the original Anglo-Saxons, the English, and those later groups which had substantially assimilated to the English core culture and society.

ANGLO-SAXON PROTESTANT REACTIONS TO IMMIGRANTS

Not all immigrant groups had the easy reception that nineteenth-century English immigrants had. Established groups, though descendants of earlier immigrants, were often hostile to new immigrant groups. The most important group was the English Americans, although they were by no means the only northern European group which played a role in anti-immigration agitation, or "nativism," as it is often termed. Nativism goes back far into American history, but the term was apparently first used in the 1840s and 1850s. Nativists were nationalists who saw themselves as the only true Americans. Higham notes three themes in reactions to immigrants: anti-Catholic, antiforeign, and racist (Anglo-Saxonism).[30]

At an early stage some immigrants were discouraged from entering the colonies—certain religious groups (such as Catholics), paupers, and convicts.[31] In the earliest period, concern was centered on religious and moral desirability. Historically, antiforeign sentiment surfaced first in actions and practices directed primarily at non-English immigrant groups. French Huguenot refugees are one example. Virginia tried to prohibit their immigration, and other colonies placed restrictions on them. At least one Huguenot community was violently attacked.[32]

The Huguenots were followed by the Irish and Germans as targets. As Jordon notes, "in the early years Englishmen treated the increasingly numerous settlers from other European countries, especially Scottish and Irish servants, with condescension and frequently with exploitative brutality."[33] Many resented the intrusion of new peoples onto English soil. In Virginia and Maryland discriminatory duties were placed on non-English servants coming into the colonies. In the rank order of discrimination, the Scottish faced the least, the Irish more, and the blacks the most. The Catholics among the Irish were "doubly damned as foreign and Papist."[34]

There was some ambivalence about the new immigrants. On the one hand, immigrants provided needed labor, ship captains profited from immigration, and new immigrants were encouraged to settle in frontier areas to increase frontier security. On the other hand, immigrants were often seen as a threat, and English American mobs occasionally tried to prevent their landing. In 1734 a "Scotch-Irish" Presbyterian church was destroyed by a mob in Worcester, Massachusetts.[35]

Fear of Foreigners

Antiforeign sentiment took legal form in the late 1700s with Federalist concern for immigrant radicalism and fear of the growth of Jeffersonian Democrats who were supported by non-British immigrants. The 1798 Alien Act empowered the president to deport immigrants considered a threat to the new nation. The period of residence required for citizenship was raised from two to five years in 1795 and to fourteen years in 1798. Attempts were also made to set an exorbitant fee for naturalization. These strategies were designed to limit the political power of the new immigrants.[36]

Numerous attempts were made to reduce the influence of foreigners by pressuring them to assimilate to the English core institutions. When Benjamin Franklin set up a Pennsylvania school in the 1740s, he was concerned with the many foreigners who did not know the language and customs.[37] A Swedish Moravian minister visiting the colonies in 1745 complained of the interaction of Swedes with the English: "The English are evidently swallowing up the people and the Swedish language is so corrupted, that if I did not know the English, it would be impossible to understand the language of my dear Sweden."[38]

The pressure of the English language was great, accelerating the acculturation process for many northern European immigrant groups. Homogeneity was clearly the goal of the English founding fathers and prominent educators of the eighteenth century. George Washington believed in a homogeneous citizenry. Thomas Jefferson and Benjamin Rush expected those who were educated to fit into a culturally homogeneous mass of citizens. But such unity could only be had by the subordination of other ethnic identities to that of the core society.[39]

Anti-Catholic sentiment was at the core of nativist agitation. The Irish and German influx of the 1840s and 1850s generated a burst of agitation, including a variety of secret societies seeking to combat immigration and Catholicism, sometimes termed the Know-Nothing movement. (When questioned, supposedly members of these societies would say, "I don't know nothing.") Some have viewed this movement as a Puritan revival because of its concern for the moral training of immigrants. In the 1850s avowed and suspected Know-Nothings were elected to state legislatures, Congress, and state executive offices. Know-Nothings stimulated numerous violent attacks against immigrants and Catholics, attacks which apparently had some negative impact on the immigration flow itself.[40]

Race-oriented nativism was a theme developed in the second half of the nineteenth century, with other north European Protestants now joining in with the English Americans. From this perspective American development was seen as the perfect example of what could be accomplished by the Anglo-Saxon "race." Higham notes the source of these notions: "By another irony, the Americans who attributed the uniqueness and distinction of their nation to the Anglo-Saxon race were simply echoing the prior claims of the English. Proud appeals to Anglo-Saxon origins and ancestors came into vogue in England in the seventeenth and eighteenth centuries among the champions of Parliament."[41]

This Anglo-Saxonism, arising in the United States by the 1840s, was picked up by the expansionists who lusted after Mexican land in California and Texas. The vigorous thrust into those areas was seen as directed and legitimated by a racial mandate to colonize the inferior races. One expansionist commented as follows: "The Mexican race now see in the fate of the aborigines of the north, their own inevitable destiny. They must amalgamate or be lost in the superior vigor of the Anglo-Saxon race, or they must utterly perish."[42] Anglo-Saxonism was to play an important role in racist thought in the decades after the Civil War, for it provided the rationalization for U.S. imperialistic efforts in places like the Philippines.

The upper classes in the United States became a stronghold of the ideology of Anglo-Saxonism after the Civil War. One influence, "scientific" historians in England, argued for the superiority of the Anglo-Saxon background which lay behind England's greatness. Anglo-Saxons were viewed as God's Chosen People. There was an Anglo-Saxon school in the United States among social scientists, whose guiding idea was that democratic institutions in this country had come from England, whose institutions had in turn derived in part from early Germanic tribes.[43] These social scientists were convinced that English ways, institutions, and language were the most civilized in the world. American intellectual thought came under the influence of social Darwinism, replete with notions of racism based on "survival of the fittest." There was a strong movement to expand the teaching of the Anglo-Saxon language in colleges and universities, with some suggestion it should be taught at lower levels of public education. One prominent intellectual advocate of biological evolution, John Fiske, celebrated the superiority of English civilization and claimed it was the destiny of the English people to populate the world's empty spaces.[44] Even more influential were popular writers such as Josiah Strong, a Congregationalist clergyman whose book *Our Country* (1885) sold thousands of copies. Strong was a vigorous advocate of the Anglo-Saxon myths in combination with attacks on Catholics and other white immigrants. The English peoples were rapidly multiplying, he argued, and the United States was destined to be the seat of a great Anglo-Saxon "race" approaching, by the 1980s, a billion strong. Survival of the fittest, he argued, dictated the ultimate superiority of the Anglo-Saxon race throughout the world.[45]

Racism and Nativism Since 1890

The increase in immigration from southern and eastern Europe and from Asia in the decades around the turn of the twentieth century focused anti-immigration sentiment on these groups. The economic and political troubles facing late-nineteenth-century America moved some intellectuals and other leaders away from their confidence that new immigrants could readily be assimilated. Henry Cabot Lodge, an English American from New England, was fiercely determined to defend the English "race" against immigrant threats in the 1890s. A prominent political figure of his day, Lodge did a study of entries in a biographical listing to prove the dominance of the English over all others. English American aristocrats from Boston formed the Immigration League to fight the flood of southern and eastern European migrants. The league worked diligently for a literacy test, which easily passed Congress, and associated itself with the eugenics movement started by Sir Francis Galton, a prominent English Darwinist. The Eugenicists argued that heredity shaped moral, as well as biological, characteristics, and that perpetuation of the unfit could thus lead to the destruction of the superior race. A basic idea was that the unfit should be eliminated.[46]

Perhaps the most prominent American to contribute to the development of racial nativism was Madison Grant, an American of English extraction. An amateur scientist, Grant fused various racist ideas in his influential book, *The Passing of the Great Race*, around 1920. Particularly worried about the influence of certain newer European groups, Grant claimed that interbreeding various "races" would lead to mongrelization. The northern Europeans, the so-called "Nordic race," were the superior "race."[47]

Such "scientific" racism eventually resulted in the restrictive immigration legislation of the 1920s, legislation which discriminated against virtually all non-British groups. Various "national origin" quotas were spelled out to restrict immigration, with Britons allowed to comprise nearly half the total.

The 1920s saw an outpouring of racial nativism on many fronts. Journalists such as Kenneth L. Roberts continued to write about racial mongrelization.[48] Nativist organizations such as the revived Ku Klux Klan provided a social outlet to express such views, both in subordinating black people and in preserving the Anglo-Saxon race against "niggers, Catholics, and Jews."[49] Anti-Catholic, anti-Semitic, antiforeign, anti-black—all these attitudes were expressed in the Klan. Nor did opposition die after the Depression and World War II. Opposition to foreign immigration again surfaced after World War II, when various members of Congress and so-called "old stock" organizations spoke up in opposition to legislation permitting displaced persons, such as Jews and Catholics, to migrate to the United States. In the 1970s and 1980s nonwhite immigrants from Asia, Latin America, and the Philippines became the targets of modern-day nativists, including those in the again revived Ku Klux Klan.

THE IMPACT ON BASIC INSTITUTIONS

Virtually all analysts of the American scene have assumed a core culture and society basically English or Anglo-Saxon. During the first century of colonial development an English heritage integrated the colonies, and the English core culture adapted to the new physical environment. The set of political, legal, and economic institutions was based on familiar English models. This is not to say that American institutions were identical to England's institutions; they were not. The dominant Anglican Church in the colonies soon gave way to a moderate amount of religious liberty. There was also no hereditary ruling class, as was found in England. The availability of land, the basis of wealth, guaranteed greater democracy in the colonies. The wilderness gave settlers greater freedom and mobility; traditional English ways and laws were modified to take into account these new conditions.[50]

Language

The lasting dominance of the English language in America makes conspicuous the impact of the English. The central language is not a blend of early immigrant languages. Language sets off ethnic groups in fundamental ways. Language can be thought of as a critical characteristic shaping the basic cultural tone.[51] The pressures on non-English-speaking immigrants first took the form of language pressures. Anglo-conformity pressures on non-English speakers could be great. Warner and Srole conclude that "our customary way of life is most like the English, and our language is but one of the several English dialects. The ethnic people most like us are English-speaking Protestants with a body of customary behavior no more deviant from our way of life than their language and religion."[52]

Religion and Basic Values

The English religious influence on the United States has been of great importance. For the first two hundred years English churches, or derivatives thereof, dominated the American scene. The Anglican Church even received some government support, but this privileged position was lost in the Revolution. The disproportionate number of Anglican and Congregational churches was obvious even at the time of the Revolution, although Baptist and Presbyterian churches were by then more numerous than Anglican churches. Gradually, in the century after 1776, English dominance of American religious institutions gave way in face of numerous Catholic, Presbyterian, and Jewish groups which grew as a result of later immigration.[53]

Herberg argues that the Catholic and Jewish faiths, as well as non-British Protestantism, have been distinctively shaped by the "American way of life," his phrase for the Anglo-Saxon core culture.[54] For example, one important study of Judaism has shown the substantial impact of the Protestant institutional framework on eastern European Judaism. Sklare found that the immigrant synagogue made major changes over time in response to the core culture. Religious school adaptations were made in scheduling and in format, with Torah schools replaced by congregational schools. Among Reform Jews, English came to be the language of worship, and worship itself was modified with the introduction of Friday night services. However, strong continuities with the past also persisted, particularly among Orthodox Jews.[55]

The impact of the core culture on the non-Protestant religions of later immigrants was mixed. The immigrant has been expected to adapt in language and in many other areas, but some preservation of religious heritage has been maintained. One area where "cultural pluralism" has descriptive accuracy in regard to the American scene is religion.

Perhaps more important than religious organization has been the impact of certain basic English Protestant values. The importance of ascetic Protestantism which many of the English settlers brought early to the colonies cannot be underestimated. Puritanism was important in establishing the Protestant work ethic at the center of the American value system. Basic was the idea of work as a duty of every person. Originally, the idea was that to work hard is to glorify God. Richard Baxter, an important English Puritan divine, exemplified this important perspective in his advocacy of hard work and abstinence from personal pleasures.[56] "Continuous work was seen as a major defense against the sinful temptations of the flesh; the primary objective of work was to glorify God. Idleness was regarded as sin."[57]

This view fostered the dominance of the work ethic so distinctive of the United States. The emerging capitalistic system in the late 1700s and 1800s was pervaded by a drive to "pursuit of profit, and forever *renewed* profit, by means of continuous, rational, capitalistic enterprise."[58] Benjamin Franklin personified this spirit of capitalism with his famous comments about "time is money," about punctuality, and about the virtues of hard work.[59]

There is much one could add here about the influence of the English on general American culture, on such features as music and art, but we have the space for only a few tantalizing comments. Musical and artistic developments were initially linked to the English religious tradition. The first book published in the New England colonies was the *Bay Psalm Book* in 1640, drawing on English tradition.[60] "Yankee Doodle" was probably an English tune, originally with lyrics satirizing rag-tag colonial soldiers. Only when the Revolution began did American soldiers take it over from the British. Thus before, during, and after the Revolution English melodies were the basis of most popular and political songs.[61] Even our national anthem, "The Star-Spangled Banner," draws on an English drinking song for its melody.

Education

English and other British Americans took advantage of what few educational opportunities were available in the colonial period; better-off parents sent their children to the few private schools and colleges established before 1800. With the public school movement, which began in earnest in the first decades of the nineteenth century and spread throughout the nation, English and other British dominance of the public schools became a fact of life. Working-class and middle-class British Americans took advantage of these public schools. Public schools in urban areas were seen as a particularly important means of socializing non-Protestant immigrants into Anglo-Saxon Protestant values and of socializing them to fit in with the emerging industrial system. British American industrialists and educators usually established the public schools, shaped their curricula and teaching practices, and supervised their operation. Although some educators, such as John Dewey, saw education as giving greater opportunity to poor immigrants, many educators emphasized the social control aspects of the schools. In many of the schools the Americanization pressures on immigrant children were intense; whether the children were Irish, Jewish, or Italian did not seem to matter. Anglicization of the children was designed to ferret out the harmful non-Anglo-Saxon ways, to assimilate the children in terms of manners, work habits, and the Protestant Ethic.[62]

Political and Legal Institutions

American political and legal institutions have been shaped in critical ways by the English and British heritage. We can think of this impact in two basic ways: in terms of laws inherited from the English and in terms of the influence which English immigrants and their descendants have had in important political organizations and government institutions.

Given the near-monopoly of English settlers among the early colonists of the eastern seaboard, it is not surprising that English-type legal institutions were dominant. A concern for governance under law and for the "rights of Englishmen" was manifest in the first settlements. The famous Mayflower Compact, which set up a political framework theoretically providing for equality and justice under law, has often been praised. New

England, with its Puritan institutions, provided the model for later political and legal developments.[63]

Interestingly, Huntington has argued that the North American colonies took on a very distinctive set of political institutions—those characteristic of sixteenth-century England. Although many of these constitutional features were being *abandoned* in England, they became part of the political structure on this side of the Atlantic. The basic ideas in this system include unity of government and society, subordination of government to law, a balance of power between the legislature (Parliament in England) and the executive (the king), and substantial reliance on local governmental authorities.[64] American political and legal institutions, including the U.S. Constitution itself, have reflected these ideas ever since. Authority and power were centralized in England, while in the United States there was a separation of basic authority into three governmental branches—the executive, the judicial, and the legislative branches. There is the unusual position of the president. The United States, unlike almost every other modern political system, does not distinguish between the head of government and the (often nominal) chief of state. In the 1970s the Watergate scandal of the Richard Nixon Administration made this executive power clear. America was a new society, but an "old" political state.

One of the most important English influences can be seen in the representative assemblies in the colonies and in the United States. By the 1600s the British Crown had begun to establish representative assemblies in the English colonies based on the parliamentary model.[65] Gradually these assemblies grew in power vis-à-vis the London government. Eventual Crown infringements on the operations of these assemblies were among the critical issues leading to the Revolution. Here the English heritage can be seen.

The American legal framework reflected English influence. Prior to the Revolution, English common law was asserted to be "the measure of rights of Americans."[66] The colonies had similar legal frameworks, but negative feeling arose over English common law because of the tension between the new United States and England. Some wanted a new American code, "but," as Pound notes, "most lawyers sought to reshape or add to the existing stock of authoritative legal materials."[67] While there was variation in the way English statutes were incorporated into the legal systems of the colonies and later of the states, "the use of English statutes was provided for at an early stage in twenty-six of the twenty-eight jurisdictions organized between 1776 and 1836."[68]

Sometimes these statutes were incorporated by direct action of the new state governments, sometimes by indirect action which had the effect of continuing previous statutes. While the American legal system has been patched many times, the basic cloth has remained English common law. The legal system in England, in which some colonial leaders were trained, had a direct impact on the development of American law.[69]

Officeholding

In addition to their impact on the laws and political institutions, the English have had an impact on the operation of institutions. There is the participation of English Americans in offices in various political contexts over the course of United States history. Only a few studies have examined the English, or British, influence on sectors of the political structure. Davie notes that "the colonial assemblies were almost exclusively English in make-up, and the English were inclined to look upon other ethnic groups as inferior."[70] The founding fathers were also quite distinctively English. The Declaration of Independence was signed by fifty-six European males, thirty-eight of whom were English by background or birth, nine Scottish or "Scotch-Irish," three Irish, five Welsh, and only one Swedish.[71]

This predominance of Englishmen among the new nation's political leaders is found in numerous other political gatherings of that period. Indeed, the Constitution clearly reflects the interests of the Englishmen of wealth. The Constitutional Convention was predominantly English, judging from the last names. Most men of wealth in the new nation—merchants, financiers, shippers, wealthy farmers, and their allies—supported the Constitution out of economic self-interest. Slaves, indentured servants, poor farmers, laborers, and women had no say in the framing of the Constitution. The framers of the Constitution perpetuated the class lines which were the substance of English social structure.[72]

Studies of national political leaders—Presidents, Supreme Court justices, and members of Congress—have revealed a distinctive pattern persisting to the present. Presidents and presidential candidates have been "required" to possess ancestry qualifications, preferably British American or northern European origins. Of the thirty-six presidents from Washington to Nixon, about 60 percent had English origins; all but six had English, British, or Scotch-Irish backgrounds; and all the remainder have had northern European backgrounds.[73] A study of the ethnic origins of Supreme Court justices from 1789 to 1957 found that over half were English or Welsh. In all time periods English Americans have been heavily represented on the nation's highest court.[74]

Analysis of the 1901–1910 period provides additional data on office-holders. One study of 162 prominent political leaders (including presidents, representatives, senators, and Supreme Court justices) in this period found that over half were of English or Welsh origin. Most were at least fourth-generation, with family lines going back before the Revolution.[75]

Baltzell has traced the rise of English American leaders such as Robert Todd Lincoln, the son of Abraham Lincoln, at the turn of the twentieth century. Educated at Phillips Academy and Harvard, Robert Todd Lincoln became a millionaire corporation lawyer at the heart of the ruling elite in Chicago and Washington. In 1901, the year of Queen Victoria's death, the Lincoln heir was part of a British and British American establishment that dominated much of the world. A northwestern European Protestant, Theodore Roosevelt, was in the White House; and J. P. Morgan, a leader in the (Protestant) Episcopal Church, had just put together the first billion-dollar corporation. The Senate of the United States was a Protestant millionaires' club. British American influence extended throughout all institutional sectors.[76]

Baltzell further argues that in the next few decades of the twentieth century this establishment developed into a rigid caste. Even when the new immigrants managed to break into politics, as in the case of Irish and Italian Americans, they were usually subservient to Protestant leaders. The Irish Catholic Kennedy administration in 1960 marked a brief shift from a homogeneous political establishment. Yet Kennedy was soon followed by more men of so-called "old-stock" lines.[77] However, as can be seen from the studies just reviewed, only a little research has been undertaken on explicit English political dominance in the mid-twentieth century.

What of the English impact on local government? One study of New Haven, Connecticut has pointed up English dominance. The old patrician elite there "completely dominated the political system. They were of one common stock and one religion, cohesive in their uniformly conservative outlook on all matters, substantially unchallenged in their authority, successful in pushing through their own policies, and in full control of such critical institutions as the established religion, the educational system (including not only all the schools but Yale as well), and even business enterprise."[78]

Even the nineteenth-century entrepreneurs and industrialists who succeeded the old patrician elite in New Haven could trace their lineage back to the Mayflower. Moreover, a study of the mayors of Cleveland, Ohio, in the 1836–1901 period found that most were part of an Anglo-Protestant elite, with strong family and friendship ties to New England. Their governing framework was guided by the "New England creed," proposition one of which was "The good society is white and Protestant."[79] Presumably some local Anglo-Saxon Protestant dominance has persisted into the decades of the mid-twentieth century.

Economic Institutions

The English heritage is reflected in U.S. economic institutions, in the values which shape institutions and the actual dominance of English individuals. Just as the legal system incorporated portions of the English legal system, the colonies developed initially under a combined mercantilist-capitalistic economic system which dominated much of Europe at the time; the attempt was made to increase the raw materials and the markets available for the king's control. The first English colonies were set up by state-chartered trading companies. Others were proprietary colonies set up by men of wealth and power. While the colonies generally did not have the payoff that these speculators had hoped, they did bring significant economic benefits.

Mercantile capitalism, the economic system which existed in the colonies at the time of the Revolution, was a type of state-directed capitalism closely linked to a vigorous nationalism which worked constantly for a favorable balance of trade for one's own country—in this case, England. The American Revolution was basically a clash between English and English (or British) American commercial interests, a clash which unified the colonies and brought a political break between two virtually identical economic systems.[80]

While the development of full-fledged industrial capitalism in the U.S.

took place several decades later, its guiding philosophy had intimate connections with the English system. The basic ideas for U.S. industrial development arrived through English channels, and many English capitalists and skilled workers provided much of the knowhow for American capitalistic development. After the Revolution, as before, Britain and the United States formed a single Atlantic economy, so close and important were their economic connections. In the decades from 1820 to the Civil War about half of United States exports went to British ports; 40 percent of American imports came from those same ports. Cotton exports to Britain were particularly significant, as were British textiles in the return flow.[81]

Direct Participation in the Economy

The English have had a significant impact on the operation of the U.S. economy through their participation in critical positions. In the beginning they established the colonies and controlled the land, and thus the wealth. Colonial society was not a democratic utopia. In the early period economic and political control of the colonies was primarily in the hands of English (and other British) landowners and merchants.[82] Morison has argued, however, that in many of the colonies the men who eventually came to dominate in the late pre-revolutionary period were yeoman farmers.[83] While the founders included English aristocrats, they had died or returned to England by the mid-1650s.

Whatever their background, men with some land and wealth needed labor, and the demand for labor was tremendous. The eighteenth-century Atlantic migration was spurred primarily by the labor demand.[84] Because there was no surplus population for economic enterprises in the colonies themselves, labor from Europe and Africa was imported.[85] By the 1730s a substantial Irish migration had begun. German immigration picked up starting in 1720 and reached its peak in the mid-eighteenth century. A large proportion of these immigrants were indentured servants. The African slave trade eventually supplanted the trade in white servants.[86]

As we move on toward the Civil War period and then into the twentieth century, we again find few specific studies on the dominance of the economy by English (or British) Americans. A recent study of the wealth of males living in the United States in 1860 concludes only that the wealth of "native-born males" was about twice that of "foreign-born males." Males born in certain New England states were better off than the others. "There is the implication that these Yankees were more likely to have had ancestors with American experience and heritage."[87] If one assumes these Yankees were predominantly English—the study is silent on this point—then the conclusion is that the English Americans were the most prosperous.

The industrialization in the nineteenth century was partially fueled by imported English and Dutch capital. American railroad development was bankrolled by English capital, which produced fortunes for several English investors. English capital also played a role in the development of agriculture (for instance, wheat farming) in the Mississippi Valley.

In U.S. industry capitalistic elites were substantially dominated by

Americans of British descent. In the nineteenth century the most famous leaders were the chief industrialists and financiers of the new industrial nation, many of whom have been regarded as "robber barons." Most were relatively young men at the time of the Civil War: John D. Rockefeller, Leland Stanford, J. P. Morgan, Jay Gould, and Jim Fisk. All were men of great wealth and power. Their ethnic heritages were typically English, with a few other northern Europeans scattered among them. Most were well versed in the Protestant ethic that stressed hard work and the private accumulation of profit. Political influence was theirs as well. Many of these men, or their associates or family members, became senators, representatives, and governors. The impact of these men and their descendants on the economy and the political sphere is incalculable. Their economic system became one of increasing exploitation of immigrant labor.[88]

A study of top executives and entrepreneurs in the late nineteenth century iron and steel industry found that few came from immigrant families recently arrived in the United States. Most were native-born and had fathers with capitalistic or professional backgrounds. Most did *not* fit the rags-to-riches image of a poor immigrant "making good," such as the famous steel magnate Andrew Carnegie, who came to America as a poor Scottish boy. Over half were of English or Welsh ancestry; most of the rest were either Scottish or (early) Protestant Irish. Another study of the social origins of a broader group of business leaders in the late nineteenth century also found that 90 percent were of English, Scottish, and Welsh ancestry. They too were from relatively prosperous Anglo-Saxon Protestant backgrounds. In both studies the English Americans were dominant.[89]

One study of persons of wealth and influence (millionaire and multimillionaire manufacturers, bankers, and merchants) in the first decades of the twentieth century found that the backgrounds of about half were English, with a significant percentage of the rest Scottish or Irish. In another study twentieth-century executives in major business organizations were found to be predominantly of northern and western European ancestry. A substantial majority of the major European-origin business executives belonged to Episcopalian, Presbyterian, or Congregational churches. Newcomer concludes that "for the most part, the religious preference is inherited from the family, and the dominance of British family backgrounds is sufficient in itself to account for the large proportion of executives belonging to these churches."[90] Yet another survey of two hundred major executives (presidents, board chairmen, and partners) in the largest companies and corporations from 1901 to 1910 found that 53 percent were of English or Welsh origin, 7 percent were Scottish, 14 percent were Irish, and 8 percent were Canadian or British (unspecified).[91]

Local Economies

A few studies bearing on American towns and cities have made clear the extent of English (or British) dominance in local economies. Thernstrom's study of nineteenth-century Newburyport, Massachusetts, for example, revealed the dominance of Yankees, New Englanders presumably of English or British origin. In the mid-nineteenth century the English and Scottish workers had significant advantages over Irish and other immigrants. "The immigrant workman in Newburyport," writes Thernstrom, "was markedly less successful than his native counterpart in climbing out of the ranks of the unskilled in the 1850–1880 period."[92] One reason was that immigrant workers such as the Irish were discriminated against by the factory owners. A later examination of Newburyport in the 1930s found half the population still to be Yankee. This predominantly Yankee group was found still to dominate the upper classes in Newburyport.[93]

Burlington, Vermont, was dominated in the 1930s by so-called "Old Americans"—those who had been in the United States for four generations, probably heavily English and English Canadian. These were in control of banking, manufacturing, and the university there, although they had given way to newer ethnic groups in certain other commercial areas. They constituted a disproportion of professional and political officials. "Old Americans" were the model for the community, a model with a racist dimension. Anderson underscores this point: "Traditions of family and name, of power and influence, in the financial and civil life of the community, of race-consciousness, plus a very deep conviction that the Protestant traditions of their forefathers are basically important to the development of free institutions in America, set the Old Americans apart as a group distinct from other people."[94]

A few studies have been done of economic influentials since the 1930s. The "proper Philadelphians" about whom Baltzell has written typically have English or British backgrounds. The English and their descendants long had a heavy influence on the development of this middle colony. This is suggested, for example, by the heavy dominance of Episcopalians and Presbyterians in the Philadelphia *Social Register* for the year 1940. Of the 147 with religious affiliations listed, most were Episcopalian or Presbyterian. And of the 513 Philadelphians in *Who's Who*, well over half were Episcopalian or Presbyterian.[95]

These Philadelphians were persons of great power and influence in the 1940s, particularly in banking, law, engineering, and business. To sum up, a typical member of the Philadelphia elite in 1940 would be "of English or Welsh descent" and "his great-great-great-grandfather would have been a prominent Philadelphian in the great age of the new republic."[96]

In an analysis of the 1950s and 1960s, Baltzell has underscored the continuing dominance of English and other British Americans at the national level as well. While there has been significant penetration by non-British groups in the economic and political system, as in the case of the Irish Catholics, this desegregation has usually not penetrated the executive suites of large corporations, where the leadership is "still mainly composed of managers of Anglo-Saxon Protestant background."[97] In the 1950s Dalton's impressive study of one large industrial corporation found ethnic stratification; 60 percent of the management was of British American origin.[98]

A Study of Elites

A recent study by Dye of the top decisionmakers in the United States identified 4,000 people in the top positions in major employment areas, including the corporate sector (industry, communication, banking), the government sector, and the public interest sector (education, mass media, law). Dye concludes that "great power in America is concentrated in a tiny handful of men. A few thousand individuals out of 200 million Americans decide about war and peace, wages and prices, consumption and investment, employment and production, law and justice, taxes and benefits, education and learning, health and welfare, advertising and communication, life and leisure."[99]

Decisions of importance are reached at the middle and lower levels of the society, but it is a few thousand people in these top positions who make the most critical decisions affecting major aspects of the lives of members of all racial and ethnic groups. Dye's research revealed that the social origins of the 4,000 people in elite positions were not typical. They were generally affluent, white, Anglo-Saxon males. There were only a few blacks in the whole group. There were virtually *no* Mexican Americans, Native Americans, or Japanese Americans among the top 4,000. Dye has estimated that the top institutional elites were "at least 90 percent Anglo-Saxon" and noted that "there were very few recognizable Irish, Italian, or Jewish names" there.[100]

In looking at obvious social and economic mobility one must be careful to distinguish the reality from Horatio Alger rags-to-riches myths. For all their movement from the lower levels of the working class to the higher levels of the working class over several generations, Catholic and Jewish Americans still do not seem to be significantly represented at the very top of the economic and political pyramids of power.

A number of critics, usually representing emerging white non-British ethnic groups, have been particularly outspoken about the persisting influence of Anglo-Saxon Americans. The following is Michael Novak's intriguing assessment:

> In the country clubs, as city executives, established families, industrialists, owners, lawyers, masters of etiquette, college presidents, dominators of the military, fundraisers, members of blue ribbon committees, realtors, brokers, deans, sheriffs—it is the cumulative power and distinctive styles of WASPs that the rest of us have had to learn in order to survive. WASPs never had to celebrate Columbus Day or march down Fifth Avenue wearing green. Every day has been their day in America.[101]

ENGLISH AMERICANS IN MODERN AMERICA: A PROBLEM OF DATA

A few scholars have suggested that there is an extensive literature on English Americans in the twentieth century—in novels, religious studies, and community studies.[102] But actually this is not the case. The literature they have in mind explicitly deals with whites—white Protestants, white south-erners, Christian Scientists, and so on—not specifically with the modern-day English (or British) Americans. Very few researchers have specifically examined these English Americans in modern times. Perhaps one reason for this is the dominant position of things English in the core culture and society. What is core is taken for granted.

Numerous studies of whites loosely mix large non-English groups such as the so-called "Scotch-Irish" and the Dutch with English Americans. In such discussions one cannot be sure about the experiences or impact of English Americans. In order to illustrate this problem, and in order to emphasize the regional variation in white-Protestant America, we can turn briefly to the case of whites who live in what was once the old Confederacy.

White Southerners

One of the interesting books on whites in the South is Lewis Killian's *White Southerners*, a study of a distinctive regional group. Killian speaks of white southerners, and occasionally of white Anglo-Saxon Protestants; it is clear that he is grouping many large white ethnic groups besides English Americans under these labels. A particularly large segment of the southern white population consists of the descendants of early Irish immigrants, those often called "Scotch-Irish." There are also large proportions of the southern white population of French, Spanish, and German descent. Killian notes that English and other British Americans have become submerged in a much larger and ethnically diverse white population which has, nearly unanimously until the last two decades, emphasized "white-ness" above all else. "For a southerner, the salient fact was and is whether he was white or black; all else was secondary."[103] While it is possible that white southerners of English descent remain influential in southern politics and the southern economy, they are not examined by Killian as a specific group.

What Killian in fact provides is an important portrait of white south-erners as a distinctive regional group. White southerners are distinctive because of the role of race in their history. After the Civil War and Re-construction southern whites rapidly rebuilt a dismantled slave-plantation society, and the New South was intentionally structured to keep black south-erners "in their place." The New South has long been riddled with a massive array of discriminatory practices, legal and informal, aimed at handicap-ping blacks, and the rationale for these practices has been a racist ideology. Killian notes that whites, and their leaders, have "offered apologies for indefensible practices," such as lynchings and segregation. The weight of this racist system has shaped the cultural system of whites in fundamental ways, even retarding literary and intellectual developments. Ever resent-ful of the regional dominance of the North in the economy, loyal sons and daughters of the white South have clung to "the belief that there is some mystical superiority in 'the southern way of life.' "[104] Even the recent economic resurgence in the Sunbelt in the 1970s and 1980s has not eliminated southern racial problems or the southern resentment of the North.

Books such as Killian's lead us to think about regional diversity in the United States and about the ethnic diversity of the South, and even lead us to questions about the role of English Americans among white southerners. But, unfortunately, Killian provides no answers to those questions; a specific history of English Americans in the South has apparently not yet been published.[105]

Religion and Ethnicity

In recent years there has been a debate over whether Catholic Americans have exceeded the socioeconomic achievements of Protestant or Anglo-Saxon Protestant Americans. For example, in one study Andrew Greeley found that Catholic American groups such as the Irish had occupational and income achievements comparable to or exceeding those of Protestants as a group, and even those of British Protestants. Greeley concludes that U.S. society has in recent decades "bestowed economic, occupational, and educational success" on its British Protestant and Irish Catholic populations. However, one difficulty here is that British Protestants include Americans of Welsh and Scottish backgrounds, as well as the English. Comparisons of English Protestant and Irish Catholic achievements are not presented.[106]

Moreover, other recent research suggests that Catholic Americans have not yet surpassed the educational, income, and occupational achievements of the elite white Protestant groups. Using 1970s survey data, Clark Roof has demonstrated that Americans in elite white Protestant groups (the Episcopalians, Presbyterians, and Congregationalists) rank substantially above white Catholic Americans, including Irish Catholics, in family income level, educational achievement, and occupational prestige. Roof concludes that, even with the upward movement of Catholic Americans, "upper-class Protestants maintain a hold on their [top] position too, and are not likely to be displaced any time soon in the status hierarchy."[107] Again, however, the data are not available in terms of English Protestants taken separately, but rather in terms of broader groups which include large numbers of Americans of English and British descent. These interesting data suggest, but do not prove, continuing Anglo-Saxon-American dominance at the top. They also suggest the dramatic upward mobility of non-English Catholic Americans.

SUMMARY

The purpose of this chapter has been to examine that most neglected of all white ethnic groups, English Americans. Their blending into the background makes it difficult to assess the power, location, and achievements of these first immigrants and their descendants. It was the English who first colonized on a large scale the area now known as the United States. In this chapter we have spelled out in some detail just what the original English colonization and migration have meant for American institutions, past and present. *Dominance* would seem to be the appropriate term, for the basic influence on American religious, economic, and political institutions has been English.

The colonization migration of the English led to a dominant core culture and society to which subsequent groups were required to adapt. The study of assimilation begins here. For several centuries English migrants and their descendants have been disproportionately represented in key social, economic, and political positions. Between the 1600s and the 1860s they were slowly joined in their dominant position by certain other Protestant groups.

If we had the space, we would have explored the class and regional diversity of this Anglo-Saxon grouping more than we have. The tremendous impact of Anglo-Saxon Protestant Americans does not mean that substantial segments did not stay working-class or even poor, in the past or the present. There have long been regional and denominational differences within the Anglo-Saxon Protestant group. Episcopalians are a bit different from Congregationalists, and southerners are rather different from New Englanders.

In recent decades Anglo-Saxon dominance has been seriously and vigorously challenged by Catholic Americans, Jewish Americans, and numerous nonwhite groups. Some have argued that its influence, particularly its artistic influence, is on the wane. Schrag has argued that Anglo-Saxon Protestants are on the road to cultural demise.[108] According to this view, white Anglo-Saxon Protestant domination came to an end in the post–World War II period; reflecting the "decline of the WASP" is the increasing non-Anglo-Saxon dominance of American music, writing, and art. But even Schrag modifies his overall estimation for the economic sphere: the Anglo-Saxon Protestant "elite still controls its own corporate offices, its board rooms, its banks and foundations."[109] In this estimation, Schrag probably comes closer to the truth; the demise of Anglo-Saxon Protestant influence seems exaggerated. And Americans of English descent remain, disproportionately, at the center of that influence.

NOTES

[1]Cleveland Amory, *The Proper Bostonians* (New York: E. P. Dutton, 1947), p. 11.

[2]Carl Wittke, "Preface to the Revised Edition," in *We Who Built America*, rev. ed. (Cleveland: Case Western Reserve University Press, 1967).

[3]Milton M. Gordon, *Assimilation in American Life* (New York: Oxford University Press, 1964), p. 72.

[4]Will Herberg, *Protestant–Catholic–Jew*, rev. ed. (Garden City, N.Y.: Doubleday Anchor Books, 1960), p. 21.

[5]Rowland T. Berthoff, *British Immigrants in Industrial America* (Chicago: University of Chicago Press, 1953), p. 1.

[6]Wilbur S. Shepperson, *British Emigration to North America* (Oxford: Basil Blackwell, 1957), p. 3.

[7]Conrad Taeuber and Irene B. Taeuber, "Immigration to the United States," in *Population and Society*, ed. Charles B. Nam (New York: Houghton Mifflin Co., 1968), p. 316.

[8]Immigration and Naturalization Service, *1975 Annual Report* (Washington, D.C.: U.S. Government Printing Office, 1975), pp. 62–64.

[9]Alice Marriott and Carol K. Rachlin, *American Epic* (New York: Mentor Books, 1969), p. 105.

[10]Samuel Eliot Morison, *The Oxford History of the American People* (New York: Oxford University Press, 1965), pp. 48–49.

[11]Klaus E. Knorr, *British Colonial Theories, 1570–1850* (Toronto: University of Toronto Press, 1944), p. 126.

[12]Marriott and Rachlin, *American Epic*, p. 106.

[13]Ibid., pp. 104–6; Winthrop D. Jordan, *White Over Black* (Baltimore: Penguin Books, 1969), p. 89.

[14]Quoted in John Collier, *Indians of the Americas,* abridged ed. (New York: Mentor Books, 1947), p. 115.

[15]The next three paragraphs draw on Morison, *Oxford History of the American People*, pp. 50–154; and Maldwyn A. Jones, *American Immigration* (Chicago: University of Chicago Press, 1960), pp. 10–38.

[16]Morison, *Oxford History of the American People*, p. 74.

[17]Ibid., p. 131. The Dutch colony in the New York area was taken over by force.

[18]Henry P. Fairchild, *Immigration* (New York: Macmillan, 1920), p. 32; Leonard Dinnerstein and Frederic C. Jaher, "Introduction," in *The Aliens*, ed. Leonard Dinnerstein and Frederic Jaher (New York: Appleton-Century-Crofts, 1970), p. 4.

[19]*Proceedings of the American Historical Association,* vol. 1 of *Annual Report of the American Historical Association* (Washington, D.C.: U.S. Government Printing Office, 1932), p. 124.

[20]Jones, *American Immigration*, pp. 34–35.

[21]Berthoff, *British Immigrants in Industrial America*, p. vii.

[22]Ibid., p. 5.

[23]Shepperson, *British Emigration to North America*, p. 20.

[24]Berthoff, *British Immigrants in Industrial America*, pp. 28–29; Charlotte Erickson, "English," in *Harvard Encyclopedia of American Ethnic Groups*, ed. Stephan Thernstrom (Cambridge, Mass.: Harvard University Press, 1980), pp. 324–32.

[25]Shepperson, *British Emigration to North America*, pp. 27–32, 84; Berthoff, *British Immigrants in Industrial America*, pp. 46–87, 122; Charlotte Erickson, "Agrarian Myths of English Immigrants," in *In the Trek of the Immigrants,* ed. O. Fritiof Ander (Rock Island, Ill.: Augustana Library Publications, 1964), pp. 59–64.

[26]Berthoff, *British Immigrants in Industrial America*, p. 125.

[27]Ibid., p. 210. See also pp. 143–83.

[28]Erickson, "English," pp. 335–36.

[29]This section draws heavily on Charles H. Anderson, *White Protestant Americans* (Englewood Cliffs, Ń.J.: Prentice-Hall, 1970), pp. 28–71, 79–87. See also Ian C. Graham, *Colonists from Scotland* (Ithaca, N.Y.: Cornell University Press, 1956); and Albert B. Faust, *The German Element in the United States* (New York: The Steuben Society, 1927).

[30]John Higham, *Strangers in the Land* (New York: Atheneum, 1963), p. 4.

[31]Fairchild, *Immigration*, p. 47.

[32]Jones, *American Immigration*, p. 44.

[33]Jordan, *White Over Black*, p. 86.

[34]Ibid., p. 87.

[35]Jones, *American Immigration*, pp. 41–46.

[36]Fairchild, *Immigration*, pp. 57–58.

[37]Quoted in Michael Kammen, *People of Paradox* (New York: Knopf, 1972), p. 66.

[38]Quoted in Jordan, *White Over Black*, p. 338.

[39]Kammen, *People of Paradox*, p. 74; Jordan, *White Over Black*, p. 339.

[40]Higham, *Strangers in the Land*, p. 6; Marcus L. Hansen, *The Immigrant in American History* (New York: Harper Torchbooks, 1964), pp. 111–36; Wittke, *We Who Built America*, p. 505.

[41]Higham, *Strangers in the Land*, p. 9.

[42]Quoted in Richard Hofstadter, *Social Darwinism in American Thought*, rev. ed. (Boston: Beacon Press, 1955), pp. 171–72.

[43]Higham, *Strangers in the Land*, p. 32; Hofstadter, *Social Darwinism in American Thought*, pp. 173–74.

[44]Higham, *Strangers in the Land*, p. 33.

[45]Hofstadter, *Social Darwinism in American Thought*, pp. 178–79; and Lewis H. Carlson and George A. Colburn, *In Their Place* (New York: Wiley, 1972), pp. 305–8. Carlson and Colburn provide excerpts from the writings of Strong.

[46]Higham, *Strangers in the Land*, pp. 96–152.

[47]E. Digby Baltzell, *The Protestant Establishment* (New York: Vintage Books, 1966), pp. 96–98; and Higham, *Strangers in the Land*, pp. 148–57.

[48]Kenneth L. Roberts, excerpt from *Why Europe Leaves Home*, in *In Their Place*, ed. Lewis H. Carlson and George A. Colburn (New York: Wiley, 1972), p. 312.

[49]David M. Chalmers, *Hooded Americanism* (Chicago: Quadrangle Books, 1965), pp. 28–38.

[50]Jones, *American Immigration*, pp. 36–38.

[51]Jordan, *White Over Black*, pp. 338–39.

[52]W. Lloyd Warner and Leo Srole, *The Social Systems of American Ethnic Groups* (New Haven: Yale University Press, 1945), p. 287.

[53]Edwin S. Gaustad, *Historical Atlas of Religion in America* (New York: Harper & Row, 1962), pp. 1–20.

[54]Herberg, *Protestant–Catholic–Jew*, p. 82.

[55]Marshall Sklare, *Conservative Judaism* (Glencoe, Ill.: Free Press, 1955), pp. 31–117.

[56]Max Weber, *The Protestant Ethic and the Spirit of Capitalism* (New York: Charles Scribner's Sons, 1958), pp. 158–60.

[57]Joe R. Feagin, *Subordinating the Poor* (Englewood Cliffs, N.J.: Prentice-Hall, 1975), p. 22.

[58]Weber, *The Protestant Ethic*, p. 17.

[59]Ibid., p. 50.

[60]David Ewen, *History of Popular Music* (New York: Barnes and Noble, 1961), pp. 1–4.

[61]Ibid., pp. 5–10.

[62]See Samuel Bowles and Herbert Gintis, *Schooling in Capitalist America* (New York: Basic Books, 1976).

[63]Morison, *Oxford History of the American People*, p. 55.

[64]Samuel P. Huntington, "Political Modernization: America Versus Europe," *World Politics* 18 (April 1966): 147–48.

[65]Jack P. Greene, *The Quest for Power* (Chapel Hill: University of North Carolina Press, 1963), pp. 1 ff.

[66]Roscoe Pound, *The Formative Era of American Law* (Boston: Little-Brown, 1938), pp. 7–8.

[67]Ibid., p. 12.

[68]Elizabeth G. Brown and William W. Blume, *British Statutes in American Law, 1776–1836* (Ann Arbor: University of Michigan Law School, 1964), p. 44. See also Lawrence M. Friedman, *A History of American Law* (New York: Simon & Schuster, 1973), pp. 96 ff.

[69]Pound, *The Formative Era of American Law*, p. 81.

[70]Maurice R. Davie, *World Immigration* (New York: Macmillan, 1939), p. 36.

[71]Henry J. Ford, *The Scotch-Irish in America* (Princeton: Princeton University Press, 1915), p. 491.

[72]Charles A. Beard, *An Economic Interpretation of the Constitution of the United States* (New York: Macmillan, 1947), p. 17.

[73]This tabulation was drawn from the profiles in Joseph N. Kane, *Facts About the Presidents*, 3rd ed. (New York: H. W. Wilson, 1974).

[74]John R. Schmidhauser, "The Justices of the Supreme Court: A Collective Portrait," *Midwest Journal of Political Science* 3 (February 1959): 1–57.

[75]William Miller, "American Historians and the Business Elite," *Journal of Economic History* 9 (November 1949): 202–3.

[76]Baltzell, *The Protestant Establishment*, pp. 10–12.

[77]Ibid., p. 21.

[78]Robert A. Dahl, *Who Governs?* (New Haven: Yale University Press, 1961), pp. 15–16.

[79]Matthew Holden, Jr., "Ethnic Accommodation in a Historical Case," *Comparative Studies in Society and History* 8 (January 1966): 172.

[80]Rowland Berthoff, *An Unsettled People* (New York: Harper & Row, 1971), p. 13; Oliver C. Cox, *Caste, Class, and Race* (Garden City, N.Y.: Doubleday, 1948), pp. 338–39; Barrington Moore, Jr., *Social Origins of Dictatorship and Democracy* (Boston: Beacon Press, 1966), pp. 112–13.

[81]Frank Thistlewaite, *The Anglo-American Connection in the Early Nineteenth Century* (Philadelphia: University of Pennsylvania Press, 1959), pp. 5–11.

[82]Jesse Lemisch, "The American Revolution Seen from the Bottom Up," in *Toward a New Past*, ed. Barton J. Bernstein (New York: Random House, 1968), p. 8; J. O. Lindsay, ed., *The Old Regime*, vol. 7 of *The New Cambridge Modern History* (Cambridge: Cambridge University Press, 1957), pp. 509–11.

[83]Morison, *Oxford History of the American People*, p. 89.

[84]Abbot E. Smith, *Colonists in Bondage* (Chapel Hill: University of North Carolina Press, 1947), p. 25.

[85]Jordan, *White Over Black*, p. 47.

[86]Howard Zinn, *The Politics of History* (Boston: Beacon Press, 1970), p. 68; Smith, *Colonists in Bondage*, p. 336.

[87]Lee Soltow, *Men and Wealth in the United States, 1850–1870* (New Haven: Yale University Press, 1975), p. 149.

[88]Matthew Josephson, *The Robber Barons* (New York: Harcourt, Brace and World, 1934), pp. 32–35, 315–452.

[89]John N. Ingham, *The Iron Barons* (Westport, Conn.: Greenwood Press, 1978), pp. 14–16; Francis Gregory and Irene Nau, "American Industrial Elite," in *Men in Business*, ed. William Miller (New York: Harper and Row, 1962), p. 200.

[90]Pitirim Sorokin, "American Millionaires and Multi-millionaires," *Social Forces* 3 (May 1925): 634–35; Mabel Newcomer, *The Big Business Executive* (New York: Columbia University Press, 1955), p. 46.

[91]Miller, "American Historians and the Business Elite," p. 202.

[92]Stephan Thernstrom, *Poverty and Progress* (Cambridge: Harvard University Press, 1964), pp. 99–101.

[93]W. Lloyd Warner and Paul S. Lunt, *The Social Life of a Modern Community* (New Haven: Yale University Press, 1941), pp. 213–25; Samuel Koenig, "Ethnic Groups in Connecticut Industry," *Social Forces* 20 (October 1941–May 1942): 105.

[94]Elin L. Anderson, *We Americans* (Cambridge: Harvard University Press, 1937), p. 137. See also pp. 21–247.

[95]E. Digby Baltzell, *An American Business Aristocracy* (New York: Collier Books, 1962), p. 267.

[96]Ibid., p. 431.

[97]Baltzell, *The Protestant Establishment*, p. 321.

[98]Melville Dalton, *Men Who Manage* (New York: John Wiley, 1959), pp. 183–84.

[99]Thomas R. Dye, *Who's Running America* (Englewood Cliffs, N.J.: Prentice-Hall, 1976), pp. 3–8, 150–53; see also Thomas R. Dye, *Who's Running America? The Carter Years* (Englewood Cliffs: Prentice-Hall, 1979), pp. 171–77.

[100]Letter to author from Thomas R. Dye, April 11, 1977.

[101]Michael Novak, "The Nordic Jungle: Inferiority in America," in *Divided Society*, ed. Colin Greer (New York: Basic Books, 1974), p. 134.

[102]Harold J. Abramson made this argument in a letter to the author, July 26, 1979.

[103]Lewis M. Killian, *White Southerners* (New York: Random House, 1970), p. 16.

[104]Ibid., p. 42.

[105]Ibid., pp. 130–38.

[106]Andrew M. Greeley, *Ethnicity in the United States* (New York: John Wiley, 1974), pp. 63–89; Andrew M. Greeley, "Catholics and the Upper Middle Class: Comment on Roof," *Social Forces* 59 (March 1981): 824–30.

[107]Wade Clark Roof, "Socioeconomic Differentials among White Socioreligious Groups in the United States," *Social Forces* 58 (September 1979): 285–89.

[108]Peter Schrag, *The Decline of the WASP* (New York: Simon and Schuster, 1970) p. 18.

[109]Ibid., p. 164.

Irish Americans

CHAPTER 4

In the last decade numerous discussions of ethnicity have often focused on the "white ethnics," a term for Catholic and Jewish Americans. Anglo-Saxon Protestant Americans have, on occasion, blamed these groups for corruption and racial discrimination in American cities. Anglo-Saxon Protestant commentators have spoken of white ethnic "hard hats" as though they were uneducated buffoons with a corrupt, racist, or authoritarian bent. Not surprisingly, white ethnics gradually counterattacked, arguing that hypocritical Anglo-Saxon Protestants have little care for and consciousness of the history or day-to-day experiences of white Catholic and Jewish Americans. It is the purpose of this chapter on the Irish, and the two following chapters on Italian and Jewish Americans, to depict and probe the neglected experiences of, and the rising consciousness of, non-Anglo-Saxon white Americans.

The Irish are one of the major groups that come to mind when white ethnic groups are mentioned, especially in the cities. The traditional view of the Irish conjures up images of parading leprechauns in funny suits, shamrocks, Saint Patrick's Day, and big-city political machines. The Irish, furthermore, are supposed to be among the most conservative and racist of white Americans, with greater alcoholism problems than other Americans. This superficial imagery is an inaccurate portrayal of the past and present realities of the Irish American experience. The Irish contribution to the development of the United States has been major.

We can now turn to some basic questions about the Irish. How did the Irish come to these shores in the first place? What was their immigration experience? What proportions were Protestant and Catholic? What conflicts have occurred? How does the assimilation model fit the Irish experience? How successful have the Irish been?

IRISH IMMIGRATION: AN OVERVIEW

On the migration continuum running from slave importation to voluntary immigration, the Irish migration to North America would be placed toward the voluntary end. The voluntary character of this movement was less than for some other European groups, for there was great economic and political pressure to leave Ireland. Yet there was choice involved, in regard to the countries chosen as points of destination. Perhaps 200,000 to 300,000 Irish left for the colonies prior to 1787; between 1787 and the 1820s approximately 100,000 migrated.[1] The decades between 1841 and 1860 saw the heaviest migration, with about 1.6 million immigrants. Migration peaked again in the 1880s and 1890s, but then dropped off sharply in subsequent decades to a trickle after World War II. From 1941 to 1980 the total number of immigrants was less than 170,000.[2]

The Eighteenth-Century Migration

The first Irish came prior to 1700, in small numbers. In the 1650s Captain John Vernon was employed to supply 550 persons from southern Ireland as servants and workers for the English colonists in New England, and by 1700 a few Irish Catholic families had settled in Maryland.[3] Not until the 1700s did large numbers of Irish arrive on North American shores. A significant proportion of these were from northern Ireland (Ulster) and had Scottish ancestry, but many were from southern Ireland and could trace their ancestry back into ancient Irish history.

There were push and pull factors. The image of North America as a land of opportunity was for most immigrants a major factor, but domestic pressures were also important. In the 1600s Ireland had been conquered by the English. Scots, in increasing numbers, were encouraged to migrate across the channel to the North of Ireland and to develop lands given to English and Scottish landowners by the king of England. Subsequently the English drove the native Irish off the land.[4]

As a result of this English colonizing of Ireland, the Ulster (northern) Irish who migrated to North America contained a significant number of persons of Scottish ancestry. Yet those who migrated were the fourth or fifth generation in Ireland. They had become Irish; Ireland was their home.[5] There is some debate among scholars as to how much the Scottish settlers blended together with the Irish, but it is clear that some intermixture, cultural and marital, did occur. Their nationality, as they themselves would say, was not Scottish but Irish.

To what extent were the migrants from northern Ireland in the 1700s joined by large numbers from southern areas? To what extent were these migrants Celtic* or Catholic? These are questions debated by scholars. The traditional view has been that virtually all the immigrants before 1800 were "Scotch-Irish," Presbyterians from northern Ireland. Ford and Leyburn

*"Celtic" refers to those inhabitants of Ireland whose ancestry dates far back before the Roman and English invasions of the island.

claim that the immigrants were generally persons from the North with Presbyterian backgrounds.[6] Yet other authors have provided evidence of a very large southern (and thus Catholic) component to this migration. O'Brien argues that "there is unquestionable proof that every part of Ireland contributed to the enormous emigration of its people, and while there are no official statistics now available—for none were kept—to indicate the numerical strength of those Irish immigrants, abundant proof of this assertion is found in authentic records."[7]

For example, tens of thousands of people with old Celtic names appear in the records. Evidence of the significant quantity of non-Ulster immigrants is suggested by data on passenger ships. Of 318 such ships sailing between 1767 and 1769, 60 percent neither came from nor ended up in northern Irish ports; in the 1771–1774 period, the figure was 57 percent for 576 ships. Such evidence is only suggestive, however, since an unknown number of ships from northern Ireland stopping in southern ports for provisions apparently gave the latter as their points of departure.[8]

O'Brien argues that southern Irish migrants gave up the traditional faith, in part because there were few Catholic churches already in the colonies, in part because in many areas (in Ireland and in the colonies) practicing the Catholic faith was dangerous because of the hostile Protestant environment.[9] Local laws often required children to be baptised as Protestant, and there was great antagonism towards "papists." Conversion of the Catholic Irish to Protestantism was apparently common in the early migration. One Episcopalian clergyman wrote to a missionary society that "there were many Irish Papists in Pennsylvania who turn Quakers and get into places as well as Germans."[10]

It is clear that the northern Irish in the first waves of immigration regarded themselves as "Irish" rather than as "Scotch-Irish." In the first two centuries of Irish presence the term "Scotch-Irish" was seldom used. The new migrants gave Irish names to their settlements and joined organizations such as the Friendly Sons of Saint Patrick rather than Scottish American societies.[11]

This debate over the percentages of northern and southern Irish in the immigration may seem minor. Yet understanding the controversy adds to our insight into ethnic relations. The term Scotch-Irish came into heavy usage in the decades after 1850, when some Irish Protestant immigrants and their British friends sought to distinguish themselves from Irish Catholic immigrants who were then the focus of much discrimination.[12] The issue of the "Scotch-Irish race" and its impact became a heated one by the late nineteenth century. Prominent politicians praised the members of the "Scotch-Irish race" as great pioneers and democrats, while they damned the "Catholic Irish race." Consider Henry Cabot Lodge writing in an 1891 issue of *Century Magazine*: "I classified the Irish and the Scotch-Irish as two distinct race-stocks, and I believe the distinction to be a sound one historically and scientifically."[13]

In his famous book *Winning the West*, Theodore Roosevelt dramatized the contributions of the Scotch-Irish frontier people. We had not understood, Roosevelt argued, the important part "played by that stern and virile people," the brave "Puritans" of the West.[14] In the early 1900s scholars argued that the Scotch-Irish were not really Irish, that they saw themselves as Scots resident in Ireland, a distinct and superior racial type with a distinctively different "type of frame and physiognomy."[15]

The view that the Scotch-Irish were part of the Anglo-Saxon or Teutonic "race" was so vigorously propounded that it became an absurd myth which saw no Celtic (i.e., Catholic) Irish part in the early Irish mixture: "Whatever blood may be in the veins of the genuine Scotch-Irishman, one thing is certain, and that is that there is not mingled with it one drop of the blood of the old Irish or Kelt."[16] Thus the data supporting the presence of large numbers of Celtic Irish in the early migration pose serious questions for this racist glorification of the Protestant Irish.

Early Life

What was life like for the Irish settlers in an English-dominated society? Perhaps half became indentured servants; others became farmers or farm workers, often in frontier areas. The English treated Irish servants as lowly subordinates, even to the point of brutality. Discriminatory import duties and longer indenture terms were placed on Irish servants.[17] Irish Catholic servants suffered because of both their nationality and their religion. As early as 1704 heavy taxes were placed on Irish Catholic immigrants. Laws were passed excluding them or discouraging their importation.[18] With times as hard as this, significant numbers of the Irish gave up their Catholicism. Not all converted, however. Irish immigrants in some Pennsylvania counties were predominantly Catholics. A few Catholic churches are recorded as having been established under their auspices. Pressing for religious tolerance, several prominent Irish Catholics wrote President Washington in the late 1700s asking that the full religious rights of Catholics be protected.[19]

Pennsylvania and New England received the first waves of Ulster Irish migration, in the decades before 1740. After 1740 many migrated to the inland valleys of Virginia and the Carolinas. Many of these, perhaps half, also were indentured servants; others became farmers. Immigrants' letters to Ireland reveal that America was considered a land of hope.[20] Many eighteenth-century Irish immigrants, encouraged to settle in frontier areas as a barrier against the Native Americans, often came into conflict with the latter, as well as with British landowners on whose land they sometimes squatted.[21]

By 1790 almost 10 percent of the white United States population of 3.2 million was Irish.[22] The Ulster Irish, somewhat more numerous, comprised large proportions of the Georgia, Pennsylvania, and South Carolina populations, while those from the southern provinces of Ireland were most substantially represented in Maryland, Virginia, Delaware, and North Carolina. The Irish were the second largest white nationality group at the time of the new nation's birth.

The Nineteenth-Century Migration

In the decades after 1790 migration picked up, although a dramatic increase was not to occur until the 1840s, when a torrent of new workers and their families began to change the overwhelming English, Protestant, rural character of the U.S. population.

The pull factors motivating millions of Irish Catholics to cross the Atlantic after 1840 were the same as those that attracted European immigrants for centuries to North America, which was, often in exaggerated terms, portrayed as the land of golden opportunity. "Push" factors loomed even larger. A potato blight led to terrible food shortages and widespread starvation lasting for a decade; this, together with continuing English political and economic oppression, triggered the migration of more than 1.6 million Irish in just two decades.[23]

The Atlantic crossing was dangerous. Few ships arrived which had not lost a number of their poorly accommodated passengers to starvation or disease. Survivors usually chose urban destinations. New York became a major center, eventually housing more Irish than Dublin.[24] Like most urban migrants the new immigrants went where relatives or fellow villagers had settled.

Residential segregation for Irish Americans in the nineteenth century had a distinctive form. Huge ghettos, such as black Americans now live in, were not the rule. Rather, the Irish newcomers found housing wherever they could, usually in the little houses and shanties on the side streets and alleys beside or behind the fashionable homes of affluent Anglo-Saxon urbanites. As blue-collar workers, they often lived within walking distance of manufacturing jobs. They clustered in smaller, more dispersed settlements than would be the case for later immigrant groups.[25]

These scattered settlements were reinforced by a second, equally large, wave of immigrants from Ireland between 1870 and 1900, and by significant but declining numbers of immigrants from 1900 to 1925. These later immigrants were not forced out by famine, but poverty and the hope for a better life were important "push" factors. In New York, Boston, and Philadelphia, slum housing was frequently their lot, with its attendant disease. An analysis of New York revealed that the 1877 death rate for the Irish-born was quite high, as was the mortality rate for their American-born children. Whole families were consigned to a single room in very crowded apartment houses called "rookeries." The Irish were overrepresented in the almshouses of some cities. The same was true for Irish crime rates, which although high for some categories of minor offenses were nonetheless exaggerated by nativists. The rate for *serious* offenses was low.[26] This poverty was the result of a number of factors. Many of the immigrants had few skills, although major reasons were hard jobs, low wages, and direct discrimination against the Irish.

STEREOTYPING THE IRISH

The resistance of English Americans to the Irish immigration dates back to the seventeenth and eighteenth centuries. "Papists" were often the targets of open hatred. Protestant and Catholic Irish Americans suffered from early nativistic concern over their political persuasions, as in the conflicts in the 1790s between the Federalists and the Jeffersonians. Yet it was the nineteenth-century Irish, poor Catholics from the famine-ridden Emerald Isle, who were attacked the most. Nativists harped on anti-Catholic themes. "Scotch-Irish" were singled out as more civilized. Attacks on Irish Catholics took the form of absurd cartoons which stereotyped the Irish using outrageous symbols—an apelike face, a fighting stance, a jug of whiskey, a shillelagh. The influential political caricaturist Thomas Nast published cartoons of this type in *Harper's Weekly* and other magazines. One of his caricatures shows a stereotyped southern black man and a nasty, apelike Irishman, both being viewed as ignorant voters and a threat to orderly politics. "New York's leading cartoonists of the 1870s and 1880s," notes Curtis, "certainly did not refrain from simianizing Irish-American Paddies who epitomized the tens of thousands of working-class immigrants and their children caught up in urban poverty and slum conditions after their flight from rural poverty and famine in Ireland."[27] Popular and scholarly stereotypes of the Catholic Irish, increasingly distinguished from the superior "Teutonic-origin Scotch-Irish," pictured them as ignorant, lazy, violence-oriented peasants.

The Ape Image

Not surprisingly, the apelike image of the Irish was imported from England. With the rise of debates over evolution in England, the poor Irish came to be regarded by many in England and in America as the "missing link" between the gorilla and the stereotyped Negro. With the constant threat of Irish rebellion on the one hand and the press of Darwinism on the other, "it was comforting for some Englishmen to believe—on the basis of the best scientific authority in the Anthropological Society of London—that their own facial angles and orthognathous features were as far removed from those of apes, Irishmen, and Negroes as was humanly possible."[28] In the process of rationalizing the exploitation of the Irish and of black Africans, dehumanizing stereotypes developed on both sides of the Atlantic.

Notice the comparable position of black and Irish Americans in this mythology. Greeley has underscored parallels in prejudice and stereotyping: "Practically every accusation that has been made against the American blacks was also made against the Irish: Their family life was inferior, they had no ambition, they did not keep up their homes, they drank too much, they were not responsible, they had no morals, it was not safe to walk through their neighborhoods at night, they voted the way crooked politicians told them to vote, they were not willing to pull themselves up by their bootstraps, they were not capable of education, they could not think for themselves, and they would always remain social problems for the rest of the country."[29] Early stage shows made fun of the Irish using these stereotypes, just as they did with blacks. In the nineteenth century the Catholic Irish were often socially defined by those in dominant groups as physically different, and thus as a "race." Later on, in the twentieth century, the emphasis on this alleged physical distinctiveness would disappear, so that exclusive emphasis would come to be placed on cultural or nationality distinctiveness.

In recent decades Irish Catholic Americans have been seen by some popular and scholarly analysts as a particularly antiblack and racist group of white Americans. This too is false. Compared with most other groups of white Americans, Irish Catholics are relatively liberal. A review of recent opinion polls came to this conclusion:

> Surveys in the 1970s revealed that in the North Irish Catholics were more sympathetic to integrated neighborhoods, integrated schools, and interracial marriages than other white Catholics and white Protestants. Among whites only Jews are more liberal on racial issues than Irish Catholics.[30]

Moreover, Irish Catholics in the northern United States are more likely than other whites to live in racially integrated neighborhoods. Of course, relatively liberal racial attitudes sometimes do not carry over into actual behavior, for Irish Catholics, like other whites, have played their role in discrimination against nonwhite Americans. The point here is that Irish Catholics have been more liberal and progressive on racial matters than many other white Gentile groups.[31]

PROTEST AND CONFLICT

From their first decades in North America, Irish Americans have suffered not only from verbal abuse and stereotyping but also from intentional discrimination and violent attacks. Irish Americans have on occasion retaliated, even to the point of violence. In other situations they have inaugurated conflict. As noted in Chapter 2, ethnic conflict means a struggle over resources and can be generated by inequality. Conflict can take both nonviolent and violent forms, and it often involves groups with differing power and resources.

Assimilation theorists have seriously neglected the conflict which is a recurrent feature of interethnic and interracial relations. Indeed, some views of American history embody a myth of "peaceful progress." In this view, common in recent decades, the members of each white ethnic group have advanced higher on the social ladder by pulling themselves up by their bootstraps—by hard work and diligent effort, not by active protest and collective violence. This image is incorrect. As with other white groups, in the case of the Irish the struggle for their "place in the sun" has been with many groups, running from established Anglo-Saxon Protestant groups to Native Americans. The Irish have been involved in conflict with groups above and below them in the social hierarchy.

Early Conflict

The first major conflict was with the established groups which were in control of the major institutions in the North American colonies at the time of the initial Irish migration. A few eighteenth-century Irish settlements were damaged or destroyed by attacks. British Americans attacked and destroyed an Irish community in Worcester, Massachusetts in the eighteenth century.[32] There was a great deal of vigorous opposition from the colonists to both Catholic and Protestant Irish migrants. Puritans such as Cotton Mather saw those of the Presbyterian religion as a threat and attacked proposals to bring the Irish in as the work of the Devil.[33]

Conflict arose between the Irish Protestant farmers in the frontier areas and the plantation gentry of British connections in the coastal areas. In the early period, the back-country Irish were sometimes seen as crude frontier people. Settling in frontier areas, the Ulster Irish defied laws made by eastern interests and engaged in aggressive protest and collective violence in the Whisky Rebellion and the Regulation movement, movements to extend their control when it suited their own ends. North Carolina saw violent conflict. Predominantly Irish frontier settlements, protesting high taxes, formed a Regulation movement, whose members were pledged to resist eastern influence. Violence against authorities was met by the sending of troops to crush the Regulation rebellion.[34]

Conflict with Native Americans was also an early part of the Irish immigrants' experience. The Irish were encouraged to settle the frontier areas of the colonies so that the dominant eastern interests would be protected from Native Americans. Scalping was institutionalized by English and Irish settlers. Placing bounties on the scalps of Native American men and women became a common practice in New England and in the middle colonies. Conflict between the Irish who were taking Native American lands and the Native Americans who were protecting their way of life became widespread in Virginia and the Carolinas.[35]

In the 1790s there were violent attacks on Irish Catholics in Maryland and elsewhere. In 1798 there was a "Federal Riot" at Saint Mary's Church in Philadelphia: opponents of the new Alien Law who had come to the church with a petition for the congregation to sign were beaten up by a group of Federalist rioters.[36] While the Irish had a valid reputation for aggressiveness, much of the rioting in the period after 1800 was directed against them because they were immigrants and Roman Catholics. Most "Irish riots" were triggered by anti-Irish incidents, often by anti-Catholic acts. An 1806 riot in New York was generated by Protestant attempts to break up a Catholic religious service.[37] Anglo-Saxon Protestant attacks on Irish Catholics took many forms. Homes were stoned in Boston in the 1820s; a convent was burned in the 1830s.

Churches were destroyed in several cities.[38] By 1850 most large cities had seen anti-Catholic demonstrations and riots. Philadelphia became a center for anti-Irish-Catholic violence. There, in 1844, two major riots "resulted in the burning of two Catholic churches. . . . ; the destruction of dozens of Catholic homes; and sixteen deaths."[39] In the 1850s new nativist groups such as the Know-Nothings played a major role in the conflict with the Irish. There were open battles in cities from New York to St. Louis. After the Civil War nativists renewed their attacks on Catholics, particularly on the Irish. The American Protective Association movement was a major example of nativist action after 1870.[40]

Later Group Conflict

Conflict in the mine fields was a major feature of the Irish experience in the latter half of the nineteenth century. The Irish workers and better-paid English workers often did not get along.[41] Old feuds were renewed. In the early days of copper mining in Michigan, English and Irish miners fought in a struggle for jobs.[42] Similar struggles characterized the coal-mining areas of Pennsylvania, where the Irish had played a major role in developing the anthracite coal mines. Here they found English and Welsh owners and English control of skilled work.[43] Conditions were oppressive. Pay rates were low, perhaps $20 to $30 a month. Often pay was in the form of "bobtail check"; that is, money owed to the company for groceries and rent equaled one's wages, a situation of wage slavery.[44] Such oppression and poverty led to violent conflict between predominantly British Protestant owners and superintendents and Irish Catholic miners.

As early as the Civil War, trouble between the Irish and the older groups flared up in Pennsylvania. There was opposition to the Union cause and to the draft among Irish workers who saw it as "a rich man's war." Many feared blacks would come north and take their jobs away from them. The use of troops against Irish groups protesting the war was narrowly avoided.[45]

The coal strike of 1875, called the "Long Strike," forced many miners into near-starvation conditions. The owners broke the strike and finished off attempts at unionization.[46] As a result, secret Irish organizations linked to the Ancient Order of the Hibernians (AOH) resorted to assassination and sabotage tactics. The owners used violence against AOH groups. Numerous shootings were engineered by the Anglo-Saxon establishment, and the miners replied with armed defense and guerilla warfare of their own.[47] Although called "Molly Maguires" (after older organizations in Ireland), the protesting miners were not part of that secret organization. The miners were members of miners' organizations who went underground when moderate protests failed.

Rather than yield to the reasonable requests of the miners for better wages, the owners hired a private army of private detectives to put down the workers' rebellion. One detective, sent into the fields to spy, gathered information used in court cases; twenty Irish miners were publicly hanged for engaging in protest. The owners' counterattack in the courts was reinforced by nativism which portrayed the members of the secret societies as undisciplined, violent Irishmen.[48] This was clear in the trials of the miners, whose convictions were influenced by Irish stereotypes. Broehl suggests that "it was, plainly, more than a labor-management squabble, . . . for behind the case were fundamental ethnic, religious, and personal tensions that mirrored the pressures of American life in the second half of that century."[49]

Violence and Rioting

Irish Americans, on occasion, have found themselves competing economically with groups lower on the socioeconomic ladder, as we have already seen in the case of Irish Protestants and Native Americans on the frontier. As early as the 1840s, Irish competition with black Americans in northern cities engendered substantial distrust and hostility between the two groups. Between the 1840s and the 1860s Irish workers attacked black workers in several cities in the North. During the Civil War Irish hostility toward black Americans increased, for the two groups were major competitors in the struggle for the dirty, low-paying jobs at the bottom of the employment pyramid. Irish opposition to blacks was basically economic: "they feared the competition of the hordes of freed slaves who might invade the North, and valued the security that came from the existence in the country of at least one social class below them."[50]

Excluded from unions, blacks sometimes were used as strikebreakers. The use of black strikebreakers spurred the 1863 Irish riot, usually termed the "Draft Riot," the most serious American riot before or since. Perhaps four hundred rioters were killed in the streets, together with some black freedmen and some white police and soldiers. Rioters attacked Yankees, the police, and black freedmen.[51] At the front of the rioters were Irish longshoremen who were upset at the recent use of black strikebreakers. Even into the present this tension has persisted in the cities. Irish and other white ethnic frustration at black gains in the 1960s and 1970s was a familiar topic of conversation in the mass media. Many felt that blacks were receiving a disproportional share of government benefits, more than the urban white ethnics were themselves receiving. Today there are serious tensions between black and Irish residents in a few cities, such as Boston and Chicago.

On the West Coast the Irish fought to maintain their economic position in the mid-nineteenth century. Competition from Chinese laborers led to anti-Chinese attacks in Irish papers, as well as meetings and parades demanding prohibition of further Chinese immigration. Anti-Chinese protest was led by Irish immigrants and their descendants.[52]

By 1900 competition with the new immigrants from southern and eastern Europe had become a problem for some Irish workers. This migration confronted Irish Americans with a new type of economic competition. In Chicago and Boston, Irish control of the Church and of political parties was also a major source of friction with these new immigrant groups.[53]

POLITICS AND POLITICAL INSTITUTIONS

When the Irish began arriving in the seventeenth century, much of the political framework was already fashioned by the English. Those Irish who came in the eighteenth century played a minority role as participants in the steps taken to shape the nation's basic institutions.[54] Some

Irish were to be found among the founding fathers. There were a number among the signers of the Declaration of Independence—altogether eight of the fifty-six, five from the North and three from the South of Ireland.[55]

Only four men born in Ireland were members of the Constitutional Convention, together with three other men of Irish descent. Several were Catholics. At least two Irishmen were members of the first U.S. Senate, and two were members of the first U.S. House. Before 1800 a few of the Irish could be found participating at state and local government levels, as governors of territories and states and as mayors.[56]

Most of the Irish migrating after the Revolutionary War settled in eastern cities, where they became involved in politics. The Irish, not unexpectedly, were anti-Federalist and supported the democratic factions. Here again was interethnic competition. The Federalist-sponsored Alien and Sedition Acts of 1798 were directed in part against them. Irish immigrants taking offense at such actions led to the downfall of the Federalists, for Irish voters turned out en masse to help elect Jefferson. In this period the Irish from the south and north of Ireland were united. A few years later the same Irish vote would play an important role in electing a first Irish (Protestant) president, Andrew Jackson.[57]

Political Organization in the Cities

Traditionally discussion of the Irish in politics has focused on the Irish Catholics. The common terms are *boss* and *machine*. The theme of corrupt urban machines has been tied to hostile views of immigrants. Protestant views have tended to be pious: "In general, the Irish Catholic political machines in the United States have been notoriously and flamboyantly corrupt—a disgrace to Catholicism, to American democracy, and to the Irish people."[58] Commenting on the Irish machine in New York, William Adams argued that "the 'horrible example' of New York politics combined with a rapid increase of pauper immigrants to check the advance of liberal ideas."[59] The tone of such analyses is that the Irish were more unscrupulous and corrupt in their political activities than other ethnic groups. In fact the Irish entered a political system with many weaknesses, including no secret ballot and much political corruption. Machines existed before the Irish ever controlled them. Political organizations by which those in power secured their poor constituents jobs, housing, and food were already the rule in cities.

Why then the strong Irish involvement in local politics? Politics was one means to social mobility, a means of achieving power in the face of great Anglo-Saxon Protestant opposition. The dominant perspective in the nineteenth and early twentieth centuries tended toward a hands-off view, with government staying out of economic affairs as much as possible. It was against this do-nothing background that desperate urban residents, plagued with unemployment, low income, and poor housing, reacted by joining large-scale urban political organizations. Taking control of local party organizations, immigrant leaders shaped government programs benefiting the poor. Providing jobs—for example, in real estate and transportation construction—was one of the machines' most critical functions. While the political elite could make a great deal of money as brokers of construction, acting illegally, poor immigrants were less concerned about corruption than with jobs.[60]

One of the first great machines was in New York City. In 1817 a group of Irishmen, incensed at discrimination at the hands of New York's political machine, the Tammany Society, broke into a meeting, demanding the nomination of an Irish person for Congress. Although they were driven away this time, a few decades later the Irish penetrated the New York political organization. Irish political power brought new leadership to Tammany Hall in the 1860s and 1870s. One major figure, William M. Tweed, better known as "Boss Tweed," has long been cursed by many writers for his alleged greed and corruption. Numerous articles and textbooks have heralded this image of "Boss Tweed." Yet this image is largely myth. In reality, William M. Tweed was a political leader who represented the underdog, including the Irish and the Jews, in nineteenth century New York. He was tolerant of religious beliefs, a family man, and ambitious. He identified with New York's poor immigrants and worked to build schools and hospitals. He was hated by Anglo-Saxon Protestant Republicans because of his identification with immigrants. Yet Tweed's own ethnic background remains unclear; he was apparently of Scottish or Irish descent. Because of growing Irish political power, Tweed became a powerful New York political leader and rewarded Irish and other immigrant constituents with jobs, schools, and social services. Recent research on Tweed indicates that he may well have been less corrupt than many traditional Anglo-Saxon Protestant politicians who have much dominated urban politics before and since.[61]

New York City finally elected an Irish mayor in the 1880s; and the Irish have played a major role in New York politics to the present. Not surprisingly, heavy Irish representation in appointed public jobs has characterized New York politics up to the present, although this representation is on the decline.[62]

With large Catholic proportions in their populations, over time numerous cities have seen the Irish gain important positions. In vigorous fights with English and other British Americans, the Irish gradually won a place in the political sun in Boston, Brooklyn, Philadelphia, New Haven, and Chicago. For example, after initial Irish Catholic occupancy of the mayor's office in 1899 in New Haven, the Irish became an increasingly significant political force.[63]

The Irish political organizations, except in Chicago, were gone by the 1960s. The paramount Irish boss, even into the 1970s, was Mayor Richard J. Daley. In 1962 the Irish comprised about 10 to 15 percent of Chicago's population, but had a quarter of the fifty aldermanic positions, the mayor's chair, and 42 percent of the fifty ward committee seats.[64] There are complexities to the Chicago machine: tremendous urban development and renewal, allowing friends to get city construction contracts, keeping old people on the payrolls even when their work ability has diminished. A policy rewarding friends and punishing enemies has been a way of life for political organizations like that in Chicago.[65]

Pragmatism in Politics

For the Irish, politics is an honorable profession. Family and friends provide the necessary entry networks into political positions.[66] The Irish developed a political style based on a concern for individuals and a personal loyalty to leaders.[67] Individual charity is a major feature. One Irish official is quoted by Levine: "When a man is ill in government and without enough time for retirement or health benefits, an efficient man fires him. Yet the Irish administrator says, 'What the hell, he has two kids,' and keeps him on. He knows this is a risky thing, letting him come in at ten and leave at two. So what happens? He gets a little more work out of the others to make it up."[68]

In recent decades Irish politicians have been influenced by reform movements to clean up blatant corruption. Some Irish politicians have been reformers, playing a major role in bringing down the corrupt leaders of political machines in New York and other cities. Yet the personal, pragmatic, nonideological style of Irish politics remains.[69]

Pragmatic politics is a major Irish contribution to American politics, with its coalition and compromise themes. One principle is that a city is a mosaic of different racial and ethnic groups and the machine is a broker, balancing off groups so that a coalition can hang together. The leaders believe in balanced tickets, for they know that people vote along ethnic lines: they are aware of the hopes and fears of the voters. Such politicians are also aware of a tendency toward trust, rationality, and a sympathy for humanistic reforms in these same groups.[70] The Irish politicians have been critical to urban coalition building. In addition, Irish organizations have made a major contribution to the bricks-and-mortar development of cities. Without the Irish contractors tied to the machines, one can speculate as to who would have met the need for public buildings, streets, and subways in many cities.[71]

With suburbanization and intermarriage with other Catholic Americans, this Irish political style has begun to fade, but it has by no means disappeared. A recent study of 51 cities by Clark found that the cities with larger Irish populations were more likely than other cities to have a local government (often Irish-dominated) which provided a high level of public services for city residents. There was more responsiveness to poorer groups, including blacks, in these Irish-populated cities than in other cities. Irish political machines may be fading, but their humane, services-oriented, patronage approach to government persists. Even in the suburbs Irish Catholicism undergirds Irish ethnicity. Some analysts have attempted to link the upward mobility of the Irish to a growing "conservatism." Since the 1960s the Irish electorates in New York and Connecticut have tended to prefer the more conservative political candidates in mayoral, gubernatorial, and senatorial races. Elsewhere, however, they continue to vote for liberal and moderate Democrats.[72]

Taken as a whole, Irish Americans are generally more liberal than numerous other white Gentile groups. Irish Catholic Americans have a progressive, sometimes radical, political tradition. Today they are heavily Democratic, with a large proportion of liberal Democrats among them. And they have been central figures in labor unions fighting for workers' rights, as in the United Steel Workers and the United Mine Workers unions.

National Politics

After 1840 the Irish electorate was increasingly sought after by presidential and congressional candidates. Grant, the Republican presidential candidate in 1868, wooed Irish votes; after he was elected he made a few Irish appointments to his administration. In most succeeding elections the Irish vote has been sought by presidential candidates of both parties.[73]

One study of the 1901–1910 period found that 13 percent of 162 prominent political leaders, including presidents, senators, representatives, and Supreme Court justices, were Irish, compared to 56 percent who were English (or Welsh).[74] Irish *Catholic* influence at the national level was weak. In a letter sent to Theodore Roosevelt, a prominent Irish writer, Finley Peter Dunne, commented on the lack of Irish influence: "As for the point about Irishmen holding office, I simply wanted to emphasize the fact that Irishmen are the most unsuccessful politicians in the country. Although they are about all there is to politics in the North between elections, there is not, with one exception, a single representative Irish man in any important cabinet, diplomatic, judicial or administrative office that I know about."[75] Penetration at the city level did not necessarily lead to important positions in the federal executive or judicial branches for Irish Catholics.

Most research literature on the Irish in politics at the national level, as well as at the local level, focuses on Irish Catholics. Millions of Irish Protestants, many in rural and southern areas, have received very little attention in political science analysis of the last century's politics. Ironically, the one prominent Scotch-Irish president in the first decades of the twentieth century, Woodrow Wilson, was not sympathetic to Irish national consciousness or Irish Catholic causes. Wilson was opposed by the Irish Catholic press because of his background and lack of support for the Irish fight against England. Irish Americans, primarily Catholics, have periodically reacted to the oppression of their brothers and sisters in Ireland. Numerous Irish nationalist groups came to public attention in the last decades of the nineteenth and the first decades of the twentieth centuries and attempted to shift American foreign policy away from its pro-English stance.[76]

Some Irish American sympathy in World War I lay with Germany. Meetings protesting Wilson's "unneutral neutrality" were held in cities across the nation. Numerous Irish Americans opposed the reelection of Wilson not only because of his pro-British stance but also because of his attack on "hyphenated" Americans, those Americans who wished to retain their ethnic heritage.

After World War I, a critical issue was Wilson's, and many other Protestants', stand on the question of Ireland's independence. In the 1918

British elections several dozen Irish representatives were elected to Parliament, but they met separately, set up an Irish Republic, and were arrested by the British. Widespread guerilla warfare developed, the rebellion was brutally suppressed, and its leaders executed. The brutality and the other issues surrounding independence racked Irish communities in the United States, again leading to organization and protest meetings. In subsequent decades the issue of an independent, united Ireland became less important, but it continued into the 1980s as a cause which can periodically generate financial and political support among Irish Americans. In 1971 Senator Edward Kennedy of Massachusetts introduced a U.S. Senate resolution asking for the removal of the British soldiers from Irish soil.[77]

The controversy over Ireland not only illustrates the interethnic struggle up to the present, in this case over foreign policy within the traditional political arena, but also shows the way in which external events in the country of origin for a segment of the population can long affect interethnic relations within the United States. This thematic pattern, the reader should note, will occur periodically in the chapters which follow, as, for example, in the effect of events in Italy on Italian Americans or in Japan on Japanese Americans.

An Irish Catholic President

By the late 1920s Irish Catholics had become increasingly visible at the level of national politics. Alfred E. Smith was the first Irish Catholic to carve out an important role in presidential politics. In 1928 he became an unsuccessful Democratic candidate for president. His Catholic religion, his calls for modification of Prohibition, his lack of knowledge of much of the United States—all these factors counted against him in this first Irish Catholic presidential campaign. He nevertheless managed to equal or exceed the Republican vote in eleven of the nation's twelve largest cities, pulling the new urban immigrants into a national voting bloc in the Democratic party for the first time. No candidate could again ignore the growing importance of the non-Protestant vote in the booming cities.[78]

By 1930, with the exception of one Supreme Court justice, there were no Irish Catholics holding major positions in the judicial and executive branches of the federal government. Franklin Roosevelt was the first president to choose Irish Catholics for important appointive positions, including ambassador to Great Britain, postmaster general, and attorney general. In the New Deal electoral landslides many were sent for the first time to Congress. Both Roosevelt and Truman appointed far more Irish Catholic judges and executive officers than any previous president.[79]

Not until 1960, three hundred years after the first few Irish Catholics had come to the United States and more than a century after there were sizeable Irish Catholic communities, was the first and only Irish Catholic president elected. Conventional ethnic descriptions of American presidents indicate that six of the thirty-six (17 percent) from Washington to Nixon had an Irish nationality background, although with the exception of Kennedy this background has been termed "Scotch-Irish" or "Protestant Irish."

President John F. Kennedy was a descendant of Irish Catholic politicians in Boston; Kennedy was elected on the "backs of three generations of district leaders and county chairmen."[80] His grandfather had been mayor of Boston; his father was the first Irish Catholic to serve as ambassador to Great Britain. John Kennedy came from the small, wealthy elite. Yet he was a pragmatic politician. Immediate day-to-day problems of food and shelter were critical issues to him. In the 1960 presidential election Irish Catholic votes in New England, New York, and Pennsylvania helped to shape Kennedy's victory. Nationwide he received an estimated 75 percent of the Irish vote, but only 50.1 percent of the total vote. As president, Kennedy acted to some extent on behalf of America's newer and emergent urban groups, appointing the *first* Italian American and the *first* Polish American to a presidential cabinet and the first black American to head up an independent government agency.[81]

THE IRISH IN THE ECONOMY

As we noted in Chapter 2, one type of structural assimilation involves large-scale movement by members of an immigrant group into the secondary-organization levels of a society, such as governmental agencies. Another critical movement is into the economic organizations—the farms, businesses, and factories—of the core society. Such movement is termed *social mobility*.

The majority of Irish immigrants started out at the bottom of the economic pyramid, filling the hard, dirty, laboring jobs on farms and in cities. The eighteenth-century Irish migrants, among whom were a large number of northern Irish, contributed significantly to the economic development of the colonies, and of the new nation beginning in 1787, by providing low-paid agricultural labor. They contributed to fledgling industries with weavers for the textile industry and laborers for the road and canal transportation systems. In New England they were important in commerce; in the South they became farm laborers, farmers, and owners of small businesses. Few data are available on the mobility patterns of these Irish immigrants or their descendants over the next century or two. Many moved from indentured service to their own farms. Most seem to have moved up the economic ladder over the next few generations, sometimes at the expense of later Catholic immigrants.[82]

The Irish after 1830

Irish immigrants after 1830 typically became urban workers or laborers in mining or transportation. Irish Catholic labor was critical to industrial and commercial development. Hard, dirty, low-paying work was the lot of most immigrants. They had migrated looking for work. Irish men found it in unskilled jobs, on the docks, and in the factories of large cities, and Irish women found it as servants in Anglo-Saxon Protestant homes. In an 1855 census of New York City three-quarters of the domestics (the maids and other servants) were Irish. Yet the Irish were only one-quarter of the population. Many immigrants were single females unattached to family groups. Impoverished and alone in an alien land, they moved into domestic work where they could live with a family. Later immigrant women, such as Italians and Jews, were not as likely to go into domestic work. This had little to do with differences in cultural backgrounds, but resulted simply from the different character of later migration—Jewish and Italian women generally came with their families. Irish women came alone not by choice but because of the terrible economic conditions in Ireland under English rule.[83]

Male Irish immigrants became farm laborers, canal and railroad laborers, miners, and textile workers. Many died in the process of building American transportation systems, as the old saying "There's an Irishman buried under every railroad tie" indicates. As late as 1876, half of Irish-born Americans were still in the worst-paid, dirtiest jobs, compared to 10 to 20 percent of other ethnic groups.[84]

Irish Catholics encountered direct discrimination in employment. Few employers would hire them except for unskilled positions. By the 1840s Boston newspapers carried advertisements with the phrase "None need apply but Americans."[85] The Irish in Boston were relegated to the least-skilled occupations. Stereotyped as unskilled or rowdies, Irish men and women were denied jobs by Protestant employers.

Numerous observers have blamed these Irish immigrants for the emergence of urban poverty problems. Against the contributions of such immigrants, argues Adams, "must be set certain intangible social burdens on the whole community and some definite expenditures, of which poor relief through almshouses, hospitals, and dispensaries was most costly."[86] Many among the Irish became dependent on charity or public aid. But local and state governments in that period actually provided rather little in the way of support for the poor—the majority of whom were not Irish.

Few among the millions of immigrants and their children moved from rags to riches. Many did save some money, sending a great deal back to Ireland. This charitable impulse reduced their own chances for mobility in the United States. Other factors retarded economic development. One study of Newburyport, Massachusetts, revealed that Irish working-class families were more likely than was commonly thought to have accumulated some property (housing) holdings. But one price of accumulated property of this particular type was a spartan life and the early employment of children, so that the education of this latter generation was reduced. Economic advance in one generation did not necessarily mean upward mobility for subsequent generations. In addition, building a separate church and parochial school system meant some drain on resources.[87]

Even with these burdens, in the decades after the Civil War some Irish Catholics had begun to move up the socioeconomic ladder. For example, in Newburyport, Massachusetts, structural movement upward in the economy came early for a small group.[88] The Irish in Philadelphia, by the decade after the Civil War, had already begun to move into middle-income residential areas. While most still found themselves in segregated, inferior housing, a significant number had begun to move to better housing. Philadelphia had become a major eastern center for manufacturing and transportation. The concentration of the Irish in unskilled labor later gave way to semiskilled and skilled positions in Philadelphia manufacturing concerns. New economic gains were reflected in the erection of churches, parochial schools, and charitable institutions. Contrasts with the Boston Irish suggest that Irish economic advancement there came more slowly than it did in Philadelphia because of Boston's slower business growth.[89]

Significant numbers of the Catholic Irish became upwardly mobile near the turn of the twentieth century. A major reason was the point at which they entered an ever-expanding, labor-hungry capitalism. New cities emerged as capitalists centered new types of manufacturing in the industrial heartland, from Pittsburgh to Chicago and Detroit. In the late nineteenth century occupational success for the Irish seems to have come a bit more rapidly in midwestern cities than in older East-coast cities.

Powerful urban political machines facilitated mobility by providing some economic resources, at least menial jobs, to begin the upward trek. Machines channeled money into building projects, facilitating the emergence of a business elite. By the end of the nineteenth century the Irish in Philadelphia could boast of twice the proportion of contractors and builders as other immigrant groups. The growing number of worker organizations aided Irish mobility. As early as the 1850s the Irish had control of a few labor organizations in Massachusetts and New York. By the early 1900s unions among longshoremen, construction workers, and miners emerged, some providing, as we have seen, the base for protest. To the present day, the Irish have been prominent in labor organizations, including the AFL-CIO.[90]

The Irish, especially Irish Protestants, had begun to penetrate business and professional areas by the middle of the nineteenth century. A few wealthy entrepreneurs could be found among the Irish Protestants. A study of the handful of native-born U.S. millionaires in the 1761–1924 period found that 8 percent were Irish, apparently Protestant Irish. Of course, this was a considerably smaller proportion than the English and Scottish contingent among men of wealth in this period.[91]

By the turn of the century some progress was obvious for rank and file Catholics. One study of Irish-born immigrants in 1890 Boston revealed them to have an occupational distribution with 0 percent in the professions, 10 percent in other white-collar jobs, and 65 percent in low-skilled jobs. This contrasted greatly with the native-born Boston residents, mostly non-Irish, 47 percent of whom were in white-collar jobs. While the second-generation Irish fared better, they too did not do nearly as well as the native Yankees. Discrimination and poverty were still having an impact. The 1890 Census showed a small proportion of the foreign-born Irish population in professional positions—only 1.7 percent for males.[92]

Mobility in the Twentieth Century

A study of Philadelphia's Irish population in 1900 found that 70 percent were in manufacturing, laboring, and domestic service jobs. Less than 10 percent of employed men and women held professional or managerial jobs. By 1900 the Irish had begun to move slowly up the social and economic ladder, with some holding political office in the urban political organizations, a small but growing middle-income group, and a few prosperous brethren in business, mining, and construction. But a majority were still rather poor. Interestingly, this middle-income group continued to grow, to the point of being stereotyped as "lace curtain" Irish. (The term comes from the prosperity which enabled this group to put up lace window curtains.) The stereotyping of the Irish as drunken, apelike scoundrels was beginning to change.[93]

The little information available on Irish mobility, Catholic and Protestant, for the decades after 1900 suggests increasing economic security for a growing segment of that population. Apparently the Irish Protestant descendants of pre-1840 immigrants were still disproportionately concentrated in farming areas, in towns, and in southern and border states. In the decades of the late nineteenth and early twentieth centuries, and probably in later decades as well, a significant proportion had become relatively prosperous farmers, owners of small businesses, and skilled blue-collar workers, as well as part of the growing clerical-job category. Many were blending into the Anglo-Saxon Protestant mainstream. Whether the overwhelming majority were moving up the socioeconomic ladder is unclear, for many also remained poor and isolated in rural areas. The data we have for these Protestant Irish, unfortunately, are only impressionistic.

By contrast, some concrete data are available on the Irish Catholics. By the 1930s they certainly had not blended into the Anglo-Saxon Protestant mainstream. In their study of Newburyport, Massachusetts, in the 1930s Warner and Srole found that the Irish were moving ever closer to native Yankee residents in socioeconomic status. None, however, could be found at the top. The Depression hit the Irish hard, probably postponing for a decade the major economic breakthrough for the Irish that was just within reach. Baltzell's study of Philadelphians in 1940 revealed that at that point in time few people of wealth and influence were Catholic; at the very top white Protestants still dominated.[94]

Commenting on the business situation in the 1950s and 1960s, Baltzell suggested that business leadership was still British American Protestant. In recent decades Irish Catholics have been less conspicuous in the ranks of leading scientists and industrialists than expected. This may be due in part to the fact that their ancestors brought little scientific or management experience from the homeland. Some have suggested that modest representation in scientific fields may be due to Catholic education, with its classical emphasis. But it is also because of anti-Catholic discrimination at higher levels in business and industry.[95]

Recent Successes and Problems

Irish Catholics have often been employed in politics, in police and fire departments, in the courts, and in colleges and schools. Government employment has been central. A 1964 study of a large urban police department revealed that about 25 percent of the police sergeants were second-generation Irish, although as one might expect by this time very few were first-generation Irish.[96]

In the last two decades Irish Catholics have moved up economically in comparison with other ethnic groups. The Irish are now one of the most prosperous of the white ethnic groups. One analysis of opinion poll data revealed that Irish Catholic males had increased significantly in proportion in low- and high-level white-collar positions compared to their fathers. The proportion for the respondents was 66 percent white-collar, while the proportion for their fathers was 38 percent white-collar. In both generations the Irish Catholics were more likely to be found in better-paying white-collar positions than most other Catholic groups. Particularly in the last decade many Irish Catholics have moved up into the better-paying white-collar jobs. In a 1977–1978 national survey of Irish Catholics, one-third were found to be in professional and managerial positions, which was above the national average of one-quarter and equal to the proportion among British Protestants in that survey.[97]

In many discussions of the Irish, the human symbols of success have typically been athletes, entertainers, politicians, or, more recently, entrepreneurs such as Joseph Kennedy. But another group of Irish heroes has received little notice—the growing group of Irish Ph.D.'s and academics. Catholics now make up one-fourth of faculty members in top state colleges and universities, and about half of these are *Irish*. Irish Catholics are heavily represented in numerous humanities departments. Moreover, many graduate-trained Irish Catholics have moved into local, state, and federal government positions where they now serve as lawyers, administrators, researchers, and elected officials.

Recent surveys of the U.S. population by the National Opinion Research Center have found that the incomes of Irish Catholic families are among the highest of all white American groups. In a late 1970s survey, 47 percent of Irish Catholic families reported incomes over $20,000. The percentage of Irish with incomes over $20,000 was higher than the 26 percent of *all* American families with incomes above that level.[98]

It is difficult to get current mobility data on Irish Protestants; they still make up at least half of the Irish group. Many are still in farming and in the South, where they are disproportionately represented. One exploratory reanalysis of opinion poll surveys has come up with rough figures on occupational prestige and family income for Irish Catholics and Irish Protestants. On occupational prestige the Irish Protestants in the sample surveys scored lower than other Protestant and Catholic groups examined, while Irish Catholics as a group were second only to British Protestants in occupational prestige. Irish Protestants as a group were at the bottom of the twelve groups on family income, while Irish Catholics as a group were at the top. It is clear that the majority of Irish Catholic Americans, and possibly of Irish Protestants, are solidly located in Middle America and are close to British Americans in *average* economic position.[99]

However, as we noted in the last chapter, penetration of the middle-income levels of the society, blue-collar or white-collar, does not guarantee representative participation at the highest levels in business or in government.

EDUCATION

Organized education on a significant scale for the Irish Protestants probably began after the Civil War. In the South, public schools spread in the Reconstruction period; and by the early twentieth century many of the Protestant Irish had apparently taken advantage of public school systems.

The Catholic Irish, in contrast, relied heavily on parochial and public schools in urban areas of the North for organized education. Because of the heated anti-Catholicism of the period, no Catholic schools of any kind existed in 1790. Apart from a few scattered seminaries, it was not until the 1820–1840 period that numerous parochial schools were established. In cities some Irish Catholic children were also beginning to receive public educational instruction, although the intense Americanization pressures in the public schools gave strong impetus to the development of a separate network of church-related schools as a means of retaining their ethnic indentity. By the late 1800s and early 1900s the center of the Irish Catholic community in numerous cities was a large-scale church and parochial school system, attached to which were hospitals and charitable organizations.[100]

By 1960 there were nearly 13,000 elementary and secondary Catholic schools, with an enrollment of five million children. At the center of this immense network are Irish Catholic Americans. In recent decades Catholic parochial schools have become a center of controversy in the United States. Financed by Catholic Americans, these private schools have gradually come to receive some public aid as well. This aid has brought extensive opposition from Protestant and Jewish groups and not a few court cases.[101]

Even today, Irish Catholics are stereotyped by many outsiders as a relatively unsuccessful group in terms of educational and occupational achievement. Yet the reality is a true success story. Even in the 1920s Irish Catholics were going to college in large numbers, above the national average for all whites. By the 1920s the educational achievements of Irish Catholic Americans were impressive, with Catholic colleges being built and college attendance for Irish Catholics on the increase. The Presbyterian Irish had already made important contributions in the area of education, including the establishment of institutions such as Princeton to provide an educated ministry for local Presbyterian churches. One recent study of opinion poll data found that Irish Catholics as a group had an average level of educational attainment about the same as that of British Protestants as a group. The survey found that the average number of years of schooling for Irish Catholics was 12.6, above the U.S. average but below that of Jewish Americans.[102]

RELIGION

In the political and economic spheres the Irish have been pressured to assimilate, more or less in a one-way, nonreciprocal manner, to the established Anglo-Saxon Protestant core society and culture. But in the religious sphere the Irish played the major role in firmly establishing what may well be the most important non-Protestant institution in the United States, the Roman Catholic Church.

While the Presbyterians from northern Ireland seem to have gradually blended into the Protestant religious institutions from the eighteenth century onward, since the same time Irish Catholics have fought intense anti-Catholic prejudice and discrimination to plant securely the Catholic Church in Anglo-Protestant soil. New churches sprang up wherever Catholic laborers went. Priests had long suffered with the poor in Ireland and in the United States, so the Church was respected. In addition to church organizations there were related community organizations of great consequence, including benevolent and charitable organizations, of which the Ancient Order of Hibernians is perhaps the most famous.[103]

The Catholic Church's hierarchy has long been disproportionately Irish. After the heavy immigration of millions of Catholics, Irish influence became great. One analysis of Catholic bishops from 1789 to 1935 revealed that 58 percent were Irish. While 17 percent of the total Catholic population was Irish in the 1970s, a third of the priests and half of the upper hierarchy were Irish. Nonetheless, Irish influence now seems to be declining. In recent years some Irish church leaders have been replaced by Polish, Portuguese, and Italian prelates.[104]

While the Catholic Church has had to adapt to some extent to the preexisting Protestant system, it has had its impact, forcing a sharpening of the separation of church and state in the United States and reinforcing the right of all Americans to choose any faith. The strong tie between the Irish and the Catholic Church has a historical basis. The longtime English oppression in Ireland had burned Catholic loyalty into Irish immigrants.

Parishes and Irish Neighborhoods

In northern cities Irish neighborhoods often are strong and are built around the parish church. Local politics blends together with church and school, as do the local grocery stores and taverns:

> Among Irish Americans, that particular part of the urban turf with which you are identified and in which live most of the people on whom you have a special claim . . . is virtually indistinguishable from the parish; when asked where they are from, Irish Catholics in many cities give not the community's name but the name of the parish—Christ the King, St. Barnabas, All Saints . . . and so forth.[105]

Today in suburbs of cities such as Chicago the Irish Catholic parish survives. Loyalty to the church remains relatively strong; one recent survey found that over half of Irish Catholics go to mass every week.

Irish Catholic priests have dominated U.S. Catholicism. This has shaped the U.S. Church in a number of distinctive ways, some conservative and some progressive. Irish archbishops and cardinals have mostly been a conservative lot, but priests and bishops have led many progressive fights. For example, the longtime president of Notre Dame University, Father Theodore M. Hesburgh, symbolizes the liberalism in Irish Catholicism. For many years, including his service as head of the U.S. Commission on Civil Rights, Father Hesburgh has been outspoken in his support for civil rights laws, for antisegregation action, and for affirmative action benefiting black Americans. A Catholic priest with an Irish mother and honorary degrees from ninety U.S. universities, Father Hesburgh symbolizes the pragmatic liberalism that has come forth out of American Irish Catholicism.[106]

ASSIMILATION THEORIES AND THE IRISH

Now we can examine how the theories and concepts discussed in Chapter 2 help illuminate the experiences of Irish Americans. As we have seen, some power-conflict (such as internal colonialism) analysts specifically omit immigrant groups such as the "white ethnics" from their analyses, preferring to focus on nonwhite groups because most nonwhite groups have endured much greater violence and repression in the process of being subordinated in the North American colonies and in the United States.

With only one or two exceptions the newer white ethnic groups have been allowed much greater structural assimilation. Thus the assimilation theories of Gordon and Greeley are perhaps the most relevant for analysis of groups such as the Irish, Italians, and Jews. Yet in looking at them from the assimilation perspective we must keep in mind something assimilationists tend to forget—the substantial conflict and ethnic stratification which has also characterized the experiences of white ethnic Americans.

Compared to many other ethnic and racial groups, the Irish are several steps up on the ladder of economic success and dominance. Among Irish Americans each new generation has become more incorporated in the core culture and society than prior generations.

The eighteenth-century Irish apparently moved up the social and economic ladders quietly but surely; they were typically Protestants. Substantial assimilation on a number of dimensions apparently came by the late nineteenth century for many of the descendants of eighteenth-century Irish Protestants. One observer argues that this group blended in rather quickly, for "their social and political activities have mixed freely and spread freely through the general mass of American citizenship.[107] While the Scotch-Irish propagandists have exaggerated the rapidity of this cultural and structural assimilation, there is doubtless truth to the view that the early Irish immigrants and their descendants assimilated relatively rapidly at the level of culture, slowly but surely at the level of structural integration into the economy and the polity, and gradually into more intimate social ties and even identification with English and other British American families. Sometime in the last century they became a difficult-to-distinguish part of the

Anglo-Saxon Protestant mainstream. Research on these Irish Protestants is so sketchy that these assertions about rapid assimilation remain tentative and deserve further research.

Assimilation came more slowly for Irish Catholics, who entered in increasingly large numbers after 1840. Some degree of immediate adaptation to the core culture, particularly in learning the language and basic values, is necessary to movement within United States institutions. In regard to language and certain work values, assimilation had to come at an early point for most Irish immigrants. Clark argues that the Irish Catholic adjustments were not as difficult as some have argued. American cities offered hope for escape from the oppressive conditions of Ireland. There was the greater chance for mobility, the expanding industrial environment. The customs had some similarities. While assimilation at all levels did not come quickly and often took several generations, cultural assimilation did proceed.[108]

Religion was an exception. Most Irish Catholics did not become Protestants. In new Irish communities external hostility and a common background reinforced a protective separatist reaction. Conflict with the nativists intensified Irish commitment to the Catholic Church.[109] The core culture eventually came to accommodate Protestant, Catholic, and Jewish religious communities. Yet the Catholic division did make some adjustments to the English-dominated milieu in language and church organizations. Such adaptation made the Catholic Church and school system an important medium within which new immigrants began their acculturation and even structural assimilation (for example, priests helped in securing employment).

Did commitment to the Catholic religion decline in later generations of Irish Catholics? Writing in recent decades, some have claimed that there has been a decline in religious commitment in later generations, and thus that cultural assimilation will soon be complete. Recent studies have not found this to be the case. As a group, the Irish are among the most likely to attend mass of all the Catholic groups studied. In his recent book, Andrew Greeley reviews information on Irish Catholics that indicates an increase in religious devotion—particularly among those in their thirties—over the last two decades.[110]

In regard to the dimensions Milton Gordon calls behavior-receptional assimilation and attitude-receptional assimilation—in effect, discrimination and prejudice—there have certainly been substantial changes since the mid-nineteenth century for the Catholic Irish. Stereotyping has declined substantially since the days of the apelike image, although there is still some negative feeling directed against Irish Catholicism and urban machine politics. Discrimination has declined significantly, although it is still felt at the very highest levels of the U.S. economy and government. The U.S. has had only one Irish Catholic president.

Patterns of Structural Assimilation for the Irish

At the structural assimilation (secondary group) levels the Irish made slow but significant movement into the Anglo-Saxon Protestant core society. We have seen the steady movement of the Irish from unskilled work into white-collar occupations and the relatively high income and occupational levels of the Irish Catholics in recent decades. Housing upgrading has paralleled these developments, although voluntary self-segregation still persists in the East and Midwest. After a century of struggle in the political sphere, Irish Catholics are now substantially integrated at local and state levels; in the last two or three decades they have moved significantly into the judicial, legislative, and executive levels of the federal government, if not yet in large numbers to the top. At the local level, in a number of cities, the Irish have shaped urban politics.

Some have argued that with their economic assimilation, their movement into higher economic status, the Irish have of late been moving away from the Democratic party. Looking at the period since the 1940s, Glazer and Moynihan have argued that the "mass of the Irish have left the working class, and in considerable measure the Democratic party as well."[111] Yet voting data for roughly the same period suggest that the Irish were and still are heavily tied to the Democratic party. Urban politicians, particularly Democrats, still pay great attention to this ethnic community, and many liberal Democratic leaders are still Irish. This suggests that one assimilation theory of ethnic politics—that economic mobility weakens traditional ethnic voting patterns—is not necessarily correct. Absorption into the Republicanism of many Anglo-Saxon Protestants has not happened for the Irish Catholics as a group.[112]

As for structural incorporation at the level of primary-group ties, data on informal groups and voluntary associations point up some interesting trends. Ethnic clubs and organizations, since World War II if not before, have apparently declined in importance for the Irish Catholics. Benevolent societies have declined in numbers; so have the great fund drives to support Irish causes. This indicates increasing integration into the voluntary associations of the larger society. There has also been a decline in Irish attendance at Catholic parochial schools over the last two decades, which may well mean that Irish children are making more friendships across ethnic lines than ever before.[113]

Intermarriage may be the ultimate indicator of adaptation at the primary-group level. Abramson's study points up an increasing intermarriage rate for Irish Catholics. Yet there is still substantial endogamy for Irish Catholics, with 65 percent of respondents with Irish fathers in one national survey also having Irish mothers; 43 percent of men who had married had a wife with an Irish father. Given the several generations that the majority of Irish Catholic families had been in the United States by the 1960s, the extent of in-marriage may be surprising. Marital assimilation with older Protestant groups has been slower to occur than one might have expected. Still, just over half were married to a non-Irish spouse. The trend does seem to be in the direction of increased out-marriage. Yet when the Irish do intermarry, it is often to persons in related Catholic ethnic groups.[114]

Is There Irish Ethnic Identity Today?

Among the final stages of assimilation is what Gordon and Greeley have seen as identificational adaptation. Ultimately, this type of adaptation would mean a loss of a sense of Irishness and the development of a sense of peoplehood which is solely American or Anglo-Saxon Protestant American. One's personal sense of identity would no longer be Irish. While this may have happened for many Irish Protestants, most Catholics still have a feeling of Irishness, although for many it may be a vague sense.

Some Irish Catholic writers, such as Daniel P. Moynihan, have argued that the Irish are losing their ethnic identity because of the decline in immigration. In her recent book, *Irish Americans: Identity and Assimilation*, Marjorie Fallows argues vigorously that the American Irish are fully acculturated to the core culture. Irish Catholicism has become "Americanized" and fully in line with the Protestant ethic. In her view distinctive ethnic traits that are culturally significant are rare among the American Irish today, except in isolated ethnic enclaves. Scholars such as Fallows have argued that even though there are still a few ethnically distinctive Irish Catholic communities in northern cities, this does not mean that most Irish Catholics live in such communities. Indeed, they argue that cultural and structural assimilation is all but complete for those Irish Catholics living outside ethnic neighborhoods.[115]

Other scholars emphasize the persistence of ethnic distinctiveness. The Irish Catholic group changed over generations of contact with the school system and media, but it retained enough distinctiveness to persist as an ethnic group into the last third of the twentieth century. The theory of ethnogenesis discussed in Chapter 2 seems appropriate to Irish Catholic Americans. This Irish ethnic group has been more than a European nationality group. The Irish who came in large numbers after 1840 forged, over several generations, a distinctive American ethnic group. Ethnicity was an important way for the Irish Catholics to attach themselves to the new scene, a way of asserting their own identity in a buzzing confusion of diverse nationality groups. For Irish Catholics, because of nativisitic attacks and discrimination, ethnic identity was less voluntary in the first few decades than it was to become later. In the beginning the Irish group had a cultural heritage which was distinctly different from that of the British-dominated host culture. Over several generations of sometimes conflictual interaction the Irish adapted substantially to the host society. In this process was created a distinctive Irish ethnic group which reflected elements *both* of its nationality background and of the host culture.

The research studies of scholars such as Andrew Greeley confirm the persistence of ethnic distinctiveness today, particularly in northern cities:

> On the basis of the evidence available to us, the Irish-American subculture is likely to persist indefinitely. The Irish Catholic Americans will continue to be different in their religion, their family life, their political style, their world view, their drinking behavior, and their personalities.[116]

Drawing on his extensive analysis of survey research data, Greeley further concludes that, seen as a group,

> The Irish will continue to be affluent and probably will become even more affluent as they settle down securely amidst the upper crusts of the middle class with a firm foothold in the nation's economic and political, if not intellectual and artistic, elites.[117]

Furthermore, Greeley and associates even see evidence of a return to higher levels of self-conscious identification among the young Irish.[118] Whether this trend will continue remains to be seen. Whatever happens, however, it is clear that the impact of the Irish background on Irish behavior remains strong.

An example of the persistence of Irish ethnicity and its positive and negative functions can be seen in the desegregation struggle which has taken place in Boston since the 1970s. There a working-class Irish community, South Boston, was involved in a judge's school desegregation plan; the plan was vigorously, even violently, opposed by the Irish. As one reporter noted:

> Antibusing demonstrators, wearing tam-o'shanter hats in the neighborhood high school colors, have broken up rallies of women's groups and dogged Senator Edward M. Kennedy's appearances. The usually jovial St. Patrick's Day parade was a procession of antibusing floats.[119]

This is more than a legal desegregation struggle. Different views of schooling and of urban communities are reflected in the controversy; the South Boston Irish see the central city schools as a socializing force, reinforcing traditional family and community values, whereas frequently nonwhites and suburban whites view them as avenues of upward mobility for nonwhite minorities. Irish resistance to the racial desegregation of central city neighborhoods is based in part on racial prejudice. But perhaps most of all, for good or ill, it is based on protecting their ethnic community against all intruders, whoever they may be.

SUMMARY

The Irish began moving to North America quite early, with indentured servants and farmers entering in the 1700s. The earlier migration apparently included far more southern or Celtic Irish than the exaggerated accounts about the Scotch-Irish have suggested. The majority of the descendants of these early migrants did become Protestants, settling disproportionately in the rural South and in frontier areas. The descendants of these early settlers, over the next several generations, often became part of the Anglo-Saxon mainstream. However, a significant proportion have remained poor. The Protestant Irish in particular have received little attention in recent decades from scholars.

After the 1840s large numbers of Catholic immigrants moved to the cities of the North, where many suffered violence at the hands of Catholic-hating nativists and discrimination at the hands of employers. Poverty-stricken, Irish Catholics slowly began the movement toward economic equality with older groups. Conflict, sometimes violent, marked their trek up from poverty. Political innovators, the Irish Catholics shaped the political organizations of the cities to facilitate their integration into the core institutions.

Economic mobility between 1890 and 1980 became so dramatic as to place Irish Catholics in a position of near parity in regard to established Protestant groups on a number of important dimensions. Irish Protestant mobility since 1900 has received little attention, although at least one recent study suggests that those still identifying themselves as Irish Protestants have lagged behind Catholics in economic and educational attainments in the last decade. Today Irish American Catholics and Protestants constitute major segments of Middle America.

NOTES

[1]U.S. Department of Justice, Immigration and Naturalization Service, *Annual Report* (Washington, D.C.: U.S. Government Printing Office, 1973), pp. 53–55. The figures for 1820–1867 represent "alien passengers arrived"; for later periods they represent immigrants arrived or admitted.

[2]Cited in William Peterson, *Population*, 2nd ed. (New York: Macmillan, 1969), p. 260.

[3]Philip H. Bagenal, *The American Irish* (London: Kegan Paul, Trench and Co., 1882), pp. 4–5.

[4]Henry Jones Ford, *The Scotch-Irish in America* (Princeton: Princeton University Press, 1915), pp. 125–28.

[5]James G. Leyburn, *The Scotch-Irish* (Chapel Hill: University of North Carolina Press, 1962), pp. 142–43.

[6]Ford, *The Scotch-Irish in America*, pp. 183–86; Leyburn, *The Scotch-Irish,* pp. 160 ff.

[7]Michael J. O'Brien, *A Hidden Phase of American History* (New York: Devin-Adair Co., 1919), pp. 249, 287–88.

[8]For this type of critique, see Robert J. Dickson, *Ulster Immigration to Colonial America, 1718–1773* (London: Routledge and Kegan Paul, 1966), pp. 66–68.

[9]O'Brien, *A Hidden Phase of American History*, p. 267.

[10]Cited in ibid., p. 254.

[11]Thomas D'Arcy McGee, *A History of Irish Settlers in North America* (Boston: Office of American Celt, 1851), pp. 25–34.

[12]Leyburn, *The Scotch-Irish*, pp. 331–32.

[13]Quoted in Ford, *The Scotch-Irish in America*, pp. 520–21.

[14]Theodore Roosevelt, *The Winning of the West* (New York: Review of Reviews Co., 1904), 1:123–25.

[15]Ford, *The Scotch-Irish in America*, pp. 522, 539.

[16]John W. Dinsmore, *The Scotch-Irish in America* (Chicago: Winona Publishing Co., 1906), p. 7.

[17]Winthrop D. Jordan, *White Over Black* (Baltimore: Penguin Books, 1968), pp. 86–88.

[18]Edwin S. Gaustad, *Historical Atlas of Religion in America* (New York: Harper & Row, 1962), pp. 34–35; Dennis Clark, *The Irish in Philadelphia* (Philadelphia: Temple University Press, 1973), p. 8.

[19]Quoted in McGee, *A History of Irish Settlers in North America,* p. 79.

[20]Ford, *The Scotch-Irish in America*, pp. 180–240; E. R. R. Green, "Ulster Immigrants' Letters" in *Essays in Scotch-Irish History*, ed. E. R. R. Green (London: Routledge and Kegan Paul, 1969), pp. 100–102.

[21]Leyburn, *The Scotch-Irish*, pp. 262–69.

[22]American Historical Association, *Annual Report* (Washington, D.C.: U.S. Government Printing Office, 1932) 1:255–70.

[23]Arnold Shrier, *Ireland and the American Emigration, 1850–1900* (Minneapolis: University of Minnesota Press, 1958), pp. 13–16.

[24]Carl Wittke, *The Irish in America* (Baton Rouge: Louisiana State University Press, 1956), p. 24.

[25]Ibid., p. 27; Theodore Hershberg et al., "A Tale of Three Cities," in *Majority and Minority*, 3rd ed., ed. Norman Y. Yetman and C. Hoy Steele (Boston: Allyn and Bacon, 1982), pp. 184–85.

[26]Bagenal, *The American Irish*, p. 72. The statistics are found on pp. 70–71; Wittke, *The Irish in America*, p. 46.

[27]Lewis P. Curtis, Jr., *Apes and Angels: The Irish in Victorian Caricature* (Washington, D.C.: Smithsonian Institution Press, 1971), p. 59.

[28]Ibid., p. 103.

[29]Andrew M. Greeley, *That Most Distressful Nation* (Chicago: Quadrangle Books, 1972), pp. 119–20.

[30]Andrew M. Greeley, *The Irish Americans* (New York: Harper and Row, 1981), p. 167.

[31]Ibid., pp. 167–68.

[32]Leonard Dinnerstein and Frederic C. Jaher, "Introduction," in *The Aliens,* ed. Leonard Dinnerstein and Frederic C. Jaher (New York: Appleton-Century-Crofts, 1970), p. 4.

[33]Leyburn, *The Scotch-Irish*, p. 328.

[34]Ibid., pp. 234, 301–16.

[35]Ford, *The Scotch-Irish in America,* pp. 291–324; Leyburn, *The Scotch-Irish*, pp. 225–30.

[36]Nathan Glazer and Daniel P. Moynihan, *Beyond the Melting Pot* (Cambridge, Mass.: MIT Press and Harvard University Press, 1963), p. 220; McGee, *A History of Irish Settlers in North America*, p. 88.

[37]Wittke, *The Irish in America*, pp. 47 ff.

[38]Ibid., p. 119; Wayne G. Broehl, Jr., *The Molly Maguires* (Cambridge, Mass.: Harvard University Press, 1964), p. 75.

[39]Clark, *The Irish in Philadelphia*, p. 21.

[40]Wittke, *The Irish in America*, p. 120.

[41]Rowland T. Berthoff, *British Immigrants in Industrial America* (Cambridge, Mass.: Harvard University Press, 1953), pp. 190–93.

[42]Ibid., p. 187.

[43]Broehl, *The Molly Maguires*, p. 85.

[44]Leonard P. O. Wibberly, *The Coming of the Green* (New York: Henry Holt and Co. 1958), pp. 101–3.

[45]Broehl, *The Molly Maguires*, pp. 87–90.

[46]Ibid., pp. 198–99.

[47]Anthony Bimba, *The Molly Maguires* (New York: International Publishers, 1932), pp. 70–73.

[48]Broehl, *The Molly Maguires*, pp. vi, 361.

[49]Ibid., p. 359.

[50]Handlin, *Boston's Immigrants*, p. 137.

[51]See James McCague, *The Second Rebellion* (New York: Dial Press, 1968).

[52]Wittke, *The Irish in America*, pp. 191–92.

[53]See Shrier, *Ireland and the American Emigration*, p. 34.

[54]Ford, *The Scotch-Irish in America*, p. 462.

[55]Ibid., p. 491.

[56]Ibid., p. 246; McGee, *A History of Irish Settlers in North America*, p. 71; Shane Leslie, *The Irish Issue in its American Aspect* (New York: Charles Scribner's Sons, 1919), p. 8.

[57]Maldwyn A. Jones, "Ulster Emigration, 1783–1815," in Green, *Essays in Scotch-Irish History*, p. 67.

[58]Paul Blanshard, *The Irish and Catholic Power* (Boston: Beacon Press, 1953), p. 282.

[59]William F. Adams, *Ireland and Irish Emigration to the New World* (New Haven: Yale University Press, 1932), p. 377.

[60]Wittke, *The Irish in America*, p. 104; Edward M. Levine, *The Irish and Irish Politicians* (South Bend, Ind.: University of Notre Dame Press, 1966), pp. 6–9.

[61]Leo Hershkowitz, *Tweed's New York* (New York: Anchor Books, 1978), pp. xiii–xx.

[62]Glazer and Moynihan, *Beyond the Melting Pot*, pp. 218–62.

[63]Robert A. Dahl, *Who Governs?* (New Haven: Yale University Press, 1963), p. 41.

[64]Levine, *The Irish and Irish Politicians*, p. 146.

[65]Mike Royko, *Boss: Richard J. Daley of Chicago* (New York: E. P. Dutton and Co., 1971).

[66]Levine, *The Irish and Irish Politicians*, pp. 145–55.

[67]Ibid., p. 155.

[68]Quoted in ibid., p. 174.

[69]Wittke, *The Irish in America*, pp. 110–12.

[70]Greeley, *That Most Distressful Nation*, pp. 206–9.

[71]Dennis J. Clark, "The Philadelphia Irish," in *The Peoples of Philadelphia*, ed. Allen F. Davis and Mark H. Haller (Philadelphia: Temple University Press, 1973), p. 145.

[72]Terry N. Clark, "The Irish Ethnic and the Spirit of Patronage," *Ethnicity* 2 (1975): 305–59; Mark R. Levy and Michael S. Kramer, *The Ethnic Factor* (New York: Simon and Schuster, 1972), pp. 130–35; Greeley, *The Irish Americans*, pp. 168–69.

[73]Maldwyn Jones, *American Immigration* (Chicago: University of Chicago Press, 1960), p. 236.

[74]William Miller, "American Historians and the Business Elite," *Journal of Economic History* 9 (November 1949): 202–3.

[75]Finley Peter Dunne, quoted in Elmer Ellis, *Mr. Dooley's America* (New York: Alfred A. Knopf, 1941), p. 208.

[76]Donald H. Akenson, *The United States and Ireland* (Cambridge, Mass.: Harvard University Press, 1973), pp. 40–42.

[77]Wittke, *The Irish in America*, pp. 281–91.

[78]Shannon, *The American Irish*, pp. 151–81.

[79]Ibid., pp. 332–52; Samuel Lubell, *The Future of American Politics*, 2nd rev. ed. (New York: Doubleday Anchor Books, 1955), pp. 83–84.

[80]Glazer and Moynihan, *Beyond the Melting Pot*, p. 287.

[81]Shannon, *The American Irish*, pp. 395–411; Levy and Kramer, *The Ethnic Factor*, pp. 126–127; Glazer and Moynihan, *Beyond the Melting Pot*, p. 287; cf. John R. Schmidhauser, "The Justices of the Supreme Court: A Collective Portrait," *Midwest Journal of Social Science* 3 (February 1959): 1–57.

[82]Leyburn, *The Scotch-Irish*, p. 322 et passim.

[83]Stephen Steinberg, *The Ethnic Myth* (New York: Atheneum, 1981), pp. 160–64.

[84]Bagenal, *The American Irish*, p. 69.

[85]Oscar Handlin, *Boston's Immigrants, 1790–1865* (Cambridge, Mass.: Harvard University Press, 1941), p. 67.

[86]Adams, *Ireland and Irish Emigration to the New World*, p. 358.

[87]Stephan Thernstrom, *Poverty and Progress* (Cambridge, Mass.: Harvard University Press, 1964), pp. 154–58.

[88]Ibid., p. 184.

[89]Clark, *The Irish in Philadelphia*, pp. 59, 167–75.

[90]Greeley, *That Most Distressful Nation*, p. 120; Clark, "The Philadelphia Irish," p. 143; Wittke, *The Irish in America*, pp. 217–27.

[91]Pitirim Sorokin, "American Millionaires and Multi-Millionaires," *Social Forces* 3 (May 1925): 634–35. Data are based on fathers' stock.

[92]Stephan Thernstrom, *The Other Bostonians* (Cambridge, Mass.: Harvard University Press, 1973), p. 131; Berthoff, *British Immigrants in Industrial America*.

[93]Hershberg et al., "A Tale of Three Cities," p. 190.

[94]W. Lloyd Warner and Leo Srole, *The Social Systems of American Ethnic Groups* (New Haven: Yale University Press, 1945), pp. 93–95; E. Digby Baltzell, *An American Business Aristocracy* (New York: Collier Books, 1962), pp. 267–431; idem, *The Protestant Establishment* (New York: Vintage Books, 1966), pp. 320–21.

[95]Shannon, *The American Irish*, pp. 436–37.

[96]Quoted in James Q. Wilson, "Generational and Ethnic Differences Among Career Police Officers," *American Journal of Sociology* 69 (March 1964): 527.

[97]Harold J. Abramson, *Ethnic Diversity in Catholic America* (New York: John Wiley, 1973), pp. 41–44; Levy and Kramer, *The Ethnic Factor*, p. 125; Greeley, *The Irish Americans*, p. 111.

[98]Greeley, *The Irish Americans*, pp. 108, 111.

[99]Andrew M. Greeley, *Ethnicity, Denomination and Inequality* (Beverly Hills, Calif.: Sage Publications, 1976), pp. 45–53; Levy and Kramer, *The Ethnic Factor*, p. 125.

[100]John T. Ellis, *American Catholicism* (Garden City, N.Y.: Doubleday Image Books, 1965), p. 62; Clark, *The Irish in Philadelphia*, p. 123.

[101]David O. Moberg, *The Church as a Social Institution* (Englewood Cliffs, N.J.: Prentice-Hall, 1962), p. 193.

[102]Greeley, *Ethnicity, Denomination and Inequality*, p. 45; Greeley, *The Irish Americans*, pp. 110–12.

[103]Wittke, *The Irish in America*, pp. 52–61, 205.

[104]Owen B. Corrigan, "Chronology of the Catholic Hierarchy of the United States," *Catholic Historical Review* 1 (January 1916): 267–389; Gaustad, *Historical Atlas of Religion in America*, p. 103; John T. Ellis, *American Catholicism* (Garden City, N.Y.: Doubleday Image Books, 1965), p. 56; Wittke, *The Irish in America*, p. 91; Greeley, *That Most Distressful Nation*, p. 93.

[105]Greeley, *The Irish Americans*, p. 145.

[106]Ibid., pp. 130–32.

[107]Ford, *The Scotch-Irish in America*, p. 538.

[108]Clark, *Philadelphia Irish*, p. 178.

[109]Thernstrom, *Poverty and Progress*, p. 179.

[110]Abramson, *Ethnic Diversity in Catholic America*, p. 111; Greeley, *The Irish Americans*, pp. 149–51.

[111]Glazer and Moynihan, *Beyond the Melting Pot*, p. 219.

[112]Raymond E. Wolfinger, "The Development and Persistence of Ethnic Voting," *American Political Science Review* 60 (1965): 907.

[113]Joseph P. O'Grady, *How the Irish Became American* (New York: Twayne Publishers, 1973), p. 141; Marjorie R. Fallows, *Irish Americans: Identity and Assimilation* (Englewood Cliffs, N.J.: Prentice-Hall, 1979), p. 147.

[114]Abramson, *Ethnic Diversity in Catholic America*, p. 53.

[115]Fallows, *Irish Americans*, pp. 148–49; see also Richard D. Alba, "Social Assimilation among American Catholic National-Origin Groups," *American Sociological Review* 41 (December 1976): 1032.

[116]Greeley, *The Irish Americans*, p. 206.

[117]Ibid.

[118]Ibid.; cf. Andrew M. Greeley, *Ethnicity in the United States* (New York: John Wiley, 1974), p. 311.

[119]John Kifner, *New York Times*, May 18, 1975.

Italian Americans
CHAPTER 5

For many decades Italian Americans have found themselves to be targets of Anglo-Saxon Protestants. In recent years this Catholic group has been attacked for being prejudiced against blacks and for being superpatriotic "hard hats" with little sophistication or with connections to the "Mafia." By the late 1960s a counterattack was developing. Many white ethnic leaders, including Italian Americans, came to view Protestant intellectuals and officials negatively: "The ethnic American is sick of being stereotyped as a racist and a dullard by phony white liberals, pseudo black militants and patronizing bureaucrats. . . . He pays the bill for every major governmental program and gets nothing or little in the way of return."[1] Richard Gambino, an Italian American scholar, complained that "the white elite has shown little understanding of Italian-American history, culture, or problems and less empathy with them."[2] Here then is a renewed militancy among Italian Americans, reflecting pride in their backgrounds and accomplishments.

It is ironic that a people whose ancestors gave the world the Roman Empire and the Italian Renaissance must press for recognition of their worth. It is ironic that they must defend their importance, given the fact that no other group can boast of a more impressive stream of geniuses of the character of Leonardo da Vinci, Michelangelo, Raphael, Galileo, and Marconi. Indeed, it was an Italian, Cristoforo Colombo, whose voyage to the Americas opened up a major era of development for the Western Hemisphere.

ITALIAN MIGRATION

Italian explorers, including Colombo, played a major role in opening the Americas to European exploitation. An Italian navigator, Amerigo Vespucci, made a number of voyages to the Americas shortly after Colombo's voyages. Because of his early maps the continents came to be named after him.[3]

Numbers of Immigrants

A few Italians migrated to the colonies prior to the 1800s, some working for English companies, some as settlers in the Catholic-tolerant colony of Maryland, and some engaged in glass manufacturing and agriculture in Virginia. Schiavo notes that "in Virginia, a small group of Italians settled with Filippo Mazzei in 1774 in order to introduce the wine and Italian agricultural methods."[4] Thomas Jefferson was so impressed that he relied on Mazzei's intellectual talents and also invited other Italian agricultural experts and crafts workers to Virginia.

Between 1820 and 1980 more than five million Italians migrated to the United States.[5] Until 1860 the migration was quite small.[6] Between 1861 and 1880 migration picked up a little, reaching 67,500 in these decades.[7] In the four decades leading up to 1920, Italian immigration became heavy, with more than four million recorded immigrants. Prior to 1880 most immigrants were from northern Italy; now they came in very large numbers from the south.[8] The heavy proletarian migration of poor farmers and laborers had begun just after the formerly independent regions of Italy were unified into one state.[9]

Certain factors are relevant to study of this migration: the point of origin, the point of destination, the migrating units, and the larger context. At the beginning of the migration there were three major social classes in Italy: a small elite of wealthy landlords, a small group of professionals, and a huge group of landless, poverty-stricken peasants. As with the Irish, land and agricultural problems triggered much of the Italian outmigration. National unification, with the new Italian government controlled by northern Italians, had brought heavy taxes to southern Italy. Low incomes, poor soil and weather, poor health conditions, a feudal land system, unreasonable taxes, corruption in government—these were the important "push" factors at the point of origin. However, not all areas of Italy sent large numbers of migrants. Areas with a large and militant working class population sent fewer migrants in spite of their poverty. Agricultural organization and labor militancy in Italy significantly lowered out-migration rates.[10]

The main "pull" factor at the point of destination was the image of the United States as an economic and political paradise. Emigration was a means of expanding opportunity. Many came to stay. Others came with the idea of building capital for enterprises back home; of these, some returned, while others remained. Most who came were poor. Many migrated as a result of labor recruiting in Italy; a considerable portion of the immigration had been stimulated by aggressively expanding industrial capitalism in the United States.[11]

Traditionally migration has been seen as a large-scale disorganizing experience, as a trail of broken homes and social networks. Yet many analysts have underestimated the structure of the international streams from Europe, South America, and Asia. Migration along family and kinship networks, typical for poor and working-class migrants from most countries in Europe, has considerably lessened the pain of migration. Italians migrated in large numbers from the same village areas. Italian men often would migrate first.[12] There were chains of kin migration across the Atlantic Ocean linking areas in Italy and America. Immigrant men worked hard, saved their money, and brought over their relatives.[13]

Most immigrants headed for urban points of destination; like the Irish, they had had enough of farm life. Cities of the industrialized East Coast, such as Boston, New York, and Philadelphia, were popular points of destination. Migration was to the "Little Italies" in larger cities, where fellow villagers from Italy resided. Today most Italian Americans live in the larger cities of the northeastern and north-central regions.

Remigration was an important feature of the migration. Between 1908 and 1920 the number returning to the homeland occasionally reached 60 to 70 percent of the number of new immigrants coming in, placing the Italians well above other groups in terms of remigration.[14] Relative to the total foreign-born Italian population in the United States, however, the proportion leaving was small. A small portion of these were temporary sojourners, sometimes termed "birds-of-passage," whose aim was to make money in the United States and then to return to Italy to invest it in enterprises at home.[15]

Between 1924 and 1965 Italian immigration was sharply curtailed by laws passed under pressure of nativist agitation. Previous Italian immigration was one of the factors that precipitated anti-immigration legislation. Beginning in 1897, numerous attempts were made to legislate restriction of immigration. In 1921 the first quota restrictions, setting specific numerical limits on immigrants, were established, with Italy's annual quota initially set at a fairly high level (42,000).[16]

The Immigration Act of 1924 changed that situation and established a much smaller discriminatory quota for Italians. By 1929 an annual quota of 5,802 Italians was established, compared to quotas of 65,721 for Great Britain and 25,957 for Germany. (These discriminatory quotas were altered very little, several decades later, by the 1952 Walter-McCarran Act.) The quota system was based on the prejudiced notion of the Anglo-Saxon nativists that those countries which had furnished the largest numbers of so-called "good American citizens"—that is, citizens prior to the immigration waves after 1880—should be the ones with the most substantial quotas. The British, Germans, Irish, and Scandinavians were given 76 percent of the total, although the demand for admission from those countries had slackened considerably by that time.

Pressure on Italy's small quota was great. A huge backlog of applicants developed. Not until 1965 was a new Immigration Act passed, replacing the discriminatory national-origin quota system in two stages. In the first stage the quota system was modified so that the unfilled quotas of some countries could be used to augment the filled quotas of certain other countries. As a result, the number of Italian entrants increased significantly. In 1966 some 26,447 Italian immigrants were admitted; in 1967 the total reached a high of 28,487. However, the 1965 Immigration Act dictated that after 1968 no country should exceed a limit of 20,000 in any one year, again increasing the backlog of Italians trying to migrate to the United States. In the last decade or so that migration has increased significantly, to the point that years such as 1972 and 1973 saw twice as many entrants from Italy as from any other European country.

Life for the Immigrant

What was life like for the large waves of Italian immigrants who entered in the peak 1880–1920 period? Their lives were economically circumscribed. Times were hard. Work took the form of unskilled labor on transportation systems such as canals and railroads and on city water and sewer systems. Pay was typically low, and individuals as well as families were poor. The immigrants and their children were discriminated against in many ways, economically, politically, and socially. Italian immigrants found themselves segregated in "little Italies," ghettos within cities.

There is a bit of irony here, since *ghetto* is thought to be an Italian (Venetian) word first applied to the practice of segregating Jews in Italy in the sixteenth century. In the United States it was the Italian Catholics who found themselves in ghettos. In many cities the Italians replaced earlier groups as part of an invasion-succession process. Other groups would follow on the heels of the Italians.[17]

Some analysts have viewed working-class communities in cities as disorganized "slum" areas with little positive social life. This was certainly not true for such Italian communities. As with the Irish before them, Italians responded to discrimination by developing their own extensive friendship and kinship circles, political clubs, avenues for mobility, and community celebrations. Central to Italian communities were indigenous organizations and festivals, including clubs and mutual benefit societies—societies involving small monthly payments in order to ensure a proper funeral and a decent burial on one's demise. In 1927 there were two hundred mutual aid societies in Chicago and many other clubs and lodges.[18] Legal agencies developed; Italian newspapers flourished.

Italian communities were laid on the bedrock of extensive kinship networks. Kinship was important in areas such as the North End of Boston, where extended family members lived near one another. As a result, and contrary to some nativist propaganda, relatively few among first-generation Italians ended up in almshouses for the poor. As they had been in Italy, Italian families in the United States tended to be patriarchal; kinship solidarity was emphasized. A high value was placed on home ownership. The community was a critical factor in cementing Italians to certain northern and midwestern cities; it was instrumental in reinforcing their commitment to fundamental family and community values.[19]

STEREOTYPING THE ITALIAN AMERICANS

Nativist images of the Irish had been harsh, but by the end of the nineteenth century the apelike-Irish image was fading and being replaced by stereotyped images of southern and eastern Europeans. Italian Catholics were one target of prejudice and stereotyping. The stereotype of the Italian American was strong and frequently absurd:

> It is urged that the Italian race stock is inferior and degraded; that it will not assimilate naturally or readily with the prevailing "Anglo-Saxon" race stock of this country; that intermixture, if practicable, will be detrimental; that servility, filthy habits of life, and hopelessly degraded standard of needs and ambitions have been ingrained in Italians by centuries of oppression and abject poverty; that they are incapable of any adequate appreciation of our free institutions and the privileges and duties of citizenship; that the greater part are illiterate and likely to remain so.[20]

Such indictments appeared in national magazines. In the 1888 *North American Review*, T.V. Powderly alleged that southern and eastern Europeans were an inferior, even barbarian, stock that lived immoral lives centered on liquor. Major themes in the press of the day were presumed inferiority, poor character and morality, illiteracy, mental problems, and crime.[21]

Myths of Biological Inferiority

Nativist concern with immigrants from eastern and southern Europe was linked to fear of biological inferiority. Popular writers, scholars, members of Congress—all warned of the peril of allowing inferior stocks from Europe into the United States. This was the era in which the "Nordic race" was praised exultantly. Kenneth L. Roberts, a prominent journalist of the first decades of this century, wrote of the dangers of the newer immigrants making Americans a mongrel race: "Races can not be cross-bred without mongrelization, any more than breeds of dogs can be cross-bred without mongrelization. The American nation was founded and developed by the Nordic race, but if a few more million members of the Alpine, Mediterranean and Semitic races are poured among us, the result must inevitably be a hybrid race of people as worthless and futile as the good-for-nothing mongrels of Central America and Southeastern Europe."[22] The "Alpine, Mediterranean, and Semitic races" generally covered countries of heavy emigration other than those of northern Europe; the Italians and Jews were foremost examples in the minds of prominent writers. Novels and popular magazines picked up these themes and circulated them widely.

Half-truths about disease and illiteracy were circulated about the southern and eastern European immigrants. It was true in some years between 1880 and 1920 that half the adult Italian immigrants could not read and write, although in other years the overwhelming majority were literate.[23] But in no year were the broadside charges of total illiteracy leveled at Italian Americans by the press and politicians accurate.[24] Particularly hostile was the leap from the proportions illiterate to assumptions of low intelligence. The stereotyping of these immigrants as of low intelligence was reinforced by the views of prominent social scientists.

In the first three decades of the twentieth century intellectual inferiority stereotypes were based in part on misreading the results of the new psychological tests, which were inaccurately labeled "intelligence (IQ) tests."

The term *intelligence test* is inaccurate because the tests measured selected, learned, verbal and quantitative *skills*, not a broad or basic intelligence. In 1912 Henry Goddard gave Binet's diagnostic test and related tests to a large number of immigrants from southern and eastern Europe. According to his analysis the data showed that 83 percent of Jewish and 79 percent of Italian immigrants were "feeble-minded," a category naively defined in terms of low scores on the new tests. Such pseudoscientific data contributed to the clamor for restrictions on immigration.[25]

With the coming of World War I some prominent psychologists became involved in large-scale testing of draftees. Verbal and performance tests were developed. While the results were not used for military purposes, detailed analyses were published in the 1920s and gained public and Congressional attention because of the racial-inferiority interpretation placed on test results of southern and eastern Europeans by some psychologists.[26]

In 1923 Carl Brigham, a Princeton psychologist who would later play a role in developing college entrance tests, wrote a detailed analysis of the intellectual inferiority of immigrant groups, including Italians, drawing on data from Army tests.[27] The average scores for foreign-born draftees ranged from highs of 14.87 for English and 14.34 for Scotch draftees, to an average of 13.77 for all white draftees, to lows of 10.74 for Polish draftees and 11.01 for Italian draftees. The low test scores for such groups as the Italian Americans were boldly explained in racial terms. Those groups with lower test scores were considered to be inferior racial stocks. These "scientific" results were interpreted by psychologists such as Brigham as support for the prevalent ideology of "Nordic" intellectual superiority being espoused by racial theorists such as Madison Grant. Brigham went on to argue that the sharp increases in southern and eastern European immigrants had lowered the overall level of American intelligence.

The political implications of Brigham's analysis were boldly proclaimed: immigration limitations were necessary. Political means should be developed within the United States to prevent "the continued propagation of defective strains in the present population." Here was pseudoscientific support for such government action as passage of the 1924 Immigration Act, which would soon restrict Italian and other southern European immigration. Here too was pseudoscientific support for those who would smear immigrants as persons without intelligence, a position taken by foremost scholars and politicians.[28]

The "intelligence" differences measured by these psychological tests were considered to reflect the inferior or superior genetic background of European "racial" stocks. In these early decades few seriously considered the possibility that the linguistic (English), cultural (northern European–American), and educational bias in the tests and in interpretive procedures could account for the differentials found. It is interesting to note that these debates over the inferiority of European "racial" groups are now a historical curiosity. No social scientist today would advance these arguments of inferiority on the basis of such test data. Yet it is odd that today similar arguments, based on similar tests, are being made for test score differences between black and white Americans. We will return to this issue in a later chapter.[29]

Some leaders representing immigrants developed strategies for dealing with concern over "blood" lineage. One prominent Italian leader, Fiorello La Guardia, suffered personal attacks which incorporated stereotyped images. For his criticism of officials such as President Herbert Hoover he received letters like the following: "You should go back where you belong and advise Mussolini how to make good honest citizens in Italy. The Italians are preponderantly our murderers and boot-leggers."[30]

La Guardia's countertactic was often biting humor. When he was asked to provide material on his family background for the *New York World*, he saw the ghost of "blood" inferiority behind the request and commented: "I have no family tree. The only member of my family who has one is my dog Yank. He is the son of Doughboy, who was the son of Siegfried, who was the son of Tannhäuser, who was the son of Wotan. A distinguished family tree, to be sure—but after all he's only a son of a bitch."[31] Such humor has been one response to hostile stereotyping.

The Mafia Myth

The most persistent aspect of the stereotyping of Italian Americans has been the criminality image. The immigrant criminal is a "beast" which nativist whites have spied in virtually every new wave of immigrants. But the image has perhaps been most prominent, and most painful, for the Italian immigrants and their descendants. As early as the 1870s Italians were depicted as lawless, knife-wielding thugs looking for a fight.[32] A report of the influential United States Immigration Commission argued that certain types of criminality were "inherent in the Italian race."[33]

Existing data raise questions about the validity of the criminality stereotype in the early period. For example, the arrest rate for drunkenness and disorderly conduct for the Italian foreign-born in 1910 was quite low—158.1 per 100,000 people, while the American-born figure was 202.6. The arrest rate for prostitution was very low, and the imprisonment rate in 1910 was much lower than public stereotypes would suggest: 527.3 prisoners per 100,000 for Italian-born, 727.4 for the English and Welsh foreign-born, and 371.3 for the white American-born population.[34]

Small-scale crime was a problem in urban Italian ghettos, but it did not involve a sinister national criminal conspiracy, an organization later known by the term "Mafia." As with other groups, Italian crime in the cities began on a small scale. Poverty and discrimination were part of the fostering milieu. The onset of Prohibition catapulted Italian Americans into organized crime, which at that time was controlled by Irish and Jewish Americans. For such immigrant groups organized crime was an avenue of mobility. Increasingly, the Sicilian term *Mafia* was used to describe these gangsters, whether Sicilian or not, and in spite of the fact that many were not even Italian. The presence of identifiable criminal societies in Italy, such as the *Mafia* and the *Camorra*, made it easier for the mass media to stereotype Italian Americans as criminals. Yet Italian Americans had low crime rates in the 1920s and 1930s. What data there are suggest that foreign-born

Italian Americans had relatively low crime rates, close to those for all native-born Americans.[35]

In recent decades the image of Italian criminality has taken on a widespread mythological character; the stereotype of the Italian American as one of a mafia hoodlum committed to crime and violence still persists. A Louis Harris opinion poll found that 78 percent of the national sample reported a belief in a secret organized crime organization called the Mafia.[36] Contemporary writers, politicians, and scholars continue to view Italian Americans as though they have a unique attachment to criminality. Moreover, the mass media have perpetuated the Mafia and Italian criminality stereotypes.[37]

That organized crime continues to exist as a major enterprise cannot be disputed. That a small proportion of Italians play a role in it is not disputed. That these Italians control a nationwide organized crime syndicate with no help from other racial and ethnic groups can be disputed; and that the Italian (Sicilian) term *Mafia* should be used to describe it can be rejected. Many law-enforcement officials and mass media people have assumed that organized crime was, and is, primarily an Italian conspiracy. The hearings conducted by Senator Estes Kefauver in 1950 resulted in this very conclusion. Smith has argued that a major reason for perpetuation of this myth is the desire of law-enforcement officials to divert public attention away from their own incompetence by picturing organized crime as a sinister, foreign conspiracy too powerful for their agencies to deal with using conventional methods.[38] All Italian Americans are made to bear the burden not only for the sins of a small minority, but also for the shortcomings of law-enforcement agencies seeking to displace the blame for their failure. And beyond that issue of who controls organized crime today, there is the persisting criminality image which continues to plague Italian Americans. To put the matter simply, there is no evidence that current Italian American crime rates are higher than those of other major ethnic groups. With far less than 1 percent of Italian Americans falling into the "gangster" category, the ludicrousness of that stereotype is evident. Crime in the United States, organized or otherwise, remains a multi-ethnic phenomenon.[39]

A Television Study: Today's Stereotypes

A recent study of the portrayal of Italian Americans on prime-time network television examined a six-week sample of 263 programs in the 1980–1981 season. The study found that negative images of Italian Americans outnumbered positive images by two to one. Most of the 96 Italian characters in the shows studied were males and had low-status jobs. A significant percentage were portrayed as criminals, and many were pictured as "lovable or laughable dimwits who worked in jobs that offered little pay and less prestige." The majority of Italian Americans portrayed on television made grammatical errors, misunderstood English words, or spoke broken English. This broken English was often used to make jokes, thus perpetuating stereotypes in questionable TV attempts at ethnic humor.[40]

CONFLICT

Italian immigrants faced vigorous, sometimes violent, opposition to their communities. The myth of peaceful progress is again dispelled by the history of struggles of Italians with Anglo-Saxon Protestant nativists, Irish Catholics, and black Americans. Northern Italian immigrants came first and suffered first. Irish and Italians were fighting it out on the streets of Boston by the 1860s, and Italian parents often accompanied their children to school for protection. In the 1870s Irish workers on strike in New York attacked Italian strike-breakers; and four Italians were killed in Pennsylvania in a clash with striking Irish miners.

By the 1880s immigrants from southern Italy had become major targets of nativist attempts at social and economic control, sometimes under the guise of "legal action" to prevent alleged Italian crime, sometimes in the form of vigilante action. In the 1880s in Buffalo, New York, more than three hundred Italians, most of the local Italian population, were detained by the police after an incident in which one Italian had killed another; only two of the three hundred were found holding weapons. Protests by the Italian community were even made to the Italian government. Replying to the governor of New York, the police chief of Buffalo explained that he thought that Italians as a rule carried concealed weapons and were a threat to social order.[41] Much violence was directed against southern Italians; several dozen were lynched or killed by mobs in numerous places in the South and a few northern areas. Four were killed in Buena Vista, Pennsylvania, in 1874; six were murdered by a mob in Walsenburg, Colorado, in 1895. There were multiple lynchings in Louisiana, Mississippi, North Carolina, and Florida between 1896 and 1910, and hundreds of other Italian Americans were threatened, injured, or driven from local areas by force.[42]

Attacks in the South were motivated by a variety of reasons, ranging from labor competition to maintaining racial lines. Italian Americans were more likely than other whites to support black political rights. Thus Italian immigrants were a threat to white solidarity in the South. They worked alongside blacks as laborers or sold to them as small shopkeepers. In one town five Sicilian shopkeepers were lynched for this reason. Elsewhere, Italian children were required to go to segregated black schools.[43]

A widely publicized attack occurred in New Orleans after the 1891 murder of a police superintendent who was investigating crime among Italians. When a number of Italians were jailed for the deed, the jail was stormed by a large group led by prominent citizens. There was no police interference; eleven of the Italians were killed. Newspapers praised the deed, as did major political figures, with most developing the theme of stereotypical criminality. Theodore Roosevelt made negative comments about Italian Americans, calling the 1891 lynchings in New Orleans "a rather good thing." Even the *New York Times* defended the lynchings as a solution for the crime problem.[44]

More Legalized Killings

Italians were fired on and forced to leave Marksville, Louisiana, because of violating southern racial taboos. Two hundred were driven out of Altoona, Pennsylvania, in 1894. In some areas, Italians were able to mount a substantial, sometimes effective, counterattack. In 1899 one Italian agricultural community in Arkansas suffered vandalism and the burning of its schoolhouse at the hands of other whites. Groups of Italians armed themselves and patrolled their area, effectively ending the attacks.[45] Mining areas saw conflict between owners and Italian workers. In 1914 in Ludlow, Colorado, a struggle with mine operators over wages and working conditions resulted in state troopers being sent in to suppress striking miners. Italian women and children were killed in the conflict.[46]

Sometimes killings were legalized. One of the most famous murder trials of all time was that of Nicola Sacco and Bartolomeo Vanzetti, Italian-born workers who were tried for robbery and murder in Massachusetts. Numerous witnesses testified that the defendants were elsewhere at the time of the crime, but the testimony of Italian-born witnesses was dismissed by the court. Anti-Italian prejudice was evident in the trial and in the presiding judge. Whether guilty or innocent, they clearly did not receive a fair trial. As suspected political radicals, they were executed in 1927 in the midst of an era of hysteria over left-wing and un-American activities.[47] Fifty years later, in 1977, the governor of Massachusetts issued a proclamation to the effect that they did not receive a fair trial.

Conflict With Blacks

Since the 1930s conflict between Italian Americans and groups lower on the ladder has been part of the urban scene. Conflicts between blacks and Italian Americans have accelerated in recent years. "Law and order" has been a major issue, as have school desegregation and busing, in the large metropolitan areas of the North.[48] Italian leaders and writers have sometimes complained that blacks are the "darlings" of the white Protestant liberals, and that blacks get disproportionate press coverage and federal aid. They have alleged that government programs are biased, that jobs in special federal programs in cities too often go to nonwhite groups.

Italian Americans in such cities as Newark and Philadelphia have found themselves surrounded by large numbers of migrating blacks. With these new poor immigrants came increased crime and drug problems. Realistic fears about crime became coupled with exaggerated views of blacks.[49]

A number of surveys have shown a significant level of antiblack prejudice and strong opposition to neighborhood desegregation among Italian Americans. One survey found that 70 percent of Italians would object if a black family moved into their area, a figure higher than for whites in general.[50] In addition, some civil rights demonstrations by blacks in the cities have provoked hostile verbal, or physically violent, attacks by white ethnics, including Italian Americans, particularly attacks on demonstrations tied to housing and school desegregation. Yet such data must be interpreted in a broader context. Italian Americans have been among the few white groups with a strong inclination to remain in central city areas. They are also among those most likely to own their own homes there. Thus Italian Americans, along with other southern and eastern Europeans, have been found in recent research studies to be more likely to live in naturally integrated neighborhoods, or at least integrated areas of cities, than are members of British American groups. Consequently, "the daily news reports generally stress the conflicts between Negroes and the most recently arrived ethnic groups, while the WASPs . . . do not have the same kinds of public conflicts that make news. Further reflection suggests, however, that public conflict between the newer ethnic groups and Negroes exists because they are in competition for the same housing as well as for economic and political power."[51]

POLITICS

In part because of late entry, Italians have not played as important a role in U.S. political institutions as earlier groups. The first meaningful Italian influence on American politics was Filippo Mazzei, a friend of Thomas Jefferson who came to the colonies to help with agricultural development. As it turned out, he helped Jefferson bring legal reforms to Virginia. Mazzei's writings speak vigorously of freedom and equality and include phrases similar to those Jefferson later used in the Declaration of Independence—for example, the phrase "All men are by nature created free and independent."[52]

Interestingly, Italian Americans first moved into politics in a significant way in the South. John Phinizy, son of an American army captain, became mayor of Augusta in 1837, and Gumersindo Pacetti was mayor of St. Augustine in 1861. Andrew Longino was even Governor of Mississippi in 1900, a time of growing anti-Italian sentiment in the South. The Italian contribution to Southern politics has been forgotten in most history books.

Italians in City Politics

During and after the great migration of 1880 to 1920, southern Italians were recruited into the Democratic party by Irish Americans. In Chicago, Italians benefited from the political patronage system; many were employed by the city in the 1890s, mostly in menial positions such as street sweeping. By 1905 Italians there had been hired in small numbers by the police and fire departments, but this type of public service came slowly. Irish leaders were slowly grooming Italian politicians as go-betweens to deal with Italian voters; by this method some were able to move up the political ladder. In Chicago, Italians had elected an alderman by 1892, and they had a few representatives in the Illinois legislature by the mid-1890s. Italians began to be elected to office in New York by 1900; by 1920 Italians were central to city politics, in passing out life-sustaining job favors.[53]

By the time of the Depression a few Italian Americans had begun to penetrate the upper political structure. By the late 1930s a few cities like

New York, San Francisco, and New Orleans had Italian mayors. Nonetheless, the typical picture was of an Italian community governed by non-Italian politicians.[54]

Substantial political gains were made in the next few decades. A number of smaller cities, particularly in New Jersey, elected Italian mayors. In 1947 New York City's political machine fell under the control of Italian Americans. In New Haven Irish control of local government had kept Italians from moving up for a number of decades, and as late as 1940 they were still underrepresented. Yet by the late 1950s Italian Americans were well represented in city government positions. Over the next two decades, the number of Italian political leaders became conspicuous in many northern cities, as mayors and members of city councils.[55]

As happened with the Irish, Anglo-Saxon Protestant reform movements often reduced the benefits going to the Italian working class. Progressive reform movements were aimed at ridding urban politics of the machine bosses and corruption. But defeating the machine meant decreasing political (and economic) power for working-class ethnics.[56]

Reform in the guise of urban renewal and urban redevelopment has also had a negative impact on Italian and other working-class communities. For example, the West End of Boston once contained a large, viable, Italian working-class community with relatively little political clout. In the late 1950s the area was officially designated a "slum" by the politically powerful city fathers and razed for urban renewal. New apartment buildings were built, development which was expected to improve the tax base of the central city. But several thousand Italians had been forced to relocate, a move that brought them great pain and grief.[57]

Some analysts have underscored the historical background of Italian Americans in explaining the relative lack of participation in politics: immigrants from the south of Italy were half-hearted participants because of their centuries-long experience with government as an exploitative oppressor.[58] Also militating against Italian involvement in urban politics, especially in the pre-World War II period, was the pressure placed on them by public stereotyping of their alleged radicalism and criminality. At an early stage, Italian immigrants gained the image of being radicals and socialists. The 1886 Haymarket Square riot, which involved a bomb thrown at police trying to break up a labor rally in Chicago, helped generate this national image of the new southern and eastern European immigrants.

Italians particularly suffered during the 1919–1922 "Red Scare." The infamous "Palmer raids" conducted by the attorney general in this period were largely aimed at immigrant families, often Italian, thought to be "radical" or "subversive." Many aliens were illegally detained or arrested, and some were deported as a result.[59] All this had a dampening effect on political participation.

State and National Elections

Increased participation in state and national politics also came slowly. Few Italians served in state and national legislatures in the North prior to 1900. One of the few was Francis Spinola, a brigadier general in the Union

Army, a member of the New York legislature, and a member of the U.S. House of Representatives. After 1900 the few successes which did come at state and national levels were often based on the concentration of voters in urban ghettos. Prior to 1950 a major state like New York had only had six Italian representatives in Congress. Perhaps the most famous of these was Fiorello La Guardia, a man quite proud of the Italian part of his heritage. La Guardia capitalized on ethnic issues and won elections in part on the strength of the Italian vote. In Congress he became the most vigorous supporter of Italian immigration, attacking Anglo-Saxon nativism and the anti-Italian quota system it had fostered. He was the first Italian American to make it up through the ranks of Irish politics in New York City, where he later served as mayor in the 1930s. First elected mayor in 1934, La Guardia showed that Italians and other white ethnics could support reform movements aimed at urban machines, in this case Tammany Hall, and promote efficient, honest government.[60]

Vito Marcantonio was one of the most vigorous representatives Italian Americans ever had in Congress, "an inveterate radical, an accomplished iconoclast, and a fiery exponent of socialist philosophy."[61] Serving in the 1930s, he was a vigorous advocate of the rights of Italians and other immigrants, as well as of blacks and Puerto Ricans.

International politics affected Italian American political activities, just as the Ireland-Britain struggle has affected Irish Americans. During the Depression Mussolini became a hero for many Italian Americans, as well as for many non-Italian Americans. Yet anti-Fascist activity was also a significant force in many Italian communities. When anti-Fascism caught on by the late 1930s, the entire Italian community was accused of being in Mussolini's pocket. As a result, during World War II Italian Americans suffered some discrimination. There was much talk about alleged Italian subversion, although the action taken against Italian (and German) Americans was far less substantial than was that against Japanese Americans. The use of the Italian language was prohibited on the radio in New York and Boston. Several thousand Italians were arrested, and nearly two hundred aliens were placed in internment camps after the U.S. declaration of war. Some industries connected with war materials limited the employment of Italian Americans. Italian American patriotism eventually managed to overwhelm this nativist fear, but the attacks did make Italians distinctive and probably slowed the process of economic and political assimilation.[62]

Coupled with this has been the persisting Anglo-Saxon Protestant fear that Italian American politicians are linked to organized crime. Political opponents only have to hint that an Italian American candidate is tied to the Mafia in order to reduce their chances of being elected. Many Italian American politicians, past and present, have had to live with smear campaigns of this type, including Mayor Joseph Alioto of San Francisco and Senator Dennis De Concini of Arizona.[63]

Since the Great Depression Italian Americans have slowly penetrated the middle levels of state and federal government, including the judicial system. Italian Americans finally made it into the judiciary in New York state by the 1930s; it was not until Franklin Roosevelt's administration that the first Italian American judge was appointed in the federal courts. Later, President Harry Truman appointed two Italians to the federal judgeships, only the second and third ever to be appointed. As of this writing no Italian American has ever served on the Supreme Court.[64] Progress in congressional representation has been a bit more substantial. By the late 1940s there were eight Italians in Congress; by the 1950s Italians were serving in ever larger numbers in state legislatures. John Pastore of Rhode Island became the first Italian governor in 1946 and the first senator shortly thereafter. In 1962 Anthony Celebrezze became the first Italian American to serve in a presidential cabinet. In 1968 Governor John Volpe of Massachusetts was considered a likely vice-presidential choice for the Republicans; and Mayor Joseph Alioto was seriously considered for the same position on the Democratic ticket. By 1973 another Italian, Volpe, had served in the cabinet.[65]

In recent years Italian movement into the Republican column has been noted, if exaggerated. Since the 1968 and 1972 presidential elections Republican strategists have worked hard for the white ethnic vote, including the Italian vote. Fears about civil rights and antiwar protests fueled discontent. Not surprisingly, there were a few successes resulting from this strategy, most notably the 1972 presidential election. Yet in most contests the votes of Italian Americans have continued to go for the Democratic party. Approximately two-thirds of Italian Americans have identified themselves as Democrats in recent surveys. A study of eighty-five state-wide elections found that the Republicans carried the Italian vote in only eight of them; moreover, the Republicans who garnered the most Italian votes were moderates. Many commentators since the Eisenhower years have claimed Italian Americans were becoming Republicans on an ever-increasing basis. Yet the data do not support this point of view, at least for the 1950–1968 period. The proportion of the Italian Republican vote went from 50 percent for Eisenhower, to 25 percent for Nixon in 1960, to 23 percent for Goldwater, to 40 percent for Nixon in 1968. Presidents Kennedy and Johnson did very well in Italian precincts.[66] Surprisingly, George Wallace had appeal for only a small minority of Italian American voters.

Persistent among Italian Americans has been the strong devotion to family and neighborhood. Attitudinal surveys have shown Italians to be somewhat less enthusiastic about government and democratic political activities, such as circulating petitions or speaking out against government, than groups such as the Irish or British.[67]

This has sometimes led to an image of Italians as incapable of community or political organization in their own behalf. An example of this would be the 1950s urban renewal process in the West End of Boston discussed earlier, when Italians were unable to organize politically to defend their neighborhood against the urban renewal desired and carried out destructively by the city fathers. But this view has been exaggerated, for there are also examples of political organization. Thus in 1968 East Bostonians organized to prevent their local neighborhoods from being further encroached upon by Boston's Logan International Airport, preventing construction of a new runway. More recently, East Bostonians have worked to prevent inroads by other outsiders. In 1972 a "Save East Boston" organization was established to protect the community from a number of external threats to its integrity. In 1976 the National Italian American Foundation was created; from its headquarters in Washington, D.C., this organization operates as a clearing house providing information on Italian politicians and on political issues of importance to Italian Americans.[68]

ITALIANS IN THE ECONOMY: MOBILITY SINCE 1880

Structural adaptation includes the movement of immigrant groups into secondary organization levels of the core society—into the economic, as well as the political and educational, organizations of the society. Economic mobility entails the penetration of higher levels of employment and attendant economic benefits. The Italian Americans started out at the bottom of the ladder. The immigrants prior to 1880 were small in number, mostly artisans, street sellers, and political exiles, and primarily from northern Italy. The southern Italian immigrants, those who came in large numbers after 1880, were economically oppressed. There was a tremendous demand for unskilled labor for canals and railroads by the late nineteenth century; southern and eastern Europeans provided much of that labor.[69]

Large numbers came to the United States with the aid of padroni, the labor bosses or work sponsors, who served as brokers linking the new immigrants to employment, food, and housing. Some claim this system was imported from Italy, but others have argued that it was a normal part of the United States' industrialization process, which virtually devoured immigrant workers. The padroni acted primarily as agents to secure cheap labor for transportation, construction, and manufacturing enterprises within the United States. Exploitation often resulted from the padroni system. Exorbitant prices were charged by the labor bosses for housing and food; labor abuses were heaped on workers isolated in camps.[70]

By 1909, because of legislation passed in several states, contractors and other business operators began to change from extra-legal padroni to legitimate agents. The greater size of Italian communities also decreased the need for the padroni. The labor boss system was in effect gone by the second decade of the twentieth century.[71]

Poverty and Discrimination

Urban poverty was the lot of most Italian immigrants. Coupled with this were dangerous working conditions, so bad that workers were killed or disabled. Stella sums this up: "The Italian immigrant may be maimed and killed in his industrial occupation without a cry and without indemnity. He may die from the 'bends' working in the caissons under the river, without protest; he can be slowly asphyxiated in crowded tenements, smothered in dangerous trades and occupations (which only the ignorant immigrant pursues, not the native American); he can contract tuberculosis in unsanitary factories and sweatshops."[72] A number of studies documented poor community conditions—overcrowding and exorbitant rents in run-down housing, as well as inadequate water and sewage facilities. In cities such as New York, death rates from infectious diseases were high.[73]

Lack of skills affected the first generation. While some were semi-skilled workers, they had among them the highest percentage of unskilled laborers among major immigrant groups in this period. One study found the immigrants around 1900 were 0.2 percent professional workers, 12.7 percent trade or industrial workers, and 64.9 percent farmers or farm workers, with the rest being women and children.[74] Poor farmers and their families made up the majority. As a result many found themselves doing the "dirty work" of the rapidly industrializing society. One study of Italian-born males in the United States found few employed in agriculture, but a high proportion employed as unskilled workers, miners, laborers, and fishermen. Many were laborers replacing the Irish in building roads and railroads. Few were in clerical fields or the professions. In the domestic and personal service area they were mostly barbers and restaurant workers. Italian women were primarily in the trade area.[75]

Background handicaps such as a poor command of English and lack of vocational skills were not the only factors restricting occupational opportunity. Discrimination played an important role. Isolate, small group, direct and indirect institutionalized discrimination—all types outlined in Chapter 1—played a role in holding Italians back. From the first years of heavy migration the new Italian residents were, Higham asserts, "abused in public and isolated in private, cuffed in the works and pelted on the streets, fined and imprisoned on the smallest pretext, cheated of their wages, and crowded by the score into converted barns and tumble-down shanties that served as boarding houses."[76] Direct discrimination was well institutionalized; the discrimination in wages was often blatant. Thus when a major New York City reservoir was built in 1895, ads for laborers listed the daily wages as $1.30 to $1.50 for "whites" and $1.15 to $1.25 for "Italians."[77] Just as important was indirect discrimination in the form of recruitment practices with a built-in bias. Informal social networks were a major means of circulating job information. Anglo-Protestant and Irish sponsors were important in job networks where they protected their own kind and discriminated against Italians.[78]

Italians in Unions

One additional factor operating against Italians, at least in the beginning, was discrimination by worker organizations. Such discrimination kept Italians from moving into many blue-collar jobs. Some poor Italians became strikebreakers because of that discrimination and because their poverty-striken conditions led them to be hired as scabs by employers seeking to destroy unions. In their first decades in the cities southern Italians were not as active in unions as native whites, in part because they had no prior experience with unions.

However, some Italian Americans later became very active in labor unions, bringing radical working class ideas with them from Italy. Some became union leaders and took part in major strikes such as that in Lawrence, Massachusetts, in 1912. Joseph Ettor, Italian American organizer of the Industrial Workers of the World (IWW), was asked to assist textile factory workers, including Italian women, in their strike over reduced wages. The woolen company there refused arbitration; the ensuing strike was sometimes violent. The state militia, made up of native-born white-collar workers, was called in, and one woman striker (Anna La Pizza) was killed in clashes between the militia and 25,000 strikers. The 7,000 Italian Americans were the largest nationality group among the strikers; and Italian Americans were prominent leaders.[79] By the early 1900s there was extensive Italian involvement in unions as members and leaders. Italians have been among the strongest union members for several decades.[80]

Upward Mobility

Progress for the great mass of Italian Americans, who numbered in the millions by the 1920s, came slowly but steadily. An early study of Italian workers found that while half were still laborers in 1916, only 31 percent were laborers fifteen years later. Data on occupation showed a decline from 33 percent in unskilled positions in 1916 to 11 percent in 1931. Small-business and skilled blue-collar positions were more common by 1931.[81]

Mobility was evident, but so was the persisting differential between Italians and others. A study in Newburyport, Massachusetts, in the early 1930s revealed that Italians there were lower than other whites on the social "prestige" ladder and somewhat lower on the occupational ladder. As with other ethnic groups, the Depression delayed economic advancement for a decade; yet even in these difficult years slow progress continued. By 1939 Italians had begun to supplant Jews as the major group represented in a number of important unions of skilled workers. They had become numerous as workers in the garment industry and in building trades. The Italians paralleled the economic pattern of the Irish, moving up from unskilled to skilled blue-collar positions in a few generations.[82]

With a number of traditional avenues of mobility essentially blocked, some Italian Americans opted for less legitimate avenues for mobility—one, destined to give the entire group a bad image, being that of "organized crime." Since the 1920s organized crime has provided better-paying jobs for some Italians in northern cities. The non-Italians, the "good citizens" of the cities, kept bootlegging, prostitution, and gambling operations going with their patronage.[83] Later on, money from organized crime would flow to legitimate enterprises, just as it had in earlier decades for other ethnic groups. Members of families successful in organized crime would move out of illegitimate enterprises altogether.[84] This trend, according to Ianni, supports "the thesis that for Italian Americans, as for other ethnic groups, organized crime has been a way station on the road to ultimately respectable roles in American society."[85] But only a few Italian Americans ever made it up this way. The line between legitimate and illegitimate business, moreover, has often been fuzzy in this society, and not just in the case of white ethnics in organized crime. The Anglo-Saxon Protestant heroes of industry were involved in a variety of economic and political activities, including illegal activities. Illegal business is a game many groups have played.[86]

A few Italians became nationally prominent business entrepreneurs and scientists. One was Amadeo Giannini, founder of the Bank of America. He made his fortune in California, bankrolling generations of small businesses and ranchers; he even permitted his poor depositors a voice in bank management. A number of Italians, with names like Di Giorgio and Gallo, had begun to play a major role in restaurant, agricultural, and contracting businesses. Nobel Prize winners Fermi and Kuria would be included among the prominent names in science. As with groups before and after them, Italians also found chances for upward mobility in sports, as is indicated by the careers of such men as Rocky Marciano, Joe DiMaggio, and Yogi Berra.[87]

By the 1950s further upward mobility had become evident, although Italians were behind major Protestant groups. One urban study conducted in the 1950s suggested that second-generation Italian Catholics fell well behind white Protestants in the proportion possessing higher-level white-collar jobs.[88] Similarly, 1950 comparisons of eight European ethnic groups in Detroit showed second-generation Italian men as having the next-to-lowest percentage in white-collar positions, the next-to-highest percentage in service-labor jobs, and the highest unemployment rate.[89]

By the 1960s and 1970s there were signs of greater mobility gains. National figures on income and occupational attainment indicate the great strides that Italian Americans have made against the widespread discrimination and hostility leveled against them. One study using 1960 Census data examined first- and second-generation white groups.[90] Foreign-born Italians fell consistently below the total native-born white figures on occupational and income levels. However, the 1960 data on American-born Italians of foreign or mixed parentage, primarily the second generation, revealed a somewhat higher average occupational level and a significantly higher average income than was reported for all native-born whites. By the general white standard, Italian Americans had done remarkably well. Recent Census data indicate that Italian Americans continue to rank at or above the national average in terms of occupation and income. March 1972 figures showed an impressive median income figure of $11,646 for Italian American families, a figure somewhat above that for the English Americans taken as a group, and above the national median income. Data on occupational levels indicated that the proportion of Italian American men employed in white-collar jobs was generally below the proportions for English and Russian Americans, but at or above the proportions for other major white ethnic groups. The proportion of men in blue-collar positions, both skilled and unskilled, was still greater than that for English and Russian Americans.

In a recent analysis of survey data, Greeley found that the income levels for Italian Catholics (under 40 years of age) were $1600 above the average for a few white Protestant groups, such as white Methodists. However, in another analysis, Roof found that Italian Catholics still ranked well below elite Protestant groups (such as white Episcopalians and Presbyterians) in terms of income. Italian American achievement is impressive; but ethnic stratification, with elite Protestant groups at the top, still persists in the United States even into the 1980s.[91]

Persisting Problems of Poverty and Discrimination

Discrimination against Italian Americans is still a problem at the highest levels of society; direct and indirect discrimination operate as barriers to higher-level managerial, administrative, and professional positions. Italian Americans are heavily represented among rank-and-file workers in city police, fire, and sanitation departments and in public utilities. Yet higher-level administrative positions in city departments often have a low representation of Italian Americans.[92] A recent New York City study found that 25 percent of New Yorkers and 22 percent of the city's professional-manager white-collar category are Italian. But these proportions have not been reflected in higher-level employment in the City University of New York. The study concludes: "In decision-making positions of Dean, Director and Chairman of the system's 18 colleges, there are only 20 Italian Americans out of a total of 504 positions."[93] A small percentage of the faculty was Italian, and these faculty members tended to be at the lowest ranks.

Exclusive residential areas and top business clubs still discriminate against Italian Americans, if subtly. Into the 1970s and 1980s some important private clubs barred Italian Americans. One finds relatively few Italian Americans in the top management ranks of major corporations. One study of the 106 largest Chicago-area corporations compared the Italian percentage in the Chicago population (4.8 percent) with the numbers of Italians among directors (1.9 percent) and officers (2.9 percent).[94] In addition to being generally underrepresented, *no* Italians were found in these positions in *most* of the major corporations studied: 79 percent of the corporations had no Italian directors at all, while 71 percent had no Italian officers. The majority of these industrial firms, retailers, utilities, transportation companies, and banks are national businesses, many among the top national companies.

We have previously underscored Dye's study of several thousand members of important elites in the United States in the 1970s, predominantly Protestant elites with few Italians to be found among them. Earlier studies noted a similar pattern; Whyte's 1940 study of Boston found that because of discrimination and prejudice there were no Italian names among the "leading officers of the old established businesses."[95]

While recent data indicate that many Italian Americans have moved up to white-collar levels, many remain in the blue-collar group. Italian Americans may now inhabit two different worlds: many who have stayed in central cities fit the blue-collar image and appear to be at somewhat lower socioeconomic levels than Italians residing elsewhere, particularly those white-collar families who have moved to suburban areas. One study of the central areas of Connecticut's cities in the 1960s found that 64 percent of the Italians there were in blue-collar jobs, a figure substantially higher than the figures for white Protestants and Irish Catholics in the same areas. More recently, a 1977 study of Italian Americans in both the city of Bridgeport and its suburban areas found that one-third were in blue-collar jobs. This study suggests a significant shift into white-collar jobs over the past two decades.[96]

However, recent data for New York City indicate that there is a difference between those living in cities and those living in suburbs. The advances into professional, managerial, clerical, and sales work seem to be most dramatic in the suburbs. For example, in New York City the majority of Italian Americans, about 57 percent, are still working in blue-collar jobs; they are construction workers, truck drivers, mechanics, plumbers, and the like. Only one-quarter of Italian Americans in New York City hold professional, managerial, or technical jobs.[97]

Moreover, poverty remains a serious problem for a portion of Italian American communities. With many of the 20,000 Italian immigrants who entered every year in the 1970s coming into New York City, Italian communities faced a growing number of poverty-stricken residents. Investigating Census tracts with 50 percent or more foreign-born Italians, one report found significant percentages of Italians living in poverty throughout the city.[98] From 15 to 18 percent of families in these tracts had incomes below the federal poverty level.

Yet it would be a mistake to exaggerate the problems of poverty. The overall picture of recent occupational and income mobility for a white ethnic group oppressed on a large scale just sixty years ago is impressive. Compared to their past, the majority of Italian Americans have made strides up the socioeconomic ladder, so much so that on some indices they are at least at parity with the Anglo-Saxon Protestants taken as a group. Stereotypes of fatalistic, low-achievement Italians are contradicted by this economic success.

EDUCATION

Organized education for large numbers of Italian Americans began toward the end of the nineteenth century. Many of the immigrants came from areas in Italy where the poor were provided with little schooling. As a result, half could not read or write. In the United States many adopted a pragmatic approach to education, valuing it greatly but asking, "What is the practical value of this for jobs, for later life?" Many poor families made sacrifices to get their first child through elementary school. And the first children were expected to help, with a job, to get later children through school.

One additional hurdle was thrown up by the Protestant Establishment. As with the Irish, Protestant educators were very concerned about the alleged corruption and cultural inferiority of Italian Americans; many sought to Americanize them as quickly as possible, teaching them Anglo-Saxon ways. Schools became pressure cookers of Americanization. Anglo-Saxon Protestant norms about health, dress, manners, work values, and language were pressed on Italian immigrants and their children. Discrimination was a fact of life. These pressures were especially strong in the case of second-generation children, most of whom went to public schools. (Conflict with the Irish, as well as economic problems, kept many Italian parents from sending their children to parochial schools). The adaptation pressures did *not* mean that public schools took all poor Italian immigrants and gave them the necessary skills to make it in American society. Public schools were Procrustean beds shaped in Anglocentric form, with the effect that many children left school rather than give in to hostile pressures. As a result, mobility for many immigrants and their children was actually slowed by these schools.[99]

Over the next few decades Italian Americans overcame these barriers in a dramatic way. Progress could be seen in rising educational levels between the 1920s and the 1950s, and in the most recent decades educational attainments have been impressive. According to 1960 Census data, educational attainment went up from six years for the foreign-born to eleven years for the second generation, nearly the same as for all second-generation Americans. The Census Bureau data showed that for those over age 35 the median level was 11.1 for Italians, compared to an English figure of 12.4 and a national figure of 12.1 years. The below-35 group, however, had the same average as that for the nation as a whole, although it was still below that of English Americans. In the 1960s Italian American children began attending college in ever-increasing numbers. Driven by the work ethic of hard labor and saving, families sacrificed to put their children through school. Today this trend continues. Attendance at college has increased significantly over the last decade or two.[100]

Serious educational problems remain. Italian American educators have emphasized a range of problems. Stephen Aiello, president of the New York City Board of Education, put it this way:

> The dropout rate among Italian high-school students is still too high. Coupled with this, many if not most of the student dropouts are not prepared with any marketable skills once they leave school and therefore, a number of our children are faced with the dilemma of dead-end jobs and a life of frustration and unhappiness. . . . Also for too many of our young people, the problem of a negative self-image and self-concept continues to plague.[101]

Documenting this point, a recent Rhode Island study found a great deal of diversity among young Italian males, with over half of young males not completing high school. At the same time, however, the proportion of young men attending college is increasing, even doubling to a figure of one-fifth in recent years. Some youths may be left behind as others progress, posing a serious educational problem for Italian American communities.[102]

RELIGION

The Catholic Church has been important in the lives of many Italian Americans. The male peasant in southern Italy infrequently attended mass, actively participating primarily on feast days, holy days, or certain other ceremonial occasions. Older women were the most active church members. There the Church was associated with the oppressive landlord system. In the United States, Protestant opposition to Catholicism was an obstacle to the free practice of religion. For Protestants, urban political machines and Catholicism conjured up images of immigrants from southern and eastern Europe. Protestant social workers in settlement houses attempted to Americanize the new Catholic population. One Protestant minister argued that "public schools, mission schools and churches will do the work to evangelize the immigrants. And it must be done, business pleads for it, patriotism demands it, social considerations require it."[103]

Many Irish Catholic churches were overwhelmed by large numbers of Italian immigrants. For the Italians, the Irish were too orthodox. For the Italian immigrant, religion was not an intimate part of political identity, while for the Irish, religious expression was tied to a nationalist heritage of anti-English agitation. Italian immigrants were Catholic, but not fanatically so. Saints were dear to Italians, as were religious festivals which played an important role in cementing together the Italian community.[104]

Irish pastors often saw the new parishioners in a negative light. They were not considered to be as serious as the Irish. Sometimes this tension escalated. Once ethnic parishes for Italians had developed, Italians were warned away, on occasion forcefully, from Irish parishes. Italians reciprocated with reactions of their own. Many first-generation Italian Americans preferred to send their children to public schools rather than to the Irish-dominated parochial schools, a reaction that would not be as vigorous in later generations.[105]

Gradually, Italian Catholicism, with its distinctive festivals and ceremonies, took its place alongside Irish Catholicism. By 1900 there were fourteen Italian parishes in New York; by 1924 there were fifty-three; by 1961 there were seventy-four.[106]

Italian Catholicism persisted. However, a 1964 study found that among seven major Catholic ethnic groups, the parents of Irish respondents were among the highest in mass attendance, while the parents of Italians, particularly fathers, were among the lowest. Italian parents were much less likely to have had any parochial schooling than any of the other groups.[107]

A study of Italian and Irish Catholics in New York City suggests the controversial conclusion that third-generation Italians may be becoming more "Irishized" in their religious practices, because the data show less emphasis on the Virgin Mary, fewer Masses said for deceased relatives, and more emphasis on generous contributions to the Church than in earlier generations.[108] Adaptations to a multiethnic Church may be coming most rapidly in suburban areas, where even Italian men are playing a more active role in church life. Upward mobility has brought a concern with the social milieu of the suburbs, one part of which is organized church life. Yet even in the suburbs Italians differ from other groups. Lopreato notes that "the Italians' tradition of secularism and skepticism toward church authority . . . has not disappeared and remains ingrained in the younger generations of the suburbs."[109] This is evident, for example, in the widespread use of banned contraceptives among Italians. The Italian immigrants and their descendants have forced the American Church to take into account different ethnic brands of Catholicism.

ASSIMILATION OR ETHNOGENESIS?

Acculturation pressures came early for southern and eastern European immigrants. Unlike the British before them, they spoke no English, nor were they familiar with the customs of Anglo-Saxon Protestant society. Concentrated in "Little Italies," Italian immigrants had to learn Italian dialects other than their own, but most could get by with minimal English. The ethnic community, the family, and the kinship network were the critical context of much daily living. Cultural adaptation was slowed by factors other than language and community: poverty, the intention of some to return home, and hostility in the new environment.[110]

Over time the intrusion of external caretakers—settlement workers, missionaries, and the police—began to exert pressure for cultural assimilation on Italians. Settlement houses and churches were centers of citizenship training. Protestant educators became heavily involved in Americanization strategies. As a result of school and other pressures for adaptation, Italian families experienced internal stress. The first-generation family was in transition, cross-pressured between old Italian and new American ways. Families became less patriarchal and kin solidarity weakened somewhat, as did ties to religion. Children were more on their own. Speaking Italian at home was a point of intergenerational conflict, since the younger members felt school pressures to speak only English.[111]

A second point of intergenerational conflict was marriage. First-generation parents saw it as a family matter, while the children tended to see it as an individual matter. Given this tension, it is not surprising that second-generation families adapted in different ways. One type abandoned the old ways, changing the Italian name and moving out of an Italian residential area. This was rare. A second type rejected the old ways in part, perhaps by moving out of the Little Italy but remaining near enough to maintain close ties to the first generation. A third type stayed in the old community and retained many of the old ways. Doubtless, the largest group was those who moved away somewhat from the parental neighborhood but retained many of the old ties. Taken as a group, the second generation was moving significantly in the direction of cultural assimilation, adopting the language and in part the family and other values of the core culture.[112]

Structural Assimilation: Progress and Limits

Structural assimilation can be seen as movement into the secondary organizations—the businesses and bureaucracies—of the larger society, as well as into its primary social networks: social clubs, neighborhoods, and friendship circles. Structural movement of Italian Americans over the first several decades came with considerable violence and resistance on the part of earlier groups. Positioning at the lower socioeconomic levels was a fact of life for a time.

In recent decades Italian Americans have made impressive gains in the areas of employment, income, and education, and lesser gains in the political sphere. Ongoing structural assimilation in terms of voluntary associations and clubs may be suggested in the decline of distinctively Italian organizations in many communities in recent decades. One study of Italian Americans in Bridgeport, Connecticut, in the 1950s found evidence that the second and third generations were not participating actively in Italian social and mutual benefit associations, a situation characteristic of Italian Americans in other cities.[113]

Residential movement into the suburbs has been seen as indicative of at least partial movement into the primary social networks of the larger Catholic community, if not the Protestant core society. We have already noted the multi-ethnic character of suburban Catholic religion. Suburbanization accelerated during and after World War II. Moving out of the ethnic community in the central city may be indicative of primary-group assimilation into the core society, or at least into some part thereof. In Firey's analysis of Boston's North End those Italians least tied to Italian associations and kinship networks were the most likely to emigrate to outlying areas. But there is another perspective. Some who moved out, including some in the 1970s and 1980s, maintained ties to the central city community, and some families moved out in groups. An affluent Italian might buy up adjacent dwellings for relatives in a suburban area, or parents might purchase a home in the suburbs, after which their children would move there as well.[114]

Many Italian American families, both in suburban areas and in central cities, have remained enmeshed in kinship-friendship networks substantially composed of other Italian Americans. Contemporary studies have revealed the persisting importance of these networks, particularly in working-class communities. In his 1962 classic study Herbert Gans wrote about an "urban village" in Boston, a blue-collar Italian American community with intimate interpersonal ties between relatives and friends. Today these ethnic enclaves can still be found in many American cities, but many, if not most, Italian Americans now live outside large ethnic enclaves. However, primary group ties remain strong. A study of Italian Americans in New York City found that most preferred Italian American neighborhoods and that primary-group relationships in all generations tended to be with other Italians. Structural assimilation at the primary level had not occurred for this small but representative sample of Italian Americans. And survey data on neighborhoods in a number of cities, collected in 1967, indicated that of all the ethnic groups studied, Italians were the most likely to live near their parents and siblings and the most likely to see their parents weekly. This family orientation has persisted into the 1980s.[115]

Even in Sunbelt cities Italian American communities thrive. In a recent study of Phoenix, Phylis Martinelli found several thousand Italian Americans participating in an ethnic community centered around social clubs (such as the Amico Club and the American-Italian Club), Italian delis and groceries, churches, celebrations and festivals, and family visitation. These Italian Americans live scattered throughout the city but maintain community ties nonetheless. Widespread assimilation at the primary-group level may be on its way, but it has not occurred.[116]

Complete marital assimilation is probably the last stage. Studies of marriages in New Haven in 1870 and in Chicago in 1920 found high rates of in-marriage for Italians; 94 to 98 percent of all marriages were endogamous. In the intervening decades in-marriage decreased: the New Haven figure was 77 percent by 1950. A recent study based on data from a number of cities suggests a similar pattern. While 93 percent of the Italian respondents' parents were in endogamous marriages, only 66 percent of the married Italian respondents were married to Italians. Still, a substantial majority could be found in endogamous marriages, the highest proportion for any immigrant group which had arrived in great numbers before 1920. The data showed that almost all of the non-Italian partners in the mixed marriages were from other Catholic groups—Irish, German, or eastern European.[117]

An Italian Identity?

Identificational assimilation involves giving up one's ethnic identity for that of the core culture. This has not happened for most Italian Americans. Interviews with Italians in one New York City study found that most saw themselves as Italians or Italian Americans. Another project in Providence, Rhode Island, found that a majority of those interviewed also saw themselves as Italian, with greater pride in ethnicity being expressed among third-generation respondents than among earlier generations.[118] A prominent historian of immigration, Marcus Lee Hansen, once argued that there is inevitably an increase in ethnic awareness in the third generation of an immigrant group; this substantially assimilated generation vigorously searches out its roots. Whether or not this rise theory is correct, it is true that many white ethnic Americans have by the third generation developed an ethnic consciousness which their fathers and grandfathers perhaps could not afford to articulate. As a result, they are more articulate in assessing and expressing the needs of their ethnic communities.[119]

Italian outspokenness in regard to cultural background and pride has increased. Such groups as the Italian-American Civil Rights League and the Americans of Italian Descent have worked vigorously to protect the Italian heritage. Part of the resurgence has been directed at stereotypes of Italian Americans, as well as their treatment by law-enforcement agencies. In the 1970s a number of demonstrations were directed at Justice Department harassment and stereotyping of Italian Americans. As a result of these and other pressures, the Justice Department formally stopped using "Mafia" and "Cosa Nostra" as equivalents for "organized crime."[120]

This concession does not mean the disappearance of the criminality stereotype prevalent among rank-and-file Americans, as well as among many law-enforcement officials. The persistence of this stereotype indicates that Italian Americans have not reached what Gordon calls complete attitudinal-receptional assimilation—the stage where prejudice and stereotyping have evaporated. Yet prejudice has declined; and direct discrimination, except at the highest levels, appears to be on the wane.

The ethnogenesis model seems to fit the Italian experience. Italians came to the United States with significant differences from the dominant British group, but they shared some historical background and a Christian tradition with that group. By virtue of interaction in the public schools and the influence of the mass media, the gap narrowed substantially, but by no means completely. Italian Americans became in some ways similar to the host culture, but in other ways they retained their distinctiveness. Over time, because of their heritage, together with segregation and strong community and kinship networks, a distinctive American ethnic group was spawned. No longer an Italy-centered group dominated by its heritage, neither has it simply become British-Protestant American or simply American. Substantial adaptation without complete assimilation characterizes Italian Americans. Even the third and fourth generations retain their Italian American-ness, particularly in their commitment to the family and Italian community.

SUMMARY

Today most descendants of Italian immigrants who entered around the turn of the century live in cities on the East Coast and in the Midwest. Most remain Catholics. These Americans play an important role in the United States. We have focused primarily on the descendants of the 1880–1920 and earlier waves of migration, examining the beginnings of this migration and tracing out its impact. Poverty and hard working conditions greeted these immigrants. They were least prepared for the intense nativist attacks, which falsely stereotyped them as an inferior, immoral, and corrupt people. IQ testing in this early period seemed to be aimed at proving their inferiority. The "mafia myth" further stigmatized their communities. Even violent attacks were suffered.

Political avenues, for a time, were closed; the economy consigned them to low-paying jobs; schools tried to make carbon-copy Anglo-Saxons out of them. Yet in spite of these problems the immigrants and their descendants persevered and prospered. By the post-war decades, in politics, in the economy, and in education, they had begun to make the mark. Their mobility makes them another American success story, although a considerable price was exacted for that success. Nonetheless, Italian Americans have retained a considerable degree of ethnic distinctiveness.

With the demise of discriminatory quotas, Italian immigration to the United States increased sharply in the late 1960s and 1970s, remaining relatively high into the 1980s. Many of these later immigrants are relatives of earlier immigrants. Some are technical workers, part of Europe's "brain drain," while others are farmers. That the experiences of this diverse group will be the same as that of earlier immigrants seems unlikely, given the more tolerant contemporary context; it is too early to judge fully the differential impact of this society on these new immigrants.

NOTES

[1]From *The New York Times*, June 17, 1970, p. 31. © 1970 by the New York Times Company. Reprinted by permission.

[2]Richard Gambino, *Blood of My Blood* (Garden City, N.Y.: Doubleday Anchor Books, 1975), p. 344.

[3]Giovanni Schiavo, *The Italians in America Before the Civil War* (New York: Vigo Press, 1934), pp. 55–180.

[4]Ibid., p. 135.

[5]U.S. Department of Justice, Immigration and Naturalization Service, *Annual Report* (Washington, D.C.: U.S. Government Printing Office, 1973), pp. 52–54. Figures for 1820 to 1867 represent alien passengers arrived; for 1868–1891 and 1895–1897, immigrant aliens arrived; for 1892–1894 and 1898–1973, immigrant aliens admitted.

[6]Schiavo, *The Italians in America*, p. 204

[7]Carl Wittke, *We Who Built America*, rev. ed. (Cleveland: Case Western Reserve University Press, 1964), p. 441.

[8]Humbert S. Nelli, *The Italians in Chicago, 1880–1930* (New York: Oxford University Press, 1970), p. 5.

[9]Grazia Dore, "Some Social and Historical Aspects of Italian Emigration to America," in *The Italians*, ed. Francesco Cordasco and Eugene Bucchioni (Clifton, N.J.: Augustus M. Kelley, 1974), p. 7.

[10]Joseph Lopreato, *Italian Americans* (New York: Random House, 1970), pp. 23–27; John S. MacDonald, "Agricultural Organization, Migration, and Labor Militancy in Rural Italy," *Economic History Review*, 2d ser., 16 (1963–1964): 61–75. I am indebted to Phylis Cancilla Martinelli for her useful suggestions on revising the sections which follow. I draw on her suggestions in this paragraph and in the rest of this chapter.

[11]Luciano J. Iorizzo and Salvatore Mondello, *The Italian-Americans* (New York: Twayne Publishers, 1971), pp. 57–59; Lopreato, *Italian Americans*, p. 36.

[12]Antonia Stella, *Some Aspects of Italian Immigration to the United States*, reprint ed. (San Francisco: R and E Associates, 1970), p. 33.

[13]Rudolph J. Vecoli, "Contadini in Chicago," in *Divided Society*, ed. Colin Greer (New York: Basic Books, 1974), p. 220.

[14]Data cited in William Petersen, *Population*, 2d ed. (New York: Macmillan, 1969), p. 260.

[15]Stella, *Some Aspects of Italian Immigration*, p. 15; Lopreato, *Italian Americans*, pp. 14–16.

[16]John Higham, *Strangers in the Land*, rev. ed. (New York: Atheneum Press, 1975), pp. 312–24.

[17]See Stanley Lieberson, *Ethnic Patterns in American Cities* (Glencoe, Ill.: Free Press, 1963), pp. 209–18.

[18]William F. Whyte, *Street Corner Society*, 2d ed. (Chicago: University of Chicago Press, 1955), pp. 272–73; Walter Firey, *Land Use in Central Boston* (Cambridge, Mass.: Harvard University Press, 1947), pp. 187–88; Wittke, *We Who Built America*, p. 446.

[19]Firey, *Land Use in Central Boston*, p. 193; Paul J. Campisi, "Ethnic Family Patterns: The Italian Family in the United States," in Cordasco and Bucchioni, *The Italians*, pp. 311–14; Lopreato, *Italian Americans*, pp. 51–53; Whyte, *Street Corner Society*, p. 274.

[20]Eliot Lord, John J. D. Trenor, and Samuel J. Barrows, *The Italian in America* (San Francisco: R and E Associates, 1970), pp. 17–18.

[21]Powderly is quoted in Iorizzo and Mondello, *The Italian-Americans*, p. 64.

[22]Kenneth L. Roberts, *Why Europe Leaves Home*, reprinted in "Kenneth L. Roberts and the Threat of Mongrelization in America, 1922," in *In Their Place*, ed. Lewis H. Carlson and George A. Colburn (New York: John Wiley, 1972), p. 312.

[23]Mary F. Matthews, "The Role of the Public School in the Assimilation of the Italian Immigrant Child in New York City, 1900–1914," in Silvano Tomasi and M. H. Engel, *The Italian*

Experience in the United States (New York: Center for Migration Studies, 1970), p. 127; Stella, *Some Aspects of Italian Immigration to the United States*, p. 54.

[24]Stella, *Some Aspects of Italian Immigration*, p. 38.

[25]Leon J. Kamin, *The Science and Politics of I.Q.* (New York: John Wiley, 1974), pp. 15–16.

[26]Ibid., pp. 16–19.

[27]Carl C. Brigham, *A Study of American Intelligence* (Princeton, N.J.: Princeton University Press, 1923), especially pp. 124–25, 177–210. Later Brigham recanted.

[28]See Woodrow Wilson, *History of the American People* (New York: Harper's, 1901), 5: 212–14.

[29]See Kamin, *The Science and Politics of I.Q.*, p. 30.

[30]Quoted in E. Digby Baltzell, *The Protestant Establishment* (New York: Random House Vintage Books, 1966), p. 30.

[31]Quoted in ibid.

[32]Iorizzo and Mondello, *The Italian-Americans*, pp. 35–36.

[33]Nelli, *The Italians in Chicago, 1880–1930*, p. 126.

[34]Stella, *Some Aspects of Italian Immigration*, pp. 60–61, 73.

[35]Gambino, *Blood of My Blood*, pp. 293–98; Lopreato, *Italian Americans*, p. 126; Nelli, *The Italians in Chicago, 1880–1930*, pp. 154–55.

[36]Reported in Francis A. Ianni, *A Family Business* (New York: Russell Sage Foundation, 1972), p. 194.

[37]Dwight C. Smith, Jr., *The Mafia Mystique* (New York: Basic Books, 1975), p. 13.

[38]Ibid., pp. 289 ff.

[39]Ibid., p. 324; Gambino, *Blood of My Blood*, pp. 300–301.

[40]Robert Lichter and Linda Lichter, "Italian-American Characters in Television Entertainment," report prepared for the Commission for Social Justice, Order of Sons of Italy, May 1982.

[41]William F. Whyte, "Race Conflicts in the North End of Boston," *New England Quarterly* 12 (December 1939): 626; Iorizzo and Mondello, *The Italian-Americans*, pp. 35, 66.

[42]Luciano J. Iorizzo, "The Padrone and Immigrant Distribution," in Tomasi and Engel, *The Italian Experience in the United States*, pp. 49–51.

[43]Gambino, *Blood of My Blood*, p. 119; Higham, *Strangers in the Land*, p. 169.

[44]Gambino, *Blood of My Blood*, pp. 118, 280–81.

[45]Ibid., pp. 104, 119; Higham, *Strangers in the Land*, p. 90.

[46]Andrew F. Rolle, *The American Italian* (Belmont, Calif.: Wadsworth, 1972), p. 78.

[47]Ibid., pp. 110–11; Gambino, *Blood of My Blood*, pp. 120–21.

[48]Iorizzo and Mondello, *The Italian-Americans*, p. 207; Gerald D. Suttles, *The Social Order of the Slum* (Chicago: University of Chicago Press, 1968), pp. 102–3.

[49]Richard Krickus, *Pursuing the American Dream* (Garden City, N.Y.: Doubleday Anchor Books, 1976), p. 280.

[50]Cited in Mark R. Levy and Michael S. Kramer, *The Ethnic Factor* (New York: Simon & Schuster, 1972), p. 174. Other data on racist attitudes can be found in Andrew M. Greeley, *Why Can't They Be Like Us?* (New York: Dutton, 1971), pp. 67 ff.

[51]Norman M. Bradburn, Seymour Sudman, and Galen L. Gockel, *Racial Integration in American Neighborhoods* (Chicago: National Opinion Research Center, 1970), pp. 147–49.

[52]Schiavo, *The Italians in America Before the Civil War*, pp. 163–66.

[53]Nelli, *The Italians in Chicago, 1880–1930*, pp. 75–76; Wittke, *We Who Built America*, p. 447; Lopreato, *Italian Americans*, pp. 113–17; Giovanni Schiavo, Italian American History (New York: Vigo Press, 1947), 1:499–504.

[54]Rolle, *The American Italian*, p. 85; William F. Whyte, *Street Corner Society*, p. 276.

[55]Samuel Lubell, *The Future of American Politics*, 2d ed. (Garden City, N.Y.: Doubleday Anchor Books, 1955), p. 70; Lopreato, *Italian Americans*, p. 114.

[56]Joel H. Spring, *Education and the Rise of the Corporate State* (Boston: Beacon Press, 1972), pp. 86–87.

[57]Herbert J. Gans, *The Urban Villagers* (Glencoe, Ill.: Free Press, 1962), pp. 285–87.

[58]Lopreato, *Italian Americans*, pp. 113–14.

[59]See Gambino, *Blood of My Blood*, p. 117.

[60]Salvatore J. LaGumina, "Case Studies of Ethnicity and Italo-American Politicians," in Tomasi and Engel, *The Italian Experience in the United States*, p. 147; Krickus, *Pursuing the American Dream*, pp. 174–81.

[61]LaGumina, "Case Studies of Ethnicity and Italo-American Politics," p. 152.

[62]Wittke, *We Who Built America*, p. 450; Iorizzo and Mondello, *The Italian-Americans*, pp. 200–205; Iorizzo and Mondello, *The Italian-Americans*, p. 208; Gambino, *Blood of My Blood*, p. 316.

[63]Phylis Cancilla Martinelli, personal communication, July 26, 1982.

[64]See Lubell, *The Future of American Politics*, pp. 83–84; John R. Schmidhauser, "The Justices of the Supreme Court: A Collective Portrait," *Midwest Journal of Political Science 3* (February 1959): 19–20.

[65]Lubell, *The Future of American Politics*, p. 70; LaGumina, "Case Studies of Ethnicity and Italo-American Politics," p. 145.

[66]Levy and Kramer, *The Ethnic Factor*, pp. 165–89. See also Krickus, *Pursuing the American Dream*, pp. 6–11.

[67]Andrew M. Greeley, *Ethnicity in the United States* (New York: John Wiley, 1974), pp. 94–101.

[68]Krickus, *Pursuing the American Dream*, p. 92; Sylvia Pellini MacPhee, *Changing Perspectives of Italian Americans* (Cambridge, Mass.: Center for Community Economic Development, 1974), pp. 10–15.

[69]Iorizzo, "The Padrone and Immigrant Distribution," p. 43.

[70]Nelli, *The Italians in Chicago, 1880–1930*, pp. 56–60; Anonymous, "The Philanthropists' View of the Italian in America," in *The Italian in America: The Progressive View*, ed. Lydio F. Tomasi (New York: Center for Migration Studies, 1972), p. 79. This article is reprinted by Tomasi from an early journal of social and settlement workers termed *Charities*.

[71]Iorizzo and Mondello, *The Italian-Americans*, pp. 138–58; Nelli, *The Italians in Chicago, 1880–1930*, pp. 64–66.

[72]Stella, *Some Aspects of Italian Immigration*, p. 94.

[73]Nelli, *The Italians in Chicago, 1880–1930*, pp. 13–14; Antonio Stella, "Tuberculosis and the Italians in the United States," in Cordasco and Bucchioni, *The Italians*, p. 449 ff.

[74]Gambino, *Blood of My Blood*, p. 85; Leonard Covello, "The Influence of Southern Italian Family Mores upon the School Situation in America," in Cordasco and Bucchioni, *The Italians*, p. 513.

[75]Lord, Trenor, and Barrows, *The Italian in America*, pp. 16–19; E. P. Hutchinson, *Immigrants and Their Children, 1850–1950* (New York: John Wiley, 1956), pp. 137–38.

[76]Higham, *Strangers in the Land*, p. 48.

[77]Gambino, *Blood of My Blood*, p. 77.

[78]Stephan Thernstrom, *The Other Bostonians* (Cambridge, Mass.: Harvard University Press, 1973), p. 161.

[79]Elizabeth Gurley Flynn, "The Lawrence Textile Strike," in *America's Working Women*, ed. R. Baxandall, L. Gordon, and S. Reverby (New York: Random House Vintage Books, 1976), pp. 194–99.

[80]Nelli, *The Italians in Chicago, 1880–1930*, pp. 78–85; Gambino, *Blood of My Blood*, pp. 115–17.

[81]John J. d'Alesandre, "Occupational Trends of Italians in New York City," *Italy-America Monthly* 2 (February 1935): 11–21.

[82]W. Lloyd Warner and Leo Srole, *The Social Systems of American Ethnic Groups* (New Haven: Yale University Press, 1945), pp. 96–97; Gambino, *Blood of My Blood*, p. 101; Wittke, *We Who Built America*, p. 443.

[83]Nelli, *The Italians in Chicago, 1880–1930*, pp. 211–14. In *The Mafia Mystique*, p. 322.

[84]Francis A. J. Ianni, *A Family Business* (New York: Russell S؛ ۽e Foundation, 1972), p. 151.

[85]Ibid., p. 193.

[86]Smith, *The Mafia Mystique*, p. 323.

[87]Rolle, *The American Italians*, pp. 89–93.

[88]Thernstrom, *The Other Bostonians*, p. 171.

[89]Carol Agocs, "Ethnicity in Detroit," in *Ethnic Groups in the City* (Lexington, Mass.: D.C. Heath, 1971), p. 92.

[90]Leonard Broom, Cora A. Martin, and Betty Maynard, "Status Profiles of Racial and Ethnic Populations," *Social Science Quarterly* 52 (September 1971): 384–85.

[91]U.S. Bureau of the Census, *Characteristics of the Population by Ethnic Origin, March 1972 and 1971, Current Population Reports*, Series P–20, No. 249 (April 1973), pp. 23–26; Andrew M. Greeley, "Catholics and the Upper Middle Class: Comment on Roof," *Social Forces* 59 (March 1981): 824–30; Wade Clark Roof, "Unresolved Issues in the Study of Religion and the National Elite," *Social Forces* 59 (March 1981): 831–35.

[92]Gambino, *Blood of My Blood*, p. 89.

[93]The study is reported in *National Center for Urban Ethnic Affairs Newsletter*, 1 (no. 5); the quotation appears on p. 8.

[94]Iorizzo and Mondello, *The Italian-Americans*, p. 215; National Center for Urban Ethnic Affairs, "The Representation of Poles, Italians, Latins, and Blacks in the Executive Suites of Chicago's Largest Corporations," *Minority Report*, no date, pp. 2–5.

[95]Whyte, *Street Corner Society*, p. 273.

[96]Harold J. Abramson, "Ethnic Pluralism in the Central City," in *Ethnic Groups in the City*, ed. Otto Feinstein (Lexington, Mass.: D.C. Heath, 1971), pp. 19–25; *National Center for Urban Ethnic Affairs Newsletter* 1 (October 1975); James A. Crispion, *The Assimilation of Ethnic Groups: The Italian Case* (New York: Center for Migration Studies, 1980), pp. 43–44.

[97]Stephen R. Aiello, "Italian-Americans and Education," *Italian Americana* 5 (Spring/Summer, 1979): 227.

[98]Congress of Italian-American Organizations, *A Portrait of the Italian-American Community in New York City* (New York: 1975), pp. 7–10, 49–51.

[99]Lawrence A. Cremin, *The Transformation of the School* (New York: Knopf, 1961), pp. 67–68; Colin Greer, *The Great School Legend* (New York: Basic Books, 1972), pp. 3–6; Aiello, "Italian-Americans and Education," pp. 225–26.

[100]The 1960 data are cited in Lopreato, *Italian Americans*, p. 161. The 1972 data are from Bureau of Census, *Characteristics of the Population by Ethnic Origin, March 1972 and 1971: Current Population Reports*, Series P-20, No. 249 (April 1973), p. 23.

[101]Aiello, "Italian-Americans and Education," pp. 224–25.

[102]Frances Korbin and Calvin Goldschneider, *The Ethnic Factor in Family Structure and Mobility* (Cambridge, Mass.: Ballinger, 1978), pp. 17–18.

[103]Silvano M. Tomasi, "The Ethnic Church and the Integration of Italian Immigrants in the United States," in Tomasi and Engel, *The Italian Experience in the United States*, p. 168.

[104]Rudolph J. Vecoli, "*Contadini* in Chicago: A Critique of *The Uprooted*," in *The Aliens*, ed Leonard Dinnerstein and Frederic C. Jaher (New York: Appleton-Century-Crofts, 1970), p. 226; see Harold J. Abramson, *Ethnic Diversity in Catholic America* (New York: John Wiley, 1973), pp. 136–39.

[105]Tomasi, "The Ethnic Church and the Integration of Italian Immigrants in the United States," p. 167.

[106]Ibid., pp. 187–88; Nelli, *The Italians in Chicago, 1880–1930*, p. 195.

[107]Abramson, *Ethnic Diversity in Catholic America*, pp. 111–15.

[108]Nicholas J. Russo, "Three Generations of Italians in New York City: Their Religious Acculturation," in Tomasi and Engel, *The Italian Experience in the United States*, pp. 200–6.

[109]Lopreato, *Italian Americans*, p. 93; cf. Gambino, *Blood of My Blood*, p. 239.

[110]Leonard Covello, "The Influence of Southern Italian Family Mores Upon the School Situation in America," in Cordasco and Bucchioni, *The Italians*, p. 515.

[111]Paul J. Campisi, "Ethnic Family Patterns: The Italian Family in the United States," *American Journal of Sociology* 53 (May 1948): 443–49; Leonard Covello, "The Influence of Southern Italian Family Mores Upon the School Situation in America," pp. 525–30.

[112]Irvin L. Child, *Italian or American?* (New Haven: Yale University Press, 1943). A critical excerpt can be found in *The Italians*, pp. 321–36; Ware, *Greenwich Village, 1920–1930*, pp. 179–93.

[113]Anthony J. Tomanio and Lucille N. LaMacchia, *The Italian-American Community of Bridgeport*, mimeographed (Bridgeport, Conn.: University of Bridgeport, 1953); Lopreato, *The Italian Americans*, pp. 106–7.

[114]Firey, *Land Use in Central Boston*, pp. 211–24.

[115]Herbert Gans, *The Urban Villagers*, rev. ed. (New York: Free Press, 1982), pp. 412–13; Greeley, *Why Can't They Be Like Us?*, p. 77; see note 118 below.

[116]Phylis Cancilla Martinelli, "Beneath the Surface: Ethnic Communities in Phoenix, Arizona," (Unpublished paper, Arizona State University, March 1980).

[117]Francis X. Femminella and Jill S. Quadagno, "The Italian American Family," in *Ethnic Families in America*, ed. Charles H. Mindel and Robert W. Habenstein (New York: Elsevier, 1976), pp. 74–75; Ruby Jo Reeves Kennedy, "Single or Triple Melting Pot? Intermarriage in New Haven, 1870–1950," *American Journal of Sociology* 58 (July 1952): 56–59; Nelli, *The Italians in Chicago, 1880–1930*, p. 196; Abramson, *Ethnic Diversity in Catholic America*, p. 53.

[118]P. J. Gallo, *Ethnic Alienation* (Rutherford, N.J.: Farleigh Dickinson University Press, 1974), p. 194; John M. Goering, "The Emergence of Ethnic Interests: A Case of Serendipity," *Social Forces* 49 (March 1971): 381–82. A recent study by John P. Roche found some support for a slight decline in "ethnic closeness" among third-generation Italian Americans in two Providence, R. I. suburbs. However, even among third-generation, white-collar suburbanites more than 80 percent reported no decline in closeness with other Italian Americans. See John P. Roche, "Suburban Ethnicity," *Social Science Quarterly* 63 (March 1982): 149–51.

[119]Marcus Lee Hansen, "The Third Generation," in *Children of the Uprooted*, ed. Oscar Handlin (New York: Harper & Row, 1966), pp. 255–71; Krickus, *Pursuing the American Dream*, p. 362.

[120]Ianni, *A Family Business*, p. 4.

Jewish Americans
CHAPTER 6

Stereotyped as inferior, Jews have been the scapegoats for the hatreds of dominant peoples in countries around the globe for thousands of years. As oppressed wanderers, Jews have been forced to become sojourners in many countries. From the Egyptian and Roman persecutions in ancient times, to the massacres and expulsions in Spain in the late 1400s, to the brutal pogroms of the Russian tsar in the 1880s, to the German Nazi massacres, Jews might be regarded as the most consistently and widely persecuted ethnic group in world history. Residing in many lands, the constantly harassed ancestors of Jewish Americans forged distinctive traditions.

The definition of who is Italian or Irish is relatively easy, because country of origin, language, and self-identification generally coincide. This is not true for the Jewish Americans, whose major countries of origin and languages have run to a half dozen or more. Under the ancient law of the rabbis, a Jew is defined as a person whose mother is Jewish—a definition of ethnicity with an accent on ancestry. Many Jewish writers define Jews as those who identify themselves as Jews. Non-Jews have often regarded as Jews those who have Jewish ancestry, whose names or looks seem Jewish, or whose cultural practices are Jewish. In the last century Jews have been regarded by some non-Jews as a religious group, a racial group, and an ethnic group. They have been socially defined on the basis of real or alleged physical characteristics or cultural characteristics. In the early 1900s, in the 1930s and 1940s, and even to the present, they have been considered by some non-Jews to be a biologically inferior "race." Today Jews are generally considered by social scientists to be an ethnic group, a group distinguished by others and by themselves primarily on the basis of cultural characteristics, including for many some form of Jewish religion.[1]

MIGRATION: AN OVERVIEW

Jewish immigration to the United States can be divided into three major periods: (1) the Sephardic (Spanish and Portuguese) migration, (2) the central European (German) migration, and (3) the eastern European (Polish and Russian) migration. The Sephardic migration was triggered by late-fifteenth- and sixteenth-century oppression in Europe. A Spanish government decree forced thousands of Jews to emigrate or convert on penalty of death. A chief sponsor of Columbus at the Spanish court had been Luis de Santangel, a Jew who had converted to Christianity. Santangel and his associates, sometimes called Marranos, were doubtless hoping that these exploratory voyages would open up lines of escape for Jews. In the 1500s and 1600s a few thousand Sephardic migrants came to the European colonies in North America. Yet by 1820 there were only five thousand Jews in the United States.[2]

In the 1840s, coinciding with the Irish Catholic influx, the migration stream became larger. Push and pull factors were important. Between 1800 and the 1840s European persecution of Jews increased; letters espousing the economic prosperity of the United States attracted migrants. Many settled in the Midwest. They were peddlers, merchants, and craftsworkers, such as tailors and shoemakers. Synagogues and other distinctive Jewish institutions were adapted to the English language and core culture. By 1880 eight of every ten Jewish Americans were of German descent. The size of the Jewish population grew slowly from a still modest 15,000 in the early 1840s to more than 250,000 by 1880.[3]

The third period of migration was eastern European. By the 1880s and 1890s waves of immigrants from Russia, Poland, Rumania, and other eastern European countries had migrated west. The overwhelming majority among the turn-of-the-century Jewish immigrants came from Russia or Russian-controlled areas. Direct discrimination in education and the economic sphere, as well as government-sponsored beatings and killings of Jews, generated large-scale emigration from Poland and western Russia. In the 1880s a chief adviser to the Russian Tsar Alexander III recommended that the official "Jewish solution" should be to force one-third to leave the country, one-third to convert to Christianity, and one-third to starve or be killed.[4]

This Jewish immigration from 1881 to 1920 has been estimated at more than 2 million. Most migration occurred in the years between 1890 and 1914 and in the five years following World War I. These eastern European immigrants were different in that, unlike the German Jews, who were a small part of the German migration, they constituted a large proportion of those leaving East European countries. Also unlike the Germans, they were concentrated at a few points of destination, the large East Coast cities. As peddlers, street vendors, and unskilled workers they became part of the growing urban working class. The pull of economic prosperity at the point of destination seems to have been less important to their moving than the push factors at the European points of origin. Oppression had driven them abroad. These new immigrants brought with them a distinctive

Yiddish language and culture, an Orthodox Jewish religious orientation, and an emphasis on scholarship and literature. Most had resided in Yiddish-speaking communities in Europe.[5]

In the 1920s a sharp decrease in immigrants occurred. After the restrictive 1924 Immigration Act, an act aimed at limiting eastern and southern European immigration, the numbers began to decline rapidly. (The Act went into full effect in the late 1920s.) Between 1921 and 1936 fewer than 400,000 Jews entered the country. During the Great Depression there was a sharp reduction in the number of immigrants coming from all parts of the globe. President Franklin Roosevelt's administration did permit some increase in Jewish refugees from Germany, yet Roosevelt, and particularly his state department, did less than they could have to allow Europe's persecuted Jews to flee to the United States. Generally, immigration quotas remained as restrictive as ever, including those for eastern European Jews.

The numbers of Jewish refugees allowed in by the U.S. government were small compared to the numbers desiring to leave Nazi-ravaged Europe. But among the 150,000 refugees who did enter between 1935 and the early 1940s were many educated and talented people. One-fifth were professionals, and many of the rest had trade and commerce skills. They set up businesses from New York to San Francisco; contrary to the then prevailing stereotype, they were no burden on their new homeland. Among these refugees were some of the world's most talented scientists and artists, including scientists such as Albert Einstein, Leo Szilard, and Edward Teller—men who played a critical role in the U.S. nuclear research program—and scholars such as Eric Fromm, Erik Erikson, Herbert Marcuse, and Bruno Bettelheim. The number of Jews, however, was far lower than it might have been because of the persisting restrictive immigration policies.

Migration Since World War II

After the arrival of thousands of postwar refugees, Jewish migration again tapered off significantly. By the 1950s and 1960s only an estimated 8,000 or so were entering each year. However, by the 1970s a significant number of Israelis—estimated at 300,000 or more—had come to the United States. How many would return to Israel was still unclear; large numbers were officially "illegals." By the 1980s the American Jewish population was estimated at six million, approximately half the world's total Jewish population. After World War II many Jewish Americans participated in the internal migration from cities to suburbs in the United States. Even with some shift to the Sunbelt in the 1980s, a majority of Jews in the United States reside in the East in larger cities and their suburbs, with a large number still in the New York City area.[6]

By the early twentieth century the various American Jewish streams were coalescing into one ethnic group. The 1840s' German immigrants coalesced with earlier groups, substantially acculturating to the core culture within a generation or two. Then came the eastern Europeans. The new group of Russians and other eastern Europeans eventually coalesced and were called "Russians," a group predominantly Yiddish in culture. Rosenberg has argued that in each case the earlier immigrant groups had already become American Jews by the time of the next group, that is, they had given up much of their European nationality character by the time the new Jewish group came in. This made for easier absorption of later immigrants. The synagogue sometimes brought Germans and eastern Europeans together; fraternal and communal organizations played an important role in mutual adaptation. Increasing contacts, as well as the intensifying attacks on Jews at home and abroad, brought increasing ethnic coalescence.[7]

As Herberg notes, by the 1920s "American Jewry, despite all internal divisions, already constituted a well-defined ethnic group."[8] However, this coalescence of Jewish groups did not eradicate entirely the distinctiveness of German and East European Jews. Some distinctiveness persisted in region of residence and religious affiliation into the 1970s and 1980s. In these decades Jewish Americans became ever more distributed across the nation, with sizeable communities in western cities such as Los Angeles and San Francisco and in southern cities such as Miami. Once attached only to the East Coast, they today make up a national community.

STEREOTYPING AND PREJUDICE

No white group in history has suffered under a broader range of stereotypes for a longer period of time than have the Jews. For centuries, Jews have been the targets for intensely held prejudices. This complex of hostile attitudes has its own name—*anti-Semitism*. Anti-Semitism has rocketed tragic political movements into prominent positions in history. Anti-Semitism has been used to refer both to attitudes and to discriminatory behavior.

Religious anti-Semitism has an ancient heritage. For almost two thousand years Jews have been cursed and killed because they were seen as "Christ-killers" deserving the cruelest treatment. From the earliest Christian period to the present, the writings and liturgies of Christendom have been rife with anti-Semitism. Incredibly, Jews as a group have been held by many Christians as culpable for the death of their Christ and as deserving of torture and death for their religious uniqueness. (Ironically, Jesus himself was a Jew, not a Christian.)

Some scholars have argued that the anti-Semitism of Hitler's Germany was grounded in the religious anti-Semitism in German Protestantism. Christian religious groups in the North American colonies, beginning in the earliest period, brought the "Christ-killers" view with them. Ministers and priests passed along these views to each new generation. Even as late as the 1970s, studies of teaching materials used in a variety of Protestant and Catholic groups showed the significant extent to which this religious stereotyping persisted, including stories of "wicked Jews" who killed Christ. Efforts to get rid of the most hostile stereotyping in religious writings and liturgy were attempted in some Protestant and Catholic groups by the mid-1960s. Nonetheless, one survey of California church members in the 1960s found that "the Jews" received greater blame than the Romans for crucifying Jesus. About 40 percent of the Catholics and Protestants interviewed agreed with, or were uncertain about, the statement that "the reason Jews have so much trouble is because God is punishing them for rejecting Jesus."[9]

Anti-Semitism has accented a number of other themes. One old cliché is the notion that the Jews are major examples of economic deviousness and cunning. Jews are stereotyped in different terms than blacks and Native Americans, who are frequently stereotyped as unintelligent. Jews have been seen as *too* hard-working, *too* intelligent, *too* crafty. McWilliams has suggested that this stereotype developed to rationalize a situation where Jews have been relatively successful as "middlemen" merchants and brokers. Because of rampant discrimination, Jews sought out the crevices—the marginal businesses—where they were allowed to operate. Success was downgraded as having been gained by cheating. By the 1850s, "to Jew" had become a phrase meaning "to cheat." The painful burden of this stereotyping lingers.[10]

After the Civil War the stereotype developed of Jews as social climbers. Parodies in the media of the day, including vaudeville, sometimes put clumsy Jewish figures speaking inflected English in high-society positions. By the 1880s newspaper and magazine cartoons, as well as business cards, had caricatures of Jews as long-nosed, garishly dressed merchants speaking in broken English.

Though some early leaders, such as John Adams, wrote tributes to the achievements of the Jews, such positive comments did not predominate in the next few generations. Even Adams's distinguished grandson, the intellectual Henry Adams, upset with the rapidly industrializing United States, was openly anti-Semitic. For him the Jew was a symbol of the money-grubbing world he so disliked. In particular, he saw some financial operations as part of a Jewish conspiracy. These themes would persist through a long line of non-Jewish intellectuals and other leaders to the present day. Even as late as the mid-1970s the head of the Joint Chiefs of Staff made some anti-Semitic remarks picked up by the media, including, "They own, you know, the banks in the country, the newspapers; you just look where the Jewish money is in the country."[11]

The Politics of Stereotyping

Political stereotypes were bedfellows with these economic prejudices. By the late nineteenth century Jewish Americans were seen as radicals with a genius for organizing. In the decades to follow Jewish people would be stereotyped as radical or "Communist" sympathizers. In the 1900–1920 period political cartoons with these themes appeared often in the mass media. A common theme was that Jews were taking over the government. By 1941 hatred of the Jews rose to a fevered pitch, with Jews being falsely accused of bringing the United States into the war with Germany—accusations coming from members of Congress, the press, and prominent citizens. After that war a *Fortune* magazine poll found that three-quarters of those who felt some groups had more power than was good for the country's economy cited the *Jews*; the corresponding figure for a question on the country's political sphere was about half. Subtle stereotypes of Jews cropped up in attacks by prominent politicians on the "Eastern liberal" press as late as the 1970s and 1980s.[12]

Just before and after 1900, such writers as Madison Grant and such journalists as Kenneth Roberts were mythmakers who helped foster a climate of anti-Semitism. Analysts such as these developed a vigorous rationale for protecting the "Nordic race" from biologically "inferior" nationalities. Jews from eastern Europe were a target for such analysts. In the early 1920s Brigham's book on IQ testing and immigrant soldiers accented not only the low scores of Italians but also the lower-than-average scores of the Russians, most of whom were probably Jews. Brigham argued that the test data disproved arguments for the high intelligence of Jews and supported the superiority of British Americans.[13]

Modern Anti-Semitism

Opinion surveys have confirmed the persisting support for anti-Semitism among U.S. citizens. During World War II the famous book *The Authoritarian Personality* reported questioning of samples of Californians which showed substantial support for stereotypes: the Jew as clannish, the Jew as parasitic, the Jew as revolutionary. Two decades later an opinion survey, analyzed by Selznick and Steinberg, found that from 10 to 54 percent of a representative cross-section of 2,000 non-Jewish Americans still accepted traditional views of the Jews:

	Percent saying "true"
Jews have too much power in the U.S.	11
International banking is pretty much controlled by Jews	30
Jews are more willing than others to use shady practices to get what they want	42
Jews stick together too much	52

Even in the late twentieth century this survey found as large a proportion as 50 percent of non-Jewish Americans opting for age-old stereotypes. The survey found that support for anti-Jewish *discrimination* was not expressed by most respondents, a fact which lead the researchers to conclude that while present-day anti-Semitism in the United States is not the most dangerous form, the acceptance of stereotypes provides a potential which could be manipulated in the future by unscrupulous leaders. Political anti-Semitism is not a dusty relic of some ancient past.[14]

In the 1980s there has been some resurgence of anti-Semitism, as seen in the rise of the Ku Klux Klan and in the 400 anti-Semitic episodes (such as defacing synagogues) occurring in 1980 alone. In 1980 the president of a major Baptist organization publicly stated that God does not hear the prayers of Jews; and a leader of the Moral Majority, a right-wing group, repeated the age-old stereotype that Jews had a "supernatural" ability to make a lot of money. Anti-Semitism still plagues America.

VIOLENT OPPRESSION AND CONFLICT

Many eastern European immigrants were fleeing oppression in the form of pogroms directed at Jewish communities. A *pogrom*, from Yiddish-Russian words for "destruction," is an organized massacre conducted with the aid of government officials. This and similar experiences led to what has been termed an "oppression mentality" for Jewish Americans, the acute awareness that anti-Jewish oppression "can happen again" even in the United States.

In the 1880s Jewish merchants in the South suffered violent attacks from poor non-Jewish farmers who blamed them for economic crises. In the 1890s the farms and homes of Jewish landlords and merchants were burned in Mississippi. In the early 1900s there were riots against workers brought into factories in New Jersey. Just before World War I in Georgia, Leo Frank, the Jewish part-owner of a pencil factory, was convicted of killing a girl employee, though much evidence pointed elsewhere. Beaten up in prison, he was taken from the prison hospital and lynched by an angry crowd.[15]

Southern demagogues such as Tom Watson used the Frank case to fuel the flames of anti-Semitism for political purposes. About this time the Ku Klux Klan was revived and waged violence against blacks, Jews, and Catholics. In the 1920s and 1930s crosses were burned on Jewish property; synagogues were desecrated and vandalized. On occasion, immigrants fought back. In the 1920s immigrant crowds, including Jews and Catholics, stoned or otherwise attacked parades and gatherings of Ku Klux Klan members in Ohio and New Jersey.[16]

Oppression in this period also took the form of the federal government restricting the entry of Jewish refugees fleeing violence in Europe. The 1924 Immigration Act sharply reduced the numbers of immigrants from eastern Europe.

Organized and Other Anti-Semitism: Violence and Vandalism

Between 1932 and 1941 the number of openly anti-Semitic regional and nationwide organizations grew from only one to well over a hundred. Two dozen organizations were large-scale operations holding numerous anti-Semitic rallies, some drawing thousands. Millions of vicious anti-Semitic leaflets, pamphlets, and newspapers were distributed across the United States. Among the more prominent groups were the German-American Bund and the Silver Shirts. Father Charles Coughlin's organizations, the National Union for Social Justice and the Christian Front, became active in anti-Jewish agitation in the 1930s.[17]

Force-oriented groups grew up under the auspices of these organizations. Early in 1940 the FBI arrested more than a dozen members of a Christian Front group which reportedly intended to kill "Jews and Communists, 'to knock off about a dozen Congressmen,' and to seize post offices, the Customs House, and armories in New York. In the homes of the group were found 18 cans of cordite, 18 rifles, and 5,000 rounds of ammunition."[18] Coughlin himself did not openly advocate violence, but he defended those who did, and he alluded to the use of force "as a last resort." From the 1930s to the present, fascist organizations have attacked Jewish Americans and their property.

One important factor feeding anti-Jewish attacks was the increase in anti-Semitism in Nazi Germany. Germans had long portrayed their Jewish neighbors in terms of negative stereotypes. This horror story began with economic and political restrictions on Jews in the Nazi sphere, soon to be followed by deportation to forced-labor camps, and culminating in the extermination of millions by means of starvation, epidemics, and mass killings.[19] These days of infamy would be etched in the minds of Jews and non-Jews alike. No one knows for certain how many were killed; estimates suggest six million died in many countries. Extermination and forced migration reduced the Jewish population in countries like Poland and Germany to 10 percent of the former numbers. The magnitude of Nazi savagery has had a profound and long-lasting effect on Jewish Americans.

The term adopted by American Jews to describe these horrors is *Holocaust.* The oppression mentality was reinvigorated not only by newspaper reports and stories of European refugees but also by the growing knowledge that the *United States government* was actually *aiding* these actions in Germany, at first by continuing normal economic and diplomatic relations and later by turning its back on thousands of desperate refugees. When it became evident in the 1930s that violence was being used against the Jews in Germany and its occupied territories, neither Congress, nor President Franklin Roosevelt, nor the State Department intervened to permit the large-scale refugee immigration necessary. The Department of State put critical blockades in the way, citing the quotas and restrictions of earlier immigration legislation and economic competition problems. A cruel example of this type of oppression can be seen in the fate of the Wagner-Rogers bill, which proposed allowing 20,000 Jewish children to come into the United States outside the national origin quota system. The bill was sabotaged in Congress, and the children were left to the ravages of the Nazis. Numerous civic organizations pressured Congress to oppose the admission of Jewish refugees, because they saw them in stereotyped terms as unfit citizens. The result was moral involvement by the United States in the Holocaust.[20]

Violent attacks on Jewish Americans, on their property, and on their synagogues were common after World War II. More than forty such incidents were reported in 1945–1946 in the United States. Between the mid-1950s and the 1980s there were numerous attacks across the United States, including the painting of Nazi swastikas on synagogues and violent attacks on the homes and stores of Jewish Americans. Some Jews were harassed or beaten. There were bomb threats. Well over eight hundred such incidents of violence or vandalism have been recorded for each year in the 1979–1982 period.[21]

Jews Fight Back

Since the 1960s there has been conflict between Jewish Americans and blacks. Jewish liberalism in central cities declined somewhat as black rioters attacked Jewish businesses in black ghetto areas, businesses which they saw as exploitative, and as black street criminals came to be seen as responsible for destroying the peace of Jewish neighborhoods. Fear of street crime led to the formation of militant self-protective associations in the late 1960s.

In 1968 Rabbi Meyer Kahane in New York City organized the Jewish Defense League (JDL) to deal with threats against Jewish communities in the cities. The JDL's goals included an attempt not only to reinvigorate the sense of Jewish pride but also to physically defend citizens wherever threatened. The JDL organized armed citizen patrols of city streets in New York specifically to protect Jewish communities from street crime. Chapters were established in a half-dozen cities from Boston to Los Angeles. In the 1970s disruptions of Soviet diplomatic activities were undertaken by JDL members to protest the treatment of Jews in the Soviet Union. Gerald Strober argues that the movement touched a "middle-class nerve" and that for many the traditional organizations appeared too unwilling to vigorously defend Jewish interests. Though most Jews disapproved of the JDL's tactics, many were supportive of many of its aims.[22]

POLITICS

The colonies limited voting and holding office to Christians (except for South Carolina in 1702–1721). Five of the new states had removed these restrictions by 1790; six others carried Christians-only provisions for political participation as late as 1869 (North Carolina) and 1876 (New Hampshire).[23]

The substantial Jewish contributions to the revolutionary cause did not bring them political freedom. While no anti-Semitism is reflected in the founding documents, some Federalist officials engaged in anti-Jewish practices. Federalist support for the Alien and Sedition Laws guaranteed that Jews would support the more liberal Jeffersonian party, later to become the Democratic party. Though Jews supported Democrats for decades, their votes eventually gravitated to the new pro-Union, antislavery Republican party. President Abraham Lincoln fostered Jewish allegiance to the Republican party by blocking General Grant's order to expel Jewish traders in the Tennessee area during the Civil War.[24]

It was not until after the Civil War that Jewish Americans became significant in the sphere of office-holding. In New York City Jewish Americans became active in Republican organizations; one became that state's Republican candidate for lieutenant governor in 1870.[25]

As Jews became more concentrated in northern cities, voting power increased. While some Socialist candidates sometimes received strong support, most eastern European Jews remained Republicans or began to gravitate to the Irish-dominated Democratic machines, which provided jobs and shelter. Soon Jewish workers in Tammany Hall in New York were given patronage positions; many became active as party district captains and poll watchers, and a few in New York and elsewhere eventually became leaders.[26]

Eastern European Jews became famous for exercising the franchise and undertaking volunteer political activity. While the Irish used politics to advance their interests—to create jobs and patronage—Jews, though concerned with bread-and-butter matters, were more issue-oriented, particularly in their commitment to civil rights causes. Jews played a role in progressive movements in the first decades of the twentieth century, pressing for industrial reform, minority rights, and urban reform.[27]

Jews and the Democratic Party

Yet in spite of their conscientious activity, by the 1910s few Jews were able to win electoral office; and few were appointed to high-level positions. An occasional city councilperson, one or two members of the state legislature, one judge—this was the extent of their clout. At the national level, since many Jews voted for Republicans, the impact was modest as well. When an internationalist Democratic candidate, Woodrow Wilson, came along, a majority of Jewish votes flowed to the Democrats for the first time in decades. Wilson appointed a few Jews to important positions, including Bernard Baruch to the War Industries Board and Louis Brandeis to the Supreme Court.[28]

After Wilson, Jewish voters generally supported Republican presidential candidates until the late 1920s, although they were shifting to Democratic candidates at local, state, and congressional levels. In 1920 there were eleven Jewish members of Congress, ten of them Republicans; but by 1922 a majority of the Jewish members of Congress were Democratic. Al Smith, New York's governor of poor Irish background, attracted a lot of Jews to the Democratic party and received substantial Jewish support in his 1928 bid for the presidency.[29]

Although Jews have become increasingly more suburban and middle-income since the 1920s, their vote has not shifted heavily to the Republican party. Franklin Roosevelt brought Jews firmly into the Democratic fold in 1932. Roosevelt's anti-Nazi rhetoric and liberalism on domestic matters and his support of social security and union organization won over many Jewish liberals and Socialists. Until Roosevelt, few Jews had served in the executive or judicial branches of the federal government. Jewish Americans Benjamin Cohen, Felix Frankfurter, and Louis Brandeis served as close advisers to Roosevelt. Anti-Semitic organizations attacked Roosevelt for these associations and appointments.

Yet Roosevelt's strong regard among Jewish Americans did not lead him to take the dynamic action in regard to refugees from Nazi-dominated Europe. One reason for Roosevelt's failure to take stronger action may have been fear of the intense political anti-Semitism prevailing in the United States during the 1930s and 1940s. Anti-Jewish discrimination was common in politics, social affairs, education, employment, jury selection in certain states, and residential restrictions.[30]

In the decades after World War II, anti-Jewish organizations declined. Yet even in recent decades at least one nationwide survey has revealed that 5 percent of Americans would like to vote for an anti-Semitic candidate for Congress and 33 percent said *it would not matter* to them if a candidate were anti-Semitic. Though such attitudes do not currently surface in political discrimination, the possibility exists that they will, given crisis conditions. It may well be that an awareness of these attitudes, coupled with a fear that oppression such as that in Nazi Germany can happen again, has kept Jewish Americans so strongly committed to liberal, civil-rights-oriented causes and politicians, a commitment documented in numerous opinion surveys since the 1940s. Recent concern among Jewish Americans for "law and order" has not kept them from remaining the most liberal of the white ethnic groups.[31]

In the post-World War II period Jewish Americans have played an important political role at local, state, and national levels. Since they are concentrated in certain large cities and states, such as New York and New Jersey, their voting strength has been magnified. They continue to vote in large numbers. At all levels, Jewish Americans continue to have the highest voter turnouts of all major race and ethnic groups.

The proportion of that vote going to Democratic candidates at all levels has remained substantial. Though in 1948 this vote fell off from Roosevelt's 90 percent landslides, three-quarters of Jewish voters still supported Harry Truman. Three-quarters voted for Stevenson during the Eisenhower landslides, and more than three-quarters supported John Kennedy in 1960. Considerably more than three-quarters voted both for Lyndon Johnson in 1964 and for Hubert Humphrey in 1968. George McGovern got 65 percent of the Jewish vote in 1972—an achievement, considering that Richard Nixon attempted to capitalize on Jewish American alienation from the old coalitions in the wake of the 1960s' "backlash" against radical militancy.

In 1976 the Democratic candidate, Jimmy Carter, received 70 percent of the Jewish vote, up from the 1972 Democratic percentage. However, in 1980 one poll found that in his second bid for the presidency Carter received only 45 percent of the Jewish vote, with the rest split between the Republican and the independent candidates. This was the lowest percentage given to a Democratic candidate since Franklin Roosevelt and apparently reflected Jewish concern over President Jimmy Carter's attempts to build new bridges to the Arab world. Jewish Americans feared that Israel's security might be jeopardized by Carter's peace initiatives in the Middle East. As a result, many writers started writing about a "swing to the right" among U.S. Jews. Yet at the same time opinion polls still showed very strong support among Jewish Americans for civil rights progress and for liberal causes such as women's rights movements. Jewish Americans still were generally progressive in their political views.[32]

Historically, Jewish Americans have been underrepresented among elected and appointed officials. Just over a hundred Jews have been Senators, members of Congress, and governors. The current scene shows an improvement. By 1981 there were 33 Jewish Americans in Congress, most of whom were Democrats. So far, however, only a half dozen Jewish Americans have served on the United States Supreme Court, although perhaps a fifth of the nation's lawyers in recent decades have been Jewish. By 1976 only nine Jews had served in presidential cabinets, including Oscar Straus under Theodore Roosevelt, Henry Morgenthau under Franklin Roosevelt, Lewis Strauss under Eisenhower, Abraham Ribicoff under Kennedy, Arthur Goldberg and Wilbur Cohen under Johnson, and Henry Kissinger under Nixon and Ford. A half dozen more served under the Ford, Carter and Reagan administrations. In addition, Jewish Americans have served in significant (although still less than representative) numbers in local and state executive and legislative offices. It was not until 1974 that Abraham Beame became the first Jewish mayor of New York City. He was succeeded by another Jew, Edward Koch. Also in the 1970s, Diane Feinstein became the first Jewish woman chosen mayor of a major city, in this case San Francisco.[33]

While statistics on members of Congress and governors are impressive when compared to the limited political clout of nonwhite groups, they still reflect discrimination. Currently, the proportion of Jews in elected office is less than one might expect, given their high proportion (perhaps 15 to 20 percent) among political activists. Isaacs has underscored the fact that although there are more Jews than Presbyterians or Episcopalians in the United States, Jewish Americans have not held a fifth the congressional offices held by those white Protestant groups in recent years. Discrimination plays a role in limiting the number of Jewish Americans who would otherwise occupy the political front lines. Because of discrimination and the oppression mentality, many Jewish Americans have preferred to work behind the scenes rather than seek elected offices. They have been very active as political advisers, consultants, fundraisers, and speechwriters.[34]

Union and Civil Rights Protest

Jewish Americans have participated in protest activities other than those associated with traditional electoral politics. Large-scale protest against oppressive economic and political conditions was first mounted by eastern European Jews. By the 1890s they were organizing to fight sweatshop working conditions—long hours, child labor, low pay, and unsafe working conditions. Tens of thousands of workers struck the garment industry; the 1910 strike, called the "Great Revolt," lasted two brutal months, with heavy costs to the "bosses" and destitution for workers. The New York strikers inspired union militants elsewhere.[35]

Jews were very active in the labor movement over the next several decades. Figures on unions in the 1930s for New York City show large numbers of Jewish workers in food, entertainment, clothing, and jewelry unions. Jewish union leaders went beyond the problems of wages and working conditions to grapple with broader issues. Jewish unions pioneered health, pension, and educational programs which would in the coming years be imitated by all major unions.[36] Many working-class Jews played an important role in the growth of the Socialist party between 1905 and 1912, and of other labor-liberal parties later on. A Jewish Socialist in New York was elected to Congress in 1914 and 1916, and a few other Jewish Socialists also won local elections.[37]

By the 1930s there were several civic and civil rights organizations among Jewish Americans which would persist in importance: the Anti-Defamation League of B'nai B'rith, the American Jewish Congress, the American Jewish Committee (AJC), and the United Jewish Appeal. Since 1906 the AJC has fought vigorously to combat anti-Semitic prejudice and discrimination in the United States. Toward this end it has generated numerous publications, including the journal *Commentary*. By the 1970s the AJC had a large budget and forty thousand members. The American Jewish Congress, established in the 1910s by eastern European Jews, has fought for civil rights of Jewish Americans, but it has been more pro-Israel in its orientation than the American Jewish Committee. By 1980 it had a large budget and thousands of members. The Anti-Defamation League, a branch of the fraternal and service organization B'nai B'rith, was set up in 1913. It has carried out perhaps the most vigorous campaign, attempting to root out anti-Semitism in the United States. The United Jewish Appeal, established in 1939, has been an extraordinarily successful fundraising organization aiding Jewish causes, including war refugees and the state of Israel. All four organizations have played a critical role in protecting the civil rights of Jewish Americans.[38]

Israel was established, and has continued to survive, with substantial financial and political support from Jewish Americans. During the Eisenhower administration Jewish American pressure to support Israel often went unheeded, but by the 1960s sharply increased American political support for Israel required less Israeli lobbying and indigenous pressure. In the 1970s and 1980s Jewish political pressure has been mobilized for other causes, such as laws supporting Soviet Jews and the punishment of liberal political candidates who took a tolerant position toward those Arab nations hostile to Israel. In the 1970s and 1980s American policy seemed to be becoming more flexible and sympathetic to the Arab position. As a result, many Jewish leaders began to worry about the apparently declining support of such Jewish causes—and, by inference, of Jewish Americans—in the United States.[39]

The important Jewish civil rights groups have not focused exclusively on anti-Semitism. Several have sought to eliminate all racial and ethnic prejudice and discrimination and to keep church and state separate. From the beginning of the black civil rights movement to the 1980s, Jewish commitment has been strong and enduring. Numerous Jewish congregations, together with their rabbis, were active in the black civil rights protests of the 1950s and 1960s. They provided substantial money for the movement and swelled the ranks of demonstrators in large numbers in cities across the South. Young Jewish Americans were active in youth and antiwar movements. Jewish students have also been active in New Left movements, although the extent of their participation has been exaggerated in the mass media.[40]

By the late 1960s, however, militant black criticism of Israel and Zionism had alienated a significant number of Jewish Americans from active participation in the black cause. A few militant black leaders were broadcasting anti-Semitic statements as part of their rhetoric aimed at the white merchants and landlords they saw as exploiting their ghettoized brothers and sisters. In addition, Jewish leaders and rank-and-file participants were being crowded out of some civil rights organizations by black militants. Jewish commitment to black civil rights also came in conflict with black inner city programs for police reform, school reforms, and desegregating schools. For example, in a 1966 New York City referendum, Jews voted in the majority against establishing a police review board desired by non-whites; in 1968 a new community-controlled school board in a black area of Brooklyn fired a number of teachers, including more than a dozen Jewish ones. A teachers' strike ensued, pitting protesting Jews against blacks.

Affirmative Action programs since the late 1960s, seeking to improve job chances for minorities and women, have come under attack by Jewish leaders. One organization led by Jewish and other white ethnic intellectuals, the Committee on Academic Nondiscrimination and Integrity, vigorously lobbied in the mass media and the halls of Congress for abolition of Affirmative Action programs. Objections to Affirmative Action have taken two tacks. One objection seems to be that these programs' "goals" become quotas benefiting certain groups and violating the principle of "merit." Memories of quota restrictions in higher education against Jews in the 1930s and 1940s are a major reason for this commitment to abolition of affirmative action programs. A second reason stems from the fact that Jewish Americans have made a disproportionately heavy commitment to higher education, so that in a situation where there are a limited number of job openings requiring college or graduate degrees, preferences for non-Jewish minorities will disproportionately affect Jewish Americans. Since this commitment to securing college and professional degrees partially reflects the earlier reactions of Jews to anti-Semitic discrimination in the business world, affirmative action programs preferring non-Jewish minorities and cutting down the chances for Jews to be hired "perpetuate in a subtle way the effects of past discrimination."[41] For many Jews affirmative action programs for nonwhites are very troubling. Indeed, some Jewish organizations have supported court suits against affirmative action programs, such as that of Alan Bakke, who sued a University of California law school.

Even so, the conflicts between blacks and Jewish Americans have not been severe enough to change one striking aspect of their relationship. Opinion surveys continue to show that, among *all* whites, Jewish Americans are *the most sympathetic* to the civil rights struggle of black Americans and to the economic problems of black Americans. Jews remain supportive of racial progress in the United States.

THE ECONOMY

Three centuries ago a few Jewish merchants contributed to the increase in Dutch prosperity in America when two dozen Sephardic Jews came to New Amsterdam in the 1650s. A Polish Jew, Haym Salomon, came to the colonies before the American Revolution and played a critical role in financing the Revolution with a large loan to the struggling revolutionary government; Salomon worked hard to secure European aid for the revolutionary cause. Organized Jewish communities were important in major cities at the time of the Revolution.[42]

The opening up of commerce in the Americas presented a golden opportunity for European Jews, because exclusion from land ownership and skilled-worker guilds had forced them into commercial pursuits in Europe where they excelled. Their trading networks made it relatively easy for them to establish a modest but important role in the emergence of the European system of commercial capitalism. For centuries in Europe a critical "middleman" or "trading" minority was the Jewish group. Because of intentional discrimination they were limited to taking on the risky or marginal tasks that developing economies require. Because they have been so successful in this "middleman" position, Jews have been an accessible scapegoat for the non-Jewish poor, who see them as exploiters, and for the non-Jewish rich, who view them as a political threat. The marginal nature of their enterprises, as well as outside hostility, fostered the growth of an *ethnic economy*, where Jews would turn to other Jews for economic aid, whenever possible, in order to maintain their enterprises and communities.[43]

Establishing an Economic Niche: A 'Middleman Minority'?

The rate of penetration of a new immigrant group into the core society depends on its own economic background as well as the economic conditions at the point of destination. German Jews entered the American economy just as frontier development and industrial growth were beginning to explode. The urban and commercial backgrounds of this new wave of immigrants were useful in establishing a niche. Itinerant peddlers roamed city streets and the countryside in the South and West engaging in trade and commerce.[44] Such services were much needed in an expanding agricultural society.

By 1889 Census figures showed 58 percent of employed Jews in trading or financial occupations, with 20 percent as office workers and 6 percent as professionals. The rest were blue-collar workers or farmers. Jewish entrepreneurs were concentrated in clothing, jewelry, alcohol, meat, and leather businesses. By the 1890s a majority of German Jews seemed to be moving up.[45] Though they had prospered by the second generation, they had come in when British American entrepreneurs firmly controlled the central enterprises in the industrial economy. Never a large group, German Jews came, as Lestschinsky notes, "without capital, with the natural consequence that they have remained to this day outside the top positions of the economic life of the country."[46]

The influx of Jewish migrants from eastern Europe hit the expanding industrial system at a particularly appropriate time. They entered with considerable experience in coping with discrimination and oppression and with a cultural heritage replete with strategies for finding those economic niches in which they could survive. It was in the industrial cities that these poor Jewish immigrants settled. Many who had been small merchants in eastern Europe continued as such in the United States. Polish, Rumanian, and Russian groups, Jewish and non-Jewish, in U.S. cities relied on Jewish merchants and professionals. These Jewish immigrants were a "middleman minority." A few eventually worked their way up to the head of clothing firms; by 1905 a proportion of the clothing industry in New York City was under eastern European Jewish management. A number went into the professions; by 1905 eastern European Jews had a toe-hold in law, medicine, and dentistry in New York. Some chose teaching positions in elementary and secondary schools, taking the role of acculturation agents for southern and eastern European children.[47]

Most went into working-class occupations, such as carpentry and manual labor. Tabulations for 1900 indicate that the occupational distributions of Russians (mostly Jews) in larger cities showed 60 percent in manufacturing, which usually meant blue-collar labor in factories. Another 8 percent were servants, while the rest were in clerical or public service jobs. Scholars have estimated that one-third of eastern European Jews were workers in clothing industries and another one-quarter were manual workers in industries such as jewelry and liquor.

Though many eventually moved out of manual occupations, new immigrants kept filling their places—until the discriminatory quota restrictions finally ended Jewish migration in the 1920s. These new residents were generally at the bottom rungs of the mobility ladder. Men, women, and children—whole families—were engaged in manufacturing work bringing in wages of $10 to $12 a week for men in 1900. Hours were long; poor conditions resulted in employment settings becoming known as "sweatshops," as indeed they were. Reform and union movements were generated in part by the agitation of these workers against such conditions. These immigrants were the targets of virulent prejudice and discrimination by employers and co-workers in the first decades of the twentieth century.[48]

Many eastern European wage earners set their sights on a business career. Some would move up on the economic ladder from junk peddler to scrap metal yard owner, or from needle worker to clothing entrepreneur. But those in the second generation were encouraged by their parents to go into clerical and sales work.[49] By the 1930s Jewish mobility had become conspicuous. More and more were in business for themselves, or in clerical or professional positions.

From the Depression to the 1950s

About one-quarter of Jews in Detroit and in Pittsburgh in the mid-1930s were in the owner or manager category, compared to 9 percent of the total population in 1930. A study in Newburyport, Massachusetts, found that Jews were moving into the middle-income levels there; the proportion was estimated at just under half. Moreover, as in the case of Japanese Americans (see Chapter 11), the solidarity of the Jewish community and the heavy involvement in small and medium-sized businesses brought aid to the unemployed in the Great Depression. Whenever possible, Jewish businesses dealt with one another. Unemployed relatives were hired to do a variety of jobs, even if they were low-paying. Here the ethnic economy provided a basis for survival. Operating within a community based on solidarity, they sometimes developed monopolies or took advantage of legal loopholes to survive. A few even became employed in organized crime in the 1920s and 1930s.[50]

The ethnic economy provided a fallback position for those who faced anti-Jewish discrimination in the 1930s. One of the goals of anti-Semitic organizations was to reduce the number of Jews in private and public employment. Discrimination became rampant as Jewish Americans moved into white-collar jobs. Non-Jewish whites in the teaching, banking, medical, legal, and engineering professions sought to prohibit Jews from employment in their sectors. In many areas, securing skilled blue-collar jobs and clerical jobs became difficult. The Depression accentuated the problem; anti-Jewish prohibitions or token quotas became commonplace. "No Jews need apply" signs were omnipresent, particularly in larger businesses and professional institutions.

Placement agencies throughout the Midwest, to take just one example, reported that from two-thirds to 95 percent of job listings specifically *excluded* Jews from consideration. A study of the teaching profession found discrimination directed against Jews, particularly in smaller cities and at colleges. Discrimination from 1900 to the 1950s was also rife in the housing sphere. Numerous real estate developments excluded Jews. Real estate agents discriminated against Jews from Philadelphia to Boston to Chicago, while neighbors made life miserable for those who managed to pioneer in desegregating an area. Later on, even those who managed to move into the suburbs in significant numbers found Protestant-oriented organizations and recreational facilities off-limits to them.[51]

One of the fears of anti-Semites has been alleged Jewish dominance of banking. Yet a famous *Fortune* magazine survey reported in February 1936 found that very few Jews were in banking and finance; nor were they to be found in significant numbers in heavy industries such as steel or automobiles or in the public utilities. (A later survey similarly found that only 600 of the 93,000 banking officials in the United States were Jewish.) Their representation was even small in the press and in radio. The *Fortune* survey found that the only sectors Jews dominated were clothing, textiles, and the movies. Even in law and medicine the *Fortune* report found that Jews had little representation in powerful positions. The author of the 1936 *Fortune* article seemed puzzled at the clustering in certain industrial and business areas and explained the situation in terms of Jewish clannishness.

Such patterns were by no means mysterious; they reflected the extent to which Jews had to work outside mainstream industries and businesses because of institutionalized discrimination. As McWilliams has noted in *A Mask for Privilege*, discrimination forced Jews to become "the ragpickers of American industry." Jews were channeled into economic spheres marginal to the mainstream economy, areas filled with greater risk.[52]

In the years after World War II extensive employment discrimination continued to be directed at Jews. Job advertising included restrictions, and many employment agencies required applicants to list their religion or ethnicity, listings used to discriminate among applicants. In spite of this, many Jews were able to share in postwar prosperity, particularly in new and thus more risky industries such as television and plastics, and finally succeeded in overcoming discrimination in areas such as engineering. Lestschinsky notes that the postwar economic pyramid for Jewish Americans has a small working-class base and no significant wealthy elite at the top. Jews remained primarily concentrated in trade, clothing, and jewelry manufacturing; commerce; merchandising; certain light industries; mass communications; and certain professions.[53]

One survey tabulation in the 1950s on occupations of household heads by religious group showed that Jewish household heads were concentrated in three white-collar categories, exceeding the total U.S. percentages there, but were sharply underrepresented in blue-collar and agricultural occupations.[54]

Research on major corporation and business executives, presidents, and board chairmen found that in 1900 just under 2 percent were Jews, while in 1925 and 1950 the figures were still between 2 and 3 percent. Given the preponderance of Jews in commercial and business employment, these proportions are much lower than they would be if there had been no anti-Jewish discrimination. The same study discovered that Jews were still concentrated in certain types of manufacturing and mass communications businesses. Very few were in transportation or heavy industry. A very large proportion of the Jewish executives—just under half—made it to the top in the ethnic economy, in *Jewish* businesses.[55]

Jews in Today's Economy

Data on incomes in the 1950s showed a very sizable proportion (30 percent) of Jewish household heads with incomes above $7,500, compared with 13 percent of the total population. This generally advantaged economic position continued into the 1960s, 1970s, and 1980s. Family incomes remained above average. Income levels in the mid-1960s are suggested in the median family income figures in one reanalysis by Glenn and Hyland of data in four opinion surveys: the total sample figure was $5,856; the figure for Jews was $7,990. At that time Jewish families averaged higher incomes than the total population. Moreover, a 1970s study estimated median family incomes at $12,600 for Jews and $10,300 for the total population. Yet this apparent Jewish affluence is not quite what it appears. There are a number of wealthy Jewish families, but not one—in spite of stereotypes to the contrary—can be found among the nation's superrich families, those worth over a billion dollars in 1982. One should also keep in mind that hundreds of thousands of Jewish families continue to fall below the poverty level.[56]

Continuing occupational mobility has characterized the last two decades. In the 1960s an estimated one-quarter of male Jewish workers were still in blue-collar occupations in New York City. The blue-collar proportions in studies of other cities were lower. In five major cities (New York,

Providence, Milwaukee, Detroit, and Boston) occupational data showed that 20 to 32 percent of Jewish males were in professional positions and 28 to 54 percent were in managerial-official positions. Over half of all Jewish workers in each city were in these two categories, while most of the rest were in other clerical or sales positions. These figures can be compared to the total employed populations in those cities, a majority of which were in blue-collar positions. The 1981 *American Jewish Yearbook* reports 1970 data on the occupational distribution of Jewish men and women nationwide. Seventy percent of the men and 40 percent of the women held professional, technical, managerial, or administrative positions. Most of the rest were in other white-collar (clerical and sales) jobs. Few were in blue-collar jobs. Surveys of local communities have found similar concentrations of Jewish Americans in white-collar occupations.[57]

Studies of financial and banking institutions have found no Jews in the top jobs in forty-five of the fifty largest banks; Jews made up only one percent of senior executives in major banks. The pattern was similar for the thousands of executives below the top level—in New York as well as in other cities. Jews owned none of the twenty largest banks. Jews, contrary to the widely believed stereotype, have never controlled banking in the United States. This is true of agriculture, mining, and heavy industry as well. Jews were never concentrated in the extractive industries such as mining or agriculture; and they were to be found only certain manufacturing industries. Within a few generations they became heavily centered in clerical and professional occupations. Except in a few Jewish enterprises, Jews are rarely to be found at the top ranks of the nation's major corporations. Jews are not an economic elite in this sense. They still are scarce in the executive suites of basic industries such as oil, steel, and autos. In recent decades Jewish entrepreneurs and executives have been common only in certain industries which they entered at an early point in time; they have been successful in radio, TV, and publishing. In 1980 Random House and Simon and Schuster were Jewish-owned businesses.

Today many Jewish professionals are in colleges and universities. Many of the nation's writers, scholars, and professors are Jewish. Jews are well represented among distinguished scholars at major universities and among top literary figures. They include Nobel laureate Saul Bellow and socialist intellectuals such as Irving Howe. They have been the backbone of literary and critical magazines such as the *Partisan Review, Dissent,* and the *New York Review of Books.* The impact of the ethnic economy can still be seen in Jewish America.[58]

The effects of anti-Semitism tend to keep many Jewish Americans in what has been termed "the gilded ghetto," economically successful but isolated from the social recognition and power that success should have brought. Ghettoization in recent decades has been a subtle process, but it is nonetheless real. Much discrimination has been hidden by secrecy at higher economic levels. Exclusion from private social clubs and private schools creates economic and political disabilities in other spheres, a classic example of the indirect discrimination discussed in Chapter 1 (page 16).[59]

Discrimination and conformity to the dominant culture have exacted a heavy price in cultural creativity, identity, and continuity. This price was heaviest for those whose mobility has carried them into professional, managerial, or clerical white-collar occupations. White-collar Jews have been forced by informal job requirements to spend much of their time in the non-Jewish world. Since non-Jews were already in the dominant positions in the corporate and business world, it was the mobile Jews who had to conform. Non-Jews are the critical gatekeepers. The possibility of anti-Semitic rejection pressures a Jewish white-collar worker to dispense with cultural distinctiveness and, to a certain extent, traditional connections. Sklare suggests that the Jewish success brought serious problems of identity.[60] The core society again sought a re-creation or cloning process, in the form of an Anglo-Saxon Protestant model. To put it another way, what would Jews have achieved, what creativity would have blossomed, and what would American society be like if the Jews had not been restricted by anti-Semitism?

While many Jewish Americans have prospered, others have not. For example, there are still sizable poor populations in some areas of New York City, as well as in other cities. There are still many working in blue-collar occupations. One 1973 study found that one-sixth of the Jews in New York, 272,000 people, were poor or near-poor by official standards, including a large number of elderly people. Large numbers of poor and moderate-income Jews were also found in Chicago, Philadelphia, and Miami. A national study estimated that 700,000 to 800,000 of America's six million Jews were still poor.[61]

EDUCATION

In education Jews not only faced acculturation pressures, but also anti-Semitic attitudes and discrimination. Significant participation in schools came with the surge of Russian and Polish Jewish immigrants who brought an ancient tradition of respect for education. Numerous religious schools were established; thousands of adults attended evening schools, established by philanthropic organizations, in an attempt to learn English after work. They sought acculturation at the level of language.[62]

When public schools spread toward the end of the nineteenth century, school attendance of eastern European Jewish immigrant children became remarkably high in spite of poverty. By the early 1900s there were three dozen de facto segregated public schools in New York City with an estimated 61,000 Jewish pupils. The situation in other cities was similar except that Jewish children were less likely to be segregated. Educational mobility for second- and third-generation Jews came swiftly. It was not long before large numbers of students were graduating from high schools in northern cities, with a significant number pursuing college educations. By 1920 the proportion of Jewish students in New York City colleges and universities was estimated to be *greater* than the proportion of Jews in the general population. Overall educational levels had increased to a remarkable level by the late 1930s. One survey revealed that in New York City just under

50 percent of Jewish students managed to complete high school, compared to only one-quarter of other students. Of the 1.1 million students in more than 1,300 colleges, 9 percent were Jewish, a considerable overrepresentation.[63]

Discriminatory Quotas for Jewish Students

Yet the highest levels of the educational system were far from living up to their ideals. Restrictive quota systems limiting the number of Jewish students were imposed at numerous colleges and universities from the 1920s to the 1950s. In a notorious 1922 graduation address President A. L. Lowell of Harvard University openly called for discriminatory quotas on Jewish students; many schools followed his advice. In the 1920s, at one major medical school in New York, three-quarters of non-Jews applying were admitted, compared to a percentage of Jews which peaked at half but eventually dropped to one-fifth. (Apparently both pools contained equal numbers of eligible persons.) In the 1920s restrictions were placed on Jewish admissions to law schools and to the bar in various states. Fraternities and sororities excluded eastern European Jews from membership; for many decades fraternities and sororities were important screening and grooming institutions whereby students from the "right" racial and ethnic backgrounds were given a boost onto the elevator to success.[64]

In the Great Depression it was difficult for Jewish students to gain admission to certain colleges and universities. Some continued to restrict Jewish students to a zero or token quota. Few would admit they had quotas for Jews, but data on admissions to major East Coast colleges showed clearly that blatant discrimination was practiced. Professional schools continued such policies as well. Percentages of Jewish enrollments at prominent institutions such as Columbia, Syracuse, and Cornell medical schools dropped very sharply between the 1920s and the 1940s. Prominent schools were at the top of the list in rigidly enforcing an exclusion policy. If they gained admission to medical school despite quotas, Jewish students faced yet another hurdle: restrictions on hospital internships. These patterns of anti-Jewish discrimination continued into the 1940s, and to a lesser extent in the decades since. Discrimination extended to privileges and benefits such as scholarships.[65]

Coupled with anti-Semitic discrimination against students was discrimination against faculty members. Between the 1920s and the 1940s it was very difficult for Jewish Ph.D.'s, however distinguished, to get appointments at Anglo-Saxon-dominated universities. For example, when the brilliant scholar Lionel Trilling was appointed to the English department faculty at Columbia University, he was the first Jew ever in that department. Other universities prided themselves on never having appointed a Jewish scholar.

Recent Achievements in Education

Severe discrimination was on the decline by the 1950s and 1960s, and educational attainment was reaching ever-higher levels. An analysis of 1963–1965 national data revealed that 36 percent of those adults identifying themselves as Jews had some college education, compared to 17 percent in the total adult sample. In those years median educational attainment was 12.6 years for Jews and 11.4 years for the total group. As of 1971, over half of Jewish Americans over the age of 24 were estimated to have had some college work, compared to less than a quarter of the general population. In recent decades the average educational attainments of Jewish Americans have remained significantly higher than in the population as a whole. In the 1970s and 1980s the educational aspirations and concrete achievements of Jewish Americans have remained at a high level, with eight in ten among Jewish young people going to college. Moreover, one-tenth of faculty members in U.S. universities were Jewish in the 1970s and 1980s.

Problems remain, however. In New York City the average educational level of foreign-born Jews has been lower than in the population as a whole. This suggests that older Jews and recent immigrants have not done as well in terms of education as second and later generations. Moreover, the rapid rise in secular education has created serious problems for Jewish Americans. Conformity pressures have had serious implications for Jewish creativity and identity.[66]

This concern for identity can be seen in the growth of Jewish schools and Jewish studies programs after World War II. In recent decades surveys have found strong support among Jewish parents for some type of Jewish education for their children. Between 1900 and World War I many second-generation eastern European Jews received some instruction in weekday religious schools. By 1918 about one-quarter of Jewish children in New York City got at least a little Jewish schooling, usually in inadequate facilities. Jewish schools could not compete with public schools. Yet by the late 1970s an estimated eight in ten Jewish children had had some religious schooling, a proportion up sharply from earlier decades. Recent figures indicate that of the more than 540,000 Jewish children in Jewish schools, 13 percent were in all-day schools, 44 percent were in weekday afternoon schools, and 42 percent were in Sunday schools.

The renewed emphasis on formal learning of one's heritage and religion in the lower grades has carried over to colleges and universities. By the 1960s there were more than five dozen positions in Jewish studies; by the 1970s there were more than three hundred positions. Jewish studies programs were accelerated by the general student push for expanded college race and ethnic studies.[67]

RELIGION AND ZIONISM

The Sephardic immigrants in the seventeenth century introduced the first non-Christian tradition carried from Europe to the colonies. The Sephardim founded Orthodox synagogues, which became community centers. In the earliest decades Jews were seldom found in the Puritan-dominated colonies because of persecution. Religious freedom in the colonies was variable, and most colonies had restrictions limiting Jewish participation in colonial life. After 1790 there was considerable support in the new nation, particularly among Jefferson and his followers, for maximizing religious freedom.[68] Yet it was evident that the new nation and its component states were fundamentally Christian. Gradually, religious freedom became law in each of the new states, in most by 1850.

With the German influx Judaism began to thrive. Jewish Reform movement leaders began to question ancient religious traditions and to call for adaptations. The Reform movement accelerated with the waves of German migration and became organized in the union of American Hebrew Congregations in the 1870s. A third tradition, Conservative Judaism, also grew up in the nineteenth century, a movement making some concessions to the core culture, as in language and weekend time schedules for religious services, but at the same time retaining more of the traditional belief and ritual systems than the Reform movement considered necessary. By 1900, Orthodox Judaism, the oldest and most orthodox group, had received a major infusion from the eastern European immigrants, whose religious commitments were closely tied to Orthodox culture. The synagogues of the eastern Europeans were ethnic centers where different nationalities came together in a religious context.[69]

In recent years substantial research has been focused on Orthodox Judaism. Many refugees fleeing the Nazis and turmoil in Europe in the 1930–1950 period were active members of Orthodox Judaism: they remained highly committed to it in the United States. Research on Jewish Americans in the 1970s and 1980s has demonstrated that commitment to Orthodoxy persists among the children of these immigrants. Highly visible, these traditional Jewish Americans have proudly asserted their religious traditions—and have rejected calls for cultural assimilation. The persistence of Orthodoxy has triggered a debate among Jewish scholars, with some arguing that Orthodox Jews are dealing with the challenges of American modernity by compartmentalizing their lives—that is, they largely separate family and ritual spheres from their workaday lives. Conflicts between these two different areas of their lives are rationalized away. Yet other scholars view Orthodoxy as a synthesis of modernity and traditional Judaism. They argue that Orthodoxy has already made major compromises with modern American culture.[70]

By the 1920s there were three divergent streams of religious commitment, with more than three thousand Jewish congregations divided into Reform, Orthodox, and Conservative groups. The authority of the rabbi, as well as the traditional ritual and theology, became less important as one moved from Orthodox to Conservative to Reform congregations. Cooperative activities linking the three branches of Judaism date back several decades, beginning in earnest with the 1917 Jewish Welfare Board. Community centers and charitable associations became settings for increasing interaction. The coordination of activities has varied considerably over the years and has often been limited to specific issues rather than indicative of a general trend toward a merger of the divergent groups. It was during the 1920s and 1930s that a secular movement away from religion began to occur. A prominent scholar, Will Herberg, has argued that many of the second-generation eastern Europeans tended to turn away from all branches of Judaism; many became ardently secularist, Zionist, or radical unionist. Secularism and labor radicalism became the new "religions" of many younger Jews during the crises of the Depression and World War II.[71]

Trends in Jewish Religion

With expanding suburbanization after World War II came a growth in the number of congregations relocating, or newly developing, in the rings around central cities. Suburbanized third-generation eastern European Jews came to accept their Jewishness more than their parents did, showing a greater interest in the ways of their grandparents—the famous "third-generation return." Herberg underscores the point that this interest is actually in a more secularized version of Judaism, one without much in the way of traditional ritual or other religious trappings.

Yet the current picture of Jewish religion is more complex, with substantial evidence of interest in the traditional heritage and in maintaining the synagogue as a community center, and at the same time evidence of a decline in home religious practices and indications of a changing religious organizational structure. In recent years the suburban synagogues have moved more in the direction of the Protestant religious core, with Sunday schools, men's clubs, women's groups, and general synagogue organization similar to that of Protestant churches. Much traditional ritual has been retained, but regular participation in ritual has played a decreasingly important role in the lives of many. Kelman suggests that by the 1950s and 1960s active synagogue membership for many was more or less confined to the childrearing periods, when attendance at Jewish school and certain rituals such as Bar Mitzvah were important.[72]

A research study of a suburb in the Midwest discovered that most respondents retained at most six of the many traditional home rituals of Judaism (lighting candles on Hanukkah, for instance), a decrease from the number of traditional observances the same respondents reported for their parents' homes. A similar pattern was found in Providence, Rhode Island. This decline in observances has been interpreted as part of a growing secularization, a slow movement away in everyday life from the religious center of the Jewish heritage. National surveys in 1957 and 1958 showed Jews to be the least regular religious service attenders among Protestant, Catholic, and Jewish adults. Nonetheless, few *never* attended. While attendance may be relatively low, except on special days, synagogues have remained the major Jewish organizations in suburbia, providing an anchor for Jewish identity and the fountain of the Jewish heritage. Synagogues have remained centers for recreational and social programs.[73]

J. L. Blau has suggested that much Jewish religion has had a flexible character. It has become denominational in the United States, with a tolerance for three or four different "denominations" of Judaism. In this regard it is like American Protestantism. Modern American Judaism is also a "voluntary" faith; Jews can choose to reject it or to accept it to varying degrees. Moreover, much American Judaism is a "cardiac" religion, one which emphasizes the heart or one's morals, rather than a rigid emphasis on ritual and theological doctrine. Judaism has become one of three American religious traditions. Of course, Blau's analysis does not apply to the Jews who are Orthodox. Today Judaism seems to be split between two different trends—denominationalism and Orthodoxy.[74]

Over the last three or four decades the importance of Christian anti-Semitism in shaping the context of America's Jews has persisted. Few Christian churches and organizations during the 1930s and 1940s took any position condemning the Nazi treatment of the Jews. Incredibly, after that war a few Christian groups even characterized the Holocaust as the *just retribution* for Jews having persistently refused to accept Jesus Christ as "savior." This interpretation of Jewish "sin" and of retribution was propounded even into the 1970s and 1980s, particularly among fundamentalist Christian groups. Fundamentalist groups have been eager to convert the "heathen" Jews. In recent decades a number of Christian evangelical missionary organizations, such as the American Board of Missions to the Jews, have sought to convert Jews to the Christian faith.[75]

Religious discrimination against Jews has been involved in a number of federal court cases. In the late 1950s and early 1960s Orthodox Jewish business owners fought local Sunday "blue laws" requiring businesses to be closed on Sundays; they argued that such laws violated their First Amendment right not to be penalized for religious practices. The Supreme Court rejected their case and upheld the "blue laws." In addition, Christian religious observances, such as reciting the Lord's Prayer, were once standard in public schools. The imposition of these practices on Jewish children was opposed in courts from New York to California. When a New York case reached the Supreme Court, the court ruled against officially sanctioned religious practices in the public schools. Sounding overtones from the past, after the decision some Christian leaders and publications, including the Jesuit magazine *America,* questioned whether Jewish leaders pressing such court cases were not themselves triggering anti-Jewish feelings among Christians.[76] The recent movement to bring prayers back into public schools often has anti-Jewish overtones. Similarly, interfaith tensions mounted in the 1970s when a number of Jewish leaders voiced criticism of the middle-of-the-road position that liberal Protestant groups (including the National Council of Churches) and numerous Catholic leaders were taking on Arab-Israeli problems.[77]

The Jewish press remained strong in the 1970s and 1980s, with thirty journals of scholarship and opinion. Several dozen Jewish communities put out their own newspapers. In the early 1980s the one Yiddish daily left (the *Forward*) became a weekly paper. This Jewish press, although slowly declining in numbers in recent decades, remains central to movements to reinvigorate Jewish religious and secular traditions.[78]

Zionism

At the heart of modern Jewish political-religious commitments is the commitment to the prosperity of the state of Israel. Whether active in religious Judaism or not, most American Jews share this Zionist commitment. Some social commentators have suggested that Zionism is like a religion, especially in its fervor. This Zionist commitment has affected not only Jewish voting patterns (as in the case of former president Jimmy Carter) and black-Jewish relations (because of pro-Arab sentiments among some blacks) but also Jewish American philanthropy. Jewish American financial support has been critical to Israel's survival in the face of hostility from surrounding Arab countries.

In the last decade there has been growing debate in Jewish communities across the nation over the government of Israel and its actions, such as the 1982 invasion of Lebanon. While most in the debate remain strongly committed to Israel, many Jews in America have raised questions about the direction of Israel's development and the wisdom of recent Israeli leaders. A growing number have expressed the view that the "overriding challenge facing Western Jewry today is essentially that of discovering how it can contribute to Israeli-Arab reconciliation."[79]

ASSIMILATION

Two different theoretical perspectives have been used to interpret the experiences of Jewish Americans—assimilation perspectives and cultural pluralism views. Most scholarly analyses of Jewish Americans have reflected some type of assimilation perspective.[80] A dominant perspective among Jewish Americans themselves has been at least partially assimilationist: the view that some rapid defensive adaptation to the surrounding culture was critical to avoiding anti-Semitic prejudice and discrimination.[81]

Partial cultural assimilation came relatively quickly for each of the three major waves of Jewish immigrants and their children. Many German Jews rapidly adapted to their new environment, picking up English and basic values; but they maintained a commitment to Judaism. Then came the waves of eastern Europeans. Completely separate Jewish communities survived only for a while; where they were close geographically the German and eastern European cultures and communities began blending together. Indeed, the German Jews often pressed the new immigrants to Americanize rapidly. In such cities as New York German social workers and others came "downtown" to help assimilate the new eastern Europeans.[82]

Soon Sephardic and German distinctiveness seemed to have been all but lost in the overwhelming numbers of the eastern Europeans. Among the Eastern European immigrants many were committed to fighting acculturation pressures, with the strongest commitment to the retention of Judaism. Some were committed to the retention of Yiddish culture. Among the latter there was a heavy emphasis on the crucial role Yiddish culture could play in perpetuating the Jewish heritage. The majority of the first generation adopted a partial commitment to cultural assimilation which was at bottom a survival strategy, a means of coping with anti-Semitic discrimination. In one sense, the eastern European immigrants were already partially acculturated when they stepped ashore: they came with a strong commitment to education, an urban-commercial background, and a desire to "make it" in North America.[83]

The second generation was more affected by assimilation pressures and rapidly picked up the language and values pressed on them in the media and the public school system. Like young Italian Americans they were caught between the culture of their parents and the core culture, a situation guaranteed to create family tensions. The proportion of Jews speaking Yiddish declined substantially. Yiddish schools and newspapers decreased in number.[84]

Judaism, particularly the Reform and Conservative branches, was partially Americanized over the decades after 1900—with its Sunday schools, English-language services, and Protestant-like associational activities. The third east European generation, according to Herberg, was secure in the United States and eager to accent its "Jewishness," but without some of the religious trappings. What Herberg has in mind is a return to a secularized "Jewishness." The Yiddish religious heritage was weakening by the mid-twentieth century, replaced to a substantial extent by a composite Jewish secularism.[85]

However, the decline of certain traditional religious values and practices has not meant the demise of Judaism or of the synagogue as a community center. And the resurgence of Orthodox Judaism in recent years suggests that at least a minority of Jewish Americans are rejecting Jewish secularism entirely. Recent research makes it clear that Orthodox Judaism is alive. A significant number of Jews, previously unaffiliated and raised in secular families, have become active in Orthodox religion, with its anti-assimilationist ideology and traditions. Liebman has suggested that Jews are going in two directions at the same time, with most more or less assimilating culturally and with a minority rejecting cultural assimilation as much as possible.[86]

Patterns of Assimilation

In the sphere of structural assimilation at the secondary level of economics and politics, we have seen the rise of German and eastern European Jews up the ladder. Eastern European Jews moved from a blue-collar concentration to a white-collar concentration in three generations. The original occupational concentration in certain blue-collar and entrepreneurial categories largely reflected discrimination as well as the skills that Jewish workers brought with them. For many an ethnic economy was critical, with concentrations of Jews in "middleman" positions, where they prospered. Hard work and mastery of the core culture's educational system facilitated upward movement. Yet their present occupational distribution underscores the point that even prosperous Jewish Americans are not fully integrated. Indicative of discrimination is the absence of Jewish Americans at the very top in most spheres of the economy. Penetration of Jewish Americans in the political sphere has come slowly; substantial representation in the political sphere is recent. Even today anti-Semitism can be found in the economic and political spheres.

Jews have, over a few generations, been very successful in moving up to the middle rungs of the economic ladder in the United States. Most came in poor; most today are part of middle-income America. Yet a question has often come up in ethnic analyses: Why were the Jews able to move up the ladder so successfully? Some have explained this in terms of basic values and religious traditions. Nathan Glazer has argued that "Judaism emphasizes the traits that businessmen and intellectuals require, and has done so at least 1,500 years before Calvinism . . . . The strong emphasis on learning and study can be traced that far back, too. The Jewish habits of foresight, care, moderation probably arose early."[87] Many authors have emphasized that Jewish values enabled them to succeed in spite of their lack of skills and education.

Others disagree. This image of Jewish success growing out of traditional religious values has been called by Stephen Steinberg the "myth of Jewish progress." Steinberg has demonstrated that Jewish success had less to do with supernatural and religious factors than with historical and structural factors. Jewish immigrants were not illiterate peasants with no urban experience. Jewish immigrants in the 1880–1920 period came mostly from the urban areas of eastern Europe, where they had already worked in a variety of urban occupations, such as manufacturing, craft work, and small-scale commerce. Many had experience as small merchants. Others were textile workers. Compared with other immigrants coming in at this time, their literacy level was high. Jews migrated to the United States at a time of expanding manufacturing and trade. Their urban backgrounds, their skills, and their education fit in well with the new needs of U.S. capitalism, especially in the expanding textile industry. Steinberg concludes that, contrary to what Glazer and others have argued, Jewish immigrants did not need to rely only on their religious values; they came in with "occupational skills that gave them a decisive advantage over other immigrants." The fit between Jewish skills and economic circumstances at the critical point in time was also better than it would be for later nonwhite immigrants (such as blacks and Puerto Ricans) to the big cities.[88]

Substantial integration into the non-Jewish core society has not come as yet in the sphere of primary relations. Because of ongoing discrimination, as well as Jewish choice, structural assimilation has not proceeded far at the informal level. Considerable concentration of informal social life still goes on within the Jewish community. Lenski found this to be true of most Jews in Detroit; the study by Sklare and associates of a midwestern surburb found that even affluent Jews chose, nearly exclusively, other Jews as close friends. And one study of a Minnesota city suggested that the Jewish community there is focally organized around friendships and family.[89]

Discrimination against Jews has taken not only economic but also social form. From the late nineteenth century onward Jewish Americans have been excluded from hotels, restaurants, social clubs, voluntary associations, and housing. Such discrimination has persisted into the present. The social ties of Jewish Americans have been firmly cemented together, partially, for defensive reasons. The Jewish community and extended family have provided the critical defensive context for survival in the face of anti-Semitism.

The "Jewish mother" stereotypes are built around a nucleus of truth found in the protective actions taken by Jewish mothers—and fathers—in defending their children from the onslaughts of non-Jews. In recent decades Jewish families have remained cohesive.

Even in cities such as Los Angeles, where the large Jewish community has a reduced birthrate and a more dispersed housing pattern in the 1980s than in previous decades, there is still a strong group life. As a recent study of Los Angeles Jews put it, "the picture that emerges from the survey is of a vibrant people whose closest personal associations are with other Jews in the family, friendship, and occupational groupings."[90]

In recent decades the intermarriage rate has not been as high as some have predicted, given the high level of acculturation of Jewish Americans. The rate of cross-national marriages *within* the Jewish group has increased to the point of significant blendings. A survey in the late 1950s found that only 7 percent of Jewish marriages (that is, marriages in which at least one partner is Jewish) involved a non-Jew. Other studies in the 1950s and 1960s found variable rates: about 17 to 18 percent of Jewish marriages involved a non-Jewish partner in New York and San Francisco. Rates have been found to be highest among third-generation Jews and in smaller Jewish communities. In a study in Providence, Rhode Island, it was discovered that less than 5 percent of Jewish marriages were intermarriages, and virtually all of these involved a non-Jewish wife. By the 1970s and 1980s the rate of intermarriage seemed to be growing again, but still remained at a modest level, with perhaps 20 to 30 percent of Jewish marriages including a non-Jewish partner, particularly among younger families. Yet even among intermarried Jews there is reportedly a tendency for the children to be raised as Jews and for the non-Jewish partner to convert to Judaism.[91]

One reason for this preponderance of in-marriages over out-marriages is the strength of Jewish families. Recent opinion surveys have demonstrated that Jewish Americans remain family-oriented. They are generally liberal on issues such as premarital sex and providing youths with birth control information, but Jewish respondents have been very opposed to extramarital sexual relations. Heilman points up the significance of this: "By and large American Jews, for all their liberalism toward sex, continue to view the Jewish family as an institution that must be protected."[92]

Intentional discrimination played a major role in frustrating the rise of first-generation Sephardic, German, and eastern European Jews. Even the acculturated children of these immigrants faced anti-Semitic barriers, barriers which would stall structural assimilation. Massive discrimination channeled the eastern Europeans into familiar ghetto communities. In spite of the affluence of later generations, subtle economic and social discrimination still seems to be part of the contemporary scene. In the 1960s Gordon argued that while Jewish Americans are partially assimilated at the behavior-receptional level (that is, discrimination has declined), there has been less assimilation at the attitude-receptional level because of the persistence of substantial anti-Semitism. Indeed, we have seen the persistence of anti-Semitic stereotypes among non-Jews surveyed in opinion polls even in the last few decades.[93]

Modern Jewish Identity: Is It Changing?

While a substantial segment have disguised their Jewish identity when in the presence of non-Jews as a protective response, only a small minority have forsaken commitment to the Jewish heritage. In the World War II period large numbers of Jewish Americans changed their names. For example, in Los Angeles right after World War II, just under half of all those petitioning for name changes were Jewish, although Jewish residents made up about 6 percent of the population. Most of those changing their names were native-born. For some this may have been the final act of Jewish identity rejection. For most, however, it may not have signified movement away from their ethnic group but rather an action instrumental in securing a job, in facilitating structural mobility. This was a tactic east European Jews in particular could use to avoid discrimination. Numerous researchers have noted the continuing strength of Jewish identification, even though that is coupled with a declining commitment to a specifically German or Yiddish heritage. Substantially middle-income, third and fourth generations have become more Americanized than their parents; at the same time many have resisted what Gordon terms identificational assimilation.

Most Jewish parents have provided some education for their children in Hebrew schools. One 1970s study found that more than eight in every ten young Jewish males had attended Jewish parochial schools, as had seven in ten young Jewish women. Most want to preserve the Jewish ethnic identity. In recent years there seems to be some resurgence of ethnic consciousness. A Minnesota study found that only a small minority of a sample there denied their Jewish backgrounds when asked. And a study by Sklare, Greenblum, and Ringer of affluent suburbanites discovered that most Jews there were committed to the maintenance of their heritage—and to the state of Israel. Israel has been a central focus of Jewish identity and consciousness, a focus reducing the possibility of identificational assimilation.[94]

An alternative to the traditional Anglo-conformity assimilation approach, cultural pluralism can be seen in the views of many ethnic group leaders since the early 1800s. Interestingly, it was a Jewish immigrant to the United States, of Polish and Latvian origin, who best formulated this alternative perspective. A democratic philosopher, Horace Kallen (1882–1974) argued that membership in ethnic-cultural groups was not a membership one could readily give up. Writing in *The Nation* in 1915, he argued that ethnic groupings had a right to exist in their own right—that is, democracy applied to ethnic groups. He argued against the ruthless Americanization of some nativists. By the 1920s he had given the name *cultural pluralism* to the view that each ethnic group has the democratic right to retain its own heritage, to live without forced Americanization pressures. However, other scholars have argued that cultural pluralism is not a useful perspective for understanding the United States, since massive acculturation and assimilation have in fact been facts of life for immigrants.[95]

Greeley's *ethnogenesis* perspective is in part a call for a recognition of the reality of cultural differences among contemporary ethnic groups. As in the cases of Irish Americans and Italian Americans, the ethnogenesis model seems to fit the Jewish experience. Jewish Americans have certainly been far more than a European nationality group. Indeed, they are a composite group of Sephardic, German, and eastern European origin. In the United States those groups forged a distinctive ethnic group, partially shaped by the European cultural heritage and partially shaped by the core culture. Substantial changes have come, but ethnic distinctiveness, including some cultural distinctiveness, remains. Today one can still speak accurately of a Jewish ethnic group.

Heritage, tradition, and socialization of children by parents still have a strong impact on and shape the behavior and beliefs of American Jews. Beyond this ethnic impact there is a question of ethnic identity. How strong is that identity? Is it, as Herbert Gans argues, only a "symbolic ethnicity," without much deep-lying significance? History suggests that Gans is probably wrong both for the present and for the future. The sense of "Jewishness" is likely to remain strong for the majority of Jewish Americans for the foreseeable future.[96]

SUMMARY

Jewish Americans, most of whom are descendants of eastern Europeans, have become partially assimilated in the culture sphere. An economically prosperous group, an ethnic group which made dramatic progress up the mobility ladder, Jews fought great discrimination and some violence. Here is a success story. Here too a price was paid for success; and today significant anti-Semitism persists, limiting movement to the top. Coupled with vertical progression has come horizontal mobility in the form of suburbanization. The first-generation eastern European Jews were concentrated in central city ghettos, while second and third generations began moving into suburban areas, though often into predominantly Jewish suburban areas. In the last few years some have even suggested that this trend toward suburbanization has ended, that there may even be a drift back to the cities. If so, the shape of Jewish communities may again change.

Central to an adequate understanding of Jewish Americans today is an understanding of the close ties to Israel. Periodic Arab-Israeli flare-ups have generated among American Jews a renewed commitment to Israel, philosophically and financially. Whatever its problems, Israel continues to be seen as the hope for a people which has survived the Roman persecution, the Spanish Inquisition, the Russian pogroms, and the Nazi Holocaust. Related to this hope has been the flow of thousands of Jewish Americans to the work camps, towns, and cities of Israel. Yet in recent years we have also seen the dramatic flow of an estimated 300,000 Israeli immigrants to the United States to escape the threat of war or to seek new economic opportunities. Many of these new Jewish immigrants settle in the United States. They provide a contemporary reminder of the continuing sojourner character of the Jewish experience. They also "pose a problem for the Jewish community: they have chosen to leave the land that every Jewish American has learned to regard as a haven, the guardian of Jewish survival, and the center of Hebraic culture."[97]

NOTES

[1]See David Sidorsky, "Introduction," in *The Future of the Jewish Community in America*, ed. David Sidorsky (New York: Basic Books, 1973), pp. xix–xxv; and Stephen D. Isaacs, *Jews and American Politics* (Garden City, N.Y.: Doubleday, 1974), pp. ix–x.

[2]George Cohen, *The Jews in the Making of America* (Boston: Stratford Co., 1924), pp. 35–39.

[3]Carl Wittke, *We Who Built America*, rev. ed. (Cleveland: Case Western Reserve University Press, 1967), pp. 324–30; Will Herberg, *Protestant–Catholic–Jew*, rev. ed. (New York: Doubleday Anchor Books, 1960), pp. 175–77.

[4]Lucy S. Dawidowicz, *The War Against the Jews: 1933–1945* (New York: Holt, Rinehart & Winston, 1975), p. xiv; Wittke, *We Who Built America*, pp. 329–31.

[5]Jacob Lestschinsky, "Economic and Social Development of American Jewry," in *The Jewish People*, vol. 4 (New York: Jewish Encyclopedic Handbooks, 1955), p. 56; Herberg, *Protestant–Catholic–Jew*, p. 178; Maurice J. Karpf, *Jewish Community Organization in the United States* (New York: Arno Press, 1971), p. 34; Samuel Joseph, "Jewish Immigration to the United States from 1881 to 1910," *Studies in History, Economics, and Public Law* 56 (1914): 509–12.

[6]Karpf, *Jewish Community Organization in the United States*, p. 33; Sidney Goldstein, "American Jewry: A Demographic Analysis," in Sidorsky, *The Future of the Jewish Community in America*, p. 71; Alvin Chenkin, "Jewish Population in the United States," *American Jewish Yearbook*, 1973, vol. 74 (New York: American Jewish Committee, 1973), pp. 307–9; Arthur A. Goren, "Jews," in *Harvard Encyclopedia of American Ethnic Groups* (Cambridge, Mass.: Harvard University Press, 1980), pp. 591–92.

[7]Herberg, *Protestant–Catholic–Jew*, pp. 170–80; Stuart E. Rosenberg, *The Search for Jewish Identity in America* (New York: Doubleday Anchor Books, 1965), pp. 47–68.

[8]Herberg, *Protestant–Catholic–Jew*, p. 182.

[9]Charles Y. Glock and Rodney Stark, *Christian Beliefs and Anti-Semitism* (New York: Harper & Row, 1966), p. 64 et passim.

[10]Carey McWilliams, *A Mask for Privilege* (Boston: Little, Brown, 1948), pp. 164–65, 170–73; John Higham, "Social Discrimination Against Jews in America, 1830–1930," *Publication of the American Jewish Historical Society*, 47 (September 1957): 5.

[11]Higham, "Social Discrimination Against the Jews in America, 1830–1930," pp. 9–10; Carey McWilliams, *Brothers Under the Skin*, rev. ed. (Boston: Little, Brown, 1964), pp. 302–3; Brown is quoted in the *Los Angeles Times*, November 24, 1974, p. 1.

[12]Gustavus Meyers, *History of Bigotry in the United States*, rev. ed. (New York: Capricorn Books, 1960), pp. 277–313; McWilliams, *A Mask for Privilege*, pp. 110–11; Isaacs, *Jews and American Politics*, pp. 51, 98.

[13]See Carl C. Brigham, *A Study of American Intelligence* (Princeton, N.J.: Princeton University Press, 1923), pp. 177–210.

[14]T. W. Adorno et al., *The Authoritarian Personality* (New York: Harper & Brothers, 1950), pp. 69–79; Gertrude J. Selznick and Stephen Steinberg, *The Tenacity of Prejudice* (New York: Harper & Row, 1969), pp. 6–8, 184.

[15]Henry L. Feingold, *Zion in America* (New York: Twayne Publishers, 1974), pp. 143–44; C. Vann Woodward, *Tom Watson* (New York: Oxford University Press, 1963), pp. 435–45.

[16]Rufus Learski, *The Jews in America* (New York: KTAV Publishing House, 1972), pp. 290–91; John Higham, *Strangers in the Land* (New York: Atheneum, 1975), pp. 298–99.

[17]Milton R. Konvitz, "Inter-group Relations," in *The American Jew*, ed. O. I. Janowsky (Philadelphia: Jewish Publication Society of America, 1964), pp. 78–79; Donald S. Strong, *Organized Anti-Semitism in America* (Washington, D.C.: American Council on Public Affairs, 1941), pp. 14–20.

[18]Strong, *Organized Anti-Semitism in America*, p. 67.

[19]Dawidowicz, *The War Against the Jews*, p. 148; see also pp. 164, 403.

[20]Lewis H. Carlson and George A. Coburn, "The Jewish Refugee Problem," in *In Their Place* (New York: John Wiley, 1972). pp. 290–91; see also the excerpt from the congressional hearings on pp. 292–94, 295–96.

²¹McWilliams, *A Mask for Privilege*, p. 161; Glock and Stark, *Christian Beliefs and Anti-Semitism*, p. xi; Konvitz, "Inter-group Relations," pp. 79–80.

²²Gerald S. Strober, *American Jews* (Garden City, N.Y.: Doubleday, 1974), pp. 149–76.

²³Lawrence H. Fuchs, *The Political Behavior of American Jews* (Glencoe, Ill.: Free Press, 1956), pp. 23–25.

²⁴Mark R. Levy and Michael S. Kramer, *The Ethnic Factor* (New York: Simon & Schuster, 1972), p. 101; Feingold, *Zion in America*, pp. 83–89; William R. Heitzmann, *American Jewish Voting Behavior* (San Francisco: R and E Research Associates, 1975), pp. 27–28.

²⁵Heitzmann, *American Jewish Voting Behavior*, p. 29.

²⁶Irving Howe, *World of Our Fathers* (New York: Simon & Schuster, 1976), pp. 362–64; Emanuel Hertz, "Politics: New York," in *The Russian Jew in the United States*, ed. Charles S. Bernheimer (Philadelphia: John Winston and Co., 1905), pp. 256–65.

²⁷Edward M. Levine, *The Irish and Irish Politicians* (South Bend, Ind.: University of Notre Dame Press, 1966); Isaacs, *Jews and American Politics*, pp. 23–24; Feingold, *Zion in America*, p. 321.

²⁸Hertz, "Politics: New York," pp. 265–67; Heitzmann, *American Jewish Voting Behavior*, p. 37; Fuchs, *The Political Behavior of American Jews*, pp. 57–58.

²⁹Levy and Kramer, *The Ethnic Factor*, pp. 102–3; Howe, *World of Our Fathers*, pp. 381–88.

³⁰Heitzmann, *American Jewish Voting Behavior*, p. 49; Fuchs, *The Political Behavior of American Jews*, pp. 99–100.

³¹Selznick and Steinberg, *The Tenacity of Prejudice*, p. 54; Fuchs, *The Political Behavior of American Jews*, pp. 171–91.

³²Isaacs, *Jews and American Politics*, pp. 6, 152; Heitzmann, *American Jewish Voting Behavior*, pp. 56–58; Gerald S. Strober, *American Jews* (Garden City, N.Y.: Doubleday, 1974), pp. 186–88; Levy and Kramer, *The Ethnic Factor*, p. 103; Milton Plesur, *Jewish Life in Twentieth Century America* (Chicago: Nelson Hall, 1982), pp. 134–52.

³³Isaacs, *Jews and American Politics*, pp. 23, 201; Levy and Kramer, *The Ethnic Factor*, p. 118; *Time*, March 10, 1975, p. 25; Plesur, *Jewish Life in Twentieth Century America*, pp. 143–45.

³⁴Isaacs, *Jews and American Politics*, pp. 12, 118–19.

³⁵Bernard Cohen, *Sociocultural Changes in American Jewish Life as Reflected in Selected Jewish Literature* (Rutherford, N.J.: Fairleigh Dickinson University Press, 1972), pp. 183–85; Learski, *The Jews in America*, pp. 158–59; Rudolph Glanz, *The Jewish Woman in America*, vol. 1, *The East European Jewish Women* (New York: KTAV Publishing House, 1976), pp. 48–57.

³⁶Nathan Reich, "Economic Status," in Janowsky, *The American Jew*, pp. 70–71; Karpf, *Jewish Community Organization in the United States*, pp. 11–12.

³⁷Howe, *World of Our Fathers*, pp. 391–93; Feingold, *Zion in America*, pp. 235–36.

³⁸Karpf, *Jewish Community Organization in the United States*, pp. 62–65; *Time*, March 10, 1975, p. 23; Naomi Cohen, *Not Free to Desist* (Philadelphia: Jewish Publication Society of America, 1972), pp. 3–18, 37–80, 433–52.

³⁹*Time*, March 10, 1975, pp. 18–28; Arnold Foster and Benjamin R. Epstein, *The New Anti-Semitism* (New York: McGraw-Hill, 1974), pp. 155–284; Strober, *American Jews*, pp. 7–42.

⁴⁰Wolfe Kelman, "The Synagogue in America," in Sidorsky, *The Future of the Jewish Community in America*, pp. 171–73.

⁴¹Strober, *American Jews*, pp. 120–30; Maurice R. Berube and Marilyn Gittell, "The Struggle for Community Control," in *Confrontation at Ocean Hill–Brownsville*, ed. Maurice R. Berube and Marilyn Gittell (New York: Praeger, 1969), pp. 3–12 et passim; Joe R. Feagin and Harlan Hahn, *Ghetto Revolts* (New York: Macmillan, 1973), pp. 327–28; Nathan Glazer, *Affirmative Discrimination* (New York: Basic Books, 1975), pp. 33–76, 196–221.

⁴²Wittke, *We Who Built America*, pp. 39–40; Cohen, *The Jews in the Making of America*, pp. 73–80.

⁴³Feingold, *Zion in America*, p. 12; McWilliams, *Brothers Under the Skin*, pp. 305–6.

⁴⁴Wittke, *We Who Built America*, p. 325; Cohen, *The Jews in the Making of America*, pp. 120–22.

⁴⁵Lestschinsky, "Economic and Social Development of American Jewry," pp. 78–79.

⁴⁶Ibid., p. 78.

⁴⁷Ibid., pp. 74–77; Isaac M. Rubinow, "Economic and Industrial Condition: New York," in Bernheimer, *The Russian Jew in the United States*, pp. 103–7.

⁴⁸Nathan Goldberg, *Occupational Patterns of American Jewry* (New York: Jewish Teachers Seminary Press, 1947), pp. 15–17; Marshall Sklare, *America's Jews* (New York: Random House, 1971), p. 61; Rubinow, "Economic and Industrial Condition: New York," pp. 110–11.

⁴⁹Cohen, *The Jews in the Making of America*, pp. 139–40.

⁵⁰Karpf, *Jewish Community Organization in the United States*, pp. 9–14; Lestschinsky, "Economic and Social Development of American Jewry," pp. 91–92; W. Lloyd Warner and Leo Srole, *The Social Systems of American Ethnic Groups* (New Haven: Yale University Press, 1945), p. 112.

⁵¹McWilliams, *A Mask for Privilege*, pp. 38, 40–41; Karpf, *Jewish Community Organization in the United States*, pp. 20–21; Higham, "Social Discrimination Against Jews in America," pp. 18–19.

⁵²The report on the February 1936 *Fortune* survey is taken from Karpf, *Jewish Community Organization in the United States*, pp. 9–11, and McWilliams, *A Mask for Privilege*, pp. 143–50; see also Lestschinsky, "Economic and Social Development of American Jewry," p. 81.

⁵³Lestschinsky, "Economic and Social Development of American Jewry," pp. 71, 87: McWilliams, *A Mask for Privilege*, p. 159; Reich, "Economic Status," pp. 63–65.

⁵⁴Donald J. Bogue, *The Population of the United States* (Glencoe, Ill.: Free Press, 1959), p. 703. I have taken these data from a table in Reich, "Economic Status," p. 56.

⁵⁵Mabel Newcomer, *The Big Business Executive* (New York: Columbia University Press, 1955), pp. 46–48.

⁵⁶Bogue, *The Population of the United States*, p. 706: Norval D Glenn and Ruth Hyland, "Religious Preference and Worldly Success," *American Sociological Review* 32 (February 1967): 78; the 1971 study is reported in *Time*, March 10, 1975, p. 24; Thomas R. Dye, *Who's Running America* (Englewood Cliffs, N.J.: Prentice-Hall, 1976), pp. 41–42.

⁵⁷Goren, "Jews," p. 593; Sklare, *America's Jews*, pp. 61–62; Sidney Goldstein, "Jews in the United States: Perspectives from Demography," in *American Jewish Yearbook, 1981* (New York: American Jewish Committee, 1980–1981), p. 54.

⁵⁸The Banking data are from American Jewish Committee reports summarized in Melvin L. DeFleur, William V. D'Antonio, and Louis B. DeFleur, *Sociology: Human Society*, 2d ed. (Dallas: Scott, Foresman, and Co., 1976), p. 268; Reich, "Economic Status," p. 74; Sklare, *America's Jews*, p. 65; Goren, "Jews," p. 593.

⁵⁹Sklare, *America's Jews*, p. 65; McWilliams, *Brother Under the Skin*, pp. 310–11.

⁶⁰Sklare, *America's Jews*, pp. 67–69.

⁶¹Naomi Levine and Martin Hochbaum, *Poor Jews* (New Brunswick, N.J.: Transaction Books, 1974), pp. 2–3, 36.

⁶²Cohen, *Sociocultural Changes in American Jewish Life as Reflected in Selected Jewish Literature*, pp. 158–59; Abraham Cahan, "The Russian Jew in the United States," in Bernheimer, *The Russian Jew in the United States*, pp. 32–33.

⁶³J. K. Paulding, "Educational Influences: New York," in Bernheimer, *The Russian Jew in the United States*, pp. 186–97; Cohen, *The Jews in the Making of America*, pp. 140–41; Karpf, *Jewish Community Organization in the United States*, p. 57.

⁶⁴Higham, "Social Discrimination Against Jews in America, 1830–1930," p. 22; Karpf, *Jewish Community Organization in the United States*, p. 19; McWilliams, *A Mask for Privilege*, pp. 128–29.

⁶⁵McWilliams, *A Mask for Privilege*, pp. 136–38; Karpf, *Jewish Community Organization in the United States*, pp. 18–19; Goren, "Jews," p. 590.

⁶⁶Glenn and Hyland, "Religious Preference and Worldly Success," p. 79; *Time*, March 10, 1975, p. 24; Sklare, *America's Jews*, pp. 54–55; Goren, "Jews," p. 593.

⁶⁷Cohen, *Sociocultural Changes in American Jewish Life as Reflected in Selected Jewish Literature*, pp. 163–67; Oscar I. Janowsky, "Achievements," in Janowsky, *The American Jew*, pp. 129–30; Walter I. Ackerman, "The Jewish School System in the United States," in *The Future of the*

Jewish Community in America, pp. 177–79; Robert Alter, "What Jewish Studies Can Do," *Commentary* 58 (October 1974): 71–74.

[68]Rosenberg, *The Search for Jewish Identity in America*, pp. 171–74; Anita L. Lebeson, *Pilgrim People*, rev. ed. (New York: Minerva Press, 1975), pp. 162–66; Feingold, *Zion in America*, pp. 29–31.

[69]Learski, *The Jews in America*, pp. 110–23; Marshall Sklare, *Conservative Judaism* (Glencoe, Ill.: Free Press, 1955): Rosenberg, *The Search for Jewish Identity in America*, pp. 174–75.

[70]Samuel C. Heilman, "The Sociology of American Jewry," in *Annual Review of Sociology*, ed. Ralph Turner, vol. 8 (Palo Alto, Calif.: Annual Reviews, 1982), p. 145.

[71]Wolfe Kelman, "The Synagogue in America," in Sidorsky, *The Future of the Jewish Community in America*, pp. 157–58; Herberg, *Protestant–Catholic–Jew*, pp. 185–96; Louis Lipsky, "Religious Activity: New York," in Bernheimer, *The Russian Jew in the United States*, pp. 152–54.

[72]Kelman, "The Synagogue in America," pp. 158–59; Herberg, *Protestant–Catholic–Jew*, pp. 190–93.

[73]Marshall Sklare, Joseph Greenblum, and Benjamin B. Ringer, *Not Quite at Home* (New York: Institute of Human Relations Press, 1969), pp. 13–23; Goldstein and Goldscheider, *Jewish Americans*, pp. 195–97 et passim; Herberg, *Protestant–Catholic–Jew*, p. 197; Bernard Lazerwitz and Louis Rowitz, "The Three-Generations Hypothesis," *American Journal of Sociology* 69 (March 1964): 532.

[74]J. L. Blau, *Judaism in America* (Chicago: University of Chicago Press, 1976), as summarized in Heilman, "The Sociology of American Jewry," p. 147.

[75]Strober, *American Jews*, pp. 73–75, 83–98.

[76]Konvitz, "Inter-Group Relations," in Janowsky, *The American Jew*, pp. 85–95.

[77]Strober, *American Jews*, p. 83.

[78]Goren, "The Jews," p. 595.

[79]Noah Lucas, "Is Zionism Dead," in *The Sociology of American Jews*, 2d ed., Jack N. Porter (Washington, D.C.: University Press of America, 1980), p. 261.

[80]Robert Blauner, *Racial Oppression in America* (New York: Harper & Row, 1972), pp. 60–66.

[81]Howe, *World of Our Fathers*, p. 645; Karpf, *Jewish Community Organization in the United States*, pp. 37–39, 49–50.

[82]Cohen, *Sociocultural Changes in American Jewish Life as Reflected in Selected Jewish Literature*, pp. 47–49; Charlotte Baum, Paula Hyman, and Sonya Michel, *The Jewish Woman in America* (New York: Dial Press, 1976), pp. 29–33; Learski, *The Jews in America*, pp. 37–38.

[83]Herberg, *Protestant–Catholic–Jew*, p. 183; Charles S. Liebman, "American Jewry: Identity and Affiliation," in Sidorsky, *The Future of the Jewish Community in America*, p. 133.

[84]Goldstein and Goldscheider, *Jewish Americans*, p. 226.

[85]Herberg, *Protestant–Catholic–Jew*, pp. 183–87.

[86]Goldstein and Goldscheider, *Jewish Americans*, pp. 8–10; Howe, *World of Our Fathers*, pp. 644–45; Milton M. Gordon, *Assimilation in American Life* (New York: Oxford University Press, 1964), pp. 190–94; C. Liebman, "Orthodox Judaism Today," *Mainstream* 25 (1979): 12–36; Heilman, "The Sociology of American Jewry," p. 139.

[87]Nathan Glazer, "The American Jew and the Attainment of Middle-class Rank: Some Trends and Explanations," in *The Jews*, ed. M. Sklare (New York: Free Press, 1958), p. 143, as quoted in Stephen Steinberg, *The Ethnic Myth* (New York, Atheneum, 1981), p. 93.

[88]Steinberg, *The Ethnic Myth*, pp. 94–102.

[89]Gerhard Lenski, *The Religious Factor* (Garden City, N.Y.: Doubleday Anchor Books, 1963), p. 37; Arnold Dashefsky and Howard M. Shapiro, *Ethnic Identification Among American Jews* (Lexington, Mass.: D.C. Heath, 1974), pp. 117–18.

[90]Quoted in Goldstein, "Jews in the United States," p. 28; cf. Isidore Chein, "The Problem of Jewish Identification," *Jewish Social Studies* 17 (July 1955): 221; Marshall Sklare, ed., *The Jews: Social Patterns of an Ethnic Group* (Glencoe, Ill.: Free Press, 1958), passim; Dashefsky and Shapiro, *Ethnic Identification Among American Jews*, pp. 115, 123–26.

[91]U.S. Bureau of the Census, "Religion Reported by the Civilian Population of the United

States," *Current Population Reports*, Series P-20 (February 1958), p. 8; the New York, San Francisco, and Providence studies are cited in Goldstein and Goldscheider, *Jewish Americans*, pp. 152–55; *Time*, March 24, 1975, p. 25.

[92]Heilman, "The Sociology of American Jewry," p. 152.

[93]Gordon, *Assimilation in American Life*, pp. 76–77.

[94]Leonard Broom, Helen Beem, and Virginia Harris, "Characteristics of 1,107 Petitioners for Change of Name," *American Sociological Review* 20 (February 1955): 33–35; Dashefsky and Shapiro, *Ethnic Identification Among American Jews*, pp. 120–21; Sklare, Greenblum, Ringer, *Not Quite at Home*, pp. 82–83.

[95]Milton R. Konvitz, "Horace Meyer Kallen (1882–1974)," in *American Jewish Yearbook, 1974– 1975* (New York: American Jewish Committee, 1974), pp. 65–67; Gordon, *Assimilation in American Life*, pp. 142–59.

[96]Herbert J. Gans, "Symbolic Ethnicity," *Ethnic and Racial Studies* 2 (1979): 1–20.

[97]Goren, "Jews," p. 597.

Native Americans ("Indians")

CHAPTER 7

It was the summer of 1977. Navaho medicine men came to Sante Fe, New Mexico, to take back religious and other ceremonial "artifacts" that a museum had collected. For the museum and its white visitors, these prayer sticks, medicine bundles, and other items were curiosities provided to entertain and perhaps inform white residents and tourists. But for the Navahos these "artifacts" were sacred objects which had been taken or stolen from their rightful Native American owners. After holding a ceremony with chants of joy, the medicine men reclaimed the sacred objects. One said, "We will take them home and teach the younger generation what these things mean." So far, few museums have followed the lead of this enlightened museum. Many sacred objects belonging to Native American tribes remain in white hands.[1]

With this chapter we begin to consider several groups whose ancestry is substantially non-European and nonwhite. Some among them, such as the Native Americans, predate European entry into this continent. European colonization and expansion processes were the social processes which brought subordination to non-European groups. In subsequent chapters we will see critical differences in the past and present life experiences of white and nonwhite Americans. We will see the greater role that race plays in the experiences of nonwhite America. We will discover the great relevance of power-conflict theories in interpreting the past and present of these subordinated groups.

The first victims of the European colonization process were those the Europeans called "Indians." Long erroneously called by this name, Native Americans have suffered from a variety of stereotyped images, from the wooden cigar-store figure to the bloodthirsty savage of the movies to the noble primitive of novels. Tomahawks, scalping, feathered headdresses, colorful dancing, and red men on wild ponies—such images have been vividly impressed on the Euro-American mind by a long tradition of mass-media sensationalism, including distorted images in magazines, newspapers, movies, and television.

Tourists have clamored for "Indian" dances. White children have killed thousands playing "cowboys and Indians." Sports teams have fought it out under the banner of the "Redskins," while automobile companies have used labels like "Cherokee Chief" for their wares.

Coupled with this has been a tendency to ignore the past and present reality of Native American life. The history of Native Americans is filled with strange ironies and popular distortions. Reflect for a moment on Europeans "discovering" an ancient continent *already* peopled by several million inhabitants. Europeans were latecomers in discovering the continent. The ancestors of the tribes encountered by the fifteenth-century explorers had discovered the continent at least twenty thousand years earlier, when they probably migrated across the Alaskan land bridge from Asia. Reflect too on the strange name these people have had to bear ever since, the "Indians" (*los Indios*), a name given to them by Europeans. Yet this name reflected a colossal error, generated by the assumption that the early expeditions had found the Asian Indies they were seeking.

"Discovered" by latecomers, named out of ignorance, militarily weaker, Native Americans soon found themselves faced with European policies of exploitation. The next few centuries would bring a sordid struggle for native lands.

CONQUEST BY EUROPEANS

Migration has been viewed as varying across a continuum from voluntary migration to slave importation. Such a migration framework typically includes a dominant race-ethnic group that is already established within certain boundaries and is assimilating a new human group into its demographic mix. But the situation of Native Americans points up the need to look at the migration of the dominant group itself, in this case Europeans moving into the territories of Native American groups. *Colonization migration* is an apt term for this process. This type of migration, unlike the others mentioned above, involves the conquest and domination of a preexisting group by outsiders. This process illustrates what some call *classical colonialism.*

How many Native Americans were there at the time Europeans came into North American history? The estimates vary considerably. Anthropologists and other analysts have estimated the native population of North America in 1600 at between 500,000 and 1,150,000 persons. Recently, the estimated number has been revised upward sharply, on the grounds that previous estimates did not take into account such factors as the number of native deaths due to disease in the initial contact period. A considered estimate by Dobyns puts the number in North America alone at nearly ten million at the time of conquest, with tens of millions in Central and South America as well. While this figure may be high, it may be closer to the number than earlier figures. Older estimates have often been used for the purpose of legitimating the European conquest of an allegedly unoccupied land.[2]

European diseases and firepower sharply reduced the number of Native Americans in North America from one to ten million at the time of first contact to approximately 200,000 by 1850. The number of Native Americans remained between 200,000 and 300,000 from the low point in the mid-nineteenth century until the 1930s, when it began to grow again. By 1980 there were more than 1.4 million persons counted as Native Americans by the Census, many of whom were counted as living on or near reservations by the Bureau of Indian Affairs.[3]

The term "Indian" and most major tribal names are terms of convenience applied by European American settlers. The naming of Native American societies by outsiders reflects their subordination, for not one of the major tribes is recorded in most history books under its own name. This suggests one difference between colonized nonwhites and European immigrants: Colonized peoples have had less control over the naming process. For example, the "Navahos" called themselves, in their own language, *Diné*, which meant "The People." Such misnomers point up the difficulty of getting the Native Americans' point of view on historical events.[4]

Native American Societies: Are They Tribes?

Native Americans have for centuries been a diverse collection of societies, with dramatic differences in numbers, languages, economies, polities, and customs. Some define the common term *tribe* as a group of relatives with a distinctive language and customs who are tied to a definite territory. Yet such a definition tends to obscure the great variety in size and complexity of Native American groups, which have ranged from very small hunting and gathering societies to the large, well-organized tribes suggested by this definition. While it is difficult to get away from the common usage of the term *tribe* for all groups, we will also use the term *society* for Native American groups in order to suggest that not all groups were well-organized tribes with definite territories.

There were perhaps 200 distinctive groups at the time of the European invasion. Traditionally, Native American societies have been grouped into geographical areas, including: (1) the societies of the East, who hunted, farmed, and fished, and whose first encounters with whites were with English settlers; (2) the Great Plains hunters and agriculturalists, whose first encounters were with the Spaniards; (3) the fishing societies in the Northwest; (4) the seed gatherers of California and neighboring areas; (5) the Navaho shepherds and Pueblo farmers in the Arizona–New Mexico area; (6) the desert societies of southern Arizona and New Mexico; and (7) the Alaskan groups, including the Eskimos.

This geographical breakdown has been linked to differences in economies, ranging from agricultural to hunting. In this chapter we will sometimes be speaking of the two hundred past and present societies as though they were one group; at other times we will be speaking of one distinctive group within this larger category. The reader should keep the great cultural diversity of Native American groups in mind as an implicit qualification to many generalizations about Native Americans.[5]

Forced migration at gunpoint was the lot of some native groups after they had been defeated. Among the famous forced marches was the one imposed on thousands of Cherokees, Creeks, Chicasaws, Choctaws, and Seminoles, who in the 1830s were forced to move to the Oklahoma Territory from their eastern lands. Other tribes in the West, such as the Navahos, were rounded up after military engagements and forced to migrate to barren reservations. In the twentieth century, moreover, internal migration from rural areas to the cities has been very important. As Native American populations began to recover from the high mortality rates of the nineteenth century and as population growth pressed hard on the economic resources of reservations, federal government policy moved to support urban relocation. In the 1950s, under the active policy of President Eisenhower's Secretary of the Interior, an earlier urban relocation program was expanded to cover more tribal groups and cities; a specific Bureau of Indian Affairs (BIA) branch was set up to oversee relocation services. The scale of this internal migration can be seen in these numbers: 200,000 Native Americans moved to the cities between the late 1950s and the 1970s, settling in poverty-stricken areas. By 1970 at least seven cities were estimated to have more than 10,000 residents from at least 10 different tribes.[6]

Why did they move to cities? Analysts have pointed to voluntary choice, triggered by the push factors of poverty and unemployment on reservations, and the pull factor of expanding economic opportunities which were concentrated in the cities.[7]

THE COLONIAL PERIOD

Various strategies were developed by the Europeans to deal with those Native Americans whose land they coveted. These ranged from honest treaty making with equals, to deceptive treaty making to defraud, to genocidal forays aimed at exterminating the "Indian menace," to enslavement in a form similar to that of Africans, to imprisonment in barren prison camps called reservations. A small number of Spanish explorers, followed by missionaries and colonists, had penetrated North America by the sixteenth century. In the process large native populations in the lands of the Caribbean and the Southwest were wiped out by enslavement, murder, and European diseases. The Spanish approach was different from that of later conquerers, for the Spanish sought to "civilize" and Catholicize the native population and to concentrate it in agricultural colonies. Military force and physical punishment were used to keep the "Indians" in line.[8]

On the East Coast in the 1600s, the Dutch established several communities. Several native groups were displaced or wiped out by Dutch settlers. A Dutch governor was one of the first to offer a government bounty for Native American scalps, used as proof of death; Europeans played a major role in spreading this bloody practice conventionally attributed only to Native Americans.[9] The English settlers gained superiority over the Native Americans, forcing them back into the frontier areas or killing them off.[10] Few seemed to be concerned for the genocidal consequences of their expansion. In spite of the often-noted reliance of English settlers on friendly Native Americans in surviving the first devastating years, the new settlers soon turned on their neighbors. A war with the Pequots in 1637 ended when several hundred Native Americans in a village were massacred by whites, with the survivors sent into slavery. The 1675–1676 King Philip's War with the Wampanoag tribe and its allies, precipitated by the oppressive tactics of the New England settlers, resulted in substantial losses on both sides. English retaliation was brutal. Hagan notes that the Native American leader, King Philip, was "captured, drawn, and quartered: his skull remained on view on a pole in Plymouth as late as 1700."[11] Survivors were sold as slaves. Similarly violent struggles took place in other colonies.

The enslavement of Native Americans—a forgotten episode—was a major source of friction. One 1708 report mentioned 1,400 Native American slaves in the Carolina area. By the mid-eighteenth century the Native American proportion among slaves was between 5 and 10 percent. As late as the 1790 Census, 200 of the 6,000 slaves in Massachusetts were Native Americans. Native Americans were replaced by Africans, in part because escape was a constant problem with Native Americans.[12]

After a ten-year war the English defeat of the French resulted in the French withdrawal from the continent in the mid-1700s, a move that brought many tribes into contact with the less sophisticated policy of the English. Uprisings resulted in a 1763 Royal Proclamation officially proclaiming the rights of Native Americans to their lands and requiring fair compensation for land taken; an Imperial Department of Indian Affairs was established. An official boundary between the settlers and the indigenous peoples was set at the Appalachian mountains. The proclamation was unenforceable because of the tremendous pressure of westward-moving settlers; Native American rights were compromised in the press of land-hungry whites. White colonists' frustration over the Crown's attempts to protect Native Americans played a role in generating the Revolution.[13]

Treaties and Reservations: Of Utmost Good Faith?

With the coming of the new republic, Native Americans found themselves in a new position. The U.S. Constitution briefly mentions Native Americans in giving Congress the power to regulate commerce with the tribes. And the 1787 Northwest Ordinance made the following solemn governmental promises:

> The utmost good faith shall always be observed towards the Indians; their land and property shall never be taken from them without their consent; and in their property, rights, and liberty, they shall never be invaded or disturbed, unless in justified and lawful wars authorized by Congress; but laws founded in justice and humanity shall from time to time be made, for preventing wrongs being done to them, and for preserving peace and friendship with them.[14]

Washington's Secretary of War, whose department had responsibility for "Indians," moved to adopt a policy of peaceful adjustment. Supreme Court decisions in the early 1800s laid out the principles that Native American societies had a right to their lands and that they were nations with a right to self-government. Chief Justice John Marshall argued that the United States government must take seriously the treaties with Native Americans. By the late 1700s the executive and legislative branches became actively involved. In 1790 an act licensing "Indian traders" was passed. A treaty was signed with the Senecas in 1794; and in 1796 government stores were established to provide Native Americans with supplies on credit.[15]

Federal officials, by action or inaction, supported the recurrent theft of lands. In practice, these officials approved of ignoring Native American boundary rights wherever necessary.[16] A distinguished French observer of the 1830s noted the hypocrisy: "But this virtuous and high-minded policy has not been followed. The rapacity of the settlers is usually backed by the tyranny of the government."[17] The procedure was usually not one of immediate expropriation of land, but rather of constant encroachment by settlers, a process sanctioned after the fact by the government and legitimated by treaties. Force was not always necessary. Early contacts often brought disease, reducing tribal numbers; the encroachment of farmers drove the game away and hunting tribes were faced with starvation. In this situation a treaty providing some compensation made the process seem legitimate.

After the inauguration of Andrew Jackson the subordination of Native Americans was encouraged by a president critical of treaty making, who even encouraged the states to defy Supreme Court rulings on Native Americans. Gradual displacement gave way to forced marches over hundreds of miles at gunpoint, in order to rid entire regions of "red savages." Congress passed the Indian Removal Act in 1830, and within a decade many of the tribes of the East voluntarily or forcibly migrated to lands west of the Mississippi under the auspices of "negotiated" treaties. Atlantic and Gulf Coast tribes, such as the Cherokees, as well as midwestern tribes, such as the Ottawas and Shawnees, were forcibly removed to the Oklahoma Territory. Resisters were exterminated. This migration became known as the "Trail of Tears." In addition to the large number of deaths in the forced march, there were problems in the new lands, with new agricultural techniques required and new animals to hunt. The tribes forced to move westward soon found their new lands, whose boundaries were "guaranteed" by the government, full of white settlers.[18]

Westward-moving settlers precipitated a bloody struggle with the Plains societies, many of whom had by that time given up agriculture for a nomadic hunting and raiding lifestyle. While most Native American groups in the region had participated in periodic intertribal raiding, the genocidal actions of federal troops and settlers were a new experience. It was the nomadic, horse-oriented Plains peoples who forever after came to symbolize "the Indian" in the public imagination. Yet the wars on the Plains were not as they have been pictured in the mass media. They usually did not involve glorious chiefs in feathered warbonnets on mighty stallions facing, on a sunswept plain, a brave collection of Army officers in dashing uniforms backed by their heroic men. The Plains wars were different from the legend, as Andrist underscores:

> As in all wars, men died unpleasantly, and often in extreme agony. Women and children suffered along with warrior and soldier, and the Army made it a part of strategy to destroy the enemy's food and possessions in order to leave him cold, hungry, and without the will to resist.[19]

Myths about Conflict

Native Americans suffered by far the most in the struggle over western lands. The movies and television have helped to create images of wagon trains moving across the West and have portrayed the 1840–1860 era of white overlanders as one of constant conflict with western tribes. Wagons in a circle, whooping Indians on ponies, thousands of dead settlers and Indians, treacherous "red men" who cannot be trusted—the movies and television have created many unforgettable images of the West. However, these images are largely mythological. Recent histories by John D. Unruh and others have made this clear. For example, between 1840 and 1860 approximately 250,000 white settlers made the long journey across the plains to the West Coast. Yet far less than 1 percent of those migrants died at the hands of the native inhabitants. Indeed, between 1840 and 1860 a total of only 362 white settlers and 426 Native Americans died in all the recorded battles between the two groups along wagon train routes. There is only *one* documented attack by Native Americans on a wagon train in which there were two dozen casualties for the white settlers. Most of the legendary accounts of massacres of whites by "wild Indians" are fiction or greatly exaggerated accounts of minor encounters. Many white Americans, it would seem, need such incredible exaggerations to rationalize the theft of aboriginal lands and the near extermination of many native peoples.[20]

Unruh's research also highlights the cooperation between Native Americans and settlers. Native Americans provided food and horses for travellers. Some served as guides. Moreover, Unruh and other historians make clear the crucial role of the federal government and of federal troops in "pacifying" the native tribes. By the 1850s an army of federal agents was assisting migrants westward, from the famous Indian agents to surveyors, road builders, and treaty agents.

There was a recurring pattern to the growing conflict between whites and natives. Settlers would settle down on native lands to farm. Land for the resettlement of the Native American group affected would be provided by the federal government under the auspices of a treaty involving threat or coercion. More settlers, prospectors, and hunters moving along migratory paths from the East would gradually intrude on these tribal lands. The land theft would then be legitimated by yet another treaty, and the process might begin again. Or perhaps a treaty promise of supplies or money to those living in their restricted area would not be kept, and some Native American men would leave their area seeking food or revenge.

Such actions resulted in the Army taking repressive action, sometimes intentionally punishing an innocent group and thus precipitating further uprisings.

The legal process involved the making of treaties by the president and ratification by the Senate. The treaties, part of United States law, were often masterpieces of fraud: consent was gained by deception or threat. Three hundred treaties with Native American tribes were made between 1790 and the Civil War. As time passed, treaties established regulations governing tribal behavior and provided restricted areas called "reservations." Tribes became dependent on the federal Bureau of Indian Affairs and on Congress, which by the time of the Civil War could change treaties without the consent of Native Americans. This treaty process was abandoned by 1871.[21]

Massacres of Native Americans

Treaty violations led to conflict. For example, in an 1862 uprising in Minnesota the eastern Sioux massacred settlers after losing much of their land and suffering at the hands of white "Indian agents." Delays in payment of promised supplies resulted in warriors burning and killing throughout the Minnesota Valley; massive white retaliation followed. About the same time conflict occurred in Colorado between local tribes and the militia left in charge when the Army had been withdrawn to fight in the Civil War. The guerrilla warfare of the tribes was met by savage retaliation. In 1864 Colonel John Chivington, a minister, and his Colorado volunteers massacred nearly two hundred Native Americans in a peace-seeking band at Sand Creek.[22] The massacre was one of the most savage in the annals of western history. Meyer's summary is brutally graphic: "Children carrying white flags were slaughtered and pregnant women were cut open. The slaughter and mutilation continued into the late afternoon over many miles of the bleak prairie."[23]

After the Civil War the extension of railroads gobbled up millions of acres. The buffalo were slaughtered by the millions, and the economy of the Plains tribes was destroyed. In the late 1860s a federal Peace Commission met with numerous tribes at Medicine Lodge Creek in Kansas. Reservations were worked out for all the Plains tribes. But there would still be two decades of battles before all the bands would agree to settle on reservations designated by the government.[24]

Settlers, miners, and the Army violated treaties with the Sioux and moved into the Dakota Territory. Controversy over the invasion escalated; troops were sent in to force Sioux bands onto a smaller reservation, even though the bands were already on what the government regarded as "unceded Indian territory." In this force was Colonel George A. Custer. In 1876, the most widely known battle of the Plains struggle occurred at Little Big Horn, when an arrogant Custer and the soldiers under his command were wiped out by a group of Sioux and allied tribes which had refused to settle on the reservation.

Fourteen years later, one of the last engagements was the massacre at Wounded Knee Creek. Attempting to round up the last few Sioux bands, the Army intercepted one group near the Dakota Badlands and forced them to camp. The colonel in command ordered a disarming of the camp, which was carried out in ruthless fashion. One young Sioux shot into a line of soldiers; the troops replied by shooting at close range with rifles and machine guns. Perhaps three hundred Native Americans were killed on the spot and while running from the camp by bloodthirsty soldiers running amok.[25]

In the Southwest, Native American resistance was substantial. Even after the United States took over the region by military conquest in the 1840s, slave raids on the Navaho by New Mexican settlers continued for a decade or two. Military expeditions were conducted in the Southwest against the scattered Navaho and Apache communities in an attempt to hem them in. Colonel Kit Carson succeeded in getting the Mescalero Apaches to agree to reside on a reservation. Establishing headquarters in Navaho territory, Carson began a "scorched earth" program, destroying fields and herds. Carson herded his captives three hundred miles to a small reservation, the famous "Long Walk" central to Navaho history. By 1890 virtually all the remnants of Native American tribes had been forced onto reservations.[26]

Toward the end of the nineteenth century native groups outside the (eventually) contiguous forty-eight states also came under white American control. Native Hawaiians, previously subordinated by European plantation owners seeking cheap labor, came under United States jurisdiction with the acquisition of Hawaii in 1898. The purchase of Alaska in 1867 led to thousands of Eskimo, Athabascan, and Aleut peoples being brought under the control of the United States. Many of the same problems, such as new diseases and genocidal forays by settlers and miners, had a substantial impact on them as well.

STEREOTYPING NATIVE AMERICANS

Stereotypes of Native Americans developed between the 1500s and the 1800s; stereotypes played a role in rationalizing enslavement and land theft. One early myth, a mixture of positive appreciation and prejudice, was that of the primitive "child of nature" or "noble savage." French philosophers such as Montaigne and Rousseau had read of European contacts with the "primitives" and utilized scanty data to argue for a golden age of human existence where there was only the unsophisticated "primitive" unspoiled by European civilization. The "child of nature" image, with its emphasis on *child* as well as *nature*, played an important role in the expectations of missionaries who saw their task as bringing Christianity to the "Primitives."[27]

European settlers were shocked by the unwillingness of the indigenous residents to submit to the "civilizing" pressures of missionaries and farmers seeking land. Fierce resistance reinforced new stereotypes of the "cruel savage." The "bloodthirsty savage" image became common after the first battles with Native Americans resisting encroachment on their lands. By the mid-1600s Europeans in New England and Virginia were writing that the Native Americans were wild beasts who should be hunted down like other savage animals. Puritan leaders such as Cotton Mather saw them as agents of the Devil.[28]

Settlers moving westward parroted these negative views. It was the era of westward expansion that imprinted on the public mind the image of a "savage race" attacking helpless settlers, in "dime novels" and later in movies and TV programs. Yet the savagery of the settlers has seldom been accented in the mass media. Carlson and Coburn have wondered aloud about the staggering number of Native Americans killed in the mass media: "The Indian, who had been all but eliminated with real bullets, now had to be resurrected to be killed off again with printer's ink."[29] The distorted image of Native Americans as savages standing in the way of civilization can be found in many textbooks which are still being used in U.S. schools.

Biased Euro-American accounts partly explain the exaggerated generalization that all Native Americans were savages. However, one must not err and romanticize the practices of Native American societies. There was brutality manifest in the customs of some tribes, particularly in the treatment of prisoners captured by warlike tribes. A proper evaluation of this "savagery" requires an evaluation also of the practices of European settlers. The fate of Native Americans who were massacred or forced onto reservations suggests that brutality was part and parcel of European "civilization." The example of scalping, whose expansion was a result of European actions, suggests how stereotypes can be turned upside down. Native Americans—who, it must be remembered, were fighting in defense of their ancient territory—were certainly no more savage than their European judges.[30]

Another erroneous but persisting image is that of the "primitive hunter" who made little use of the land. In fact, most tribes who were forced off lands or killed off were *not* composed of nomadic hunters but of part-time or full-time farmers. Tribes such as the Cherokee had by the removal period of the 1830s developed their own mills and other enterprises. Alexis de Tocqueville, that acute French observer of American life in the 1830s, accepted the myth, noting in his writings that it would be difficult to "civilize" the "Indians" without settling them down as agriculturalists. There is hypocrisy in European American theories about the right to use undeveloped land, for only in the case of European expansion into Indian lands was the principle of seizure of unused private property enunciated.[31]

Another stereotype prevalent since the nineteenth century has been that of low intelligence. As early as the 1830s Dr. Samuel G. Morton argued that Native Americans were anatomically savage. In his 1931 book, *Race Psychology*, Thomas R. Garth argued for the intellectual inferiority of Native Americans, basing his conclusions on the fact that they achieved the lowest average scores of any minority group on the omnipresent IQ test of the time. Racial inferiority theories have been aimed at Native Americans, who were increasingly defined after 1850 as a "racial group."[32]

A number of studies of elementary, high school, and college social-science textbooks have found stereotypes about Native Americans. Most school texts have dealt briefly with the Native American, with a few references to Pilgrim or pioneer days and occasional use of derogatory terms such as *squaw* and *buck*. Recent studies of the mass media have pointed up grossly exaggerated images. One study of cartoons in the once widely read *Saturday Evening Post* found that virtually every Native American had feathers in his or her hair; one-third of the cartoons showed Native Americans with bows and arrows. No modern-day Native Americans were to be found in the thousands of cartoons surveyed in this study. The "Indian warrior" remains a common mass media image.[33]

Opinion poll studies of white attitudes have been rare. One study in the 1970s found that white views of Native Americans mixed romantic stereotypes with traditional negative stereotypes. The study updated earlier studies by Bogardus, who studied the social-distance attitudes directed at Native Americans. White college students were asked how close, on a scale from 1 ("would marry") to 7 ("would not allow them in nation"), they would allow a given racial or ethnic group to themselves. Among two dozen groups, Native Americans ranked fairly low in negative attitudes in Bogardus's 1926, 1946, and 1956 studies. These white students rejected all close contacts (such as friendships) with Indians. A recent study using the same attitude scale found Native Americans still being rejected by white respondents in regard to primary-group relations, such as intermarriage and club membership.[34]

POLITICS

European communities at first dealt with Native Americans as independent nations; with growing strength came a shift in policy, so that tribes were treated as groups to be exterminated or as dependent wards. By the 1830s the eastern tribes were weak enough for the government to force them to move westward. About the same time, the Bureau of Indian Affairs (BIA) was established to coordinate federal relations with tribes, from supervision of reservations and land dealings to provision of much-needed supplies. Until the end of battles in 1880s the position of the BIA was strange, since its attempts to protect Native Americans were in conflict with the military policy of extermination.

Chiefs were set aside and replaced by Courts of Indian Offenses. Tribal religions were suppressed, and Christian missionaries were imported by the carload. BIA rations were usually provided to those who remained on reservations, while troops chased those who did not. Limited attempts were made to educate Native Americans to European ways in health and agriculture. With the termination of treaty making in 1871 and the reduction of all major groups to reservations by the 1890s, Native Americans entered into a unique relationship with white America. Here was the only subordinate group whose life was to be administered by a bureaucratic arm of the federal government.[35]

From the Dawes Act to the New Deal

A major policy shift in regard to land took place in the late nineteenth century. Native Americans, liberal reformers argued, should be taught new rules of land use. The Dawes Act of 1887 provided that reservation lands would be divided up among individual families. The European tradition of private ownership and individual development of land, for many Native American groups an alien value system, was dropped like a bomb from the sky. The hope was that small individual allotments (40 to 160 acres) would convert Native Americans into farm entrepreneurs. Unallotted lands left over could then be sold to white outsiders. The upshot of this new government policy was large-scale land sale to white Americans; through means fair and foul the remaining 140 million acres of Native American lands were further reduced to 50 million acres by the mid-1930s.[36]

In 1884 a Native American named John Elk went to the city (Omaha, Nebraska), adapted to the white ways, and attempted to vote. Denied this right, Elk took his case to a federal court where he argued that the Fourteenth Amendment made him a citizen and that the Fifteenth Amendment guaranteed his right to vote.[37] The court ruled he was not an American citizen—that he was in effect a citizen of a *foreign* nation and thus not entitled to vote. Under the land allotment approach of the 1887 Dawes Act, the "wards" of the government could become citizens if they showed themselves competent in managing their individual land allotments. Some Native Americans were issued "certificates of competency" by special "competency commissions" which decided if they could function well in the white world. In 1924 Congress finally passed the Indian Citizenship Act, granting citizenship, including voting rights, to all Native Americans. Native Americans were kept subordinate for an extraordinarily long period.

The U.S. Supreme Court continued to hold that Native Americans were wards of the federal government, a status not changed by the Citizenship Act. As a result, many state governments refused to provide services or allow Native Americans to vote. On the other hand, the federal government on occasion tried to break off its services on the ground that Native Americans were officially citizens. They were caught in a political "no man's land."[38]

It was not until the New Deal that major changes were made in federal policy. The new policy was imbedded in what was viewed as reform legislation—the 1934 Indian Reorganization Act. Native American groups were to vote on whether or not they wanted to come under the act, which ended the land allotment process and sale of lands without careful supervision. Provisions were made for federal credit, for economic development, and for preferential hiring in the BIA. The changes seemed progressive. Very important was the new provision for tribal governments somewhat independent of the federal government. Here was some recognition of the principle of self-government. As a result, many Native American groups incorporated themselves; many developed a central council, with constitutions reflecting the values of white culture. Others operated under traditional customs. Gradually, numerous tribes began some self-government, managing their own property, raising their own tax revenues, and governing their own affairs under federal supervision.[39]

Yet the New Deal policy had negative features. Oklahoma tribes were excluded; the Papago tribe lost control of its mineral resources; and great power was put in the hands of the Secretary of the Interior, who became what some called the "dictator of the Indians." The secretary made rules for elections, could veto constitutions, supervised expenditures, and made the regulations for land management on the reservations. As progressive as the law appeared, it ignored many problems, and, basically, the ward relationship to the government was maintained.[40]

Fluctuations in Federal Policies

In the 1950s another shift in policy toward Native Americans could be seen in House Concurrent Resolution 108, which called for the *termination* of federal supervision of Native American groups. The intent of the resolution was to reject the 1934 Indian Reorganization Act and return to the policy of forced conformity to individualistic values of land use. Coupled with the termination resolution was Public Law 280, which gave certain states the right to overturn or to replace reservation laws and customs with state laws. Supporters of "termination" included land-hungry whites outside reservations and members of Congress seeking to cut government costs, as well as some tribal members no longer on reservations. Between 1954 and 1960 several dozen groups were "terminated"; they were no longer under federal guardianship. Because of the resulting negative effects, including the problems of dealing with often unfriendly local officials and white land entrepreneurs, termination came to be viewed as a failure. In the famous case of the Menominee tribe, which became a new political unit under state law, per capita payments exhausted their joint funds and thus their development capital, their hospital had to be closed because it did not meet state standards, and their power plants were sold to an outside company. The termination process has been costly for many such tribes unprepared to deal with the complexity and treachery of the outside white world.[41] In effect, BIA control was the lesser of two evils.

From the 1960s to the 1980s federal policy began to move away from termination. President Nixon sent a message to Congress calling for maintenance of the tie of Native Americans to the federal government and for no termination without consent. Some of Nixon's specific proposals were soon legislated by Congress and put into effect, including the restoration of Blue Lake to the Taos Pueblo and the passage of an Indian Financing Act making credit available for business purposes. Congress passed an act settling certain land claims of Alaskan natives; and Congress passed self-determination legislation in 1974, establishing a procedure for tribes to take over some of the administration of certain federal programs existing on reservations. In the late 1970s some Native American groups began to run their own schools and social-service programs.[42]

The most important government bureaucracy has been the Bureau of Indian Affairs. The BIA defines who is a Native American. The BIA has kept records of "blood" lines in order to determine who is an "Indian" eligible for benefits. The BIA still supervises tribal government, banking, utilities, and highways, as well as millions of dollars in tribal trust funds. The Bureau still supervises leasing and selling of lands. And until quite recently, all control of social services, including education, was strictly in the hands of the BIA or allied federal agencies. Not surprisingly, the reservations have been viewed as colonies under the near-totalitarian rule of a complex outside bureaucracy.

By the 1980s there were in effect nearly 400 treaties and other governmental agreements, 5,000 federal statutes, 2,000 federal court decisions, 500 attorney general's decisions, and 30 volumes of BIA regulations covering federal relations to Native Americans. A large bureaucracy sits on top of a complex system of regulations.[43]

Today the BIA is regarded by many Native Americans as the lesser of two evils. To some extent, it has protected them against predatory exploitation from the outside. To terminate the BIA would be to terminate what protection now exists. Outside interests would have one less barrier. Even the Interior Department's other major branches have opposed the interests of Native Americans because of pressure from private ranching, lumbering, farming, and mineral interests. For example, the Bureau of Commercial Fisheries opposed Native American fishing rights in the Northwest. By the 1970s, the BIA, with growing numbers of representative Native American administrators, had begun to provide significant protection from whites, coupled with the greatly expanded self-determination and community control.[44]

Growing Pressures for Political Participation

Most Native American political participation has been limited to reservation elections and service in tribal governments. With some exceptions reservations have been exempt from outside state control and taxation, and tribes have made their own laws and regulations, subject to BIA approval. Tribal governments have often combined legislative and executive functions in one elected tribal council. Voter turnout for tribal elections has been substantial; one study of voting in forty-nine tribes for the years 1958 to 1960 found half the eligible voters voting.[45] Still, numerous tribal governments have been under the thumb of federal authorities.

To what extent have native Americans participated in electoral politics outside the reservation? It was not until the 1924 Indian Citizenship Act that Native Americans got the right to vote in elections outside the reservation. Even this right required protest for its implementation in states such as Utah, Arizona, and New Mexico, where reservation Indians were barred from voting until the 1940s; and as late as the 1960s and 1970s some states made voting and jury participation difficult. Subtle mechanisms of direct and indirect discrimination, such as state literacy tests and the gerrymandering of district lines, have reduced the voting power of Native Americans in western states. Voter participation has been low in many areas. One study found only 40 percent of Native Americans of voting age registered, and only 17 percent voting in that year. By the 1960s and 1970s these figures were rising to substantial proportions in some areas. Leaders were talking about the Native American vote as a "swing vote" (a bloc that can throw close elections one way or another) and calling for increased voting.[46]

Because of increased voter turnout, Native Americans from predominantly Navaho counties in New Mexico were elected to the legislature there for the first time in 1964; attempts to bar them from the legislature failed. In the mid-1960s the first Native American was elected to the state legislature in Arizona. By 1967 there were an estimated fifteen Native Americans serving in legislatures in six western states. At least a dozen others were elected to local positions. This trend continued into the 1970s and 1980s.[47]

While trends in western states suggest signs of modest change in representation, a broad reading of the situation in the first decades of the twentieth century suggests that the oldest Americans have had little access to American politics. Only a handful have served in state and federal legislatures, most of these since the 1950s. Two dozen have served in state legislatures since 1900. Very few have served in Congress—perhaps a half-dozen representatives and two senators with some, often modest, Native American ancestry. The most famous, Charles Curtis, was born on the Kaw reservation in 1860. One-eighth Native American, Curtis was a representative for fourteen years, a senator for twenty, and vice-president under President Herbert Hoover. Since that time, there has seldom been more than one Indian representative at any one time.[48]

The lack of representation in state legislatures and Congress is paralleled in town and city governments. In the 1950s and 1960s tens of thousands of Native Americans were encouraged to leave reservations for the greener employment pastures of the cities, so that by 1980 about half of all Native Americans were living in metropolitan areas. Native Americans have suffered at the hands of urban whites; towns near reservations and areas of larger cities to which migrants have traditionally gone have frequently been strongholds of prejudice and discrimination. Nonetheless, by the 1970s and 1980s, in some of these local areas Native Americans were elected to city councils, school boards, and county governments. For example, in the early 1970s there were 631 Native Americans serving on school boards in 232 districts; many of these districts were predominantly Native American. Progress in electing other city and county officials has been less dramatic.[49]

The extent of representation seems to vary by state and area. For example, a recent report of the South Dakota Advisory Committee to the U.S. Commission on Civil Rights reported that few Native Americans have ever served as elected officials in that state, even though 5 percent of the population is Native American. In 1981 only one Native American was serving in that state legislature. Very few had ever served there. Moreover, only one was mayor of a city, and a very small number were serving on school boards, even where there was a large Native American population.

Much research on Native Americans has focused on deviance, particularly on alcohol-related offenses. These problems are serious and reflect to a substantial degree the critical employment crisis migrants face in cities. Moreover, a few studies on the role of government in the lives of Native Americans in urban areas have focused on the police system. One study done in Minneapolis and St. Paul found that Native Americans were underrepresented as employees in city government, including the criminal justice system, but heavily overrepresented among those arrested. A disproportionately small percentage of the Minneapolis police force was Native American. Recent complaints by Native American leaders in numerous cities centered on the lack of efforts to recruit Native Americans as police and parole officers and government attorneys, as well as discriminatory treatment and unnecessarily high arrest rates. [50]

PROTEST AND CONFLICT

Native American protest against subordination has doubtlessly been the most sustained of any group in the history of North America. Violent resistance between 1500 and 1900 produced some of the greatest protest leaders the continent has seen.[51]

Yet the end of this period did not end protest, although the character of protest changed. By the late nineteenth century a number of protest organizations had sprung up. One of the most important was the Indian Rights Association, founded by Quakers concerned with protecting and "civilizing" Native Americans. By exposing the corruption and oppression on reservations, such early groups laid the basis for reforms in policy. One of the first organizations formed by Native Americans was the Society of American Indians, created in the early 1900s. A major pan-Indian organization (drawing together representatives of different tribes), it was self-help-oriented; a goal was to develop pride and a national leadership and to work for improved educational and job opportunities. In the decades which followed, the organization did reach the important goals of developing a pan-Indian alliance and grooming a new leadership which pressed for citizenship legislation and argued for tribal self-determination.[52]

In the 1920s a prominent white defender of Native Americans, John Collier, organized the militant American Indian Defense Association to fight the attempts by Republican officials to establish "executive order reservations," not covered by treaty and accessible to greedy whites who wished to extract minerals. The National Congress of American Indians (NCAI) was formed in the 1940s and pressed for education, legal aid, and legislation. An influential organization, the NCAI worked vigorously against the termination policy of the 1950s and 1960s and for the War on Poverty policy of the 1960s and the self-determination policy of the 1970s and 1980s. In 1961 the National Indian Youth Council was created. It has fought vigorously for the civil rights of Native Americans, has organized civil disobedience, and has developed a "Red Power" ideology. The Youth Council has been active in education and has taken up causes critical to the protection of Native American lands. For example, one newsletter of the organization urged all to fight the development of coal-gasification plants on the Navaho reservation.[53]

Since the 1960s a number of protest actions and civil disobedience movements have been organized. One analysis of protest activities between 1961 and 1970 found 194 instances reported. Of these, 141 fell into the category of "facilitative tactics," such things as legal suits and formal complaints. This type of activity continues a long tradition of trying to seduce or coax established institutions into making concessions, the great strength of organizations like the National Congress of American Indians. The other 53 involved civil disobedience, such things as delaying dam construction, occupying offices or other government facilities, picketing, and sit-ins. Over the last few decades there has been significant increase in the number of protest actions, many of which have brought changes.[54]

In one widely publicized action, students began a long occupation of California's Alcatraz Island late in 1969; they were replaced later by one hundred Native Americans claiming *unused* federal lands under provisions of an old treaty. Their intent was symbolic and concrete—to dramatize the plight of Native Americans and to establish a facility there where Native Americans could preserve tribal ways. Government agents forcibly removed the occupying group in the summer of 1971. In the same period a number of other attempts were made to seize other unused federal property, including Ellis Island in New York Harbor, and BIA offices across the country were occupied in protest against BIA policies.[55]

In the midwest the Alexian Brothers' novitiate building was occupied by armed Menominees in 1975. A year earlier an even larger-scale occupation and siege took place under the auspices of the American Indian Movement (AIM), a group organized to deal with problems ranging from police brutality to housing and employment. An Indian Patrol was established to supervise contacts between Native Americans and the police and was reportedly successful in improving police behavior. The movement spread until there were more than a dozen groups in cities and on reservations. Some leaders and several hundred members played an important role in the occupation and seige of Wounded Knee on the Pine Ridge reservation in the spring of 1973. Reform-minded leaders were upset with the white-dominated tribal government and began an armed occupation of Wounded Knee in an attempt to correct the situation. Federal agents were sent in. Members of U.S. Army units occupied the reservation in civilian disguise, an illegal operation since there was no congressional authorization for it.

There was an armed struggle which ended after a seventy-one-day siege. In its attempt to convict AIM leaders the federal government, with President Nixon's encouragement, used illegal wiretaps, altered evidence, and paid witnesses—which led to dismissal of the case against the AIM leaders by a federal judge. Afterward, some government agents apparently participated in a campaign to destroy the movement, probably including a dozen suspicious murders and accidents involving AIM members. Two hundred AIM members were harassed and arrested, but only a dozen or so were ever convicted. Here was a not-so-nonviolent confrontation between militant Native Americans and the Indian Establishment propped up by white officials.[56]

Fishing Rights and Land Claims

At the heart of conflict between Native Americans and whites have been issues of law enforcement, fishing rights, and land claims. Law enforcement has been an issue across the country, but it is particularly important in the Midwest, as the AIM movement demonstrates. Fishing rights have been a source of conflict on the West Coast. In the State of Washington, Native American nations have struggled with whites for a century over fishing rights. There have been shootings and court battles over tribal rights to catch fish, particularly salmon and trout—rights guaranteed by treaties between the nations and the federal government more than a century ago. White anglers and commercial fishing companies object to Native Americans exercising their ancient treaty rights because this reduces white fishing opportunities significantly. In a major court decision, *U.S. vs. State of Washington* (1974), the judge ruled that the treaties did indeed reserve fishing rights for Native Americans that are different from those allowed whites. The court ordered the State of Washington to protect Native American fish catchers and recognized the tribal right to manage fishing resources.[57]

The court's decision was openly defied by white fish catchers, who protested that the decision discriminated against them. The federal government became heavily involved, spending millions of dollars to increase the fish available in the area and to compensate whites who suffered economic hardship. Knocking down a white legal challenge, a 1979 U.S. Supreme Court decision upheld the lower court ruling. Government enforcement has gradually reduced illegal fishing by whites. Slowly the government moved to uphold ancient treaties.

In the last decade or two a major controversy has grown up over land claims by eastern tribes. A recent report by the U.S. Commission on Civil Rights underlined the root cause of the land claims conflict:

> The basic Eastern Indian land claim is that Indian land in the East was invalidly transferred from Indians to non-Indians in the 18th and 19th centuries because the Federal Government, although required to do so, did not supervise or approve the transactions.[58]

The historical record is one of the taking of Native American land without adequate compensation and in violation of laws which require the federal government to supervise transfer of land. Native American groups, such as the Oneida in New York and the Passamaquoddy in Maine, have gone to court to press land claims. A number of these cases have been won by tribal members, restoring some lands illegally taken.

The land claims have caused whites to become alarmed. Thus a Maine congressperson said that one court suit "threatens to bring the State of Maine to its knees. . . . Already there is a revolt beginning among the non-Indian citizens." A *Time* magazine essay entitled "Should We Give the U.S. Back to the Indians?" took a hostile view and argued that court decisions awarding land to Indians would mean "the unthinkable unraveling of society." Bills have been introduced in Congress to extinguish the land claims. The federal government, including President Jimmy Carter, became heavily involved in working out a settlement in the Maine case. An agreement providing for the acquisition of 300,000 acres of land (to be held in trust for Indians by the federal government) plus a $27 million trust fund was signed by President Jimmy Carter in 1980. A number of other land claims have also been settled in recent years, often involving the return of lands to Native American tribes.[59]

Because of Native American land claims, fishing claims, and other militant protest, a white backlash developed, even including the creation of a national organization called the Interstate Congress for Equal Rights and Responsibilities. In the late 1970s Senator Mark Hatfield of Oregon publicly noted that "We have found a very significant backlash that by any other name comes out as racism in all its ugly manifestations." Members of Congress, supporting the backlash, introduced bills to break the treaties, to overturn court decisions, and to exterminate Indian land claims. These whites argued that the excessive demands by Native Americans had soured the longtime "friendly relations" with whites. Yet Native Americans argued that they were seeking what was legally theirs and that they were not seeking special privileges. Whites were hostile because living up to U.S. law was becoming costly in terms of dollars and property. And whites were also hostile, as one tribal leader noted, because of ignorance, "because of the lack of educational systems to teach anything about Indians, about treaties." White stereotypes about Indians and ignorance of treaties have played a critical role in recent struggles over social justice.[60]

Since the 1960s Native Americans have won a number of other legal battles over tribal law and jurisdiction. For example, in a 1959 case, *Williams v. Lee*, the U.S. Supreme Court ruled that a non-Indian doing business on a reservation was subject to tribal law and courts. In a 1973 case the Supreme Court invalidated an Arizona state tax which had been applied to reservation Indians. In addition the other branches of the federal government recognized some Native American rights in the 1970s and 1980s. The Menominee Tribe in Wisconsin was restored to tribal status in 1975 (it was legally terminated earlier). And in 1975 a distinguished federal commission, the American Indian Policy Review Commission, ruled that tribes are sovereign political bodies with power to enact and enforce their own laws and that a special trust relationship still exists between the tribes and the federal government.[61]

THE ECONOMY

Structural assimilation can involve upward movement into ever-higher levels of the economy. This movement has been modest for Native Americans. The colonialism model points up the way in which a group such as Native Americans can be incorporated in some fashion into the U.S. economy without getting on the escalator to ultimate equality. Prior to being forced onto reservations, most groups were self-sufficient; there was diversity, ranging from the Pueblo agriculturalists of the Southwest to a few hunting societies on the Plains to the many mixed agricultual-hunting societies across the continent. Many of the first contacts between white settlers and Native Americans led to agricultural exchange; early settlers learned from Native Americans how to cultivate a variety of crops.

Land was the basis of the Native American economies; yet by the

1880s the native tribes had lost millions of acres which once belonged to them. With the new policy of breaking up the remaining lands under the 1887 Dawes Act came the loss of millions more. Native American lands were frequently reduced to those which had the least appeal to white entrepreneurs. Many reservations have faced problems such as poor natural resources, utilities, roads, and transportation facilities. They have an unskilled work force. Those that retained important natural resources have typically not had the trained workers or capital to make use of them. Explaining this situation, numerous white observers have accented cultural isolation, language problems, the propensity for drunkenness, and unwillingness to live by the time clock. Indeed, the explicit rationale for the 1887 individual land allotment policy was to move Native Americans away from the allegedly negative influence of traditional Indian culture.[62]

Yet such cultural explanations of land use are insufficient. Native Americans have not been in isolation. Beginning with the first conquests and continuing to the present, all tribes have become linked to the larger economy in a subordinated position. With the growth of industrial capitalism and urbanization in the late nineteenth century came waves of economic exploitation.

The encroachment on Indian lands by lumbering, ranching, farming, and railroad interest redirected resources from rural Native American lands to growing urban centers. Killing off the bison and other game for skins for people in Eastern cities and the taking of lands by white ranchers for cattle raising and by farmers for raising crops hastened the impoverishment of Native Americans in the West. Rural poverty increased as corporations reached out from metropolitan centers to exploit more and more land; this in turn put pressure on many to migrate to cities. Jorgensen argues that the poverty of rural Native Americans is "not due to rural isolation nor a tenacious hold on aboriginal ways, but results from the way in which United States' urban centers of finance, political influence, and power have grown at the expense of rural areas."[63] This was true in the nineteenth century and has continued to be true in the twentieth century.

Poverty and Land Theft

The poverty of reservation life has come from the destruction of tribal economies, the constant encroachments on remaining lands, and the mismanagement and corruption of BIA officials. Testifying before a congressional committee on events in the winter of 1883, one member of the Assiniboine tribe made the point that tribal members were healthy until the buffalo were killed off, and that the substitute BIA rations were not adequate:

> They gave us rations once a week, just enough to last one day, and the Indians they started to eat their pet dogs. After they ate all their dogs up they started to eat their ponies. All this time the Indian Bureau had a warehouse full of grub.

He went on to describe the result:

> Early that spring, in 1884, I saw the dead bodies of the Indians wrapped in blankets and piled up like cordwood in the village of Wolf Point, and the other Indians were so weak they could not bury their dead; what were left were nothing but skeletons.[64]

By the 1880s many government agents, who were officially responsible for supplies, instruction in farming, and supervision of lands, were notorious for their corruption and incompetence. Many had gone into this work with the desire to make their own fortunes at the expense of those for whom they were responsible. "Agency towns" were growing up on reservations—towns that developed a stratified system in which there was little equitable contact between Native Americans and paternalistic white officials. After the 1890s attempts were made by the BIA to expand farming on some reservations. Yet white officials usually built paternalistic systems in which Native Americans had little part other than that of unskilled laborers or small farmers.[65]

The reorganization policy of the 1930s, which provided for tribal governments, put a partial brake on outright corruption and blatant land theft, but economic problems persisted. Federal policy fluctuated between tribal self-determination and forced individualism. Termination experiments have thrown some tribes to the "outside wolves." Lands have been sold to pay taxes, and tribes have fallen deeper into poverty as resources have been further depleted.

Native American lands have been taken for dams, reservoir projects, national parks, and right-of-ways for roads. The sale of lands to private lumbering and mineral interests—200,000 acres in the year 1970—continues. Attempts by tribes to control the use of their lands have led ranchers and other white interests to argue that self-government by Native Americans is an unreasonable threat to "rational" development. What substantial money is made in agriculture or ranching on reservations has frequently flowed to the whites who lease the lands. Large proportions of the usable land on reservations have been leased to whites.[66] By the late 1960s the gross income from agricultural activities on reservations was $300 million a year, but Native Americans received only a third of that; whites earned the majority. Facing discrimination, and with limited technical schooling, little available technical assistance, and little capital to buy seeds, livestock, or machinery, the Native American farmer is faced with suffering a low yield or else leasing to outsiders.[67]

Land, Minerals, and Federal Policy

In recent decades the federal government has taken some action to deal with the economic problems of reservations. War on Poverty programs came to the reservations in the 1960s, bringing some job and training benefits, mostly temporary. A major BIA strategy has been the urban relocation and employment assistance program. Thousands of Native Americans have moved to cities.[68] Studies have found that urbanites earn more than those on reservations but are dissatisfied with urban life. One-half to three-quarters of urban relocatees return to the reservation areas after a few years. Lack of economic success seems to be the major reason. Studies of the relatively high urban arrest rates have shown a relationship between the negative economic experiences of migrants, such as low wages and unemployment, and arrest rates. A basic problem is that Native Americans in cities continue to face poverty and discrimination; they find themselves in residential ghettos and in low-wage, dead-end jobs.[69]

Government attempts to attract industrial plants to reservations were ineffective in the early 1960s but improved with the tighter labor market of the late 1960s and 1970s. Where there were only three such factories in 1959, by 1968 there were 110, and by 1972 there were 200. Yet many jobs (often half) in the plants built on or near reservations went to workers other than Native Americans. In effect, these government funds have expanded corporate profits, with only modest gains for tribal members. The BIA has also encouraged "cottage industries," the revival of Native American arts and crafts; this revival has helped improve the financial situation on some reservations, although it does not integrate workers into the economic mainstream.[70]

In the last decade or so a major issue for reservation Indians has been the development of coal, oil and other mineral resources. Recent investigations have found that tribes have not received the correct amount of royalties from the energy companies which leased their lands. Not surprisingly, then, three dozen tribes made national headlines in the 1970s when they announced the creation of the Council of Energy Resources Tribes (CERT) and hired a former Iranian oil minister to help them get better contracts with white-owned companies. Many whites worried that tribes were going to behave like OPEC and seek to be completely independent in making contracts with energy corporations. CERT was created because tribal leaders felt they were being cheated by energy companies and by the federal government. CERT researchers estimated that Native American lands included nearly one-third of the coal available for strip mining in the West and one-half of the uranium outside public lands.[71]

As a result, the federal Department of Energy has tried to co-opt CERT by providing several million dollars in grants. CERT has used the money to secure technical assistance and to develop proposals to industrialize reservations using royalties from resource development. CERT has also provided technical assistance to various tribes and has worked to increase engineering and other technical skills among Native American youths. Yet the close ties between CERT and the federal government have led to internal conflict. Several tribes pulled out of CERT because of its stand for extensive uranium mining on Indian lands. Indian activists in groups such as the American Indian Movement (AIM) have criticized expanded mining on the traditional lands as a "destruction of Mother Earth." Many Indians fear that such new economic coalitions as CERT have adopted white ways of unthinking resource exploitation and environmental destruction. The how, where, and why questions about resource development and the issues of "raping nature" and curing unemployment with resource development will pit Native Americans against whites, and Native Americans against Native Americans, in the future.[72]

Persisting Economic Problems

Over the last few decades, just how poor have Native Americans been? How much upward mobility has there been? The urban economy has been viewed as divided into two major sectors, a core (or primary) labor market and a peripheral (or secondary) labor market. The primary labor market has been composed predominantly of white workers and has been characterized by skilled jobs, high stability, high wages, highly profitable companies, and significant mobility. The secondary labor market, on the other hand, has been composed predominantly of nonwhite workers and of white workers who have recently immigrated and has been characterized by instability, low wages, less profitable companies, and little job mobility. Typically, the secondary labor market involves unskilled, semiskilled, and service-type low-wage jobs.

Native Americans have been disproportionately concentrated in the secondary labor market. Seasonal employment and high unemployment rates demonstrate this. In 1940 one-third of all Native American males were unemployed, a figure far higher than that for white males. By 1960 the rate was even higher, 38 percent, compared to 5 percent for all males. This reflected, in part, the move to urban areas, out of agriculture. By 1970 the rate had gone down to 12 percent for males, still three times the national figure. In 1980 the unemployment rate was more than double that of whites. These recent rates, one should note, do not include the large proportion of Native American workers who have given up looking for work. Rates for Native American women have also been high. Up to the present, Native Americans find themselves facing perhaps the longest "Great Depression" of any racial or ethnic group in the United States.[73]

Compare Census data on occupational distribution for the decades since 1940:[74]

	NATIVE AMERICAN MEN			NATIVE AMERICAN WOMEN	
	1940	1960	1970	1960	1970
Professional, technical	2.2%	4.9%	9.2%	9.1%	11.1%
Managerial, administrative	1.4	2.8	5.0	2.0	2.3
Clerical, sales	2.0	4.9	8.0	17.8	29.1
Craft workers	5.7	15.5	22.1	1.2	2.1
Operatives	6.2	21.9	23.9	15.2	18.7
Nonfarm laborers	11.4	20.2	13.2	1.7	1.3
Farmers, farmworkers	68.4	23.5	8.0	10.5	2.3
Service workers	2.6	6.3	10.5	42.6	33.0
	99.9%	100.0%	99.9%	100.1%	99.9%

At all three dates, men and women were heavily concentrated at the lower occupational levels—those levels with substantially less income. In 1940 most men were poor farmers or unskilled workers. By 1960 the impact of the urban migration had become clear, with a drop in farm occupations. (Some of this drop may reflect problems in data collection.) In 1960 men and women were heavily concentrated in the unskilled and semiskilled categories. Between 1960 and 1970 there seems to be significant evidence of upward mobility for men and women, with substantially higher proportions at the white-collar levels for men and women and at the skilled blue-collar level for men.

Yet the conclusion of significant economic mobility should be a cautious one. First, there is the problem of the Census *omission* of large numbers of labor force dropouts who have given up looking for work, largely those on farms and the urban unskilled. Second, between 1960 and 1970 the Census definition of "Native American" changed, with more emphasis on self-designation in 1970, so the total number employed increased sharply in that decade; this probably means that more people with partial Native American ancestry opted for that designation, many of whom were already at higher occupational levels. Third, even in these understated data there is concentration at lower levels. For 1970 men and women are overrepresented at the level of unskilled workers, while they are very underrepresented at the higher white-collar levels. (The 1980 distribution of Native Americans by occupation will not be made available by the U.S. Census until the mid-1980s.)

For decades Native Americans on reservations have had perhaps the lowest incomes of any race or ethnic group. In 1939 Native American males on reservations had a median income of only $500, compared with $2,300 for all U.S. males. And that great imbalance was found for 1949, 1959, and 1970 as well. In 1970 the median income for Indian males was $2,749, compared with $6,614 for all U.S. males. The income level of Native American male earners was around one-quarter that of all males until 1970, when it surged to 42 percent, still under half of the national figure. The 1970 figure for Native American individuals in urban areas was better: $4,568, or about 69 percent of the national figure.

In 1970 the median income for Native American families was only $5,800, well below the median for all U.S. families. While one in ten among all U.S. families fell below the government poverty line in 1970, fully one-third of all Native American families were officially classified as poor, including nearly half of all those in rural areas. Native Americans in rural areas face the worst economic and housing situation of any race and ethnic group, although the situation of rural blacks is not greatly different. Native Americans face the worst housing conditions in the United States. In the early 1970s, 6 percent of those in urban areas and 29 percent of those in rural areas lived in severely crowded conditions; and 9 percent and 48 percent, respectively, had no toilet facilities. Two-thirds of those in rural areas had no plumbing in their houses. Death rates from accidents and illness remain high. Into the 1980s Native American health conditions are among the worst in the United States. Native Americans die, on the average, younger than any other group in the population—20 years younger for Navahos. On several reservations infant mortality rates are extremely high—comparable to rates in poor Third World nations. Inadequate medical care facilities, coupled with poor nutrition resulting from low incomes, constitute a major part of the problem. Cutbacks in federal government health programs in the 1980s, under the guidance of the Ronald Reagan Administration, have reduced access to medical care for Native Americans.[75]

EDUCATION

The formal educational experience of subordinated Native Americans began in the reservation period. Some influential whites were committed to the idea of education as the channel of forced acculturation. In the white-controlled school the "wild Indians" could be civilized. After the Civil War a number of government schools were provided.[76]

By 1887 the congressional appropriation for the education of Native Americans was $1.2 million, with 14,300 children enrolled in 227 schools, most of which were operated by the BIA or by religious groups with government financial aid. By the end of the nineteenth century some attempt was being made to provide higher-level vocational training, with the establishment of Haskell Institute (Kansas) and Carlisle Indian School (Pennsylvania).

By 1900 only a small percentage of Native American children were in any type of formal school; for most, schooling took place within tribal circles. In the Southwest perhaps one-quarter of the school-age children in the four decades after 1890 had some experience with boarding schools; a small percentage of the rest were in public schools. From the beginning the BIA and mission schools were run strictly; students were punished for speaking native languages, and an Anglo-conformity approach was taken to schooling.[77]

By the mid-1930s some boarding schools were replaced by day schools closer to home, and a bilingual educational policy was at least being discussed. Increasingly, public schools became the context for Native American education. In the 1930s the Johnson-O'Malley Act provided some federal aid for those states developing public schools for Native Americans. Yet after World War II large proportions of Native Americans were not in formal schools—including, for example, three-quarters of those in the largest tribe, the Navahos. From the 1960s to the 1980s aid to primary, adult, and vocational education expanded substantially. Pressure mounted from Native Americans for improvement.[78]

Renewed government attention was focused on schools. In many federal schools there was a development of advisory school boards composed of Native Americans. With the aid of War on Poverty funds, the first reservation community college opened on the Navaho reservation. By 1970 there were 141,000 Native American children recorded in public schools, with 52,000 in BIA schools and 11,000 in private schools. Less than half the BIA schools were now boarding schools. Federal aid was increasingly provided for local public schools with significant numbers of Native Americans. By 1980 several thousand Native American students were in college. Moreover, some BIA schools were being operated by new tribal corporations. The shift away from heavy dependence on Anglocentric boarding schools was the result of two factors: (1) parental pressures for schools closer to home, and (2) the movement of many Native Americans to the cities, where they used local public schools.[79]

Educational attainment levels have increased since the 1960s. The percentage of urban male Native Americans with fewer than nine years of schooling decreased from 46 percent in 1960 to 30 percent in 1970; for women this figure also went down. The rural figures were much higher, but they too were declining—from 66 to 50 percent for men and from 65 to 47 percent for women. In all cases these were well above national figures. The gap at the high-school level has persisted, even in the youngest groups. In 1970 two-thirds of the total U.S. male population aged 16 to 24 years had finished high school, compared to only half of young Native Americans in urban areas and 26 percent in rural areas. The pattern for young women was similar.[80]

Research studies document continuing problems. One 1960 study found that Native Americans had the lowest rate of school enrollment of any race or ethnic group. Several studies have found large proportions of Native American children with problems of low achievement scores, low grades or dropping out. In a study of dropouts on a Sioux reservation, Wax suggested the high rates were due to a "pushout" process whereby students were driven out of school because of white-oriented school regulations conflicting with the norms of their own Native American peer groups.[81]

For nearly a century now critical reports on the boarding schools have underscored the colonized position of Native Americans. Even in recent decades the remaining boarding schools have sometimes been described as oppressive environments. In most the facilities and staff have been inadequate, so that 100 children may find themselves under the care of one matron in a bleak dormitory with little in the way of recreational facilities. Children have been pressured not to speak their native language and not to practice native traditions. Children have even died from exposure attempting to run away from boarding schools. Here is an example of educational isolation unique in the annals of United States history.[82]

The issue of enforced acculturation goes beyond the boarding schools. Native American cultures have long been viewed as a major problem by public school administrators as well. Conventional explanations of educational problems have zeroed in on cultural differences, emphasizing that the distinctive (seen as inferior) values and patterns of thought and expression of Native Americans contrast with those of white Americans. Heavy pressure has been placed by teachers attempting to make their pupils "less Indian."[83] Little has been provided in school textbooks to make the child feel a link to his or her own culture. Most texts have devoted little attention to Native Americans or have reinforced the stereotypes of bloodthirsty savages and simple primitives.[84] As a result, those Native Americans who "succeeded" in public, BIA, and mission schools have sometimes lost touch with their roots.[85]

RELIGION

Pressures for acculturation have been clear in the case of religion. The Spanish conquerors brought Roman Catholic priests to reduce southwestern tribes to a mission-centered life. Later white settlers sometimes attempted to convert the "heathen Indian" to Christianity. Religion was a partner in the conquest process. Some Native Americans have said of the Christian missionaries that "when they arrived they had only the Book and we had the land; now we have the Book and they have the land."[86]

With the reservation period came a jockeying among Christian denominations for control; reservations were divided up so that Episcopalians got one, Methodists another, and Catholics yet another. "Home mission" efforts by a dozen denominations were developed. Religious boarding schools and missions were placed alongside BIA operations. For a number of reasons, including fear, many Native Americans became affiliated with some Christian denomination. Many denominations still have "mission" programs, sending white missionaries to serve on reservations. A Native American ministry has often been discouraged.[87]

Millenarian Movements as Protest

From the beginning, indigenous religious movements coexisted with missionary invasions. From the Pacific Islands to Africa to the U.S. colonized peoples have lashed out at European oppressors in millenarian movements. Such movements are often oriented to a radical "golden age" in which supernatural events will change oppressive conditions. Often the movements have been led by a visionary prophet. From the beginning of conquest on the Atlantic coast, such prophets have emerged periodically among Native American tribes.

Perhaps the most famous were the Ghost Dance groups which emerged on the Great Plains. In the 1870s the prophet Wodziwob told of a vision of Native American ancestors coming on a train to Earth, with an explosive force, and of the swallowing up of the whites by the Earth. Members of a number of tribes joined in the movement in hope of salvation from white oppression. But when no cataclysm came, the movement died down. In the late 1880s there was a resurgence; the prophet called Wovoka experienced a vision ordering him to found a new Ghost Dance religion. The religious fervor spread through the Plains tribes. Trancelike dances were a central part of the ritual; whites, it was said, could be driven out by means of the circle dance. Cooperation among all Native Americans was preached in this movement; it had an impact on intertribal cooperation. Government officials were disturbed at the resurgence of millenarianism and tried to suppress it. The Sioux massacred at Wounded Knee in 1890 had gathered for Ghost Dance ceremonies.[88]

Peyotism surfaced as the Ghost Dance movement was being destroyed, reflecting another way of protesting white pressures. Long used by individual practitioners to deal with sickness, peyotism did not become a group religion until 1880. Between 1880 and 1900 it spread throughout the Plains. The new religion reflected an ambivalence toward Christianity. Peyote rituals involved singing and praying, but were distinctive in the eating of peyote and in the visionary experiences this induced. Devoted to meditation, peyotism did not aspire to armed rebellion, but rather to using Christian and/or traditional religious ways to build up an intertribal religion.[89]

Attacks by Christian missionaries and officials welded believers together strongly. By 1918 intensive white opposition to peyote led to the introduction by a member of Congress of a bill to prohibit its use; although the bill passed the House, it went no further. Growing white opposition provoked formal organization. In the same year the Native American Church was formally incorporated as an association of Christian groups with the Sacrament of Peyote. With the new name and the development of its own offices, it became more difficult to attack the movement because of the First Amendment guarantee of freedom of religion. Nonetheless, by the 1920s seven states had passed antipeyote laws, and proclamations were issued by the BIA banning its use. Again, the opposition only seemed to stimulate its growth, for in 1934 the Oklahoma Native American Church amended its charter to include those churches in other states, a major step in the direction of national unity. By the 1930s the attempts to prohibit the use of peyote died down. The new commissioner of Indian Affairs, the progressive John Collier, came to the defense of indigenous expressions of religion and allowed the resurgence of the old ways, although this brought charges that the government was fostering "paganism."[90]

Since World War II there has been a resurgence of tribal religions. The attempt to restrict the peyotism movement did not have much effect. Membership continued to increase. On some Sioux reservations, 40 percent were Native American Church members by the 1960s.[91]

Also by the 1960s a number of leaders were openly criticizing Christianity as a crude religion stressing blood, crucifixion, and bureaucratized charity rather than practicing sharing and compassion for people. The American Indian Historical Society requested that federal museums return thousands of Native American religious and art objects, particularly those illegally acquired. "God is Red" bumper stickers signaled a movement away from Christianity by younger Native Americans. Closely tied to religious criticism is the resurgence of criticism of the European core culture, stressing such themes as the following. The white Europeans are newcomers to the continent. They sharply accelerated war on the continent. They killed off many animal species. They betrayed the Native Americans who had aided them in establishing a place on the continent. They destroyed the ecosystem and polluted the environment. They became slaves to technology. Given this, many Native Americans now argue that the solution lies in recognizing the *superiority* of Native American values, including a respect for the environment and a strong sense of community.[92]

ASSIMILATION AND COLONIALISM

Theoretical analyses in the field of race and ethnic relations have neglected Native Americans. Native Americans are distinctive among race and ethnic groups in that the classical (external) colonialism model is relevant to certain contacts with Europeans. In the earliest period Native American tribes on the Atlantic Coast saw their lands seized and their members driven off the lands or killed off by outsiders. For some tribes the European strategy was genocide, the killing off of those indigenous peoples who stood in the way of settlement by people with greater firepower. This process would periodically recur as European Americans moved westward from the Atlantic in the next several centuries. Sometimes, as in the case of Plains tribes, genocide was the informal policy. Yet genocidal policy coexisted with a reservation policy. Even in the earliest periods some whites felt that subordination of Native Americans and restricting them to limited areas, later called reservations, made for a better policy than killing them off. With the reservation period of the nineteenth century came a new oppression for Native Americans. No longer were there wars and treaties with outsiders. The Native American "race," as they were termed, was now a subordinate segment of a larger U.S. stratification system, a segment placed at the very bottom. Movement up that ladder, or the lack thereof, can be viewed from both assimilation and power-conflict perspectives.

Applying Assimilation Theories

Some white observers have argued that the "option to assimilate is far more open for Indians than for almost any other minority."[93] In the 1920s and 1930s even a few Native American professionals argued that Native Americans should voluntarily follow the lead of white immigrant groups and blend into the dominant white culture.

It is thus meaningful to ask how assimilation theorists today might view the past and present adaptations of Native Americans. Applying an assimilation model to Native Americans, one might accent the extent to which their traditional cultures have already undergone Europeanization. Schools and missions in the nineteenth century brought changes in religion, language, and dress styles. Other cultural changes have also been substantial, ranging from language changes to changes in land ownership values. Assimilationists have argued that the major barriers to Indian acculturation are the Native American traditions. Assimilation analysts can seize on the cultural adaptations that many Native Americans have made as evidence of their substantial movement in the direction of inclusion in the larger society. Yet some critics would note that much acculturation was forced, often taking place only because the police power of white America lay behind Native American decisions. In addition, some data on acculturation suggest that it has only been partial, particularly for certain larger tribes.

The persistence of Native American languages has been significant. In the 1970 Census, fully one-third gave a Native American language as their mother tongue, with proportions varying from 76 percent in Arizona to 13 percent in the State of Washington. The intensive acculturation process has not resulted in the demise of Native American cultures. Certain larger tribes, such as the Navaho and the Sioux, by cementing together internal groups have welded together sizable groups which retain to a considerable degree their indigenous culture.[94]

Structural assimilation at levels above the lowest in the economy has come slowly for Native Americans. Isolated on reservations until the 1950s and 1960s, many are poor farmers or rural laborers. Not until the urban migration of the last few decades could many Native Americans even be viewed as moving up into the better-paying levels of the dominant economy. Yet urban integration has largely been limited to less-well-paid positions in the blue-collar job market and to ghetto housing. Integration into major political spheres has been very limited.

Structural assimilation at the primary-group level seems to have been limited as well. One study in the Spokane, Washington, area found little social integration of Native Americans into voluntary associations in that area. A few studies of urban migrants have accented their somewhat greater social integration with outside whites when compared to rural dwellers. A shift can be seen in certain family values, with less emphasis on extended families in the urban area. Increases in marital assimilation have occurred. One Los Angeles study found that one-third of the married respondents had white spouses; 1970s Census data showed the same pattern among urban Native Americans nationwide, while the rural rate of intermarriage is about half that in urban areas.[95] In-marriage still seems the dominant pattern. Structural assimilation at the primary level, while greater in urban areas than on the reservation, has come very slowly. Many urban migrants sooner or later return to the reservation.[96]

Other dimensions of assimilation suggested by Gordon—attitude-receptional, behavior-receptional, and identificational assimilation—reflect relatively little adaptation. Some movement can be glimpsed in the area of public attitudes; recent data point to some decline in negative stereotyping of Native Americans in the white population. Discrimination too is less than in the past, although as we have seen in the economy, education, and politics, many types of direct and indirect discrimination still hamstring Native Americans.

Attachment to tribal identity seems quite strong, particularly for those who have predominant Native American ancestry. Some West Coast tribes have exemplified perhaps the weakest sense of identification. One study of the Spokane tribe in the late 1960s found over half identified themselves in interviews as definitely Native American, while a third identified themselves as "definitely more white." Many Native American tribes persist as cultural islands; their tribal identification has been very resistant to change.[97]

Because of the low level of overall assimilation of Native Americans, some have persuasively argued that power-conflict models have greater relevance to the Native American experience. Analysts such as Blauner cite Native Americans as the most clear-cut case of an externally colonized minority in United States history. After three hundred years of bloody violence, the colonizers gained complete economic and political control of the country and subordinated the original inhabitants—except for a small elite allowed to develop as go-betweens. Then came the reservation period. Outside administrators, soldiers, and missionaries—these have been the main bearers of the European way of life to the various Native American tribes. The original inhabitants were segregated on reservations where there was a systematic attempt to root out their native cultures.[98]

Power-Conflict Perspectives

Power-conflict analysis accents the deception and force involved in the subordination process. Much assimilation rhetoric—"civilizing the Indians"—was a cover for exploitation by land-hungry settlers. There was great pressure, even force, involved in treaties and laws providing for individual Native Americans to become "citizens" by taking individual land allotments and making other adaptations. In 1879 the commissioner of Indian Affairs stated the government position clearly:

> Indians are essentially conservative, and cling tenaciously to old customs and hate all changes: therefore the government should *force* them to scatter out on farms, break up their tribal organizations, dances, ceremonies, and tomfoolery; take from them their hundreds of useless ponies, which afford the means of indulging in their wandering, nomadic habits, and give them cattle in exchange, and compel them to labor or to *accept the alternative of starvation.*[99]

On the reservations forced acculturation has been practiced in missions and boarding schools, where children are isolated from families. In recent decades the acculturation pressures from educational and religious sources have remained intense. Unlike assimilation analysts, power-conflict analysts would look at the broad sweep of the acculturation process and see the *force* behind it. Ultimately, the police power of white governments lies behind the decisions of many Native Americans to depart from traditional customs, to learn the English language, to migrate, or to change landholding systems.

In the 1970s and 1980s serious problems of forced assimilation to white values and behavior remained. One major problem is the taking of Native American children from their homes and placing these children in white foster homes or institutions. In some areas 25 to 40 percent of all children are taken from their homes. Social workers argue the homes of poor Native Americans are not "fit" places for children and place the children in white homes. According to Shirley Hill Witt, one Mormon child placement program has reportedly been one of the most aggressive in seeking the placement of Indian children. In a newspaper interview the president of the Mormon church reportedly commented in this way:

> When you go down on the reservations and see these hundreds of thousands of Indians living in the dirt and without culture or refinement of any kind, you can hardly believe it. Then you see these boys and girls [placed in Mormon homes] playing the flute, the piano. All these things bring about a normal culture.[100]

Here again we see the white culture held up as the "normal" culture against which Native Americans are judged. This is sadly ironic, for the poverty and "dirt" in the lives of Native Americans are fundamentally the result of the destruction of Native American resources, the taking away of land, the rank discrimination in urban areas over hundreds of years of colonial oppression. It is white society that continues to create the problem of poverty.

Native American children face tremendous assimilation pressures; many capitulate, adopting white stereotypes of themselves and dressing and behaving in Anglo-preferred ways. But this stylized behavior, notes anthropologist Shirley Hill Witt, damages "the inner self" and creates great stress for many. Caught between their native culture and Anglo pressures, some commit suicide. An Oklahoma study found that young male suicide rates have been increasing; those with the highest rate were those who were the most assimilated to white culture. Traditionally, suicide has been rare among young Native Americans.[101] Other young Native Americans, however, are fighting back aggressively against the vestiges of colonialism. The renaissance of Native American culture can be seen in the many protest movements in recent years.

A power-conflict analyst might also stress that many Native Americans remain isolated geographically on the reservations, in rural areas, or in urban ghettos. They remain colonized on their own lands, while European Americans prattle on about the "vanishing red man." For example, in Oklahoma there has been a prevalent white misconception to the effect that the reservation Cherokee tribe is dying out. Yet the tribe is one of the largest in the nation, clinging tenaciously to its language and values. Wahrhaftig and Thomas have suggested that this white "fiction serves to keep the Cherokees in place as a docile and exploitable minority population."[102] In effect, by denying the existence of viable and enduring Native American communities, whites can ignore the problems of their neighbors.

Perhaps the strongest argument for the relevance of a power-conflict (colonialism) model can be found in data on Native American income, employment, housing, education, and political participation. Although there have been some gains, Native Americans as a group remain on the lower rungs of the socioeconomic ladder. Poverty characterizes life for most in rural areas and many in cities. In urban areas, Native Americans, like blacks, Mexican Americans, and Puerto Ricans, have had to face, to a disproportionate degree, low-wage jobs, absentee landlords, and widespread discrimination. A system of ranked race and ethnic groups, with Native Americans generally at the bottom, is the social reality. Native Americans are latecomers to the industrial structure of the cities and have found their "place" defined by whites as in the secondary labor market and in urban ghettos. The image of an *internal* colony remains highly appropriate for Native Americans on reservations.

SUMMARY

Native Americans remain a subordinate group. They are the descendants of the only group which did *not* immigrate to North America in the last five hundred years. They were brought into the European American sphere over a long period during which they fought bloody battles with the invaders. After the battles came a long reservation era, a long line of bureaucrats and officials seeking to dominate or exploit. Even social scientists got into this act. This is illustrated by the quip: "What is a Navaho family?"

Answer: "Three matrilineal generations and one white anthropologist living together in an extended family."

Stereotyped as inferior or savage, Native American tribes have suffered exploitation and discrimination in the economic, political, religious, and educational spheres. In the economic sphere they have seen their lands taken, their young forced by job circumstances to relocate in inhospitable cities, and their upward mobility limited by continuing discrimination. Recent decades have seen some positive changes. Yet the economic progress, however slow, has yet to be matched by substantial political progress, particularly off reservations. The BIA, although becoming more progressive and "Indianized," remains an outside governmental bureaucracy.

Protest organizations, secular and religious, have underscored the discontent of these subordinated peoples. In recent years "Red Pride" advocates have pointed up the cultural uniqueness of the Native American respect for community and for ecology. Groups have organized to regain fishing rights and lands that were stolen. Calls for maintaining cultural distinctiveness and recognizing the superiority of Native American values have also been heard. Some Native Americans have accented the uniqueness of their colonized position. Native Americans have a unique position in regard to citizenship, since they existed in America prior to any European government. Indeed, some in groups such as the Iroquois have continued to argue that they are *not* citizens of the United States, and that they do not want to be citizens. They predate the European invasions, so they are citizens of their own nations.

NOTES

[1] Stan Steiner, "Sacred Objects, Secular Laws," *Perspectives* 13 (Summer-Fall, 1981): 13.

[2] Henry F. Dobyns, "Estimating Aboriginal American Population," *Current Anthropology* 7 (October 1966): 395–416; Virgil J. Vogel, "How Many Indians Were There When the White Man Came and How Many Remain?" in *This Country Was Ours*, ed. Virgil J. Vogel (New York: Harper & Row, 1972), p. 250.

[3] D'Arcy McNickle, *The Indian Tribes of the United States* (London: Oxford University Press, 1962), p. 1; Murray L. Wax, *Indian Americans* (Englewood Cliffs, N.J.: Prentice-Hall, 1971), p. 221; U.S. Bureau of the Census, *U.S. Census of Population, 1960* (Washington, D.C.: Government Printing Office, 1960); Alan L. Sorkin, *American Indians and Federal Aid* (Washington, D.C.: Brookings Institution, 1971), pp. 4–5.

[4] Edward H. Spicer, *Cycles of Conquest* (Tucson: University of Arizona Press, 1962), pp. 20–23; Clyde Kluckhohn and Dorothy Leighton, *The Navaho*, rev. ed. (Garden City, N.Y.: Doubleday Anchor Books, 1962), pp. 23–27 et passim.

[5] U.S. Bureau of Indian Affairs, *The American Indians: Answers to 101 Questions* (Washington, D.C.: Government Printing Office, 1974), pp. 2–3.

[6] Howard M. Bahr, "An End to Invisibility," in *Native Americans Today*, ed. Howard M. Bahr, Bruce A. Chadwick, and Robert C. Day (New York: Harper & Row, 1972), pp. 407–9; James E. Officer, "The American Indian and Federal Policy," in *The American Indian in Urban Society*, ed. Jack O. Waddell and O. Michael Watson (Boston: Little, Brown, 1971), pp. 45–60.

[7] Bahr, "An End to Invisibility," p. 408.

[8] Spicer, *Cycles of Conquest*, pp. 5, 306–7; Wax, *Indian Americans*, pp. 6–7; Lynn R. Bailey, *Indian Slave Trade in the Southwest* (Los Angeles: Westernlore Press, 1966), pp. 73–140.

[9]Leo Grebler, Joan W. Moore, Ralph C. Guzman, *The Mexican-American People* (New York: Free Press, 1970), pp. 320–21; Spicer, *Cycles of Conquest*, pp. 4–5; Carey McWilliams, *North from Mexico* (New York: Greenwood Press, 1968), pp. 20–33; Herbert Blatchford, "Historical Survey of American Indians," Appendix H in Stan Steiner, *The New Indians* (New York: Harper & Row, 1968), pp. 314–15.

[10]McNickle, *The Indian Tribes of the United States*, pp. 13–17; Alice Marriott and Carol K. Rachlin, *American Epic* (New York: Mentor Books, 1969), pp. 104–8; John Collier, *Indians of the Americas* (New York: Mentor Books, 1947), p. 115.

[11]William T. Hagan, *American Indians* (Chicago: University of Chicago Press, 1961), p. 14. The history of these wars is taken from ibid., pp. 12–15.

[12]Almon W. Lauber, *Indian Slavery in Colonial Times Within the Present Limits of the United States* (New York: Columbia University Press, 1913), pp. 107–69.

[13]McNickle, *The Indian Tribes of the United States*, pp. 23–28; Ruth M. Underhill, *Red Man's America* (Chicago: University of Chicago Press, 1953), pp. 321–22; Wax, *Indian Americans*, p. 13.

[14]Quoted on title page of Vine Deloria, Jr., *Of Utmost Good Faith* (New York: Bantam Books, 1972).

[15]McNickle, *The Indian Tribes of the United States*, pp. 32–35; National Indian Youth Council, "Chronology of Indian History, 1492–1955," in Steiner, *The New Indians*, pp. 318–19.

[16]Blatchford, "Historical Survey of American Indians," pp. 316–18; Hagan, *American Indians*, pp. 41–44.

[17]Alexis de Tocqueville, *Democracy in America*, vol. 1 (New York: Vintage Books, 1945), p. 364.

[18]Virgil J. Vogel, "The Indian in American History, 1968," in Vogel, *This Country Was Ours*, pp. 284–87; McNickle, *The Indian Tribes of the United States*, pp. 40–41.

[19]Ralph K. Andrist, *The Long Death* (London: Collier-Macmillan, 1964), p. 3.

[20]John D. Unruh, *The Plains Across* (Urbana, Ill.: University of Illinois Press, 1979), p. 185 et passim.

[21]Vogel, "The Indian in American History," p. 285; Wendell H. Oswalt, *This Land Was Theirs* (New York: John Wiley, 1966), pp. 501–2.

[22]Andrist, *The Long Death*, pp. 31–68, 78–91.

[23]William Meyer, *Native Americans* (New York: International Publishers, 1971), p. 32.

[24]Andrist, *The Long Death*, 140–48.

[25]Ibid., pp. 240–50, 350–53; Alvin M. Josephy, *The Indian Heritage of America* (New York: Bantam Books, 1968), pp. 284–342; Theodora Kroeber and Robert F. Heizer, *Almost Ancestors* (San Francisco: Sierra Club, 1968), pp. 14–20.

[26]Spicer, *Cycles of Conquest*, pp. 216–21, 245–70.

[27]Robert F. Spencer et al., *The Native Americans* (New York: Harper & Row, 1965), pp. 495–96; David Miller, "The Fur Men and Explorers View the Indians," in *Red Men and Hat Wearers*, ed. Daniel Tyler (Fort Collins, Colo.: Pruett Publishing Co., 1976), pp. 26–28.

[28]Peter Farb, *Man's Rise to Civilization as Shown by the Indians of North America from Primeval Times to the Coming of the Industrial State* (New York: Dutton, 1968), pp. 246–49; Tyler, *Red Men and Hat Wearers*, passim.

[29]L. H. Carlson and G. A. Colburn, *In Their Place* (New York: Wiley, 1972), p. 44.

[30]Farb, *Man's Rise to Civilization*, pp. 122–24.

[31]Vogel, "The Indian in American History, 1968," in *This Country Was Ours*, pp. 288–89; Tocqueville, *Democracy in America*, 1: 355–57.

[32]Carlson and Colburn, *In Their Place*, pp. 32–33; Thomas R. Garth, *Race Psychology* (New York: McGraw-Hill, 1931), pp. 73–82.

[33]U.S. Senate Subcommittee on Indian Education, *Hearings on Indian Education* (Washington, D.C.: U.S. Government Printing Office, 1969), passim; Jeanette Henry, "Text Book Distortion of the Indian," *Civil Rights Digest* 1 (Summer 1968): 4–8; Kathleen C. Houts and Rosemary S. Bahr, "Stereotyping of Indians and Blacks in Magazine Cartoons," in Bahr, Chadwick, and Day, *Native Americans Today*, pp. 112–13 (see also p. 49).

[34] Emory S. Bogardus, *Immigration and Race Attitudes* (Boston: D. C. Heath and Co., 1928); "Introduction: Patterns of Prejudice and Discrimination," in Bahr, Chadwick, and Day, *Native Americans Today*, pp. 44–45; Beverly Brandon Sweeney, "Native American: Stereotypes and Ideologies of an Adult Anglo Population in Texas" (M.A. thesis, University of Texas at Austin, 1976), pp. 125–33.

[35] U.S. Bureau of Indian Affairs, *Federal Indian Policies* (Washington, D.C.: U.S. Government Printing Office, 1975), p. 6.

[36] Ibid., p. 7; Spicer, *Cycles of Conquest*, p. 348.

[37] *Elk v. Wilkins*, 112 U.S. 94 (1884). See also Deloria, *Of Utmost Good Faith*, pp. 130–32.

[38] U.S. Bureau of Indian Affairs, *Federal Indian Policies*, p. 7; S. Lyman Tyler, *A History of Indian Policy* (Washington, D.C.: U.S. Government Printing Office, 1973), pp. 95–107 et passim; Jack Forbes, *Native Americans of California and Nevada* (Berkeley, Calif.: Far West Laboratory for Educational Research and Development, 1968), pp. 79–80.

[39] Spicer, *Cycles of Conquest*, pp. 351–53; McNickle, *The Indian Tribes of the United States*, p. 59; U.S. Bureau of Indian Affairs, *Federal Indian Policy*, p. 9.

[40] Vogel, "Introduction," in Vogel, *This Country Was Ours*, pp. 196–97.

[41] W. A. Brophy and S. D. Aberle, *The Indian* (Norman: University of Oklahoma Press, 1966), pp. 179–93.

[42] U.S. Bureau of Indian Affairs, *Federal Indian Policy*, p. 12.

[43] Forbes, *Native Americans of California and Nevada*, pp. 80–82; Sorkin, *American Indians and Federal Aid*, pp. 48–65; Vogel, "Introduction," in Vogel, *This Country Was Ours*, p. 205.

[44] E. S. Cahn, *Our Brother's Keeper* (New York: World Publishing, 1969), pp. 157–58.

[45] Brophy and Aberle, *The Indian*, pp. 33–44.

[46] Stan Steiner, *The New Indians* (New York: Harper & Row, 1968), pp. 235–36.

[47] Ibid., pp. 232–34.

[48] Vogel, "Famous Americans of Indian Descent," in Vogel, *This Country Was Ours*, pp. 310–51.

[49] Theodore W. Taylor, *The States and Their Indian Citizens* (Washington, D.C.: U.S. Government Printing Office, 1972), pp. 82–84.

[50] U.S. Commission on Civil Rights, Minnesota Advisory Committee, *Bridging the Gap: The Twin Cities Native American Community* (Washington, D.C.: U.S. Government Printing Office, 1975), pp. 65–67.

[51] Vogel, "Famous Americans of Indian Descent," pp. 310–51.

[52] Hazel W. Hertzberg, *The Search for an American Indian Identity* (Syracuse: Syracuse University Press, 1971), pp. 20–21, 42–76, 180–200.

[53] Ibid., pp. 200–208, 291–93; I have also drawn from a fall 1976 newsletter of the National Indian Youth Council.

[54] Robert C. Day, "The Emergence of Activism as a Social Movement," in Bahr, Chadwick, and Day, *Native Americans Today*, pp. 516–17.

[55] Vogel, "Famous Americans of Indian Descent," pp. 310–51.

[56] Meyer, *Native Americans*, p. 88; "Pine Ridge After Wounded Knee: The Terror Goes On," *Akwesasne Notes* 7 (Summer 1975): 8–10.

[57] U.S. Commission on Civil Rights, *Indian Tribes: A Continuing Quest for Survival* (Washington, D.C.: U.S. Government Printing Office, 1981), pp. 61–99.

[58] Ibid., p. 103.

[59] Ibid., pp. 118–19, 133.

[60] Ibid., pp. 1–2.

[61] Ibid., pp. 4–7.

[62] Sar A. Levitan, Garth L. Mangum, and Ray Marshall, *Human Resources and Labor Markets*, 2d ed. (New York: Harper & Row, 1976), p. 441.

[63] Joseph G. Jorgensen, "Indians and the Metropolis," in *The American Indian in Urban Society*,

ed. Jack O. Waddell and O. Michael Watson (Boston: Little, Brown, 1971), p. 85; this paragraph draws on Jorgensen's theory.

[64]"Early Reservation Days: Martin Mitchell Fort Peck, Assiniboine Indian," in Deloria, *Of Utmost Good Faith*, pp. 380–81.

[65]Hagan, *American Indians*, pp. 126–27; Spicer, *Cycles of Conquest*, pp. 349–56.

[66]Cahn, *Our Brother's Keeper*, pp. 69–110; Rupert Costo, "Speaking Freely," *Wassaja* 4 (Nov.–Dec. 1976): 2.

[67]Sorkin, *American Indians and Federal Aid*, pp. 70–71; Jorgensen, "Indians and the Metropolis," pp. 96–99; Cahn, *Our Brother's Keeper*, pp. 90–109.

[68]Sorkin, *American Indians and Federal Aid*, pp. 105, 136–39.

[69]Ibid., p. 201; Levitan et al., *Human Resources and Labor Markets*, p. 443: Theodore D. Graves, "Drinking and Drunkenness Among Urban Indians," in Waddell and Watson, *The American Indian in Urban Society*, pp. 292–95.

[70]Levitan et al., *Human Resources and Labor Markets*, p. 443, Jorgensen, "Indians and the Metropolis," p. 83; Brophy and Aberle, *The Indian*, p. 99.

[71]Michael Parfit, "Keeping the Big Sky Pure," *Perspectives* 13 (Spring 1981): 44.

[72]Jeff Gillenkirk and Mark Dowie, "The Great Indian Land Power Grab," *Mother Jones* 7 (January 1982): 47–48.

[73]U.S. Department of Health, Education, and Welfare, *A Study of Selected Socio-economic Characteristics of Ethnic Minorities Based on the 1970 Census*, vol. 3, *American Indians* (Washington, D.C.: U.S. Government Printing Office, 1974), p. 49; Sorkin, *American Indians and Federal Aid*, p. 12. The 1970 figures are for males 16 years and over; earlier figures are for those 14 years and older.

[74]U.S. Bureau of the Census, *1970 Census: American Indians* (Washington, D.C.: U.S. Government Printing Office, 1973); U.S. Bureau of the Census, *Population, 1960: Nonwhite Population by Race* (Washington, D.C.: U.S. Government Printing Office, 1963), p. 104; U.S. Bureau of the Census, *Population, 1940: Characteristics of the Nonwhite Population by Race* (Washington, D.C.: U.S. Government Printing Office, 1943), pp. 83–84: The data do not include those not reporting or, in 1960, states with less than 25,000 Native Americans. Census data sometimes do not include Alaskan natives.

[75]U.S. Department of Health, Education, and Welfare, *A Study of Selected Socio-economic Characteristics*, pp. 59–78.

[76]U.S. Bureau of Indian Affairs, *Federal Indian Policies*, p. 5.

[77]Ibid., pp. 5–6; Spicer, *Cycles of Conquest*, p. 349; Forbes, *Native Americans of California and Nevada*, passim.

[78]U.S. Bureau of Indian Affairs, *Federal Indian Policies*, p. 9.

[79]Tyler, *A History of Indian Policy*, pp. 228–29; Taylor, *The States and Their Indian Citizens*, pp. 83–85.

[80]U.S. Department of Health, Education, and Welfare, *A Study of Selected Socio-economic Characteristics*, pp. 38–39, 43.

[81]The study by Rosalie Wax is cited in Bruce A. Chadwick, "The Inedible Feast," in Bahr, Chadwick, and Day, *Native Americans Today*, pp. 133–36; James S. Coleman et al., *Equality of Educational Opportunity* (Washington, D.C.: U.S. Government Printing Office, 1966) pp. 1–100, 449–52.

[82]Cahn, *Our Brother's Keeper*, pp. 29, 32–34, 37–40.

[83]Brophy and Aberle, *The Indian*, p. 142; Chadwick, "The Inedible Feast," p. 141; Murray L. Wax, Rosalie H. Wax, and Robert V. Dumont, "Formal Education in an American Indian Community," in *The Emergent Native Americans* (Boston: Little, Brown, 1972), pp. 638–40.

[84]American Indian Historical Society, "Textbooks and the American Indian," reprinted in U.S. Senate, *Hearings Before the Special Subcommittee on Indian Education, 1967–1968*, part 1 (Washington, D.C.: U.S. Government Printing Office, 1969) pp. 397–405; Cahn, *Our Brother's Keeper*, pp. 35–36.

[85]Leo W. Simons, ed., *Sun Chief* (New Haven: Yale University Press, 1942), p. 134.

[86]Quoted in Vine Deloria, Jr., *Custer Died for Your Sins* (London: Collier-Macmillan, 1969), p. 101.

[87]Ibid., pp. 108–16.

[88]Vittorio Lanternari, *The Religion of the Oppressed* (New York: Mentor Books, 1963), pp. 110–32; Spencer and Jennings, *Native Americans*, pp. 498–99; Wax, *Indian Americans*, p. 141.

[89]Lanternari, *The Religions of the Oppressed*, pp. 99–100; Hertzberg, *The Search for an American Indian Identity*, pp. 239–40, 251, 280.

[90]Hertzberg, *The Search for an American Indian Identity*, pp. 246, 257, 271–74, 280–84; Elaine G. Eastman, "Does Uncle Sam Foster Paganism?" in Carlson and Colburn, *In Their Place*, pp. 29 ff.

[91]See Deloria, *Of Utmost Good Faith*, pp. 177 ff; idem, *Custer Died for Your Sins*, pp. 110–15.

[92]Deloria, *Custer Died for Your Sins*, pp. 122–24; Cahn, *Our Brother's Keeper*, pp. 175–90.

[93]Lurie is quoted in John A. Price, "Migration and Adaptation of American Indians to Los Angeles," *Human Organization* 27 (Summer 1968): 168–75.

[94]U.S. Department of Health, Education, and Welfare, *A Study of Selected Socio-economic Characteristics*, p. 48; Price, "Migration and Adaptation of American Indians to Los Angeles," p. 435; Cahn, *Our Brother's Keeper*, p. 27.

[95]Prodipto Roy, "The Measurement of Assimilation: The Spokane Indians," *American Journal of Sociology* 67 (March 1962): 541–51; Price, "Migration and Adaptation of American Indians to Los Angeles," pp. 169–74; U.S. Department of Health, Education, and Welfare, *A Study of Selected Socio-economic Characteristics*, pp. 35–37.

[96]Price, "Migration and Adaptation of American Indians to Los Angeles," pp. 170–74; Oswalt, *This Land Was Theirs*, pp. 513–14.

[97]Lynn C. White and Bruce A. Chadwick, "Urban Residence, Assimilation, and Identity of the Spokane Indian," in Bahr, Chadwick, and Day, *Native Americans Today*, p. 243; Brophy and Aberle, *The Indian*, p. 10; Spicer, *Cycles of Conquest*, p. 577.

[98]Robert Blauner, *Racial Oppression in America* (New York: Harper & Row, 1972), p. 54; Spicer, *Cycles of Conquest*, pp. 573–74.

[99]Quoted in Francis McKinley, Stephen Bayne, and Glen Nimnicht, *Who Should Control Indian Education?* (Berkeley, Calif.: Far West Laboratory for Educational Research and Development, 1969), p. 13. Italics added.

[100]Quoted in Shirley Hill Witt, "Pressure Points in Growing Up Indian," *Perspectives* 12 (Spring 1980): 31.

[101]Ibid., pp. 28–31.

[102]Albert L. Wahrhaftig and Robert K. Thomas, "Renaissance and Repression: The Oklahoma Cherokee," in Bahr, Chadwick, and Day, *Native Americans Today*, p. 81.

CHAPTER 8

Afro-Americans have a history running back a dozen generations. The majority of black Americans have family trees in the United States extending back before 1800, which theoretically should put them in good stead for applying for membership in such lineage-oriented organizations as the Daughters of the American Revolution. There is a tragic irony here. That a people who have been here as long as the first European settlers should still find themselves in a subordinate position is a fact problematical both for assimilation theory and for public policy in this democratic nation. For centuries dominant white groups have seen to it that black-white relations are characterized by prejudice, discrimination, and subordination.

MIGRATION AND SLAVERY

White immigrants came to North America voluntarily, for the most part. For most Africans no choice was involved; they came in chains. They exemplify the slave-importation end of the migration continuum we have discussed. The points of destination were predetermined by the slave traders.

At first, Europeans attempted to enslave the Native American populations, but a number of factors, including ease of flight, made this difficult. For a time poor whites such as the Irish, brought in as indentured servants, helped meet the need for agricultural labor. But runaways were a problem, and terms of service eventually ran out. The enslavement of black Africans was a solution to the problem of cheap labor, chiefly in the agricultural South. Why were Africans the ones enslaved? Some have accented the demands of colonial agriculture and the accessibility of Africans with their weaker military technology. Others have emphasized the European view of African peoples. Prior to enslavement, the residents of Africa were seen as a heathen people, as unbelievers whose failure to practice Christianity was rationale enough for enslavement.[1]

Dutch and French companies early dominated the forcible importation of Africans, although England came into the slave trade in the late 1600s. Fed by European piracy, the slave trade soon saw the institutionalization of trading alliances between certain African chiefs, who wanted horses and manufactured goods, and white slavers, who wanted human beings to sell. Some African coastal chiefs, out of greed or fear, succumbed to the slave trade pressure and established themselves as go-betweens in Western Africa.[2] A vicious cycle of wars and raids was created by the European intrusion.

Europeans justified the trade in religious and ethnocentric terms; they were not buying and selling their own kind, but rather "outsiders" and "unbelievers." The result was a violent, exploitative system. The impact on African points of origin cannot be fully calculated, but the slavers obviously took many vital young citizens. The internal disruption generated by the European slave trade weakened the coastal states to the point that by the late 1800s direct European colonization was easy.[3]

The slave trade ranked high in barbarity. Once captured, slaves were chained in corrals called *barracoons*, where they were branded and held for transportation. The voyage was a living hell. Slaves were chained together in close quarters, with little room for movement and no sanitary facilities.[4] The horror was summed up by a young slave:

> I was soon put down under the decks, and there I received such a salutation in my nostrils as I had never experienced in my life: so that with the loathsomeness of the stench, and crying together, I became so sick and low that I was not able to eat, nor had I had least desire to taste any thing.... On my refusing to eat, one of them held me fast by the hands, and laid me across, I think the windlass, and tied my feet, while the other flogged me severely.... One day, when we had a smooth sea and moderate wind, two of my wearied countrymen who were chained together (I was near them at the time), preferring death to such a life of misery, somehow made through the nettings and jumped into the sea.[5]

Protest took various forms. Suicides were common, and uprisings brought death to slaves and sailors alike. They myth of Africans' passive acquiescence is contradicted by the 155 recorded shipboard uprisings by slaves between 1699 and 1845, with many other attacks going unrecorded. At the points of destination in North and South America conditions did not improve significantly. Diseased slaves were left to die; the rest were sold directly to a plantation owner or channeled through dealers to other buyers.[6]

In 1619 twenty blacks were brought to Jamestown by a Dutch ship. There has been a scholarly debate over the status of these Africans. Some were apparently treated as indentured servants, receiving land when their terms expired; existing records show the presence of free blacks in the colonies in the first decades. Yet by the mid-1600s the slave status of Africans had been fully institutionalized in the laws of several colonies. For the next two-and-a-half centuries virtually all African immigrants were brought in to serve in involuntary servitude. The most careful estimates of the number of slaves seem to be those of Curtin, who puts the total at 9.6 million for this period, with most brought to the West Indies and South America and only 5 percent to North America.[7]

The major receiving areas in colonial America were Virginia, Maryland, the Carolinas, and Georgia. Relatively few slaves were brought into New England and the Middle Atlantic colonies; yet these colonies played a major role nonetheless, for their port towns and aggressive shipowners prospered on the slave trade. Prior to 1790 an estimated 275,000 African slaves were brought into all the colonies; between 1790 and the end of the legal slave trade in 1808 another 70,000 were imported.[8] The total for the entire slave period was approximately half a million Africans.

A number of founding fathers, including the slaveholders Washington, Madison, and Jefferson, spoke of the problems of slavery and envisioned its eventual demise. In strong language in his draft of the Declaration of Independence, Thomas Jefferson went so far as to attack slavery by blaming it on King George. As a result of southern slaveowning opposition, his antislavery language was *not* included in the final draft.[9]

Slave interests also forced an official recognition of slavery in provisions of the United States Constitution. Slavery was officially recognized in the section which provided for the counting of each slave as three-fifths of a person, in a fugitive-slave section, and in a section postponing prohibition of slave importation to 1808. The slave trade was officially abolished as of 1808, but the ban was not enforced. Thousands were imported illegally. In addition, an extensive domestic breeding system and internal slave trade developed to provide for the growing demand for slaves in the cotton kingdom and in the developing areas to the West. Slavery was a well-established and enduring system in the new capitalist nation.[10]

What was slavery like? In 1860 an estimated one-quarter of the 1.6 million southern white families owned 4 million slaves. Most slave owners had fewer than 10 slaves; and there were only 46,000 white families with 20 or more slaves. Most white farmers, both poor and yeoman farmers, had no slaves.[11] A majority of the slaves were chained to the larger farms or plantations, which produced the surplus agricultural products to be marketed. Plantation owners, tied into trade with the North and England, were agrarian capitalists attuned to commercial trade and a money profit. Recently, there has been debate over the profitability of the slave system, with some arguing that slavery was unprofitable because it was less efficient than a free-labor system. However, a slave system can be less efficient and still be profitable. By any standards the wealth, as well as power, of the white gentry rose as a result of slave agriculture.[12]

Slave Life

There has long been a magnolias-and-mint-julep mystique concerning the slave system, which lingers on, particularly in the South. According to this mythology a paternalistic master cared kindly for contented, happy slaves. A big, white plantation house with multiple columns and surrounded by magnolia trees was at the center of this idyllic existence. Black house-servants were treated like members of the family. Numerous popular writers and scholars have painted sugar-coated views of slavery, conveniently overlooking brutality and oppression, as well as violent rebellions.

Comparisons have often been made with the living conditions of slaves in South America or poor workers in Europe, the point being that in terms of food and housing slaves in the South were apparently somewhat better off. Yet the apologists conveniently ignored such issues as personal freedom; with regard to such matters southern slaves were worse off.[13] The South's Anglo-Saxon Protestant religious and legal tradition had no prior experience with slavery. In the South there was little recognition of the slave as a person.

Slave autobiographies describe the oppressiveness of living conditions. Most slaves rose before dawn, then worked in the house or the fields until dark. Food was often insufficient. Clothing and housing were crude and inadequate. Social control in this system—the maintaining of slaves in subordination—depended to some extent on value consensus between slaves and masters, but even more on force. That many slaves came to accept the system was an important factor in its perpetuation. A racist ideology legitimated (for whites) the position of slaves. Whites controlled the state militias and the courts. Control also took the form of ministers prosyletizing among the African slaves.[14]

The whip and the chains were mechanisms in the control system. Some masters were extremely cruel, such as the owner of one slave who told about moving from Georgia to Texas:

> Then he chains all the slaves round the necks and fastens the chains to the hosses and makes them walk all the way to Texas. My mother and my sister had to walk. Emma was my sister. Somewhere on the road it went to snowing, and Massa wouldn't let us wrap anything round our feet. We had to sleep on the ground, too, in all that snow.[15]

Other slaveowners earned a reputation for kindness; they provided better material conditions and were less likely to use the whip. But most owners fell in between the two extremes, taking some care for their "property" but willing to resort to cruel punishment when necessary.[16] The legal system backed up the slaveowner. Slave codes were established throughout the South to control the growing numbers of slaves. Severe restrictions were placed on slaves. They could not make economic decisions, testify in court, or leave plantations without permission. The owner's power was absolute: "Behind the owner stood an elaborate and complex system of military control. In the cities were guards and police, for the countryside there were the ubiquitous patrols, armed men on horseback."[17]

The subordinate place of the slave was reinforced from childhood onward by etiquette. At a tender age young slaves encountered a system of enforced deference to all whites and learned that docility was a virtue. White southerners developed an extensive racist ideology to back up the etiquette of deference. They liked to believe that slaves were happy with their lot. Stereotypes consistent with the alleged inferiority of blacks were developed by intellectuals and popular writers.[18]

So comprehensive was the system of social control that some scholars have compared the slaves' situation to that of prisoners in concentration camps, such as those of the Nazis. Elkins has argued that slavery in the South was a "total institution," a thought-control and behavior-control system which cut off slaves from communication with the rest of society, detached them from their cultural traditions, relegated them to a subhuman status, and treated them in a barbaric way. The alleged typical slave reaction, the docile, fawning "Sambo," was similar to the white concentration camp inmate who also became a docile "Sambo" licking the boots of the Nazi guards.[19]

Others have taken a different view, arguing that slavery can best be described as a strange mixture of cruel despotism and control by paternalistic benevolence. Reviving an earlier tradition, Genovese sees slavery as such a paternalistic system, although he also stresses the role of violent oppression. For the masters, fatherly paternalism rationalized the subordination of other human beings; for the slaves, it meant some recognition of material needs. Yet a paternalistic system can be dangerous for the oppressed, for it tends to foster individualism among the oppressed and thus to make organization for resistance more difficult.[20] Genovese has been criticized for exaggerating the paternalistic aspects of slavery, but his view remains important, for both accommodation and violent resistance were part of the slave reaction to an alternately despotic and paternalistic system.

This paternalistic context may help make sense out of family life. Slave families have been a concern of social scientists; contemporary problems of poverty and broken families have frequently been traced back to the assumed constant break-up of family units in slave days. Supportive family life has been viewed as unimportant for the great majority of Afro-American slaves. Yet recent research suggests that this view is half-true, for there is considerable evidence of paternalistic slaveowners actually fostering families. Slave families were protective environments and provided support which helped slave communities to survive. Slaves often deserted as family units; and a frequent cause of desertion had to do with the attempt to find lost loved ones.[21]

In an extensive analysis of families on large plantations, Gutman found that women were expected to have their children by one man; that the names of fathers were given to sons; that adoption was a mechanism used to ease the disruption of death within and break-up of families; and that there was a continuity in many families over several generations.[22] Yet the threat to the slave family was also great. Slave marriages were likely to be broken up at some point, most often by death but frequently by masters. Black children received less care than they needed, because their mothers were forced to work. An accurate picture of the slave family must, it seems clear, include both the stability and the disruption.[23]

Slave Resistance

What was the slave reaction to slavery? Apologists for slavery have emphasized the submissive response, picturing a docile "Sambo."[24] In recent scholarly debates over slavery a similar theme has received attention. Numerous scholars have underscored the severe impact of slavery on personality. As we have noted, Elkins argues that the major personality type created by the oppressive "total institution" was the childlike, docile type.[25]

Yet some scholars have criticized this perspective and argued that submissiveness was only one response. Most slaves did not adopt the "Sambo" personality in order to survive. The "Sambo" perspective captures an important aspect of slave personality, but it overlooks the assertive aspect that existed as well. Both aspects are likely to have been important components of a given slave's personality. Depending on the circumstances, one aspect or the other might come to the forefront. Slaves used their wits to escape as much forced work and punishment as possible and observed the servile etiquette when necessary, but many also reacted with rebellious or attacking behavior where that was possible.[26]

Rebellious behavior took different forms, including flight, suicide, and psychological withdrawal. Fugitive slaves were a serious problem for slaveowners; a fugitive-slave provision was incorporated in the Constitution because of this problem. Perhaps the most famous route of escape was the "Underground Railroad," the network of antislavery citizens who secreted and passed along tens of thousands of slaves to the North between the 1830s and the Civil War.[27] Thousands fled shorter distances. Southerners committed to the "happy Sambo" view of their slaves sometimes went to absurd lengths to explain runaways. Physician Samuel Cartwright seriously attributed the problem to a strange black disease, "drapetomania," by which he meant the unhealthy tendency to flee one's owner.[28]

Nonviolent slave resistance took the form of a slow working pace, feigned illness, and strikes. Violent resistance was directed at the property and persons of slaveowners or overseers. Black resistance could be seen in the destruction of tools, livestock, fields, and farmhouses. Masters and overseers were killed. Collective resistance could also be seen in revolts and conspiracies to revolt. In his research, Aptheker found evidence of 250 slave revolts or conspiracies to revolt, a count that did not include numerous mutinies aboard slave ships. There is considerable evidence, in the newspapers of the day, of extensive white fear of uprisings.[29]

The first major conspiracy in English-controlled areas was in Gloucester County, Virginia, in 1663, where a conspiracy to revolt by slaves and servants was betrayed by an informer. Numerous revolts and conspiracies occurred prior to the Revolution, but the most widely heralded revolts took place later. In 1800 a group of slaves led by Gabriel Prosser in Henrico County, Virginia, gathered weapons and planned to march on Richmond. Governor Monroe took defensive action to protect the state capital. A thousand armed slaves rendezvoused, but a heavy rain cut them off from the city and they went away. Betrayed, the leaders were quickly arrested;

at least thirty-five, including Prosser, were hanged. Perhaps the most serious slave revolt took place in 1811 near New Orleans; after several hundred armed slaves attacked whites on local plantations, white troops suppressed the rebellion. Several dozen slaves were killed during the encounter; others were executed later by a firing squad and their heads were displayed along the route to New Orleans. An 1822 conspiracy led by Denmark Vesey, an African who had purchased his freedom, involved a planned attack on Charlestown, South Carolina, by several thousand armed slaves. Several hundred weapons were gathered, but the plans were betrayed by informers. Vesey and thirty-six others were hanged.[30]

The most famous rebellion took place in Southampton County, Virginia, in 1831. Nat Turner, the leader, was a self-taught slave with mystical-religious leanings. Turner recruited seventy slaves in a single day; his revolutionaries attacked, and dozens of white members of slaveholding families in the area were killed. Delaying a planned attack on the county seat, the rebels were attacked and defeated by hundreds of militiamen and army soldiers. Turner, who had escaped, was executed several months later.[31]

Such slave revolts intensified fears of whites, many of whom were near panic following a revolt. Here was irrefutable evidence contradicting the apologist's notion of happy slaves. Given the opportunity, slaves would resist violently. Slavery, and the fears surrounding it, had a severe impact on whites in the South. Southern whites lost much of their humanity, as well as much of their own freedom of speech, press, and assembly, because of the slave system.[32]

Outside the Rural South

Information on city and town life in the nineteenth century is sketchy, but we do know that as southern cities grew the number of free and enslaved blacks there increased. However, cities were too dynamic for slavery to fit in easily. Social control there was a problem, for contacts with free blacks proved corrosive for the bonds of slavery. There free blacks had some freedom of activity; they married, owned property, and formed associations. With the weakening of traditional controls came a system of formal *segregation* which made no distinction between free and enslaved blacks. This developed because of the problem of blacks moving about in their work and leisure without a master nearby. Public transportation, churches, hospitals, theaters, and jails had separate facilities. Housing segregation was part of the trend.[33]

Jim Crow laws (legally enforced segregation) had already been given a boost in the states and cities of the North. North of slavery, "free" blacks were not in reality so free. There were few slaves in the North, but direct discrimination was fully institutionalized in hundreds of Jim Crow laws. Legal segregation was in fact "invented" by the North, not the South. Free blacks were segregated in public transportation, hospitals, jails, schools, churches, and cemeteries. Jim Crow railroad cars were early established in Massachusetts, the citadel of abolition. All the major northern cities had their black ghettos at a time when there were no comparable ghettos in southern cities. Few states allowed blacks to vote; before 1855 none allowed them to serve on juries.[34] Even the "Great Emancipator," President Abraham Lincoln, opposed civil and social equality for black Americans. The Frenchman Tocqueville, visiting in the 1830s, noted that "the prejudice of race appears to be stronger in the states that have abolished slavery than in those where it still exists."[35]

STEREOTYPING BLACK AMERICANS

Dominant groups develop beliefs to rationalize their domination. Racial theories of biological, mental, and moral inferiority were early devised by theologians, intellectuals, and other southern leaders to rationalize the exploitation of blacks as slaves.

Negative views of African peoples existed in Europe before the founding of Jamestown, but these did not develop into full-blown racist ideologies until the late 1700s. Thomas Jefferson personified the moral dilemma of whites in the eighteenth century: He wrote a stinging indictment of slavery in the original draft of the Declaration of Independence; yet he was a major slaveowner. He wrote vigorously of his opposition to interracial sex and miscegenation; yet he apparently had a black mistress who bore him children. He wrote of the inferiority of blacks; but he also expressed his views that they should be free. In his 1786 *Notes on Virginia*, Jefferson argued that what he saw as the ugly color, the offensive odor, and the ugly hair of blacks were signs of the physical inferiority of blacks and that what he alleged to be their inability to reason or produce imaginative creations was a sign of mental inferiority.[36] Jefferson's views on the inferiority of Afro-Americans gave a boost to popular stereotyping of blacks in the eighteenth and nineteenth centuries. Many of these themes have been part of white thinking to the present.

Black Color as Badge of Inferiority

At an early date, black people's dark color was singled out as unusual or ugly. By 1800 blackness was seen as a critical distinguishing factor useful in sorting out people; the terms *black* or *Negro* underscored the importance of color.[37] As with the Irish, black Americans were early stereotyped as evolutionary inferiors. The absurd linkage of Africans and apes was part of a pseudoscience which saw all beings in a great hierarchy, with the apes just below the lowest of *Homo sapiens*, the Africans. By the mid-1800s proslavery advocates were arguing for acceptance of the supposed apelike characteristics of the Afro-American, a stereotype applied by Anglo-Saxons to Irish Americans a decade or two earlier. Thus Samuel Cartwright, in a famous article published in the 1850s, wrote that Africans were a different species than Europeans "because the head and face are anatomically constructed more after the fashion of the simiadiae [apes]."[38]

By the turn of the century this way of insulting black Americans had taken on ludicrous forms. The low point was probably reached in 1906 when the New York Zoological Society put an African pygmy, Ota Benga, in a cage in the monkey house of the Bronx Park Zoo as part of an exhibit. Thousands came to view the African's new home. Some black clergypersons protested the degrading exhibition, but white officials as well as the white populace thought it great sport.[39]

Blacks were often depicted as having an offensive odor by southerners in the 1840s and 1850s. Sex stereotyping, to the point of fantasy, was part of the process. Black women were seen as immoral, while black men were regarded as oversexed and potential rapists.[40] Since there was significant miscegenation between white men and black women slaves, this absurd fear of black sexuality reflected guilt over interracial sex. Intermixing in the South had become a permanent feature of the sexual landscape, a point testified to by the lighter color of some black Americans.[41]

Afro-Americans were also charged with being mentally and morally inferior. Proslavery advocates tried hard to depict slaves as childlike, happy-go-lucky "Sambos"; this stereotype did not die with slavery. Between 1900 and World War II, prominent scientists, such as geneticist Edward East of Harvard University, took the position that "mentally the African negro is childlike, normally affable and cheerful, but subject to fits of fierce passion."[42] Naive white ideas about blacks' childlike emotionalism, often linked to notions of an excessive black love for music and dancing, were to last to the present. To racists of the nineteenth and twentieth centuries slavery and segregation were God-given; southern slave owners and segregationists were the agents of God's will.[43] This view of segregation can still be found today.

Early discussions of blacks' inferiority saw them as having a small brain and a lower mental capacity than Europeans.[44] Southern apologists for slavery embraced views of racial inferiority, views legitimated in the "scientific racism" of nineteenth century writers in Europe. A burst of interest in this mental inferiority argument occurred around 1900, when a number of American scientists argued for inferiority of racial groups, including Americans of African descent. As we noted in Chapter 5, many observers, relying heavily on IQ tests, attempted to "prove" the mental inferiority of southern and eastern Europeans; others used the same tests to "prove" the inferiority of black Americans. Psychologists such as George Oscar Ferguson, who found average test differences of 25 points favoring whites, used these findings in his writings to support theories of racial inferiority. Scholarly journals and popular magazines parroted this theme. Antiblack thought was coupled with theories of "Aryan" or "Teutonic" (northern European) racial superiority over a variety of other groups, south European as well as African. Even American presidents participated in the crude racial theorizing of the first decades of the twentieth century.[45]

"IQ" Testing and Race: Pseudoscience?

The theme of intellectual inferiority has received renewed attention since World War II—as, for example, in response to the 1954 Supreme Court decision desegregating public school systems. Social scientists Audrey

Shuey and Henry Garrett wrote and spoke in support of inferiority theories, drawing on the extensive IQ-testing literature and alleging that blacks are so significantly different in mentality that they should not be educated with whites. Popular writers such as columnist James J. Kilpatrick and magazines such as *U.S. News & World Report* spread these arguments throughout white America.

In the 1960s and 1970s a new group of social scientists were again attempting to resurrect the old inferiority arguments, based on the psychological test results available for blacks and whites. Arthur Jensen and Richard Herrnstein, among others, have recently pressed the argument that there are inherited IQ differences among racial groups. Groups at the lower social and economic levels are seen as being intellectually and genetically inferior to those at higher ones. In the past, as we have noted in earlier chapters, this perspective was centered on those *white* immigrant groups considered to be inferior to Anglo-Saxons, while in the last decade the focus has been primarily on *nonwhite* Americans.[47] Jensen has argued that IQ test score differentials reflect genetic differences between blacks and whites and that the two groups have different types of intelligence, perhaps requiring different educational techniques. Racial differences in mental ability, he has argued, are not just environmentally determined. Citing earlier studies by "scientific" racists, Jensen has expressed concern about the higher birth rates of blacks and the alleged lowering of the national IQ.[48]

Since the 1930s scientific opposition to these views has developed. In the 1930s a number of social psychologists began questioning whether IQ test results could be used as evidence of genetically determined racial differentials. Citing data on the oppressive conditions suffered by blacks, they argued that black-white differences in IQ test scores reflected education and income differences. A number of studies showed that IQ test scores of black children improved with better economic and learning environments, as when black children from segregated southern schools attended integrated northern schools.[49] Results from large-scale IQ testing have even shown blacks in some northern states scoring *higher* than whites in some southern states. Otto Klinberg retabulated data for selected states from World War I tests:

White Scores (Median)		Black Scores (Median)	
Mississippi	41.25	New York	45.02
Kentucky	41.50	Pennsylvania	42.00
Georgia	42.12	Ohio	49.50
Arkansas	41.55	Illinois	47.35

Reprinted by permission of Louisiana State University Press from CHALLENGE TO THE COURT by I. A. Newby, copyright © 1967 and 1969.

Using the same logic analysts from Brigham to Jensen, one would be forced to conclude that southern whites in certain states are mentally (and thus racially) inferior to northern blacks. Of course, these writers avoid such an interpretation—obviously they, as whites, do not wish to argue for black intellectual superiority. A few interpreters have used test data consistently showing lower scores for southern white children than for northern white children to make the tongue-in-cheek argument that southern whites are "racially inferior" to northern whites.[50] Not even "scientific" racists would argue any longer for the racial inferiority of certain groups of white Americans, but rather would accept the environmental explanation for uncomplimentary regional differentials. So too, overall IQ score differentials between blacks and whites can reasonably be interpreted as reflecting environment. Yet another problem has arisen for racial inferiority interpretations of IQ tests. In 1982 one psychologist reported that the IQ test scores for Japanese children, measured in Japanese schools, averaged 11 points higher than the average IQ score for U.S. students. The study triggered a reaction from U.S. scholars, who argued that the real difference was *only* 5–7 points between the children of the two countries. Yet no one in these debates used the higher Japanese scores to argue for the racial superiority in intelligence of the Japanese over, for example, white Americans. Yet using the logic of analysts such as Brigham and Jensen, one might be forced to that conclusion.

Some analysts focused on the cultural bias—specifically, the white middle-class bias—in the makeup of traditional U.S. achievement and other psychometric tests (including IQ tests). Most psychometric tests measure *learned* skills and *acquired* knowledge (such as linguistic, literary, or geographical subjects), skills and knowledge not available to the same degree to all racial groups. Researchers have found that test-taking itself is a skill white children are more likely to possess. White children with generations of middle-income experience take the tests with a built-in advantage over black children. IQ scores do seem to predict success in school, but this may well be because those children who have been trained to do well on tests are also trained in the same skills necessary for success in schools.[51]

The most fundamental problem is the equation of *intelligence-test results* with *intelligence*. From the beginning intelligence tests have been misnamed. These tests are only measures of certain verbal, mathematical, and/or manipulative *skills*. A number of scholars have argued that intelligence is something much broader than what paper-and-pencil tests can measure. More broadly, intelligence can be viewed as a complex ability to deal creatively with one's environment. Only a small portion of that ability can be revealed, even under the best testing conditions, on the typical test. Even the most vocal advocates of racial differentials admit the very large overlap in scores on the tests, with a large number of blacks scoring as well as or better than many whites. Given this overlap, some have asked how it is possible to argue for placing black children in different educational tracks or programs, as Jensen and others have suggested.

Opinion Polls, Prejudice, and Stereotyping

To what extent does the white public still accept the various negative stereotypes of black Americans? A number of surveys have revealed that large numbers of whites believe in the inferiority of blacks.[52] As recently as 1966, half of a randomly selected national white sample felt that blacks had a different odor, were morally inferior, and laughed a lot. Few polls have asked white Americans about biological- and mental-inferiority stereotypes. A 1963 Harris survey found that 30 percent of white Americans believed that blacks had lower intelligence than whites. Belief in inferiority was also revealed in a 1965 survey of whites in Los Angeles: 31 percent felt blacks had "less native intelligence than whites," while 27 percent felt that some races are "superior because of the contribution they have made to civilization throughout time."[53] While the majority of whites no longer publicly express racial superiority views, a minority of whites still do.

Moreover, when whites were asked about segregated schools for blacks in 1972 and 1976 public opinion polls, three-quarters said they favored desegregated schools. The proportion of those interviewed who said whites do not have a right to keep blacks out of their neighborhoods was a bit lower, at just over half. About the same proportion thought laws banning racial intermarriages were not a good idea. Support for traditional segregation of blacks is no longer publicly expressed by a majority of whites. However, a large minority of whites still express the traditionally segregationist views.

Today it may be the case for many whites that subtle views of cultural and moral superiority have replaced crude theories of biological or intellectual superiority. Some evidence for this shift was found in a research study of whites' attitudes in fifteen major cities; the study revealed that the majority saw black job, education, and housing problems as resulting from black cultural inferiority, laziness, or lack of ambition rather than from discrimination by whites.[54]

Moreover, surveys of whites in the last decade have found a new type of racial prejudice and hostility, what John McConahay has called "modern racism": the view that blacks are illegitimately challenging cherished white values and are making illegitimate demands for changes in U.S. race relations. McConahay and his associates have demonstrated in a number of studies of whites that old-fashioned race prejudice, which opposes all desegregation and which includes extreme negative stereotypes of blacks, has declined in rigor, although many whites still cling to it. But the research has also found strong support among whites for these "modern racist" views:

1. That government and the news media have shown more respect to blacks than they deserve;
2. That blacks, over the last few years, have gotten more economically than they deserve;
3. That blacks are too demanding in their push for equal rights.

Other opinion polls have found resentment among whites of gains blacks have made, a strong feeling that blacks are too pushy and demanding, and a view that blacks are not playing by the rules that earlier white immigrant groups played by.[55]

Many whites believe that blacks *do not deserve* the gains they have made. Most of these whites believe that blacks should have freedom of opportunity, unlike older racists who believed in across-the-board segregation;

but the modern racists also feel that "blacks are too pushy, too demanding, too angry; things are moving too fast and blacks are getting more than they deserve."[56] Much of this modern racism targets certain symbols of recent racial change (such as affirmative action, busing, and fair housing laws) in its hostility. This resentment can be found in the North and South. Whites holding such views do not see themselves as racist. Most whites no longer publicly express the once commonplace views that "all Negroes are lazy" or that "all Negroes have less intelligence than whites." They realize that these views have been branded as racist and are thus no longer fashionable. In contrast, however, many whites today accept the modern racism which views black demands for equality as illegitimate or radical and which sees current black progress as unfairly penalizing whites. These modern racist beliefs are directly linked to discrimination. Measures of this modern racism have been found to be related to antiblack voting by whites in Los Angeles and to white opposition to school desegregation in Louisville, Kentucky.[57]

VIOLENT CONFLICT BETWEEN WHITES AND BLACKS

White Violence Targets Blacks

Intergroup conflict was at the foundation of the slave trade. Just behind the slave system's veneer of civility were the bloody instruments of social control—the whip, the dogs, the guns. Slaves on occasion retaliated, countering force with force. Free blacks also suffered at the hands of whites. Before the Civil War, white-dominated race riots directed at free blacks occurred a dozen times in northern cities. The most serious race riot in American history, measured in terms of human casualties, was the 1863 antidraft riot in New York City staged by a group of immigrant rioters. Among the targets of their attacks were blacks. The end of the Civil War brought an increased threat of violence against the legally free Afro-Americans. As long as a slave was worth several hundred dollars, he or she was relatively safe from lynching. After the war, freed slaves became the victims of lynching. Lynching became a means of keeping blacks "in their place." Recorded lynchings show the following pattern:[58]

	White	Black
1882–1891	751	732
1892–1901	381	1,124
1902–1911	76	707
1912–1921	53	553
1922–1931	23	201
1932–1941	10	95
1942–1951	2	25
1952–1956	0	3

Most killings took place in the South. In the first decade more whites than blacks were put to death. In the decades between 1892 and 1921, the peak period of segregation, nearly 2,400 black Americans lost their lives. Cash points out that there was a growing

> inclination to abandon such relatively mild and decent ways of dispatching the [lynch] mob's victim as hanging and shooting in favor of burning, often roasting over slow fires, after preliminary mutilations and tortures . . . a disposition to revel in the infliction of the most devilish and prolonged agonies.[59]

Research studies have documented the fact that at least one-third of black victims of white vigilante action were falsely accused and that the lynchers involved were seldom punished. Local police officers were on occasion involved in lynchings, and in most other cases they winked at the crimes. There were spurts in lynchings after World War I and World War II, as "uppity" black servicemen were kept in line by this method. The sharp decrease in lynching statistics since World War II is somewhat misleading, since "legal" and secret lynchings had by then replaced public lynchings. Unnecessary killings by police officers have taken many black lives. Secret attacks resulted in hundreds of deaths of blacks and of white civil-rights workers in the South between the 1940s and the 1960s. Moreover, numerous white-supremacy groups, such as the ever-present Ku Klux Klan, have periodically played an important role in violence directed against blacks.[60]

Many blacks left the South for northern cities to escape oppressive conditions, but the movement north itself sometimes resulted in violent conflict, often with white workers concerned with the new job competition. Labor recruitment in the South by northern industry generated resentment of black migrants among the northern white workers. Clashes with whites became frequent as blacks moved into the central-city areas of border and northern cities. A white riot in 1900 in New York City saw a predominantly Irish police force encouraging working-class whites, who attacked blacks wherever they could be found. A similar case was the 1917 East St. Louis riot, one of the most serious white-dominated race riots of this century. East St. Louis's white workers, who saw blacks as an economic threat, pressed local government for action. Union organizers placed a newspaper advertisement announcing that Negro labor was being brought into the community by local industries in order to reduce white wages. In the attack on the black ghetto that resulted, thirty-nine blacks and nine whites were killed; ghetto residents had fought back, killing some of their white attackers. This riot was followed in 1919 by a string of riots from Chicago to Charleston, South Carolina. Most were one-sided white attacks on blacks, with few white casualties.[61]

In the decades which followed, blacks in both the North and the South faced the threat of violence from such white groups as the Ku Klux Klan, which gained strength in the 1920s and again in the 1970s and 1980s. In early 1983 the number of white Americans in the various Klan factions was estimated at 10,000. Newspaper reports have documented Klan activities, including violence against minorities and paramilitary training camps where Klansmen are preparing for what they call a "race war." In the last decade Klan members have been involved in hundreds of antiblack and anti-Jewish incidents; several have been convicted of the murder or assault of blacks and white liberals. In November 1979 a group of Klan and Nazi Party members in Greensboro, North Carolina, were accused of the murders of five demonstrators who were protesting the Klan. TV cameras captured the killings on film, but a local jury acquitted the accused Klansmen and Nazis in a long court trial. The resurgence of the century-old Klan, with its historical commitment to subordinating blacks, signals that virulent forms of white racism remain alive in the United States.[62]

Recent Black Rioting: Structural Causes?

With increased urbanization in the 1930s and 1940s bringing large numbers of blacks to the cities, a new potential for riots developed. A few times in the 1930s and 1940s, particularly in New York City, there were black riots involving pitched battles between black residents and the police. Such rioting revealed the feelings of blacks toward a nonresponsive economic and political system. In the North, by the mid-1960s, more and more cities saw ghetto residents rioting against the symbols of white oppression: the police, local businessmen, and absentee landlords. Between the early 1960s and the early 1970s there were black riots throughout the United States. Large-scale uprisings occurred in Los Angeles (Watts) in 1965, in Detroit and Newark in 1967, and in Washington, D.C., in 1968. Even as late as 1970–1971 there were 250 race-related riots of various size taking place across the United States. The impact was felt across the nation, which was confronted by a militant new generation of proud black Americans willing to engage in the ultimate type of protest. Ameliorative action came on the heels of the riots in the 1960s and early 1970s, sometimes in the significant form of direct economic aid, sometimes in the form of the appointment of investigative riot commissions.[63]

But the problems remained. A few years later in the late spring of 1980 there was another major riot in Miami in which black ghetto residents again lashed out against the police and the larger white society with extensive burning and looting. The three days of angry rioting there took 16 lives, caused 400 injuries, and entailed more than $100 million in property damage. In a *Newsweek* magazine poll conducted after the Miami riot, a nationwide sample of black Americans were asked if they thought the rioting was justified. Twenty-seven percent said "yes" and another 25 percent replied "don't know" or "not sure." Half also said that whites don't care about what happens to blacks or want to "keep blacks down." Black anger at the discrimination and lack of concern of white America broke out in other cities as well. Several cities faced rioting in the early 1980s, from Chattanoga, Tennessee, to Washington, D.C. In the fall of 1982 there was a small riot in Washington, D.C., involving angry blacks and others who were protesting a Ku Klux Klan demonstration. And there was yet another riot in Miami late in 1982.[64]

Rioting has been interpreted by media analysts, police officials, and politicians as a wild rampage by ghetto "riff-raff." Criminals, teenage delinquents, and recent migrants have been blamed. Yet research has shown this view to be a myth, for rioters are typically under 30 years of age but are not for the most part young teenagers. The majority are native-born or long-term local residents of the areas they rioted in; most are not convicted criminals. The role of white officials and the police in generating and accelerating rioting, while overlooked by most white Americans, has been significant; police brutality in particular has often precipitated or accelerated rioting by black Americans.

Police brutality remains a problem. In a 1980 nationwide opinion poll, 26 percent of black Americans said there was substantial police brutality in their areas; another 24 percent said either that there was a little or that they were not sure. Significant numbers still view brutality as a problem. In 1981, *Time* magazine ran a major news report about two blacks who had recently been killed while in police custody in the cities of Los Angeles and Milwaukee. Under pressure from blacks and other citizens, officials in both cities decided to prosecute the police officers involved in the deaths. In recent years many black communities have reported similar "mysterious" deaths of black youths in police custody.[65]

THE ECONOMY

An assimilation framework includes the idea of structural assimilation, one aspect of which is the upward movement of members of racial groups into higher levels of the economy. The ultimate result of structural assimilation is equality with dominant groups. Whether this assimilation framework can be applied to black and other nonwhite Americans has been disputed by power-conflict analysts, who point to the mass of blacks more or less permanently locked into the lower regions of the economy. A test of the optimistic assimilation theories is the economic progress, or lack of progress, of black Americans since their emancipation from slavery.

Prior to the Civil War the relatively few free blacks sometimes found themselves in competition with white immigrants, such as the Irish. In some northern areas blacks found themselves displaced from unskilled- and skilled-job categories by white immigrants. These patterns continued after the Civil War had released large numbers of blacks for the free labor market. After the Civil War blacks began to compete directly with whites in the South. Increasingly blacks were segregated in unskilled "Negro jobs" and were prohibited from taking skilled employment in the newly expanding industrial sectors in the South.

With no major land reform accompanying the shift to free status, most blacks were forced to sell their labor to those controlling the agricultural system, their old slavemasters. Semislave farm labor became the lot of many. Black laborers in particular were often tied to one farm or one area because of the debts they built up in an exploitative, white-controlled system. With less money and less legal protection and facing discrimination in land and consumer-product dealings, it is no wonder that blacks failed to become independent farmers.[66]

The black population in 1900 was still centered in the South; nine blacks in every ten lived there. But the bustling economy developing in the northern and border cities, especially by World War I, the declining significance of "King Cotton" in the South, and southern oppression in the form of segregation stimulated the migration of blacks to northern cities. With the cessation of massive foreign immigration resulting from anti-immigrant legislation, the demand for black laborers in northern industries increased. Thousands of poor black farmers, unable to finance the technological innovations necessary to circumvent the pestilence of the boll weevil, were driven from their farms to the cities. The major push factors, then, were segregation and the declining importance of cotton; the major pull factor was ready employment.[67]

The Great Urban Trek to the "Promised Land"

The urban trek began in earnest around World War I; by the mid-twentieth century millions of black Americans had migrated to what they saw as the economic "promised land." What were their points of destination? Large cities in the Northeast, Midwest, and West. Representing the younger and better-educated segments of the black population, these migrants have often been misrepresented. They were not the dregs of the South that some whites have pictured. Indeed, such an outflow meant a skill loss for the South just as it was undergoing industrialization; those blacks educated in the South became capable workers in other regions.[68]

What was the effect on cities? Recent migrants generally were forced to settle in low-income areas already occupied by blacks, swelling the size of ghettos. A traditional view of this migration, one fostered by optimistic assimilation theorists, is that it has brought great opportunities for economic mobility: Blacks can be viewed as another immigrant group in a long line of immigrant groups (such as the Irish and the Italians) successfully seeking their fortunes in the city. Given this view, one would have expected occupational and income gains between 1900 and 1980 dramatically closing the black-white gap. The reality has, however, been quite different.[69]

A persisting division of labor was established in the cities, enforced at first by coercion and by discriminatory law, then by subtle institutional factors. The urban economy has been viewed as divided into at least two major sectors. The primary labor market has been composed predominantly of privileged white workers and has been characterized by skilled jobs, high wages, and significant mobility ladders. The secondary labor market has traditionally been composed of nonwhite (or earlier by white immigrant) workers and has been characterized by instability, low wages, and few mobility ladders.[70] The dramatic rise of corporate capitalism in the decades after 1900 resulted not only in enormous corporate units, but in unionism as well. One method of dealing with the organized expression of worker discontent was to make concessions to the large segment of white workers, separating them from less privileged nonwhites. Secondary labor market positions would be for nonwhite minorities. Here we see the racially split labor market that has been emphasized by Edna Bonacich, a view we examined in Chapter 2.

The growing number of black workers moving out of farm occupations found themselves channeled into the secondary labor market of cities. There was a slow but steady shift away from tenant farming and share-cropping to unskilled jobs in the industrial sector. In cities the principal occupations of black men became porter, truck driver, janitor, and cook; black women served as maids, restaurant workers, and dressmakers. By 1930 the dominance of agricultural and domestic service jobs could still be seen in Census Bureau figures. Of every 1,000 black workers, 648 were in agricultural or domestic service jobs, compared to 280 of every 1,000 whites. Most of the remainder of blacks were in other unskilled blue-collar positions. Only 7 in 1,000 held clerical positions, compared to 104 in every 1,000 whites. Most blacks in the relatively small professional category were teachers, ministers, and physicians serving the black community; blacks in business usually served a black clientele.

As a result of such occupational concentration, black incomes were sharply lower than those of whites. For example, the median annual income of black families in Atlanta in the mid-1930s was about one-third that of whites ($632 versus $1,876), a typical situation. In the North, black median incomes were only 40 to 50 percent of the incomes of whites. Most blacks, North and South, were poverty-stricken.[71]

One hopeful sign in the Depression era was the slow opening up of labor unions. Most labor unions had traditionally been segregated. By the late 1930s black pressure and federal legislation forced many American Federation of Labor (AFL) unions to begin to reduce discrimination in attempts to secure critical black votes. The new Congress of Industrial Organizations (CIO) began with an officially nondiscriminatory policy in order to attract blacks in the automobile, steel, and packing industries. In 1930 at least twenty-six major unions officially barred blacks from membership; by 1943 the number had dropped to fourteen.[72]

From 1940 to the 1980s: How Much Mobility?

The 1940 Census continued to show a heavy concentration of blacks in agriculture and the secondary labor market of cities. Seventy-three percent of black male workers were in blue-collar jobs, with a heavy concentration in the laborer category and virtually all the rest in unskilled or semiskilled positions or in farming. Sixty percent of black women were employed in the domestic-service category, and most of the rest were in service, laborer, or farming positions. During World War II some industries were forced because of severe labor needs to make significant concessions. In war-related industries the proportion of blacks employed increased from 3 to 8 percent over the war years. Race discrimination there had been lessened by executive orders issued by President Roosevelt. At the end of the war this interlude came to an abrupt end; layoffs at the end of the war hit blacks much harder than whites.[73]

Occupational gains have been made by black Americans over the last two decades, with the most rapid gains coming in the 1960s. Bureau of Labor Statistics data on the proportions of nonwhites among employed persons in specific categories indicate the following changes:[74]

	1955	1961	1972	1980
Professional, technical	4%	4%	7%	9%
Managerial, administrative	2	2	4	5
Sales	4	5	4	5
Clerical	2	3	9	11
Craft and kindred workers	4	5	7	8
Operatives	11	12	13	15
Nonfarm laborers	28	26	20	17
Service workers	29	26	19	18
Private household workers	49	43	41	33
Farm workers	14	16	15	13

The proportions of nonwhites in white-collar categories have grown since 1955, with the largest increase in the job category the Census Bureau calls "clerical." There has been little increase in nonwhite representation in the sales category, and the growth in the proportion of nonwhites in the higher-level categories was most rapid in the 1960s, but slowing down in the 1970–1980 period.

Some of these gains at first seem impressive, but they are not quite what they seem. There are several reasons for this. First, these are data for nonwhites, not just for blacks. The Census Bureau includes certain more prosperous Asian American groups (such as Japanese Americans) in this category. If the data were available for blacks by themselves, the proportions of blacks in white-collar jobs would probably be somewhat lower than these figures for nonwhites. These data, while they are the best available, somewhat exaggerate black progress. Second, nonwhites in white-collar categories are disproportionately concentrated in jobs with lower pay and status than are whites in the same category. For example, within the professional-technical category, nonwhites today are most commonly found in such fields as social and recreation work, kindergarten teaching, vocational counseling, personnel, dietetics, and health-care work. They are least often found among lawyers and judges, dentists, writers and artists, engineers, and university teachers. Within the managerial-administrative category nonwhites are most commonly found among restaurant and bar managers, health administrators, and government officials; they are least commonly found among office managers, bank and financial managers, and sales managers. And among clerical workers nonwhites are most often seen among file clerks, shipping clerks, postal clerks, key punch operators, and typists. Yet another problem is that nonwhites who have moved into better-paying, nontraditional jobs find not only better pay but also new forms of entrenched discrimination, including tokenism.

Blacks are still disproportionately concentrated in the low-paying, lower-status work categories for instance, as private household workers (such as maids), other service workers, nonfarm laborers, and operatives (such as local truckdrivers). Brimmer analyzed employment data for the 1960–1975 period and found that the major part of the gains for blacks came between 1960 and 1969, with stagnation in the 1970's. In the 1970s blacks' "occupational center of gravity remained anchored in those positions requiring little skill and offering few opportunities for advancement."[75] The greatest gains came for those young blacks penetrating the labor force at entry level; although in recessions it is the younger workers who are the most likely to be fired. Gains for black women have come faster than gains for black men workers; but the significance of this is reduced by the fact that the positions attained, such as white-collar jobs typically held by white women workers, are relatively low-status and low-paying.

Traditional discrimination has not disappeared from the American economy. All the types of discrimination which we discussed in Chapter 1 have been documented in research studies and federal court cases dealing with employment practices. An example of isolate discrimination is the white personnel officer in an industrial firm who expresses stereotyped views of blacks by personally defying the company's merit regulations and hiring less-qualified whites over better-qualified blacks. This type of discrimination is common.

Small-group discrimination has also been a common problem, North and South. Small-group conspiracies, arranged by prejudiced supervisors or union officials to subvert company or union regulations that require the hiring or promotion of qualified black employees, continue to be an omnipresent but hard-to-document problem. Direct institutional discrimination refers to organizationally prescribed actions carried out routinely by people in companies and businesses. Examples of this type are still common; they include practices that relegate blacks to inferior job categories or retard the job mobility of blacks beyond the entry level. Today they also include discriminatory disciplinary practices. For example, in 1982 U.S. Postal Service figures were released showing that black postal workers were being fired or suspended four times as often as white workers. Although Post Office officials publicly said that these dismissals and other disciplinary practices were based only on performance, it is highly likely that such a dramatic racial discrepancy means that there is much racial discrimination in this federal government agency.

Indirect institutional discrimination is illustrated in now-common practices which have a negative impact on blacks even though the actions are carried out with no intent to harm. A major example can often be seen in employment screening procedures, where the use of credentials (such as high-school or college degrees) in employment decisions has a negative impact on blacks. Intentional institutional discrimination in education, past and present, often handicaps blacks when they attempt to compete for jobs for which screening requirements include unnecessarily high educational requirements. Moreover, many blacks have suffered because of seniority practices, which have usually been established with no intent to harm them. In plants which were intentionally segregated in the past, and where as a result blacks have not been able to build up the necessary seniority, such practices act to restrict black employment mobility. Recent federal court cases document these persisting discriminatory practices.

Unemployment, Income, and Poverty

Unemployment has been a recurrent problem for white workers, but it has been a much more serious problem for blacks. The nonwhite (or black) unemployment rate has consistently been about twice the white unemployment rate in recent decades:[76]

	NONWHITE (OR BLACK)	WHITE	RATIO
1949	8.9%	5.6%	1.6
1959	10.7	4.8	2.2
1964	9.6	4.6	2.1
1969	6.4	3.1	2.1
1975	13.8	7.8	1.8
1980	13.0	5.9	2.2
1982 (Last quarter)	20.4	9.5	2.1

In recent recessions blacks have continued to lose jobs at twice the rate for whites, and they have been recalled at a slower rate than whites have. Indeed, in the 1981–1982 recession black unemployment went above 20 percent, the highest rate recorded to that point in time.

In addition, government unemployment figures seriously underestimate joblessness and related employment problems. Much higher than the unemployment rate for black Americans is the *subemployment* or *underemployment rate*, which includes those with no jobs, those working part-time, and those making poverty wages. One nationwide study in 1980 found that in addition to the blacks who were unemployed, many more had part-time work but wanted full-time work, had very low-wage jobs, or were discouraged workers who had given up looking for work. In 1980, 3.5 percent of black workers were discouraged workers, 5.4 percent were "involuntary part-time" workers, and 9.5 percent worked for poverty wages. Altogether nearly one-third of black workers fell into these troubled-worker categories; the figure for whites was much less. Over the last decade or so the proportion of blacks in most troubled-worker categories has increased. In terms of unemployment and underemployment, conditions for blacks worsened between the late 1960s and the early 1980s.[77]

Since the 1950s black family income has remained at about 55 to 60 percent of white income. Over this period blacks have not made consistent gains in income relative to whites; black family income as a percent of white family income fluctuated slightly during the 1950s, rose significantly in the late 1960s, then dropped over the 1970s.[78]

BLACK (OR NONWHITE) INCOME AS A PERCENT OF WHITE INCOME FIGURE	
1950	54%
1954	56
1959	52
1964	54
1969	61
1974	58
1980	58

And there is a dollar gap as well. In 1980 the median family income for whites was $21,904. Black family income, however, was just over $12,600, or about 58 percent of the white figure. Between 1970 and 1980 the real income (actual income adjusted for inflation) of white families went up a little, but black income actually declined in real terms. Moreover, in 1959 the number of black families below the poverty line was 1.9 million; in 1981 fully 2 million fell below the line.[79]

The most severe income differential is between black and white families where there is only one parent. In those families black income is only half that of whites. Unemployment for black women has been particularly serious. As Robert Hill has concluded from extensive research, "families headed by black women are primarily poor, not because they do not have husbands, but because they do not have jobs."[80] Black women face both race and sex discrimination in employment.

Whatever the type of family, blacks pull in fewer dollars than whites and are much more likely than white families to live in poverty. Indeed, in the early 1980s *one-third* of all black families were classified as *poor* by official government standards, compared with only *one-tenth* of whites. Many whites suppose that government programs such as welfare, unemployment assistance, and Medicaid are used especially by the black poor. A major survey by the National Urban League of 3,000 black households in 1979 revealed that

1. Seventy percent of the unemployed never get unemployment benefits;
2. Over half of poor blacks get *no* welfare aid such as Aid to Families with Dependent Children (AFDC);
3. Half of all black families on welfare get no Medicaid assistance.[81]

And this situation worsened further with federal cutbacks in the early 1980s.

Remedying Racial Discrimination?

What has government done to eliminate discrimination against black and other nonwhite Americans? Government action has been a hotly debated issue in recent years, with some arguing that it has gone too far, even to the point of large-scale "reverse" discrimination favoring nonwhites, while other analysts argue that federal policies have had little impact on discrimination.

Significant government action in regard to employment discrimination began with President Franklin Roosevelt's establishment of a Fair Employment Practices Commission (FEPC) in 1941, an action taken because of heavy pressure from black leaders. The FEPC was at first ineffective because of opposition from employers, so a second executive order was issued in 1943 and a new commission was established. Modest gains in war-related employment resulted from FEPC actions, but after the war attempts to make it a permanent agency were unsuccessful and blacks lost some of what they had gained. It was not until executive orders were issued by President Johnson in the 1960s requiring government contractors to act to desegregate that the pressure became significant. However, federal government contract compliance agencies, those that are supposed to implement the executive orders, have reviewed only a minority of contractors under their supervision. Progress there has in fact been modest.[82]

The 1964 Civil Rights Act and its later amendments prohibited discrimination in employment by employers. The Equal Employment Opportunity Commission (EEOC) was created to enforce the 1964 Act, primarily to deal with employment discrimination by labor unions, private employers, state and local governments, and educational institutions. The EEOC has the responsibility of investigating complaints, seeking conciliation, and—since 1972—filing suit to end discrimination. For example, in the fiscal year 1974 nearly 57,000 persons filed complaints, a sharp increase over previous years; two-thirds of the complaints were by blacks. However, because of management problems and a lack of staff a very large backlog of cases (100,000) had built up in the 1970s, to the point that many complainants could find no practical remedy through this procedure; indeed, the average complaint was taking more than two-and-a-half years to resolve.

By 1982 EEOC had substantially reduced its backlog of discrimination complaints. Yet the backlog was still estimated at five thousand to ten thousand cases, many of them several years old. Moreover, operating under the conservative philosophy of the Ronald Reagan Administration in the early 1980s, EEOC drew back from an aggressive position on discrimination. EEOC reduced the number of class action complaint investigations and other broad institutionally-focused investigations. These broad civil rights investigations have the potential to liberate large numbers of blacks and other nonwhites from discriminatory employment practices. The cutbacks, black leaders argued, signaled a government retreat from protecting the employment rights of black Americans.[83]

There is no systematic evidence available on the impact of this type of government activity on black job mobility. What data we do have indicate increased pressure on employers—from small business to corporations to universities—to desegregate their work forces. Thousands of Affirmative Action forms are filled out annually. The data on actual changes in the work force reveal a mixed picture. For example, those large firms (one hundred or more employees) covered by the EEOC reporting requirements reported greater percentage gains in black employment in the 1966–1974 period than did all employers in the economy, but the gains were limited to such positions as clerical, craft, and service workers. Percentage gains in the professional and managerial areas for the same firms were *less* than in the economy as a whole. In addition, as of the mid-1970s, the black proportion of employees in these firms was generally lower than in the economy as a whole in the white-collar and the skilled blue-collar categories. It is clear from a number of research studies that economic gains in the 1960s began *before* significant EEOC, Labor Department, and other federal court actions had been taken in the area of Affirmative Action, gains actually reflecting growing black militancy and the economic prosperity generated by the Vietnam War economy of the 1960s. We will return to these issues in Chapter 12.[84]

The old phrase "the poor pay more" has long been appropriate to the situation of ghetto consumers, both nonwhite and white. The poor in urban ghettos have historically faced serious problems with credit, with shoddy merchandise, high prices, few stores, and the like. Small independent stores are common in ghetto areas, for large chains have been less willing to operate there; such stores are typically less efficient, have less to offer, and charge more. Studies of food stores have often found higher prices and lower quality in ghettos, although a few studies have found little or no difference. Ghetto stores have been found to have lower-quality merchandise. Some merchants deal in off-brand merchandise and use bait-and-switch advertising, illegal interest, exorbitant markups, and high-pressure salespersons. Many merchants have come in from outside the community, a situation viewed as exploitative and described as "business colonialism." The ghetto consumer is faced with restricted housing choices and typically a dismal housing situation. According to Census data, blacks are less likely than whites to own their own homes and more likely to live in overcrowded housing lacking some or all plumbing facilities.[85]

PARTICIPATION IN POLITICS

Walton has distinguished four levels of political participation by black Americans: (1) nonparticipation, where blacks are excluded; (2) limited participation, where a few privileged blacks participate; (3) moderate participation, where the majority of blacks participate and where demands are being made; (4) full participation, where black priorities become imbedded in public policy. In the slavery period the situation was close to his first category, one of very limited participation by a few free blacks. Between the 1660s and the 1860s some black Americans petitioned legislatures and executive officials for redress of grievances; numerous petitions were submitted and, as a rule, ignored.[86] The Civil War period brought an end to slavery and a beginning for increased black participation in electoral politics. The 1866 Civil Rights Act made all blacks citizens and proclaimed their civil rights. The Thirteenth Amendment abolished slavery, and the Fourteenth Amendment spelled out the doctrine that blacks are citizens whose rights cannot be denied by the states. The Fifteenth Amendment guaranteed blacks (males) the right to vote. Legislative action had at last dealt with the civil rights of the largest group of nonwhite Americans.

From the Reconstruction Era to the 1920s

The Reconstruction era came to the South as a breath of fresh air. Reconstruction was precipitated by a South unwilling to make major changes in its treatment of blacks and insisting that the leaders of the Confederacy be allowed to rule. A brief period of limited federal occupation resulted. While Reconstruction has often been pictured as a tragic period in southern history—and there were abuses of federal power—it was actually a period of some progress for black and white alike, at least for the majority in the poorer classes. *Whites* dominated all the state governments. Remarkable gains came to the South: dueling and whipping were banned; public schools, prisons, and hospitals were developed; state constitutions and courts were reformed.[87]

During Reconstruction, blacks made political gains, although the gains were nowhere near as great as southern apologists have suggested. Moderate political participation, to use Walton's term, became the order of the day. After the Civil War, black men gained the right to vote in all states. Southern state constitutional conventions included black delegates, although in most states native white southerners were the majority of delegates. These progressive constitutions brought the South into a new era, with most abolishing the rule that only property owners could vote or hold office. Black voters turned out in large numbers, political organizations flourished, and significant numbers of blacks were elected to political office for the first time.

Between 1870 and 1901 twenty blacks served in the U.S. House of Representatives and two in the U.S. Senate. Hiram R. Revel and Blanche K. Bruce served the state of Mississippi between 1870 and 1881 as senators, the first two to serve there and two of the three blacks that as of the early 1980s had *ever* served there. Blacks served in state legislatures, but they attained a legislative majority only for a brief period in the lower house in South Carolina.[88]

The overthrow of white Reconstruction governments by conservative southern forces came swiftly; the so-called "Redemption" period began with the Hayes Compromise of 1877, which removed federal troops from southern states and abandoned federal protection of blacks. During the Reconstruction period there was considerable segregation, although it was not the all-encompassing system it would become by the early 1900s. In the first decade the Redeemers kept the existing patterns of segregation but did not seem eager to expand it. In many areas blacks still voted and continued to hold public office. Sometimes public accommodations, such as hotels, were open to blacks. Freedom here, segregation there, mixing here, exclusion there—such was the fluidity of the period, a fluidity long neglected by social scientists and popular writers.[89]

But this era of what Van Woodward calls the "forgotten alternatives" did not last long. The threat of black-white coalitions among farmers became too great for the conservative gentry to endure. Agrarian populist movements binding poor black and poor white together reflected an awareness of common problems, but the conservative opposition roared an ugly response. Conservatives appealed to the poor whites' sense of racial superiority; populist voters were intimidated by Ku Klux Klan-type violence; election fraud was common. The white populist was attacked as a Negro-loving traitor to the white race, a "renegade to Southern womanhood, the Confederate dead, and the God of his fathers."[90] Unable to withstand such pressure, working-class whites bailed out on their black allies. Thus came an era with increasingly rigid walls of segregation.

Supreme Court decisions nailed the lid on the coffin of southern racial progress. The decision in *Plessy v. Ferguson* (1896) was the major blow, with its doctrine of "separate but equal" facilities for blacks in a case involving the racial segregation of railroad cars. The Court reasoned that "legislation is powerless to eradicate racial instincts or to abolish distinctions based upon physical differences, and the attempt to do so can only result in accentuating the difficulties of the present situation." Moreover, "if one race be inferior to another socially, the Constitution of the United States cannot put them upon the same plane."[91]

By the early 1900s the South was well on its way to an absurd complex of segregatory laws. In 1922 Mississippi passed a law requiring segregated taxicabs; in 1932 Atlanta passed a law requiring black and white baseball teams to play at least two blocks apart; and Birmingham, Alabama, even prohibited interracial domino playing![92]

Disenfranchisement of black voters was achieved by the rigorous enforcement of discriminatory literacy test laws, poll tax laws, and "grandfather clause" laws limiting the vote to those who had voted prior to 1861 and their (white) descendants. Between 1896 and 1900 the number of black voters in Louisiana decreased from 130,000 to 5,300.[93] All other southern states followed this lead. The first decade of the twentieth century was a low point in the political history of black Americans. Political exclusion of free citizens was directly institutionalized. A slow upward trend began in the second decade of the twentieth century. The Supreme Court began a slow swing back to the protection of civil rights in 1915 by declaring "grandfather clauses" unconstitutional. Voter registration increased very slowly.

By the 1920s the movement to the cities brought a few blacks to the political forefront, particularly in the North. Independent political organizations were constructed in a few cities, but the only major success was that of Adam Clayton Powell, Jr., in New York City. In 1945 Powell became the first black elected outside Chicago to Congress in several decades. Blacks generally lacked clout in many northern cities because of such discriminatory techniques as gerrymandering, which has persisted into the 1980s as a way of reducing the impact of black votes. In the North the black vote was at first strongly tied to the Republican party, but by the 1930s this had begun to change. As Republicans became more conservative and Democrats more concerned with health and welfare issues, the black vote shifted dramatically.[94]

The Limits of Black Progress

By 1940 the political situation still looked bleak; in that year only 90,000 of the 3.7 million adult blacks in the Deep South voted in the general election. The segregated white primary had become one of the most effective devices keeping blacks from voting in the South. In 1942 there were only a dozen black state legislators and a few blacks on school and tax boards; none were serving in the South, except for a few in small all-black towns.[95] Blacks benefited little from southern government programs; schools, hospitals, parks, and other public facilities for blacks were inadequate or nonexistent, a situation that would hold true in the South for several more decades.

By the late 1940s blacks were again voting in some numbers in the South, with an estimated 600,000 registered. Voter registration increased sharply in the South between the 1940s and the 1970s, from 250,000 to 4 million voters. A big jump came in the years after passage of the Voting Rights Act in 1965, an act with a demonstrable impact on participation. Conventional wisdom among social scientists has sometimes suggested that because of inadequate civic training and lower educational levels blacks would not be able to organize in an effective way. Yet this conventional wisdom has been proven wrong. With their new enfranchisement blacks have developed effective political organizations and campaigns in some areas of the South. The results are proof enough of growing organization. In 1965 there were approximately 70 black elected officials in the South. By February 1968 the figure was 248; by 1980 the figure had increased to 2,457. Blacks were even being elected in some areas where black populations were minorities, most typically from black wards or districts in those areas. Yet blacks have still attained proportional equality in *very few* areas of the South. Their proportion among all elected officials was in the neighborhood of 3 percent. At the current rate of increase, blacks can achieve equality late in the twenty-first century.[96]

Have black officials in the South been able to accomplish anything? Some argue, with the late Rev. Martin Luther King, Jr., that black votes and officials can end segregation and alleviate poverty. Others see blacks as unable to gain much through the electoral process. Mack Jones has argued that black elected officials have not been able to reorder white priorities significantly in regard to employment, housing, and education.[97] So far the accomplishments of black office-holders in the South have been more than the pessimists would expect, although much less than justice would require. Relying heavily on federal and private foundation aid, rather than local or state money, black officials have increased public services and expanded economic opportunities somewhat for their constituents. Even where they are in the minority, some have succeeded in improving services as well as in increasing the number of blacks hired.

The number of black elected officials in the nation as a whole increased sharply between 1964 and 1980, from about 100 to more than 4,900. Since 1967 blacks have won mayoral elections in a number of major cities with large black populations: Washington, D.C., Newark, Detroit, Chicago,

Cleveland, Los Angeles, Atlanta, and Gary, Indiana. Yet, even on a nationwide basis, black officials have been a tiny percentage of all elected officials, indicating continuing substantial underrepresentation. A study of black officials by Conyers and Wallace found them as effective in the North as in the South: the election of blacks typically brought some concrete payoff, usually at the local or state level, in terms of black employment in government, expanded services, and some increased respect for black rights by government officials.[98]

With the New Deal in the 1930s came a new recognition of the contribution blacks could make at the federal level. Between 1933 and 1940 President Roosevelt appointed more than one hundred black Americans to federal positions below the top levels. Benefits flowing from New Deal actions nonetheless benefited whites considerably more than blacks. New Deal agencies such as the Agricultural Adjustment Administration (AAA) and the National Recovery Administration (NRA) did little to make sure that blacks received their fair share of government aid. Because of direct discrimination, AAA and NRA dollars did not flow freely to black farmers and workers. Black Americans did receive aid from agencies concerned with temporary relief, but the more important recovery agencies favored white constituents.[99]

Between World War II and the 1980s, black voters began having a greater impact on the legislative, executive, and judicial branches of the federal government. A small number of blacks were elected to Congress. In the 1950s a third black was finally elected to Congress, joining the two others from New York and Chicago. By the early 1980s there were 21 black representatives, but no black senators, in Congress. The first black *ever* to serve in a presidential cabinet was Robert Weaver, who in 1967 became secretary of housing and urban development. In the mid-1960s President Lyndon Johnson appointed Andrew Brimmer as the first black on the Federal Reserve Board, Thurgood Marshall as the first black Supreme Court Justice, and Patricia Harris as the first black ambassador. Yet even in the Johnson administration few black Americans served at the top in any major executive department or on federal commissions other than the civil-rights agencies. Moreover, only a small percentage of federal judgeships have been held by black Americans. The overall pattern in federal legislative, executive, and judicial positions can still be described as one of sharp and continuing discrimination and underrepresentation.[100]

The growing black vote has sometimes been important in close elections. At the local levels moderate whites sensitive to black needs have, with the aid of the black vote, beaten more openly conservative or racist whites. In federal elections the black vote has from time to time loomed large. In the 1944 election black voters played a role in Roosevelt's election; in the late 1940s they were important to the Truman election. And the black vote in a few key states reportedly decided the Kennedy election in 1960. Black voters played a key role in electing Lyndon Johnson president in 1964 and Jimmy Carter president in 1976. The black vote has also kept white liberal members of Congress in office when they otherwise would not have survived conservative trends among their white constituents. And in the 1982 congressional elections blacks increased the number of black representatives in Congress to 21, the largest number in U.S. history. Black voters turned out in record numbers for that off-year election and helped elect a Congress more sympathetic to civil rights issues than the preceding Congress.[101]

The future of black political participation in the North and South is unclear. Recent gains are a first step. Whether the southern developments will be nipped in the bud or will lead to larger-scale change is open to debate. The future of black political power in the North is tied to the fate of the cities. Numerous observers see increasing black political control of the large central cities; but a decline in the financial strength of those cities may well result in blacks ruling bankrupt fiefdoms. Nonetheless, recent black electoral victories in cities such as Chicago and Los Angeles have caused white politicians to pay more attention to the black vote in national elections. Some have calculated that no less than 220 of the electoral college votes can depend on black votes at the state level. Democratic Party successes at the national level depend on these votes.[102]

Nonviolent Protest

Black protest ranges from legal strategies, to the ballot, to nonviolent civil disobedience, to violent attacks on the system. Criticizing the accommodationist position of such leaders as Booker T. Washington, W. E. B. DuBois and other black and liberal white leaders formed the Niagara movement in 1905. Legal and voting rights, as well as economic issues, were the focus of their activities. Not long thereafter, some of these leaders played a role in creating the National Association for the Advancement of Colored People (NAACP).

Organizations directed at self-help and philanthropic activity, such as the Urban League, were also created in the early decades of the twentieth century. The efforts of the new black organizations began to pay off, in providing more philanthropic aid for the poor in cities and in chipping away at the legal edifice of segregation. One of the first major NAACP legal victories was a 1917 Supreme Court decision, *Buchanan v. Warley*, which knocked down a Louisville, Kentucky, law requiring residential segregation and took a first step in reversing the segregationist position the Court had taken since the late 1800s. Most other High Court decisions until the 1930s, however, hurt the cause of black rights, reinforcing segregation in schools, transportation, and the jury system.[103]

In the cities large numbers of blacks were crowded together. Black consciousness grew up together with new organizations—civil rights groups, educational organizations, and a new press. There was a black renaissance in music and literature in the ghettos. There were newly elected politicians, pressed by their constituents to seek changes in discriminatory laws and practices. Against fierce resistance the NAACP began a large-scale attack on segregation in schools, voting, transportation, and jury selection. Beginning in the 1930s NAACP lawyers, together with other lawyers, won a series of cases which over the next several decades expanded the legal

rights of black defendants, eliminated the all-white political primary, protected the voting rights of blacks, reduced job discrimination by unions,
voided restrictive housing covenants, and desegregated schools and public
accommodations. The separate-but-equal doctrine of *Plessy v. Ferguson* increasingly came under attack. Dramatically reversing its position in the
1896 case, the Supreme Court in a famous decision in *Brown v. Board of
Education* (1954) ruled that "in the field of public education the doctrine
of 'separate but equal' has no place."[104]

Other organizations have pursued different protest strategies. One
was the separatist strategy. Black nationalism blossomed in the 1920s and
1930s in such organizations as Marcus Garvey's Universal Negro Improvement Association (UNIA), as well as in new black business and professional
groups. Back-to-Africa schemes were part of Garvey's movement. The UNIA
was also a black self-help organization which involved thousands of black
Americans in black businesses, including a black steamship line. Garvey
articulated a philosophy of black nationalism and attracted large numbers
of followers.[105]

Black-white relations in the United States have alternated between
periods of relative calm and bursts of sustained fury. In the quiet phases
expectations rise and preparations are made for new action. By the 1940s
and 1950s more militant strategies were being generated in black communities. During World War II a threatened large-scale march on Washington, D.C., to be led by A. Phillip Randolph and other black leaders,
forced President Roosevelt to issue an employment desegregation order.
After World War II, Randolph and other leaders organized against the
peacetime draft on the basis that blacks should not serve in a Jim Crow
army. After unsuccessful attempts to get black leaders to back down on
this issue, President Truman set up an agency to get rid of discrimination
in federal employment and a committee to oversee desegregation in the
armed forces.[106]

The 1950s and 1960s saw an increase in nonviolent civil disobedience.
First came major boycotts such as the boycott of segregated buses in Montgomery, Alabama, in the 1950s, a successful movement which brought the
Reverend Martin Luther King, Jr., into national prominence. In 1960 black
students began the sit-in movement at a whites-only lunch counter in
Greensboro, North Carolina, touching off a long series of similar actions
by thousands of black southerners and their white allies throughout the
South. The Freedom Rides on buses came in 1961; blacks and whites were
testing federal court orders desegregating public transportation and demonstrating the lack of compliance throughout the South. Near Anniston,
Alabama, the first bus of Freedom Riders was burned; in Birmingham the
riders were attacked by a white mob.

Thus began a series of major demonstrations. There were mass marches,
prayer vigils, and arrests in Albany, Georgia, in 1962. In the spring of 1963
Martin Luther King, Jr., and his associates launched a series of demonstrations against discrimination in Birmingham, Alabama. Fire hoses and
police dogs were used against the demonstrators, many of whom were
young children, gaining much national publicity. An agreement desegre-

gating businesses and employment ended the protests, but another round of more aggressive demonstrations was touched off when a black home and motel were bombed. Then came the massive 1963 March on Washington, in which King dramatized rising black aspirations in his famous "I have a dream" speech.[107]

Direct action against segregation in the North began in earnest in the 1960s. There were boycotts in Harlem, sit-ins in Chicago, school sit-ins in New Jersey, and mass demonstrations in Cairo, Illinois. The Nation of Islam ("Black Muslims") was aggressively pressing for black pride and black-controlled businesses. The Congress of Racial Equality (CORE) accelerated protest campaigns against housing and employment discrimination. School boycotts, picketing at construction sites, and rent strikes became commonplace. In 1964 blacks in New York tried to stop traffic by staging a sit-in on a bridge and threatened a stall-in to disrupt the opening of the World's Fair. New organizations sprang up. Under the leadership of Stokeley Carmichael, the Student Nonviolent Coordinating Committee (SNCC) had germinated the "black power" movement. There was a growing group of militant organizations oriented toward a black power ideology, including the Black Panthers. In this period pride and consciousness grew in all segments of the black community in the North, particularly among the young.[108]

Progress and Retreat

During the Johnson administration the civil rights movement brought about three major pieces of legislation prohibiting discrimination in employment, voting, and housing—the Voting Rights Act of 1965 and the Civil Rights Acts of 1964 and 1968. In the 1970s these important pieces of legislation were amended and expanded and more effort was put into enforcement.

Yet many of these advances were threatened in the 1980s with the arrival of the Ronald Reagan administration. The conservative president radically increased military spending but cut back federal social programs, such as job training and food stamp programs, on which many poor blacks and other nonwhites depend. In addition, there were cuts in funding for federal agencies which enforce civil rights laws. Between 1980 and 1983, according to the U.S. Commission on Civil Rights, there was a 25 percent drop in support for enforcement agencies, with inflation taken into account. The Commission analyses indicate that most civil rights agencies were reducing their enforcement activities, such as class-action suits aimed at discriminatory employers and compliance reviews of government contractors, because of the budget cutbacks and the new conservative policy of the Reagan Administration. As a result, black civil rights organizations protested; some staged demonstrations in Washington, D.C., and in other cities protesting budget cutbacks. A Gallup poll late in 1981 found that while 61 percent of whites approved of President Reagan's performance at that point in time, only 13 percent of blacks expressed similar approval. A majority of blacks seemed to feel that the federal government had again turned its back on an oppressed nonwhite group in need.[109]

EDUCATION

The Reconstruction period saw the establishment in the South of numerous schools for ex-slaves under the sponsorship of the federal government or private organizations. The end of Reconstruction did not bring an end to black schools. Religious organizations and white philanthropists took up the slack left when federal government aid subsided; schools and colleges increased in number. By 1900, however, overt institutionalized discrimination was clear in grossly inferior public educational facilities and programs for blacks; all southern states had legally segregated schools operating on a "separate but equal" doctrine.

Yet schools were anything but equal. For many decades little public money was spent on black children. In 1900 some counties in the South were spending *ten* times as much per capita for the education of white children as for education of black children. As late as the 1930s one study found that the average expenditure per pupil in elementary and secondary schools in ten southern states was $49.30 for white children but only $17.04 for blacks, a ratio of nearly three to one for the entire area. A racial discrepancy in expenditures persists in some areas in the 1980s.[110]

In spite of discrimination, blacks pressed onward in the direction of the educational dream. By the early 1900s a million-and-a-half black children were in schools. There were thirty-four black colleges in the South. In the late nineteenth century, the nationally known black leader Booker T. Washington advocated vocational education for black youths in the South. He played a significant role in expanding schooling opportunities. Specialized education became a dominant tradition, with a focus on industrial skills suitable for an agricultural economy, which was unfortunately declining. Moreover, well-trained blacks had difficulty being accepted by white agriculturalists, who preferred low-level tenant farmers.[111]

After 1900 the proportion of black children attending school in the South continued to increase; sharp improvements in black literacy occurred. Segregated education notwithstanding, between the 1940s and the 1970s blacks continued to make significant educational progress. Median educational attainment for those over 25 years of age went from 5.7 years in 1940 to 9.9 years in 1970. Most of this gain came prior to 1960. By 1980 the black-white differential had narrowed significantly: 12.5 years for whites and 12.0 years for blacks. The black-white educational gap is narrowing much more quickly than the economic gap.[112]

Are increases in educational attainment translated into commensurate occupational and income achievement? Since the late 1800s a chorus of opinion has pressed the view that education is *the* solution to black problems. Yet research studies in recent years have come to the conclusion that educational differences account for little of the differences in black and white incomes. One study of poverty areas in the twelve largest metropolitan areas in 1966–1967 found that education and training had a much greater economic payoff for whites than for blacks: "In central city poverty areas, whites earn on the average well over *twice as much per extra year of schooling as nonwhites.*"[113] Increased education significantly reduced the likelihood of unemployment for whites—but not for blacks. This study, together with others, raises serious questions about the traditional assumption that education can easily bring about economic benefits for blacks just as it has for whites.

The Desegregation Struggle

The black struggle for education has created a significant body of law. Early civil rights activity in the twentieth century was directed at improving that education. One of the NAACP's early objectives was the inauguration of a drive to equalize opportunity. The slow movement toward school desegregation began in earnest in the 1930s, with the NAACP legal attack. Graduate school cases were the first to show up the "separate but equal" doctrine for the sham it was. In the mid-1930s, the decision in *Murray v. University of Maryland* forced the desegregation of Maryland's law school. Later cases forced the desegregation of the University of Missouri, University of Oklahoma, and University of Texas law schools. A suit against the University of Oklahoma forced the dismantling of a segregated graduate school program. Then in 1954 black parents won the most famous school case of all, *Brown et al. v. Board of Education of Topeka.* Nonetheless, school desegregation came very slowly, with most systems ignoring or circumventing the *Brown* decision. Private white academies were set up to avoid school desegregation. Collective resistance and even violence were used by some whites in attempts to forestall desegregation. In 1956 in Little Rock, President Eisenhower was forced to federalize the Arkansas National Guard to desegregate a Little Rock high school.[114]

A series of court cases over the next two decades in response to these subtle and not-so-subtle resistance techniques expanded the attack on segregated schooling. In *Swann v. Charlotte-Mecklenburg Board of Education* (1971) the Supreme Court upheld the use of limited pupil transportation ("busing") as legal means of disestablishing a dual school system. In *Keyes v. Denver School District No. 1* (1973) the Court, for the first time in a northern case, ruled that evidence of government-imposed segregation in part of a school district, by such means as selective attendance zones and school-site selection, is sufficient to prove segregation and to require desegregation, including pupil transportation, as a remedy. (Nonwhites other than blacks were considered.) Segregated schools included those in which local white authorities had taken any significant action to keep nonwhite and white children separate, such as by gerrymandering districts or locating new schools so as to reinforce segregation lines. In decisions made in the 1970s, however, the Supreme Court rejected the inclusion of suburban districts in city desegregation plans except where the outlying suburban districts could be shown to have played a role in perpetuating segregated school systems.[115] By the late 1970s and early 1980s the newly conservative Court was moving away from requiring massive desegregation except in the most blatant situations of direct discrimination.

School desegregation has become a heatedly discussed white-black issue. As a result of a long series of court-ordered desegregation actions, large numbers of black children are attending school with whites in formerly dual systems throughout the South. Indeed, desegregation was more extensive in the South than in the North in the 1970s and 1980s. Northern school systems, such as that in Boston, Massachusetts, were under court order to desegregate; and resistance to such orders—including white violence—was building in the North. Some liberal social scientists and politicians who had been vigorous advocates of desegregation were now alleging that court-ordered desegregation was accelerating the suburbanization of whites, North and South, and thus creating natural dual systems, with blacks in the central city and whites on the periphery. A common conclusion was that school desegregation policy was either a threat or a failure.[116]

Yet such arguments are problematical, for the suburbanization of white families had been going on for several decades prior to school desegregation. The urban situation—sometimes described as a "black neck in a white noose"—would have occurred even without court-ordered desegregation. It is not possible to massively desegregate schools in many of the largest cities without involving the suburbs. Moreover, one crucial point missed in much of the debate over white flight to the suburbs and busing is that most American cities have populations well below 1 million. Desegregating formerly segregated schools in a city of 100,000 or 200,000 involves much less in the way of organization and transportation problems than it does in the largest cities. Many school boards could do a great deal more to desegregate their public schools without engaging in large-scale pupil transportation. For example, they could redraw gerrymandered districts or locate all new schools on the boundaries of segregated residential areas so as to maximize natural desegregation; or they could develop more central learning centers which would draw children from all over the city. Desegregation of a school's staff, extracurricular activities, or curriculum would not require "massive busing."[117] The failure of many school systems to make these changes suggests that much of the debate over busing is calculated to obscure the real issue—white opposition to white and black children going to school together.

The issue of busing for desegregation has seldom been placed in the necessary historical context. School busing dates back many decades prior to the desegregation of schools—in fact, to the beginning of public schools. Even in the early 1970s at least 44 percent of all schoolchildren rode to school on school buses, and perhaps as many as 65 percent rode on school or public buses, while less than 4 percent were being bused for the purpose of school desegregation.[118]

Another important issue in the debate over desegregation has been the question of results. While there is agreement among researchers that whites in majority-white schools have not suffered a loss in achievement after desegregation, debates have raged over black gains or losses. A majority of research studies with the most careful methodologies show some gains in achievement for black children as a result of desegregation, but the results have not been as favorable or as dramatic as supporters had hoped. One review of 120 research studies found that black achievement improvement in desegregated settings was most likely to be found in earlier grades, in 50-percent-or-more-white schools, and in arithmetic. Some studies have found few or no achievement gains. The very limited research on aspirations, interracial attitudes, and social mixing in desegregated schools has shown mixed results.[119]

One result of school desegregation may be housing desegregation. In a recent study, Diana Pearce reported that cities with metropolitan-area school desegregation plans had experienced much more rapid desegregation of housing patterns than cities that were not desegregating their schools on a metropolitan-area-wide basis. Cities of similar size and racial mix differed greatly in the extent of housing desegregation as a result of differences in the scope of their school desegregation programs. Cities with school desegregation plans only for central cities did not have as much housing desegregation as cities which desegregated both central cities and suburban areas. Pearce concluded from this that busing for school desegregation purposes need not be a long-term program, since metropolitan desegregation of schools may eventually reduce housing segregation— and that in turn means that in the future schools can be naturally desegregated without busing.[120]

Important too is the way in which desegregation is implemented. Much school desegregation has taken place in the context of a rather hostile community and school administration, a situation which might in the short term reduce the positive results. Perhaps most important of all, in virtually all school settings *comprehensive* school desegregation is a long way from being achieved. Students may be mixed, but seldom has desegregation been systematic enough to cover all the following features: (1) desegregation of students; (2) desegregation of internal tracking systems; (3) desegregation of teachers and administrators; (4) desegregation of extracurricular activities; (5) desegregation of formerly white-oriented textbooks and curricula; (6) two-way pupil transportation so that nonwhite children do not bear the burden alone; and (7) sharply increased school funding to cover the costs of the innovative programs required.

The political scene in the 1970s and 1980s made these issues difficult to cope with. White opposition to large-scale desegregation was mounting to the point where even the Supreme Court began backing away from a metropolitan desegregation approach and even from desegregation other than the most necessary kind. It remains unclear whether the Supreme Court will continue to order dismantling of segregated school systems in the face of growing opposition. That black children will face segregated education for generations to come is a sad prediction not likely to be in error.

In the 1980s the Reagan administration proposed tuition tax credits for parents who send children to private schools. If this plan were to become law, it would mainly benefit the more affluent—and thus mainly white— families who have the money to send children to private schools. Most black families would not benefit from tuition tax credits. These tax subsidies might eventually mean a reduction in government expenditures for public schools, which expenditures were sharply reduced by nearly one-third in the first years of the same Reagan administration. Black children (and less affluent white children) would doubtless suffer from a tuition tax credit program. In this way, the American school system could become more racially segregated than it now is.

College Attendance

Since the 1950s black students have gone to college in ever-increasing numbers. Once limited to segregated all-black colleges, by the 1970s and 1980s three-quarters of black college students were going to predominantly white colleges. Yet many black students face racial problems on white campuses. There is a higher drop-out rate and a lower rate of enrollment in advanced degree programs than for whites. Walter Allen has reported that "black students often find it necessary to create their own social and cultural networks" because of their exclusion from white networks. In a 1980 University of Michigan study, half the black students questioned said they did not feel part of general campus life. Lack of support from white students and teachers creates severe adjustment problems for many black students, particularly when there is only a token number on campus. Many black students have poor relations with white faculty members and get inadequate counseling. Many report they are disenchanted with their college environments. Most blacks come to white campuses as the victims of institutional and personal racism. And, Allen has noted, "after their entrance, such incidents of discrimination evidently do not cease and black students subsequently experience adjustment and academic performance difficulties."[121] In the University of Michigan survey cited above, 85 percent of black students questioned reported that they had run into racial discrimination on campus, including subtle forms of discrimination such as comments by professors that "black students aren't very bright" and blatant forms of discrimination such as "KKK" and "nigger" being painted on a house owned by a black organization.

Black students are often blamed by whites for their failure to adjust. In fact, it often is the white administrators, faculty members and students at the colleges who have failed to adjust their white-oriented college environments to students from different racial and income backgrounds. Institutionalized racism may be more subtle in higher education today, but it is nonetheless real.

RELIGION

The first major stereotyping of black Africans was in terms of what Europeans saw as un-Christian, uncivilized savagery. The irony of militaristic, slave-trading, warring Europeans seeing Africans as "savage" has been lost on white Europeans since that period. The slaves imported into the colonies brought an array of religions with them. At first slaveowners feared that "Christianizing" the Africans would put notions of freedom into their heads; but missionaries were instructed and laws were passed making it clear that conversion to Christianity did not bring freedom along with it. Devout slaveowners encouraged missionaries, particularly Baptists and Methodists, to convert slaves. Only certain parts of the Christian tradition were considered appropriate for instruction. That obedience was divinely ordained was a central lesson. So too was the promise of eternal life in heaven as the payoff for obedience as a slave. Slaveowners came to recognize the advantages of religion as a way of reinforcing physical subordination.[122]

Yet it was impossible to hide the profreedom and antiauthoritarian aspects of the biblical tradition. The Christianity of the slaves sometimes became linked to protest. The view of God that many slaves held—stressing a God who led the Israelites out of slavery—was different than that slaveholders had hoped for. In spirituals there was, hidden by symbolism, a religion of yearning to be free. Regular meetings were encouraged by the new religion, some of which were held secretly. In these gatherings slave conspiracies to revolt were sometimes hatched. Blacks were permitted to preach to gatherings; and many of these preachers became leaders, including leaders of slave revolts.[123]

Formal church organizations grew up among slaves and free blacks in the cities, a result of exclusion from white churches. Absalom Jones and Richard Allen were black leaders in Philadelphia who, after being mistreated at a white Methodist church, established their own Free African Society in 1787. Later, Jones established the first Negro Episcopal Church, and Allen played a role in the emergence of the African Methodist Episcopal Church.[124]

After the Civil War, churches played an important role in black communities. Churches were mutual-aid societies, ministering to those facing sickness and death; and churches played a role in the pooling of economic resources. Education often came as religious education. After the Civil War, new schools were established, many under religious auspices, with some training of ministers as black leaders. Black churches continued as community and schooling centers, since few such centers were provided by local or state governments.[125]

With migration to the cities came a shift for some urbanites to a less otherworldly religious style. Social welfare and civil rights activity were an ever-increasing part of black religious life, particularly in the mainline churches. One sect-church grew up on the urban scene to become a major force. Popularly known as the "Black Muslims," the Nation of Islam sharply broke with the Christian background of black Americans, pressing hard for a black-oriented theology suffused with major doses of black pride and self-help. Thousands of black Americans rejected white Christianity and turned to a distinctive American version of an ancient non-Western religious tradition. Prominent black leaders have come out of this non-Christian movement, foremost among whom was Malcolm X.[126]

Black Religion as Protest?

Has black religion been excessively otherworldly? Has black religion fostered or stifled protest? In an influential analysis of these issues, Gary Marx has argued that otherworldly religion and protest orientations are not compatible. Basing his arguments on an opinion survey of several hundred black Americans in major cities, Marx showed that support for civil rights militancy among these blacks declined as religiosity increased. Religion, acting as an opiate, reduced the tendency for protest.[127] Other scholars have taken issue with his arguments. First they have noted that the public image of black religionists as more religious and otherworldly than whites has not been supported in recent research. One major study by the Nelsens found no black-white differences in reports of religious experience, in prayer frequency, or in conservative theology. Moreover, the same study found that blacks were more likely than whites to feel that their ministers should speak out on social and political issues, an attitude which seems to contradict the opiate-of-the-masses theory of black religion. A reanalysis of Gary Marx's data concluded that it was not black religion in general or black church participation that reduced militancy, but rather a sectarian religious orientation reflecting a heavy subjective commitment to religion.[128]

The protest motif has been part of black religion from the beginning; religious gatherings and leaders have played a role in spreading protest since the days of slavery. Ministers have long been political leaders. Black ministers have been torn between being protest leaders and defenders of a discriminatory status quo; many have supported protest. The nonviolent civil disobedience movement from the mid-1950s to the 1970s had religious underpinnings.[129]

Most prominent among the minister-leaders was the Reverend Martin Luther King, Jr. Raised in an intensely religious family with a record of fighting for black rights, King came naturally to his essentially religious view of the legitimacy of nonviolent protest as a way of winning concessions and at the same time healing the wounds of oppressed and oppressor. He led blacks in effective protests and died an assassinated hero.[130]

Afro-American music and literature have often emerged out of this religious background. The slave spirituals used religious symbols to capture the grief of oppression; other slave songs reflected the severity of slave life and the desire to escape. Songs like "Steal Away," "We Shall Be Free," "I Am Bound for the Promised Land," and "Go Down Moses" probably had double meanings—a traditionally religious dimension and a protest dimension. Yet the main purpose of the songs and spirituals was to tell of suffering and deliverance. This creative music might be viewed as America's first major body of folksongs contributed by a native-born racial or ethnic group.[131] This black tradition saw subsequent expression in distinctively American music, a long series of musical inventions ranging from syncopated ragtime to blues and jazz.[132]

ASSIMILATION FOR BLACKS?

Both assimilation and power-conflict frameworks have been used to interpret the experiences of black Americans. Milton Gordon argues that his theory of assimilation is applicable to both ethnic and racial groups. Gordon briefly applies this schema to black Americans, whom he sees as substantially assimilated at the cultural level in terms of English language and the Protestant religion, with some black-white differences remaining because of "lower-class subculture." Acculturation came more slowly because of antiblack discrimination. Beyond acculturation Gordon sees modest integration at the structural (primary-group) level, little intermarriage, little erosion of prejudice or discrimination, and no demise of group identity. While Gordon does not go into detail on these later dimensions, his basic view seems clear. Substantial acculturation has taken place, but assimilation at the other levels has come slowly. In his recent work Gordon is optimistic about assimilation, a trend he sees as evident in the growing black middle class.[133]

Assimilation Theories: An Evaluation

Optimistic assimilation-oriented analysts have underscored black progress in terms of cultural, economic, and social integration. Talcott Parsons argued that the race-ethnic inclusion process is a basic process internal to U.S. society, one aspect of which is the increasing inclusion of black Americans in the institutions of the society. Parsons viewed this ongoing inclusion process as operating earlier for white immigrants; but inclusion for him does not mean slavish Anglo-conformity assimilation. In his view even white ethnic groups have not been prevented by inclusion from maintaining a distinctive ethnic identity. From Parson's inclusion perspective, given the basic egalitarian values of the United States, "the only tolerable solution to the enormous [racial] tensions lies in constituting a single community with full membership for all."[134] Other recent analysts such as Nathan Glazer have taken the position that there has been a major collapse in traditional racial discrimination, that structural (secondary-group) assimilation of black Americans into the core society is well under way. What they view as dramatic black economic progress, particularly in the last decade, is cited as proof of the ongoing assimilation process.[135]

While discrimination is recognized as a serious barrier for black Americans, some assimilationists have in effect blamed black Americans themselves for their slower economic and social mobility, particularly in the last few decades. In a famous government report in the 1960s, Daniel P. Moynihan viewed the broken black families headed by females as a serious retardant to progress. Others have pointed to a subculture of poverty among low-income blacks as a major barrier. This general theme of scholars and popular analysts boils down to "Why can't they be like us?" The suggestion is that blacks are similar to earlier urban, white immigrant groups in their likelihood of moving up through the various levels of the economy, society, and polity—if they will only put their effort to that end. If white ethnic Americans can pull themselves up by their own bootstraps, so can black Americans.[136]

Power-conflict analysts reject this optimistic assimilationist view. According to this perspective, the current condition of black Americans is more rigidly hemmed in, more segregated than that of white ethnics because of the character of African incorporation into the English colonies and later into the United States. Once a system of extreme racial subordination is established historically, those in the superior position in the hierarchy continue to monopolize economic and social resources. Blauner convincingly argues that there are major differences between blacks and white immigrant groups.[137]

Africans were enslaved and brought across the Atlantic Ocean in chains. Blacks were incorporated into the economy against their will, providing the hard labor at the lowest occupational levels, first as slaves, then as tenant farmers, then as urban laborers. Even with the northward migration this status was not altered; blacks became a subordinate part of the growing urban economic system. In one sense, they were brought into established economic arrangements. Yet they were incorporated at the bottom levels of the economy. This point underscores a major problem in traditional assimilation frameworks, for although incorporation into the society might occur, it might be at the lowest level with modest chances of mobility. Nonwhite minorities suffer destruction of their original cultures. Africans were forced to give up their traditional ways as part of their incorporation into the American work patterns, the Protestant religion, and the English language. The contrast with the assimilation view can be seen in the emphasis on forced acculturation among power-conflict analysts.

Barriers to Assimilation

The power-conflict perspective takes a different view of the failure of blacks to move up economically and socially. Little relevance is assigned to the black church, matriarchal families, or a subculture of poverty as barriers, while direct and indirect institutionalized discrimination is given great emphasis. For example, when white ethnic groups such as the Irish began coming in, they did *not* make it on an equal-opportunity or fair-competition basis: they often displaced free blacks who were relegated to the lowest-paying jobs. Prior to the Civil War black workers could be found in a number of skilled trades in northern and southern cities. By the mid-nineteenth century white immigrant workers were crowding blacks out of many occupations. Blacks were increasingly forbidden by law from entering such craft occupations as blacksmithing, bricklaying, and mechanics. From Mobile to New York, Irish and German immigrants had begun to fill jobs once filled by blacks. Only the very lowest-level jobs were now open to skilled and unskilled blacks. After the Civil War most blacks remained as poor tenant farmers and sharecroppers, for the new industrial machine drew workers from southern and eastern Europe, not from the South.[138] The structural assimilation process failed in the face of well-institutionalized discrimination.

With the urban trek northward blacks increasingly filled low-level jobs in industry, but it was not until World War II, with its huge labor demand, that a large proportion of blacks encountered the industrial machine for the first time. Yet by the end of that war a decline in demand for black labor had begun, and with it a growing unemployment problem. Thus a second major barrier to mobility for black Americans has been time of entry. Unlike the European immigrants who came in prior to World War I, in a boom period of small businesses and of unskilled labor demands, black migrants after the World War II boom found a declining demand for their labor. Just as the children of the white immigrants had begun to move up dramatically, blacks were moving into cities in very large numbers. Black migrants found the opportunity was much paler than the promised-land image which had drawn them cityward. Since World War II the demand for black labor in cities has also been reduced by automation, which has reduced the number of relevant jobs.[139]

A third barrier maintaining blacks' subordinate position has been the political situation. Irish, Italian, and other nineteenth- and twentieth-century European immigrants benefited from urban politics; urban political organizations played an important role in providing jobs and thus in facilitating upward mobility. When blacks came in during World War II, the period of great public construction in the cities was over. Indeed, because of reform movements the urban machines were on the decline. Blacks were never able to benefit much from the political patronage system in most cities.[140]

In the United States it has been possible for an individual of low status to attain high-status roles, even though for members of nonwhite groups it has not been probable. There is a strong individualistic ethic emphasizing the mobility possible through individual effort. Inequality in society is legitimated by this ethic, for those who fail—those who remain in subordinate positions—have only themselves to blame. Those blacks and other subordinate group members who do rise sometimes become defenders of the system and thus help legitimate the poverty of the majorities in their racial groups.

Yet even those blacks moving up into better-paying jobs in this society face race discrimination and a new kind of colonialism. A new type of sophisticated discrimination has become widespread in recent years—tokenism. Tokenism has been one of the most successful devices in slowing down the dismantling of institutionalized discrimination. Reluctantly tearing down the traditional exclusion barriers over the last two decades, many officials in organizations have retreated to a second line of defense called tokenism. Part of the tokenism strategy is to hire nonwhite minorities for nontraditional jobs and put them in conspicuous and/or powerless positions. Following this strategy, officials must be careful not to place too many blacks in one particular unit of their organization. A management consultant, Kenneth Clark, has noted that blacks moving into nontraditional jobs in corporate America have frequently found themselves tracked into "ghettos" within organizations, such as a department of "community affairs" or of "special markets." Many professional and managerial blacks end up in selected staff jobs such as equal opportunity officer rather than in line managerial jobs. Clark notes that "they are rarely found in line positions concerned with developing or controlling production, supervising the work of large numbers of whites or competing with their white 'peers' for significant positions."[141] Black "tokens" in managerial and professional jobs are frequently put into staff jobs with little power. They must rely on white line managers to implement their suggestions. Moreover, decisions by those blacks in staff positions dealing with affirmative action may be irritating to white line managers, who ignore such decisions because they see the equal opportunity programs as interfering with their production goals.

Tokenism can become a self-perpetuating cycle. Isolated and alone, unable to draw on white networks for routine assistance, some black employees have difficulty in coping with the tensions of these higher-level jobs. As a result, turnover may increase. White managers and supervisors, then, may cite the difficulties of these tokens in arguing against more aggressive affirmative action and equal opportunity programs.

The movement of black Americans up into positions of power has come excruciatingly slowly, with two steps forward, one step backward. Indeed, the progress of blacks has been so slow that assimilation theories seem weak when applied to their centuries-long history in the United States.

SUMMARY

In this chapter we have probed the experiences of America's largest non-white group—Afro-Americans. The social progress of this group of Americans was severely restricted by slavery, even though at the time of the first great waves of white European immigrants blacks were already tenth-generation Americans. The slave period was followed by a long epoch, not yet ended, of legal and informal segregation. Jim Crowism frustrated the lives of freed slaves and generations of their descendants. The urban, northward trek reflected protest against southern oppression, protest "by the feet." Other types of black protest against subordination, nonviolent and violent (early petitions and recent demonstrations, slave revolts and ghetto revolts), have periodically punctuated the long course of black-white relations to the present.

In the early 1980s most black Americans were living in cities, especially metropolitan areas. Many lived in northern cities. The net migration of blacks from the South had reached a zero point: no more were leaving the South than were coming in from the North and the West. A trend in the direction of southern migration is now being established. Yet, wherever they live, black Americans face the apparent paradox of declining white prejudice but continuing discrimination and inequality. Attitude surveys between the 1940s and the 1980s have found that white support, at least openly expressed support, for racial integration is growing, while support for the old racial stereotypes is declining.[142] While the decline in prejudice to some extent reflects a subtle concealment of white American views, it is so steep a decline that it probably reflects a real change from the blatantly racist attitudes of the recent past. At the same time, the data on economic inequality along racial group lines, taken as a whole, show no radical improvements for blacks since the 1950s. Recent debates over black progress in the economic and political spheres really seem to be between advocates of "no changes" and advocates of "rather modest changes." Most blacks are not at income, occupational, or political parity with whites.

The civil rights movement and other protests since the 1950s have revealed the depth and character of racial inequality in a society that often seems on the surface to be moving toward inclusion and greater equality. Racial inequality seems firmly entrenched. A fundamental question regards how many *generations* it will take for this process to reach the goal of complete inclusion for black Americans.

NOTES

[1]John Hope Franklin, *From Slavery to Freedom*, 4th ed. (New York: Alfred A. Knopf, 1974), pp. 35–36; Winthrop Jordan, *White Over Black* (Baltimore: Penguin Books, 1969), pp. 91–98.

[2]Basil Davidson, *The African Slave Trade* (Boston: Atlantic Monthly Press, 1961), pp. 81 ff.

[3]James H. Dorman and Robert R. Jones, *The Afro-American Experience* (New York: Wiley, 1974), pp. 72–74; Thomas R. Frazier, "Preface to Chapter 1," in *Afro-American History: Primary Sources*, ed. Thomas R. Frazier (New York: Harcourt, Brace, and World, 1970), pp. 3–5.

[4]Dorman and Jones, *The Afro-American Experience*, pp. 78–80.

[5]Olaudah Equiano, "The Interesting Narrative of the Life of Olaudah Equiano," in Frazier, *Afro-American History: Primary Sources*, pp. 18, 20.

[6]Dorman and Jones, *The Afro-American Experience*, pp. 80–82.

[7]Philip D. Curtin, *The Atlantic Slave Trade* (Madison: University of Wisconsin Press, 1969), pp. 87–93.

[8]Ibid.; U.S. Bureau of the Census, *Historical Statistics of the United States* (Washington, D.C.: U.S. Government Printing Office, 1960), p. 770.

[9]Carl N. Degler, *Out of Our Past* (New York: Harper & Row, 1959), pp. 161–63; Franklin, *From Slavery to Freedom*, p. 88.

[10]Ibid., pp. 132–33.

[11]U.S. Bureau of the Census, *Historical Statistics of the United States*, p. 11; Degler, *Out of Our Past*, pp. 163–64; Ulrich B. Phillips, *Life and Labor in the Old South* (Boston: Little, Brown, 1929), pp. 339 ff.

[12]Degler, *Out of Our Past*, pp. 164–66; Kenneth M. Stampp, *The Peculiar Institution* (New York: Random House Vintage Books, 1956), pp. 383–418.

[13]Phillips, *Life and Labor in the Old South*, pp. iv–v; Eugene G. Genovese, *Roll, Jordan, Roll* (New York: Random House, 1974), pp. 56–57. See Gilberto Freyre, *The Masters and the Slaves* (New York: Alfred A. Knopf, 1956); Marvin Harris, *Race Patterns in the Americas* (New York: Walder and Company, 1964), pp. 65–90.

[14]John W. Blassingame, *The Slave Community* (New York: Oxford University Press, 1972), pp. 155–60.

[15]Ben Simpson, "Ben Simpson: Georgia and Texas," in *Lay My Burden Down*, ed. B. A. Botkin (Chicago: University of Chicago Press, 1945), p. 75.

[16]See Blassingame, *The Slave Community*, pp. 165–66.

[17]Herbert Aptheker, *American Negro Slave Revolts* (New York: International Publishers, 1943), p. 67.

[18]Blassingame, *The Slave Community*, p. 160; Aptheker, *American Negro Slave Revolts*, pp. 56–58.

[19]Stanley M. Elkins, *Slavery* (Chicago: University of Chicago Press, 1959), pp. 72–127.

[20]Genovese, *Roll, Jordan, Roll*, pp. 5, 362–64.

[21]Ibid., p. 451.

[22]Herbert Gutman, *The Black Family in Slavery and Freedom, 1750–1925* (New York: Pantheon Books, 1976); Stanley Elkins, "The Slavery Debate," *Commentary* 46 (December 1975): 46–47.

[23]Blassingame, *The Slave Community*, p. 103.

[24]Stampp, *The Peculiar Institution*, p. 86.

[25]Elkins, *Slavery*, pp. 84–85.

[26]Blassingame, *The Slave Community*, pp. 203–14; Genovese, *Roll, Jordan, Roll*, p. 588.

[27]Aptheker, *American Negro Slave Revolts*, pp. 140–41.

[28]Cited in Genovese, *Roll, Jordan, Roll*, p. 650.

[29]Aptheker, *American Negro Slave Revolts*, pp. 12–18, 162.

[30]Ibid., pp. 165, 220–25, 249–50, 267–73.

[31]Herbert Aptheker, *Essays in the History of the American Negro* (New York: International Publishers, 1945), pp. 39, 49–51.

[32]Harriet Martineau, *Society in America* (Garden City, N.Y.: Anchor Books, 1962), p. 228.

[33]Richard C. Wade, *Slavery in the Cities* (New York: Oxford University Press, 1964), pp. 243–49.

[34]C. Vann Woodward, *The Strange Career of Jim Crow*, 3d ed. (New York: Oxford University Press), pp. 19–21.

[35]Alexis de Tocqueville, *Democracy in America* (New York: Vintage Books, 1945), 1:373.

[36]Thomas F. Gossett, *Race* (New York: Schocken Books, 1965), pp. 42–43.

[37]Jordan, *White Over Black*, p. 257.

[38]Samuel Cartwright, "The Prognathous Species of Mankind," in *Slavery Defended*, ed. Eric L. McKitrick (Englewood Cliffs, N.J.: Prentice-Hall, 1963), p. 140.

[39]Lewis H. Carlson and George A. Colburn, *In Their Place* (New York: John Wiley, 1972), p. 99.

[40]Duncan J. MacLeod, *Slavery, Race, and the American Revolution* (London: Cambridge University Press, 1974), p. 158.

[41]Tocqueville, *Democracy in America*, p. 345.

[42]Edward East, "Excerpt from *Heredity and Human Affairs*," in Carlson and Colburn, *In Their Place*, p. 103.

[43]I. A. Newby, *Jim Crow's Defense* (Baton Rouge: Louisiana State University Press, 1965), pp. 98–99.

[44]Tocqueville, *Democracy in America*, p. 344.

[45]Newby, *Jim Crow's Defense*, pp. 19–23, 41.

[46]Thomas F. Pettigrew, *A Profile of the Negro American* (Princeton, N.J.: Van Nostrand, 1964), pp. 100 ff.

[47]See also Richard J. Herrnstein, *IQ in the Meritocracy* (Boston: Little, Brown, 1973).

[48]Arthur R. Jensen, "How Much Can We Boost IQ and Scholastic Achievement?" *Harvard Education Review* 39 (1969): 1–123.

[49]Pettigrew, *A Profile of the Negro American*, pp. 123–26.

[50]Otto Klineberg's data are cited in I. A. Newby, *Challenge to the Court* (Baton Rouge: Louisiana State University Press, 1967), p. 74. See also M. F. A. Montague, "Intelligence of Northern Negroes and Southern Whites in the First World War," *American Journal of Psychology* 58 (1945): 161–88. More recently, see Horace M. Bond, "Cat on a Hot Tin Roof," *Journal of Negro Education* 27 (Fall 1958): 519–23.

[51]This section on intelligence draws on Leon J. Kamin, *The Science and Politics of IQ* (New York: John Wiley, 1974), pp. 175–78; and N. J. Block and Gerald Dworkin, "IQ, Heritability, and Inequality," in *The IQ Controversy*, ed. N. J. Block and Gerald Dworkin (New York: Random House, 1976), pp. 410–540.

[52]William Brink and Louis Harris, *The Negro Revolution in America* (New York: Simon and Schuster, 1964) pp. 140–41; William Brink and Louis Harris, *Black and White* (New York: Simon and Schuster, 1967), p. 136.

[53]Richard T. Morris and Vincent Jeffries, "The White Reaction Study," in *The Los Angeles Riots*, ed. Nathan Cohen (New York: Praeger, 1970), p. 510.

[54]Angus Campbell, *White Attitudes Toward Black People* (Ann Arbor, Mich.: Institute for Social Research, 1971), p. 14.

[55]John B. McConahay and Willis D. Hawley, *Is It the Buses or the Blacks?* (working paper, Center for Policy Analysis, Duke University, 1981), pp. 35–38.

[56]John B. McConahay and Joseph C. Hough, "Symbolic Racism," *Journal of Social Issues* 32 (1976): 38.

[57]Ibid., pp. 23–45; John B. McConahay, Betty Hardee, and Valerie Batts, *Has Racism Declined?* (working paper, Institute of Policy Sciences, Duke University, n.d.), p. 21.

[58]U.S. Bureau of the Census, *Historical Statistics of the United States*, p. 218.

[59]N. J. Cash, *The Mind of the South* (New York: Vintage Books, 1960), p. 125.

[60]Note a 1940 pamphlet written by a white southerner for U.S. senators and congressmen, quoted in Gunnar Myrdal, *An America Dilemma* (New York: McGraw-Hill, 1964), 2:1198.

[61]Gilbert Osofsky, *Harlem: The Making of a Ghetto* (New York: Harper & Row, 1963), pp. 45–51; Arthur I. Waskow, *From Race Riot to Sit-In, 1919 and the 1960s* (Garden City, N.Y.: Doubleday, 1966), pp. 209–10 et passim; Elliot M. Rudwick, *Race Riot at East St. Louis* (Carbondale: Southern Illinois University Press, 1964), pp. 3–30.

[62]John Turner, *The Ku Klan Klan: A History of Racism and Violence* (Montgomery, Ala.: Southern Poverty Law Center, 1982), pp. 48–56.

[63]Joe R. Feagin and Harlan Hahn, *Ghetto Revolts* (New York: Macmillan, 1973), p. 134.

[64]"The Mood of Ghetto America," *Newsweek*, June 2, 1980, pp. 32–34.

[65]Ibid., p. 33; "Accidents or Police Brutality?" *Time*, October 26, 1981, p. 70.

[66]Ray Marshall, *The Negro Worker* (New York: Random House, 1967), pp. 7–12; MacLeod, *Slavery, Race, and the American Revolution*, pp. 151–53; Pete Daniel, *The Shadow of Slavery: Peonage in the South* (London: Oxford University Press, 1972); Myrdal, *An American Dilemma*, 1:228.

[67]Karl E. Taeuber and Alma F. Taeuber, *Negroes in Cities* (Chicago: Aldine, 1965), pp. 12–13; Thomas D. Clark, *The Emerging South* (New York: Oxford University Press, 1961), pp. 42–44.

[68]Charles Tilly, "Race and Migration to the American City," in *The Urban Scene*, ed. Joe R. Feagin (New York: Random House, 1973), p. 35. This essay has influenced the view of black migration in this chapter.

[69]Taeuber and Taeuber, *Negroes in Cities*, pp. 144ff.

[70]Bennett Harrison, *Education, Training, and the Urban Ghetto* (Baltimore: Johns Hopkins University Press, 1972).

[71]U.S. Bureau of the Census, *Negroes in the United States, 1920–1932* (Washington, D.C.: U.S. Government Printing Office, 1935), p. 289; Myrdal, *An American Dilemma*, 1:304 ff.

[72]Marshall, *The Negro Worker*, pp. 23–24, 56–57.

[73]U.S. Bureau of the Census, *Population*, vol. 3, *The Labor Force* (Washington, D.C.: U.S. Government Printing Office, 1943). See also Sidney M. Wilhelm, *Who Needs the Negro?* (Cambridge, Mass.: Shenkman Publishing Co., 1970), p. 57.

[74]U.S. Bureau of the Census, *Statistical Abstract of the United States: 1980* (Washington, D.C.: U.S. Government Printing Office, 1980), pp. 416–19; U.S. Bureau of the Census, *The Social and Economic Status of the Black Population in the United States, 1974* (Washington, D.C.: U.S. Government Printing Office, 1975), p. 73. The next three paragraphs draw heavily on Joe R. Feagin, *Social Problems* (Englewood Cliffs, N.J.: Prentice-Hall, 1982), pp. 121–22.

[75]Andrew F. Brimmer, *The Economic Position of Black Americans, 1976* (Washington, D.C.: National Commission for Manpower Policy, 1976), p. 17.

[76]U.S. Bureau of the Census, *The Social and Economic Status of the Black Population in the United States, 1971* (Washington, D.C.: U.S. Government Printing Office, 1972), p. 52; Brimmer, *The Economic Position of Black Americans*, p. 13; U.S. Commission on Civil Rights, *Unemployment and*

Underemployment among Blacks, Hispanics, and Women (Washington, D.C.: U.S. Government Printing Office, 1982), p. 5.

[77]Wilhelm, *Who Needs the Negro?* p. 155; U.S. Commission on Civil Rights, *Unemployment and Underemployment among Blacks, Hispanics, and Women*, pp. 5–8; C. Clogg and T. Sullivan, "Labor Force Composition and Underemployment Trends," *Social Indicators Research* (forthcoming, 1983).

[78]U.S. Bureau of the Census, *The Social and Economic Status of the Black Population in the United States, 1971*, p. 29; Brimmer, *The Economic Position of Black Americans: 1976*, p. 37; and data from U.S. Bureau of the Census for 1980 reported in Spencer Rich, "New Data Show Blacks' Income Outgained Whites' in 1970s," *Washington Post*, June 3, 1982.

[79]Rich, "New Data."

[80]Robert B. Hill, "The Economic Status of Black Americans," in *The State of Black America, 1981*, ed. J. D. Williams (New York: National Urban League, 1981), pp. 5–6, 33.

[81]Ibid., p. 37. This is drawn from Feagin, *Social Problems*, p. 123.

[82]Marshall, *The Negro Worker*, pp. 120–24; U.S. Commission on Civil Rights, *The Federal Civil Rights Enforcement Effort, 1974*, vol. 5, *To Eliminate Employment Discrimination* (Washington, D.C.: U.S. Government Printing Office, 1975), pp. 291–92.

[83]U.S. Commission on Civil Rights, *The Federal Civil Rights Enforcement Budget: Fiscal Year 1983* (Washington, D.C.: U.S. Government Printing Office, 1982), pp. 53–59.

[84]Brimmer, *The Economic Position of Black Americans*, 1976, p. 27; see also Commission on Civil Rights, *The Federal Civil Rights Enforcement Effort*, 1974.

[85]U.S. Bureau of the Census, *The Social and Economic Status of the Black Population, 1974*, pp. 135–38; Frederick D. Sturdivant, *The Ghetto Marketplace* (New York: Free Press, 1969), pp. 3–6, 146–49.

[86]Hanes Walton, Jr., *Black Politics* (Philadelphia: J. P. Lippincott, 1972), pp. 14–15, 26.

[87]This discussion draws on a course given by Thomas F. Pettigrew at Harvard University.

[88]Ibid.; Franklin, *From Slavery to Freedom*, pp. 252–53; Chuck Stone, *Black Political Power in America*, rev. ed. (New York: Dell Publishing Company, 1970), pp. 30–31.

[89]C. Vann Woodward, *The Strange Career of Jim Crow*, 2d rev. ed. (New York: Oxford University Press, 1966), pp. 31 ff.

[90]Cash, *The Mind of the South*, p. 174.

[91]*Plessy v. Ferguson*, 163 U.S. 551–552.

[92]Woodward, *The Strange Career of Jim Crow*, pp. 115–18.

[93]Cited in Stone, *Black Political Power in America*, p. 35.

[94]Walton, *Black Politics*, pp. 100, 119.

[95]Myrdal, *An American Dilemma*, 1: 475–501.

[96]David Campbell and Joe R. Feagin, "Black Politics in the South: A Descriptive Analysis," *Journal of Politics* 37 (February 1975): 129–62.

[97]Martin Luther King, Jr., in the *New York Times*, February 2, 1965, p. 1; Mack Jones, "Black Office Holders in Local Governments of the South: An Overview" (Paper presented at the 68th annual meeting of the American Political Science Association, Los Angeles, September 6–12, 1972), p. 38.

[98]James E. Conyers and Walter L. Wallace, *Black Elected Officials* (New York: Russell Sage Foundation, 1976), p. 159; see also pp. 8, 137–40.

[99]Myrdal, *An American Dilemma*, 1: 503; Raymond Wolters, *Negroes and the Great Depression* (Westport, Conn.: Greenwood Publishing Corporation, 1970), p. xi et passim.

[100]Stone, *Black Political Power in America*, pp. 68–72.

[101]Ibid., p. 47. Stone is drawing here on Henry L. Moon, *Balance of Power* (Garden City, N.Y.: Doubleday, 1948).

[102]Campbell and Feagin, "Black Politics in the South," p. 151.

[103]Feagin and Hahn, *Ghetto Revolts*, pp. 81–85; Loren Miller, *The Petitioners* (New York: Random House, 1966), pp. 250–56.

[104]Miller, *The Petitioners*, pp. 260–347.

[105]Feagin and Hahn, *Ghetto Revolts*, pp. 88–89.

[106]Lerone Bennett, Jr., *Confrontation: Black and White* (Baltimore: Penguin Books, 1966), pp. 164–69.

[107]Ibid., pp. 223–34; Bryan T. Downes and Stephen W. Burks, "The Historical Development of the Black Protest Movement," in *Blacks in the United States*, ed. Norval D. Glenn and Charles Bonjean (San Francisco: Chandler, 1969), pp. 322–44.

[108]Feagin and Hahn, *Ghetto Revolts*, pp. 92–94; Bennett, *Confrontation: Black and White*, pp. 234–37; Inge P. Bell, *CORE and the Strategy of Nonviolence* (New York: Random House, 1968), pp. 13 ff.

[109]U.S. Commission on Civil Rights, *The Federal Civil Rights Enforcement Effort: Fiscal Year 1983*, pp. 5–7.

[110]Franklin, *From Slavery to Freedom*, pp. 280–81; Myrdal, *An American Dilemma*, 1: 337–44; Henry A. Bullock, *A History of Negro Education in the South* (New York: Praeger, 1967), pp. 1–99.

[111]Bullock, *A History of Negro Education in the South*, pp. 170–86; Franklin, *From Slavery to Freedom*, pp. 284–86.

[112]U.S. Bureau of the Census, *Statistical Abstract of the United States*, 1981 (Washington, D.C.: U.S. Government Printing Office, 1981), p. 142.

[113]Harrison, *Education, Training, and the Urban Ghetto*, p. 67; italics added.

[114]Bullock, *A History of Negro Education in the South*, pp. 211–12, 225–30; Miller, *The Petitioners*, pp. 347–58.

[115]U.S. Commission on Civil Rights, *Twenty Years After Brown* (Washington, D.C.: U.S. Government Printing Office, 1975), pp. 11–41.

[116]See Glazer, *Affirmative Discrimination*, and the interview with James Coleman, "Busing Backfired," *National Observer*, June 7, 1975.

[117]See the numerous articles on innovative desegregation strategies in the 1966–1976 issues of the journal *Integrated Education*.

[118]Nicolaus Mills, "Busing: Who's Being Taken for a Ride," in *The Great School Bus Controversy*, ed. Nicolaus Mills (New York: Columbia University, Teachers College Press, 1973), p. 7. See also U.S. Commission on Civil Rights, *Your Child and Busing* (Washington, D.C.: U.S. Government Printing Office, 1972).

[119]Nancy H. St. John, *School Desegregation: Outcomes for Children* (New York: John Wiley, 1975), pp. 119–21.

[120]Diana Pearce, "Breaking Down Barriers: New Evidence on the Impact of Metropolitan School Desegregation on Housing Patterns" (Unpublished research report, School of Law, Catholic University, November 1980), pp. 48–53.

[121]Walter R. Allen, "Correlates of Black Student Adjustment, Achievement, and Aspirations at a Predominantly White Southern University," in G. E. Thomas, ed., *Black Students in Higher Education* (Westport, Conn.: Greenwood Press, 1981), pp. 128–37; Walter R. Allen, "Black and Blue: Black Students at the University of Michigan" (unpublished research report, University of Michigan, n.d.), pp. 8–12.

[122]Stampp, *The Peculiar Institution*, pp. 156–62; Aptheker, *American Negro Slave Revolts*, pp. 56–60.

[123]Aptheker, *American Negro Slave Revolts*, pp. 56–70.

[124]Wade, *Slavery in the Cities*, pp. 161–63; Jordan, *White Over Black*, pp. 422–25.

[125]E. Franklin Frazier, *The Negro Church in America* (New York: Schocken Books, 1964), pp. 35–39; Myrdal, *An American Dilemma*, 2: 938–39.

[126]Frazier, *The Negro Church in America*, p. 51; E. U. Essien-Udom, *Black Nationalism* (New York: Dell, 1964).

[127]Gary T. Marx, *Protest and Prejudice* (New York: Harper & Row, 1967), p. 105.

[128]Hart M. Nelsen and Anne Kusener Nelsen, *Black Church in the Sixties* (Lexington: University of Kentucky Press, 1975), pp. 81–123.

[129]Frazier, *The Negro Church in America*, p. 44; Joseph R. Washington, Jr., *Black Religion* (Boston: Beacon Press, 1964), pp. 2–29.

[130]David L. Lewis, *King* (Baltimore: Penguin Books, 1970), p. 390.

[131]Miles M. Fisher, *Negro Slave Songs in the United States* (New York: Citadel Press, 1953), pp. 170–90; John Greenway, *American Folksongs of Protest* (New York: Perpetua Books, 1960), p. 78; Ben Sidran, *Black Talk* (New York: Holt, Rinehart and Winston, 1971), pp. 16–17.

[132]Sidran, *Black Talk*, pp. 16, 27–33; cf. Le Roi Jones, *Black Music* (New York: William Morrow and Company, 1970), p. 12.

[133]Milton Gordon, *Assimilation in American Life* (New York: Oxford University Press, 1964), p. 78.

[134]Talcott Parsons, "Full Citizenship for the Negro American? A Sociological Problem," in *The Negro American*, ed. Talcott Parsons and Kenneth B. Clark (Boston: Houghton Mifflin Co., 1965), p. 740; see also pp. 714–15.

[135]Glazer, *Affirmative Discrimination*, pp. 40–76.

[136]Daniel P. Moynihan, *The Negro Family* (Washington, D.C.: U.S. Government Printing Office, 1965); Frazier, *The Negro Church in America*; Myrdal, *An American Dilemma*.

[137]Robert Blauner, *Racial Oppression in America* (New York: Harper & Row, 1972), pp. 51–110.

[138]Wade, *Slavery in the Cities*, pp. 273–75; Herman D. Bloch, *The Circle of Discrimination* (New York: New York University Press, 1969), pp. ix–xiii.

[139]Wilhelm, *Who Needs the Negro?*; Robert L. Allen, *Black Awakening in Capitalist America* (Garden City, N.Y.: Doubleday Anchor Books, 1970), pp. 4–6; *Report of the National Advisory Commission on Civil Disorders* (New York: Bantam Books, 1968), pp. 278–79.

[140]*Report of the National Advisory Commission on Civil Disorders*, pp. 279–80.

[141]Kenneth B. Clark, "The Role of Race," *New York Times Magazine*, October 5, 1980, p. 30.

[142]See Herbert H. Hyman and Paul B. Sheatsley, "Attitudes Toward Desegregation," *Scientific American* 211 (July 1964): 16–23.

Mexican Americans
CHAPTER 9

One stereotypical view of Mexican Americans is of sleepy peons under big sombreros, moustachioed banditos, lazy farmworkers, a diet of tortillas and tacos, and, perhaps, a fatalistic version of folk Catholicism. Such popular caricatures are supplemented by treatments of Mexicans and Mexican Americans in schoolbooks which distort the past and present history of the Southwest, as in the southwestern myths which glorify achievement-oriented, freedom-loving, heroic Texans confronting a backward and cowardly Mexican people. Typical too in popular and scholarly accounts of life in the Southwest* is the omission of references to Mexican American contributions to the development of life and culture in the United States.

Yet the Mexican American role has been critical in the development of the United States. How did Mexicans initially become incorporated? What has life in the economy and the polity been like for them? How do the assimilation and power-conflict models relate to their experience?

THE CONQUEST PERIOD (1500–1853)

Like Native Americans, the first Mexican citizens did not migrate to the United States. Their land and persons were brought into the United States by force. No choice was involved.

Early European expansion touched not only the Atlantic Coast of North America but also the Gulf Coast and the West. When the Spaniards arrived, there were dozens of Native American groups. The Spanish sought

*"The Southwest" refers primarily to the states of California, Arizona, New Mexico, Colorado, and Texas.

to Catholicize the native population and to concentrate it in agricultural and mining communities for labor exploitation. The Spanish language and the Catholic religion were part of the acculturation pressures bearing down hard on the native population. A five-level system of European-born Spanish, Criollos (native-born Spanish), Mestizos (mixed Spanish and "Indian"), Mulattoes (mixed Spanish and black) and Negroes, and Indios was established. Because of the relatively small number of Spaniards, the native contribution was dominant in the population mix then as it is today.[1]

Mexico won its independence from Spain in 1821.[2] Prior to the 1830s Mexicans had established numerous communities in the Southwest. These were centered in a Mexican way of life. Along the Rio Grande in what would become southern Texas there were several thousand inhabitants living on land grants with a self-sufficient economy. There were an estimated four thousand Mexican settlers in the Texas area in 1821. Soon thousands of European American* settlers from the United States flooded the area. In a few years the new settlers outnumbered the Mexican population. By the 1830s there were twenty thousand such new migrants.[3]

The Texas Revolt: Myth and Reality

The Texas province, both its Mexican population and its new United States immigrants, strongly supported a decentralized system of Mexican government. By 1830 some Mexican residents there had joined the new settlers to protest actions by the central government in Mexico City. Some actions, including freeing slaves and placing restrictions on immigration, angered the new European American settlers from the east. The causes of the much-publicized Texas revolt are complex, but they include not only government policies in Mexico City but also the racist attitudes of the new Euro-American immigrants toward Mexicans, the resentment of white slaveholders toward Mexican antislavery laws, and the growing number of Euro-American immigrants coming in *illegally* from the north. Until recently, few analysts have been inclined to see the Texas revolt as territorial aggression by United States citizens against another sovereign nation, which in the end it was, but rather have excused the behavior of the new Texans and blamed an oppressive Mexican government.[4]

The Texas revolt has been portrayed in persisting myths about heroic Texans. The legend of the Alamo portrays about 180 principled native-born Texans courageously fighting thousands of Mexican troops. But the reality was different. Most men at the Alamo mission, in what is now San Antonio, were not native Texans, but newcomers. White adventurers and fortune seekers had poured into Texas. Many in the Alamo were not men of principle defending their homes but adventurers or brawlers such as James Bowie, William Travis, and Davy Crockett. In addition, the myth-makers do not mention that the Alamo was one of the best-fortified sites

---

*In this book the terms *European American* and *Anglo* are used to designate persons whose predominant ancestry is European. The common term *Anglo* is not fully satisfactory, because many of those involved in subordinating Mexican Americans had non-English European ancestry. Here *Anglo* is used in the broad sense of European American.

in the West; the defenders had twice as many cannons, much better rifles, and much better training in riflery than the poorly equipped and poorly fed Mexican recruits, including untrained Indian recruits. Another part of the myth suggests that all the defenders died fighting heroically. In fact, several defenders surrendered. After a series of further skirmishes General Sam Houston managed a surprise attack which wiped out much of the Mexican army in the north.[5]

The Texas rebellion was a case of U.S. settlers going beyond an existing boundary and intentionally trying to incorporate new territory into the United States. Texas was annexed in 1845, an action which precipitated the Mexican War. Provocative American troop actions in a disputed boundary area generated a Mexican attack and a declaration of war by the United States. The poorly equipped Mexican army lost. Some historians have questioned the view of this war as an honorable war, citing substantial evidence that Mexico fell victim to a U.S. conspiracy to seize its territory by force. The murder of innocent civilians and other atrocities were committed by U.S. soldiers and Texas Rangers in occupied areas of Mexico. In 1848 the Mexican government was forced to cede the Southwest for $15 million. Mexican residents had the choice of remaining there or moving south; most stayed, assured on paper of the protection of their rights by Article IX of the Treaty of Guadalupe Hidalgo, which gave them "the enjoyment of all rights of citizens of the United States."[6]

By the 1850s the population of Texas had grown to two hundred thousand, most of whom were in-migrants. Gradually, much of the land owned by the original Mexican occupants was taken away by the outside invaders, particularly by ranchers and farmers who used means legal and illegal, including force, to gain new lands. Most Mexican landowners lost their lands.

Prior to conquest the California situation was one of Mexican-run ranches and missions, with perhaps 7,500 Mexican residents. After the 1849 gold rush they too were outnumbered by incoming Euro-American settlers. The new settlers, particularly a small elite of large Anglo landowners, took over lands and political control from the Mexicans. The means of takeover ranged from lynching to armed theft to quasilegal and legal means, such as bringing expensive litigation in American courts to force Mexican landowners to prove land titles.[7]

In New Mexico, villages provided the organization to withstand some of the new onslaught. The villages there are quite old—Sante Fe was established in 1609. By far the most numerous Mexican population in the newly conquered region, the fifty thousand New Mexicans had long maintained their own traditions. The richest 2 percent owned most of the land, while the poor made up the rest. Many landholders did fairly well under United States rule, continuing to play an important role in commerce and politics in the region for many decades. Nonetheless, most Mexicans eventually suffered great losses of private and communal lands.[8]

By the mid-nineteenth century the new United States system of private land ownership was replacing an older Mexican system which emphasized communal lands. The old land grants were ignored in spite of treaty promises and treated as U.S. government land; Mexican landholders were faced with a variety of tactics which ultimately resulted in the loss of most of the land. The invasion of the Southwest was not a heroic period in which United States settlers liberated unused land. It was in fact a period of imperalistic expansion resulting in the colonization of a communal people who already lived in the area. This coercive colonization alone makes the Mexican American experience distinctive.[9]

THE IMMIGRATION PERIOD

Estimates of the number of Mexicans brought by force into the new territorial limits of the expanding United States range up to 118,000 for the year 1850. In the decades to follow, millions of Mexicans entered the United States, with their points of destination being rural counties and cities. Two major push factors shaped this immigration: regular political upheavals and changing economic conditions. On the pull side were expanding opportunities and the tremendous demand for unskilled labor in the fields and factories north of the border. On the pull side too were family ties to persons in what was once old Mexico.

Millions of Mexicans have migrated to the United States since the late nineteenth century. The peak periods have been the decades between 1910 and 1930 and the three decades since 1950. Over the course of this immigration there have been five major categories of immigrants: (1) those with official visas ("legals"); (2) undocumented immigrants ("illegals"); (3) braceros (seasonal farm workers on contract); (4) "green-card" commuters with official alien visas who live in Mexico but work in the United States; and (5) "border crossers" with short-term permits, many of whom become maids.[10] With the exclusion of the Japanese immigrants by federal government action (see Chapter 11) and the industrialization of the World War I era came a sharp decline in the number of laborers available for agricultural work. Mexican labor was drawn into the Southwest by the demand for cheap labor. During World War I more than seventy thousand Mexican workers were legally brought in, with immigration restrictions waived by federal authorities because of U.S. employer pressure.[11]

This Mexican migration increased in the 1920s, with 500,000 workers and their families entering on visas. Improved canning and shipping technologies opened new markets for agricultural produce, as did refrigeration. Cities such as San Antonio had labor recruitment agencies which specialized in recruiting Mexican workers for agriculture as well as for jobs in the steel, auto, cement, and meat-packing industries—in the North as well as in the South. Business opposition to serious restriction of the immigration of Mexicans was intense; temporary work-permit programs were periodically expanded. Mexicans were not excluded by the Immigration Act of 1924, which did exclude most southern and eastern Europeans. Mexico had become a main source of cheap labor for the Southwest and the Midwest. Those in favor of this migration continued to stress the benefits of cheap Mexican labor for agriculture; those against argued for limiting immigration out of fear that Mexican culture would dilute the Anglo-Saxon core culture.[12]

In the 1920s the Border Patrol of the Immigration and Naturalization Service was created; and in 1929 legislation made it a felony to enter the United States illegally. The Border Patrol came to play a larger and larger role in the lives of Mexicans and Mexican Americans. Although it has had the formal authority to keep out all undocumented workers, it has not always used this authority. Rather it has regulated the flow of Mexican workers so that the number coming in has been sufficient to meet the work demand but less than the number which would cause political problems. In times of depression and recession between the 1920s and the 1980s, the Border Patrol has conducted vigorous exclusion and deportation campaigns, while in better times restrictive activity has often been less rigorous.[13]

During the Great Depression the demand for Mexican labor decreased as a result of "dust bowl" agricultural problems; a large number of the U.S. unemployed were willing to do agricultural work. Between 1931 and 1940 there were only 22,000 immigrants, 5 percent of the number in the previous decade. During the Depression federal enforcement of literacy tests and the prohibition against poor immigrants becoming public charges greatly reduced the flow of immigrants. There was, moreover, considerable pressure to get Mexicans who were already here, whether citizens or not, to leave the country. Some left voluntarily; undocumented workers (that is, those without papers) were forcibly deported in massive border campaigns; thousands of others, including U.S. citizens, were expelled in organized caravans by social agencies eager to reduce their costs.[14]

Braceros and Undocumented Workers

World War II changed the labor situation. In 1942 an Emergency Farm Labor ("bracero") Agreement between the United States and Mexico was made providing workers for agriculture. Under this program, seasonal workers were brought in on a temporary basis to work in the fields. In its two decades of existence nearly five million braceros were brought in under contract. Some have argued that a key feature of these workers was that they were not militant; employers wanted non-union workers.

This bracero program helped to generate an increased migration of undocumented workers, due to contract laborers going home with tales of prosperity; and many employers became eager for the cheaper "illegals." The undocumented immigration from Mexico has been so large that the legal figures are only a small portion of the total. Approximately two million documented immigrants have come in since the 1860s, while between the 1920s and the 1980s somewhere between four and seven million undocumented immigrants entered. Many of these were only temporary migrants who returned to Mexico.[15]

Considerable opposition to this large-scale migration has been generated, particularly since World War II. Union officials, including a few Mexican Americans, have called for restrictions to protect the jobs of citizens. But the issue is a very difficult one. The Mexican government has made little effort to stop the undocumented migration, for it relieves severe poverty and population pressures on that side of the border. A worker often decides that going north is the solution to keeping his or her family alive. One study of 493 workers in three detention centers in Texas and California provides a profile of the "illegals." The study found that most had come in without papers. Most were males under 30 years of age, with poverty backgrounds and less-than-sixth-grade educations. Their poverty had driven many to desperate measures. Many had come in under the auspices of labor smugglers, who charge $300 to $1,100 per person for bringing persons in. Recent research has also made it clear that a significant number of those who have crossed the border are women and children. Although they do not comprise a majority, families of undocumented workers have been neglected in public policy discussions.[16]

Growing opposition led to new restrictions in the 1960s, when legal immigration from Mexico was for the first time curtailed. The 1965 Immigration Act which removed the discriminatory quotas directed primarily at southern and eastern Europeans incorporated a new limit of 120,000 persons from the Western Hemisphere in an attempt to restrict "inferior" migrants from Mexico. Stricter labor certification restrictions were also instituted. And in 1976 a restrictive limit of just 20,000 immigrants per year was placed on Mexican immigration. Attempts to deal with undocumented Mexican immigrants have focused on intensified Border Patrol policing and legislation on visas. Until quite recently there were no legal penalties for employers who knowingly hired such workers—only penalties for the workers. In the 1970s several attempts were made to pass legislation to make the employment of undocumented workers a criminal offense. These have been repeated in the 1980s. In 1982 the U.S. Senate passed a restrictive immigration bill which would have imposed fines and jail sentences on employers who hired illegal aliens. The bill would also have made it easier to deport undocumented workers. In addition, the bill provides "amnesty" for all undocumented workers who came before 1980, making it easier for them to become legal residents and citizens. However, when the legislation came before the U.S. House late in 1982, intensive opposition was directed at it. Hispanic groups protested that employers would discriminate against Hispanic Americans, that they would be afraid to hire them because they look just like illegal aliens. Black groups protested that the easier deportation rules would make it too easy to deport black migrants such as Haitian refugees. Civil liberties organizations protested the bill's provision requiring identity cards for citizens, designed to enable employers to distinguish citizens from illegal aliens.[17]

Because of continuing economic troubles in Mexico, such as poverty and unemployment, a substantial flow of undocumented workers continued in the 1970s and 1980s. The best estimates for the number of undocumented Mexican workers in the United States in the early 1980s were *substantially less* than the official estimates of 5 to 10 million. Careful research estimates suggest that the real number is closer to 1.5 to 4 million. Public officials, particularly in election campaigns, have exaggerated the estimates for political purposes. Moreover, recent research has revealed that the undocumented workers do not place a burden on the U.S. taxpayer by going on welfare and using social services for which they have not paid. Numerous studies have shown that they have very low rates of utilization of tax-supported programs such as welfare, the food stamp program, and unemployment compensation. They pay out considerably more in income and other taxes than they ever receive back in benefits. In numerous ways illegal aliens subsidize U.S. society, providing the cheap, dirty labor most Americans are no longer willing to provide and paying taxes they seldom recover in services.[18]

Official Census estimates of the Mexican-origin population show an increase from 1.3 million to 1930 to 4.5 million in 1970 and 8.8 million in the early 1980s. These figures are likely to reflect undercounts, perhaps by as much as 500,000. By 1980 most Mexican Americans lived in urban areas, especially in the southwestern states. Most were native-born. A common although incorrect notion that Mexican Americans reside only in the Southwest has pervaded much of the popular and scholarly literature. Many now reside in other regions, particularly the Midwest.[19]

STEREOTYPING MEXICAN AMERICANS

Mexican Americans have suffered from more than their share of negative images. In the process of competing with and subordinating the Mexican residents of the Southwest, European Americans early came to believe that laziness, backwardness, and poverty were fundamental to the character of the Mexican "race." The Protestant work ethic of the new Anglo settlers contributed to the distorted view that Mexicans were poor because they desired to be that way, because they did not like to work hard. The slave-holders who came in already had a well-developed race prejudice rationalizing the subordination of black Americans, so for many it was natural to stigmatize dark-skinned Mexican Americans as an inferior racial group.

"Greaser" has been a contemptuous term applied to Mexican Americans at least since the Mexican war, perhaps deriving from the activities of Mexicans who greased wagon axles. Cowardice was a stereotype which grew up after the defeat of the Mexican army in the 1840s.[20] So too was the idea of political incompetence. In the 1850s John Monroe reported to Washington that the people of New Mexico "are thoroughly debased and totally incapable of self-government, and there is no latent quality about them that can ever make them respectable."[21] In his racist view, their "Indian blood" made them suspect. Imperialistic Americans saw themselves fulfilling their national destiny by taking and developing an area the allegedly lazy Mexicans had failed to develop. Ironically, it was these Mexicans whose knowledge of ranching, agriculture, and mining had laid the foundation for development of the Southwest.

The heavy Mexican immigration after 1900 triggered attacks on Mexicans by racists and nativists. Mexican labor camps were raided by the Ku Klux Klan and other white groups who tore up tents and beat Mexican workers. Some workers were beaten to death or lynched. Even the 1911 federal Dillingham Commission on immigration alleged that Mexicans were unskilled, and thus undesirable. In the 1920s a prominent U.S. congressperson viciously stereotyped the Mexican as a mixture of Spanish and "low-grade Indians who did not fight to extinction," plus some slave "blood," a mongrelized and undesirable people. A prominent expert for the House Immigration Committee testified to the racial inferiority of Mexicans in 1928, branding the "Mexican race" a threat to the "white race."[22] In line with their views of other groups, nativist scholars and popular writers alike expressed fear of "race mongrelization" as a result of contact with Mexicans. In 1925 a Princeton economics professor spoke fearfully of the future elimination of Anglo-Saxons by interbreeding in "favor of the progeny of Mexican peons who will continue to afflict us with an embarrassing race problem." Racist notions could be found at the highest levels.[23]

A criminal stereotype emerged as well. Much literature since the 1920s has pictured the Mexican American in stereotypical terms as a crime-oriented villain with shifty eyes, a knife in the pocket, and a wild desire to slash out. This image has been proclaimed by government officials. For example, a report by a lieutenant in the Los Angeles Sheriff's Department after the 1942 "zoot-suit" riots alleged that the Mexicans' desire to spill blood was an "inborn characteristic," a view endorsed by the local Anglo police chief. Two decades later another Los Angeles police official publicly spoke of Mexicans as being genetically "not too far removed from the wild tribes" in the interior of Mexico.[24] Much stereotyping has linked alleged social traits to genetic inferiority: "The Mexican was 'lawless' and 'violent' because he had Indian blood; he was 'shiftless' and 'improvident' because that was his nature."[25]

Since the 1920s the results of IQ testing have been used to argue for the intellectual and racial inferiority of Mexican Americans. As in the case of Jews, Italians, and black Americans, scientists have argued on the basis of paper-and-pencil tests that Mexican American children are of lower intelligence.[26]

Modern Stereotyping

By the 1960s some aspects of the harshest stereotypes were beginning to fade from public view, but prejudicial attitudes were still expressed. One study in a Texas city found that the "dirty" image was quite prevalent; drunkenness, immorality, and criminality were charges leveled at Mexican Americans. Another study in a central California city found one-quarter of Anglos reporting they would find it distasteful to eat with a Mexican; over half said they would find it distasteful to be at a party where most people were Mexican. Such attitudes often reflect stereotypical views. The statement that "generally speaking, Mexicans are shiftless and dirty" was accepted by 37 percent of the respondents.[27]

The mass media have played a role in perpetuating anti-Mexican attitudes. Movies have cast Mexicans as banditos. Movies of Pancho Villa's raids in Texas, to take one example, play up the criminal image and ignore the relationship of banditry to prior exploitation by U.S. settlers.[28] With the advent of television a new medium for circulating the stereotypes became available. In television serials the men could be seen as "lazy, fat, happy, thieving, immoral creatures who make excellent sidekicks for white heroes."[29] The women have been portrayed as flirting señoritas playing up to non-Mexican actors.

Comedians on television and in night clubs get laughs for stereotyping Hispanic Americans as buffoons who talk with a "funny accent." To be fair, one should note that one or two television comedy series, such as *Chico and the Man,* have tried to portray Hispanic figures in terms other than the traditional stereotypes, but these attempts have not offset the prevailing negative stereotypes aired on other shows, not to mention those in movie reruns. Media advertising has also played a role in perpetuating stereotypes. One study found that there were numerous major advertisers still showing Mexican Americans in a negative light, as lazy, funny, or dirty. Frito Bandito ads suggested that Mexicans were odd criminals. One deodorant company used a grubby-looking Mexican bandit in an ad which said, "If it works for him, it will work for you." Tequila advertisements in college campus newspapers had a "game" with characters representing aspects of negative stereotypes of Mexicans, the lazy peon in a large sombrero sleeping on a burro, the border-town prostitute, the sleepy border guard, and the thieving bandito.[30]

Mexican Americans have also had positive stereotypes aimed at them, though many have negative implications. For example, since the late nineteenth century there has been a positive image of things called "Spanish": unique foods, colorful fiestas, architecture, enjoyment of life. Yet the positive view has often been used to distinguish these things from things "Mexican," even though they are in fact often the same.

George Murphy, once a senator from California, alleged that "Mexicans are ideal for 'stoop' labor—after all, they are built close to the ground."[31] Here a biological characteristic is linked to menial jobs. In 1969 one California judge, ruling against a Mexican American youngster in an incest case, asserted in court:

> Mexican people, after 13 years of age, think it is perfectly all right to go out and act like an animal. We ought to send you out of the country—send you back to Mexico. . . . You are lower than animals and haven't the right to live in organized society—just miserable, lousy, rotten people. Maybe Hitler was right. The animals in our society probably ought to be destroyed because they have no right to live among human beings.[32]

Here again is the criminality image, with genocidal and racist overtones.

Numerous government officials have assumed the passivity and fatalism of Mexican Americans. Thus officials sometimes explain Hispanic activism in terms of outside agitators.[33] Such a view is based on a sophisticated type of stereotype originating in some social science studies—those that adopted the perspective of a Mexican American culture of passivity, lack of protest, resignation and fatalism, hypermasculine "machismo," and extreme family orientation. Some anthropological studies conducted since the 1940s by such scholars as Robert Redfield and Oscar Lewis have portrayed what they thought was a folk culture of fatalism and familism in the villages of Mexico, a view extended to Mexican American life. Such views have been expressed in studies such as that by Madsen on Mexican Americans in Texas.[34]

Since the 1960s other social scientists have criticized these distortions in the traditional views of Mexicans and Mexican Americans and the errors in assuming that life in villages decades ago was the same as life in Mexican American communities today. Their point is that the great diversity of Mexican American life and culture in areas from southern Texas to New Mexico to California has been overlooked.[35]

In the views of outsiders Mexican Americans have been seen both as a racial group and as an ethnic group. Some have accented their cultural characteristics as the major indicators of their distinctiveness. Others have seen them as an inferior race, accenting dark skins and "Indian" features thought to be typical of the group.

VIOLENT CONFLICT

The Early Period

Beginning with the Texas revolt of 1836, the transfer of resources from Mexican settlers to Euro-American settlers did not come without bloodshed. Coercion was a fundamental factor in the establishment of Anglo domination in the Southwest. Mexican agricultural development was taken over by chicanery and force. The competition for land led to a new system of inequality. Both elite and rank-and-file Mexicans became subordinate to the invaders' control. The struggle over resources resulted in much conflict.

The Mexicans resisted. The reaction sometimes took the form of rebellion, termed by dominant groups "banditry." Numerous Mexican "bandits" raided the Anglo settlers' farms and towns, often retaliating for settler actions. Such resistance began with the expropriation of Mexican lands in the 1830s and 1840s. Throughout history there have been bandits whose praises have been sung in folk ballads. Many have been social rebels unwilling to bear quietly the burdens imposed on their peoples. Typically they commit acts regarded as crimes by the authorities in the dominant group, but *not* by people in the subordinate group; thus they are protected by the common people, in some cases becoming legends.[36]

Among the heroes in Mexican legends are Juan Cortina and Pancho Villa. Cortina has been typed as an "outlaw" and "cattle thief," but he became something of a Robin Hood figure to many Mexicans. He was certainly more than a thief, for he fought against the oppression of poor Mexicans in the Texas borderlands. In a series of guerilla-type raids along the border, his followers clashed with the local militia and the Texas Rangers; in the 1850s and 1860s Cortina fought the injustice of the European American intruders. He issued formal statements of grievances detailing such actions as the stealing of lands and the setting up of biased legal systems. Colonel Robert E. Lee was sent to put down the Cortina rebellions, but was successful only in limiting Cortina's activities. There were numerous other raids and clashes along the Texas border from El Paso to Brownsville. Between 1910 and 1925 there were many killings of both Mexicans and Euro-Americans in the Texas border area, with estimates of the dead ranging from five hundred to five thousand. Far more Mexican civilians than others were killed, often without provocation.[37]

Lynching and public whipping became ways of keeping Mexicans in line; numerous lynchings were recorded in the nineteenth century. Much of the lawlessness against Mexicans in the Southwest had an official or semiofficial status. Law-enforcement officers such as the Texas Rangers became a kind of "Gestapo" force used to terrorize and subordinate Mexican Americans. The image of the Texas Rangers has been sugar-coated in exaggerated stories of heroism. Paredes has demonstrated that the myth covers up the oppressiveness of a police force traditionally used by Anglos to exploit the Mexican population in Texas. The European American rancher and farmer often became rich with the aid of the Texas Rangers. In New Mexico the expansion of Anglo ranches at the expense of Mexicans did not come peacefully. Vigilante groups such as *La Mano Negro* (The Black Hand) used whatever means necessary to protect Mexican livestock and land; village organization there formed the basis for protest groups operating between the 1890s and the 1920s.[38]

More Anglo Attacks

Later decades in the twentieth century also saw open conflict. The so-called zoot-suit riots began in June 1943 in Los Angeles with attacks by Anglo sailors on Mexican American youths, particularly on those who dressed in baggy "zoot suits" and who wore their hair long. Groups of white sailors and other whites roamed the Los Angeles area beating up young zoot-suiters. Mexican groups organized retaliatory attacks on the sailors. Why did these riots occur? After Japanese Americans were forced out of southern California, local officials and newspapers began to focus on Mexican American crime and youth. Police harassment increased, sometimes to the point of flagrant brutality. Newspapers and other media played a critical role in shaping intense anti-Mexican sentiment in the Los Angeles area.

A few biased but well-publicized court trials involving Mexican youths stirred up local prejudices. Their unusual dress became a focus of attention; youth groups were called "gangs" whether they involved criminals or not. One study found that in the three years leading up to the riots there was a sharp decline in the *Los Angeles Times's* use of the term *Mexican* and a corresponding increase in use of the term *zoot suit* (in connection with Mexican Americans) in an unfavorable way. So intense was paranoia that during the rioting the Los Angeles City Council seriously discussed making the wearing of zoot suits a criminal offense.[39]

Recent Protest

In the 1960s and 1970s groups of young Chicanos, such as the Brown Berets, took to the streets and fought back against police actions they saw as oppressive.* There were three dozen Mexican American protest-oriented riots in southwestern cities. Among the most important were the East Los Angeles riots. In 1970 a Los Angeles riot involved 100 persons attacking stores owned mainly by Anglo absentee owners; and an August riot took place when 20,000 Mexican Americans went to Los Angeles for a National Chicano Moratorium March on the Vietnam War. During the march, according to the police, some deputies along the route were attacked by the demonstrators. The marchers were later attacked by police at a park at the end of the route. Four hundred persons were arrested; dozens were injured; 25 police cars were damaged. Another riot later occurred along the route of a Mexican Independence Day parade, with 100 injuries and 68 arrests.[40]

These riots were similar to the black riots of the same period. Police-community confrontations preceded the riots. Police forces, with no or few Chicanos in them, have long been used, sometimes illegally, as a force to end legal strikes and protests by Mexican American workers. Some cases have resulted in deaths to innocent civilians. Between 1965 and 1969 the U.S. Justice Department received 256 complaints of police malpractice from persons with Spanish surnames; in the late 1960s the American Civil Liberties Union received 174 such complaints in California alone. The common practice of preventive police patrolling in ghetto areas, with its "stop and frisk" and "arrest on suspicion" tactics, often leads to unfavorable police contacts for Mexican American males. Harassment of this type intensifies negative attitudes toward the police. Inadequate police protection is another serious problem. One study of three California cities found that most Mexican Americans interviewed felt the police did not care about protecting their property and lives and were hostile regarding their needs. Such relations laid the groundwork for rioting.[41]

THE ECONOMY

We have already traced the outlines of the incorporation of Mexicans into the U.S. economy, first by violent conquest and later by the takeover of lands. The scale of the land ripoff has not been fully documented, but it involved millions of acres. An estimated 2 million acres of private lands and 1.7 million acres of communal lands were lost between 1854 and 1930 in the New Mexico area alone. A study of Taos County in New Mexico pointed up what had happened to Chicano lands by 1940: two-thirds of the county's private acreage had originally been land grants made to Mex-

---

*The term "Chicano" has been preerred to the term "Mexican American" by some activists, particularly in the 1960s and early 1970s. By the late 1970s there was debate over its use, even among militant activists.

ican communities and families, but this land had been lost to Anglo settlers or the federal government. Mexican Americans were driven off their lands by action by the federal Departments of the Interior and Agriculture when they developed major irrigation and flood-control districts.

This dramatic loss of lands laid the basis for the current poverty-stricken nature of many Mexican American communities. Across the Southwest those who lost their lands, as well as the descendants of such people and new immigrants, became landless laborers. Industrial and commercial operations increasingly came to predominate in the expanding capitalist economy of the region, while agriculture was developed in a commercial large-farm direction. One south Texas study found that in the 1850–1860 period, one-third of Mexican Americans in the rural labor force were ranch and farm owners, one-third were skilled laborers or professionals, and one-third were manual laborers. However, by 1900 the proportion of ranch and farm owners had dropped to 16 percent, while the proportion of manual laborers—many working for large Anglo ranches and farms—had climbed to two-thirds of all workers. A similar shift took place in the urban labor force, from a predominantly skilled labor force to a predominantly unskilled labor force. Many Mexican Americans were made parts of the proletariat, forced out of farming and ranching on their own or out of skilled labor into performing unskilled labor for Anglos.[42]

Overt, sometimes violent, discrimination played its part in limiting job opportunities. For example, because Mexican miners were resented by by non-Mexican miners in California, a Foreign Miners Act placing a license tax on "foreigners" was passed to force Mexicans out of mining; and in the 1850s a group of two thousand Euro-American miners attacked Mexicans in Sonora, killing dozens and destroying a community. By the 1880s manual laborers were being used extensively in the expansion of railroads. Living in tents and boxcars, Mexican workers for many years played a significant part in building these lines. Mexicans were the original vaqueros (cowboys) on the ranches across the Southwest.[43]

The continued expansion of agriculture and railroads between 1900 and 1920 from California to Texas brought a sharp demand for workers. Reliance on a supply of Mexican labor became central. In El Paso in 1908, labor recruitment agencies were placing two thousand Mexican railroad workers per month; thousands more were placed through other cities.

But the experiences of these people were not the same as those of Irish and other European immigrants, because of the ruthless dehumanization of Mexicans in the fields and in industries. Mexican peasants were viewed by agricultural and industrial capitalists as ideal workers because of their presumed docility. Yet poverty was a major reason for their doing the "dirty work" in the economy. Labor smugglers played a major role in recruiting undocumented workers. Labor contractors transported the workers and made job commitments; they took care of supplies and often watched over the work itself.[44]

Working conditions for agricultural "stoop" labor were so severe that, before the Depression, few competed with Mexicans for jobs. Mexican laborers in farming averaged $1.75 a day in Texas and $2.75 to $6.00 a day in California in the late 1920s. In mining, Mexicans averaged $2.75 to $4.00 a day; in brick work they made $2.75 to $4.00 a day. In the railroad and construction industries wages were similarly quite low. One study of Mexican agricultural workers found that they averaged $600 to $800 per year in income.[45]

Job Discrimination Persists

Institutionalized discrimination was a major problem. It was common from the 1920s onward for agricultural operations, oil companies, mining companies, and other industries to pay different rates for "whites" and "nonwhites," under which category Mexicans were frequently listed. In the border area, discrimination was easy because of the character of the work force. Wages for citizens and noncitizens alike could be kept low because of the constant availability of undocumented workers; the presence of a large number of undocumented workers forestalled unionization.

Many unions have a record of discrimination against Mexican Americans going back to the early days of the labor movement; in the 1920s and the 1930s such unions as the California Federation of Labor worked for their exclusion. Numerous industrial unions excluded Mexican Americans from membership. Attempts to create farm labor unions date back several decades, but they were not very successful until the 1960s.[46]

By 1930 Mexican Americans were still heavily employed in manual labor in low-wage, secondary-labor-market positions. In the 1930 Census, out of nearly three million Mexican American residents only fifty-four hundred were in clerical positions, with a few hundred doctors and lawyers. In the Depression the fact that many poor Mexican Americans were on relief led to increasing Anglo hostility toward them. Forced repatriation to Mexico was tried as a solution by a number of local welfare agencies. More than eleven thousand, citizens and noncitizens, were sent back in 1932 from Los Angeles communities.[47]

The 1940s saw some improvement in the employment situation but discriminatory barriers were still severe. One study of San Bernardino, California, found rampant discrimination keeping Mexican Americans in low-wage positions, with average annual incomes in the neighborhood of $700 to $800. By 1943 Roosevelt's antidiscrimination order and the tight labor supply had finally opened up some jobs at decent wages to Mexican Americans; this development, however, was short-lived. Virtually no qualified workers moved up into skilled or supervisory positions.[48]

Poorly paid jobs meant inferior housing, a situation further sharpened by housing discrimination. With the increase in Mexican immigrants came segregated urban ghettos, called *barrios*, which were usually concentrations of deteriorating housing. Restrictive covenants in deeds kept Mexican Americans out of numerous housing areas in the Southwest in the 1930s.[49]

In the 1950s and 1960s many Mexican Americans were still in secondary-labor-market positions as farm workers, urban laborers, or service workers. Internal migrant labor streams were very important for Mexican Americans (and Mexicans), with the largest stream coming out of southern

Texas. Some families migrated to agriculture areas in other parts of Texas and in the Midwest. The average annual wage for migrant workers in 1956 was only $1,500 in Texas and $2,600 outside of Texas. Even by the late 1960s the average hourly wage for seasonal farmworkers was only $1.07 in Texas and $1.50 to $1.70 in the midwestern states. Not only was poverty their lot; several studies found high rates of disabling work injuries among farm workers.[50] Many were living in camps with totally inadequate housing, beds, and sanitation facilities. One author has described the oppressive life of a child in a farmworker's family:

> I was never a happy child; in fact I never felt that I was a child since I had to work from an early age. . . . In 1950 my father, Gustavo, bought a little one room shack behind his mother-in-law's house, here my parents and eight children lived. Dad's economic situation at the time was very bad and since he worked as a farm laborer he was only paid 60 to 70 cents an hour, hardly enough to feed eight kids much less clothe them and provide for medical attention.[51]

Other Mexican American workers were in industries located in southwestern cities, many within a few hundred miles of the border. A major problem in the border region has been that of "run-away" industries, those which have moved from higher-wage areas to this low-wage region in order to continue or increase company profits. Food-processing plants have been a major industry in the Imperial Valley of California, in southern Arizona and New Mexico, and in the Rio Grande Valley. A major garment industry also grew up, taking advantage of low wages and unemployment in the female labor force. By 1970 there were two thousand manufacturing plants in the border region employing over one hundred thousand people, primarily concentrated in the garment, food-processing, metal-smelting and metal-refining, and defense-related industries, as well as such local industries as the concrete and fertilizer industries.[52]

Large parts of the border region can be seen as one big secondary labor market, with low wages for employees and significant benefits for employers. One study of border cities found that wages were consistently lower on the border than in the interior.[53]

Farm wages in Texas and California were lowest in border areas; manufacturing wage rates were also quite low in Texas border areas. A study of Mexican commuter workers in Laredo, Texas, found that most of them were in garment manufacturing, hotels, restaurants, and retail trade; those employers with alien commuters paid lower wages than those employing U.S. citizens. Commuter and "illegal" workers, many of whom eventually return to Mexico, often make less than their productivity deserves because they cannot bargain vigorously with employers.

Many employers in the Sunbelt and the Midwest prefer undocumented workers because they can be exploited more easily than U.S. workers. If they protest oppressive working conditions, an employer can turn them in to police authorities. That threat keeps such Mexican workers more docile than U.S. workers. In the mid-1970s the *Los Angeles Times* found that 99 percent of employers refused government help in trying to find U.S. workers to replace undocumented Mexican workers who had been caught. The reason was that employers preferred to find cheap Mexican workers to replace those caught. Even the *Times* reporter noted that these employers wanted "workers who can be exploited"—that is, who can be paid less than the minimum wage, who will not organize, and who will get no significant fringe benefits.[54]

Unemployment, Poverty, and Income

Unemployment rates have been high for decades. In 1981 the unemployment rate was still relatively high for Mexican American men—8.5 percent, as compared with 5.5 percent for non-Hispanic white men. Rates were similarly high for Mexican American women. Occupational distributions were changing slowly between 1960 and 1980. We can obtain a rough idea of these changes from the data on the Spanish-surname population* tabulated in the 1960 Census for the five southwestern states and from data on the Mexican-origin population tabulated in 1970 and 1979 for the nation:[55]

	MEXICAN AMERICAN MEN			MEXICAN AMERICAN WOMEN		
	1960	1970	1979	1960	1970	1979
Professional, technical	4.1%	5.3%	5.5%	5.9%	6.4%	6.4%
Managerial, administrative	4.6	4.0	6.0	2.7	1.9	3.5
Sales workers	3.6	3.2	1.9	8.1	5.7	5.1
Clerical workers	4.8	5.8	6.0	21.8	26.0	31.1
Craft workers	16.7	21.0	21.5	1.3	2.3	1.8
Operatives	24.1	27.1	26.3	26.6	26.0	25.0
Nonfarm laborers	15.2	13.0	13.6	1.2	1.7	1.3
Farm owners, workers	19.1	9.8	6.2	4.3	4.0	2.4
Service workers	7.7	11.0	12.9	28.0	26.0	23.4

Clearly, Mexican American males were concentrated at the lower job levels, with a majority in the operative, laborer, farmworker, and service worker categories in 1960, 1970, and 1979. Working women were located primarily in the service, operative, and clerical categories. Contrary to some stereotypes, however, most Mexican Americans are not now farm workers.

Moreover, 1980 data from the Bureau of the Census revealed little in the way of changes from the 1979 data. Mexican Americans have been sharply underrepresented in the professional, managerial, and sales categories. One can see changes between 1960 and 1980 in the direction of mobility, but only the decline in the percentage of farm workers among the males seems dramatic. A majority are still concentrated in lower-paying blue-collar and white-collar jobs.[56]

According to the 1960 Census most Spanish-surname families had

*In U.S. Census tabulations the category "Spanish surname persons" is predominantly Mexican American.

incomes well below the Anglo average. By 1970, Mexican American incomes still remained relatively low compared to Anglos. At least one-quarter of all Mexican American families fell below the poverty line in that year. The proportion was even higher in rural areas. The median family income for Mexican-origin families was $6,972 in 1970, compared with the much higher figure for all families of $9,600. And family incomes have been substantially lower in Texas than in California. In the late 1970s and early 1980s the relative picture had changed little. In 1979 one-fifth of Mexican Americans still fell below the official poverty line. Family income was up but was still only 70 percent of that for Anglos.

Why are there persisting income and job differentials? A recent (1982) report by the National Commission for Employment Policy notes that discrimination, language problems (lack of ability to speak English well), and low levels of formal education are major reasons. In the job market, Mexican Americans are penalized (more than whites with equivalent fluency) for their lack of fluent English. One might expect areas with large numbers of Chicano families to show less of a negative impact because of fewer English-language difficulties. Yet one study found that Mexican American wages are lower in cities and other areas with large Mexican American communities. This is due in part to the fact that Mexican Americans are concentrated in low-wage states such as Texas. Studies have also shown that some employers discriminate against Mexican Americans because they do not want to risk hiring illegal aliens.[57]

POLITICS

Mexican American involvement in politics has been limited by discrimination. In the period before 1910 some Mexican Americans did hold office in territorial and state legislatures; usually hand-picked by Anglos, they served in the governments of California, Colorado, and New Mexico. This was a situation of political participation confined to a few privileged persons. There were no urban political organizations for Mexican immigrants coming in after 1900 to use and to take over, as there were in northern cities for the southern and eastern European immigrants. No preexisting political organizations provided the critical economic benefits to facilitate the survival and eventual mobility of immigrants.[58]

Railroads, mining interests, large ranchers, land companies—just a few powerful European American groups—have dominated local and state politics in the Southwest for decades. These interests made sure that Mexican American voting strength was kept low. While there has been considerable variation in direct discrimination from state to state, a number of devices have been used to reduce voting, including the poll tax, the white primary, gerrymandered political districts, and threats of violence. Indirect discrimination in the form of property requirements for voting have also had an effect. Between the 1910s and the 1940s few voted, because of discrimination, apathy, or fear.[59]

World War II brought hundreds of thousands out of the barrios of the Southwest into new cities and industries or into the armed forces. With this came an uphill fight to expand political participation. Numerous examples of slowly expanding, sometimes regressing, participation could be seen in the counties and cities of the Southwest from the late 1940s onward. For example, although gerrymandering continued to keep representation down, the Los Angeles city council finally saw its first Mexican American representative in 1949; but again, between the early 1960s and the early 1970s there were no Mexican Americans on the city council.

By the 1960s Chicanos had moved up significantly from a position of low representation on school boards. Among the 4,600 board members in the Southwest there were then 470 Mexican Americans. The number of state legislators with Spanish surnames increased from 20 in 1950 to 67 in 1973. By 1983 the number had increased to more than 90. The number of other state officials was also growing slowly in this period.

In spite of recent gains the percentage of *all* officials who are Mexican American remains generally low. By the late 1960s a few were serving at the federal level. In 1968 there were three Mexican Americans in the U.S. House of Representatives, one from California and two from Texas, and one U.S. senator from New Mexico; by 1972 there were only four representatives and one senator. And in 1982 there were again only four Mexican Americans in Congress, from Texas, California, and New Mexico. Expanded voting strength was brought about by legal victories in the form of the Twenty-fourth Amendment, which banned the poll tax, and a California court case knocking down an English-only literacy requirement for voting.[60]

Presidential Voting

At the presidential level, Mexican American voting has been traditionally Democratic. In 1960 Kennedy won an estimated 85 percent of Mexican American votes, which was more than enough to make the difference in New Mexico and Texas. In 1964 Johnson got 90 percent; and in 1968 Humphrey got 87 percent of the vote. These Hispanics stayed with the Democratic party in the debacle of 1972, and the 1976 and 1980 elections again saw a substantial Democratic majority among these voters. Some analysts have been critical of the relatively low turnout of Chicanos, portraying the Chicano voter as apathetic; their "culture" has been cited as the reason for this lack of political interest.

Mexican American voter turnout has on occasion been substantial, as in Los Angeles in the Kennedy election and in southern Texas elections, where Mexican Americans have won important electoral victories. Low turnouts in many elections may be due to a variety of structural factors, such as little education, lack of Spanish-language ballots, and the absence of meaningful political choices. In addition, official statistics often seriously underrepresent the turnout, because of the large numbers of recent immigrants and noncitizens included in the broad "voting-age group" (all adults) used to calculate percentages.[61]

A few War on Poverty programs of the Johnson administration focused on the plight of Mexican Americans. For example, one such program, Plans for Progress, Inc., was tied to existing Mexican American organizations; community programs in five states were supervised by this agency, which worked hard to improve job opportunities and to teach Mexican Americans how to deal with problems of discrimination in bureaucracies. Some middle-income Mexican Americans were co-opted by War on Poverty and Model Cities programs which provided, at least for them, white-collar employment.[62]

Progress in the judicial branch has also come slowly; underrepresentation has been common. The first Mexican American was appointed as a federal judge in the 1960s; and a 1969 study found that only two of the fifty-nine federal district judges in the five southwestern states had Spanish surnames. In the same year only 3 percent of the nearly one thousand state judges in the five southwestern states were Spanish-surnamed individuals, with over half of these in New Mexico. An examination of district attorneys and public prosecutors (and assistants) in twenty-two southwest cities found that only 3 percent were Spanish-surnamed. Many Hispanic applicants have been found unqualified for police positions by the indirect discrimination of height and weight requirements and English-language requirements, as well as by poor scores on conventional qualifying examinations. Moreover, few Mexican Americans have ever served at the higher levels of the U.S. Department of Justice or of other federal law-enforcement agencies.[63]

Given this serious underrepresentation, it is not surprising that widespread discrimination in the operation of the criminal justice system has been documented. Arizona, California, and Colorado have required jurors to have an ability to speak and understand English, screening out many Spanish-speaking citizens; in fact, the pool of eligible jurors in numerous states has until recently been selected by whatever method has suited (usually Anglo) jury commissioners. As a result, Mexican Americans charged with crimes have historically been judged by juries on which sit none of their peers. There is a serious language problem for some Mexican American defendants tried in courtrooms where no one, including lawyers and judges, understands Spanish. Other harmful practices have included the use of excessive bail, the poor quality of appointed legal council, the absence of Spanish interpreters in courtrooms, and the negative views of judges regarding Mexican American defendants.[64]

Chicano Politics

Improvements in political participation at the local level came during the 1960s and 1970s. Mexican Americans won major political victories in Crystal City, Texas. A small city of 10,000 people with a predominantly poor, Mexican American population, Crystal City lies in Zavala County in the heart of the profitable Winter Garden area in southern Texas. A Del Monte cannery came to the area in the 1940s, followed in the mid-1950s by the Teamsters' Union. The union gave the Mexican American workers job security and some political resources for electoral campaigns in the early 1960s. Five Mexican Americans won city council positions in 1963, displacing the establishment. Economic reprisals were taken against the Chicanos, and Anglos regained control of the council in the late 1960s. In 1969 a massive school boycott expressed the discontent of the predominantly Mexican student body in a school system not controlled by Mexican Americans. Led by José Angel Gutiérrez, the new La Raza Unida party became a leading political party in the area. In 1970 Mexican Americans won three of seven school board positions and two of five city council positions. With one already in each body, the Mexican Americans gained political control. In nearby towns victories were also recorded. Outside aid had played some role in the victories, but the main impact came from the well-organized and aggressive campaign of local people.[65]

The new elected officials saw to it that established ways were altered. Changes came in the schools with the hiring of more Mexican American teachers, teacher aides, and administrators. Bilingual programs were started, and curriculum changes included attention to Mexican American history. Sharp decreases in the dropout rate were reported. Mexican Americans were hired or promoted at all levels of the city bureaucracy, including the police department. The new city council even passed a resolution attempting to stop the Texas Highway Patrol, notorious for its harassment of Mexican Americans, from patrolling barrio areas. Attempts were made to attract new industries. Millions of dollars in new federal aid poured in, and important programs were started in health, housing, and urban renewal.[66]

The impact on the Anglo population was far-reaching. Out of power for the first time, they counterattacked. Some Mexicans lost their jobs. Anglo parents reacted by withdrawing their children from school, and teachers resigned, complaining of discrimination and a redirection of school activities in the direction of Mexican American goals. Financial resources were limited because of a boycott of school taxes. State agencies put pressure on the school district. In 1976 a Chicano group secured a $1.5 million federal grant for a large cooperative farming operation in the county. The grant was attacked by the Texas Governor, who called the project "anti-American" and "un-Texan" because he felt it was patterned on communal farms in Cuba. The governor got implementation delayed, arguing that the state government had not reviewed the project. A federal judge blocked the grant, pending this review.[67]

The impact of Crystal City's new leadership, in addition to bringing job, housing, and other material benefits, has been to increase militancy and political activity in the area. For example, a 1971 survey of high-school students in Crystal City found that those who identified themselves specifically as "Chicanos" had a higher level of political consciousness than those who chose the term "Mexican Americans." They were more critical of the legal and political system and more willing to protest. This increase in Chicano consciousness seems connected with the rise of La Raza Unida Party. With political experience and activity, however, have come divisions within the Mexican American community; tensions in leadership have developed, with a consequent decline of the La Raza Unida Party. Some of the Mexican American officials were replaced by Anglos in the late 1970s and early 1980s. And some of the Chicano militants left the community. There seemed to be a decline in Mexican American political power there by the 1980s. Most Mexican Americans were no longer identified with the militant La Raza Unida Party, but rather with the state Democratic Party.[68]

Organizations and Protest

Protest activity has a long history among Mexican Americans. Since the 1920s nonviolent protest activity has been directed at discrimination in the economic and political spheres. Much protest activity has itself been a political resource, supplementing electoral activities in bringing about changes in the system.

The docile-Mexican myth is dashed by a review of protest activity. Union organization came early. Several organizations of workers came and went between 1900 and 1927, but the first permanent organization was the Confederación de Uniones Obreras Mexicanas (CUOM), organized in California in 1927, with three thousand members. A 1928 strike by the CUOM was killed by deportation and arrests. In the 1930s coal miners, farm workers, and factory workers struck in New Mexico, Arizona, and Texas, during which time Mexican Americans were beginning to make their way into a number of mainstream unions. In the International Ladies Garment Workers Union they participated in militant strike activities. In this period police force was used to break up many union meetings and strikes. Newspapers and public officials throughout the Southwest supported this use of Anglo police to frustrate union activities.[69]

Mutual-benefit associations developed early among Mexican Americans. These included worker alliances aimed at pooling resources and providing contexts for social interaction, as well as religious brotherhoods. Such organizations often provided the social groundwork for later protest organizations. By the 1920s a number of Mexican American newspapers were being published, most of which encouraged pride in the Mexican heritage. The League of United Latin American Citizens (LULAC) was organized in southern Texas in the 1920s and pressed for a better deal for Mexican Americans. Originally oriented toward civic activities and acculturation to the Anglo-Saxon core culture, LULAC refused to call itself a protest association. However, from the 1960s to the 1980s, LULAC has worked to break down segregation and discrimination on many fronts.[70]

A number of organizations formed after World War II reflected growing militancy. After a Mexican American soldier was not permitted in a Texas cemetery and Mexican American veterans were segregated in or excluded from veterans' organizations, the American G.I. Forum was established to organize Chicano veterans and to work for expanded civil rights. In Los Angeles the Community Service Organization (CSO) worked to organize the voting strength. Two new groups, formed about 1960, more explicitly focused on political goals: the Mexican American Political Association (MAPA), a California organization, and the Political Association of Spanish-Speaking Organizations (PASSO), a Texas organization. Both fought successfully to improve political power. Mexican American protest intensified in the 1960s, in part reflecting an understanding of the effectiveness of black militancy and in part reflecting growing political consciousness. "Corky" Gonzales and his associates worked in Denver in support of school strikes and against police brutality. New youth organizations were formed throughout the Southwest, including the United Mexican American Students (UMAS), the Mexican American Youth Organization (MAYO), and the Brown Berets, a paramilitary organization that set forth a ten-point program of better education, employment, and housing. A new ideology of *Chicanismo* was here being developed, espousing a philosophy of decolonization rather than assimilation.[71]

Perhaps the most militant protest activities in the last few decades were those led by Reies Tijerina and his associates. Tijerina aimed his movement at recovering stolen land. The organization Alianza Federal de Mercedes was created in 1963 by Tijerina after he had spent a number of years researching the old Mexican land grants in the Southwest. A new strategy of collective action directed at restoring the grants emerged. An itinerant preacher, Tijerina became a secular prophet. In July 1966 a group of Alianza members marched to Santa Fe and presented a statement of land grant grievances. Another group camped out without a permit on Kit Carson National Forest land, which had once been part of a communal land grant. Forest Rangers who tried to stop them were seized and tried for violating the old land grant boundaries. Tijerina and some others were arrested and tried for this civil disobedience. Police harassment of the organization intensified. A local district attorney took it upon himself to break up a 1967 Alianza meeting in a small town in New Mexico. News broadcasts were made asking Mexican Americans not to attend, and motorists near the town were stopped by the police and given a notice that alleged the meeting was illegal. Some of the leaders of the Alianza were arrested arbitrarily and taken to the Tierra Amarilla courthouse.

This escalated the nonviolent protest to a brief violent protest. A group of armed Mexican Americans went to the courthouse to make a citizen's arrest of the district attorney for his unwarranted actions. A shootout ensued, with some officials wounded. Meanwhile, those families going to the meeting had camped at a nearby picnic ground. After the raid on the Tierra Amarilla courthouse, this group of men, women, and children were detained without due process of law at the picnic ground, without adequate shelter or water, by armed police and hundreds of National Guardsmen. Police made the incredible claim that the Alianza was planning a takeover of northern New Mexico and that their police actions were warranted. Tijerina was charged as a result of the Tierra Amarilla raid, but he was acquitted on major state charges. The federal government later put Tijerina in jail for 1966 and 1969 incidents involving forest rangers before the state government could secure a conviction. In 1969 Tijerina's wife had burned two Forest Service signs as a symbolic act. Reies Tijerina was arrested and convicted for destroying this government property. After serving some time in jail, Tijerina continued his fight for land redistribution.[72]

Unions for Poor Workers

Two major developments in unionization took place in the early 1960s—the creation of the Agriculture Workers Organizing Committee (AWOC) and Cesar Chavez's National Farm Workers Association (NFWA). By 1964 the NFWA had a thousand members and its own credit union. Several small-scale strikes brought early victories for both organizations; in 1965 the first big strike came. Pilipino* workers in the AWOC struck the Delano, California, growers in September 1965; the NFWA met in Delano and voted to go on strike too, with demands for $1.40 hourly wages. Growers refused to talk with union leaders; picket lines went up; guns were fired at pickets; police harassment was a constant problem. Chavez successfully worked to keep his own movement nonviolent in the face of provocation. A grape boycott was started in October 1965 and gradually spread across the country. Picket lines went up wherever the grapes went. National publicity came when major labor leaders visited the strikers and the Senate Subcommittee on Migratory Labor held a hearing in Delano. There was a massive march on Sacramento. Extensive support came from churches and other labor unions. In 1966 AWOC and NFWA merged into the United Farm Workers Organizing Committee.[73]

Unionization was more difficult in south Texas. The attempt by the United Farm Workers to organize in the Rio Grande Valley in the 1960s and 1970s moved slowly because of imprisonment of strikers and leaders and the intervention of the hated Texas Rangers. Attempts by the Meat Cutters Union to organize Mexican Americans in South Texas did result in some union victories, but much suffering was the price.[74]

In 1973 the largest winery in the United States, Gallo Brothers, chose not to renew its contract with the United Farm Workers and signed with the Teamsters. Several other wineries followed suit. A number of newspaper and magazine articles appeared arguing that Chavez and his union movement were dying. Yet the struggle continued. Now Governor Jerry Brown of California worked for new legislation to protect farm workers, and a labor board was established to run secret-ballot elections, with considerable protection for union activities. Some progress has been made, but funding problems for the state agency developed and many problems remain for the workers in the fields.[75]

Other action against discrimination was taken from the 1960s to the 1980s, often by high-school and college students. Of the boycotts and demonstrations, some reinforced growing electoral power, as in cities such as Crystal City, Texas, while others resulted in violent conflict with the police, as in the Los Angeles riots. Moreover, a recent survey by the University of Michigan's Survey Research Center found that 80 percent of the Mexican Americans interviewed favored mass demonstrations to protest unfair laws and discrimination; similar proportions favored pressuring employers to hire more Mexican Americans for jobs and organizing to increase voting power.

*"Pilipino" is the spelling preferred by many activists in this growing group of Americans from the Pacific.

EDUCATION

In the first three decades of the twentieth century little attention was given to the education of Mexican Americans. Mexican Americans, many Anglos argued, were better off as workers in the fields; the agricultural economy of the Southwest pressed for cheap labor without the expense of education. As a result, schooling for laborers was usually minimal—just what was needed for them to learn a little arithmetic and English, together with certain Anglo culture values. A high-school dropout (pushout) rate contributed to low educational levels. Such a situation supported the low-wage agricultural system, as well as the common Anglo stereotypes of "dumb and lazy" Mexican Americans.[76]

School segregation has been a bit different for Mexican Americans than for black Americans. As a rule, Mexican Americans were not segregated by state law; rather, segregation was maintained either by local laws or by informal gerrymandering of school district lines. In addition, discrimination in housing reinforced school segregation. Prior to World War II children were segregated in schools from Texas to California. Across the Southwest lax enforcement of school attendance laws was typical in areas where attendance zones or transfer policies did not guarantee segregated schools. Discrimination could also be seen in school personnel practices throughout the Southwest. Until the 1950s there were few Mexican American teachers, and even fewer administrators.

Rationalizations for segregation touched on the language "problem" or the alleged disease-ridden condition of Mexican American children. Not surprisingly, segregation meant inferior schools and the discouragement of those Mexican American children who excelled under such oppressive conditions from continuing on to high school or college. Schools were typically not only separate but poor as well.[77]

Where some attempt was made at providing education, there was usually pressure for Anglo-conformity Americanization. We have seen similar Americanization pressures on Native American children. In Anglo-centered schools Mexican American children have often faced hostile pressures with regard to their language and culture. To the present, children caught speaking Spanish in some schools have been punished; they may be sent to a detention class, asked to pay money to the teacher, forced to stand in a corner, or sent to the principal's office.[78]

The Problems Persist

After World War II, increased but usually token efforts were made to deal with the education of Mexican Americans. A major conference in Texas in 1946 called for ending segregation and a new Mexican-oriented curriculum, better teacher training, and better school facilities. Conferences three decades later were still reiterating these needs. Perhaps more important, a few court decisions in the late 1940s began to outlaw segregation.

Yet court decisions did not quickly change the patterns of segregation. In 1970 approximately 17 percent of the children in southwestern schools were Mexican Americans, mostly in California and Texas. Nearly half of these students attended 1,500 predominantly Mexican American elementary and secondary schools. Pupil segregation is only one type of discrimination; underrepresentation among personnel is another. A 1969 study found that only 4 percent of the 325,000 teachers in the public schools in the Southwest were Mexican American, while only 3 percent of the 12,000 school principals and 6 percent of the 9,500 nonteaching professionals (such as counselors) were Mexican Americans. Mexican Americans constituted only 6 of the 58 members of state boards of education in the five Southwestern states, the best representation figure of all these. Given this general underrepresentation, it may not be surprising that modest action has been taken to meet the educational needs of Hispanic children.[79]

Moreover, schools with high percentages of Mexican American students have often been rigid in enforcing discipline and prohibiting manifestations of Mexican subculture. Many schools have enforced an offensive dress and hair code on Mexican American students. Teachers have anglicized the names of children (for instance, Roberto becomes "Bobby"), further downgrading the cultural heritage of the children. School curricula have ignored Mexican and Mexican American history.[80]

A persisting problem is the "special education class" designed for the mentally retarded. In Texas and California Mexican American children have been greatly overrepresented in classes for the mentally retarded. Yet most of these children are "six-hour" retarded children—children quite capable of functioning in the outside world yet pigeonholed as mentally retarded in the public schools because of testing procedures, usually conducted in English. One study in Riverside, California, found that 100 percent of the Anglo children in mentally retarded classes showed behavior abnormality, but less than half (40 percent) of the Mexican American children were behaviorally retarded. Indirect discrimination in the testing procedures thus seems the major reason for this mislabeling.[81]

A disproportionate number of children are stigmatized by other student assignment policies, such as grade retention and ability grouping. Holding Hispanic children back in the same grade for two years has been common in the Southwest. Yet one recent survey found no strong research evidence that grade retention is beneficial for students. Ability grouping, common to most elementary and secondary schools, was even more likely to be practiced in schools with a proportion of Mexican Americans. As a rule, these children were overrepresented in the low-ability groups. Recent research on the usefulness of ability grouping for children in average or low-achieving groups suggests that it, too, may not benefit children academically.[82]

Certain problems in the interaction between students and teachers might well affect the performance of Mexican Americans on a broad range of tests. One study of teacher behavior in classrooms found that the average teacher praised Anglo children 35 percent more often than Mexican Americans, questioned them 20 percent more often, and used their ideas 40 percent more often. Research studies of such teacher practices have shown them to have a strong relationship to student achievement. Carter has shown that Mexican American children may act out the negative expectations of their teachers and adopt a "dumb Mexican" pattern in order to cope with teachers, thus making the teacher's expectations a self-fulfilling prophecy.[83]

Current Controversies: Bilingualism and Undocumented Workers' Children

As recently as 1973, no southwestern state had taken more than token steps in bilingual education. English-as-a-second-language programs had been tried, but they relied heavily on intensive English-language work for an hour or less a day and assumed that the children could work in English in other subjects at the same time. Bilingual programs, on the other hand, make use of a child's knowledge of the cultural background in order to link him or her more positively to the learning environment. Altogether 5 percent of the Mexican American children in the Southwest were being affected by federally funded bilingual programs in the 1972–1973 school year. This was the case even though the 1968 Elementary and Secondary Education Act passed by Congress set up a mechanism for the federal government to fund bilingual programs, and in spite of 1970 federal guidelines requiring school districts getting federal funds to set up language programs for Hispanic students.

More teeth were put into federal requirements in a 1974 Supreme Court decision (*Lau v. Nichols*) which ruled that school systems could not ignore the English-language problems of national-origin minority groups. The Department of Health, Education, and Welfare (HEW) set up a task force to lay out specific bilingual programs in line with that court decision. Unfortunately, the "Lau Remedies," as they came to be called, were still being formulated and debated into the 1980s. Today there is a debate over what kind of bilingual programs to provide for language minority students. Many school systems have only provided weak bilingual programs. One federal accounting office (GAO) study found that most local school systems had few qualified bilingual teachers and had difficulty in accurately assessing the English language needs of language minority students. Only the first tentative steps toward adequate bilingual education for Hispanics have so far been taken. Many of the programs implemented so far fall short of comprehensive bilingual education.[84]

Some researchers have accented the advantages of bicultural background and have put a positive face on what has been traditionally viewed in negative terms. The traditional view sees Mexican American children as culturally deprived. The new approach emphasizes that cultural background can play a crucial role in overcoming the discriminatory environment. The basic idea is *bicognitive-ness*, a facility which makes for creativity. From this perspective a child should learn to operate effectively in two cognitive worlds; the Mexican American background could be emphasized in aiding a child in the learning process.[85]

Median education levels for Mexican Americans increased between 1950 and 1980, but they still fell behind Anglo figures. In 1950 the median schooling for adults was 5.4 years; by 1976 the figure had increased to 9 years, decreasing but not closing the gap with the national median of 12 + years. A 1979 nationwide survey of adults found that two-thirds of those interviewed had not completed high school, and that one-quarter had less than an elementary school education. The lower attainment figures are partially the result of the lack of formal education for foreign-born immigrants in Mexico. But even native-born Mexican Americans have substantially less education than native-born Anglos. The reason for this seems to be the high dropout (pushout) rate. Over 40 percent of those aged 20 to 24 are not high-school graduates. Moreover, Mexican Americans have long been underrepresented in major colleges and universities in the Southwest. In spite of this negative picture, pressures for educational change persist, with Mexican American leaders calling for major improvements.[86]

One of the most vigorous educational debates in the 1970s and 1980s raged over the obligation of U.S. school systems to provide education for the children of illegal Mexican aliens. State officials in Texas and other southwestern states complained that educating these children was a burden on U.S. citizens. Publicly, state officials tended to exaggerate the number of such children in their schools for political reasons. In Texas a court case arose out of officials' attempts to charge illegal alien children a special tuition fee to attend schools. After an extended struggle in the courts, the Supreme Court ruled in 1982 that *all* children had to be provided with schooling and that children could not be discriminated against on the basis of parental condition, such as immigrant status.[86]

RELIGION

In the mid-nineteenth century the Catholic Church in the Southwest was fairly weak. With the great waves of Mexican immigrants in the 1900–1930 period came a resurgence of Catholicism. However, Mexican migrants to Texas were not accompanied by a significant number of Catholic priests; nor were the official (Roman) Catholic Church and its dogma major factors in the lives of these migrants. What has been termed "folk Catholicism," a blend of Catholicism and certain non-Catholic (native) beliefs, values, and rituals, did play an important role.[87]

Many of the new Mexican migrants were hostile to the established Church in Mexico; and most were not ready for a Catholic Church dominated by the Irish. In the first decades little was done for the religious schooling of Mexican Catholics; as late as the 1930s there were only seventy parochial schools in major dioceses of southern California, where there were several hundred thousand Catholics. Little was done by the Church to aid a Mexican population troubled by poverty and discrimination before the 1940s.[88] After World War II the Catholic archdiocese including Los Angeles became committed to building numerous schools.

In the 1950s and 1960s some Catholic priests took an active role in union activities. In the 1960s, War on Poverty programs were sometimes operated in connection with Church projects, and a number of "lay protest" and "priest protest" groups were formed to deal with urban problems. Yet in some areas priests have been forbidden to aid protesting Mexican Americans. The Los Angeles cardinal refused to provide priests for the Delano farmworkers on strike in the 1960s. Moreover, there has traditionally been a pattern of direct discrimination against Mexican Americans in the hierarchy of the Catholic Church. Very few Mexicans had penetrated the positions of responsibility prior to the 1960s; the first Mexican American bishop was designated, in San Antonio, in the 1970s.[89]

The Catholicism of most Mexican Americans has been described as similar to that of Italians, with a general allegiance to the Church and relatively little active participation except for women and children. Attendance at mass has been less than for other Catholic groups. Tuck's study of San Bernardino in the 1940s found that most Mexican Americans there were baptized, married, and buried with a Catholic priest in attendance, but most participated infrequently in weekly church activities. The power of priests, while often questioned, was found to be influential in affecting community attitudes on such issues as venereal disease campaigns and unionization. In recent years, however, this influence of the Church on secular issues has appeared to be on the wane; rejection of the Church position on matters of abortion and birth control has been extensive.[90]

ASSIMILATION OR COLONIALISM?

An assimilation perspective has been explicit or implicit in the prominent studies of researchers such as Tuck, Sanchez, Madsen, and Grebler. A pivotal idea is that Mexican Americans are moving up, or will move up, the mobility ladder just as the European white ethnics did, and thus will proceed surely, if a bit more slowly, into the mainstream at all the major assimilation levels.[91]

An assimilationist looking at Mexican American history might emphasize the point that only a hundred thousand Mexicans were brought into the United States as a result of military conquest. Most immigrants came later. Most of these immigrants were able to improve their economic circumstances relative to their condition in Mexico. Aspects of Mexican traditional culture began disappearing as the acculturation process proceeded.[92]

For the first generation of Mexican Americans, the impact of cultural assimilation came mainly in adjustment in language and agricultural values. Religion and basic values were less affected, and respect for Mexico remained strong. For the second and third generations there was increased structural assimilation in the economy and considerable cultural adaptation. Some acculturation could be seen in family values. The traditional view of the Mexican American family depicts a large extended, patriarchal family; this is perhaps most accurate as a description of family patterns in agricultural towns in earlier decades. Urbanization and increased incomes opened up the possibility of separate residences for nuclear families and a decline in the number of extended families living together. Fertility trends and values became similar to those of other Americans.[93]

Nonetheless, from the traditional life of rural villages to the faster-paced life of the urban barrios there has been substantial cultural persistence. Most notable in this regard has been language, which has persisted as a primary language or as part of a bilingual pattern. Closeness to Mexico and the constant movement across the border have been given as important reasons for the persistence of the Spanish language. Surveys in Los Angeles and San Antonio found that most Mexican Americans wished their children to retain ties to their Mexican culture, particularly to language, customs, and religion. There are strong pressures within the group for a bicultural pattern of adaptation which resists full acculturation. A recent survey of Mexican Americans found that 93 percent are bilingual and one-third have little or no fluency in English. Loyalty to Spanish language and culture is very strong. Three-quarters said that Spanish was a very important aspect of culture to maintain. Virtually all favor bilingual teaching in public schools. Mexican American parents want their children to know their cultural heritage.[94]

One should not exaggerate structural assimilation. Even for second and third generations structural assimilation at the economic level has come slowly, with persisting discrimination and resultant concentration of workers at the lower-wage occupation levels. Problematical too has been expanding participation in political institutions.

Gordon's dimensions of behavior-receptional assimilation and attitude-receptional assimilation have varied considerably within the Mexican-American group and over time. Widespread prejudice and severe discrimination faced the Mexicans who were conquered in the aggressive expansion of the United States, as well as the waves of first-generation migrants entering the United States since 1900. As time passed, some lighter-skinned Mexican Americans in larger cities were treated with much less prejudice and discrimination. Darker-skinned persons have often been treated just as black Americans have. There still remains considerable prejudice and discrimination directed against Mexican Americans. Assimilationists would underscore the decline in prejudice and discrimination, as well as the proliferation of civil rights laws, as signs that the movement is in the direction of assimilation on these dimensions.

The Limits of Assimilation

Structural absorption at the primary-group level and marital assimilation have not yet reached the point where one can speak of moderate-to-high assimilation for Mexican Americans as a group. Some increases in interethnic friendship contacts have been found in recent studies, particularly for children in desegregated situations, although most still have predominantly Mexican American friends. One study in the mid-1960s found that less than 5 percent of Mexican respondents in San Antonio had predominantly Anglo friends; the proportion in Los Angeles was about 15 percent. The current adult population still seems enmeshed in predominantly Mexican American primary relations, but the data on the children suggest that primary-level assimilation is underway, at least in some large urban areas.[95]

Intermarriage data indicate that a majority of marriages are within the Mexican American group. In San Antonio the proportion of Spanish-surname individuals marrying outside the group went from 10 percent in the 1940–1955 period to 14 percent in 1964, to 16 percent in 1973—a slow increase, but not much change in the last decade. In Los Angeles the proportion of individuals marrying outside the group increased from 9 percent in a 1924–1933 study to 25 percent in 1960–1961. In the small city of Edinburg, Texas, it went from 3 percent in 1961 to 5 percent in 1971. Studies in New Mexico have found that in recent years the proportion of Mexican Americans marrying outside the group has stabilized in the 14 to 24 percent range, depending on the county. The one exception to these relatively low outmarriage rates is a study for all California counties, which found outmarriage rates to be in the 34 to 36 percent range for the 1970s. Even in that study the outmarriage rates seemed to be stabilizing. The overall picture seems to indicate that intermarriage has increased since the 1940s but now seems to be stabilizing. And the rates vary substantially between Texas and California.[96]

Identificational assimilation has not proceeded very far. Most Mexican Americans remain clearly aware of their identity as persons of Mexican descent. And the young show a movement toward emphasizing ethnic identification. Pressures brought by outside oppression forced many, particularly in earlier decades, to try to hide their Mexican origin under the euphemism of "Spanish" or "Latin" Americans, but this is not necessarily a sign of identificational assimilation. It was the middle-income Mexican Americans who in the 1920s began to use such terms in an attempt to hide from prejudice. In recent years there has been a shift back to "Mexican" and "Mexican American." In a mid-1960s survey the preference was for "Mexican" or "Mexican American" in Los Angeles, while in San Antonio the preference of a majority was for "Latin American." Few in either city wanted to be called just "American." In a 1979 survey of households in the Southwest and Midwest, most respondents preferred to be called Mexican American, Mexican, or Chicano. Pride in Mexican identity remains strong.[97]

Some sociological analysts reject the assumption that all groups are, or must eventually be, completely assimilated to the outside society and culture. One basic idea is of substantial adaptation at the secondary-structural level (enough to secure jobs with decent incomes) but partial adaptation in terms of major aspects of the subculture (such as language, religion, and family values). Edward Múrguía has argued that the Anglo-Saxon, Protestant core society is presently allowing substantial portions of Mexican Americans to assimilate on a more-or-less equal-status basis. Yet in his view assimilation cannot go as far as it has for other Catholics, such as the Italians and the Irish. The differences are narrowing, but the processes will stop short of complete absorption. Mexican Americans might conceivably move into a situation of near-parity at the secondary-structural level, in the economy and the polity, although considerable separation would remain at the primary-group level and major cultural differences would be retained. Yet in Múrguía's view, something less than this pluralism is the probable future for Mexican Americans.[98]

Applying a Power-Conflict Perspective

Many power-conflict analysts would not agree with much in the assimilationist analysis. Rather, they would accent the extent to which Mexican Americans have *not* moved in the direction of incorporation in the core society. The best that assimilation analysts can argue is that the trend is in the assimilation direction, for substantial assimilation at the higher economic and political levels for the majority of Mexican Americans is not now a reality. Power-conflict analysts would suggest that the trend is so slow that a different theoretical framework is necessary.

Internal colonialism analysts tend to accent certain features of Mexican American history, particularly its origin in the ruthless colonial conquest of northern Mexico in the 1836–1853 period. The situation for the early Mexican, whose land and person were brought into the United States by force, can be viewed in terms of classical colonialism. Acuña has underscored the parallels between the Mexican American experience and that of the external colonization of other Third World populations: Land is taken by military force, the native population is subjugated economically and politically, the native culture is suppressed, and a small native elite is favored in order to maintain the subjugation.[99] Unlike European immigrant groups, initially "Mexicans were *annexed by conquest,* along with the territory they occupied, and, in effect, their cultural autonomy was guaranteed by a treaty"[100]—a treaty that was not honored.

One problem in applying the colonialism perspective to Mexican Americans lies in the fact that most entered as more or less voluntary immigrants in the postconquest period. Such voluntary immigration would seem to be similar to that of European immigrants. Colonialism analysts reply by indicating a number of critical differences between this migration and European migration. Unlike Europeans, Mexican migrants did not come into a new situation. People of their background were already here. Socially and culturally, they moved *within* one broad geographical area, all of which was originally controlled by their own people. Second, little effort or time was required to move back and forth across the border, to overcome the physical barrier—in sharp contrast to the much longer time of travel required of European immigrants.[101]

But perhaps the most significant difference was the heritage of the (external) colonial situation, with its practices of subordination, inherent in the situation of the immigrants. "The colonial pattern of Anglo domination over the Mexican people was set by 1848 and carried over to those Mexicans who came later to the Southwest, a land contiguous to Mexico and once a part of it."[102] One can even speak of subordination by force in the form of deportation, Border Patrol activities and searches, and so forth at the hands of Anglos.

Later Mexican immigrants were channeled into situations in which low wages, absentee landlords and business people, inferior schools, and across-the-board discrimination severely limited their job potential. For many decades residential segregation has reflected discrimination and exploitation. Mexican Americans are not like European immigrant groups whose level of segregation has declined significantly with length of residence in the United States. Intentional discrimination in employment and housing persists, even if it is less blatant and more subtle today.

Mario Barrera has argued that Anglo workers certainly benefit from the subordination of Mexican Americans, since they have less job competition and higher wages as a result. But Barrera also notes that historically Anglo workers "have been reacting to the racially segmented labor system created by employers precisely to undercut the wage standards, organizing efforts, and unity of workers as a whole."[103] That is, capitalist employers have created a split labor market system from which they as employers have profitted greatly; and they have focused the attention of Anglo workers on Hispanics and blacks as the threat to Anglo workers and away from capitalists themselves. Given the segmentation of the labor force by Anglo employers, it is not surprising that Anglo workers work to solidify their positions and to keep minority workers out of the privileged job categories reserved for Anglo workers. Employers benefit from having working people, Anglos and Hispanics, divided against one another. Barrera views this situation as a type of internal colonialism.

Flores, moreover, has underscored the cultural and psychodynamic aspects of the Mexican American situation. In his view the Mexican American group has been treated as much more subordinate than white immigrant groups. Psychological as well as economic benefits have accrued to the Anglo oppressors. The acculturation of Mexican American children and adults has often involved intense pressure and coercion, such as in the public schools. Racial stereotyping of Mexicans has played a major role in establishing and preserving the racial hierarchy of the Southwest. Theories of biological inferiority were introduced to justify the taking of land and the exploitation of Mexican American labor. This racial subordination provides benefits for most Anglos. It

> is a complex cultural system of racial and cultural domination which *produces* privileges above and beyond the surplus value generated solely by capitalism—privileges from which all members of the dominant social groups (despite their class) derive benefit directly or indirectly.[104]

Consequently, power-conflict analysts see the real hope for less oppression and for an improved economic, political, and cultural situation in decolonization movements, the Mexican American protest movements of the past and present.

A Still-Growing Community

A distinctive aspect of Mexican American communities today is the infusion of undocumented workers. Particularly for Chicanos in the Southwest, this provides constant renewal of ties to Mexico and a constant reinforcement of Mexican culture, including the Spanish language and Catholicism. These immigrants provide much cheap labor for the Southwest's Anglo-dominated corporations, farms, and ranches. And their presence has become the center of controversy over U.S. immigration laws and policies. This continuing influx of immigrants creates serious problems for the assimilation perspective on Mexican Americans, because the close ties to the traditional culture—the closest for any immigrant group in U.S. history—significantly slow the cultural assimilation process. For Mexican Americans the closeness to Mexico provides counter pressures to the pressures for Anglo-conformity acculturation in the United States.

A power-conflict analyst might suggest that the flow of undocumented workers shows the heavy impact of U.S. capitalism on Mexican migration. U.S. corporations have played a major role in developing large agribusiness (corporate) farms in Mexico, farms which gobble up the land of Mexico's small farmers and tenant farmers and which are highly mechanized. Mexican farmers and farm workers are no longer needed in the countryside so they migrate, looking for work, to Mexico's overcrowded cities or to the United States. Poverty in Mexico is thus in part the result of profit-seeking agribusiness corporations seeking to grow crops in Mexico for export to the United States. Moreover, many corporations and small businesses on the U.S. side of the border eagerly seek the cheap, non-unionized labor from Mexico. On both sides of the border, Mexican migration has been heavily shaped by the needs of U.S. corporate capitalists.

SUMMARY

Mexican Americans have an ancient ancestry, predominantly Native American, but with a Spanish infusion. Their cultural background is part Native American, but it is heavily shaped by a Spanish infusion which affected language, religion, and customs. With the British American conquest, Mexicans became part of the complex mosaic of race and ethnic peoples in the United States. They have suffered racial stereotyping similar to that of other groups of non-European ancestry. Racially motivated discrimination in economics, education, and politics was part of their lot, from the beginning to the present.

In the race and ethnic relations literature, it has been common to compare the situations of black Americans and Mexican Americans, groups considered the largest subordinated minorities in the United States. Both groups face a situation of declining prejudice but continuing discrimination and inequality. The apparent decline in white traditional prejudice against blacks has probably paralleled a decline in negative attitudes toward Mexican Americans. But substantial and similar discrimination continues to confront both groups in the last third of the twentieth century, although lighter-skinned, middle-income Mexican Americans sometimes face less discrimination than middle-income blacks.

At the attitudinal level, blacks and Mexican Americans are often sympathetic to one another's problems. One study of Mexican American attitudes in Texas found more positive feelings toward blacks than were found among Anglos, more sensitivity to discriminatory barriers, and more support for civil rights protest. Differences between blacks and browns appeared in the area of protest strategies. The researcher found that blacks were significantly more militant than Mexican Americans on selected issues, being more dissatisfied with civil rights progress and more approving of civil rights demonstrations.[105] This type of difference has made it difficult for the two groups to work in a coalition against the dominant groups. In some situations the two groups even find themselves competing for limited benefits granted by established groups. In recent years several attempts to build black-brown coalitions have been tried, as yet with only partial success. The future will probably see more attempts to build stronger Hispanic-black coalitions for reform.

NOTES

[1]Edward H. Spicer, *Cycles of Conquest* (Tucson: University of Arizona Press, 1962), pp. 4–7; Carey McWilliams, *North From Mexico* (New York: Greenwood Press, 1968), pp. 32–34; Tomás Almaquer, "Historical Notes on Chicano Oppression: The Dialectics of Racial and Class Domination in North America," *Atzlán* 5 (Spring-Fall 1974): 30–33.

[2]Spicer, *Cycle of Conquest*, pp. 4–5; McWilliams, *North From Mexico*, pp. 21–31.

[3]Américo Paredes, *With His Pistol in His Hand* (Austin: University of Texas Press, 1958), pp. 3–14; Rodolfo Acuña, *Occupied American* (San Francisco: Canfield Press, 1972), pp. 10–12.

[4]Acuña, *Occupied America*, p. 15; S. Dale McLemore, "The Origins of Mexican American Subordination in Texas," *Social Science Quarterly* 53 (March 1973): 665–67; Rodolfo Alvarez, "The Psycho-historical and Socioeconomic Development of the Chicano Community in the United States," *Social Science Quarterly* 53 (March 1973): 925.

[5]William Lord, "Myths and Realities of the Alamo," *The American West* 5 (May 1968): 20–25. I draw here on the summary of the article in Acuña, *Occupied America*, pp. 16–17.

[6]Carl N. Degler, *Out of Our Past* (New York: Harper & Row, 1959), pp. 109–10; Acuña, *Occupied America*, pp. 23–29.

[7]Leo Grebler, Joan W. Moore, and Ralph G. Guzmán, *The Mexican-American People* (New York: Free Press, 1970), pp. 43–44; Acuña, *Occupied America*, p. 105; Joan W. Moore, "Colonialism: The Case of the Mexican Americans," *Social Problems* 17 (Spring 1970): 468–69.

[8]Ellwyn R. Stoddard, *Mexican Americans* (New York: Random House, 1973), pp. 9–13; McWilliams, *North From Mexico*, pp. 70–76; Acuña, *Occupied America*, pp. 60–62; Grebler et al., *The Mexican-American People*, pp. 43–44; Nancie L. Gonzales, *The Spanish-Americans of New Mexico* (Albuquerque: University of New Mexico Press, 1967), pp. 204 ff.

[9]Alvarez, "The Psycho-historical and Socioeconomic Development of the Chicano Community in the United States," p. 925.

[10]Oscar J. Martinez, "On the Size of the Chicano Population: New Estimates: 1850–1900," *Aztlán* 6 (Spring 1975): 55–56; U.S. Immigration and Naturalization Service, *1975 Annual Report* (Washington, D.C.: U.S. Government Printing Office, 1975), pp. 62–64; Julian Samora, *Los Mojados: The Wetback Story* (South Bend, Ind.: University of Notre Dame Press, 1971), pp. 7–8.

[11]Leo Grebler, *Mexican Immigration to the United States: The Record and Its Implications* (Los Angeles: UCLA Mexican-American Study Project, 1965), pp. 20–21; Samora, *Los Mojadas*, p. 38.

[12]Grebler, *Mexican Immigration to the United States*, pp. 23–24; Manuel Gamio, *Mexican Immigration to the United States* (New York: Dover Publications, 1971) pp. 171–74; Gilberto Cardenas, "United States Immigration Policy Toward Mexico: An Historical Perspective," *Chicano Law Review* 2 (Summer 1975): 69–71.

[13]Samora, *Los Mojados*, pp. 48–52.

¹⁴Cardenas, "United States Immigration Policy Toward Mexico," pp. 73–75; Grebler, *Mexican Immigration to the United States*, p. 26.

¹⁵Samora, *Los Mojados*, pp. 18–19, 24–25, 44–46, 57; Joan Moore, *Mexican Americans*, 2d ed. (Englewood Cliffs, N.J.: Prentice-Hall, 1976), pp. 49–51.

¹⁶Samora, *Los Mojados*, pp. 80–92; Moore, *Mexican Americans*, pp. 49–51.

¹⁷Cardenas, "United States Immigration Policy Toward Mexico," 84–85; Cheryl Anderson, "Immigration Bill under Attack on Several Fronts," Austin *American-Statesman*, December 12, 1982, p. Cl.

¹⁸Wayne A. Cornelius, "Mexican Migration to the United States," in *Crisis in American Institutions*, ed. J. Skolnick and E. Currie (Boston: Little, Brown, 1982), pp. 154–68; Frank Bean, Allen King, and Jeffrey Passel, "The Number of Illegal Migrants of Mexican Origin in the United States," *Demography* forthcoming, February, 1983.

¹⁹This draws on critical notes from Gilberto Cardenas.

²⁰Moore, *Mexican Americans*, pp. 3–6; McWilliams, *North From Mexico*, pp. 115–32.

²¹Philip D. Ortego, "The Chicano Renaissance," in *Introduction to Chicano Studies*, ed. Livie I. Duran and H. Russell Bernard (New York: Macmillan, 1973), p. 337.

²²Cardenas, "United States Immigration Policy Toward Mexico," pp. 70–71.

²³Quoted in Ralph Guzmán, "The Function of Anglo-American Racism in the Political Development of Chicanos," in *La Causa Politica*, ed. F. Chris Garcia (South Bend, Ind.: University of Notre Dame Press, 1974), p. 22.

²⁴Ibid., pp. 25–27; Grebler et al., *The Mexican-American People*, pp. 529–30.

²⁵McWilliams, *North From Mexico*, p. 213.

²⁶William Sheldon, "Educational Research and Statistics: The Intelligence of Mexican-American Children," in *In Their Place*, ed. Lewis H. Carlson and George A. Colburn (New York: John Wiley, 1972), pp. 149–51.

²⁷Ozzie G. Simmons, "The Mutual Images and Expectations of Anglo-Americans and Mexican-Americans," in Duran and Bernard, *Introduction to Chicano Studies*, pp. 387–97; Robin M. Williams, *Strangers Next Door* (Englewood Cliffs, N.J.: Prentice-Hall, 1974), pp. 29–80.

²⁸Stoddard, *Mexican Americans*, p. 6.

²⁹Livie I. Duran and H. Russell Bernard, "Introduction to Part 2," in *Introduction to Chicano Studies*, p. 237.

³⁰Ibid.; Tomás Martinez, "Advertising and Racism: The Case of the Mexican American," *El Grito* 2 (Summer 1969): 3–13; *Daily Texan*, November 5, 1976.

³¹Cited in Guillermo V. Flores, "Race and Culture in the Internal Colony: Keeping the Chicano in His Place," in *Structures of Dependency*, ed. Frank Bonilla and Robert Girling (manuscript, Stanford, California Research Seminar, 1973).

³²Quoted in Armondo Morales, *Ando Sangrando* (Fair Lawn, N.J.: R. E. Burdick, 1972), p. 43.

³³Stoddard, *Mexican Americans*, p. 49.

³⁴See Octavio Ignacio Romano, "The Anthropology and Sociology of the Mexican-Americans," *El Grito* 2 (Fall 1968): 13–19; Oscar Lewis, *Five Families* (New York: John Wiley, 1962); William Madsen, *Mexican-Americans of South Texas* (New York: Holt, Rinehart, and Winston, 1964).

³⁵See Romano, "The Anthropology and Sociology of the Mexican-Americans"; Stoddard, *Mexican Americans*, pp. 42–44.

³⁶E. J. Hobsbawm, *Primitive Rebels* (New York: W. W. Norton and Co., 1959), pp. 15–16.

³⁷Acuña, *Occupied America*, pp. 48–50; McWilliams, *North From Mexico*, pp. 110–12.

³⁸Paredes, *With His Pistol in His Hand*, pp. 27–32; McWilliams, *North From Mexico*, p. 127; Moore, "Colonialism: The Case of the Mexican Americans," 466; Stoddard, *Mexican Americans*, p. 181.

³⁹Ralph H. Turner and Lewis M. Killian, *Collective Behavior* (Englewood Cliffs, N.J.: Prentice-Hall, 1957), pp. 125–28; McWilliams, *North From Mexico*, pp. 229–38.

⁴⁰Morales, *Ando Sangrando*, pp. 100–108.

[41]U.S. Commission on Civil Rights, *Mexican Americans and the Administration of Justice in the Southwest* (Washington, D.C.: U.S. Government Printing Office, 1970), pp. 6–10.

[42]Clark Knowlton, "Recommendations for the Solution of Land Tenure Problems Among the Spanish Americans," in *Chicano: The Evolution of a People*, ed. Renato Rosaldo, Robert A. Calvert, and Gustav L. Seligmann (San Franciso: Rinehart Press, 1973), pp. 334–35; George I. Sanchez, *Forgotten People* (Albuquerque: University of New Mexico Press, 1940), p. 61; Arnoldo Deleón, *The Tejano Community, 1836–1900* (Albuquerque: University of New Mexico Press, 1982), pp. 63–91.

[43]Almaguer, "Historical Notes on Chicano Oppression," pp. 38–39; Richard del Castillo, "Myth and Reality: Chicano Economic Mobility in Los Angeles, 1850–1880," *Atzlán* 6 (Summer 1975): 153–54; McWilliams, *North From Mexico*, pp. 127–28.

[44]Moore, "Colonialism: The Case of the Mexican Americans," pp. 468–69; McWilliams, *North From Mexico*, pp. 178–79.

[45]Gamio, *Mexican Immigration to the United States*, pp. 39–40; Charles Wollenberg, "Huelga, 1928 Style: The Imperial Valley Cantaloupe Workers' Strike," in Rosaldo, Calvert, and Seligmann, *Chicano: The Evolution of a People*, pp. 185–88.

[46]Samora, *Los Mojados*, p. 130; Grebler et al., *The Mexican-American People*, p. 91.

[47]McWilliams, *North From Mexico*, pp. 193, 220; Grebler et al., *The Mexican-American People*, p. 526.

[48]Ruth H. Tuck, *Not With the Fist* (New York: Harcourt, Brace, and World, 1946), pp. 173–83.

[49]McWilliams, *North From Mexico*, pp. 217–18; U.S. Commission on Civil Rights, *Mexican American Education Study*, report 1, *Ethnic Isolation of Mexican Americans in the Public Schools of the Southwest* (Washington, D.C.: U.S. Government Printing Office, 1970), p. 11.

[50]Anne Brunton, "The Chicano Migrants," in Duran and Bernard, *Introduction to Chicano Studies*, pp. 489–92.

[51]Jesus Luna, "Luna's Abe Lincoln Story," in Rosaldo, Calvert, and Seligmann, *Chicano: The Evolution of a People*, p. 348.

[52]Robert R. Nathan Associates, *Industrial and Employment Potential of the United States–Mexico Border* (Washington, D.C.: U.S. Department of Commerce, Economic Development Administration, 1968), pp. 50–51, 125–29.

[53]*Report of the Select Commission on Western Hemisphere Immigration* (Washington, D.C.: U.S. Government Printing Office, 1968), p. 116.

[54]*Report of the Select Commission on Western Hemisphere Immigration*, p. 120; the *Los Angeles Times* story is quoted in Mario Barrera, *Race and Class in the Southwest* (Notre Dame, Ind.: University of Notre Dame Press, 1979), p. 124.

[55]U.S. Department of Health, Education, and Welfare, *A Study of Selected Socio-economic Characteristics of Ethnic Minorities Based on the 1970 Census*, p. 63; U.S. Bureau of the Census, *U.S. Census of Population, 1960: Subject Reports—Persons of Spanish Surname*, PC (2)–1B, p. 38; U.S. Bureau of the Census, "Persons of Spanish Origin in the U.S.: March 1979," in *Current Population Reports*, series P–20, no. 354, pp. 1–10.

[56]Dale McLemore and Harley L. Browning, *A Statistical Profile of the Spanish-Surname Population of Texas* (Austin: University of Texas, Bureau of Business Research, 1964); F. Peñalosa and E. C. McDonagh, "Social Mobility in a Mexican-American Community," *Social Forces* 44 (June 1966): 498–505.

[57]Moore, *Mexican Americans*, p. 34; U.S. Department of Health, Education, and Welfare, *A Study of Selected Socio-economic Characteristics of Ethnic Minorities Based on the 1970 Census*, p. 79; National Commission for Employment Policy, *Hispanics and Jobs: Barriers to Progress* (Washington, D.C.: National Commission for Employment Policy, 1982), pp. 30–54.

[58]Moore, *Mexican Americans*, p. 33.

[59]Ibid., p. 142.

[60]Ibid., p. 156; U.S. Commission on Civil Rights, *Mexican American Education Study, Ethnic Isolation of Mexican Americans in the Public Schools of the Southwest*, (Washington, D.C.: U.S. Government Printing Office, 1971) p. 55; Grebler et al., *The Mexican-American People*, pp.

562–63; Frank Lemus, "National Roster of Spanish Surnamed Elected Officials, 1973," *Aztlán* 5 (Spring-Fall 1974): 313–410.

[61]Moore, *Mexican Americans*, p. 140; Mark R. Levy and Michael S. Kramer, *The Ethnic Factor* (New York: Simon and Schuster, 1972), pp. 77–85.

[62]Moore, *Mexican Americans*, pp. 148–58.

[63]U.S. Commission on Civil Rights, *Mexican Americans and the Administration of Justice in the Southwest*, pp. 79–86.

[64]Ibid., pp. 66–69.

[65]Michael V. Miller and James D. Preston, "Vertical Ties and the Redistribution of Power in Crystal City," *Social Science Quarterly* 53 (March 1973): 772–82; John S. Shockley, *Chicano Revolt in a Texas Town* (South Bend, Ind.: University of Notre Dame Press, 1974), pp. 28–148.

[66]Shockley, *Chicano Revolt in a Texas Town*, pp. 162–77.

[67]Ibid., pp. 169–73; *El Cuhamil*, October 22, 1976. (*El Cuhamil* is a south Texas paper put out by Chicano farmworkers.)

[68]Armando Gutiérrez and Herbert Hirsch, "The Militant Challenge to the American Ethos: 'Chicanos' and the 'Mexican Americans,' " *Social Science Quarterly* 53 (March 1973): 844–45.

[69]McWilliams, *North From Mexico*, pp. 191–93; Grebler et al., *The Mexican-American People*, pp. 91–92.

[70]Stoddard, *Mexican Americans*, p. 180; Gamio, *Mexican Immigration to the United States*, pp. 135–38.

[71]Grebler et al., *The Mexican-American People*, pp. 543–45; Stoddard, *Mexican Americans*, p. 188; Moore, *Mexican Americans*, p. 152.

[72]U.S. Commission on Civil Rights, *Mexican Americans and the Administration of Justice in the Southwest*, pp. 15–17; Rees Lloyd and Peter Montague, "Ford and La Raza: 'They Stole Our Land and Gave Us Powdered Milk,' " in *Introduction to Chicano Studies*, pp. 376–78; Frances L. Swadesh, "The Alianza Movement: Catalyst for Social Change in New Mexico," in Rosaldo, Calvert, and Seligmann, *Chicano: The Evolution of a People*, pp. 270–74.

[73]Jacques E. Levy, *Cesar Chavez* (New York: W. W. Norton and Co., 1975), pp. 182–201; Peter Matthiessen, *Sal Si Puedes* (New York: Delta Books, 1969), pp. 59–216; John G. Dunne, *Delano* (New York: Farrar, Straus, and Giroux, 1967), pp. 110–67.

[74]Shockley, *Chicano Revolt in a Texas Town*, pp. 216–17.

[75]Levy, *Cesar Chavez*, pp. 495, 522–35.

[76]Thomas P. Carter, *Mexican Americans in School* (New York: College Entrance Examination Board, 1970), pp. 204–5.

[77]Ibid., pp. 67–68; George I. Sánchez, "History, Culture, and Education," in *La Raza*, ed. Julian Samora (South Bend, Ind.: University of Notre Dame Press, 1966), pp. 1–26; Sanchez, *Forgotten People*, pp. 31 ff; Paul Taylor, *An American-Mexican Frontier* (Chapel Hill: University of North Carolina Press, 1934), pp. 196–204.

[78]U.S. Commission on Civil Rights, *Mexican American Education Study*, vol. 3, *The Excluded Student* (Washington, D.C.: U.S. Government Printing Office, 1972), pp. 18–20; Carter, *Mexican Americans in School*, pp. 10–11.

[79]Wilson Little, *Spanish-Speaking Children in Texas* (Austin, University of Texas Press, 1944); Tuck, *Not With the Fist*, pp. 185–87; Carter, *Mexican Americans in Schools*, p. 71; U.S. Commission on Civil Rights, *Ethnic Isolation of Mexican Americans in the Public Schools of the Southwest*, pp. 21–25, 41–51.

[80]Carter, *Mexican Americans in Schools*, pp. 97–102.

[81]Jane Mercer, *Labelling the Mentally Retarded* (Berkeley: University of California Press, 1973), pp. 96–189.

[82]U.S. Commission on Civil Rights, *Mexican American Education Study*, vol. 6, *Toward Quality Education for Mexican Americans* (Washington, D.C.: U.S. Government Printing Office, 1974), pp. 21–22.

[83]Ibid., pp. 1, 33–34; Thomas P. Carter, "The Negative Self-concept of Mexican-American Students," *School and Society* 96 (March 30, 1968): 217–20.

[84]Manuel Ramirez and Alfredo Castaneda, *Cultural Democracy, Bicognitive Development, and Education* (New York: Academic Press, 1974); U.S. Commission on Civil Rights, *Toward Quality Education for Mexican Americans*, pp. 6–8.

[85]National Commission for Employment Policy, *Hispanics and Jobs*, pp. 60–62, 81–82.

[86]Moore, *Mexican Americans*, pp. 67–69; U.S. Department of Health, Education, and Welfare, *Americans of Spanish Origin*, p. 47; Carter, *Mexican Americans in Schools*, pp. 30–31; National Commission for Employment Policy, *Hispanics and Jobs*, p. 11.

[87]Spicer, *Cycles of Conquest*, pp. 285–365; Patrick H. McNamara, "Bishops, Priests, and Prophecy: A Study in the Sociology of Religious Protest" (Ph.D. dissertation, UCLA, 1968).

[88]Moore, *Mexican Americans*, pp. 88–89.

[89]Ibid., p. 91; Stoddard, *Mexican Americans*, p. 93; Grebler et al., *The Mexican-American People*, pp. 459–60.

[90]Grebler et al., *The Mexican-American People*, pp. 436–39, 473–77; Tuck, *Not With the Fist*, pp. 152–54; cf. also Jane M. Christian and Chester C. Christian, "Spanish Language and Loyalty in the Southwest," in *Language Loyalty in the United States*, ed. Joshua A. Fishman (London: Mouton and Co., 1966), pp. 296–97.

[91]Tuck, *Not With the Fist*; Sánchez, *Forgotten People*; Madsen, *The Mexican-Americans of South Texas*; Grebler et al., *The Mexican-American People*.

[92]Edward Murguía, *Assimilation, Colonialism, and the Mexican American People* (Austin: University of Texas Press, 1975), pp. 4–5.

[93]Rodolfo Alvarez, "The Unique Psycho-historical Experience of the Mexican-American People," *Social Science Quarterly* 52 (June 1971): 15–29; Stoddard, *Mexican Americans*, p. 103; Benjamin S. Bradshaw and Frank Bean, "Trends in the Fertility of Mexican Americans, 1950–1970," *Social Science Quarterly* 53 (March 1973): 696–97.

[94]Grebler et al., *The Mexican-American People*, pp. 384, 430; "Maintaining a Group Culture," *Institute for Survey Research Newsletter*, pp. 7–8.

[95]Grebler et al., *The Mexican-American People*, pp. 396–97.

[96]Edward Múrguía, *Chicano Intermarriage: A Theoretical and Empirical Study* (San Antonio, Texas: Trinity University Press, 1982), pp. 45–51; U.S. Department of Health, Education, and Welfare, *Americans of Spanish Origin*, p. 46.

[97]Grebler et al., *The Mexican-American People*, pp. 385, 558; "Maintaining a Group Culture," *Institute for Survey Research Newsletter*, p. 8.

[98]Múrguía, *Assimilation, Colonialism, and the Mexican American People*, p. 112.

[99]Acuña, *Occupied America*, p. 3.

[100]McWilliams, *North From Mexico*, p. 207.

[101]Alvarez, "The Psycho-historical and Socioeconomic Development of the Chicano Community in the United States," pp. 928–30.

[102]Múrguía, *Assimilation, Colonialism, and the Mexican American People*, pp. 8–9.

[103]Barrera, *Race and Class in the Southwest*, p. 213.

[104]Flores, "Race and Culture in the Internal Colony," p. 194.

[105]Chandler Davidson and Charles M. Gaitz, "Ethnic Attitudes as a Basis for Minority Cooperation in a Southwestern Metropolis," *Social Science Quarterly* 53 (March 1973): 747–48.

CHAPTER 10

Piri Thomas, an acclaimed Puerto Rican author, tells this story about his early life:

> I remember my own mother's answer one day when I asked her. "Why can't we have a nice house like this?"—showing her a picture in a magazine. I can remember her now, laughing as she replied, "Of course; we can have it in heaven someday." And I could feel the anger inside me saying, "I want it now."[1]

One of the nation's poorest groups, Puerto Ricans have long suffered at the bottom of the U.S. economic and political pyramids. Many have raised Thomas's question, "Why can't we have a nice house like this?" And other questions have been raised as well: "Why can't we have decent paying jobs? A decent standard of living?"

Puerto Ricans make up an important part of the U.S. population, even though many other Americans are unaware of their presence. Puerto Ricans as a group have strong links to the Caribbean and the rest of the Third World.

PUERTO RICO AS A COLONY

From Spanish to U.S. Rule

Borinquén, the original native name for the island of Puerto Rico, had a population of 50,000 in 1493 when Spanish imperialism reached the island. At first, Spain used the native peoples there as forced labor in mines and fields. Forced labor, disease, and violent suppression of rebellions led to a sharp decline in the local population, so black slaves were imported to fill the gap. By 1530 imported black slaves were the majority of the population. Plantation agriculture replaced the earlier craze for gold, and slaves worked the fields. By the end of the nineteenth century there was a large multiracial, multiethnic population on the island.[2]

In 1897 Puerto Ricans successfully pressured the Spanish government into granting them some autonomy, including the right to elect their own house of representatives. In July 1898 U.S. troops landed in Puerto Rico as part of the war with Spain. In the subsequent peace treaty (1899) Spain gave the island to the United States government, which saw it as a useful refueling station for warships and a profitable agricultural enclave. Puerto Rico moved from one empire, the Spanish, to another, that of the United States, without democratic participation by the local inhabitants in the decision.[3]

A U.S. governor was appointed by the U.S. president. Acts of the local legislature were subject to veto by the U.S. Congress; and English became the mandatory language in schools. In 1917 the Jones Act awarded U.S. citizenship to all Puerto Ricans. Islanders were split over ties to the United States, with the majority party (the Unionist Party) favoring greater autonomy. The request of Unionist leaders to let the people of Puerto Rico vote on whether they wanted to become U.S. citizens was denied.[4]

In 1948 Puerto Ricans were permitted, for the first time, to elect their own governor; and in 1952 the Commonwealth of Puerto Rico, with its own constitution (approved by the U.S. Congress), was created. Considerable home rule was granted, and Puerto Ricans were allowed to elect their officials, make their own civil and criminal codes, and run their own schools. In 1948 Spanish finally became the official language in the schools, and the Puerto Rican flag was allowed to fly. However, this was only *permitted* by the U.S., as the colonial power overseeing Puerto Rican "autonomy."

Puerto Ricans were incorporated into the U.S. empire by force. Unlike most European immigrants they were not given a choice; they were transferred from one colonial empire to another. The supervising officials from the United States often saw their mission as one of converting the black and mestizo populations of Puerto Rico and the rest of Latin America to "our way of life."

Operation Bootstrap

Signs of U.S. colonialism and paternalism can be seen in the way the island's economy has been developed by external decision-makers. When the U.S. took over Puerto Rico, much of the land was owned by peasants and smaller farmers who raised coffee, sugar, tobacco, and foodstuffs. In 1899 Puerto Ricans themselves owned 93 percent of the farms, but by 1930 this was changing dramatically. A few large absentee-owned companies soon controlled 60 percent of sugar production; absentee-owned companies monopolized tobacco production and the shipping lines. The independent farmers growing coffee were driven out by the U.S.-forced devaluation of the Puerto Rican peso and the closing of European markets that came with U.S. occupation. Laws were established by military rulers. Many peasants were forced to seek jobs with the absentee-owned companies, mainly the sugar companies. Puerto Ricans thus became cheap labor for international corporations, and in the slack seasons thousands of the unemployed endured terrible poverty.[5]

Until the 1930s Puerto Rico was an agricultural colony based on the monoculture (growing of one crop) of sugar plantations; it was ruled strictly under various U.S. decrees which determined life on the island, from currency exchange to the amount of land a person could own. When the New Deal reforms came to Puerto Rico, a more progressive U.S.-imposed governor, Rexford Tugwell, envisioned a program of economic development for the island which would include both agricultural and industrial development. But after World War II, agricultural development was forgotten, as a program called Operation Bootstrap, designed to attract U.S. industrial corporations to the island, was implemented.

More conservative social scientists, such as Nathan Glazer and Daniel P. Moynihan, have seen Operation Bootstrap as a great help to Puerto Rico because it opened up "access to American investment capital."[6] Actually it was American capital that did the opening up. U.S.-dominated agribusiness took much land which could have been used for growing food locally, forcing this richly endowed island to import food. Operation Bootstrap lured multinational corporations to Puerto Rico through a system of tax breaks and other subsidy concessions. Government programs provided the necessary electricity, land, and roads for multinational enterprises. Urban industry was emphasized; agriculture was neglected, tilting the island farther away from its heritage of independent locally owned farms and pressing the rural population to migrate to urban industrial areas. The absence of taxes and the presence of cheap labor led to the development of many industries in Puerto Rico, particularly labor-intensive industries. Later, capital-intensive industries such as petrochemical and pharmaceutical plants began to migrate there. "Modernization" has brought with it massive unemployment problems. Capital investments grew from $1.4 billion in 1960 to $24 billion in 1979. Yet at the same time the official unemployment rate grew from 13 percent to 19 percent. Swift industrialization helped create large numbers of unemployed workers, even with massive migration to the mainland. By 1970, fully 80 percent of the industry on the island was owned by U.S. corporations.[7]

Recently, numerous industries have left the island, some looking for cheaper labor and new tax exemptions elsewhere. This has created new problems of even greater unemployment. One Puerto Rican immigrant said at a U.S. Commission on Civil Rights hearing that he came to the United States because the company he worked for had used up its fifteen-year exemption from taxes, and its executives had decided to move rather than pay the taxes.[8] The 1974–1975 recession brought cutbacks in the petrochemical plants, sharply increasing unemployment rates and the cost of federal payments for unemployment compensation, welfare, and food stamps. Since 1974–1975 the island has been in a more or less permanent recession, with a negative economic growth rate and very high unemployment. Operation Bootstrap has clearly failed to provide permanent industrial employment for the island.

MIGRATION TO THE UNITED STATES

This economic situation in Puerto Rico is clearly linked to the ebb and flow of migrants to the U.S. mainland. Unlike European immigrants, Puerto Ricans are one major migrant group which has migrated from one part of the U.S. empire, the island Commonwealth of Puerto Rico, to another part of that empire, the mainland.

Migration Streams

Puerto Ricans migrated to the mainland before 1900, but the number of migrants was relatively small until World War II. In 1940 there were only 70,000 Puerto Ricans on the mainland. For later periods the net number of migrants to the mainland has been as follows: 1946–1955, 406,000; 1956–1965, 179,000; 1966–1971, 121,000. At first most Puerto Ricans who went to the mainland went to New York; later they went to the other cities on the eastern seaboard; and in the 1960s they went to the Midwest and West, taking advantage of easy air travel between such places as Chicago and the island.[9]

Many a mainland tourist who has seen the island of Puerto Rico has said, "Why would anyone want to leave such a beautiful island?" A Puerto Rican author, Piri Thomas, puts the answer succinctly: "Bread, money, gold, a peso to make a living . . . Diggit, wasn't that the greatest reason all the other different ethnic groups came to America for, freedom from want?"[10] Indeed, it was the Operation Bootstrap industrialization period of the 1950s that created great pressures for migration to the mainland. One in five Puerto Ricans left. Thousands of unemployed farmworkers, forced out of work by changes in agriculture, migrated to the mainland. The Puerto Rican government even encouraged migration as a "safety valve" reducing the pressures of unemployment on the island. Pull factors were important. With the U.S. economy booming in the 1950s, corporations sent recruiters to Puerto Rico seeking cheap labor, such as workers who would work in the New York textile sweatshops. And in the late 1970s and 1980s a few technical and computer companies sent recruiters to the island seeking skilled workers such as engineers and computer programmers.[11]

In addition, temporary farm labor migration is part of the Puerto Rican back-and-forth migration; several thousand farm workers have come each year to do low-wage work for U.S. farmers. This migration is seen by federal and state government officials and U.S. farmers as providing much-needed cheap labor.

Although there was an increase in the number of factory jobs in Puerto Rico by the 1960s, the outmigration continued, at half the rate of the previous decade. But in the 1970s and 1980s the opportunity structure in the United States deteriorated; a series of recessions created a situation in which more Puerto Ricans left the United States each year than entered. Ironically, in the last decade many Puerto Rican workers who could not find work on the island because of declining industrialization there have migrated to central areas of U.S. cities, which have also been plagued with industries and high unemployment.[12]

Population Distribution

In 1900 there were fewer than 2,000 Puerto Ricans on the mainland, and the numbers grew slowly until World War II. At the beginning of the war about 70,000 Puerto Ricans resided here, but in the next two decades the number increased more than tenfold to 887,000. By 1980 the number of people of Puerto Rican descent had doubled again to nearly 2 million. Between the 1940s and the 1980s the Puerto Rican population has gradually fanned out to many cities across the nation. In 1940 most Puerto Ricans lived in the Manhattan borough of New York City, but by 1980 there were large communities in New Jersey cities as well as to the west in Chicago, Cleveland, and Los Angeles. Today Puerto Ricans make up one-sixth of all Hispanic Americans and are one of the fastest-growing segments of that group.[13]

STEREOTYPING PUERTO RICANS

Puerto Ricans have been stereotyped in ways similar to those imposed on Mexican Americans and black Americans. The first Anglo-American stereotypes were developed by U.S. military officials and colonial administrators. In the 1890s, for example, several U.S. officials wrote a number of reports on the Puerto Ricans under their control. One captain noted that "the people seem willing to work, even at starvation wages, and they seem to be docile and grateful for anything done for them. They are emotional. . . ." A lieutenant commented that the "natives are lazy and dirty, but are very sharp and cunning."[14]

Images of lazy, submissive Puerto Ricans still persist, particularly among officials and professionals who deal with Puerto Rican clients. Anglo teachers for example, have held images of Puerto Ricans as lazy, lethargic, and immoral. Lopez reports on being at a college meeting in New York where an experienced teacher from a ghetto school spoke on instilling the "middle-class values" of thrift, morality, and motivation in the children. Lopez asked the teacher about her stereotyped image of poor Puerto Rican children:

> It was when I asked what morality was and where it was practiced among middle-class people or what motivation was lacking in our people and how she had discovered this, or finally, how the hell a person could be thrifty on eighty-four dollars a week, that she began to do some thinking.[15]

Often referred to with the derogatory term *spics*, Puerto Ricans have been viewed, as were the Italians and Chicanos before them, as a particularly criminal and violent lot. For example, a 1980 Aspen Institute conference report noted that the English-language news media emphasize selected aspects of Puerto Rican and Chicano life, that the media emphasize the problems of poverty, gang violence, and illegal immigrants. Crimes by Puerto Ricans have been sensationalized in the New York City newspapers and other mass media, helping to foster the image of Puerto Ricans as criminals. Indeed, J. Edgar Hoover, former director of the FBI, promulgated this violence stereotype:

> We cooperate with the Secret Service on presidential trips abroad. You *never* have to bother about a President being shot by Puerto Ricans or Mexicans. They don't shoot very straight. But if they come at you with a knife, beware.[16]

Hoover's stereotype of Hispanic peoples as dumb-but-sinister knife-carriers is still circulating in the United States. Such a stereotype is applied to Hispanics whether they live inside or outside the boundaries of the mainland United States.

In the 1950s, when large numbers of migrants began coming to the United States, the Puerto Rican government occasionally circulated pamphlets in rural areas trying to prepare migrants for race prejudice on the mainland. One pamphlet read as follows:

> If one Puerto Rican steals, Americans who are prejudiced say that all Puerto Ricans are thieves. If one Puerto Rican doesn't work, prejudiced Americans say all of us are lazy . . . we pay, because a bad opinion of us is formed, and the result may be that they discredit us, they won't give us work, or they deny us our rights.[17]

Clearly this pamphlet recognizes the ways in which Anglo-Americans unfairly generalize from one Puerto Rican's actions to those of the entire group, and it also implies that these negative stereotypes are translated by Anglos into discriminatory actions against Puerto Ricans looking for jobs.

Stereotypic images of Puerto Rico and Puerto Ricans have been circulated by social scientists as well. For example, Nathan Glazer and Daniel Moynihan argued in 1963 that Puerto Rican society was "sadly defective" in its culture and family system. Folk arts and culture were said to be weak and defective. Families were said to be weak and disorganized. Glazer and Moynihan suggested that this alleged weak family structure was the reason why on the mainland Puerto Ricans did not move up into better-paying jobs as had other immigrants.[18]

Self-image and Racism

As with other non-European groups, today this stereotyping continues to have a severe negative impact. It is reflected in Anglo discrimination, and it is also reflected in the negative self-images that Puerto Ricans have

of themselves. Some Puerto Ricans, particularly those who do well in
U.S. society, reportedly develop a feeling of shame about being Puerto
Rican. The constant diet of negative images sometimes pressures them to
describe themselves as "Latin American" or as "white." They thus try to put
distance between themselves and their brethren. Until the brown-pride
movements began in the 1960s, some Puerto Ricans tried to cover up their
identity.[19]

Americans of white European descent tend to lump Puerto Ricans
together with black Americans or with Chicanos. They are thus seen as a
nonwhite group, as "black" or "brown." Physical distinctiveness is emphasized even more than cultural distinctiveness. The obvious racial discrimination and segregation on the U.S. mainland come as a shock to many
immigrants. Color discrimination is less blatant on the island than in the
U.S., though it does indeed exist there too. Until they come to the mainland,
most Puerto Ricans have seldom had to deal with overt and extensive color-
based discrimination.

ECONOMIC CONDITIONS: THE MAINLAND

From the first decades of this century to the present, Puerto Rican immigrants have faced unemployment, underemployment, and poverty. One
early migrant was Jesús Colon, who wrote a book on his experiences. Puerto
Ricans did the dirty work of the society, and poverty was their lot. Jesús
and his brother worked different hours, and to save money they even
shared their working clothes. Jesús notes that "we only had one pair of
working pants between the two of us."[20]

From the beginning discrimination faced the new immigrants, with
the darker-skinned immigrants usually suffering the most. Piri Thomas,
author of *Down These Mean Streets,* grew up in Spanish Harlem (El Barrio)
and eventually became well known. He recounts an interview in 1945 for
a job as a door-to-door salesperson. He went for the interview but did not
get a job, while his lighter-skinned friend who went along did get a job.
Dark-skinned Puerto Ricans, he discovered by asking other dark-skinned
applicants, were discriminated against by the white employer; they were
treated like blacks.[21]

Occupation and Unemployment

The sharp increase in migration after 1950 did not change conditions. Mainland Puerto Ricans still did the "dirty work" for other
Americans. They worked to clean up New York City as busboys and
janitors; they worked as cheap labor in sweat shops that paid low wages.
And many have faced unemployment. The occupational distribution for
employed Puerto Ricans in the continental United States has been as
follows:[22]

	MEN			WOMEN		
	1950	1970	1979	1950	1970	1979
Professional, technical	5.3%	4.7%	8.2%	3.4%	7.2%	10.4%
Managers, administrators	5.4	4.2	4.6	1.2	1.6	4.2
Clerical and sales	9.6	14.9	12.2	11.0	34.1	42.0
Skilled blue-collar (crafts)	11.2	15.7	14.4	1.7	2.4	2.2
Operatives	33.0	33.5	28.1	72.5	39.7	23.4
Service workers	25.1	17.5	⎰ 19.5	6.5	12.5	⎰ 16.1
Domestic work	0.2	0.1	⎱	2.3	1.0	⎱
Nonfarm laborers	7.3	8.0	10.1	1.0	1.1	0.8
Farmers, farmworkers	2.9	1.5	3.0	0.4	0.4	0.9

In 1950, 1970, and 1979 we find male workers concentrated in blue-collar jobs, especially in lower-paying jobs as laborers, service workers (e.g., bus-boys), and assembly-line workers ("operatives"). A major shift can be seen in the movement of Puerto Rican women into the clerical (and sales) fields by the late 1970s, particularly as lower-level typists, retail sales clerks, and keypunch operators. In many East Coast areas Puerto Rican laborers have done much of the low-paid field work that has put vegetables on American tables. For example, in the late 1970s in Vineland, New Jersey, 15,000 Puerto Rican farmworkers were working for low wages, often seven days a week and in inhumane, barracks-type housing. Nearby farmworkers were fired for attempting to organize to improve their working conditions.[23]

Many Puerto Ricans are "operatives," a category which involves factory workers and seamstresses. The proportion of Puerto Rican men and women in these jobs has declined significantly since 1950, in part because employment in these areas has declined generally in the northern states. Puerto Ricans were particularly hard-hit in the late 1960s and 1970s by decline in New York City's clothing industry, a decline which increased unemployment for apparel workers. Many men have moved into work as dishwashers, orderlies, janitors, health care aides, and recreational facility attendants. Women have moved into service jobs and into jobs as file clerks, typists, cashiers, and teacher aides. Many such jobs are relatively low-paid. Puerto Ricans in professional and other white-collar jobs tend to be at the lower-paid levels, which include such workers as teachers, librarians, and health, personnel, and recreational professionals. Many in the professional-technical category are less-well-paid technicians. Those who are managers tend to be in smaller companies. Few are doctors, lawyers, dentists, or engineers.[24]

For Puerto Ricans on the mainland unemployment has been high:[25]

	MALES			FEMALES		
	1960	1976	1979	1960	1976	1979
Puerto Ricans	8.8%	16.3%	14.3%	11.1%	22.3%	11.9%
Anglo whites	4.7	5.9	5.6	4.7	8.7	6.4

In 1976 over 16 percent of Puerto Rican men and 22 percent of women were unemployed, figures up sharply from 1970. In 1979 the figures were down a bit from their 1976 high, but the 14.3 percent and 11.9 percent figures were still far higher than those of whites. Moreover, by 1982 Puerto Rican unemployment had sharply increased again, probably approaching 20 percent. The recessions of the 1970s and 1980s have created a severe and permanent problem of large-scale unemployment.

Employment Discrimination and Other Barriers

Puerto Ricans face discrimination. Institutionalized discrimination can be seen in the restriction of Puerto Rican access to certain job categories. In New York City, for example, Puerto Ricans are very underrepresented (relative to their population percentage) in local and state government jobs. This is at least in part because of their being less well integrated into traditional job information networks dominated by white New Yorkers. In many cases, Puerto Ricans are screened out of jobs because screening tests are, unnecessarily, given only in English. This even occurs in situations where Puerto Rican applicants are quite capable of doing the jobs, but the screening tests are not job-related. Even trash collection jobs have sometimes required screening tests on which those who speak English and have a high school diploma score better—tests that have no relation to the actual jobs performed. As with Mexican Americans, many Puerto Ricans find themselves unfairly stigmatized as of "low intelligence" just because their command of English is not very good. Numerous studies have found language discrimination directed at Hispanic Americans.[26]

Oddly enough, Puerto Ricans have suffered discrimination because they, unlike some other immigrants, are U.S. citizens. As a Puerto Rican woman in California said in a 1978 Civil Rights Commission interview,

> I've had about six or seven jobs since I came here. What happens is that they hire you temporarily and get rid of you as soon as possible because you don't belong to the right race. I'd even say that bosses here prefer Mexicans [particularly illegals] because they know that unions don't represent them, so they can be exploited easier. At least Puerto Ricans have citizenship and can get into unions.[27]

Even government agencies in California have classified Puerto Ricans as Chicanos rather than as Puerto Ricans. Moreover, some Puerto Ricans have been asked by local government officials to prove that they are U.S. citizens—that is, to prove that Puerto Rico is part of the United States.

Institutionalized discrimination can be seen in height and weight requirements that have disqualified some Puerto Rican applicants for police and fire department jobs; that is, they do not fit the height and weight standards set up on the basis of white Anglo males. Moreover, several studies have found that, with only a few exceptions, the skilled blue-collar trades remain virtually all white. Less-skilled jobs, such as those of concrete laborers and mason tenders, have been carefully controlled so that only token numbers of blacks and Puerto Ricans have been hired; union, private, and governmental authorities have collaborated in these practices. Herbert Hill has detailed the persisting discrimination against Puerto Ricans and blacks in numerous unions, particularly in New York.[28]

Relatively poorer and confined by their incomes and by real estate discrimination to central city housing, many Puerto Rican workers find transportation to outlying jobs in suburban areas a difficult problem. Apart from service sector jobs, many types of jobs have increased more rapidly in outlying areas than in central areas, at the same time that many public transit systems have been deteriorating in quality and service. Chicago, for example, has little public transit beyond the city limits. And using public transportation at off hours, as many Puerto Ricans who are offered night-shift work would like to do, is difficult because of limited schedules.[29]

A new problem for Puerto Rican workers on the mainland has been corporate flight. Seeking a "better business climate," many U.S. companies have left such cities as New York for Sunbelt or Third World cities where wages are cheaper, unions are weak, and governments are more willing to assist corporate profit goals. Yet other U.S. corporations have moved to the suburbs. Non-European migrants today have a much more difficult time than earlier white European migrants did because the employment opportunity structure has changed. Today decent-paying jobs are not as plentiful or accessible; many jobs have been moved far away from the larger Puerto Rican communities in central cities.

Income and Poverty

Puerto Ricans are the poorest of American minorities except for Native Americans. Relative to the national average, Puerto Rican family incomes worsened between 1959 and 1974, declining from 71 percent of the national average to only 59 percent. The 1980 census data indicate that for the first time in 21 years Puerto Rican income has risen a little relative to whites; it is now half the national average, but it is still much lower than it was in 1959. In 1980, median family income for Puerto Ricans was only $9,900, less than half the Anglo median family income.[30]

Poverty and near-poverty are the lot of most families. With about four in ten Puerto Ricans falling below the federal poverty line, it is not surprising that many accounts graphically describe oppressive conditions.

Felipe Luciano thus describes his life as a Puerto Rican:

> You resign yourself to poverty—my mother did this. Your face is rubbed in shit so much that you begin to accept that shit as reality . . . my stomach rumbling. My mother beating me when I knew it was because of my father . . . the welfare investigator cursing out my mother because what she wants is spring clothing for her children. . . .[31]

Discrimination against Puerto Ricans is conspicuous in the area of housing. A Rutgers professor of law testified at a Civil Rights Commission hearing that Puerto Ricans have suffered even more from housing discrimination than blacks. Blacks are "steered" by real estate agents to certain housing areas. But Puerto Ricans generally have been excluded from all decent housing markets. Puerto Ricans get the "housing scraps" no one else wants. Overcrowding and deteriorating housing—these are primary characteristics of many ghetto areas.[32]

Housing displacement and blatant housing discrimination have been serious problems for Puerto Ricans. Recently the Puerto Rican Legal Defense and Educational Fund has won a major court victory over housing discrimination in four new housing developments in Brooklyn, where racial quotas limited the number of nonwhite residents. In *Williamsburg Fair Housing Committee v. New York City Housing Authority*, the court found that discrimination against Puerto Ricans did exist, and legal remedies were provided that eliminated racial quotas. Moreover, in 1977–1978 a large number of poor families, the majority of whom were Puerto Ricans, were forced to move out of a residential area in the city of Lyons, New York, as part of a downtown renewal project. A protest committee was formed which demonstrated publicly and filed a civil rights suit. Controversy developed when a fire broke out in the empty buildings, and a Puerto Rican leader was sentenced to six to eighteen years for allegedly having set the fire. There was much controversy over whether he was guilty, with local residents arguing that he was framed in an effort to destroy the Puerto Rican group's leadership.[33]

EDUCATION

In the mid-1970s, average educational attainment for Puerto Ricans was only 8.7 years, well below the national average. Most Puerto Rican children aged seven to thirteen are in school, but in the over-fourteen age group fewer Puerto Rican than Anglo young people are still in school. One Chicago study found that 71 percent of Puerto Rican children leave before they finish high school. Among Puerto Ricans only 6 percent of males and 4 percent of females have completed college, compared to a third of Anglo males. Still, the number in college has increased in recent years; for example, the percentage of Puerto Ricans in the City University of New York increased from 4 percent in 1969 to 7.4 percent in 1974.[34]

Barriers to Mobility

The high drop-out rate, or rather the *push-out* rate, for Puerto Rican children is the result of a number of factors, including the need to work to support families and a variety of discriminatory barriers present in U.S. school systems. Most such barriers are faced by other Hispanics as well. One such barrier is the relative absence of Puerto Rican role models in the schools. Few teachers are Puerto Rican or Hispanic. One study found a sharp disparity in many urban school systems between the percentage of Hispanic teachers and the percentage of Hispanic students. While 27 percent of the students in New York City were Hispanic, only 2 percent of the teachers were. In Hartford the corresponding figures were 22 percent and 4 percent. In Chicago, the figures were 11 percent and 1 percent. This disparity is found in numerous cities.[35]

The representation of Puerto Ricans among administrators is similarly small. Only a few Puerto Ricans have moved into influential positions in higher education. A few Puerto Ricans have served on local and state boards of education in New York; in 1977–1978 the school system in New York City had two Puerto Rican district superintendents and forty-five Puerto Rican principals.[36]

Another school barrier is the excessive tracking of Puerto Rican children. Puerto Rican students are often assigned to low-ability groups, to mentally retarded classes, or to lower grades. A number of New York and New Jersey studies have found racially identifiable tracking systems and placement of children in classes for the mentally retarded without sufficient justification. In New York City these classes were disproportionately made up of Hispanic children. As a recent civil rights commission report put it, "the rationale for such practices is that students will benefit from special instruction in low-level classes, but the correlation between such placement and improved academic performance is dubious. In fact, the lower level of curriculum and the absence of stimulation from higher-achieving students may be negative factors that further retard the student."[37] Such a stigma can permanently handicap students throughout the rest of their lives.

Curriculum and Language

Another barrier is the school curriculum itself. The school curriculum often seems irrelevant to many Hispanic children. The Anglo curriculum authorities frequently are insensitive to Hispanic history and cultures. This neglect of Puerto Rican culture and history by the schools contributes to a lack of self-esteem.[38]

The language barrier is a related problem. U.S. schools are generally not structured to deal with students who do not speak English. The fault is in the schools, not in the children; in Europe many schools are, in contrast, more hospitable to language diversity among students. Puerto Rican students, on the average, do not do as well on achievement tests as Anglo students. One important reason for this is that most tests are given in English. In Philadelphia one psychologist commented on the inaccuracy of English-language test scores:

> In my clinic, the average underestimation of IQ for a Puerto Rican kid is 20 points. We go through this again and again. When we test in Spanish, there is a 20 point leap immediately—20 higher than when he's tested in English.[39]

Moreover, many of the new Spanish-language achievement and "IQ" tests are translations of English-language tests into Spanish, a practice which simply passes along whatever cultural bias exists in the tests. Often the translations make use of Spanish colloquialisms more familiar to Mexican American than to Puerto Rican students.

Many Puerto Rican educators argue that children should be taught to read and write well in Spanish first, should first be taught subjects in that language, and then be taught English as a second language. Civil rights groups have been active in pressing for bilingual education programs for Hispanic children. Cultural pluralism is a goal. Herman La Fontaine, a Puerto Rican educator, phrased it this way: "Our definition of cultural pluralism must include the concept that our language and our culture will be given equal status to that of the majority population."[40]

In the 1980s bilingual programs were heavily cut by the Reagan Administration. Conservative officials viewed them as luxuries which could be dispensed with. Funds were cut by 10 percent in fiscal year 1982, with a projected 50 percent cut to come in the next year. A leader of Philadelphia's Puerto Rican Alliance argued that this showed a "blatant disregard of a right the courts have already recognized." Even greater cutbacks may come at the state government level, where most bilingual programs are funded. In such states as New Jersey and Massachusetts attempts have been made to cut back or eliminate existing bilingual education laws. In New York City major cutbacks in bilingual programs have been implemented.[41]

POLITICS

Formal participation of Puerto Ricans in the American political system is much less than their participation in the Puerto Rican political system. In Puerto Rico the voting participation rate, among those registered, runs to 60 percent or more, especially in rural municipalities. In the metropolitan areas of the island, voter participation is often high. In the United States, voting rates are as low as 20 and 30 percent in some urban areas. Since the early 1940s Puerto Ricans have participated in Democratic Party politics in such states as New York and New Jersey, but that participation has usually been token. So far in New York, Puerto Ricans have been able to dominate only one congressional seat, that originally held by Herman Badillo.[42] In 1965 Badillo became the first Puerto Rican to be elected president of a New York City borough (the Bronx); six years later he became the first voting representative in the U.S. House of Puerto Rican background. In the 1970s, however, Badillo lost the race to become mayor of New York. In 1982 there was still only one Puerto Rican holding a regular voting position in Congress, Robert Garcia, who held the House seat previously occupied by Badillo.

In 1937 the first Puerto Rican was elected to the New York state assembly; but it would be fifteen more years before another was elected to same legislative body. In 1977 New York had two state senators, four members of the state assembly, and two members of the New York city council who were Puerto Ricans. Today Puerto Ricans are also significantly underrepresented in appointed political positions, relative to their population size.[43] A U.S. Commission on Civil Rights report recently concluded that this persisting underrepresentation in elected and appointive offices reflects ongoing political discrimination against Puerto Ricans.

The effects of discrimination can be seen in New York state and city government employment, in which Puerto Ricans are significantly underrepresented.[44] As a result, Puerto Ricans frequently feel they are not part of the political system. In 1978 a Civil Rights Commission study interviewed 120 members of the Puerto Rican community in California. These Puerto Ricans felt that they were treated as "nonpersons" by government and private agencies. Government officials serving or surveying minorities are usually not Puerto Rican and seldom speak much Spanish. Government services have historically been less accessible to Puerto Ricans. Job corps, job training, and employment services have been slow in coming to Puerto Rican communities and have often been very inadequate in relation to the employment and other problems they attempt to solve.[45]

PROTEST

In Puerto Rico

In Puerto Rico the period of U.S. rule has been punctuated with vigorous protests. In the early 1930s there was a mass attack by Puerto Ricans on the colonial capital buildings, and in 1934 there were massive strikes in the sugar cane fields. The Nationalist Party, led by the Puerto Rican hero, Harvard-educated Pedro Albizu Campos, began pushing vigorously for expanded freedom and for independence. In March 1937 there was a massacre of Nationalist Party marchers who had joined a legal march in Ponce. The U.S. governor belatedly tried to stop the march. Bringing in 200 heavily armed police, the governor set the stage for violence. A shot was fired, probably by the police, and a pitched battled ensued, with 20 dead and 100 injured, mostly marchers and bystanders. The U.S. Civil Liberties Union labeled this "a massacre" that should be investigated. The Ponce Massacre became a symbol of the Puerto Rican nationalist movement.[46]

Political protests continued in the 1940s and 1950s. U.S. officials reportedly came to the island to plan the imprisonment of Nationalist Party leaders. In the fall of 1950 police raided Nationalist Party meetings and houses. This precipitated an armed revolt which spread to five cities. Hundreds of people were killed. Two thousand people were arrested for actively advocating or pressing for independence. Puerto Rican nationalists also attacked the residence of President Harry Truman and attacked the U.S. House while it was in session. From the beginning numerous Puerto Ricans have vigorously protested the colonization of their island.

Currently, the future of Puerto Rico is a major political issue on the island and on the mainland. The 1980 platforms of both the Republican and the Democratic parties supported statehood for Puerto Rico. Pro-statehood sentiment is very strong on the island; "statehood for the poor" is the slogan of this movement. But there are substantial pressures against statehood as well. On the island there is still a significant pro-independence movement, representing perhaps 10 percent of the voters. Some in this movement continue to use violence against U.S. officials and military personnel in an attempt to drive, as they see it, the colonialists from the island.[47]

Organizational Protest on the Mainland

Within the mainland Puerto Rican community there have always been service organizations which deal with community problems. In education there is ASPIRA, which tries to provide educational opportunities for youths. There are the Puerto Rican Legal Project, the Puerto Rican Legal Defense Fund, the League of Puerto Rican Women, the Puerto Rican Teachers Association, the Puerto Rican Forum, and the Puerto Rican Family Institute. The Puerto Rican Teachers Association has worked to increase the representation of Puerto Ricans among teachers and principals and to expand bilingual programs. The Forum is an older social, political, and business organization. The Puerto Rican Family Institute provides services to families with health and legal programs and provides aid to recent migrants from the island.[48]

Militant protest against mainland conditions is not new among Puerto Ricans. Puerto Ricans have been active in labor and union organizations in the United States since the late 1800s. In the 1960s and early 1970s Puerto Rican protest and political activity increased; there were riots in some Puerto Rican ghettos. Since then, there has been a growth in Puerto Rican pride; "Puerto Rican is beautiful" has become a commonplace theme.

Chicago was the birthplace of the Young Lords, which began as a street gang and evolved into a militant protest group. In the spring of 1969 the Young Lords, patterned after the Black Panthers, occupied the administration building of McCormick Theological Seminary to publicize the poverty in Chicago. They also took over a Methodist church, opening a day care center and school for the community. They broke up a meeting in order to protest the use of urban renewal land for a tennis club, and they set up a "people's park" on other urban renewal land.[49] A New York group formed the Young Lords Party. In December 1969 these Young Lords occupied the First Spanish Methodist Church in New York City for eleven days and organized a day care center, a breakfast program, and a clothing distribution program. They created a newspaper, *Palante (Forward)* and led a demonstration of two hundred Puerto Ricans protesting squalid conditions at a local hospital.[50] The Young Lords developed their own protest style. Children of poor immigrants, they articulated a thirteen-point program for a democratic socialist society. They called for "liberation and power in the hands of the people, not Puerto Rican exploiters." This U.S. protest group envisaged a multi-ethnic, democratic-socialistic society in the United States. At the peak of their influence, the Young Lords had chapters in twenty cities.[51]

Police repression came down hard on the most militant black and Puerto Rican groups. They were infiltrated; leaders were tried, sometimes in frame-up trials. Other leaders were co-opted into government anti-poverty programs. Internal divisions helped splinter the group as well. Nonetheless, there are still militant protest groups that are active in Puerto Rican communities. There are the Puerto Rican Socialist Party, which supports independence for the island of Puerto Rico, and the Puerto Rican Solidarity

Committee, with chapters in numerous cities on the mainland and in Puerto Rico. This latter group is a U.S. support group for independence which aims to build broader support among non-Puerto Ricans.[52]

Community Protests

Recently there have been community protests against discrimination. In Cleveland, Orlando Morales, a young prisoner serving two life sentences, has been viewed by community groups as innocent. Recently three hundred angry Puerto Ricans met in a protest meeting at Cleveland's Spanish American Committee Hall. Much evidence indicated that Morales did not commit the murder for which he was convicted. Many in the Puerto Rican community felt the twenty-two-year-old Puerto Rican had been railroaded for a crime he did not commit and actively protested what they saw as discrimination in the criminal justice system.[53]

Some protests have brought changes. Pressures from Puerto Rican activists led to the founding of a community college in the South Bronx and helped create an open admissions program at the City University of New York. City and state governments provided more funds for community projects. More Puerto Ricans were hired into city governments. More Puerto Rican studies and bilingual programs were added to the schools, and more Puerto Rican teachers were hired.[54]

New coalitions of grass-roots organizations and older established groups are being created in the 1980s. For example, a new organization, the National Congress for Puerto Rican Rights, was created in 1981. Through such mechanisms traditional and militant leaders have been trying to bridge the gap that has long separated them, building a coalition to work to improve the conditions of Puerto Ricans. A constant source of tension between the federal government and Puerto Ricans is Puerto Rican support for radical independence organizations. A number of grand jury investigations of the independence-for-Puerto-Rico movement have been conducted in the United States and Puerto Rico. Puerto Ricans have been jailed for refusing to talk before authorities. As a result, there have been community protests over these grand jury investigations.

RELIGION

Most Puerto Ricans are Catholic, but in the United States they have generally been led by clergypersons from backgrounds other than Puerto Rican. The supportive social framework that parishes gave to previous Catholic groups (such as Irish immigrants) has largely been missing. One exception to this dependence on non-Puerto Rican clergy is the Bishop of Puerto Rico, Artulio Parilla, who regularly visits Puerto Rican parishes on the mainland; this progressive bishop is a backer of Puerto Rican independence as well.

One scholar, Joseph Fitzpatrick, argues that Puerto Rican religion is more a religion of the community than of the church and parish. Community celebrations and processions are important, as is reverence for the Virgin Mary and the saints. As is the case for Italian Americans, formal worship is less important than communal celebrations and home ceremonies. On the mainland Puerto Ricans have shared parishes with blacks and other Latin American groups. Hispanic caucuses have developed within the Catholic Church to press for better Hispanic services and for more priests of Hispanic background. As Fitzpatrick said, "The principal demand of the Puerto Ricans and other Hispanics is for a policy of cultural pluralism in the church that will provide for the continuation of their language and culture in their spiritual life and the appointment of Puerto Ricans and other Hispanics to positions of responsibility."[55] In recent years Puerto Ricans have pressed for the regular celebration of their holy days by the U.S. church, particularly Three Kings Day (January 6).

ASSIMILATION OR COLONIALISM?

Assimilation Reconsidered

In his influential book on Puerto Ricans, Joseph P. Fitzpatrick relies on an assimilation model to interpret Puerto Rican experiences. Although in his 1964 work Gordon, the assimilation theorist, had found little or no assimilation of Puerto Ricans into the core culture and society, Fitzpatrick in this later work reports a significant degree of assimilation. Fitzpatrick notes substantial cultural assimilation, particularly for many mainland-born Puerto Ricans who identify with U.S. society and who have adopted English as a second language. This cultural adaptation creates family problems when Spanish-speaking parents must depend on English-speaking children in order to get along in mainland society. In her book *Up from Puerto Rico*, Elena Padilla notes that second-generation Puerto Ricans often have a different reference group, the mainland society rather than island society, and hide their Spanish language facility in an attempt to assimilate.[56]

The pressure to assimilate culturally has been intense, as Maldonado-Denis notes: "Regardless of what Glazer and Moynihan argue in *Beyond the Melting Pot,* the American ethic is a messianic one, and all ethnic groups are required to assimilate culturally as a condition for achieving a share in the material and spiritual goods of American society."[57] For Puerto Ricans these cultural assimilation pressures actually begin in Puerto Rico, where for several decades the U.S. colonial government pressured Puerto Ricans on the island to assimilate culturally, pressure which could be seen in the forced requirement of English as the teaching language in the schools.

Fitzpatrick also notes significant Puerto Rican resistance to Anglo-confirmity cultural assimilation. The Puerto Rican quest for identity, he notes, "is taking the form of a strong assertion of the significance of Puerto Rican culture, including language, and also the definition of Puerto Rican interests around militant types of political and community action."[58] Among Puerto Rican groups themselves the following issues are debated. Some groups argue that Puerto Ricans in the U.S. must assimilate and become

Americans in order to find better jobs and have or achieve a higher position in this society; some argue that this can be done with a minimal of soul selling—that is, with a strong persistence of Puerto Rican culture. Others worry about the heavy cost of assimilation in terms of the identities of Puerto Ricans; they worry that assimilation pressures, as with other race and ethnic groups, lead to a malignant rootlessness.

While there does seem to be some decline in blatant prejudice and discrimination against Puerto Ricans, subtle prejudice and discrimination continues in the areas of housing and employment. For the most part, the level of assimilation in this regard is relatively low. Moreover, secondary-structural assimilation at the level of higher-paying jobs has been slow, with a disproportionate concentration of Puerto Ricans in "dirty work" jobs of the society, as well as among the unemployed. Problematical too has been the low level of participation of Puerto Ricans in mainland political institutions, where they remain seriously underrepresented.

Structural assimilation of Puerto Ricans at the primary-group level and marital assimilation have not yet reached levels comparable to those of earlier European immigrants. However, outmarriage seems to be growing for the second generation. Just over half of the U.S.-born Puerto Ricans who are married have a Puerto Rican spouse, compared to over 80 percent of the island-born migrants who are married. Numerous outmarriages, however, are to other Hispanics and to black Americans rather than to Anglos.[59]

Generational conflict has been a problem for Puerto Rican families. Children grow up in U.S. culture and pick up new values which often conflict with traditional values. The traditional chaperoning of girls has given way before less restricted mainland dating patterns. And the street life of boys in large ghettos is more difficult to supervise. Moreover, identificational assimilation has come slowly for Puerto Ricans. Most, whether island-born or mainland-born, still see themselves as Puerto Rican. For all, there is the island nearby. Among the many immigrant groups coming to the United States, Puerto Ricans are among the few who have never completely severed ties with the homeland. Yet identity problems have been serious for many in the second generation. This native-born generation finds itself in a second-class citizenship on the mainland; but it is too acculturated to be comfortable in Puerto Rico. Indeed, the term "Neo-rican" has been coined to describe Puerto Ricans who are products of both the United States mainland and Puerto Rico, who are torn between two cultures.[60]

Power-Conflict Views

Power-conflict analysts would agree that there has been heavy Anglicization pressure on Puerto Ricans, but they would stress just how distinctive and colonized Puerto Rican Americans remain. Assimilation into the economic and political mainstream has moved excruciatingly slowly, which suggests that non-European migrants such as Puerto Ricans are not, contrary to the views of some assimilation analysts, like the European immigrants in earlier periods of U.S. history. Puerto Ricans live, for the most part, in segregated ghetto areas. And there seems to be a co-opted Puerto Rican elite which, like colonial elites in the Third World, has, at least in part, a parasitic or social control function.[61]

Internal colonialsm can also be seen in the "urban enterprise zone" proposals of the Ronald Reagan administration. These proposals significantly reduce taxes and regulations on corporations which decide to open plants in poverty and ghetto areas in U.S. cities. This plan recognizes nonwhite ghettos as distinctive territorial areas for special economic exploitation. The laws will even be different for these nonwhite areas, thus legally condoning exploitation of workers who will move from their unemployed status to that of low-wage workers. Bonilla and Campos have compared this "puertoricanization" of central city ghettos with the economic colonialism of Operation Bootstrap in Puerto Rico. Under Operation Bootstrap, Puerto Rico's poverty and low wages became its main asset as far as multinational corporations were concerned. In the early 1980s President Ronald Reagan's advisers explicitly used Puerto Rico as an example of the reindustrialization they have in mind for mainland "urban enterprise zones." In Puerto Rico corporations were encouraged by various incentives to come in and profit from exploiting cheap labor. The "puertoricanization" of central city ghettos makes them corporate havens of profitability similar to the island of Puerto Rico. Colonial solutions are thereby introduced into U.S. cities, showing again the close linkages between the external economic colonialism of an island such as Puerto Rico and the economic colonialism imposed on nonwhite minorities in the United States.

Bonilla and Campos note that various schemes, new and old, to exploit Puerto Rican and black workers in central cities show the logic of capitalistic expansion, which leads "not only to the introduction of the peoples and problems of colonialism into the metropolis, but also to the transfer there of colonial 'solutions' [such as urban enterprise zones] and practices."[62] Colonialism, thus, is a two-way street.

SUMMARY AND CONCLUSION

Puerto Ricans are a distinctive American group, with an ancient and diverse heritage. As with Mexican Americans they represent a fusion of Native American, Spanish, and African heritages. Puerto Ricans are a divided nation, with one foot on the mainland and one foot in Puerto Rico. The existence of an island population in a more or less external-colony situation just off the mainland complicates the picture. In recent years there has been a debate among Puerto Ricans as to whether Puerto Ricans are one nation with one set of problems with a few variations or rather are two nations with very different sets of problems.

The issue of class also comes into this debate. The Caribbean island is a self-contained society with a variety of classes, including both a local capitalist class and a local working class, as well as a small elite of U.S.-based capitalists. Some argue that island problems are different in terms of class from those on the mainland. On the mainland, Puerto Ricans tend to be primarily poor working-class people; there are few Puerto Rican capitalists on the mainland. Others play down the class divisions and accent the argument that there is only *one* Puerto Rican nation. As one Puerto Rican social scientist put it recently, "No matter how we see ourselves internally the Yanqui always sees us and deals with us as one class and one people with the same problems. Therefore we should band together and not divide ourselves to fight for our nation against the colonizer."[63]

NOTES

[1] Piri Thomas, "Introduction: 'Me, My People, Our Island,' " in "Puerto Ricans in the Promised Land," *Civil Rights Digest* 6 (no. 2, n.d.): 7.

[2] Manuel Maldonado-Denis, *Puerto Rico: A Socio-historic Interpretation,* trans. Elena Vialo (New York: Random House Vintage Books, 1972), pp. 13–19.

[3] U.S. Commission on Civil Rights, *Puerto Ricans in the Continental United States: An Uncertain Future* (Washington, D.C.: U.S. Government Printing Office, 1976), pp. 11–12.

[4] Ibid., p. 12.

[5] Maldonado-Denis, *Puerto Rico,* pp. 305–306.

[6] Nathan Glazer and Daniel P. Moynihan, *Beyond the Melting Pot: The Negroes, Puerto Ricans, Jews, Italians, and Irish of New York City* (Cambridge, Mass.: MIT and Harvard Presses, 1963), p. 95.

[7] Maldonado-Denis, *Puerto Rico,* pp. 311–12; Frank Bonilla and Ricardo Campos, "A Wealth of Poor: Puerto Ricans in the New Economic Order," *Daedalus* 110 (Spring 1981): 135.

[8] Piri Thomas, "Puerto Ricans in the Promised Land," p. 19.

[9] Adalberto Lopez, "The Puerto Rican Diaspora: A Survey," in *Puerto Rico and Puerto Ricans: Studies in History and Society,* ed. Adalberto Lopez and James Petras (New York: John Wiley, 1974), p. 318.

[10] Thomas, "Puerto Ricans in the Promised Land," p. 20.

[11] U.S. Commission on Civil Rights, *Puerto Ricans in the Continental United States,* p. 25.

[12] Ibid.

[13] Ibid., pp. 19–21; Juan Gonzalez, "Puerto Ricans on the Mainland," *Perspectives* 13 (Winter 1982), p. 10.

[14] Quoted in Frank Bonilla, "Beyond Survival: Porque Sequiremos Siendo Puertoriquenos," in Lopez, *Puerto Rico and Puerto Ricans,* p. 439.

[15] Alfredo Lopez, *The Puerto Rican Papers* (Indianapolis: Bobbs-Merrill, 1973), p. 120.

[16] Ibid., p. 211; Charles Ericksen, "From Bylines to Bottomlines," *Perspectives* 13 (Winter 1982): wl.

[17] From a "What is Prejudice?" pamphlet by the Puerto Rican government, reprinted in *The Puerto Ricans: A Documentary History,* ed. Kal Wagenheim (Garden City, N.Y.: Anchor Books, 1973), p. 291.

[18] Glazer and Moynihan, *Beyond the Melting Pot,* pp. 88–90.

[19] Lopez, "The Puerto Rican Diaspora," pp. 328–29.

[20] Jesús Colon, "The Early Days," in Wagenheim, *The Puerto Ricans: A Documentary History,* p. 286.

[21] Piri Thomas, *Down These Mean Streets* (New York: Knopf, 1967), as quoted in Wagenheim, *Puerto Ricans: A Documentary History,* pp. 314–20.

[22] U.S. Commission on Civil Rights, *Puerto Ricans in the Continental United States,* p. 54; Bonilla and Campos, "A Wealth of Poor," p. 158; Bureau of Census, *Persons of Spanish Origin in the United States: March 1979* (Washington, D.C.: Government Printing Office, 1980), p. 29.

[23]Gonzalez, "Puerto Ricans on the Mainland," p. 16.

[24]U.S. Commission on Civil Rights, *Puerto Ricans in the Continental United States*, p. 52; Bonilla and Campos, "A Wealth of Poor," p. 160.

[25]U.S. Commission on Civil Rights, *Social Indicators of Equality for Minorities and Women* (Washington, D.C.: U.S. Government Printing Office, 1978), p. 30; Bureau of the Census, *Persons of Spanish Origin in the United States: March 1979*, p. 25.

[26]U.S. Commission on Civil Rights, *Puerto Ricans in the Continental United States*, pp. 59–62.

[27]Western Regional Office, U.S. Commission on Civil Rights, *Puerto Ricans in California* (Washington, D.C.: U.S. Government Printing Office, 1980), p. 17.

[28]Herbert Hill, "Guardians of the Sweatshops: The Trade Unions, Racism, and the Garment Industry," in Lopez, *Puerto Rico and Puerto Ricans*, pp. 386–88.

[29]U.S. Commission on Civil Rights, *Puerto Ricans in the Continental United States*, p. 60.

[30]Gonzalez, "Puerto Ricans on the Mainland," p. 10.

[31]Felipe Luciano, "America Should Never Have Taught Us to Read, She Should Never Have Given Us Eyes to See," in Lopez, *Puerto Rico and Puerto Ricans*, pp. 430–31.

[32]Testimony by Jose A. Rivera, printed in "Fair Housing and the Spanish Speaking," *Civil Rights Digest* 8 (Fall 1975): 35–36.

[33]Gonzalez, "Puerto Ricans on the Mainland," pp. 15–17.

[34]Bonilla and Campos, "A Wealth of Poor," p. 163; Joseph P. Fitzpatrick, "Puerto Ricans," in *Harvard Encyclopedia of American Ethnic Groups*, ed. S. Theonstrom (Cambridge, Mass.: Harvard University Press, 1980), p. 863.

[35]U.S. Commission on Civil Rights, *Puerto Ricans in the Continental United States*, p. 104.

[36]Fitzpatrick, "Puerto Ricans," p. 863.

[37]U.S. Commission on Civil Rights, *Puerto Ricans in the Continental United States*, p. 100.

[38]Lopez, *The Puerto Rican Papers*, p. 119.

[39]Quoted in U.S. Commission on Civil Rights, *Puerto Ricans in the Continental United States*, p. 99.

[40]Ibid., p. 103.

[41]Gonzalez, "Puerto Ricans on the Mainland," p. 11.

[42]In the sections on politics and protests I draw on some insights provided by Maria Merrill-Ramirez in comments on an earlier draft of this chapter.

[43]Lopez, "The Puerto Rican Diaspora," p. 329.

[44]Fitzpatrick, "Puerto Ricans," p. 866.

[45]Western Regional Office, *Puerto Ricans in California*, p. 16.

[46]Lopez, *The Puerto Rican Papers*, pp. 55–58.

[47]Bonilla and Campos, "A Wealth of Poor," pp. 166–67.

[48]Fitzpatrick, "Puerto Ricans," p. 866.

[49]John Adam Moreau, "My Parents, They Cry for Joy," in Wagenheim, *The Puerto Ricans: A Documentary History*, pp. 327–30.

[50]Lopez, "The Puerto Rican Diaspora," p. 331.

[51]Ibid., pp. 331–32.

[52]Michael Abramson, *Palante: Young Lords Party* (New York: McGraw-Hill, 1971), pp. 34–36.

[53]Gonzalez, "Puerto Ricans on the Mainland," p. 17.

[54]Lopez, "The Puerto Rican Diaspora," p. 332.

[55]Fitzpatrick, "Puerto Ricans," p. 865.

[56]Joseph P. Fitzpatrick, *Puerto Rican Americans: The Meaning of Migration to the Mainland* (Englewood Cliffs, N.J.: Prentice-Hall, 1971), especially pp. 22–43; Milton Gordon, *Assimilation in American Life* (New York: Oxford University Press, 1964), pp. 75–77; Elena Padilla, *Up From Puerto Rico* (New York: Columbia University Press, 1958).

[57]Maldonado-Denis, *Puerto Rico*, p. 319.

[58]Fitzpatrick, Puerto Rican Americans, p. 43.

[59]U.S. Commission on Civil Rights, *Puerto Ricans in the Continental United States*, p. 29.

[60]Maldonado-Denis, *Puerto Rico,* pp. 320–23.

[61]Cf. Lopez, "The Puerto Rican Diaspora," p. 343.

[62]Bonilla and Campos, "A Wealth of Poor," p. 172.

[63]Maria Merrill-Ramirez, private communication, July 1982.

Japanese Americans

CHAPTER 11

For many non-Asian Americans, thinking about the Japanese conjures up conventional stereotyped images of crafty "Orientals," of treachery, of militaristic expansionism, of successful gardeners, or of "yellow" skins and slanted eyes. Occasionally political speeches and press conferences have in recent years included such phrases as "fat Japs" and "little Japs." Negative views are prevalent among the World War II generation of European Americans, whose memories of the Japanese enemy sometimes remain couched in the terms of war propaganda. The mass media have played a role in giving Japanese Americans a negative image from the beginning of agitation against the "yellow peril" in the nineteenth century. In the 1970s and 1980s we have seen a new stereotyping of Japanese Americans as the "model minority." We have also seen a new hostility toward all things Japanese because of growing Japanese economic competition with the United States in world trade.

MIGRATION: AN OVERVIEW

Japanese rulers set strict emigration restrictions until the 1880s; only a trickle of emigration was permitted. When Western imperialism spread to Asia by the middle of the nineteenth century, Japan was finally "opened up." In 1853 Commodore Matthew Perry sailed warships into Tokyo Bay, and with his show of *force* won a treaty granting the United States trading rights with Japan. In a few decades increased trade and labor migration would characterize the shipping lanes between the two nations.

Hawaii was the first major point of destination for Japanese migrants coming within the political sphere of the United States, where they had been preceded by the Chinese. Because of a declining native Hawaiian population, the European planters sought low-wage laborers for the sugarcane fields. At first, Chinese laborers were brought in under five-year contracts, typically but one step away from slavery, since quitting a job meant a breach of contract and a stay in jail. A change in employer attitudes toward the Chinese resulted in a shift to Japanese workers.

Between 1885 and 1894 an estimated thirty thousand Japanese laborers were brought to the Hawaiian plantations under contract labor agreements. As the weaker nation, the Japanese government agreed to this, though it had been misled as to who would pay for the passage and as to whether the migrants would be allowed to settle there. When the agreement expired in 1894, Japanese immigration decreased. Most immigrants stayed on and laid the basis for the large present-day Japanese community in Hawaii. Propertied European Americans were striving to ensure their control of the islands, with many hoping for annexation by the United States. In 1898 Hawaii came under the territorial control of the United States government, which guaranteed non-Asian control of the islands and permitted the capitalists again to recruit Japanese labor without fear and to continue taking native Hawaiian lands.[1]

The Chinese

Prior to the Japanese migration to the mainland, beginning in the 1880s, there came the Chinese. Chinese migration to the United States began in substantial numbers in the decade just before the Civil War, with the largest number, a quarter of a million, coming in during the three decades after 1860. Most entered as poor workers, brought in to do the "dirty work" along the West Coast, including mining, railroad, and service work. Many were brought in by capitalists to remedy the labor shortage in service employment, to fill menial positions in such areas as laundry and restaurant work that the European American miners and settlers did not want.

As the Chinese became more numerous and successful, increased attacks on them led to official government exclusion in the 1882 Chinese Exclusion Act. Direct immigration was prohibited. Subsequently, dozens of local, state, and federal laws institutionalized direct discrimination against Chinese Americans. Anti-Chinese prejudice developed to a fevered pitch, so that non-Asian citizens and U.S. courts alike viewed them as an "inferior race" to be segregated with other "colored" citizens. Dozens of Chinese Americans were killed by vigilante groups on the West Coast, where at an early point few legal or political rights were recognized as applying to Asians.[2]

Mainland Migration

Into this hostile situation surged Japanese migrants to the mainland. Between the 1880s and the Gentleman's Agreement in 1908 more than 150,000 immigrants entered; between then and the 1920s another 100,000 came. The immigrants to the mainland United States came under more diverse auspices than did the immigrants to Hawaii. Some came under contract to capitalists, others came under the auspices of relatives and friends, and yet others came on their own. Most entered as relatively voluntary migrants, though they might have previously served under contract in Hawaii. The pre-1908 Issei* had a harder time than those who came afterward, because the later immigrants were brought into an already well-formed Japanese American community. Many came directly from Japan, while others came in stepping-stone fashion from Hawaii to various points of destination up and down the West Coast.[3]

The demand for workers on the West Coast was the strong pull factor which attracted immigrants whose aspirations had not been met in a Japan just beginning to industrialize. Oscillation in the capitalistic economy of the United States varied the demand for workers in the late nineteenth century, but by the early twentieth century the demand for low-wage workers was again sharply increasing. With the decline in Chinese immigrants, a sharp demand for low-wage labor, particularly in agriculture, accelerated the Japanese migration.[4]

Soon agitation was sprouting anew on the West Coast. Anti-Japanese activity continued the hostile tradition begun against the Chinese. Employers often favored the continuation of the immigration, while many white workers and unions opposed the competitive threat. The mayor of San Francisco campaigned vigorously against the Japanese, arguing they were "unassimilable" and a competitive threat. In 1905 California newspapers began a campaign against the "yellow peril," which they saw as a threat to everything from public schools to white women. In the same year both houses of the California legislature passed a resolution calling for exclusion on the grounds that the Japanese would not assimilate, given their distinctive racial habits and differences. Because of this intense agitation, President Theodore Roosevelt arranged for a government prohibition on Japanese migrants coming in by way of Hawaii, Mexico, and Canada. In negotiations in 1907–1908 Roosevelt persuaded the Japanese government to agree to the infamous Gentleman's Agreement, whereby no passports would be given by the Japanese government to any workers except those who had already been in the United States and to close relatives of those already here.[5]

This agreement to limit immigration reduced the numbers entering, though not the agitation. Between 1910 and 1919 the majority of the immigrants who came in directly from Japan were former residents or parents, wives, and children of residents. The number of those leaving the United States was quite significant in the 1908–1924 period, about one-third the total number of the immigrants. In contrast to the earlier Chinese immigrants, who were virtually all male, more of the Japanese immigrants were wives and other family members. Some Japanese American men later

---

Issei, Nisei, Sansei, and *Yonsei* are Japanese terms for the first four generations of Japanese Americans. The *Issei* were (are) born in Japan.

married, often by traditional parental arrangement and to sight-unseen Japanese brides, and brought their wives to the United States. This migration was the target of further anti-Japanese agitation.

Hate groups argued that the Japanese were taking over California, that their birth rate was so high they would overpopulate California, that they were disloyal to the United States, and that they were an alien race. A fierce pamphlet and speech battle was waged over these issues, with European Americans railing against what was viewed as the "yellow peril" and a few Japanese scholars counterattacking with carefully documented pamphlets and books.[6]

Racist Agitation

The same writers and scholars who proclaimed the threat posed by southern and eastern Europeans to "Anglo-Saxon" superiority expressed fear of the Asian migration. Organized groups, including the American Legion, the American Federation of Labor, and the California Farm Bureau Association, pressed for exclusion of the Japanese. By the 1920s Congress had succumbed to the racist agitation. The 1924 Immigration Act which established racist quotas based on a formula giving preference to "Nordic" nations also *excluded* Japanese immigration with an amendment prohibiting "aliens ineligible for citizenship." An earlier Supreme Court decision, *Ozawa v. United States* (1922), had paved the way by ruling definitively that only those immigrants of white or African origin could become citizens of the United States—that is, Asians could not even become citizens. Under the leadership of Senator Henry Cabot Lodge, the Senate voted to incorporate complete exclusion of the Japanese into the 1924 Immigration Act, and the House followed suit.[7]

Government action against Asians, spurred by labor unions and hate groups, persisted. Until after World War II, much of the U.S. labor movement, fighting for survival, supported direct discrimination and exclusion, including discriminatory legislation. West Coast newspapers fostered exclusionist sentiments. During World War II the United States pressured friendly governments to take action against their Japanese immigrants. It was not until the 1950s that action was taken to provide a token quota for the Japanese; and not until 1965 were anti-Asian restrictions taken out of U.S. immigration law.[8]

In 1880 there were only 148 Japanese in the United States. By 1920 the number had grown to 111,000. By 1970 it was nearly 600,000. In 1970 Japanese Americans were the largest Asian group in the United States; and the 1965 Immigration Act has resulted in a new burst of immigrants from the Land of the Rising Sun, with thousands being admitted since 1965.[9] However, by the 1970s and 1980s other Asian and Pacific peoples predominated in the migration streams from the East. According to the U.S. Census there were 3.5 million Asian Americans in 1980, an increase of more than 100 percent from 1970 to 1980. Among these there were more than 600,000 Japanese Americans.

STEREOTYPING JAPANESE AMERICANS

The sentiments of non-Asian Americans in regard to Japanese Americans have contained both positive and negative stereotypes. Stereotypes are half-truths or gross exaggerations with little or no empirical support. Public officials have played an important role in propagating stereotypes of the Japanese, attitudes in part reflecting relations between the governments of the United States and Japan.

In the earliest years, comparisons with the negatively stereotyped Chinese immigrants led many to evaluate the new Japanese migrants more positively, as somehow less threatening and more family-oriented. This was in part a consequence of the fact that the Japanese immigrants were more likely to bring along their families. Yet early images also contained negative notions that the Japanese were docile and servile. The exaggerated docility image has lasted up to the present.[10]

Around 1900, European Americans adopted a racist set of stereotypes. Some worried about exaggerated claims of Japanese land ownership, which was growing but which never involved more than a small percentage of all West Coast farmlands (though the Japanese did dominate in a few vegetable crop areas.) Another widespread view was that the Japanese were incapable of being shaped by the Anglo-Saxon core culture because of their different customs and culture. V. S. McClatchy, a Sacramento editor and outspoken opponent of the Japanese, vigorously argued that the Japanese were "for various reasons unassimilable, and a dangerous element either as residents or citizens."[11]

Above all, their "race" was seen as problematical: "He is brown; we are white; and this difference, they insist, carried with it such psychological, social, and civilizational differences that any attempt to live together is sure to be disastrous."[12] The ultimate outcome of mixing was seen as "race degeneracy." From presidents and U.S. senators to ordinary westerners, many whites belabored the point of dramatic racial differences. James Phelan, U.S. senator from California, argued that the Japanese were a great threat to the "future of the white race, American institutions, and Western civilization."[13] These stereotyped views played a major role in anti-Japanese legislation passed by the U.S. Congress.

The nativist view of the "yellow peril" to Western civilization first began with the Chinese, but it was also applied to the Japanese. As early as 1905 some even saw a military threat, when the victories of the Japanese in the Russo-Japanese War evoked fears of an invasion from Japan. Paranoia reached a fevered extent in white fears that spies were coming in disguised as immigrants. In the 1907–1911 period western newspapers repeated rumors of outside invasion. Racists worried about vaguely defined Japanese "hordes," not necessarily armies, which would somehow destroy "Nordic" dominance in the United States.

A related stereotype targeted the alleged Japanese American disloyalty to the United States, due to a prior and overriding loyalty to the Japanese emperor. Some saw Japanese Americans as unpatriotic, as so tied to an increasingly militaristic Japan that they would aid Japan under any

circumstances. Rumors ran rampant after 1910: the Japanese were planning a naval base in Mexico, the Japanese were organizing Native Americans on the West Coast, the Japanese had charted the ocean off the California
coastline. Anti-Japanese sentiment of this type was reflected in such movies
as the 1916 *Patria,* which portrayed Japan invading California, and the
1920 *Shadows of the West,* with its Japanese spies.[14]

These movie images were part of a broader smearing of the Japanese
as treacherous, villainous, and immoral. In the formative period of the
movie industry, Chinese and Japanese characters were consistently pictured
as villains, often by white actors. The Asian was stereotyped as "inscrutable,"
as speaking little English, as cunning, and as lying and treacherous. Public
officials propagated such myths.[15]

Novelists and writers in popular magazines contributed to the visual
and verbal images. Between 1900 and the 1920s the image of the forward,
buck-toothed "Jap" exploded in the mass media. In his widely circulated
"Letters of a Japanese Schoolboy," Wallace Irwin stimulated stereotypes
about Japanese Americans, including a mode of speech parodied with
phrases such as "honorable sir" and "so sorry please."[16]

Stereotypes of uncleanliness and immorality were also prevalent. Magazines and newspapers complained about the dirty conditions Japanese
Americans allegedly lived in. Legislators spoke of their alleged immorality,
even bringing up the apelike image applied earlier to the Irish and the
blacks. As with other nonwhite groups, the threat of intergroup sex led to
much stereotyping. Officials worried openly about Japanese males in their
twenties sitting in schools ready to desecrate pale young virgins. Coupled
with this was a fear of the high Japanese birth rate. Some nativists prepared
outrageous demographic tables showing that between the years 1920 and
2000 the white population in California would be overwhelmed by the
Japanese. Some expected *10 million* Japanese Americans by the late twentieth century.[17]

Attitude surveys in the 1920s and 1930s suggested that anti-Japanese
prejudice and accompanying social-distance attitudes were widely accepted
by white Americans, although anti-Japanese feeling was most intense on
the West Coast. Whites elsewhere seemed vague in their attitudes. A survey
of white student attitudes in one county in California in 1927 found the
frequently mentioned stereotypes to be negative: dishonest, treacherous,
unfairly competitive, and having low standards of living. Another West
Coast sample of whites in the 1920s expressed very negative social-distance
attitudes toward Japanese and Chinese persons in regard to such matters
as intermarriage, friendships, and desirability as neighbors.[18]

War Propaganda

By the early 1930s there was some decline in public rabble-rousing
against the Japanese. Soon, however, the actions of the Japanese government, with its growing power in the Pacific, provoked anti-Japanese sentiment on a large scale. By 1940, *before* the attack on Pearl Harbor, West
Coast leaders were openly portraying Japanese Americans as disloyal, as

potential spies. This image escalated after Pearl Harbor, with rumors of spying and sabotage circulating by the thousands, including such stories as Japanese American farmers planting flowers in a pattern to guide attacking airplanes.[19]

Here again was the threat of the "yellow peril." Major political figures repeated these racial stereotypes to a public inclined to accept them. California's Attorney General (later U.S. Chief Justice) Earl Warren depicted Japanese Americans as dangerous and threatening. In 1943 General John L. DeWitt, the West Coast military commander, argued, "A Jap's a Jap. . . . The Japanese race is an enemy race and while many second- and third-generation Japanese born on United States soil, possessed of United States citizenship, have become 'Americanized,' the racial strains are undiluted."[20] The national press presented the image of numerous enemy agents in the "large alien population." The irony is that the reason for the large alien population was the racist *prohibition* on Japanese Issei becoming citizens in U.S. law. Movies also played their role; there Japanese soldiers tortured and raped, a stigma carried over by white viewers to Japanese Americans.

Such massive propaganda doubtless contributed to the lingering anti-"Jap" feeling lasting from the 1940s to the present. Surveys by the War Relocation Authority after the war revealed that stereotypes continued to be commonplace among whites. Yet with the changes in Japan's position from enemy to ally, the stereotypes slowly began to change in the decades after the war. By the 1960s new stereotypes had developed in regard to the Japanese, many with apparently positive aspects. Gallup polls documented attitude changes. Various magazines and newspapers praised the Japanese Americans for being highly acculturated. Some argued they were "just like whites." A related image was that of the "successful citizen" who worked hard and achieved much in a free society.

Some magazines came to see Japanese Americans as the foremost example of a nonwhite success story. However, Ogawa has argued that the "highly Americanized" and "successful citizens" stereotypes are not entirely positive, suggesting that they operate to rationalize and preserve white American dominance. The stereotypes suggest that one must become "white" in order to be a good citizen or fully human. In the "success" view, since the Japanese Americans have become English-speaking models of the Protestant ethic, they can be accepted by whites as sterilized members of the "Oriental race." This may be similar to the Japanese businessperson being made an "honorary white" in South Africa, so he or she will not suffer from segregation laws there against nonwhites. The "superior, successful citizen" image has been used to defend the U.S. record with other minorities by suggesting that other nonwhites can make it too if they become like the Japanese Americans. If the Japanese can make it, anyone can. Society's leaders thus defend themselves against charges that this is a racist society. In the view of some Japanese American critics another tragic aspect of this stereotype is that it forces young Japanese Americans to live up, or down, to the image.[21]

Textbook Distortions, Stereotypes, and Omissions

A recent study of the images of Japanese Americans in school history textbooks found not only this exaggerated success stereotype but also numerous other distortions of Japanese American history and serious omissions in the telling of that history. For example, one prominent U.S. history textbook that is used in public schools tiptoes around the circumstances of early Japanese American history, speaking of new groups of Japanese being "added" to the United States population. There is a serious omission in such textbooks concerning the fact that U.S. employers in Hawaii and California actively recruited and exploited Japanese laborers. These history textbooks also do not deal squarely with the impact of the racist 1924 Immigration Act on Japanese Americans. That Act violated the earlier Gentleman's Agreement with Japan and stopped the immigration of Japanese families to the United States entirely, over the vigorous objections of the Japanese government. In addition, the internment of Japanese Americans in concentration camps during World War II (see pp. 328–331) is not adequately portrayed. The history textbooks see the camp experience as part of the "hysteria of war" and do not discuss the long history of anti-Japanese agitation in the United States as a prelude to the illegal uprooting and imprisonment of American citizens of Japanese descent. Moreover, one textbook suggests that Japanese Americans "have forgiven the government for violating their rights during World War II." The fact is that the imprisonment is well remembered by Japanese Americans, who are still pressing the government for *fair* compensation for the great damage done. They have neither forgotten nor forgiven.[22]

Often the textbook approach to Asian Americans, including Japanese Americans, is to see them as exotic Orientals (a term resented by many Asian Americans), as "coolie" laborers fit for dirty labor, or as a "model minority" which has entirely overcome discrimination. For the most part the textbooks have very little on the real history of Japanese and other Asian Americans; these omissions are as serious as the historical distortions and vulgar stereotypes.

REPRESSION AND VIOLENT CONFLICT

Japanese Americans have suffered not only from stereotyping, but from discrimination and physical attacks as well. Unlike other groups, Japanese Americans have seldom countered violence with violence of their own. Violent attacks on Chinese immigrants were common in the decades preceding the Japanese immigration. Chinese laborers were massacred in Los Angeles and in Wyoming; riots against the Chinese occurred in a number of states and territories.

The first major acts of violence against the Japanese came within a decade of their arrival in large numbers. White groups, particularly on the West Coast, used a variety of means to stop Japanese migration and competition. Violence was a part of the machinery aimed at keeping Japanese Americans in a subordinate position.

Fear grew in the wake of crises. After the 1906 San Francisco earthquake the violence directed at Japanese and Japanese Americans increased. Scientists sent by Japan to help with earthquake relief were attacked by groups of men and boys; local newspapers condoned the actions as pranks. In the wake of growing anti-Asian hostility, Japanese businesses were boycotted; windows were broken; Japanese shopkeepers were attacked. At least two dozen Japanese were attacked and beaten on the streets and in places of business in the San Francisco area. Japanese American resistance was active but inadequate to the task, since the police seldom intervened on their behalf.[23]

The anti-Japanese exclusion movement sometimes turned to violence, as in central California in 1921, when large numbers of Japanese farm workers were driven out of certain farm areas. Japanese farm workers and farmers were harassed by exclusionists, and the farmers formed cooperative organizations for protective purposes. In the 1930s white farmers in Arizona petitioned the governor to throw out Japanese farmers. When this failed, attempts were made to drive them out violently. The threat of such violence spreading to California led the California legislature to consider a bill restricting Japanese American agricultural enterprises. At the beginning of World War II violent attacks on Japanese Americans on the West Coast escalated. In 1942 newspapers and radio broadcasts were reporting dozens of attacks on Japanese Americans and their property from Seattle to San Diego. Such attacks were cited by some as justification for removing Japanese Americans from coastal areas.[24]

Concentration Camps in the United States

The most massive exercise of force against Japanese Americans was their evacuation under military escort to guarded prison camps in the interior of the West. In this century only one U.S. racial or ethnic group has been forcibly imprisoned as a group—Japanese Americans. The military victories of the Japanese government in the 1930s and 1940s, including the attack at Pearl Harbor, sharply increased fears of a Japanese invasion of the American mainland. We have already noted the dramatic increase in negative stereotyping among whites on the West Coast at the time. Members of Congress and the news media parroted the stereotypes and rumors and escalated fear across the United States. By January 1942 evacuation and imprisonment were being suggested as the solution. The old exclusionist organizations played an active role in pressing for internment. In addition, white-dominated organizations such as the Farm Bureau and the Western Growers Protective Association seemed committed to destroying Japanese farming and business competition.[25]

Discriminatory government action was taken against Japanese Americans beginning in December 1941 and January 1942. The California legislature passed a bill aimed at reducing the presence of Japanese, including the native-born, in state government. State and federal police raids on

Japanese aliens, which had begun directly after Pearl Harbor, were intensified in a frantic search for spies; more than two thousand aliens were arrested, most without tangible evidence. California Attorney General Earl Warren speculated that the lack of confirmed cases of espionage or sabotage until then reflected the cunning of the Japanese, who were waiting for just the right time to attack. Japanese businesses were forced to close. Citizens were illegally detained by local police, evicted by landlords, and fired by employers.[26]

In the first phase of federal action a small number of Japanese, German, and Italian aliens were moved from certain sensitive military areas and their travel was restricted. Then came the second stage. On February 19, 1942, Executive Order 9066 was issued by President Franklin Roosevelt and was soon validated by Congress. It ordered the Secretary of War to establish military areas from which any person could be excluded. The West Coast military commander established the western parts of California, Washington, and Oregon, as well as the southern part of Arizona, as areas where no Japanese, Italian, or German aliens could reside. But *only* the Japanese were pressured to resettle outside coastal areas. The two hundred thousand Italian and German aliens there did *not* have to endure forced movement from their homes. Japanese Americans were forcibly detained in assembly centers and later transported under guard to barbed-wire concentration camps.[27]

The War Relocation Authority (WRA) was set up to supervise removal; the Federal Reserve Bank was ordered to protect the property of evacuees. Since the agencies encouraged the sale of property, most Japanese Americans sold their property at low prices. Businesses and farms were generally sold at losses. The evacuees were at first housed in temporary centers, then moved to permanent concentration camps. By the fall of 1942 inland areas in the West housed more than 100,000 Japanese, *two-thirds of them native-born U.S. citizens,* in ten camps watched over by armed military guards and administered by the War Relocation Authority. The camps were in barren areas. Very small monthly wages were paid evacuees who volunteered to work. Supplies were often inadequate. Barracks were bareboard buildings with few furnishings; small sections housed large families.[28]

Local camp governments were set up, usually filled by Nisei under the supervision of WRA authorities. Each block had its own manager, and a council was elected from among the prisoners. Managers and members of the council became central figures in the camps. This provided a training ground for organizational skills which would come in handy after the war. Soon political screening was implemented, under the auspices of government authorities, aimed at ferreting out the disloyal by means of background checks. As a result, protest movements, demonstrations, and riots were generated in the camps. Six thousand prisoners renounced their U.S. citizenship, many expressing a desire to leave these oppressive conditions for Japan.

A few thousand college students and workers for special agricultural assignments were released. Others were released to serve in the U.S. Army, where, ironically, many served with extraordinary valor in segregated units under white officers. In 1943 more than ten thousand were permitted to relocate to the East. By 1944 one-third had been allowed to leave the camps.[29]

Late in 1944 an order was issued rescinding the original order to evacuate Japanese Americans from the coast; the WRA planned to close all the camps within a year. In a few months most remaining evacuees returned to the West Coast, though during late 1945 and 1946 eight thousand despairing evacuees returned to Japan. Those released from camps returned home to the West Coast to find farms and businesses in ruin, household goods destroyed, and local residents hostile; some experienced violent attacks by their white neighbors. At least three dozen violent attacks have been documented; violence against property and persons included beatings, shootings, and arson.

The cost of this entire episode was enormous. The government (including the Army) spent about $250 million on the evacuation; Japanese American economic losses have been set at at least $400 million.[30]

Why the Camps Were Created

Why were the Japanese Americans forcibly imprisoned? Some emphasize the military angle. Others focus on the intensity of anti-Japanese prejudice rampant in California or on the role of business elites in their power struggle with Japanese American competitors. Yet others have accented the role of West Coast politicians such as governors and mayors who sought to gain public favor by selecting an issue supported by popular prejudices. In a number of decisions the U.S. Supreme Court upheld the military decision without investigation. Even though *two-thirds* of those evacuated were U.S. citizens, the Court cavalierly ignored this issue in upholding the concentration camps' legality. Justice Robert M. Jackson dissented in the Supreme Court decisions which upheld the presidential order to evacuate Japanese Americans, pointing out that the Court had validated "the principle of racial discrimination in criminal procedure." Here was a politically motivated action which was a violation of the rights guaranteed by the Constitution. Severe discriminatory actions were directed at a people assumed, but not proved, to be disloyal primarily because they were not of the "white race," because of their Asian extraction. (Italian and German Americans were not treated in this fashion.) This negative image lingered on after the war. A survey of Californians in the late 1960s found 48 percent still approving of the Japanese evacuation of 1942.[31]

Some have raised the question of why Japanese Americans did not protest imprisonment more than they did. Yet research has shown that the actual protest, including riots, was greater than many assessments have indicated. A number fought valiantly but unsuccessfully in the courts to prevent their forced evacuation. Vigorous public demonstrations were also held. There was a confrontation between Japanese American evacuees and authorities at the Santa Anita Assembly Center in California over the rumored appropriation of personal property. Property was destroyed and a police officer was attacked by a group of angry Japanese; 200 armed military police suppressed the rioting. As in other riots, the confrontation was escalated by the police into violence.[32]

Protest took place in the prison camps as well. At the Poston camp in the fall of 1942 there was a strike over the imprisonment of two particular Japanese Americans; more than two thousand persons met in a protest rally. In a few days the demands had escalated, calling for more rights of self-determination by the relocatees.

A similar situation occurred at Manzanar in east-central California, where there were ten thousand relocatees. Certain Nisei leaders there were given some responsibility and came to be seen by other internees as collaborators with the oppressors. The Manzanar demonstrations were aimed both at the white authorities and at subservient Nisei leaders. In December 1942 an assault on a Japanese American collaborator and the imprisonment of the attacker led to a mass meeting of four thousand people and to demands for an investigation of conditions at the camp. The camp director, escorted by military police armed with machine guns, met with the crowd. A crowd again formed at night at the jail and was fired upon when it did not disperse. Two inmates were killed and a dozen wounded. There were additional clashes with soldiers.

There was also protest at the Tule Lake camp in California after it became a segregation camp for those Japanese Americans considered especially disloyal. A series of conflicts between inmates and the authorities erupted over police attempts to break up crowds, over arbitrary work decisions, over poor working conditions, over a public funeral, and over camp living conditions. Numerous petitions were made to the camp director to deal with these problems. In 1943, as a result of a fight between a white officer and evacuees, the latter were arrested, the Army brought in tanks to restore order, and martial law was declared. It is clear from such protests in the camps that a substantial minority of Japanese Americans were willing to resist their oppression openly.[33]

THE POLITICAL ARENA

First-generation Japanese immigrants settled in ghetto communities along the West Coast, where they faced hardship and discrimination. The Japanese government watched over the Issei more than other governments watched their emigrants, pressing for better working and living conditions for workers in the United States. Japanese diplomatic officials had high status in Japanese American communities and played an active role in fighting discrimination against the Issei and Nisei.[34]

Because of the racist character of U.S. naturalization laws in the late 1800s, the Issei could not become citizens. Japanese were aliens ineligible for citizenship. In a 1922 decision the Supreme Court reaffirmed that Japanese Americans could not become citizens because citizenship was limited by law to "free white persons" and those of African ancestry. We have already discussed the intense agitation against Japanese settlers led by prominent politicians on the West Coast, culminating in Congress's passage of the exclusivion provision in the 1924 Immigration Act. (This intense agitation did not gain one political objective of nativists: passage of a constitutional amendment barring second-generation Japanese from citizenship.) Great pressure was directed against Japanese participation in U.S. electoral politics.[35]

Most second-generation Japanese did not become old enough to vote until the 1940s. Just as the Nisei were coming of age in large numbers, World War II brought a severe setback in the struggle for political participation. Because they had no leading politicians and few votes, there was no political peril involved in uprooting them.

After World War II political gains began accruing to Japanese Americans, primarily because of their growing organization. Some organization had begun in the 1930s, when many Japanese Americans rejected protest organizations and preferred to join business-oriented or civic organizations instead. Patient accommodation was the thrust. By the 1930s the Japanese American Citizens League (JACL), controlled by Nisei leaders, was pressing moderately for their own civil rights and for naturalized citizenship for the Issei. Voter registration campaigns were inaugurated, but attempts to get candidates to run generally stopped at the planning stage. The JACL has long been the largest voluntary association among the Japanese; in its beginning it reflected a break with the Issei-controlled prefectural clubs in the direction of the dominant core culture. During World War II the Nisei-controlled JACL engaged in controversial collaboration with white authorities in the prison camps. In recent decades the JACL has come under attack as too establishment-oriented and conformist, particularly from some young advocates of "yellow power."[36]

Compensation Pressures and Political Progress

In the decades after World War II the JACL, together with other Japanese American groups, played a primary role in winning some of the first major political victories for Japanese Americans. The first victories came in the area of legal and political rights. By 1946, together with newer organizations, it was pressing hard for compensation for evacuation losses, for citizenship for the first generation, and for changing discriminatory laws, including the 1924 Immigration Act. Funds were raised for a lobbying campaign in Washington, D.C. Meager compensation finally came in the form of the 1948 Japanese American Evacuation Act. By the 1950 deadline nearly 24,000 claims had been filed for $132 million. Ultimately these Japanese American victims of this unconstitutional deprivation of rights were paid only $38 million, less than 10 percent of estimated losses.[37]

However, these token compensatory payments did not mean the end to Japanese American pressures. In the last decade a number of Japanese American organizations and officials have pressed the United States government for more adequate repayment for the real economic losses suffered. Under pressure, in 1980 Congress established the Commission on

Wartime Relocation and Internment of Civilians. The Commission recommended that the 60,000 survivors of imprisonment receive compensation of $1 billion to $2 billion. And the Commission called on Congress to officially apologize to Japanese Americans for the unnecessary imprisonment. Whether Congress will follow the suggestions of the Commission yet remains to be seen.

Court decisions and legislative action began to change patterns of discrimination, ruling alien land laws unenforceable and belatedly restoring Japanese American rights in numerous areas. In 1950 an attempt to get an alien naturalization bill failed to get through Congress, while the regressive 1950 Internal Security Act provided for concentration camps to be ready in case of future need. In 1952 the Japanese *exclusion* provision of the 1924 Immigration Act was repealed; but it was replaced with racist quota restrictions; at least the Japanese now had a token quota. Finally, Asian background was removed as a barrier to naturalized citizenship. The new racist quota on Japanese immigration was not eliminated until the 1965 Immigration Act.[38]

In the early 1970s, in response to pressure from organized Japanese Americans, Title II of the 1950 Internal Security Act was finally repealed. That title permitted government imprisonment of citizens deemed potential collaborators with an enemy in time of crisis. Camps built under that law were dismantled. Gradually, other injustices were corrected. Old anti-Japanese laws and ordinances were repealed. "Tokyo Rose," a Japanese American woman who had been forced to work in the Japanese propaganda effort when caught in Japan during the war and who later served long years in federal prison on a trumped-up charge of treason, was finally pardoned in January 1977. In the mid-1970s a symbolic political gain was achieved when President Gerald Ford rescinded the infamous 9066 Executive Order which had resulted in the deportation and imprisonment of Japanese Americans during World War II.[39]

While these belated gains were being won, political activity aimed at electoral victories was increasing. Major gains came first. In Hawaii the Japanese Americans have been numerous. Some Nisei were registered to vote in Hawaii as early as 1917; and a few made unsuccessful bids for office in the territorial legislature between 1922 and 1930. In 1930 the first Japanese were elected to office, one as a county supervisor and two as members of the territorial legislature; by the late 1930s nine Japanese officials were among the nearly one hundred elected officials in Hawaii. Indeed, this modest political clout may have played some role in creating greater freedom and less oppressive conditions for Hawaii's Japanese Americans during World War II.

In the late 1940s and early 1950s returning Japanese American World War II veterans, intent on expanding their political participation, became active in Democratic attempts to overthrow the traditional Republican domination of the islands. As a result, several Japanese veterans were elected to the Hawaii territorial legislature; by the late 1950s their activities facilitated Congress's conferral of statehood, finally overcoming the anti-Asian sentiment which had long kept Hawaii from achieving this status. Daniel

Inouye, a war hero who had lost an arm in battle, was elected the first U.S. representative from the new state of Hawaii and the first Japanese American in Congress. Spark Matsunaga became the second Japanese American to serve in the House in 1962, when Inouye became the first senator. In 1964 a second House seat was won by Patsy Takemoto Mink, the first Japanese woman to serve in Congress. Between the 1960s and the 1980s local and state offices in Hawaii were seeing a growing number of Japanese occupants. Japanese Americans now made up about half of the state legislature; they hold many of the state's top executive offices.[10]

Political progress has come more slowly for the Nisei and Sansei on the mainland. Numerous mainland Nisei cut their political "teeth" serving in the prison camps of World War II, but political victories have been made difficult by the dilution of votes in the heavily European American populations of the western states. Clarence Arai made unsuccessful attempts at election to the Washington legislature in the 1930s. Only one Nisei was elected to a state legislature between that time and the late 1960s, as a Republican from Colorado. In 1953 the first Japanese American became a judge on the mainland, in a Los Angeles municipal court. In the 1960s a few Japanese were elected to city council offices in Los Angeles County, Oakland, and San Jose and to mayoral posts in two or three smaller towns. A few dozen others have served since the late 1950s in appointive positions on city boards and school boards. Nonetheless, by the 1980s there were only a handful of Japanese Americans serving in elected positions at the higher levels of local, state, and federal governments on the mainland. There were four Japanese Americans in Congress. In 1976 the aging Samuel I. Hayakawa, a Canadian-born semanticist, was elected senator from California, becoming the first Japanese American senator from the mainland, together with Norman Mineta of California, who became the first mainland representative. In 1982 Hayakawa retired from the Senate and was replaced by a non-Asian senator.[41]

Politics, Stereotyping, and Competition with Japan

Beginning in the 1970s, and escalating in the 1980s, a new form of anti-Japanese agitation was spreading across the United States. Japan's economic development was surpassing that of the United States in a number of important industries, such as steel and automobile manufacturing. As a result, the United States was importing large quantities of manufactured goods from Japan. This generated new anti-Japanese hostility. Buy-American cartoons caricatured "wily Japs," "yellow power," and "crafty Orientals." Old stereotypes of the Japanese appeared again in public conversations and in newspaper articles. Japanese American members of the U.S. Congress received hostile phone calls and letters. The growing unemployment problems in the United States fueled the tendency to make the Japanese auto and steel industries the scapegoats for U.S. economic troubles. Anti-Japanese protectionist bills were introduced in Congress. And Japanese *Americans* were blamed for the actions of the Japanese.

Yet Japan was not the major cause of recessions in U.S. capitalism;

the real causes lay elsewhere—in poor management, for example. Nonetheless, Japan—and the Japanese—again became singled out as targets of hostile political discussion and threatened political action. Such anti-Japanese agitation had a negative impact on Japanese Americans, who had to endure again a questioning of their loyalties. Japanese Americans had to endure a resurgence of racist stereotyping and of hostilities they had hoped were buried. Opposition to renewed anti-Japanese racism appeared in Japanese American communities.

Protest Organizations and Nonviolent Protest

Japanese Americans have been stereotyped as a docile Asian group incapable of vigorous protest. Yet research since the 1960s has dramatized the forgotten protests of Japanese Americans against oppression, a struggle in which political tactics other than those of the ballot box have been utilized. At the turn of the century white delegates arriving at a Chinese Exclusion Convention to debate Asian immigration were met at the door, much to their surprise, by Japanese Americans with leaflets arguing against attempts to exclude the Japanese. This was the beginning of a long series of books, speeches, and pamphlets over the next two decades by Japanese and Japanese Americans vigorously protesting exclusion attempts. A few voluntary associations, such as the Japanese Association, were formed in the early 1900s to combat white exclusion activities and other manifestations of anti-Japanese discrimination. Each sizeable community had its Association, which offered protection in times of violence.[42]

Organized worker activity was part of the early Japanese experience. Japanese workers in Hawaii participated in at least sixty work stoppages in the five decades after 1870. On the mainland there was substantial worker organizing. A few strikes occurred in the 1890s; after 1900 their number increased. A few socialist groups were formed by Japanese immigrants in the early 1900s, most of which were connected with pressure for better wages and working conditions. In 1903 more than one thousand agricultural workers, Japanese and Mexican, struck sugar beet farmers in Ventura, California. Japanese American workers were involved in agricultural and mining strikes in California, Utah, Colorado, and Washington between 1903 and 1920. Thousands participated in agricultural strikes in the 1930s. Up to the 1940s, Japanese American and Mexican American workers cooperated in strikes against exploitative white growers and farmers in southwestern states. Such strikes played an important role in generating the opposition of white farmers to the Japanese.[43]

The Japanese American Citizens League (JACL) played an important role in accommodation during the prison camp period. Others vigorously resisted imprisonment.[44] Thousands renounced their citizenship and returned to Japan. There were numerous demonstrations and even a few riots against oppressive conditions. There was the later political-rights action of JACL leaders.

Two decades later, in the 1960s, an Asian American movement developed, this time led by the Sansei. The students active in the movement were, like other non-European Americans, questioning older views and leaders. Ties to Third World peoples were seen as necessary. Asian American studies programs were established; new journals were created, such as the *Amerasia Journal,* with scholarly articles as well as papers urging collective Asian American action and a new attention to problems of that group. Other journals took even more militant positions. Sugar-coated images of Japanese and Chinese success were increasingly challenged as a new sense of group pride and collective consciousness developed. The young have been sensitive to the price paid for acculturation—a price of unthinking acquiescence to European-American values, which they see encouraging conservatism and frustrating creativity among Japanese Americans on the contemporary scene. By the 1980s some of the militancy had died down; organizations were less political. New publications were being circulated. But the concern for Asian American problems persisted.[45]

THE ECONOMY

Most immigrants to the mainland started out at the bottom levels of the economic pyramid, filling the hard, dirty jobs on farms and in cities along the West Coast. They played a critical role in economic development there by providing low-paid agricultural and urban labor. Contract labor from Japan first went to the agricultural plantations in Hawaii. On the mainland many Japanese went into agricultural work and other work in rural areas, such as logging and working for lumber mills and railroads. Most had farming backgrounds and so were receptive to this type of labor. One California study in 1909 found 65 percent of Japanese American workers in agriculture, 15 percent in domestic service work, 15 percent in small businesses, and only 5 percent in other lines of work, including white-collar positions.[46]

Wages were quite low. In the first decades the new residents worked for as little as 50 cents to a dollar a day in agriculture. Japanese workers received less than European Americans. While white sawmill laborers got $2.60 to $3.50 a day in the state of Washington, Japanese laborers got only $1.75 to $2.75. This pattern of differential wage rates was true for many, if not most, job categories along the West Coast. Here intentional discrimination can be seen.

Poverty-stricken Japanese workers did agree to work for less. Such situations gave partial support to the nativist charge that the Japanese were taking low pay. Other charges by nativists that the Japanese were generally lowering wages on the West Coast were unfounded. Wage rates in the relevant job categories increased significantly between the 1890s and the first decades of the twentieth century.[47]

In cities the Japanese became service workers and laborers. Some gained a toehold in the economy as servants in the homes of whites, at wages at around the year 1900 of $1.50 a week plus board. By 1910 there were several thousand domestics in San Francisco alone. As in the case of the Italians and Irish, the immigrants were aided in their entry by those who had preceded them. Boarding houses became both places of lodging and employment centers where contracts for cheap labor could be made.[48]

Finding an Economic Niche

Japanese laborers sought upward mobility away from the entry positions. Gradually the Issei began to buy or lease land to farm on their own. In urban areas, where direct discrimination kept the Japanese out of manufacturing and white-collar employment, some went into small businesses, such as restaurants, laundry shops, and barber shops. By World War I there were two or three thousand such businesses along the West Coast. These small businesspersons established a niche for themselves by catering to Japanese Americans or whites unwilling to do this type of work. Those who succeeded brought in relatives and others from Japan and helped them get a start. One Japanese American would start a small business, become somewhat successful, then hire other Japanese to work for relatively low wages but with great job security, a large-family environment, and room and board.[49]

Most Japanese immigrants came from eleven southern perfectures in Japan, each with its own social associations in the United States. These prefectural clubs could act as mutual-aid associations for immigrants in a hostile environment. Prefectural associations aided the movement of Japanese immigrants into the economy by providing training for workers and directing clients to businesses. Restaurants and cleaning operations succeeded because the networks could be drawn on for new workers and for economic aid. In addition, the pooling of resources in informal money-raising organizations called *tanomoshi* provided capital for entrepreneurs who could not secure funds from U.S. banks. Mutual-aid associations aided perhaps half of all foreign-born Japanese in securing the capital necessary for establishing businesses.[50]

This toehold was not achieved easily. After a brief interlude, white opposition to the Japanese built swiftly and had a clear economic thrust. In urban areas the labor movement led the opposition, even though the Japanese seldom sought jobs in unionized industries. Boycotts and anti-Japanese advertising were used by white groups, as in the 1908 Anti-Jap Laundry League attempt to drive the Japanese out of the laundry business. Japanese laborers and farmers were accused by non-Asians of every conceivable "vice." But the basic problem was simply that the Japanese immigrants were very hard-working and, frequently, successful competitors.[51]

Farming success brought them new problems. The 1913 California Alien Land Law, passed under pressure from white farmers, stipulated that aliens could not buy land or lease it for more than three years; nor could they pass on land to their children. Of course, all Issei were forced to remain "aliens" because of discriminatory naturalization laws. While this California land law did interfere with agricultural activity, some ways were found to circumvent it, such as registering ownership of lands under the names of one's children. In response, in the 1920s new discriminatory laws prohibited Issei from leasing land at all and from holding it in the name of their minor children.

The impact of these land laws was to reduce the number of Japanese farms from over five thousand in 1920 to four thousand in 1930. Census figures on land ownership in California show a sharp decrease in acreage. Those who remained in farming increasingly relied on tenant or truck farming, raising vegetables for urban markets. New organizations such as the Japanese Cooperative Farm Industry organized the flow of farm products to Japanese retailers in cities. Using ingenuity, Japanese farmers were again demonstrating their knack for success; then the evacuation destroyed their farming again.[52]

Forced out of farming by land laws, and attracted to the demand for landscaping in the booming cities of California, many displaced farmers and farm workers became gardeners or nursery operators. The gardeners hired other Japanese Americans and relied on Japanese businesses for supplies. By 1928 there were thirteen hundred Japanese American gardeners in the Los Angeles area alone, a number which would grow to about seventeen hundred in the next decade.[53] The 1930 Census for California showed that 54 percent of the male Japanese workers were still in agriculture or gardening, 25 percent were in trade or business, 2 percent were in the professions, and a large percentage of the rest were in other urban occupations. At least half of those in business were in small retail businesses such as groceries, auto dealerships, restaurants, cleaning establishments, and hotels. Most professionals, including doctors, dentists, clergypersons, and teachers, dealt with members of their own or other minority communities. Those considering technical training in fields such as engineering still had to face the grim reality of discrimination in white-controlled industries. Discrimination remained a tragic fact of life for both Issei and Nisei.[54]

By the beginning of World War II some Japanese Americans in larger cities were moving up into white-collar positions. In 1940 in the highly urbanized Los Angeles County one study estimated that 51 percent of the males there were in white-collar positions (professional, managerial, and clerical-sales occupations) and about 40 percent were in semiskilled and unskilled blue-collar positions. The proportion of professionals was growing, yet half of those classified as white-collar employees were actually self-employed in small businesses. Japanese Americans were still a class of small businesspeople.[55]

Then the bottom fell out. Median economic losses per family from the forced wartime evacuation, for Los Angeles families, were estimated at about $10,000 in goods, property, income, and expenses (in 1940 dollars). The figures were similar elsewhere. There were heavy losses to small businesses. One official estimate put total economic losses at $400 million. Returning after 1945, many of those who could not regain their businesses and farms went into contract gardening and private household work. Some groceries and restaurants were soon reestablished, and the "Little Tokyos" of West Coast cities again became vibrant areas. Surprisingly, the wartime evacuation has been credited as contributing to the progress of some Japanese. In the evacuation centers the Nisei could do a greater variety of jobs than in the outside world. Teachers could teach in the camps, even though they usually could not in the communities from which they came. Some gained experience from this variety of jobs.

The Postwar Economy

The booming postwar economy was more willing to accept Japanese workers with experience, particularly outside the West Coast—where some migrated as a result of the war period—and in professional and civil service areas. Yet social and economic discrimination continued to affect the second generation; after the war certain occupations and industries were still off-limits to them. For example, for more than a decade University of California education departments discouraged Japanese students, not always successfully, from considering the teaching profession because of the difficulty of placement.[56]

Self-employment continued to be important. By 1960 there were seven thousand Japanese-owned businesses in the Los Angeles area alone, most of which were gardening businesses. Hotels, groceries, and laundries made up the next-largest categories. One study of Nisei residing in several states found that four in ten were still self-employed, more than three times the national figure. This concentration has been referred to as an "ethnic economy." The majority not in the self-employment ethnic economy were professionals or skilled blue-collar workers. Income figures for Japanese Americans in the ethnic economy showed higher percentages making less than $10,000 and more than $20,000 than one finds in the economy as a whole, pointing up the high risks and potential gains involved in small businesses. Those in small business were found to maintain kinship ties and ties to Buddhism more than those employed outside the small business economy.[57]

Occupational Mobility and Problems

Since 1960 a number of books and articles have appeared relating the Japanese American experience as a remarkable success story of achievement in the face of enormous odds. The usual socioeconomic indicators in Census data do indicate that Japanese American progress since the 1950s has been dramatic. Note the following occupational distributions for 1960 and 1970:[58]

	JAPANESE AMERICANS			
	1960		1970	
	MEN	WOMEN	MEN	WOMEN
Professional, technical	15.4%	12.3%	21.3%	15.9%
Managerial, administrative	10.1	3.8	11.7	3.8
Sales, clerical	13.8	37.2	15.0	41.2
Crafts	20.2	1.3	19.7	1.8
Operatives	11.4	16.9	10.3	13.5
Laborers	6.1	0.8	9.9	0.8
Farm managers, laborers	17.2	6.7	5.2	2.1
Service workers	5.8	21.1	6.6	20.8
	100.0%	100.1%	99.7%	99.9%

Compared to the total U.S. male population, in 1970 Japanese men occupied white-collar levels in somewhat larger proportions. In 1960 about 40 percent of Japanese American men were in white-collar positions, a proportion which had increased to nearly half by 1970. Similarly, the majority of women were in white-collar positions in both 1960 and 1970, with the percentage also increasing over that decade. Japanese women are concentrated in two traditionally female categories, clerical and service work occupations. Moreover, in some cities, such as Los Angeles and San Francisco, Japanese (and Chinese) Americans are much more likely to hold low-status, low-income jobs (for example, as laborers, maids, or service workers) than are Americans of European descent. (Occupational breakdowns from the 1980 Census are not as yet available.)

A 1978 study by the U.S. Commission on Civil Rights found a significant degree of occupational segregation for Japanese American workers, when compared with white workers. Examining 441 major job categories, the study found that 42 percent of Japanese American males and a third of Japanese American females would have to change occupations to have the same occupational distribution as white workers. The study also found that the extent of occupational segregation from whites had increased since 1960. Even though Japanese Americans have made major occupational gains since World War II, they are still disproportionately concentrated in certain job categories. They do not hold as wide an array of jobs as do European-American workers. This clearly reflects their history of being victimized by discrimination. Even today, the niches occupied by many Japanese Americans reflect past and present exclusion from other job categories.[59]

The income picture seems generally supportive of the success argument as well. In 1970 Japanese American income distribution for working males showed a large group making less than $4,000—about 30 percent, a statistic about the same as the national figure. The income distribution for females showed 58 percent making less than $4,000, compared with a national figure of 68 percent. In 1970 the median income for Japanese American families was $12,500, compared with $9,600 for all U.S. families. In the mid-to-late 1970s Japanese Americans continued with a median family income above that of whites. The average Japanese American earned a bit more than the average U.S. worker. In 1975, for example, Japanese American males earned an average of $12,615, compared with $11,247 for white males. Japanese American women earned much less than males, about $5,880; compared with the $5,122 for white females, however, they too have higher than average incomes. Although income levels for Japanese Americans have not as yet been made available by the Bureau of the Census from the 1980 census, data for a broader category, "Asian Americans," have been released. The 1980 median income (families) for this Asian category was $22,025, slightly higher than the comparable median income figure for whites.

While these income attainments are impressive, some problems remain. These Census income figures relate to current income and do not include property and other types of wealth. Japanese American families average more workers per household than the typical white family, and Japanese American workers are concentrated in states (Hawaii, California) with both high wages and a high cost of living. Moreover, Japanese families with *foreign-born* heads, many of whom are recent immigrants, have had incomes substantially below the national median figure for families. The income levels of Japanese Americans are lower than they should be, given the high level of education. Some statistics suggest this discrepancy between occupation and education. In 1970 in the United States as a whole, for every male aged 25 to 34 with an education including at least four years of college there were 1.5 males making $10,000 or more; among the Japanese Americans the comparable ratio was much lower, only 0.9 males making $10,000 or more for every one aged 25 to 34 years. Among older males, those aged 35 to 44 years, the national ratio of 2.4 was still higher than the Japanese ratio of 1.8. For a given (high) level of education Japanese men got less on the average than non-Japanese men. Moreover, a 1975 study by the U.S. Commission on Civil Rights found the same pattern. This study calculated what Japanese American (male) workers would have been earning if they had been white (male) workers with the same level of education, state of residence, age, and level of work effort. They found that Japanese workers earned only 88 percent of the amount earned by white males with comparable characteristics. Discrimination against Japanese Americans is suggested in these imbalances between education and income. Indeed, there are many college-educated Japanese who have become small businesspeople because of discrimination. While economic success may result, the cost of broken dreams cannot be counted, although it is doubtless high.[60]

Into the 1980s Japanese Americans continued to face subtle exclusion from prominent positions in businesses, in movies and television, in politics, and in certain civil service areas, such as police and fire departments. Indirect discrimination in the form of height and weight requirements has played a role in some occupational areas. Positions at higher administrative, managerial, and professional levels are often closed to Asians, particularly on the West Coast. In recent years some Japanese have complained that whites with poorer credentials or lesser ability have been promoted at a faster rate. One recent study examined Asian American employment in private industries in the San Francisco metropolitan area. It found Asian Americans to be underrepresented in manufacturing, construction, and wholesale trade. Asian Americans were found to be underrepresented in better-paying jobs (such as managerial jobs) and overrepresented in lower-paying jobs (such as clerical jobs). These patterns held true for Japanese Americans and for other Asian Americans. In addition, a 1976 research study of state government jobs in California found a similar pattern of Japanese American overrepresentation in lower-status clerical jobs.[61]

In 1979 a civil rights attorney testified before the U.S. Commission on Civil Rights that a study of California's Blue Shield (health insurance) company found no Asian Americans among the top nineteen decision-makers, even though one-quarter of all the employees were Asian American (many of these were Japanese Americans). One in six whites held a managerial or supervisory job, compared with only one in thirty-nine Asian Americans. Yet many Asian American employees there were qualified for higher-level positions than those they actually held. A recent *Newsweek* review of Asian Americans in America noted that "Asians tend to be underemployed for their levels of education and are underrepresented in corporate executive suites." Overall trends in the U.S. economy have also affected the employment patterns of Japanese Americans, particularly the younger generations. For example, although (elementary and secondary) education has been a popular college major in the postwar period, since the 1960s demand for teaching jobs has on occasion slackened. Past discrimination channeled Asian Americans into a few occupations, such as teaching, thus setting some of them up for serious problems in times of category-specific recessions.[62]

That Japanese Americans have achieved remarkable economic success against enormous odds is clearly indicated in socioeconomic data obtained since the 1940s. What they could have achieved without direct and indirect discrimination can only be imagined.

EDUCATION

Japanese Americans have had a commitment to education, a legacy brought from Japan. Issei parents sent their children to school more often than parents in most other groups of immigrant workers. Many Issei themselves pursued formal education. Forty-five percent of a large sample of Issei who had come in the years after 1908 reported they had secured some formal education in the United States; consequently, many developed a facility with the English language at an early point.[63]

This educational commitment triggered outbursts by nativists, inasmuch as Japanese children were viewed as members of a "morally inferior race." In 1906 the mayor of San Francisco, in a move supported by influential local newspapers, pressed for and got a resolution from the board of education setting up a separate school for all Asian children. There were at the time fewer than 100 Japanese children scattered throughout two dozen schools in the city. One member of the California legislature spoke of the danger to the "pure maids of California" based on the presence in schools of a handful of older Japanese students in primary grades because of their language problems. The Japanese government protested, and the federal government took action in court in an attempt to force the San Francisco Board of Education to give Japanese children the equal rights promised to them by an 1895 treaty.

Some anti-Japanese Californians were so angered about this (rare) federal support of Japanese Americans that they began to talk about secession. A compromise was worked out between President Theodore Roosevelt and San Francisco officials. After three months out of school, most of the Japanese children were allowed to return; the compromise meant the exclusion of over-age Japanese pupils. In return, the infamous "Gentleman's Agreement" aimed at stopping migration was executed by President Roosevelt.[64]

In this period of racist agitation a common stereotype was that the Japanese were displacing other children in California schools. The fact was that in 1920 Japanese children outnumbered whites only in one village school in the small town of Florin. Even by the late 1930s Japanese children were present only in small proportions in all but two or three schools in all of California. One result of this agitation over schools was an increase in segregation pressures. Several attempts were made by California legislators to segregate Japanese children, and by 1930 there were segregated schools for Asian Americans in four school districts.[65]

Language Schools and Japanese Educational Progress

In addition to sending their children to public schools, the Japanese developed private "language schools," which focused on training in the Japanese language and in traditional virtues. Though the length of time in these schools was insufficient for fully learning the Japanese language, the schools did provide a crucial setting for the socialization of children. The schools played an important role in teaching such traditional values as intensified respect for elders, industry, and courtesy. In this way the children gained a less distorted view of their heritage than they got in public schools. Many also needed to know some Japanese for employment on Japanese farms and in small businesses.

The Issei established the language schools as a way of promoting ties between their children and themselves and of strengthening community bonds. By 1920 there were at least 54 language schools in California, with 2,000 pupils; by 1928 there were more than 4,000 pupils in 118 language schools. The schools continued to play an important role until the 1940s. Not surprisingly, the schools played an important part in the lives of a large number. One survey of California Japanese during the Great Depression found that about 70 percent had attended language schools. These schools received the venomous attention of nativists. Anti-Japanese exclusionists vigorously attacked the schools as centers of emperor worship and Buddhism aimed at making children disloyal to the United States. The California legislature passed a bill, fortunately vetoed by the governor, abolishing the schools. The exclusionists' stereotyped view of these schools was sharply out of touch with reality.[66]

By the 1930s Japanese Americans were making great strides in public education, from the primary grades to the college level, in spite of entrenched opposition. For example, at several branches of the University of California the ratio of Japanese students there to the Japanese population was a little greater than the figure for the total California population. A 1930 survey of a large number of Japanese in California showed the average educational level for Japanese males over 20 years of age born in the United States to be 12.5 years. The proportion with some college work was quite high. Female figures were also relatively high. Their educational attainments were equal to those of whites.[67]

The war evacuation intervened to interrupt sharply these educational attainments. Students were forced to leave public schools. Americanization schools were provided in the prison camps during World War II. Many second- and third-generation Japanese Americans got part of their schooling in the camps. Pressures in the direction of loyalty and superpatriotism were great in these classes held behind barbed wire. Some Nisei were released from the camps to attend selected colleges, usually church colleges, providing a basis for postwar success. After the war, educational discrimination against the Japanese relaxed further, so that major gains continued to be made. Enrollment in Japanese language schools gradually declined, though many were still functioning in the late 1970s, and public schools became ever more central to Japanese education.

By 1970 the median educational levels for Japanese American males and females (adults) were 12.6 and 12.4 years, respectively, compared to a combined national figure of 12.1 years. The proportion of Japanese Americans who had completed high school and college was larger than the proportion of the population as a whole; and school enrollments were also higher. Between 1970 and 1980 the level of Japanese educational attainment increased further. In 1960 the proportion of Japanese American youths (aged 20 to 24) completing high school was 89 percent, well above the white figure of 69 percent. By the late 1970s the Japanese American figure was close to 100 percent, higher than the white figure of just under 90 percent. The same dramatic pattern can also be seen in college completion figures. By the late 1970s well over half of Japanese American males and over one-third of females aged 25 to 29 had completed college, compared with one-third of white males and one-quarter of white females.[68]

Yet the educational picture also contains more than a few traces of discrimination. For example, Japanese Americans continue to be underrepresented in graduate programs and faculty positions at the University of California. Further, while Japanese Americans make up a representative proportion of administrators and teachers in the Department of Education in Hawaii, they remain underrepresented on the faculty of the University of Hawaii. And the education levels of Japanese Americans are higher than those of the white population, though their income levels are lower than one would predict on this basis. One major study showed that in the mid-1970s Japanese American males with college degrees had median incomes that were less than those of comparably educated whites. The financial payoffs of college vary according to race and ethnicity.[69]

RELIGION

Japanese immigrants brought Buddhism and Shintoism with them as they crossed the Pacific, religious traditions which remained strong in the United States. Those who immigrated brought religious tolerance to the United States; many became practicing Protestants, while at the same time retaining elements of Buddhism or Shintoism.

Once the Japanese had arrived in the United States, Protestant missionaries played an important role in converting many to Christian beliefs. The Protestant missions provided support for immigrants establishing themselves in a difficult environment. They have also been seen as crucibles of acculturation in which young Japanese Americans began to absorb the language and values of the core culture. When the missions grew in size they became full-scale Japanese Protestant churches segregated from other churches. By the 1920s there were thousands of practicing Japanese Protestants in California.[70]

Buddhist temples were founded in all major coastal cities in the decade after 1900. By 1920 there were two dozen temples in the West, with an active membership of approximately nine thousand. Buddhist groups made significant adaptations to the new environment, with Christian-type Sunday schools and church organization. In a fashion similar to their reaction to the Japanese language schools, exclusionists made the grossly exaggerated claim that the temples were hotbeds of emperor worship and antipatriotic teaching. Buddhism does not even involve emperor worship.[71]

A survey of Japanese Californians in the 1930s found that while three-quarters of first-generation immigrants were Buddhist, only 39 percent of the second generation were. A bare majority among the Nisei were Christian. Gradually, the Japanese were becoming a Christian group. Another study in Seattle in the 1930s found the Japanese community there roughly split between Christian churches and traditional Japanese religious groups. Yet the division was not as great as it might have appeared on the surface. Adoption of Christian practices did not entail a full break with the past, for many considered themselves both Christian and Buddhist. Indeed, Japanese American Christian churches have utilized a large measure of the traditional beliefs in their ethical teaching.[72]

Just before and during World War II there was again jingoistic agitation against Buddhism and Shintoism, branding them un-American linkages to the Japanese state and emperor. The evacuation closed churches on the mainland; Buddhist temples were closed in Hawaii, where priests were imprisoned. World War II also brought destruction to Buddhist temples; many in Los Angeles were vandalized during the war. After the war Buddhist temples grew in numbers across the United States; a few Buddhist priests even led underground movements emphasizing loyalty to Japan and sharp criticism of United States oppression, with some support among the Issei. While most Japanese Americans did not follow the militants, Buddhism did regain its important position in Japanese communities. Some Japanese Americans also joined metaphysical movements brought from Japan, such as the Sokka-Gakkai, though that movement eventually became predominantly white in membership.[73]

By 1980 there were several dozen Protestant churches in the Japanese Southern California Ministerial Fellowship, with numerous others scattered up and down the West Coast and across the country. The Jodo Shinshu Buddhist Churches of America had many churches, together with the temples of dozens of smaller Buddhist sects. Reportedly, Japanese Americans have become somewhat less involved in churches. Yet one recent study of Japanese in San Francisco found that younger Japanese American churches were second in importance only to the family in cementing the community; two-thirds of those interviewed were at least occasional participants in church activities. Buddhist groups tended to attract older, more conservative members, while younger Japanese Americans preferred Presbyterian and Methodist churches. Petersen has argued that formal religion has been less important than the broad Japanese *ethical* background tied in with that religion, with its emphasis on respect, industry, and community and its ability to foster the cohesion and moral strength of Japanese American communities.[74]

ASSIMILATION?

At the turn of the century Euro-American nativists worried about the desirability of the new immigrant groups assimilating. Contemporary assimilationists, both Japanese and some white leaders, disagreed with the nativists, arguing for the rapid cultural adaptation of the Japanese.

An assimilation perspective, moreover, has predominated in much analysis of Japanese Americans over the last few decades. Japanese Americans have been seen as the most adaptive of non-European immigrant groups. Particularly important for the assimilationist position is the view that most Japanese immigrants entered voluntarily. Cultural assimilation came at an early point for most of the Issei, although some acculturated more rapidly than others. Modell has suggested distinguishing two groups of the Issei. One group sought to survive by isolating themselves from the outside world and immersing themselves as much as possible in things Japanese; the other group sought to acculturate rapidly, at the same time maintaining their social, and some cultural, ties.[75]

Cultural assimilation, particularly in regard to language and religion, came more rapidly for later generations. Thus in one survey, although most Issei reported they could get along in English, many also reported that they had some language difficulty in communicating even with the Sansei. On other cultural dimensions many Issei have made even fewer concessions. The influence of the Issei in the Japanese community context has been wide-ranging, while their ability to cope in core culture contexts has been narrowly restricted. The Nisei have equally wide-ranging adaptive patterns in the two spheres. Several studies of the Sansei have underscored the apparent closing of the gap with the outside white culture. For example, in a 1969 study Feagin and Fujitaki found that Nisei and Sansei respondents showed substantial acculturation in regard to speaking English at home, not reading Japanese literature, and not feeling it was essential to maintain Japanese traditions.[76]

Acculturation for the Japanese has in some ways been less difficult because of a rough similarity in certain Japanese and core culture values. Certain traditional Japanese values (such as *enryo*, the deferential or self-denying behavior in a variety of situations, and the ancient Buddhist-Confucian ethic of hard work aimed at individual honor and the success of the group) have been useful for the Japanese operating in the United States context. *Enryo* was useful in coping with oppression and bears some similarity to the Protestant Ethic. As a result, Japanese Americans have sometimes been viewed as "just like whites" in many ways. Yet the basic values are still fundamentally Japanese. In this sense, then, complete acculturation has not been fully attained. What appears to be Anglo-conformity acculturation may not always be so.[77]

Structural Assimilation

Structural assimilation at secondary levels has been dramatic for the Japanese, particularly in the economic sphere. Many analysts have dramatized this particular aspect of the assimilation process. Petersen, for example, has argued that Japanese Americans represent a remarkable success story in the economic progress they have made against intense discrimination. Economic mobility has been incredible; high levels of occupation, income, and education are characteristic of the Nisei and even more characteristic of the Sansei. Explanations for this success have tended to focus on Japanese values, ethical background, and community organization. For example, Light has opted for a traditional culture explanation in examining the proliferation of successful adventures in the small business economy in the United States. He has argued that the development of the small business economy among the Japanese sets them apart from other non-European Americans such as blacks and Mexican Americans; he accents the role of a "culturally preferred style of economic organization," by which he means the rotating credit associations brought over with the immigrants from Japan. Assimilation-oriented analysts have underscored the mobility of the Japanese.[78]

What Gordon refers to as behavior-receptional assimilation and attitude-receptional assimilation showed little change until after World War II, when significant changes seemed to be occurring. Intense discrimination and prejudice marred the lives of the Issei and Nisei for the first fifty years of the Japanese experience in the United States. Since World War II, discrimination and prejudice directed at Japanese Americans has decreased, the latter more than the former. The fact that ideal adaptation has not been reached in these areas was pointed up in the 1969 study of Feagin and Fujitaki. While a majority of the respondents reported not having experienced discrimination in a variety of areas, including housing and social activities, yet substantial minorities, 20 to 43 percent, reported significant discrimination in these areas; more Sansei than Nisei reported discrimination.[79]

Assimilation at the level of primary social ties and voluntary associations is an important dimension; for the Japanese this assimilation has not proceeded nearly as far as integration in the economic sphere. The Issei often immigrated under the auspices of family members already in the United States. Employment and small business contacts were their main contacts with the non-Japanese; most remained isolated socially, in part because of discrimination. In recent decades, the still-surviving Issei have tended, much more than later generations, to reside in extended families and localize their ties within Japanese networks. A number of researchers have found that integration with outsiders, at the primary-group level, has been limited for the Nisei and modest for the Sansei. One study of 148 Japanese males looked at the primary-group level. Two-thirds had mostly Japanese as close friends; and the Sansei were only slightly more integrated with whites than were the Nisei. However, majorities in both groups reported they lived in neighborhoods where 50 percent or more of their neighbors were white. According to a major study of Japanese Americans by Montero and associates, the proportion of Japanese Americans living in heavily Japanese neighborhoods declined from 1915 to 1967. By the late 1960s over half lived in predominantly non-Japanese neighborhoods, while 40 percent lived in mixed neighborhoods. Residential segregation has declined for these Asian Americans.[80]

In their study Feagin and Fujitaki found that only a minority of the Nisei and Sansei samples preferred that their children associate only with other Japanese; most preferred mixed associations. Data since the 1960s suggest a slow movement in the direction of primary group assimilation. There does seem to be an increased movement among the Sansei into wider social circles; yet they prefer if possible to maintain numerous social ties within their own Japanese American sphere.[81]

Until the late 1940s antimiscegenation laws in western states made Asian-European marriages illegal. Aside from the Japanese war brides of returning European American soldiers, there was almost no intermarriage with outsiders until the last decade. Los Angeles data showed an out-marriage rate of 2 percent in the 1924–1933 period and a rate of 11 to 20 percent for the 1950s. Several surveys in the 1950s and 1960s showed strong but declining preferences among the Nisei and the Sansei for Japanese marriage partners. In 1967 a national survey of the Sansei discovered that one-third had out-married or were planning to out-marry, while more localized studies based on studies of marriage licenses in Los Angeles and Fresno counties found the proportions out-marrying to be closer to half. A study of the Sansei in Sacramento in the 1970s found that only 28 percent of marriages in the decade surveyed had involved non-Japanese. Studies in other cities have found higher figures—up to half—for the 1970s. By the 1970s the out-marriage rate for the Sansei may have been on the rise.[82]

Japanese Identity

When it comes to identificational assimilation, there is little doubt that few Japanese have rejected their Japanese heritage for a purely "American" identity. The sense of "Japaneseness" has been strong in all generations. Most have seen themselves as having a foot in both worlds. Feagin and Fujitaki found more than 60 percent of the Sansei and more than 80 percent of the Nisei saying they were *very proud* of their Japanese background. Indeed, in recent years some of the Sansei and Yonsei have developed a renewed interest in that heritage, to the extent of a few activists emphasizing a "yellow power" militancy.[83]

An assimilationist might well see the Japanese as well on the road to comprehensive assimilation to the outside white culture and society. On major levels there has been some movement in the direction of greater integration and inclusion, though candor would require an assimilationist to contrast the substantial integration in such areas as the economy with the more modest integration at the primary-group level.

Japanese Americans might also be viewed as a clear-cut example of ethnogenesis—partly in but partly outside the dominant white culture and society. No analyst has developed this perspective on Japanese Americans, although Petersen has argued that Japanese Americans have become a "subnation" in the United States, achieving integration in the economic sphere and making some cultural adaptation, but maintaining a distinctive and cohesive, family-centered community. Indeed, Connor's research study of three generations of Japanese Americans in Sacramento suggests the persistence of Japanese ways. Connor found that the third generation (the Sansei) still had many psychological and family traits that were characteristic of the first generation (the Issei). The Sansei had a greater sense of duty and obligation, closer family ties, and a greater tendency to be deferential than whites also surveyed. Changes were occurring in the acculturation direction, but there was substantial persistence of "Japaneseness" as well.[84]

A Power-Conflict View

Few analysts have interpreted the Japanese American experience systematically from a power-conflict point of view. One leading power-conflict thinker mentioned in Chapter 2, Robert Blauner, has suggested that Japanese Americans might be viewed as partially colonized. Many early Japanese immigrants worked in a position of debt servitude or came under substantial coercive pressure to migrate to the United States. This was particularly the case for thousands of contract laborers who went to Hawaii and later moved on to the mainland.

Lucie Cheng Hirata and Edna Bonacich have underscored the intimate economic relationship between the labor needs of capitalism and the streams of immigrant workers employed over the centuries in the United States. Asian labor filled the needs of a booming frontier capitalism on the West Coast. Chinese and Japanese laborers became the "colored" labor, with fewer rights than their white counterparts. The United States was an imperial power in the Pacific region; as a result, U.S. agents had easy entry into Asian countries and could more or less dictate treaties and labor agreements benefiting U.S. employers. U.S. capitalists actively recruited Asian laborers because they could be made to work for very low wages, wages for which European Americans would not work. U.S. employers thus had the backing of their government in securing cheap labor from countries such as Japan and China where the United States had the greatest influence. Neither China nor Japan had the clout that European nations had to protect immigrant workers. And from the U.S. capitalists' point of view immigrant labor is usually cheaper and more docile than local labor. Moreover, the Japanese immigrants could not become citizens under U.S. law, so they could easily be excluded if they later became "unsuitable" to West Coast employers.[85]

In the beginning Japanese Americans were often forced, by means of severe racially motivated discrimination to become cheap laborers in the fields, in much the same way as Mexicans were forced into this work. The alien labor laws barring land ownership for Issei, the complete exclusion of Japanese immigrants in 1924 on the grounds of race, and the massive imprisonment in World War II underscore the forcible semicolonial treatment that Japanese Americans—unlike virtually all European immigrant groups—have endured. Their structural experiences were not the same as those of most European immigrants on whose experience the assimilation models are usually grounded.

Acculturation might be viewed a bit differently in a systematic power-conflict analysis. The pressures to acculturate were coercive. Commitment to some cultural assimilation in Japanese communities can be seen as a reaction to *severe* white discrimination. By the 1910s and 1920s numerous Japanese American leaders were exhorting their constituents to be exemplary in their hard work and deference in order to command some acceptance of dominant groups. Once in the public schools, the acculturation pressures took the form of attacks on the Japanese cultural heritage. Japanese Americans, while in some ways the most integrated of non-Europeans, have many experiences essentially similar to the forcible exploitation of blacks, Mexicans, and Native Americans.

Some recent analysts have been quite critical of assimilationist perspectives. They have not as yet, however, developed a systematic alternative to put in its place. Some have raised questions about the origins of the assimilation model itself. For example, Takagi argues that the assimilation theory of Robert Park and other early social scientists emerged in a period of intense agitation over Japanese immigration and reflected their sometimes *racist* views of the Japanese. Defending against charges of a group's unassimilability even led some assimilationists to Euro-centric views of Japanese culture, views which have persisted into present-day theorizing.

Paramount among the weaknesses recently attacked in the assimilation perspective has been the success stereotype. The success of Japanese Americans, seen as rooted in their values and family styles, has been cited by numerous writers as a paramount "bootstraps" example of what other nonwhites, particularly blacks and Mexicans, could be if they would only conform to these patterns. Stereotyping that sees the Japanese as representing an Asian Horatio Alger story and as paragons of hard-working, docile, non-rocking-the-boat virtues carries a negative undercurrent. Critics of this cultural background interpretation have noted a number of other factors as important in shaping Japanese economic success: the role of the Japanese government in supporting immigrants, the availability of a ghettoized small business niche on the West Coast, and the effect of intense racial discrimination in the surrounding environment in forging group solidarity.

Bonacich has pointed out the distinctive character of this response to discrimination. Japanese Americans created small businesses to serve one another and the basic economic needs of a frontier economy. This hostile situation fostered a situation where both Japanese employers and employees saw themselves as a single "class" versus the outside world. Out of dire economic necessity, employers and employees, often with kinship or regional ties worked together against white competitors. Success came at the price of being ghettoized in the small business economy (as a "middleman minority") and, later, in certain professions. As with Jewish Americans, Japanese Americans have "made it" as a group in American society in a distinctive way, a process of adaptation not in line with idealistic assimilation models. Thus the long-term effects of past discrimination are still reflected in the concentration of Japanese Americans in the small business economy and in certain professional occupations.[86]

A recent study of minority-owned businesses found that most of those owned by Asian Americans were in retail trade (such as grocery stores and restaurants) and selected services (such as laundries). Gross annual receipts were $9,000 to $12,000 for the majority of Japanese firms, those with no paid employees. Research in the 1970s also revealed that Japanese Americans do not get as much payoff from their relatively high levels of education as do comparably educated whites. One study found that Japanese American males with four years or more of college earned only 83 percent of the incomes of white males with similar educations. For Asian American females the disparity was even worse. And these discriminatory effects were found at lower income levels as well.[87]

Smaller oppressed groups, it seems, have a better chance of establishing an *economic niche,* where they go because of widespread prejudice and discrimination, but where they can also attain some measure of success, particularly in an expanding economy. Such niches are not as readily available to larger oppressed groups, such as black Americans.

Takagi has pointed to another bias in the traditional cultural background explanation of Japanese American success: the idea that those race/ethnic groups with values closest to the dominant groups' culture are the ones who will be, and should be, successful. In this sense, success is evaluated only in terms of values prized by the dominant white culture. While Japanese Americans have acculturated in numerous ways, the price paid in conformity and lost creativity has been very great. [88]

SUMMARY

Japanese Americans are a distinctive non-European group. In the beginning, they were a severely exploited minority. Many entered as laborers, facing violence and intense discrimination. They endured complete exclusion as a result of immigration legislation. They endured laws against land ownership. They suffered the only large-scale imprisionment of U.S. citizens in concentration camps. Against these terrible odds, they moved up. Here is a non-European group whose economic mobility has been remarkable. Yet, for all their acculturation and economic assimilation, Japanese Americans have a way to go before they are fully included in North American society. Whether they will be the first non-European group to be fully included, politically and socially, as well as economically, in the dominant white culture and society yet remains to be seen.

It is important for students of racial and ethnic relations to realize that the success story of Japanese Americans is partially myth. Past and present, Japanese Americans have suffered from neglect by government and from discrimination in the private sector. Far fewer Japanese Americans than whites can fully realize the earnings levels that parallel their education levels. Few rise high in Fortune 500 corporations or in many government agencies. In general, they have been neglected by insensitive state and federal government officials. For example, recently Lionell Van Deerlin, California representative and head of the House Subcommittee on Communications, commented that Asian Americans did not need to be considered a disadvantaged minority group because they were "more prosperous than [majority] Americans." Yet in the communications industry, as of that date (1979), there was not one television or radio station owned by a Japanese or other Asian American; and a survey of four San Francisco television stations showed that Asian American males were underrepresented, relative to their proportions in the local labor force, at three of them. These data suggest that Japanese and other Asian Americans have not yet achieved equal opportunity in the communications industry or in many other American industries. In spite of hard work and impressive achievements, this so-called "model minority" continues to suffer discrimination and deprivation.[89]

NOTES

[1]Roger Daniels, *The Politics of Prejudice* (New York: Atheneum, 1969), pp. 3–6; Hilary Conroy, *The Japanese Frontier in Hawaii, 1868–1898* (Berkeley: University of California Press, 1953), passim.

[2]See the Supreme Court decisions *Gong Lum v. Rice,* 275 U.S. 172 (1927), and *Chae Chang Ping v. U.S.,* 130 U.S. 1068 (1889).

[3]U.S. Immigration and Naturalization Service, *1975 Annual Report* (Washington, D.C.: U.S. Government Printing Office, 1975), pp. 62–66.

[4]Arinori Mori, *The Japanese in America* (Japan Advertiser Press, 1926), pp. 19–21; Kaizo Naka, *Social and Economic Conditions Among Japanese Farmers in California* (San Francisco: R and E Research Associates, 1974), p. 6; John Modell, "On Being an Issei: Orientations Toward America" (Paper presented at American Anthropological Association, San Diego, Calif., November 1970), p. 4.

[5]Daniels, *The Politics of Prejudice,* pp. 21–44.

[6]T. Iyenago, *Japan and the California Problem* (New York: G. P. Putnam's Sons, 1921), pp. 100–106; Roger Daniels, "Japanese Immigrants on the Western Frontier: The Issei in California, 1890–1940," in *East Across the Pacific,* ed. Hilary Conroy and T. Scott Miyakawa (Santa Barbara, Calif.: ABC–CLIO Press, 1972), pp. 82–86; V. S. McClatchy, *Japanese Immigration and Colonization* (San Francisco: R and E Research Associates, 1970), pp. 42–44; Kiyo Sue Inui, *The Unsolved Problem of the Pacific* (Japan: Japan Times, 1925).

[7]Jacobus tenBroek, Edward N. Barnhart, and Floyd W. Matson, *Prejudice, War, and the Constitution* (Berkeley: University of California Press, 1968), pp. 42–43; *Takao Ozawa v. United States,* 260 U.S. 178 (1922).

[8]Hilary Conroy and T. Scott Miyakawa, "Foreword," in Conroy and Miyakawa, *East Across the Pacific,* pp. xiv-xv.

[9]The statistics are from U.S. Census publications.

[10]E. Manchester-Boddy, *Japanese in America* (San Francisco: R and E Associates, 1970), pp. 25–30.

[11]McClatchy, *Japanese Immigration and Colonization*, p. 42.

[12]Sidney L. Gulick, *The American Japanese Problem* (New York: Charles Scribner's Sons, 1914), p. 16.

[13]Quoted in Edward K. Strong, Jr., *The Second-Generation Japanese Problem* (Stanford, Calif.: Stanford University Press, 1934), p. 133.

[14]tenBroek et al., *Prejudice, War, and the Constitution*, pp. 26–28; Carey McWilliams, *Prejudice* (Boston: Little, Brown and Co., 1944), pp. 30–45; Dennis M. Ogawa, *From Japs to Japanese* (Berkeley: McCutchan Publishing Co., 1971), pp. 16–19.

[15]tenBroek et al., *Prejudice, War, and the Constitution*, p. 31; Haynes is quoted in Strong, *The Second-Generation Japanese Problem*, p. 145.

[16]Ogawa, *From Japs to Japanese*, p. 12; Carey McWilliams, *Brothers Under the Skin*, rev. ed. (Boston: Little, Brown and Co., 1964), pp. 148–49; Stanley Sue and Harry H. L. Kitano, "Stereotypes as a Measure of Success," *Journal of Social Issues* 29 (1973): 83–98.

[17]Ogawa, *From Japs to Japanese*, p. 13; Strong, *The Second-Generation Japanese Problem*, p. 150.

[18]C. N. Reynolds, "Oriental-White Race Relations in Santa Clara County, California" (Ph.D. dissertation, Stanford University, 1927); E. S. Bogardus, "Social Distance: A Measuring Stick," *Survey* 56 (1927): 169 ff. Both are cited in Strong, *The Second-Generation Japanese Problem*, pp. 109, 128.

[19]tenBroek et al., *Prejudice, War, and the Constitution*, pp. 69–70.

[20]Quoted in Ogawa, *From Japs to Japanese*, p. 11.

[21]U.S. War Relocation Authority, Department of the Interior, *Myths and Facts About the Japanese-American* (Washington, D.C.: U.S. Government Printing Office, 1945), pp. 7–8; Ogawa, *From Japs to Japanese*, pp. 35–54. Survey data document the attitude changes, 1942–1961; Roger Daniels, "Why It Happened Here," in *The Social Reality of Ethnic America*, ed. R. Gomez et al. (Lexington: D.C. Health, 1971), p. 236.

[22]Council on Interracial Books for Children, *Stereotypes, Distortions and Omissions in U.S. History Textbooks* (New York: Racism and Sexism Resource Center for Educators, 1977), pp. 42–46.

[23]Herbert B. Johnson, *Discrimination Against the Japanese in California* (Berkeley: Courier Publishing Co., 1907), pp. 73–74; Daniels, *The Politics of Prejudice*, pp. 33–34; Howard H. Sugimoto, "The Vancouver Riots of 1907: A Canadian Episode," in Conroy and Miyakawa, *East Across the Pacific*, pp. 92–110.

[24]Jean Pajus, *The Real Japanese California* (San Francisco: R and E Associates, 1971), pp. 164–66; Daniels, *The Politics of Prejudice*, p. 87; tenBroek et al., *Prejudice, War, and the Constitution*, p. 73.

[25]Lemuel F. Ignacio, *Asian Americans and Pacific Islanders* (San Jose, Calif.: Pilipino Development Associates, 1976), pp. 95–96; tenBroek et al., *Prejudice, War, and the Constitution*, passim.

[26]Dorothy Swaine Thomas and Richard S. Nishimoto, *The Spoilage* (Berkeley: University of California Press, 1946), pp. 5–10; tenBroek et al., *Prejudice, War, and the Constitution*, pp. 82–84.

[27]Thomas and Nishimoto, *The Spoilage*, pp. 8–16; tenBroek et al., *Prejudice, War, and the Constitution*, pp. 118–20.

[28]tenBroek et al., *Prejudice, War, and the Constitution*, pp. 120, 126–29, 130; Thomas and Nishimoto, *The Spoilage*, pp. 10–20; Edward H. Spicer et al., *Impounded People* (Tucson: University of Arizona Press, 1969), pp. 141–241.

[29]Thomas and Nishimoto, *The Spoilage*, pp. 54–71; tenBroek et al., *Prejudice, War, and the Constitution*, pp. 126–32, 149–55; Spicer et al., *Impounded People*, pp. 252–80.

[30]Leonard Bloom and Ruth Riemer, *Removal and Return* (Berkeley: University of California Press, 1949), pp. 124–57, 198–204; tenBroek et al., *Prejudice, War, and the Constitution*, pp. 155–77, 180–81.

[31]Bradford Smith, *Americans from Japan* (New York: Lippincott, 1948), pp. 10–12, 202–76; McWilliams, *Prejudice*, p. 4; tenBroek et al., *Prejudice, War, and the Constitution*, pp. 211–23; Harry H. L. Kitano, *Japanese Americans*, 2d ed. (Englewood Cliffs, N.J.: Prentice-Hall 1976),

pp. 82–88; S. Frank Miyamoto, "The Forced Evacuation of the Japanese Minority during World War II," *Journal of Social Issues* 29 (1973): 11–29.

[32]Kitano, *Japanese Americans*, p. 73.

[33]Gary Y. Okihiro, "Japanese Resistance in America's Concentration Camps: A Re-evaluation," *Amerasia Journal* 2 (Fall 1973): 20–34; Arthur A. Hansen and David A. Hacker, "The Manzanar Riot: An Ethnic Perspective," *Amerasia Journal* 2 (Fall 1974): 112–42. See also Roger Daniels, *Concentration Camps, U.S.A.* (New York: Holt, Rinehart, and Winston, 1971); Thomas and Nishimoto, *The Spoilage*, pp. 113 ff.

[34]Daniels, "Japanese Immigrants on the Western Frontier," pp. 80–81; Inui, *The Unsolved Problem of the Pacific*, pp. 291–332.

[35]Daniels, *The Politics of Prejudice*, pp. 104–105.

[36]Ivan H. Light, *Ethnic Enterprise in America* (Berkeley: University of California Press, 1972), pp. 174–79; Bill Hosokawa, *The Nisei* (New York: William Morrow, 1969), pp. 199–200; Kitano, *Japanese Americans*, pp. 55–58.

[37]Hosokawa, *The Nisei*, pp. 439–46; Kitano, *Japanese Americans*, pp. 89–90.

[38]Hosokawa, *The Nisei*, pp. 452–55.

[39]Rodolfo Acuña, *Occupied America* (San Francisco: Canfield Press, 1972), pp. 212–13.

[40]Kitano, *Japanese Americans*, pp. 174–86; Daniel Inouye and Lawrence Elliot, *Journey to Washington* (Englewood Cliffs, N.J.: Prentice-Hall, 1967), pp. 248–50; Hosokawa, *The Nisei*, pp. 460–69.

[41]Hosokawa, *The Nisei*, pp. 486–87.

[42]Daniels, *The Politics of Prejudice*, pp. 23–24.

[43]Yuji Ichioka, "A Buried Past," *Amerasia Journal* 1 (July 1971): 1–25; Karl Yoneda, "100 Years of Japanese Labor History in the U.S.A.," in *Roots*, ed. Amy Tachiki et al. (Los Angeles: UCLA Asian American Studies Center, 1971), pp. 150–57; Carey McWilliams, *North from Mexico* (New York: Greenwood Press, 1968), p. 190.

[44]Kitano, *Japanese Americans*, pp. 55–58.

[45]See the various articles in Tachiki (ed.), *Roots*.

[46]Cited in Gulick, *The American Japanese Problem*, p. 11.

[47]Japanese Association of the Pacific Northwest, *Japanese Immigration* (San Francisco: R and E Associates, 1972), pp. 22–25.

[48]Ibid.; Daniels, *The Politics of Prejudice*, pp. 7, 10–12.

[49]Kitano, *Japanese Americans*, pp. 21–24.

[50]Ibid., pp. 19–21; Light, *Ethnic Enterprise in America*, pp. 27–29; S. Frank Miyamoto "An Immigrant Community in America," in Conroy and Miyakawa, *East Across the Pacific*, pp. 223–25.

[51]Gulick, *The American Japanese Problem*, pp. 11, 32–33; Light, *Ethnic Enterprise in America*, p. 71; Daniels, "Japanese Immigrants on the Western Frontier," p. 85.

[52]Pajus, *The Real Japanese California*, pp. 147–51; Light, *Ethnic Enterprise in America*, p. 76.

[53]Bloom and Riemer, *Removal and Return*, pp. 115–17.

[54]Strong, *The Second-Generation Japanese Problem*, pp. 209–11; Pajus, *The Real Japanese California*, pp. 189–95.

[55]Bloom and Riemer, *Removal and Return*, pp. 17–20.

[56]Ibid., pp. 44, 144; Kitano, *Japanese Americans*, pp. 91, 97; Forrest E. LaViolette, *Americans of Japanese Ancestry* (Toronto: Canadian Institute of International Affairs, 1945), pp. 162–67.

[57]Al Erickson, "L. A.'s Nisei Today," *California Sun Magazine* (Summer 1968): 3, cited in Kitano, *Japanese Americans*, p. 95; Edna Bonacich, "Small Business and Japanese American Ethnic Solidarity," *Amerasia Journal* 3 (Summer 1975): 101.

[58]U.S. Bureau of the Census, *Population, 1960: Nonwhite Population by Race* (Washington, D.C.: U.S. Government Printing Office, 1963), p. 108. The "occupation not reported" data have been excluded for the purpose of calculating percentages. The 1970 data are from U.S. Department of Health, Education, and Welfare, *A Study of Selected Socio-economic Characteristics*

of Ethnic Minorities Based on the 1970 Census (Washington, D.C.: U.S. Government Printing Office, 1974), p. 83.

[59]U.S. Commission on Civil Rights, *Social Indicators of Equality for Minorities and Women* (Washington, D.C.: U.S. Government Printing Office, 1978), pp. 42–45.

[60]U.S. Department of Health, Education, and Welfare, *A Study of Selected Socio-economic Characteristics,* pp. 105–108; see also Gene N. Levine and Darrel M. Montero, "Socioeconomic Mobility Among Three Generations of Japanese Americans," *Journal of Social Issues* 29 (1973): 33 ff; U.S. Commission on Civil Rights, *Social Indicators of Equality for Minorities and Women,* pp. 48–54.

[61]The studies are cited in U.S. Commission on Civil Rights, *Success of Asian Americans: Fact or Fiction?* (Washington, D.C.: U.S. Government Printing Office, 1980), pp. 14–15.

[62]Kitano, *Japanese Americans,* pp. 92–93, 95; Levine and Montero, "Socioeconomic Mobility," pp. 45 ff; Dale Minami, "Testimony to U.S. Commission on Civil Rights," in *Civil Rights Issues of Asian and Pacific Americans* (Washington, D.C.: U.S. Commission on Civil Rights, 1979), pp. 420–22; "Asian Americans: A 'Model Minority,' " *Newsweek,* December 6, 1982, p. 41.

[63]K. K. Kawakami, *The Japanese Question* (New York: Macmillan, 1921), pp. 143–45; John Modell, "Tradition and Opportunity: The Japanese Immigrant in America," *Pacific Historical Review* 40 (May 1971): 163–82.

[64]Johnson, *Discrimination Against the Japanese in California,* pp. 3–20, 40–47; Franklin Hichborn, *The Story of the Session of the California Legislature of 1909* (San Francisco: James H. Barry Press, 1909), p. 207; Pajus, *The Real Japanese California,* pp. 170–78; Kawakami, *The Japanese Question,* pp. 168–69.

[65]Pajus, *The Real Japanese California,* pp. 180–81; Kawakami, *The Japanese Question,* pp. 162–63.

[66]William Petersen, *Japanese Americans* (New York: Random House, 1971), p. 183; Strong, *The Second-Generation Japanese Problem,* pp. 201–204; Kawakami, *The Japanese Question,* pp. 146–51; Pajus, *The Real Japanese California,* p. 181.

[67]Pajus, *The Real Japanese California,* p. 183; Strong, *The Second-Generation Japanese Problem,* pp. 185–88.

[68]U.S. Department of Health, Education, and Welfare, *A Study of Selected Socio-economic Characteristics,* pp. 70 ff; U.S. Commission on Civil Rights, *Social Indicators of Equality for Minorities and Women,* pp. 12–14.

[69]Kitano, *Japanese Americans,* pp. 93, 174–75; U.S. Commission on Civil Rights, *Social Indicators of Equality for Minorities and Women,* pp. 24–26.

[70]Ibid., p. 60; E. Manchester Boddy, *Japanese in America* (San Francisco: R and E Associates, 1970), p. 118.

[71]Petersen, *Japanese Americans,* p. 177; Boddy, *Japanese in America,* pp. 114–18.

[72]Strong, *The Second-Generation Japanese Problem,* p. 229; Shotaro Frank Miyamoto, "Social Solidarity Among the Japanese in Seattle," *University of Washington Publications in Social Sciences* 11 (December 1939): 99–102; Petersen, *Japanese Americans,* pp. 174–75.

[73]Andrew W. Lind, *Hawaii's Japanese* (Princeton, N.J.: Princeton University Press, 1946), pp. 212–57; Petersen, *Japanese Americans,* pp. 177–78, 185.

[74]Hosokawa, *The Nisei,* p. 131; Kitano, *Japanese Americans,* p. 115; Christie Kiefer, *Changing Cultures, Changing Lives* (San Francisco: Jossey-Bass, 1974), pp. 34–38; Petersen, *Japanese Americans,* p. 187; Bruce Iwasaki, "Response and Change for the Asian in America," in Tachiki, *Roots,* pp. 89–98.

[75]Modell, "On Being an Issei," pp. 1–2, 19–20.

[76]John Modell, "The Japanese American Family: A Perspective for Future Investigations," *Pacific Historical Review* 37 (February 1968): 79; Joe R. Feagin and Nancy Fujitaki, "On the Assimilation of Japanese Americans," *Amerasia Journal* 1 (February 1972): 15–17; Abe Arkoff, "Need Patterns in Two Generations of Japanese-Americans in Hawaii," *Journal of Social Psychology* 50 (1959): 75–79.

[77]Feagin and Fujitaki, "On the Assimilation of Japanese Americans," pp. 13–30; Kitano, *Japanese Americans,* pp. 121–42.

[78]Petersen, *Japanese Americans*, pp. 6–7; Light, *Ethnic Enterprise in America*, passim; William Caudill, "Japanese American Personality and Acculturation," *Genetic Psychology Monographies* 45 (1952): 3–102.

[79]Feagin and Fujitaki, "On the Assimilation of Japanese Americans," pp. 20–21.

[80]Darrel Montero, *Japanese Americans: Changing Patterns of Ethnic Affiliation over Three Generations* (Boulder, Colo.: Westview Press, 1980), p. 80; Petersen, *Japanese Americans*, pp. 220–24; Modell, "The Japanese American Family," pp. 76–79; Kitano, *Japanese Americans*, pp. 189, 196; George Kagiwada, "Assimilation of Nisei in Los Angeles," in Conroy and Miyakawa, *East Across the Pacific*, p. 273.

[81]Feagin and Fujitaki, "On the Assimilation of Japanese Americans," p. 23.

[82]Akemi Kikumura and Harry H. L. Kitano, "Interracial Marriage: A Picture of Japanese Americans," *Journal of Social Issues* 29 (1973): 67–81; Gene N. Levine and Darrel M. Montero, "Socioeconomic Mobility Among Three Generations of Japanese Americans," *Journal of Social Issues* 29 (1973): 47; John N. Tinker, "Intermarriage and Ethnic Boundaries: The Japanese American Case," *Journal of Social Issues* 29 (1973): 55; Akemi Kikumura and Harry H. L. Kitano, "Interracial Marriage," *Journal of Social Issues* 29 (1973): 69; John W. Connor, *Tradition and Change in Three Generations of Japanese Americans* (Chicago: Nelson-Hall, 1977), p. 308.

[83]Modell, "The Japanese American Family," pp. 80–81; Caudill, "Japanese American Personality and Acculturation"; Feagin and Fujitaki, "On the Assimilation of Japanese Americans," pp. 25–26.

[84]William Petersen, *Japanese Americans* (New York: Random House, 1971), pp. 214–21. Connor, *Tradition and Change in Three Generations of Japanese Americans*, pp. 304–308.

[85]Lucie Cheng Hirata and Edna Bonacich, *Labor Immigration Under Capitalism: Asian Immigrant Workers in the United States before World War II* (forthcoming).

[86]This section draws on Robert Blauner, *Racial Oppression in America* (New York: Harper & Row, 1972), p. 54–55; Paul Takagi, "The Myth of 'Assimilation in American Life,' " *Amerasia Journal* 2 (Fall 1973): 149–58; Bonacich, "Small Business and Japanese American Ethnic Solidarity," pp. 100–101; Peter Uhlenberg, "Demographic Correlates of Group Achievement: Contrasting Patterns of Mexican-Americans and Japanese-Americans," *Demography* 9, (February 1972): 119–28.

[87]Amado Cabezas, "Testimony to U.S. Commission on Civil Rights," in *Civil Rights Issues of Asian and Pacific Americans* (Washington, D.C.: U.S. Commission on Civil Rights, 1979), pp. 389–93.

[88]Takagi, "The Myth of 'Assimilation in American Life' " pp. 149–58; Ogawa, *From Jap to Japanese*, pp. 43 ff; Lowell Chun-Hoon, "Review of Ethnic Enterprise in America," *Amerasia Journal* 2 (Fall 1973): 173–79.

[89]U.S. Commission on Civil Rights, *Success of Asian Americans: Fact or Fiction?*, p. 21; Ignacio, *Asian Americans and Pacific Islanders*, pp. 119–20.

Current Issues in
Racial and Ethnic Relations
CHAPTER 12

A MELTING POT?

One image of this society has been the "melting pot." In the early 1900s Israel Zangwill made an influential statement of this idea in his popular play, *The Melting Pot*. In that play a struggling Russian immigrant vigorously argues that

> America is God's Crucible, the great Melting-Pot where all races of Europe are melting and re-forming! Here you stand, good folks, think I, when I see them at Ellis Island, here you stand in your fifty groups, with your fifty languages and histories, and your fifty blood hatreds and rivalries. But you won't be long like that, brothers, for these are the fires of God. . . . A fig for your feuds and vendettas! Germans and Frenchmen, Irishmen and Englishmen, Jews and Russians—into the Crucible with you all! God is making the American.[1]

Here is the idealistic image of the great crucible which melts divergent groups together to form the new "American blend." This is a rosy view of a mutual adaptation process in which old and new groups freely blend together on an equal basis. Yet this is a pipe dream that glosses over the reality of unequal intergroup relations in the United States. The omission of nonwhite groups such as Afro-Americans, from the boiling cauldron, just to cite one flaw, suggests how unduly optimistic the image is. The melting pot has never come to a boil.

REVIEWING RACIAL AND ETHNIC THEORIES

In previous chapters we have seen the usefulness of the assimilation perspective, particularly when the acculturation process is distinguished from structural assimilation processes. Yet our analyses in this book have revealed the need for further development of the assimilation perspective beyond its rudimentary stage. Thus a few social scientists have begun to explore a perspective which departs significantly from the traditional assimilation model in the direction of a cultural pluralism model. As we noted in Chapter 2, Greeley's ethnogenesis model incorporates features of both the traditional assimilation and cultural pluralism perspectives.

Greeley has rejected the view that homogenization is inevitable.[2] Partial "Anglo-conformity" acculturation did take place, the old immigrant cultures did change, but the white immigrant groups nevertheless became distinctive ethnic groups. The ethnic group is therefore one part host culture, one part immigrant culture, and one part unique adaptive culture. The "unique adaptive culture" refers to the distinctive customs, ways, and values that immigrant groups developed as they adapted to the core culture and society, ways fully equivalent neither to host ways nor to the ways of those at their national point of origin. Persisting cultural diversity has been documented throughout this book. Our analysis of "white ethnic" Americans in earlier chapters—the Irish, the Italians, the eastern European Jews—clearly indicates the persisting differences between these groups not just in informal social ties and intragroup marriage patterns, but also in regard to fundamental values, attitudes, and informal customs. Neither the Irish political style nor the Italian religious style nor the fierce commitment of Jewish Americans to civil liberties can be explained by a simple Anglo-conformity model of acculturation.[3]

Power-Conflict Theories

Power-conflict theory has developed in part to cope with the difficult problems encountered in applying assimilation models to groups such as black Americans. A number of authors have developed the view that conventional assimilation models are inadequate for describing what has happened to nonwhite Americans. A basic idea is that nonwhite groups were brought into the economic and political system by force. Blacks were enslaved. The conquest of North America brought Native Americans and Mexican Americans into the system by forcible annexation. This forcible incorporation began in the early stages of commercial capitalism when European powers had sailors probing into every part of the globe. A racial division of labor developed at an early point, with subordinate nonwhite groups having segregated and subordinate goals defined for them. They were not permitted to assimilate at the structural-informal level. Under duress, they were to acculturate to the dominant group's desires, language, and work values, and they were to "integrate" themselves at the lowest levels of labor in the developing capitalist system. Some surrendered their lands to the invaders, as in the case of Native Americans and the early Mexican settlers. In the initial phase of contact Asian Americans, such as the Japanese and Chinese, also did the dirty work in semislave conditions on the West Coast.[4]

Power-conflict theorists accent the point that, with the exception of some Asians, the majorities of other nonwhite groups have so far found a permanent home reserved for them at the lower levels of the economy and of the society. Some assimilationists have seen slow assimilation coming for nonwhite Americans. Eventually they will be permitted to move up into their "place in the sun." Yet power-conflict analysts underscore the persisting economic and political subordination of nonwhites. For power-conflict theories such non-European groups as Japanese Americans pose serious theoretical problems—that is, from a power-conflict point of view, how do you interpret their socio-economic success in recent decades?

Critics of power-conflict theories point out that a considerable proportion of the nonwhite groups have, in spite of centuries of labor exploitation and oppression, made it up into at least the lower echelons of middle-income America. In effect, progress that comes very slowly fits into both perspectives: assimilationists can point to the progress, while power-conflict analysts can underscore the slowness.

One area where power-conflict theory needs to probe further than it has is in regard to white ethnic groups in the United States. Power-conflict analysts can argue, with substantial evidence, that the progress and achievements of certain white groups have sometimes been exaggerated. As dramatic as they are, the success stories have a seldom-told seamy side. In a number of respects groups such as eastern European Jews still occupy "gilded ghettos." The early patterns of capitalistic exploitation and discrimination were severe enough to channel the groups into "ethnic economies," with substantial group involvement in small businesses such as groceries, restaurants, tailor shops, and junkyards. Often these distinctive niches were high-risk areas on the margins of the major sectors of the economy. To a substantial extent groups such as eastern European Jews are still disproportionately represented in their traditional employment sectors; they are by no means randomly distributed in the U.S. economy.[5]

CURRENT ISSUES AND TRENDS: IMMIGRATION

By way of conclusion we can now turn briefly to two controversial issues recently discussed in regard to race and ethnic relations in the United States. These issues can be phrased as questions: What is the scale and impact of the waves of immigrants still beating on U.S. shores? What is government affirmative action policy doing to improve the situations of nonwhite Americans? And, in regard to both questions, what is the dominant white response to these conditions and events?

Recent Immigrants: Is America Too Full?

Give me your tired, your poor,
Your huddled masses yearning to breathe free,
The wretched refuse of your teeming shore;
Send these, the homeless, tempest-tost to me,
I lift my lamp beside the golden door![6]

This is the famous inscription by poet Emma Lazarus on the Statue of Liberty in the New York City harbor. Following the light from the Statue of Liberty, and hoping its inscription means what it says, hundreds of thousands of immigrants have come to the United States in recent decades, mostly from the Americas and from Asia. The numbers of legal immigrants to the United States in the 1970s ran as follows:[7]

Mexico	625,000
Other Asia (Cambodia, Japan, etc.)	568,000
South and Central America	379,000
Philippines	349,000
Cuba	278,000
Korea	249,000
Dominican Republic and Haiti	201,000
Taiwan, Hong Kong, China	189,000
Vietnam	138,000
Jamaica	138,000

In the European migrations of the early 1900s the U.S. government and U.S. corporations played little part in generating migration from Europe. Today, however, the United States plays a political and economic role in the migration of many groups such as Mexicans, Haitians, Cubans, Vietnamese, and Koreans—at both their points of origin and their point of destination. For example, Mexican workers come to the United States seeking any kind of work so they can feed starving families back home. Yet, as we noted in Chapter 9, back at home the U.S. multinationals engaged in agribusiness for export have played an important role in driving Mexican peasants off the land and in reducing the amount of food grown for home consumption by Mexicans. Immigrants from the Caribbean, such as Haitians, face political persecution and extreme poverty at home. Yet it is a U.S.–supported regime headed by a dictator that provides the oppression driving some Haitians to emigrate; and U.S. multinationals have played their role in increasing poverty on the island by changing its economy from one emphasizing local needs to one exporting foods and products to richer nations. In the last decade about sixty thousand Haitians fled their homeland, seeking a better life in the United States; they provide much low-wage labor in states such as Florida and New York. The U.S. government, rejecting the philosophy on the Statue of Liberty, has tried to throw them out. The sixty thousand Haitians, a mostly black group, seem to be unwelcome. Yet in the same decade thousands of Cubans and Vietnamese have been accepted by the U.S. government. Why has there been such a difference in treatment? The differential treatment of immigrants is probably more political than racial. Those fleeing, for political or economic reasons, Communist dictatorship in Cuba or Vietnam are welcomed. Those fleeing, for political or economic reasons, right-wing dictatorships in Latin America are not welcomed.[8] An Attorney General in the Ronald Reagan administration emphasized this bias in recent U.S. immigration policy: "There are certain refugees who are of particular interest to the United States, either by virtue of previous association with the country or because the implementation of United States foreign policies may have placed such refugees in particularly threatening situations."[9] Immigration now takes place within an intensely political context, as well as within the traditional economic context.

The Cuban Immigration

One example of the political character of immigration is that of Cubans who have fled the Communist government of Cuba, a government that replaced a U.S.–supported right-wing dictatorship. Thousands of Cubans fled the new regime. Again overseas involvement by the U.S. government directly or indirectly generated migration to the United States.

Cuban Americans have been viewed as among the most politically conservative of the Hispanic groups. As the Cuban American marketing director of the *Miami News* recently put it, "Cuban-Americans are definitely super-conservative. Communism for us is the enemy. On domestic issues, we will be more toward the center . . . but the Cuban business community is still more in favor of Reaganomics than Mexicans or Puerto Ricans."[10] Today in Miami there are half a million Cubans, many of whom are still psychologically involved in the politics of Cuba. Some have been involved in paramilitary training and plans for terrorist acts against the existing Cuban government.

In 1980 there was a new influx of 124,000 Cubans. These recent immigrants are generally poorer and less well educated than the earlier waves of Cuban refugees, many of whom were from middle-income and professional backgrounds. Substantial federal aid was required for resettlement of these recent immigrants; many remained in detention camps for many months after arrival because the U.S. government feared that many of the new immigrants were criminals. These immigrants have created serious tensions in Cuban communities. One result of the various Cuban migrations over the last few decades is a major change in the population mix of south Florida. By 1982 about 39 percent of the people in the Miami metropolitan area were Hispanic (mostly Cuban), 44 percent were Anglo whites, and 17 percent were black. Population forecasts suggested that a majority of the population of the area would be Hispanic by 1990. The growing Hispanic population has had a number of effects on south Florida. One effect is political. For example, the 1981 Miami mayoral election pitted two Hispanics against each other, a Puerto Rican incumbent and a Cuban challenger. Another result has been economic. In 1982 the Miami area's unemployment rate was at least 13 percent, a high figure resulting in part from recent boatloads of Cuban immigrants.[11]

The 1980 Cuban migration also swelled Miami welfare aid rolls, increased overcrowding in the schools, and created $30 million in added expenses for local governments already hurting from cutbacks in federal government programs. The millions of dollars paid out to care for the new influx of Cubans angered many whites; the latter unfairly blamed all Cubans for local social problems. Tensions with blacks were also accelerating because of the growing Cuban American power in south Florida. Miami's 1980 Liberty City riot and 1982 Overtown riot by poor blacks were precipitated in part by Hispanic (and white Anglo) police officers involved in the killing of black men. After the Liberty City riot in Miami white landlords and businesses which had been damaged were replaced by Hispanic landlords and businesses. One former black school official complained bitterly that "after a generation of being Southern slaves, blacks now face a future as Latin slaves." Blacks also complained that Cuban Americans were taking jobs away from them. Indeed, many businesses in the Miami area require people to speak Spanish, to be bilingual, which effectively excludes most black applicants. Moreover the larger and more affluent Cuban American community controls many of its own businesses, small and large; Cubans are usually preferred in hiring there. Not surprisingly, then, in a recent mayoral election 95 percent of black voters voted *against* the Cuban American candidate. Intergroup rivalry and competition can be seen clearly in south Florida today, with a very old immigrant group (Afro-Americans) apparently losing out in a power struggle with a rather new immigrant group (Cuban Americans).

Cultural assimilation pressures on the new Cuban immigrants have created cross-generational problems similar to those of earlier Asian and European immigrants. For example, among Miami's Cubans the young reportedly prefer to listen to English language programs on radio and TV, while their parents switch back and forth between English and Spanish programs. The grandparents prefer to hear and speak Spanish. Parents and grandparents worry about the excessive freedom and lack of parental respect of teenagers in U.S. cities. They worry that dates between Cuban American young people are not chaperoned the way they once were in Cuba. Parents and grandparents tend to emphasize Cuban traditions and food, while children often prefer things American. Moreover, the older generations seem to be more strongly committed to overthrowing Cuba's Communist government and to returning home to Cuba. Home for the less politically active youth is the United States. Nevertheless, family and community ties remain strong; and the young are proud of their Cuban identities.[12]

The Vietnamese: Part of an Asian Migration

Between 1969 and the early 1980s the proportion of Asians in the migration to the United States increased dramatically. The end of racist quotas in the 1960s, together with special refugee admissions, was responsible for significant increases in the number of Asian migrants, particularly Chinese, Koreans, Pilipinos, and Vietnamese. By 1980 the Chinese had surpassed Japanese Americans as the nation's largest Asian group. Altogether, there was an increase from 1.5 to 3.5 million Asian Americans from 1970 to 1980. Most of the new American immigrants have settled on the West Coast.

In the last decade the United States has become home for a half million Indo-Chinese immigrants, more than two-thirds of them Vietnamese. Many

Vietnamese refugees have settled in California and along the Gulf Coast in cities from Corpus Christi, Texas, to Biloxi, Mississippi. Yet many Vietnamese refugees have suffered at the hands of U.S. nativists. Racist groups such as the Ku Klux Klan have raised questions about their "racial inferiority" and have even attacked those engaged in fishing on the Gulf Coast. For example, in Seadrift, Texas, a white fishcatcher was killed by a Vietnamese fishcatcher. The jury verdict was that the killing was justified because of harassment the Vietnamese were suffering from whites in the area. Later in the same area Ku Klux Klan members burned an effigy of a Vietnamese fishing boat, bringing new terror to the Vietnamese immigrants settling along the Gulf Coast.[13]

Suffering similar harassment, many Vietnamese were forced out of Empire, Louisiana, and as a result moved to Biloxi, Mississippi. Louisiana fishermen shot at the Vietnamese fishing boats and would not let the Vietnamese Americans dock or freely market their fish. The immigrants had been encouraged to come to Biloxi by employers looking for workers to do the dirty, mostly low-wage work in the fishing industry. Gradually, more than a thousand migrated to the area. In Biloxi they suffered some harassment in the form of verbal threats and violence directed against their nets and boats. In addition, many markets would not buy from them. The Vietnamese themselves have been confused by U.S. fishing rules, both those set by law and the informal rules established by whites. So the Vietnamese unintentionally violated the rules, precipitating conflict with whites. Nonetheless, their reception was mixed; some whites befriended them as well.[14]

Like the Cuban Americans, the Vietnamese Americans have had trouble with the generation gap. Because of school attendance, young Vietnamese know English better than their parents. As was the case with the children of immigrants in earlier decades, these children often have to deal with landlords and merchants and answer the phone for their parents. Yet the parents complain that the children are not as respectful of their parents as children are in Vietnam; children, as brokers with the public, are more active and aggressive in the United States. The Vietnamese children, in addition, suffer at the hands of white children who taunt them with derogatory racist names such as "gook." The problems of Hispanic and Asian immigrants in contemporary America in numerous ways mirror those of earlier waves of immigrants.[15]

The Revival of Anti-immigration Legislation

An amazing variety of citizens oppose these new immigrants: nativists such as members of the Ku Klux Klan, political conservatives, some unions, and even some political liberals. Some union leaders fear that immigrants will take away jobs. Political conservatives and nativists fear that immigrants are destroying the values and moral fiber of the "real America." Some liberals fear that new immigrants such as the Cubans adhere too strongly to a right-wing political philosophy and tilt American voting patterns to the right. Controversy over the new immigrants has fueled the debate over the first exclusion-oriented immigration bill to be introduced in the U.S.

Congress since the 1920s. The 1924 Immigration Act set up quotas which sharply curtailed the number of immigrants from southern and eastern Europe, as well as excluding Asian immigrants such as the Japanese. It was not until 1965 that the discriminatory quotas and exclusion provisions were eliminated. In 1982 another restrictive immigration bill, called the Immigration and Nationality Act, was passed by the U.S. Senate (80–19). It was set to come up in the U.S. House in 1983. While opposition to the bill was growing in late 1982 and early 1983, particularly among Mexican American groups, it seemed likely that most of the bill would be incorporated into U.S. law.

The proposed Immigration and Nationality Act would put a new annual ceiling on immigrants of 425,000, not including refugees. It would set up penalties for employers who knowingly hire undocumented workers, as well as an identification card system for workers so that employers can tell if they have a legal status. The bill also would also provide amnesty for illegal workers who came into the United States before 1980. The debate over this restrictive immigration legislation conjured up many anti-immigration arguments of the past. Many were worried that the United States could not absorb so many new immigrants, even though the ratio of immigrants to the native-born population was *much* higher in earlier decades than it is today. Many senators were worried about the character and values of the new immigrants. Implicit in many discussions seemed to be a concern that most of the new immigrants were not white or European.

A U.S. Senate report on the 1982 Immigration and Nationality Act sidestepped the inscription on the Statue of Liberty with the argument that "immigrants can still greatly benefit America, but only if they are limited to an appropriate number and selected within that number on the basis of immediate family unification and skills." The emphasis here on ties to families already in the United States will probably mean that whites, Europeans, and those with skills will be given preference over nonwhites, non-Europeans, and the unskilled poor. Among others Asians will be penalized. As in earlier decades, the proponents of restrictive legislation have worried about how assimilable the new "foreign" elements are. As the Senate report puts it, "if the newcomers remain 'foreign,' they may not be welcome, especially if they seek to carve out separate enclaves to embrace only their language and culture and if their numbers and the areas of the community which they directly affect are great."[16] In other words, the senators were worried that new immigrants may seek to preserve their own languages and cultures and may even seek to create their own (large) communities—like earlier European immigrant groups.

The Senate report further alleged that many new immigrants do not want to assimilate rapidly and that "they have the potential to create in America a measure of the same social, political, and economic problems which exist in the countries from which they have chosen to depart" and that the immigrants' language and cultural separateness may "seriously diminish" the "unity and political stability of the nation."[17] U.S. race and ethnic history here seems to repeat itself. These immigration issues were hotly debated once before, in the 1890s to the 1920s. In the 1980s we can again glimpse American nativism targeting new immigrants for hostility. And a racially discriminatory immigration act has emerged from these debates just as it did in the 1920s.

CURRENT ISSUES: AFFIRMATIVE ACTION AND EQUAL OPPORTUNITY PROGRAMS

Another debated topic of the last two decades has been government equal opportunity and affirmative action programs. Affirmative action programs seem to be in serious trouble in the 1980s. The white male backlash against the social progress of nonwhite minorities began in earnest in the 1970s, less than a decade after the 1964 Civil Rights Act. The backlash has grown in significance to the point that it has had articulate and powerful spokesmen at the highest levels of government. For example, a report of a Ronald Reagan administration team called for the gutting of the Equal Employment Opportunity Commission, including a freeze on new court suits challenging discrimination and a thorough reconsideration of the philosophy of affirmative action. In his book, *Wealth and Poverty,* (once called the "Bible" of the Reagan administration), George Gilder has argued that there is no need for affirmative action because:

1. It is now virtually impossible to find in a position of power a serious racist
2. It would seem genuinely difficult to sustain the idea that America is still oppressive and discriminatory
3. Discrimination has been effectively abolished in this country.

Race discrimination has been described as a "myth." Affirmative action is seen as unnecessary. Equal opportunity and affirmative action regulations are seen as destroying private enterprise. Most serious analysts of civil rights would not have predicted such a rapid acceptance of these reactionary views at the highest levels of business, government, and academia in the 1980s.[18]

What is Affirmative Action?

Before we examine arguments about affirmative action, let us first examine a bit of history, particularly in regard to employment. The phrase *affirmative action* has been used to cover at least four different types of government and private actions:

1. Any increase in nonwhite employment
2. Voluntary remedial programs
3. Court-ordered employment remedies for discrimination (such as goals in hiring)
4. Administratively (government) coerced employment remedies for discrimination (such as goals in hiring).

The first usage is the vaguest, since it covers all situations where there have been increases in the numbers of nonwhites hired, even though such increases may be the result of subordinate group (e.g., black American) pressure rather than government action programs. The second type of usage refers to voluntary business programs not ordered by government.

Two categories critics have been concerned with are (1) court-ordered programs and (2) administratively ordered programs. Court-ordered affirmative action programs are perhaps the more difficult for opponents to criticize, since in most cases *documentation* of past intentional discrimination by a company or organization has become part of the legal record. Frequently a severe imbalance in the nonwhite proportions of employees in skilled and unskilled work, compared to proportions in the available workforce, has been enough to establish a prima facie case of discrimination. Then it is the responsibility of the employer to prove that such imbalances were not due to intentional discrimination. Where such a defense has been inadequate, courts have ordered affirmative action by employers to increase the proportions of nonwhites in their work force and to take other actions to upgrade or improve the working situations of nonwhites.

Administratively ordered affirmative action has also "taken the heat." Federal administrative agencies, particularly the Equal Employment Opportunity Commission (EEOC) and the Office of Federal Contract Compliance (OFCC) have pressured employers to develop and implement affirmative action programs. The authority for the EEOC pressure stems from the 1964 Civil Rights Act. Since 1972, EEOC has been empowered to sue employers thought to be discriminating. Each year large employers must submit to the EEOC a form, sometimes called an affirmative action form, indicating the racial, ethnic, and sex composition of their work force. Yet the EEOC does not have the legal staff to examine all these confidential reports carefully for patterns of discrimination. In this respect the EEOC does seem a "paper tiger."

Another major source of administrative pressure on employers has been the Office of Federal Contract Compliance (OFCC) in the Department of Labor. Issued in the mid-1960s, two presidential Executive Orders prohibited discrimination on the basis of race, national origin, or sex by private businesses with federal contracts and gave authority to the OFCC to supervise them. The OFCC has responsibility for supervising the implementation of its contract regulations, which spell out the intent of the orders. Since the OFCC has delegated much of its enforcement authority to other agencies, the Department of Health, Education, and Welfare (HEW), for example, has responsibility for educational organizations such as colleges and universities which receive federal contracts. The OFCC regulations require federal contractors to take affirmative action to eliminate discrimination in their employment practices, from recruitment networks to hiring practices to promotion procedures. Since 1968 federal contractors have been required to submit written affirmative action plans indicating the current representation of nonwhites in detailed job categories and providing for goals and timetables for categories where underutilization of nonwhites exists. Compliance agencies such as HEW are supposed to review their contractors to see if they are taking remedial action. The effectiveness of the OFCC-fostered affirmative action has been debated. U.S. Commission on Civil Rights studies of compliance reviews have indicated that little in the way of penalties has been applied to nonconforming contractor-employers. Grossly deficient plans have been approved, and few contractors have been barred from federal contracts.

Supreme Court Cases: Voluntary Affirmative Action

Critics have also been concerned with voluntary affirmative action plans seeking to remedy the underrepresentation of members of subordinate groups. Indeed, extensive publicity has been given to a few Supreme Court decisions dealing with voluntary affirmative action programs. In the famous 1978 *Bakke v. Regents of the University of California* case, a white male applicant to a university medical school argued that he had been excluded from consideration for a small number of medical school openings which had been set aside for subordinate group (e.g., nonwhite) applicants with lesser academic credentials than his.[19] The medical school had voluntarily set aside sixteen of its one hundred annual openings for qualified candidates who were seen as victims of societal race discrimination. Bakke challenged this procedure, and the case went to the Supreme Court. The Supreme Court justices decided the case with a five-to-four vote in favor of Bakke. Bakke was ordered to be admitted to the medical school; but five of the justices also agreed that such affirmative action plans *were* constitutional if universities would show more clearly how their specific affirmative plans remedy past discrimination. This particular affirmative action plan was ruled illegal; but most carefully targeted affirmative action plans, the court seemed to be saying, were legal.

A second case, *United Steelworkers of America v. Weber,* involved a voluntary affirmative action plan, set up by the Kaiser Corporation and a union, which sought to raise black representation in skilled craft jobs from 2 percent to something closer to the black percentage (39 percent) of the local area work force.[20] The plan reserved half the positions in a small job-training program for qualified black employees, some of whom had less seniority than white male workers such as Brian Weber, who went to court to challenge the plan. The Supreme Court ruled in 1979 by a five-to-four vote that racial preferences in this affirmative action plan were legal and that the plan was a lawful means of ending the proven racial discrimination in craft jobs in that area of the country. The Court decided that race-conscious plans were necessary "to open employment opportunities for Negroes in occupations which have been traditionally closed to them."

Other Court Action

In the 1980s a number of cases involving court-ordered affirmative action plans came before federal courts. One of the more important cases was *Boston Firefighters Union v. Boston Chapter NAACP*, which was considered by the Supreme Court in 1983. In an earlier (1974) case a federal district court had ordered new affirmative action plans to remedy discrimination in the Boston fire department. (This was not a voluntary plan.) As a result, minority employment in the fire department increased from less than 1 percent to nearly 15 percent. (Boston's population is about one-third black and Hispanic.) When budget cutbacks in 1981 forced cuts in the fire department, the Circuit Court of Appeals ruled that layoffs could not be made in terms of total on-the-job seniority because recently hired minorities had less seniority than whites who had been hired under the earlier racially discriminatory hiring program. Because several hundred whites were laid off and some black and Hispanic firefighters with less seniority were kept on, the firefighter unions appealed to the Supreme Court.[21]

The Ronald Reagan Administration filed a "friend of the court" brief in favor of the position of the whites; this was the first time that the U.S. government had put its weight officially against a court-ordered affirmative action plan. The Administration rejected official letters from its own Equal Employment Opportunity Commission and Commission on Civil Rights, both of which argued that black and Hispanic percentages must be protected during layoff periods because the fire department in question had a proven record of past racial discrimination. This past record was the major reason that current black and Hispanic employees had low seniority. Seniority, some courts have noted, is just the length of time one has been an employee; it is not an untouchable "sacred cow."

Opponents of Affirmative Action

Affirmative action pressures have generated a struggle between white ethnic and nonwhite Americans. Opponents of affirmative action scored a coup by getting the mass media to discuss affirmative action in terms of the simplistic phrase "reverse discrimination." For example, in 1976 *U.S. News and World Report* ran a feature story entitled: "Growing Debate—Reverse Discrimination—Has It Gone Too Far?" and in 1977 *Newsweek* ran a cover story under a front page headline of "reverse discrimination." The cover showed a white student and a black student in a tug of war over a college diploma. Many scholarly critics have also made use of this phrase.

Yet the term reverse discrimination is an inaccurate label for the events the critics deplore. This can be seen clearly if we follow the principle of keeping traditional patterns of institutionalized discrimination in mind in assessing arguments about affirmative action. Think for a moment about patterns of discrimination against black Americans in the United States. Traditional discrimination has meant, and still means, widespread (blatant and subtle) discrimination by whites against blacks in most organizations in all major institutional areas of this society—in housing, employment, education, health services, the legal system, and so on. For three centuries now, millions of whites have participated directly in discrimination against millions of blacks, including routinized discrimination in the large-scale bureaucracies that now dominate this society. Most other whites have benefited in indirect ways, such as from less competition for better-paying jobs. Traditional discrimination has meant heavy economic and social losses for blacks in all institutional sectors for hundreds of years.

What would the *reverse* of this traditional race discrimination look like? The reverse of the traditional discrimination by whites against blacks would mean the following: For several hundred years, institutionalized discrimination would be directed by dominant blacks against most whites. Most organizations in areas such as housing, education, and employment would be run at the top by a disproportionate number of blacks; and middle- and lower-level decision-makers would be disproportionately black. These decision-making blacks would have aimed much costly discrimination at whites. As a result, millions of whites would have suffered trillions of dollars in economic losses, lower wages, unemployment, political weakness, widespread housing segregation, inferior school facilities, and lynchings. That societal condition would be something one could reasonably call a condition of "reverse discrimination." It has never existed. Whatever cost affirmative action has meant for whites, it does not total anything close to the total cost of true reverse discrimination.

What Are the Costs of Affirmative Action?

Even though the enforcement penalties backing up affirmative action in employment have often been weak, some employers have responded to the threat of enforcement. In response to affirmative action pressures, an unknown number of businesses, school systems, and colleges have occasionally established what became in effect restrictive quotas in hiring and promotions, usually favoring blacks or white women. This has especially been problematical where the job situation has been tight, where because of economic recession few people are being hired or promoted. Granting opportunity to blacks, for example, in a limited job market necessarily means disadvantages for some whites. In some cases blacks have been hired or promoted where they did not have quite the credentials (that is, degrees) or seniority (that is, experience) of white male applicants. Since credentials and seniority are major criteria used to measure merit in the United States, bending these criteria a little in order to hire more blacks or Hispanics has been vigorously criticized as violating this society's supposed meritocratic standards.

A heated fight over affirmative action has taken place in higher education, where many white Catholics and Jews have done well in recent decades. The preparation of written affirmative action plans with specific goals and time schedules for improving the hiring of nonwhites has been seen by white critics as leading to restrictive quotas. Critics assert that colleges have recruited, often at the expense of white graduate students, less qualified nonwhite graduate students to fill faculty positions. While there is some evidence for such charges, they do seem to have been exaggerated. In fact, most blacks and Hispanics hired in universities appear to be qualified for the positions they hold.

It is true that to this point in time a modest number of white males have paid a price for some affirmative action programs. If affirmative action is successful, particularly in a society with little economic growth, it will entail some cost. White male suffering will occur. But to compare the scale of that suffering to the scale of the suffering of traditionally exploited nonwhites seems unfair. A white male who suffers as an individual from remedial programs such as affirmative action programs in employment or education suffers because he is an exception to his privileged racial group. A black person who suffers from racial discrimination suffers because the whole group has traditionally been subordinated, not because he or she is an exception. Moreover, MacKinnon suggests this contrast:

> When a white charges race discrimination (for example, due to preferential admissions for blacks) he is protesting the cost on one sphere of his life of a rectification process of an entire system that has tried to destroy all blacks in every sphere of their lives for generations, and could afford to ignore their protests.[22]

Few businesses, companies, or universities have ever had federal contracts or grants canceled because of discrimination or because of their failure to implement affirmative action. The impact of government agency pressures has led to significant changes in employment patterns only in a hit-and-miss fashion. HEW (now the Department of Education), for example, has spent a generous amount of time in greatly extended negotiations with colleges over the required paperwork on affirmative action plans.

In addition, tokenism has been one of the most successful devices in slowing down the process of dismantling institutionalized discrimination, particularly at the level of the nontraditional, better-paying jobs seldom held in the past by nonwhites. Reluctantly tearing down the traditional exclusion barriers over the last two decades, many organizations have retreated to a second line of defense we can call tokenism. Part of the tokenism strategy is to hire nonwhites for nontraditional jobs and put them in conspicuous or powerless positions. Following this strategy, officials must be careful not to place too many nonwhites in one particular unit of their organization. A prominent management consultant, Kenneth Clark, has noted that blacks moving into nontraditional jobs in corporate America have frequently found themselves tracked into "ghettos" within the organization, such as a department of "community affairs" or of "special markets." Many professional and managerial blacks end up in selected staff jobs, such as that of "equal opportunity officer," rather than in line managerial jobs. Clark notes that "they are rarely found in line positions concerned with developing or controlling production, supervising the work of large numbers of whites or competing with their white 'peers' for significant positions." Nonwhite "tokens" in managerial and professional jobs are frequently put into staff jobs with little power.[23]

Tokenism can become a self-perpetuating cycle. Intentionally isolated by their peers, unable to draw on old-boy networks for routine assistance, some nonwhite employees have difficulty in coping successfully with the tensions of these higher-level jobs. As a result, job turnover may increase. Kanter makes the point that increasing the proportion of nonwhites in an organizational unit beyond token numbers is critical for equal opportunity to work in the long run. Going beyond tokenism is necessary from the point of view of social justice for nonwhite Americans. But going beyond tokenism is also critical from a practical point of view as perhaps the only way of actually dismantling the age-old structure of deeply rooted institutionalized discrimination.[24]

The Pace of Change

From the nonwhite point of view much of the progress that has come in recent years has not been the result of government remedial programs such as affirmative action; it has come from the persisting protest and hard work of nonwhites themselves. Many organizations have desegregated their work forces because of court suits started by civil rights groups or because of pressure from individual applicants. From the black point of view, progress has been made. But much more progress needs to be made. A substantial majority of black Americans questioned in a 1979 survey felt that there was a great deal of racial discrimination in this country. And the supposed beneficiaries of affirmative action (those with incomes over $20,000) were somewhat more likely than the poor to report a great deal of discrimination. There is a consensus among large majorities of nonwhites that racial discrimination remains a serious problem. In the same survey a majority of the black respondents saw a declining national commitment to equal rights. The survey asked, "Is the push for equal rights for black people in this country moving too fast, at about the right pace, or too slow?" Fully three-quarters said, "too slow."[25] This compares dramatically with the results of a similar question asked in a Harris survey in 1970. In that survey only 47 percent said, "too slow," with 41 percent saying, "about right."[26] The overwhelming majority of black Americans believe that the U.S. commitment to racial equality is eroding. Moreover, middle-income blacks are somewhat more likely than poorer whites to feel that the movement to racial equality is going too slowly. Those who have made the greatest progress in the last decade, middle-income blacks, are a bit more likely than the rest to see equal rights as moving too slowly, as well as to report a great deal of discrimination in the country.

How do black Americans see affirmative action today? According to a 1980 *Black Enterprise* survey of its middle-income and upper-income black readers, 78 percent of the respondents saw affirmative action as "somewhat effective." Virtually all (94 percent) thought affirmative action would still be needed in the 1990s.[27]

CONCLUSION: RACE, ETHNICITY, AND EQUALITY

Equality has been viewed in different ways in the years since 1776. The philosophy that "all men are created equal" held by some of the founding fathers seems to have meant equality of political participation for white, northern European, male adults with property. Even this equality of access to the political institutions was a dramatic step for its day, but such a limited view of equality obviously excluded such groups as women, black slaves, Native Americans, and to some extent Jewish and Catholic immigrants.

Over the next two centuries conceptions of equality would change, so much so that numerous commentators have seen equality as an ideal whose driving force has been extraordinarily great in American history. In this view the historical process has seen the progressive "egalitarianization" of the economic and political system. Gradually, the idea of equality came to include equality of worth among individuals, equality of opportunity for all individuals, and equality before the law (civil rights). Numerous authors have praised the egalitarian trend in the United States. A long series of poor ethnic and racial groups experienced ever-greater equality in some or all of these categories—according to this optimistic perspective. Between the early 1800s and the early 1900s economic development came dramatically and swiftly to the United States. Rapid expansion gave substantial equality of economic opportunity to millions of immigrants; they became the prospering labor for this economic miracle. Although they suffered, substantial mobility and success came to the majority of white ethnic Americans who entered as low-income individuals. From this perspective, even the white ethnics finally "made it"; and today even nonwhites are moving toward full inclusion in the society.

Such a view of the egalitarianizing society is a series of half-truths. Substantial economic and political mobility did indeed come for many white groups. But this optimistic view ignores the great poverty and misery that white ethnics and nonwhites endured as poorly paid laborers in an exploitative economic system. We have documented this exploitation for white groups such as the Italians, Irish, and Jews; this was also the picture for many white ethnic groups we have not examined. The racist immigration law aimed at restricting the entry of whites from southern and eastern Europe was not abolished until the mid-1960s. This portrait does not take into account the significant discrimination, often subtle and institutionalized, still experienced by groups such as the Italians and the Jews.

This rosy picture glosses over the continuing subordination of many nonwhite Americans in the lower social, political, and economic tiers of the society. To some extent, of course, the egalitarianizing trend has affected the majority of nonwhite Americans, especially as concerns legal rights and formal opportunity. But in terms of political and economic advancement, most run as hard as they can to keep from becoming more unequal than they currently are. It was only a century ago that a decade or two of great progress in expanding opportunities for black Americans (1865–1885), called the Reconstruction period, was followed all too soon by a dramatic resurgence of reaction, called the Redemption period. While there are major differences between then and now, it is also true that today, only fifteen to twenty years after public policy shifted significantly in favor of expanded opportunities for nonwhite Americans, we again seem to be moving in a reactionary direction. Many powerful leaders have called for cutting back or eliminating affirmative action and equal opportunity programs. The bottom line on evaluating racial progress is that two decades into affirmative action and equal opportunity programs no fundamental changes can be seen at top levels in most major institutional sectors in the United States. White males overwhelmingly dominate upper-level and middle-level positions in most major bureaucratic organizations in the United States, from the Department of Defense, to Fortune 500 corporations, to state legislatures, to local banks and supermarket chains. In the 1980s the dominant white concern has shifted away from patterns of institutionalized race discrimination. Sadly, those hurt most by the shift have been those nonwhite Americans who have long suffered from traditional institutionalized discrimination. In the best scenario one can envision, nonwhite equality or parity with whites still seems generations in the future. Equality has long been an authentic American dream. Whether it can ever be reality in the sphere of racial and ethnic relations remains to be seen.

NOTES

[1] Israel Zangwill, *The Melting Pot* (New York: Macmillan, 1925), p. 33.

[2] Milton R. Konvitz, "Horace Meyer Kallen (1882–1974): Philosopher of the Hebraic-American Idea," in *American Jewish Year Book, 1974–1975,* ed. Morris Fine and Milton Himmelfarb (Philadelphia: Jewish Publication Society of America, 1974), pp. 65–67; Horace M. Kallen, *Culture and Democracy in the United States* (New York: Boni and Liveright, 1924), pp. 124–25.

[3] Andrew M. Greeley, *Ethnicity in the United States* (New York: John Wiley, 1974), pp. 290–317.

[4] Robert Blauner, *Racial Oppression in America* (New York: Harper and Row, 1972); Guillermo V. Flores, "Race and Culture in the Internal Colony," in *Structures of Dependency,* ed. Frank Bonilla and Robert Girling (Palo Alto, Calif.: Stanford University Research Seminar, 1973).

[5] See R. A. Schermerhorn, *Comparative Ethnic Relations* (New York: Random House, 1970), for a start on some of these issues.

[6] Emma Lazarus, "The New Colossus," 1883, inscription on Statue of Liberty.

[7] These figures are calculated from Immigration and Naturalization Service, *1979 Statistical Yearbook* (Washington, D.C.: U.S. Government Printing Office, 1979), pp. 39–42 and from Frank Viviano, "The New Immigrants," *Mother Jones* 8 (January 1983): 29.

[8] U.S. Commission on Civil Rights, *The Tarnished Golden Door: Civil Rights Issues in Immigration* (Washington, D.C.: U.S. Government Printing Office, 1980), pp. 12–19; Viviano, "The New Immigrants," pp. 28–29.

[9] Quoted in Viviano, "The New Immigrants," p. 28.

[10] Quoted in "Widespread Political Efforts Open New Era for Hispanics," *Congressional Quarterly,* October 23, 1982, p. 2709.

[11] "Trouble in Paradise," *Time,* November 23, 1981, pp. 24–29.

[12] Ibid., pp. 31–32.

[13] "Asian Americans: A 'Model Minority,' " *Newsweek,* December 6, 1982, p. 39; Harvey Arden, "Troubled Odyssey of Vietnamese Fisherman," *National Geographic* 160 (September 1981): 381–86.

[14] Arden, "Troubled Odyssey," pp. 386–94.

[15] Ibid., p. 394.

[16] U.S. Senate, Committee on the Judiciary, *Immigration Reform and Control, Report on S. 2222* (Washington, D.C.: U.S. Government Printing Office, 1982), pp. 3–4.

[17] Ibid., p. 6.

[18] George Gilder, *Wealth and Poverty* (New York: Basic Books, 1981), pp. 128–39.

[19] 438 U.S. 265 (1978).

[20]443 U.S. 193 (1979). A good discussion of these cases can be found in U.S. Commission on Civil Rights, *Affirmative Action in the 1980s: Dismantling the Process of Discrimination* (Washington, D.C.: U.S. Government Printing Office, 1981), pp. 24–28.

[21]I am drawing here from a copy of the letter from the U.S. Commission on Civil Rights and from Fred Barbash, "Justice Department to Aid Suit Challenging 'Reverse Discrimination,' " *Washington Post*, December 17, 1982, p. A-1. Portions of this and the next section have been drawn from Joe R. Feagin, "Affirmative Action in an Era of Reaction," in *Consultations on the Affirmative Action Statement of the U.S. Commission on Civil Rights* (Washington, D.C.: Government Printing Office, 1982), pp. 44–61.

[22]Catharine A. MacKinnon, *Sexual Harassment of Working Women* (New Haven: Yale University Press, 1979), p. 132.

[23]Kenneth B. Clark, "The Role of Race," *New York Times Magazine*, October 5, 1980, p. 30.

[24]Rosabeth Moss Kanter, *Men and Women of the Corporation* (New York: Basic Books, 1977), pp. 186–242.

[25]"Initial Black Pulse Findings," Bulletin No. 1, Research Department, National Urban League, August, 1980, pp. 1–2.

[26]Cited in ibid.

[27]"Economics," *Black Enterprise* (August 1980), p. 64.

Index